Fodor's **2002**

W9-DCM-702

Paris

METRO

Fodor's Travel Publications • New York, Toronto, London, Sydney, Auckland
www.fodors.com

CONTENTS

MAPS

Circled letters in text correspond to letters on the photographs. For more information on the sights pictured, turn to the indicated page number Ⓐ▷ on each photograph.

DESTINATION PARIS

Stroll along formal footpaths in the Jardin du Luxembourg and lose yourself in the halls of the Louvre. Meander through Montmartre and promenade down broad boulevards off the Arc de Triomphe. Master métro lines and river curves. Immerse yourself in the city's patchwork of villages. Linger in a Left Bank café and indulge in gastronomic delights. Admire the architectural filigree—the woven metal of the Eiffel Tower and the plastic tubing encasing the Centre Pompidou. Listen to vendors hawking the season's produce in the markets of Montorgueil and Mouffetard. At every turn Paris envelops you in its spell of history, proportion, harmony, and visual delights and compels you to return.

Ⓐ▷45

ARCHITECTURE

Ⓑ▷65

It may be a heightened sense of aesthetics or just Gallic disdain, but Parisians seem to have always greeted the architectural innovations that are continually rising in their midst with skepticism—all the while assembling the most beautiful city on earth. "C'est magnifique," say some Parisians of the grandiose glass pyramid by architect I. M. Pei that sprouted in 1989 from the Cour Napoléon at their beloved Ⓓ**Louvre.** "C'est horrible," say others. The Ⓐ**Grand Palais** was tolerated only as a frothy oddity when it went up as a temporary pavilion for the World's Fair of 1900, but it's still there, a reassuring glass and iron presence on the banks of the Seine. And some Parisians sniffingly refer to the high-rise complex of Ⓔ**La Défense**

as "Houston on the Seine," though this futuristic area and such other glassy creations as the Ⓒ**Institut du Monde Arabe**, completed in 1988, continue to provide the visual theatrics with which Paris astonishes. Even the Ⓑ**Eiffel Tower** wasn't spared Parisian scorn: When the city's grace-

Ⓒ▷109

ful icon first appeared above the rooftops in 1889, naysayers quipped that they enjoyed ascending to the top because it was the only place they didn't have to look at the damned thing.

The mansard-roofed buildings lining the grand boulevards that Baron Haussmann sliced through the medieval city in the 19th century are as emblematic of Paris as the Art Nouveau entryways to métro stops such as Ⓗ**Porte Dauphine,** which have a playful elegance that you can find only in Paris. But over centuries, other familiar sights have come to represent not only the city but also all things French—the Eiffel Tower, of course, but

also the Arc de Triomphe and Ⓖ**Notre-Dame.** Perhaps the world's most famous cathedral, Notre-Dame is the symbolic center of France and, quite literally, the nation's ground zero—it sits at the point from which all distances to the capital are measured. Still, the memories you cherish most may be of burnished jewels like the Palais de Chaillot, St-Sulpice, or Ⓕ**Sainte-Chapelle.** More glass than stone, the latter is one of the supreme achievements of the Middle Ages and its heavenly light has not dimmed over the ages.

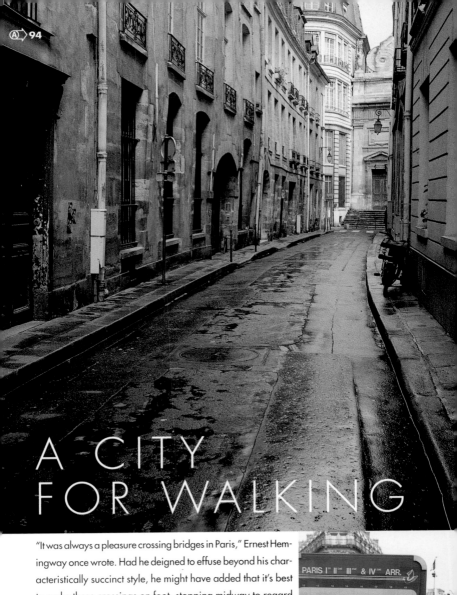

A CITY
FOR WALKING

"It was always a pleasure crossing bridges in Paris," Ernest Hemingway once wrote. Had he deigned to effuse beyond his characteristically succinct style, he might have added that it's best to make these crossings on foot, stopping midway to regard the monuments along the quais and perhaps ponder the meaning of life as one of the Ⓑ**Bateaux Mouches** slips beneath your feet. Along age-old, fabled boulevards such as the rue de Rivoli and twisting medieval streets that fan out from the banks of the Seine, Paris hides all sorts of secret trea-

Ⓑ 63

Ⓒ 94

sures that can be discovered
only on foot. In your random
wanderings you may come
upon a thrilling street market
or old men playing boules,
perhaps on Ⓓ**rue de La
Tour Maubourg** in front of
the Hôtel des Invalides, delightfully unaware that they are
fulfilling a cliché of how French
men of a certain age should
pass their time. Or you might
amble into a street market like
the one at Ⓔ**Bir Hakeim,**

Ⓓ 206

where the shoppers prove that
Parisians do spend much of the
day in pursuit of gastronomic
pleasures. The ⒶⒸ**Marais**
still resembles the neighborhood in which Molière and
La Fontaine scurried along
narrow streets to the salons of
17th-century aristocrats, who built the quarter's magnificent
hôtels particuliers, as its mansions are known. No doubt these
enlightened gentlemen of letters paused to take stock of the ur-
bane beauty all around. Few can resist the urge.

Ⓔ 256

MUSEUMS

Not just repositories of masterworks, the museums of Paris also reveal the endlessly fascinating nuances of French culture. It is fitting that the ⑩**Musée d'Orsay,** a Belle Epoque former train station, houses the city's legacy of art from 1848 to 1914: Railroads and other everyday phenomena were—shockingly so

at the time—favorite subjects of the period's artists, especially the Impressionists, who enjoy pride of place under the glass-vaulted roof. Art has always flourished in Paris; now the city benefits from French government efforts to keep its citizens' masterpieces perpetually within its borders. Near the Musée d'Orsay, the Ⓐ**Musée Rodin** bears testimony to the sculptor who, with the admirable shrewdness that Parisians have elevated to an art form, arranged to live and work at state expense in the 18th-century Hôtel Biron in return for leaving his work behind in its airy rooms and lovely gardens. The

Ⓐ▷ 121

Ⓔ 102

Ⓓ 120

Ⓔ**Musée Picasso,** occupying the 17th-century home of a financier who made his fortune collecting salt taxes, also arose from a compromise—Picasso's heirs gave France 230 paintings, 1,500 drawings, 1,700 prints, and many sculptures in lieu of paying death duties. And it was the French Revolution that opened the Ⓑ**Louvre** to the masses, so that all can now view the extraordinary collection amassed in good part by seven centuries of monarchs, while imagining the history-shaping intrigues that once fermented in these same salons. A proletarian spirit also holds sway at the Ⓕ**Centre Pompidou,** where the world's largest collection of modern art is displayed; though opened in 1977, it has been so popular that it has already needed renovating, and will go into the new millennium looking better than ever. At the futuristic Ⓒ**Parc de La Villette**, with its interactive science and musical-instrument museums and its shining spherical Géode theater, you can look into the city's future. And if the surroundings are any indication, its future will be every bit as fascinating as its past.

Ⓕ 99

Quotidian activities are elevated to high art in Paris, and shopping is no exception. Sophisticated city dwellers that they are, Parisians approach this exercise as a ritual, and an elaborate ritual at that. Picking produce at the open-air markets on rue Mouffetard or rue Montorgueil or at the Ⓐ**Marché d'Aligre**, or searching for haute couture at Jean-Paul Gaultier, Sonia Rykiel, or Ⓕ**Christian Dior**, they cast a discerning eye on the smallest detail and demand the highest quality—which may explain why

SHOPPING
AND MARKETS

the city's shopkeepers are so famously grouchy. Browsing through old books and maps in the stalls of *bouquinistes* (booksellers) on Ⓓ**quai de l'Hôtel de Ville** along the Seine, or prowling through castoffs at the Ⓔ**Marché aux Puces St-Ouen**, Parisians show their practicality, their sense of economy, and their ability to turn even a piece of junk into an inventively chic treasure. The city's lairs of consumerism are celebrated— the fashion salons, venerable antiques shops, august fashion

showrooms, and *grands magasins* such as Bon Marché, Au Printemps, and the Ⓑ Ⓒ **Galeries Lafayette,** which flaunt Belle Epoque extravagance and trendy designers. Though a short visit

Ⓕ 261

may not give you time to develop a Parisian's innate sense of taste and style, you are sure to be indoctrinated into the pleasures of worldly goods and to come home with some glittering prizes.

15

"Animals feed, men eat, but only wise men know the art of dining," wrote the French gastronome Anthelme Brillat-Savarin. Join them as they pursue their art, and abide by their rules—over a picnic of Camembert on a baguette in the Bois de Boulogne; at a meal created by the brilliant Ⓑ**Pierre Gagnaire** at his eponymous temple of gastronomy; in a chic lunch devised by Alain Ducasse at his ©**59 Poincaré**; or at a feast at Ⓐ**Guy Savoy,** whose ethereal creations remain the favorite of Parisian connoisseurs.

DINING OUT

Ⓐ▷**180**

buulanger CONFIS

Wherever you go in this world capital of good eating, one essential requirement is to toss caloric caution aside (after all, Parisians appear capable of consuming croissants by the basketful without gaining an

ounce) and throw yourself into creations that are nothing short of poetic. Another is to follow the age-old routine: End any proper meal with a cheese course, then dessert (the more decadent and creamy the better), then an *express* (taken black, with sugar). As to the wine: as Monsieur Brillat-Savarin memorably noted, "A meal without wine is like a day without sunshine." A visit to this city without partaking of all the pleasures of the table would be more dire than that.

PARKS AND GARDENS

Ⓐ 118

Every once in a while it's pleasant to regard Paris from the comfort of a chair in one of the city's parks. The experience is all the finer if it's springtime, if you're with someone you love, and if the park is as idyllic as the Ⓐ **Jardin du Luxembourg.** This Left Bank retreat and the Ⓓ **Jardin des Tuileries** across the river provide amusements that are resolutely genteel and satisfy a uniquely French craving to enjoy the great outdoors amid gravel paths, statuary, and manicured flower

beds. In contrast, and not by accident, the surroundings are uncharacteristically rusticated in the Ⓑ**Parc Montsouris**—this expanse of copses and lawns on the city's southern periphery is one of the rare Parisian parks in the English style. Understandably, King Henri IV favored a French design when commissioning the pink-brick mansions and central garden that grace the Ⓒ**place des Vosges,** once the favored in-town address of nobility (known as place Royale until the Revolution prompted a name change), but in these democratic times the gates are open so that all may enjoy the prettiest square in Paris. As for the city's most poignantly liberating outing, it's to the Ⓔ**Parc André-Citroën,** on the site of one of the famous car maker's former factories, an oasis of greenery and dancing fountains.

Ⓓ 45

Ⓔ 144

LITERARY
PARIS

Over the centuries Paris has fueled the genius of no small number of men and women of letters. You are likely to encounter the ghosts of many of them in the Ⓐ**Cimetière du Montparnasse,** where Baudelaire may well be exchanging bons mots with Maupassant, Sartre, and Beckett amid the riot of statuary that honors them, or in the Cimetière du Père-Lachaise, where rocker Jim Morrison rests alongside such luminaries as Gertrude Stein. Oscar Wilde, one of many foreign writers to have sought refuge in Paris, complained of his hotel on Ⓓ**13 rue des Beaux-Arts** in St-Germain-des-Prés, "I am dying beyond my means." A plaque commemorates his passing, shortly

©▷112
⑩▷128

before which he eyed the wallpaper and uttered one last quip: "One of us has to go." He would be pleased that the surrounding quarter still draws literati, who work in publishing houses or frequent the small bookshops such as ⑧**Shakespeare and Company,** the city's noted outpost of expat, bookish bohemia. The nearby ©**Sorbonne,** one of Europe's oldest universities, has been the nerve center of Parisian intellectual life since 1253, and any number of landmarks around the city have inspired some of the world's most noted works of literature. The 19th-century realist novelist Emile Zola found his muse in Les Halles, referring to this marketplace and gathering spot for riffraff as the "Belly of Paris." Pedestrian zones and shopping malls have since replaced the stalls of butchers and fishmongers, and one of the few vestiges of the neighborhood Zola would recognize is the church of ⑥**St-Eustache.** Even there, new statuary looks out at the ever-changing city from an unusual point of view, offering hope that novelty, and the genius it fosters, will continue to be one of Paris's most precious commodities.

⑥▷73

Parisians can sit for hours in the many wonderful neighborhood cafés like Le Vieux Colombier, Le Sancerre, and Ⓓ**Au Père Tranquille** in the heart of Les Halles, and any true Paris experience requires joining them. Cafés are perfect for a break and for people-watching. The ⒶⒸ**Café de Flore** on boulevard St-Germain is still

CAFÉS

⟩116

redolent of the 1940s and 1950s, when Jean-Paul Sartre and Simone de Beauvoir held court for a cadre of other iconoclastic writers and artists. You can't help feeling that something profound is being uttered at the next table, any more than you can resist the ultra-rich hot chocolate being served. Only Paris can muster settings as impossibly pretty as the Jardins du Palais-Royal, the Galerie Vivienne, and the Ⓑ**Cour de Rohan**; before you abandon yourself to romance at a café here, remember that the guillotine was invented nearby. Most typical of Paris is the *café du coin*, where, for the price of a cup of coffee or a glass of beer or wine, you can catch up on gossip and observe everyday life passing by—which is always a lot more interesting in Paris than elsewhere.

Café de Flore

CAFE DE FLOR

C 186

D 183

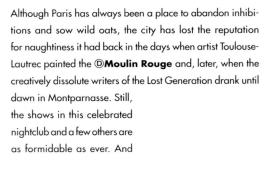

PERFORMING ARTS AND NIGHTLIFE

Although Paris has always been a place to abandon inhibitions and sow wild oats, the city has lost the reputation for naughtiness it had back in the days when artist Toulouse-Lautrec painted the Ⓓ**Moulin Rouge** and, later, when the creatively dissolute writers of the Lost Generation drank until dawn in Montparnasse. Still, the shows in this celebrated nightclub and a few others are as formidable as ever. And

though the Lost Generation is long gone, along with most of the smoke-filled *boîtes de nuit* they frequented, succeeding generations of night owls have found new venues. Clubs like Le Petit Opportun and Le Sunset in Les Halles and ®**New Morning** in the 10ᵉ arrondissement have earned Paris a reputation as one of the world's serious jazz cities, and the ®**Divan du Monde** in Pigalle is a major stop on the international rock circuit. The ®**Opéra Garnier** in the 9ᵉ arrondissement has been upstaged by the new ©**Opéra de la Bastille,** which pays homage to its address by providing grand opera at (somewhat) proletarian prices; but Garnier's sumptuous hall, built with upper-class tastes in mind, is not entirely out of fashion—it's now the home of the illustrious Paris Ballet. If you yearn

①>220

to dance in the moonlit streets like Maurice Chevalier and Leslie Caron, visit on July 13th. All Paris turns out in neighborhoods like the Marais for the ®**Bals des Sapeurs-Pompiers** (Firemen's Balls), late-night, outdoor dance parties that usher in Bastille Day on the 14th, but more than that, simply to enjoy a balmy summer evening in this most beautiful of cities.

®>332

®>226

GREAT ITINERARIES

Paris in 5 Days

A visit to Paris is never quite as simple as a quick look at a few landmarks. Each neighborhood has its own treasures, so be ready to explore—a pleasant prospect in this most elegant of cities. ⊘ So that you don't show up somewhere and find the doors locked, shuffle the itinerary segments with closing days in mind. To avoid crowds, go to museums and major sights early in the day. Note, too, that some museums and major sights have reduced entrance fees on Sunday and that many museums are closed early in the week (on Monday your best bet is the Day 2 itinerary).

Paris, a superb modern art museum. Or take a tour of the Seine on the Bateaux Mouches; these boats depart regularly from place de l'Alma. From here, walk or take the métro to the Arc de Triomphe; from the top there's a great view of the boule-

Ⓐ 71

Place Charles de Gaulle
Arc de Triomphe

Av. des Champs-Élysées
Av. Marceau

Rue du Faubourg St-Honoré
Palais de l'Élyseé
Rond Point des Champs Élysées
Av. des Champs-Élysées

Musée Guimet
Av. du Président Wilson
Place du Trocadéro
Musée d'Art Moderne de la Ville de Paris
Av. de New York
Place de l'Alma
Pont de l'Alma

Seine
Quai d'Orsay

Palais Bourbon/ Assemblée Nationale

Palais de Chaillot
Place de Varsovie
Pont d'Iéna

Eiffel Tower
Champ de Mars

Place des Invalides

Hôtel des Invalides
Rue de Varenne
Église du Dôme
Musée Rodin
Place Vauban

DAY 1

Head first to the Eiffel Tower: morning (or late evening) is the best time to avoid the crowds. The most thrilling approach is via the Champ de Mars. Afterwards consider visiting the Art Deco Palais de Chaillot, with its numerous museums. Also in the area is the Musée Guimet, with Asian art, and the Musée d'Art Moderne de la Ville de

vards emanating from L'Étoile and the noble vistas extending to the Louvre and La Défense. Then work your way along the Champs-Élysées, across place de la Concorde and the Jardin des Tuileries (with a visit, perhaps, to the Jeu de Paume museum) to the Louvre. Don't visit the museum now—wait until the next morning, when it will be less crowded. ⊘ Don't do this on a Monday if you plan to go to either the Musée d'Art Moderne or the Jeu de Paume because they are both closed then.

Ⓑ 46

DAY 2

Get to the Ⓑ Louvre early to avoid the crowds; in a morning you'll be able to see only part of the museum—it's that big. After lunch, wander along the ritzy rue St-Honoré. Here you'll find the French president's home, the Palais de l'Élysée, and the Neoclassical Ⓐ Église de la Madeleine. For good shopping and a look at Hauss-mann's 19th-century Paris and the famous Opéra Garnier, join up with the Grand Boulevards. Spend the late afternoon getting a sense

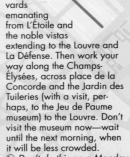

Place du Tertre

Sacré-Coeur Basilica

Moulin Rouge

Place Blanche
Blanche

St-Jean de Montmartre

Place des Abbesses
Abbesses

Bd. de Clichy

Pigalle
Place Pigalle

Rue Fontaine

Rue Pigalle

Rue Notre-Dame de Lorette

Square de la Trinité

Rue du Faubourg Montmartre

Gare St-Lazare

Bd. Haussmann

Opéra Garnier

Place de l'Opéra

Bd. Montmartre

Bd. Poissonière

Église de la Madeleine

Bd. de la Madeleine

Bd. des Capucines

Rue Royale

Rue St-Honoré

Place de la Concorde

Jeu de Paume

Jardin des Tuileries

Rue St-Honoré

Place du Palais Royal

Quai Anatole France

Seine

Pyramid Entrance

Louvre

Musée d'Orsay

⊙ This is fine any day but Tuesday, when the Louvre is closed.

DAY 3

Start the morning admiring the Impressionists in the ©Musée d'Orsay; arrive early to avoid the crowds. Then head west to the Palais Bourbon, home of the Assemblée Nationale (the French parliament), and the Hôtel des Invalides, with its impressive Église du Dôme. If you're up for another museum, visit the Musée Rodin; if not, see its rose garden, filled with Rodin's sculptures. Continue east toward the enormous church of St-Sulpice. From here it's just three stops to the Vavin métro station in Montparnasse.

⊙ This won't work on Monday, when the Musée d'Orsay and the Musée Rodin are closed.

© 12

of Paris's villagelike character by exploring Montmartre. Either walk (north along rue du Faubourg Montmartre to rue Notre-Dame de Lorette to rue Fontaine to place Blanche) or take the métro to the Pigalle or Blanche stop. On boulevard de Clichy you'll find the famous Moulin Rouge. Continue up into Montmartre, via place des Abbesses. On this square are two Art Nouveau gems: the church of St-Jean de Montmartre, and the Art Nouveau Guimard entrance to the Abbesses métro station. From here walk through the winding, hilly streets to place du Tertre, and then on to Sacré-Coeur, where there's a tremendous view of the city below.

Bd. Raspail

St-Sulpice

St-Sulpice

Rue de Rennes

Bd. Raspail

Vavin

DAY 4

Begin by visiting Notre-Dame Cathedral and Sainte-Chapelle on Ile de la Cité. Then head over to the neighboring Ile St-Louis and wander the narrow streets. Cross over the Seine to explore the Latin Quarter, using the Panthéon dome as a landmark. Set aside more time if you plan to see the Musée National du Moyen-Age or the Institut du Monde Arabe, relax in the Jardin du Luxembourg, or sip coffee in a neighborhood café. In the afternoon visit the Centre Pompidou and explore the winding streets of the Marais. The Musée Picasso is in one of this old neighborhood's

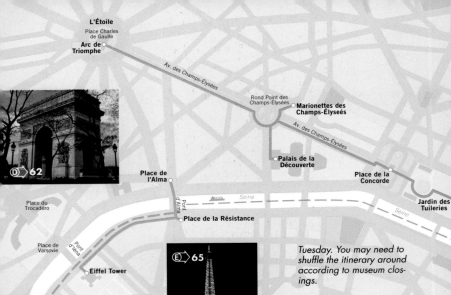

L'Étoile
Place Charles
de Gaulle
Arc de
Triomphe

Av. des Champs-Élysées

Rond Point des
Champs-Élysées

Marionettes des
Champs-Élyseés

Av. des Champs-Élysées

Palais de la
Découverte

Place de la
Concorde

Jardin des
Tuileries

Place de
l'Alma

Place du
Trocadéro

Place de la Résistance

Pont
d'Alma

Seine

Seine

D⟩62

Place de
Varsovie

Pont
d'Iéna

Eiffel Tower

To Bois de
Boulogne

To Parc
André-
Citroën

E⟩65

hôtels particuliers (mansions). The elegant place des Vosges is pleasant for a break. ☺ *Closings make this a problem on Monday (Institut du Monde Arabe), Tuesday (Musée du Moyen-Age, Centre Pompidou, Musée Picasso), and Wednesday (Musée Picasso).*

DAY 5

To get a sense of the splendor in which French royalty lived, spend most of the day visiting Versailles. ☺ *This is fine any day but Monday.*

If You Have More Time

You can attack the smaller museums like the Maillol and the Marmottan and explore the funky Bastille, elegant Passy, and up-and-coming Bercy neighborhoods. Or take the métro to see attractions on the edge of the city: Père-Lachaise Cemetery, the Parc de La Villette, or the Bois de Boulogne or Bois de Vincennes, Paris's two largest parks. Or take a day trip to Fontainebleau, Chartres, or other points of interest around Paris.

If You Have 3 Days

On a first visit, start by following the suggestions for the first two days of the 5-day itinerary above: See the Eiffel Tower, the Arc de Triomphe, Champs-Élysées, and the Jardin des Tuileries on the first day; and tour the Louvre, the Faubourg St-Honoré, the Grand Boulevards, and Montmartre on the second day. On the third day visit the Musée d'Orsay and then Ⓕ Notre-Dame; in the afternoon explore the Latin Quarter.

Paris with Kids

Paris's major museums, like the Louvre and the Musée d'Orsay, can be as engaging as they are educational—as long as you keep your visits short. Many activities and museums are designed especially for children, and some museums even have children's programs. ☺ *Note that many museums are closed on Monday or*

Tuesday. You may need to shuffle the itinerary around according to museum closings.

DAY 1

Give your kids an idea of how Paris was planned by climbing to the top of the Ⓓ Arc de Triomphe. From here work your way down the Champs-Élysées toward place de la Concorde. Stop for a puppet show at the Marionettes des Champs-Élysées, at avenues Matignon and Gabriel, halfway down the Champs. Or head to the Palais de la Découverte, just off the Champs, to catch a planetarium show. Continue walking down the Champs, to the Jardin des Tuileries, where kids can sail boats on a small pond. For an afternoon treat, head for Angélina (on rue de Rivoli), a tearoom famous for its thick hot chocolate. ☺ *If you want to see the puppet show, do this on a Wednesday, Saturday, or Sunday. Skip this on Monday when the Palais de la Découverte is closed.*

DAY 2

In the morning head to the Ⓔ Eiffel Tower for a bird's-eye view of the city. After you descend, either ride on one of the Bateaux Mouches at place de l'Alma, nearby; or brave Les Égouts, the Paris sewers (the tour takes about an hour and departs from place de la Résistance, across the Seine). Next take the métro to the Parc André-Citroën, where there's a computerized "dancing fountain," or to the Bois de

Boulogne, where you'll find a zoo (the Jardin d'Acclimatation), rowboats, and plenty of wide-open space.
☼ *This won't work on Thursday or Friday, when Les Égouts are closed.*

DAY 3

Introduce your kids to Notre-Dame Cathedral; go early so you don't have to wait to get in. Have lunch in the area, and then head nearby, then continue on foot or by bus to the Arènes de Lutèce, one of the few vestiges of the former Roman city. Not far on foot or by métro is the Jardin des Plantes, a botanical garden with the state-of-the-art Grande Galerie de l'Évolution, a museum exhibiting a collection of taxidermy of all kinds of animals. Also just a métro ride away in Montparnasse are the Catacombs, Roman quarries that served as headquarters for the and catch a magic show. Or take in the Centre Pompidou; either see an exhibit (often there are special kids' programs related to the shows) or simply ride the escalator to the top for a great view of Paris. Around the corner, on the Square Igor-Stravinsky, watch the imaginative, moving sculptures in the fountain. Another option is to take the métro from Châtelet–Les-Halles to the Porte de La Villette; in the whimsical park of the same name are an interactive science museum, a museum of musical instruments, an IMAX theater, and

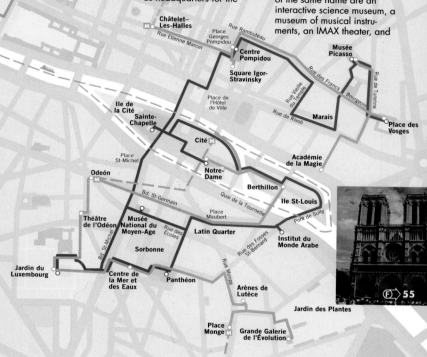

to Berthillon on the Ile St-Louis for some of the city's best ice cream. Afterward cross the Seine and walk or take the métro to the Odéon stop. From here walk around the colonnaded Théâtre de l'Odéon to the Jardin du Luxembourg, where there's a playground, a pond where kids can rent miniature boats, a café, and plenty of places to sit. Ready for more? Walk to the Centre de la Mer et des Eaux, an aquarium French Resistance during World War II.
☼ *Don't try to see the Catacombs on Monday or the Grande Galerie de l'Évolution on Tuesday, when they're closed.*

DAY 4

On Day 4, at the Musée Picasso in the Marais, show your kids the paintings and sculptures of one of France's finest artists. Nearby, pick up a sandwich to eat on a bench in the place des Vosges. If your children are up for another museum, one that's more child-oriented, head for the Académie de la Magie various innovative structures to play on and in.
☼ *Because of closings, do this between Thursday and Sunday: The Parc de La Villette is closed Monday, the Centre Pompidou Tuesday, the Musée Picasso Tuesday and Wednesday, and the Académie de la Magie every day except Wednesday and weekends.*

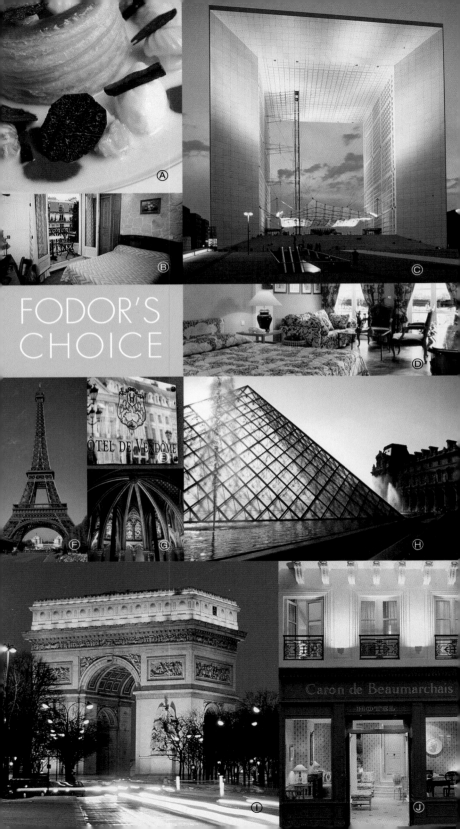

FODOR'S
CHOICE

Even with so many special places in Paris, Fodor's writers and editors have their favorites. Here are a few that stand out.

DINING

Ⓐ **Alain Ducasse.** With culinary delights so delicious even Parisians swoon, this is the most talked-about restaurant in France today, thanks to the masterpieces of superstar chef Ducasse. $$$$ ☞ p. 168

Les Ambassadeurs. Looking as if it was airlifted piece by piece from Versailles, the restaurant of the Hôtel Crillon delivers *le grand luxe* on every score. $$$$ ☞ p. 170

Le Grand Véfour. Back when Napoléon dined here, this was the most beautiful restaurant in Paris. Guess what? It still is. $$$$ ☞ p. 151

Pierre Gagnaire. Legendary chef Pierre Gagnaire brings together at least three different tastes and textures in each sensational dish. $$$$ ☞ p. 170

Taillevent. Perhaps the most traditional of all Paris luxury restaurants, this grande dame is suddenly the object of a certain uncharacteristic buzz, since the arrival of new chef Michel Del Burgo. $$$$ ☞ p. 171

Au Trou Gascon. Feast on first-rate Southwestern specialties—such as superb cassoulet—in a pretty Belle Epoque setting. $$$ ☞ p. 175

Hélène Darroze. She is Paris's newest culinary star—taste her duck fois-gras confit with a chutney of exotic fruits, and you'll know why. $$$ ☞ p. 164

La Grande Armée. The decor here—a Napoléon III bordello extravaganza—is almost more delicious than the food. $$ ☞ p. 180

Au Bon Accueil. The excellent, reasonably priced *cuisine du marché* (a menu based on what's in the markets) has made this bistro a hit. $–$$ ☞ p. 167

Les Pipos. With conversation that flows as freely as the wine, this is everything you can ask for in a Latin Quarter bistro. $–$$ ☞ p. 163

LODGING

Costes. Baron de Rothschild hasn't invited you this time? No matter—stay here at Paris's most stylishly sumptuous hotel and you won't know the difference. $$$$ ☞ p. 191

Ⓔ **Vendôme.** The Second Empire–style rooms are simply sumptuous. $$$–$$$$ ☞ p. 197

Ⓓ **Relais St-Germain.** Rooms in this hotel are named for French literary heroes and are at least twice the size of those you'll find elsewhere at this price level. $$$ ☞ p. 204

Le Tourville. Here is a rare find: a cozy, stylish hotel that doesn't cost a fortune. $$–$$$ ☞ p. 206

Ⓙ **Caron de Beaumarchais.** Beaumarchais's work is the theme of this hotel in the heart of the Marais. $$ ☞ p. 200

Esméralda. Once the ultimate Left Bank *hôtel de charme* and set in a fusty 17th-century building across from Notre-Dame, this has long been cherished for its cozy and eccentric style. $$ ☞ p. 201

Victoire Opéra. This hotel, with its very Parisian cream-color facade and wrought-iron balconies, has it all—intimacy, comfort, affordability, and a delightful location. $$ ☞ p. 198

Ⓑ **Familia.** The hospitable Gaucheron family bends over backward for you at this pleasant Latin Quarter hotel. $ ☞ p. 202

CHURCHES

Église du Dôme. Under the dome of this commanding Baroque church, part of Les Invalides, Napoléon rests in imperial splendor. ☞ p. 117

Notre-Dame Cathedral. At this historic church, climb to the towers for a glimpse of the gargoyles and for wonderful views of Paris. ☞ p. 55

Ⓖ **Sainte-Chapelle.** Built by Louis IX to house what he believed to be the Crown of Thorns from Christ's crucifixion and fragments of the True Cross, Sainte-Chapelle shimmers with stained glass. ☞ p. 58

MONUMENTS

Ⓘ **Arc de Triomphe.** Commissioned by Napoléon I as a monument to his military might, this is the world's largest triumphal arch. ☞ p. 62

Ⓕ **Eiffel Tower.** The 10,000-ton result of a contest held to design a tower for the 1889 World Exposition, the Eiffel Tower is the most-recognized landmark in Paris. ☞ p. 65

Ⓗ **The Louvre's glass pyramid.** This modern glass structure, I. M. Pei's new entrance to the museum, was extremely controversial when first unveiled. ☞ p. 55

VIEWS TO REMEMBER

The Eiffel Tower from Trocadéro. This view of the Eiffel Tower is unsurpassed and is particularly pretty when the fountains in Trocadéro plaza are on. ☞ p. 65

Ⓒ **The Grande Arche from Esplanade de la Défense.** The colossally elegant triumphal arch, shaped like a hollow cube, towers above an immense flight of white marble steps. It's even better at night. ☞ p. 144

Notre-Dame from the Pont de l'Archevêché. Standing on the bridge behind Notre-Dame, you get breathtaking views of the east end of the cathedral ringed by flying buttresses, surmounted by the spire. ☞ p. 55

Paris spread out beneath Sacré-Coeur in Montmartre. The basilica is set on the highest hill in Paris, providing extensive views of the city. ☞ p. 135

St-Gervais–St-Protais from the bottom of rue des Barres. The charming view of the flying buttresses above the roofs and cobbles of this pedestrian street is quintessential Paris. ☞ p. 104

1 EXPLORING PARIS

Radiating 2,000 years of history and culture, Paris intrigues, astonishes, provokes, overwhelms . . . and gets under your skin. It is the apex of architectural beauty, artistic expression, and culinary delight, and it knows it. As drop-dead arrogant as the Arc de Triomphe, as disarmingly quaint as a lace-curtain bistro, it seduces newcomers with Latin lover style—and its subtle siren song keeps calling you back. Wink at the Mona Lisa, look gargoyles in the eye at Notre-Dame, then be sure to take a dreamy time-out for a *café crème* at a sidewalk café.

Y OU'LL ALWAYS HAVE PARIS. Like the champagne-frosted idyll
Bogie and Bergman reminisced about in *Casablanca,* your time
in this highly charged, endlessly resonant city will remain a lifelong reference point. Over and over, as in a reverie, you'll conjure its
sensorial assault—the sting in the nostril of a fresh-lit Gitane cigarette,
the rippling of lights on the misty Seine, the confetti flutter of antique
prints over a *bouquiniste*'s stand, the aromatic bedlam of a street food
market, at the Louvre, the waves crashing on the prow of an epic Géricault canvas. And you'll go all moony again.

Revised and
updated by
Simon Hewitt

Introduction by
Nancy Coons

Whether weaned on Hemingway or Henry James, Doisneau or Cartier-
Bresson, Brassaï or Cecil Beaton, Westerners share an image of Paris
as the city of lovers, from Rodin's brawny duo to smolder-eyed apache
dancers, from *La Bohème's* Mimi and Rodolfo weeping in a chilly gar-
ret to Anaïs Nin's flappers naked under fur. Sartre and de Beauvoir!
Montand and Signoret! Belmondo and Seberg! Add the Hollywood pro-
paganda machine, and the world fell hopelessly, helplessly head over
heels: who could stand firm in the face of Leslie Caron's blushes as she
danced in Gene Kelly's arms along the Seine in *An American in Paris,*
or Audrey Hepburn's fine-boned take on the *Winged Victory* in *Funny
Face,* or the punched-in-the-gut look on Bogie's face in *Casablanca* when
the German tanks roll in?

Yet there's always a delicious glint of gaslight casting a louche pall over
the romance, a hint of the demimonde, the backstreet, the black-
stockinged knee under a naughty froth of petticoats. After all, these
people were not married. And there lies the yang to Paris's sweet, romantic yin: its sloe-eyed sophistication, its worldliness, its savoir faire.
Business as usual in a country where the love-child of the president of
the Republic publicly attends his funeral—but deliciously concentrated
in its capital city, and tantalizing to strait-laced visitors dreaming of
dalliance. . . .

The real love affair is with Paris itself, and it can play you like a violin. Around every corner, down every *ruelle,* or little street, lies a res-
onance-in-waiting. You can stand on the rue du Faubourg St-Honoré
at the very spot where Edmond Rostand set Ragueneau's pastry shop
in *Cyrano de Bergerac.* You can peruse the letters of Madame de Sévigné in her erstwhile *hôtel particulier* (private mansion), now the Musée
Carnavalet. You can hear Racine resound in the ringing, hair-raising
diction of the Comédie Française. You can breathe in the fumes of hubris
before the extravagant porphyry tomb of Napoléon at Les Invalides.
You can try to resist genuflecting in the Panthéon, where religion
bowed down before France's great post-Revolution statesmen. You can
climb into César Franck's organ loft at the church of Ste-Clothilde. You
can gaze through the gate at the Ile St-Louis mansion where Voltaire
honed his wit, and then lay a garland on Oscar Wilde's grave.

No matter which way you head, any trip through Paris will be a voy-
age of discovery. But choosing the Paris of your dreams is a bit like
choosing a perfume or cologne. Is it something young and dashing you
want, or something elegant and worldly? Something sporty or strictly
for glamorous evenings? No matter—beneath touristy Paris, historic
Paris, fashion-conscious Paris, pretentious bourgeois Paris, thrifty,
practical lower-class Paris, the legendary bohemian arty Paris of undying attraction, you will find your own Paris: vivid, exciting, often unforgettable. Veterans know that Paris is a city of vast, noble perspectives
and intimate, ramshackle streets, of formal *espaces vertes,* or green open

spaces, and quiet squares. The combination of the pompous and the private is one of the secrets of its perennial pull.

Another is its size. Paris is relatively small as capitals go, with distances between many of its major sights and museums invariably walkable. The city's principal tourist axis is less than 6½ km (4 mi) long, running parallel to the north bank of the Seine from the Arc de Triomphe to the Bastille. In fact, the best way to get to know Paris is on foot, although public transportation—particularly the métro subway system—is excellent. Serious explorers should buy a *Plan de Paris* booklet: a city map-guide with a street-name index that also shows métro stations (note that all métro stations have a detailed neighborhood map just inside the entrance).

To help you digest Paris in sensible bites, this chapter is divided into 12 neighborhood walks. For the first-timer, there will always be several "musts" at the top of the list—the Louvre, Notre-Dame, and the Eiffel Tower, among them—but a visit to Paris will never be quite as simple as a quick look at a few landmarks. Every *quartier*, or neighborhood, has its own treasures, and you should be ready to explore— a very pleasant prospect in this most elegant of cities. It is no exaggeration to say that the most assiduous explorers of Paris are the Parisians themselves. Each quartier has its own personality and unsuspected charms, which are discovered best by footpower. You can follow our suggested "good walks," but ultimately your route will be marked by your own preferences and your curiosity—or your state of fatigue. You can wander for hours without getting bored—though not, perhaps, without getting lost. By the time you have seen only a few neighborhoods, drinking in the rich variety they have to offer, you should not only be culturally replete but downright exhausted, and hungry, too. Again, take your cue from the Parisians, and plan out your next move at a sidewalk café. So you've heard stories of a friend of a friend who paid $6 for a coffee at a famous café? So what? What you're paying for is time—to watch the intricate drama of Parisian street life unfold in front of you. Hemingway knew the rules: he'd be just another sports writer if the café waiters of Paris had hovered around him impatiently.

After enjoying your ringside seat at the street theater, you're ready to explore the city as a living art gallery. Paris provides, at nearly every turn, a familiar work of art, framed in reality: *promeneurs* in the Bois de Boulogne in perfect pointillist silhouette, broad street perspectives flashing from gold to pink to silver under scudding Impressionist clouds, a woman's abstracted stare over a glass of green liquid at a Montmartre café, and fine-boned ladies in black and white sniffing delicately at Guerlain's perfume counter.

You'll learn it's all so familiar and all so terribly . . . Parisian. *Rillettes* (preserved goose spread) and *poilâne* (the ubiquitous chewy sourdough bread of baker Lionel Poilâne) and Beaujolais. Ranks of posters, eight at a time, plastered over scaffolding. The discreet hiss of the métro's rubber wheels. The street sweeper guiding rags along the rain gutters with a twig broom. The coins in the saucer by the *pissoir*. The tantalizing hidden carriage courtyards lined with boxwood, gravel, and Peugeots. The shriek of the espresso machine as it steams the milk for your café crème, the flip-lid sugar bowl on the zinc bar. The illuminated monuments looming like Maya idols. The lovers buried in each others' necks along the Seine.

Yes, you'll always have Paris. So what are you waiting for?

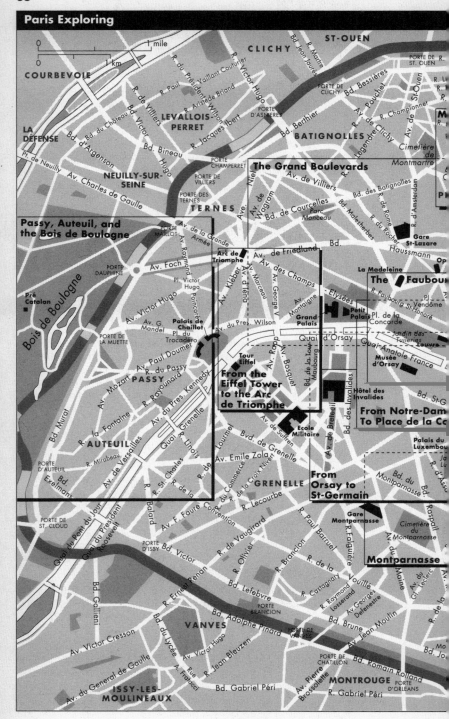

The Grand Boulevards

Passy, Auteuil, and the Bois de Boulogne

La Madeleine

The Faubou

From the Eiffel Tower to the Arc de Triomphe

From Notre-Dam To Place de la Co

From Orsay to St-Germain

Montparnasse

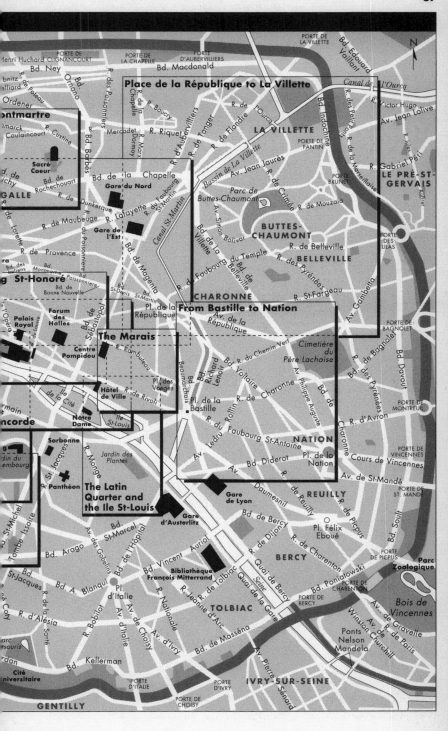

Place de la République to La Villette

From Bastille to Nation

The Marais

The Latin Quarter and the Ile St-Louis

PORTE DE LA VILLETTE

Canal de l'Ourcq

PORTE DE LA CHAPELLE

PORTE D'AUBERVILLIERS

Bd. Macdonald

PORTE DE LA VILLETTE

Bd. Ney

R. des Poissonniers

R. d'Aubervilliers

Bd. Ordener

LA VILLETTE

Victor Hugo

Av. Jean Lolive

Bd. Indochine

R. des Fêtes

R. Gabriel Péri

LE PRÉ-ST-GERVAIS

Montmartre

Caulaincourt

R. Custine

Sacré Coeur

Bd. de Rochechouart

PIGALLE

R. de Maubeuge

Bd. de la Chapelle

Gare du Nord

R. Lafayette

Bd. de Magenta

Parc de Buttes-Chaumont

BUTTES-CHAUMONT

R. de Belleville

R. de Mouzaïa

PORTE DES LILAS

R. de Provence

St-Honoré

Palais Royal

Forum des Halles

Centre Pompidou

Gare de l'Est

Canal St-Martin

BELLEVILLE

R. des Pyrénées

R. St-Fargeau

Av. Gambetta

PORTE DE BAGNOLET

CHARONNE

Pl. de la République

Av. de la République

Cimetière du Père Lachaise

Bd. Voltaire

Bd. de Charonne

Bd. des Pyrénées

Bd. Davout

PORTE DE MONTREUIL

R. d'Avron

Hôtel de Ville

Pl. des Vosges

R. de Rivoli

Île St-Louis

Notre Dame

Pl. de la Bastille

R. du Faubourg St-Antoine

R. de Charonne

NATION

Pl. de la Nation

Cours de Vincennes

PORTE DE VINCENNES

PORTE DE ST-MANDE

Sorbonne

R. St-Jacques

Panthéon

Jardin des Plantes

Bd. Diderot

Av. de St-Mandé

Gare de Lyon

REUILLY

R. de Reuilly

R. de Picpus

PORTE DE PICPUS

Gare d'Austerlitz

Daumesnil

Bd. de Bercy

Pl. Félix Eboué

Parc Zoologique

Bd. Arago

Bibliothèque François Mitterrand

BERCY

R. de Charenton

PORTE DE CHARENTON

Bois de Vincennes

Av. de Gravelle

R. d'Alésia

Pl. d'Italie

Quai de Bercy

PORTE DE BERCY

Ponts Nelson Mandela

Cité universitaire

TOLBIAC

Bd. de Masséna

IVRY-SUR-SEINE

GENTILLY

PORTE D'ITALIE

PORTE DE CHOISY

PORTE D'IVRY

Paris with Arrondissements

COURBEVOIE

LA DÉFENSE

ST-OUEN

CLICHY

LEVALLOIS-PERRET

Bd. de Villiers
Bd. du Château
Bd. Victor Hugo
Bd. Bineau
Pl. de Neuilly
Av. Charles de Gaulle

NEUILLY-SUR-SEINE

PORTE DE NEUILLY

R. du Président Vaillant Couturier
R. Paul
R. Aristide Briand
Av. Jacques Ibert
Av. Victor Hugo

PORTE D'ASNIÈRES

PORTE DE CLICHY

Bd. Bessières
Bd. Berthier
Bd. Jean Jaurès
Av. de Clichy
R. Championnet
Légende Clichy
R.

PORTE DE ST. OUEN
R. Henri
R. Liebn
R. Bell
R. O

R. Lam
R. C

BATIGNOLLES

17e

Cimetière de Montmartre

PORTE CHAMPERRET

Av. de Villiers
Bd. des Batignolles
R. de Rome
R. d'Amsterdam
R. de Rocher

Cliche

PIG

Gare St-Lazare

Opéra

8e

TERNES

PORTE DE VILLIERS

PORTE DES TERNES

Av. Niel
Av. de Wagram
Bd. de Courcelles
Parc Monceau
Bd. Malesherbes
Bd.
Haussmann

La Madeleine

PORTE MAILLOT

Av. de la Grande Armée

Arc de Triomphe

Av. de Friedland

Pl. Vendôme

PORTE DAUPHINE

Av. Foch

Pl. Victor Hugo

Av. Kléber
Av. d'Iéna
Av. Marceau
Av. des Champs - Elysées
Av. George V
Av. Montaigne
R. Faubourg St-Honoré

Grand Palais
Petit Palais
Pl. de la Concorde

Jardin des Tuileries
Louvre

Bois de Boulogne

Pré Catalan

PORTE DE LA MUETTE

16e

PASSY

Av. Victor Hugo
Av. G. Mandel
Av. Paul Doumer
R. du Passy

Palais de Chaillot
Pl. du Trocadéro

Av. du Pres. Wilson

Tour Eiffel

Quai d'Orsay
Quai Anatole France

Musée d'Orsay

7e

6e

Av. Mozart

Av. Rapp
Bd. de la Tour Maubourg

Hôtel des Invalides

Bd. St-Germ

la Fontaine

Av. du Pres. Kennedy

R. Raynouard

Av. de Suffren

Av. de Breteuil
Bd. des Invalides

AUTEUIL

R. Mirabeau
Av. de Versailles

Quai

R. Grenelle
R. Linois
R. St. Charles
R. de la

Ecole Militaire

Bvd. de Grenelle

Av. Emile Zola

Palais du Luxembourg

Jardin
Luxen

PORTE D'AUTEUIL

Bd. Exelmans

Lourmel
R. du Commerce
R. de la Croix Nivert
R. Lecourbe

GRENELLE

Bd. du Montparnasse

PORTE DE ST. CLOUD

Quai du Pont du Jour
Quai du Président Roosevelt

R. Balard

Av. F. Faure
Convention

R. de Vaugirard
R. Olivier

Gare Montparnasse

Bd.
Raspail

Cimetière du Montparnasse

PORTE D'ISSY

Bd. Victor

R. Brancion

15e

R. Paul Barruel
R. Falguière

14e

Av. du Maine

Av. du Gl. Leclerc
Av. René Coty

Bd. Galliéni

R. Ernest Renan

Bd. Lefebvre

PORTE BRANCION

R. Castagnary
R. Vouillé
R. Raymond Losserand
Av. Georges Defenestre
Bd. Brune

R. de la

VANVES

Bd. Adolphe Pinard

PORTE DE VANVES

Av. Jean Moulin

Par
Montsc
Bd. Jourd

Av. Victor Cresson

Bd. du Lycée
Av. Victor Hugo
Rue
R. Jean Bleuzen
A. Fratacci

PORTE DE CHATILLON

Bd. Romain Rolland

MONTROUGE

PORTE D'ORLEANS

Uni

ISSY-LES-MOULINEAUX

Av. du General de Gaulle

Bd. Gabriel Péri

Av. Pierre Brossolette
R. Gabriel Péri

FROM NOTRE-DAME TO
THE PLACE DE LA CONCORDE

No matter how one approaches Paris—historically, geographically, emotionally—it is the Seine River that beckons us. The city owes both its development and much of its visual appeal to the Seine, which weaves through its very heart. Each bank of the river has its own personality; the Rive Droite (Right Bank), with its spacious boulevards and formal buildings, generally has a more sober and genteel feel than the more carefree Rive Gauche (Left Bank), to the south. In between, the river harbors two tiny islands that stand at the center of the city—the Ile de la Cité and the Ile St-Louis. Both seem to be gliding downriver, as if the latter were being towed by the former. It is the Ile de la Cité that forms the historic ground zero of Paris.

It was here, for obvious reasons of defense, and in the hope of controlling the trade that passed along the Seine, that the earliest inhabitants of Paris, the Gaulish tribe of the Parisii, settled in about 250 BC. They called their little home Lutetia, meaning "settlement surrounded by water." In the year 53 BC Julius Caesar, in fact, mentioned the settlement of Lutetia, and it was to this island city that he commanded the leaders of the Gaulish tribes to pay him homage, before his general, Labienus, ruthlessly crushed them. Whereas the Ile St-Louis is today largely residential, the Ile de la Cité remains deeply historic and is the site of the first church of Paris—the great, brooding Cathedral of Notre-Dame. Napoléon was crowned here, and kings and princes married before its great altar. The cathedral is the symbolic heart of the city, if not the symbolic heart of France itself, as all roads throughout the realm converge here and are marked by a stone in the plaza before the church. Most of the island's other medieval buildings fell victim to town planner Baron Haussmann's ambitious rebuilding program of the 1860s. Among the rare survivors are the jewel-like Sainte-Chapelle, a vision of shimmering stained glass, and the Conciergerie, the former city prison where Marie-Antoinette and other victims of the French Revolution spent their last days.

If Notre-Dame represents Church, another major attraction of this walk—the Louvre—symbolizes State. This royal palace came into existence in the mid-13th century, when Philippe-Auguste built it as a fortress to protect the city's western flank. It was not until pleasure-loving François I began a partial rebuilding of this original rude fortress in the early 16th century that today's Louvre began gradually to take shape. A succession of French rulers were responsible for filling this immense, symmetrical structure, now the largest museum in the world as well as one of the easiest to get lost in, with the world's greatest paintings and works of art. Right in the middle of the Louvre's main courtyard is I. M. Pei's shimmering glass pyramid, reminding us that while Parisians take their role as custodians of a glorious heritage most seriously, they are equally intent on bequeathing something to the future.

Before you leave Notre-Dame, take a cue from Victor Hugo and climb the 387 steps of one of its towers to the former haunts of its legendary hunchback, Quasimodo. You'll be rewarded with the ultimate view of Paris—unforgettably framed by the stone gargoyles created by Viollet-le-Duc. From here, one can see how the city—like the trunk of a tree developing new rings—has spread out in circles from the island on which you now stand. To the north is the Butte Montmartre; to the west, the Arc de Triomphe at the head of the Champs-Élysées; to the south, the towers of St-Sulpice and the domes of the Invalides, the Panthéon, and the Luxembourg palace. Drinking in the view, you can remain here for hours in a pleasant state of medieval suspended animation, but don't delay—you have too much else to see ahead.

Numbers in the text correspond to numbers in the margin and on the From Notre-Dame to the Place de la Concorde map.

A Good Walk

The best approach to the Ile de la Cité is to cross the Pont au Double from quai de Montebello (St-Michel Métro stop or RER). This bridge leads to the large, pedestrian place du Parvis. To the right, lovers of Old Paris will want to explore rue du Cloître-Notre-Dame, a street lined with picturesque houses spared demolition by Baron Haussmann in the 19th century. Place du Parvis is regarded by the French as *kilomètre zéro*, the spot from which all distances to and from the city are officially measured, and makes a fitting setting for the regal cathedral of **Notre-Dame** ①. Study the magnificent facade, explore the interior, then toil up the steps to the towers for a gargoyle-framed view of the heart of Paris. History and art buffs will want to visit the **Musée de Notre-Dame** ② across the street. A walk around the outside of Notre-Dame sets the whole place in proportion, with the gardens between the cathedral and the Seine offering splendid views of the sophisticated medieval masonry. Head through the gardens to the nearby **Square Jean-XXIII** ③ and turn right to cross Pont de l'Archevêché for the best view of all, with Notre-Dame's flying buttresses (archlike structural supports enabling the walls to soar heavenward) lending the heavy apse a magical lightness.

Walk (or dance—this is where Leslie Caron and Gene Kelly so memorably pas-de-deuxed in *An American in Paris*) along quai de la Tournelle until you reach the Petit Pont, then cross back over the Seine and head straight on to rue de Lutèce. Turn left here, past the flower market, and continue on to the boulevard du Palais and the imposing **Palais de Justice** ④, the 19th-century law courts; you can wander around the buildings among the black-robed lawyers or attend a court hearing. But the real interest here is the **Sainte-Chapelle** ⑤, a medieval masterpiece tucked away to the left of the main courtyard. Turn left as you leave the Palais de Justice, then left again onto quai de l'Horloge, named for the oldest clock (*horloge*) in Paris, marking time since 1370 from high up on the **Conciergerie** ⑥, the prison where Marie-Antoinette and other blue bloods awaited their slice of history at the guillotine. Quai de l'Horloge leads to rue de Harlay and historic **place Dauphine** ⑦. Cross this old-fashioned square to **square du Vert-Galant** ⑧, with its equestrian statue of Henri IV. Steps on the right lead down to the waterside where Vedette motorboats set off for their tours along the Seine.

Cross **Pont Neuf** ⑨—actually the oldest bridge in Paris—to the Rive Droite and turn left along quai du Louvre, past the Art Deco Samaritaine department store, to reach the great **Louvre** ⑩ museum, entering through the frigidly elegant Baroque East Front designed by Charles Perrault in the 1660s. This entry portal leads into Cour Carrée, a grandiose courtyard (which has something of the assured feel of an Oxford or Cambridge quadrangle, though on a much grander scale). Through the massive archway of the domed Pavillon de l'Horloge, straight ahead, you can make out the controversial main entrance to the Louvre: I. M. Pei's famous glass pyramid. Settle in for a visit to the home of the *Venus de Milo,* the *Winged Victory of Samothrace,* and the mystifying countenance of the *Mona Lisa.* At the point when one priceless Titian painting begins to look like the next, head back to the

From Notre-Dame to Place de la Concorde

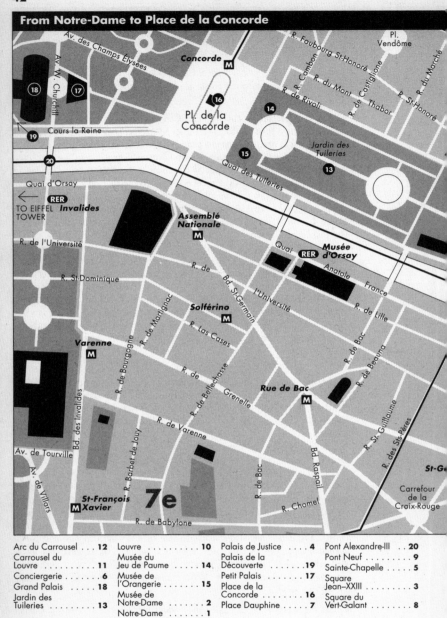

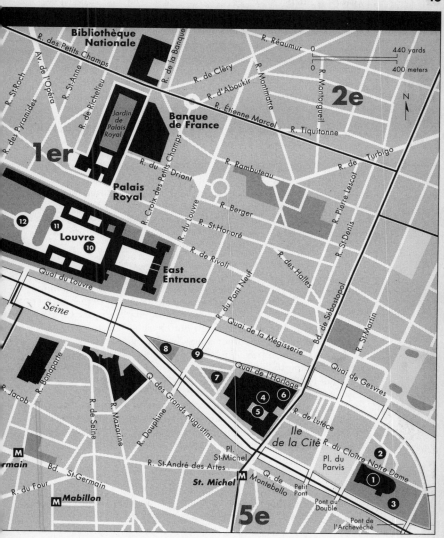

Bibliothèque Nationale

R. des Petits Champs

Av. de l'Opéra

R. St-Roch

R. St-Anne

R. de Richelieu

R. de la Banque

R. de Cléry

R. d'Aboukir

R. Montmartre

R. Réaumur

0

440 yards

0

400 meters

R. Montorgueil

2e

N

R. des Pyramides

Jardin de Palais Royal

Banque de France

R. Étienne Marcel

R. Tiquitonne

R. de Turbigo

1er

R. du Louvre

R. Rambuteau

R. Pierre Lescot

R. du Driant

R. Croix des Petits Champs

R. Berger

R. St-Honoré

Palais Royal

R. St-Denis

⑫ ⑪ ⑩ **Louvre**

R. de Rivoli

R. des Halles

East Entrance

R. du Pont Neuf

Bd. de Sébastopol

R. St-Martin

Quai du Louvre

Seine

Quai de la Mégisserie

R. Bonaparte

⑧ ⑨

Quai de l'Horloge

Quai de Gesvres

R. Jacob

R. de Seine

R. Mazarine

R. Dauphine

Q. des Grands Augustins

⑦

④ ⑥
⑤

R. de Lutèce

Île de la Cité

R. du Cloître Notre Dame

Ⓜ *rmain*

Pl. St-Michel

②

Pl. du Parvis

①

Bd. St-Germain

R. St-André des Artes

Ⓜ *St. Michel*

Q. de Montebello

Petit Pont

③

R. du Four

Ⓜ **Mabillon**

5e

Pont au Double

Pont de l'Archevêché

main concourse under the pyramid and make for the **Carrousel du Louvre** ⑪, an underground mall with its snack bars and designer boutiques fanning out from a smaller, inverted pyramid. If you exit by the **Arc du Carrousel** ⑫—a small relation to the distant Arc de Triomphe— you'll be ideally placed to assess the grand vista (aligned *almost* perfectly) that leads from the Louvre pyramid, through the Arc du Carrousel to the Concorde obelisk, Champs-Élysées, and Arc de Triomphe, with the shadowy towers of La Défense just visible behind.

Continue west, past eccentric diagonal hedges, to the **Jardin des Tuileries** ⑬, or Tuileries Gardens, with its manicured lawns, fountains, rows of trees, and regiments of statues old and new. To the north side is arcaded rue de Rivoli, built for Napoléon to honor his Italian conquests. Two smallish buildings stand sentinel by place de la Concorde, at the far end of the Tuileries. Nearest rue de Rivoli is the **Musée du Jeu de Paume** ⑭, host to outstanding exhibits of contemporary art. The almost identical building nearer the Seine is the **Musée de l'Orangerie** ⑮, containing the largest versions of Monet's *Water Lilies* (unfortunately, the museum is closed for renovation until the end of 2002).

The two museums gaze down on one of the world's most opulent squares, **place de la Concorde** ⑯, centered by its gilt-tipped Egyptian obelisk, with the Seine to the south, the Champs-Élysées and Arc de Triomphe to the west, and rue Royale and the Madeleine church to the north. If you don't have a bad case of gallery feet by now, continue up the Champs-Élysées for 500 yards and turn left onto avenue Winston-Churchill. Looming over the street corner is Jean Cardot's giant bronze statue of General de Gaulle, unveiled in November 2000. On the left is the **Petit Palais** ⑰, facing the larger, glass-roofed **Grand Palais** ⑱—two museums built for the Exposition Universelle of 1900 and currently under restoration. The back of the Grand Palais—the entrance is on avenue Franklin-D.-Roosevelt—houses the **Palais de la Découverte** ⑲, a science museum with a planetarium. A 10-ft statue of Churchill, unveiled in 1998 by Queen Elizabeth II, gazes toward the Seine and the **Pont Alexandre-III** ⑳. With luck, by the time you reach this exuberant Belle Epoque bridge, you'll be greeted with a memorable sunset to set off the gleaming, gold-leafed Invalides dome that looms up ahead.

TIMING

Allowing for toiling up towers, dancing down quays, and musing at Mona Lisa, this 5½-km (3½-mi) walk will take a full day—enabling you to reach Pont Alexandre-III just before the blue hour of dusk.

Sights to See

⑫ **Arc du Carrousel.** This small triumphal arch between the Louvre and the Tuileries was erected by Napoléon from 1806 to 1808. The four bronze horses on top were originally the famous gilded horses that Napoléon looted from Venice; when these were returned in 1815, Bosio designed four new ones harnessed to a chariot, driven by a goddess symbolizing the Restoration (of the monarchy). *Métro: Palais-Royal.*

⑪ **Carrousel du Louvre.** Part of the early '90s Louvre renovation program, this subterranean shopping complex is centered on an inverted glass pyramid (overlooked by the regional Ile-de-France tourist office) and contains a wide range of stores, spaces for fashion shows (this is Paris, after all), an auditorium, and a huge parking garage. At lunchtime, museum visitors rush to the mall-style food court where fast food goes international. Note that you can get into the museum (and avoid some lines) by entering through the mall. ⊠ *Entrance on rue de Rivoli or by the Arc du Carrousel. Métro: Palais-Royal.*

⑥ Conciergerie. Bringing a tear to the eyes of ancien régime devotées, this is the famous prison in which dukes and duchesses, lords and ladies, and, most famously, Queen Marie-Antoinette were all imprisoned during the French Revolution and ultimately carted off to the guillotine. By the end of the Reign of Terror (1793–95), countless others fell foul of the revolutionaries, including their own leaders, Danton and Robespierre. Originally part of the royal palace on the Ile de la Cité, the turreted medieval building still holds Marie-Antoinette's cell (with some objects connected with the ill-fated queen); a chapel, embellished with the initials M. A., occupies the true site of her confinement. Out of one of these windows, Toni (the queen's nickname) notoriously saw her best friend, the Comtesse de Lamballe—lover of the arts and daughter of the richest duke in France—torn to pieces by a wild mob, her dismembered limbs then displayed on pikes. Elsewhere are the courtyard and fountain where victims of "The Terror" spent their final days playing piquet, writing letters to their loved ones, and waiting for the dreaded climb up the staircase to the Chamber of the Revolutionary Council to hear their final verdict. You can also visit the guardroom, complete with hefty Gothic vaulting and intricately carved columns, and the monumental Salle des Gens d'Armes, whence a short corridor leads to the kitchen, with its four vast fireplaces. The building's name derives from the governor, or *concierge,* of the palace, whose considerable income was swollen by the privilege he enjoyed of renting out shops and workshops. ✉ *1 quai de l'Horloge,* ☎ *01–53–73–78–50.* 🎫 *35 frs/€5.34, joint ticket with Ste-Chapelle 50 frs/€7.63.* ☉ *Apr.–Sept., daily 9:30–6:30; Oct.–Mar., daily 10–5. Métro: Cité.*

⑱ Grand Palais. With its curved glass roof and florid Belle Epoque ornament, the Grand Palais is unmistakable when approached from either the Seine or the Champs-Élysées and forms an attractive duo with the Petit Palais on the other side of avenue Winston-Churchill. Both these stone buildings, adorned with mosaics and sculpted friezes, were built for the world's fair of 1900, and, as with the Eiffel Tower, were not intended to remain as permanent additions to the city. But once they were up, no one seemed inclined to take them down. Today, the atmospheric iron-and-glass interior of the Grand Palais plays host to major exhibitions but was closed for renovation in 1994 and is unlikely to reopen before 2003. ✉ *Av. Winston-Churchill. Métro: Champs-Élysées–Clemenceau.*

🦆 ⑬ Jardin des Tuileries (Tuileries Gardens). Monet and Renoir captured this impressive garden—really more of a long park—with paint and brush, Left Bank songstresses warble about its beauty, and all Parisians know it as a charming place to stroll and survey the surrounding cityscape. The planting of the Tuileries—the name comes from an ancient clay pit formerly on this spot that supplied material for many of the tile roofs of Paris—is typically French: formal and neatly patterned, with statues, rows of trees, and gravel paths, often adorned with a string quartet or jugglers entertaining large crowds on weekends. No wonder the Impressionists liked this city park—note how the gray, austere light of Paris makes green trees look even greener. *Bordered by quai des Tuileries, pl. de la Concorde, rue de Rivoli, and the Louvre. Métro: Tuileries.*

NEED A BREAK? Stop off for a snack or lunch at **Dame Tartine,** one of the two designer brasseries erected in the Tuileries in the late '90s (it's on the left as you arrive from the place de la Concorde). With its glass-paneled walls and roof and light wood and aluminum decor, the restaurant is sober and airy. The cuisine is inventive—try the lamb flan with tomato puree—and a carafe of red Ventoux from the Rhône offers good value. You can also eat outdoors in the leafy shade.

★ ⑩ **Louvre.** Leonardo da Vinci's *Mona Lisa* and *Virgin and Saint Anne,* Van Eyck's *Madonna of Chancellor Rolin,* Giorgione's *Concert Champêtre,* and Delacroix's *Liberty Guiding the People* . . . you get the picture. This is the world's greatest art museum—and the largest. In days of yore, couples would arrive at its front door, race along its miles of corridors—passing the *Venus de Milo, Winged Victory,* and the *Mona Lisa*—and forty minutes later, collapse while exclaiming, "At last, we have seen the Louvre!" Today, of course, nearly everyone respects the fact that you don't go to the Louvre to speed past major milestones in civilization. Many thousands of treasures are newly cleaned and lit, so plan on seeing it all—from the red brocaded Napoléon III salons to the fabled Egyptian collection, from the 186-carat Regent Diamond to the rooms crowded with Botticellis, Caravaggios, Poussins, and Géricaults. After three decades of renovations, the Louvre is now a coherent, unified structure and search parties no longer need to be sent in to find you and bring you out.

To get into the Louvre, you may have to wait in two long lines: one outside the Pyramide entrance portal and another downstairs at the ticket booths. You can avoid the first by entering through the Carrousel du Louvre, but you can't avoid the second. Your ticket will get you into any and all of the wings as many times as you like during one day. As enormous as the Louvre is, we've outlined a simple guide in the following pages that is broken up by location (wing, floor, collection, and room number). If you want a more exhaustively comprehensive guide, the museum bookstore sells—in addition to the general maps at the information desk—a plethora of books and leaflets in English.

The Louvre is much more than a museum—it is a saga that began centuries ago. Originally built as a fortress by Philippe-Auguste in the 13th century, it was not until the reign of pleasure-loving François I, 300 years later, that today's Louvre gradually began to take shape. Through the years, Henri IV (1589–1610), Louis XIII (1610–43), Louis XIV (1643–1715), Napoléon I (1804–14), and Napoléon III (1852–70) all contributed to its construction. Before rampaging revolutionaries burned part of it down during the bloody Paris Commune of 1871, the building was even larger. The open section facing the Tuileries Gardens was originally the Palais des Tuileries, the main Paris residence of the royal family.

The uses to which the building has been put have been almost equally varied. Though Charles V (1364–80) made the Louvre his residence—parts of the original medieval fortress have been excavated and can be seen during your visit—later French kings preferred to live elsewhere, mainly in the Loire Valley. Even after François I decided to make the Louvre his permanent home, and accordingly embarked on an ambitious rebuilding program (most of which came to nothing), the Louvre never became more than a secondary palace.

The construction of the stately Cour Carrée (Square Court), mainly during the reign of Louis XIII, marked the beginning of the Louvre as we see it today. When a competition for architects to design a suitably imposing east facade was held in 1668, a young draftsman named Claude Perrault teamed up with the seasoned illustrator and painter Charles Le Brun to produce the winning proposal. You'd have thought its muscular rhythms would have wowed the Sun King, but he left the city for Versailles in 1682. Then, during the remainder of Louis's reign, the

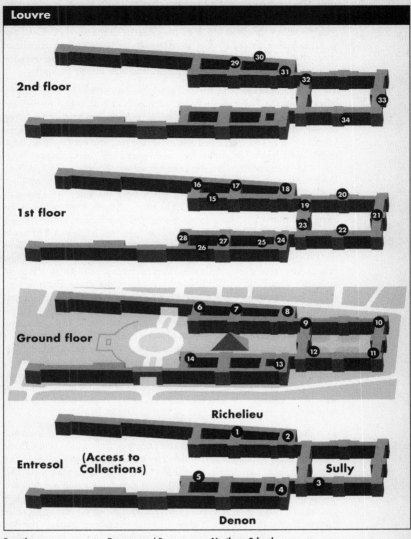

Louvre

2nd floor

1st floor

Ground floor

Richelieu

Entresol (Access to Collections)

Sully

Denon

Egyptian Antiquities: . . .11, 21

French Paintings:
14th–17th cent. **31**
18th–19th cent. **33**
19th cent. (large) **25, 34**

French Sculptures:
17th–18th cent. **1**
17th–19th cent. **7**
Middle Ages, Renaissance **6**

Greek, Etruscan and Roman Antiquities:
Bronzes and Precious Objects **23**
Ceramics and Terracotta **22**
Greek Antiquities **4, 12**

Etruscan and Roman Antiquities **13**
Venus de Milo **12**

Islamic and Asia Minor Antiquities:
Arab Antiquities . . . **10**
Iranian Antiquities **9**
Islamic Art **2**
Mesopotamia **8**
Italian Paintings: . . .**26**
Mona Lisa **27**

Italian Sculptures:
11th–15th cent. **5**
16th–19th cent. **14**
Michelangelo's The Dying Slave . . . **14**
Medieval Louvre: **3**

Northern School Paintings:
Holland, Flanders, Germany **29**

Northern Sculptures:
17th–19th cent. **14**

Objets d'Art:
17th–18th cent. **18, 20**
Galerie d'Apollon (Crown Jewels) **24**
Middle Ages, Renaissance **17**
Napoléon III Apartments **15**
19th cent. **16, 19**

Prints and Drawings:
French 17th cent. **32**
Italian School **28**
Northern Schools . . .**30**

palace underwent a rapid decline. Its empty apartments were taken over by a rabble of artists; little shacklike shops were set up against the walls; and chimneys sprouted higgledy-piggledy from the severe lines of the facades. Louis XV (1715–74), thanks in large measure to the financial shrewdness of his chief minister, Marigny, inaugurated long-overdue renovations, though this king, too, preferred to live at Versailles.

The Louvre's association with the French crown did not last much longer. It was from the Tuileries Palace that Louis XVI and Marie-Antoinette fled in 1791 (they had been under house arrest), two years after being forced back to Paris from Versailles. They got as far as Varennes, in Lorraine, only to be arrested and returned to Paris for trial and, ultimately, execution. The palace was taken over by the revolutionary leaders—the Convention first, then the Directory. Then, in 1793, during the Revolution, the National Assembly voted to turn part of the Louvre into a public museum. The galleries were stocked with nationalized art taken from the churches, the king, and other members of the French nobility, but the greatest boon to the collection came when a Corsican corporal measured his power by how much Great Art he could ransack from the rest of the world. Napoléon Bonaparte moved into the Louvre in 1800 as his armies were marching across Europe. They bravely captured the world's most famous treasures and brought them all back to the Louvre. With Napoléon's fall from grace, the new museum was forced in 1815 to return many of its works to the original owners. Napoléon's stay, however, did not prevent the three remaining French kings—Louis XVIII (1814–24); Charles X (1824–30); and Louis-Philippe (1830–48)—from making the Louvre their home. Fast forward to the 20th century. During World War II, the invading Germans looted the Louvre and used it as office space; a classical-art buff, Hitler had the *Winged Victory of Samothrace* installed near his desk. Most of the stolen pieces were recovered after the Liberation, but no large-scale changes or innovations were made until François Mitterrand was elected.

As a desire on the part of the late president to make his mark on the city, he commissioned the design and construction of I. M. Pei's **Pyramide** (or glass pyramid) surrounded by three smaller pyramids in the Cour Napoléon. Unveiled in March of 1989, it's more than just a grandiloquent gesture. The pyramid provided a new, and much needed, entrance to the Louvre; it also tops a large museum shop, café, and restaurant. Moreover, it acts as the terminal point for the most celebrated city view in Europe, a majestic vista stretching through the Arc du Carrousel, the Tuileries Gardens, across the place de la Concorde, up the Champs-Élysées to the towering Arc de Triomphe, and ending at the giant modern arch at La Défense, 4 km (2½ mi) more to the west. Needless to say, the architectural collision between the classical stone blocks of the courtyard surrounding the pyramid and the pseudo-Egyptian glass panels caused a furor. But, as time has passed, initial outrage has faded—as it once did for the Eiffel Tower.

The pyramids marked only the first phase of the Grand Louvre Project, a plan for the restoration of the museum launched by Mitterrand in 1981 for an estimated $1.3 billion. In November 1993, exactly 200 years after the Louvre first opened its doors to the public, Mitterrand cut the ribbon on the second phase: the renovation of the **Richelieu Wing** on the north side of the Cour Napoléon. Built between 1852 and 1857 by Napoléon III and grudgingly vacated in 1989 by the Ministry of Finance, the wing was renovated by Pei and his French associates and reopened to house more than 12,000 artworks, nearly a third from storage. The wing contains principally the Islamic and Mesopotamian art collections, French sculpture and painting, and Napoléon III's sumptuous apartments, now lovingly restored to their full, gilt-and-red-velvet ostentatious glory.

The third phase of the Grand Louvre Project is ongoing. By 1996 a much-needed improvement of lighting and air-conditioning had been carried out; the remaining exterior facades had been cleaned; and the adjacent Tuileries Gardens had been restored to its original splendor. By 1998, the museum had 11 new rooms of Persian and Arab antiquities; extra space for Greek, Roman, and Egyptian art; and first-time-ever public access to the balcony of the East Wing's mighty colonnade. And thanks to the controversial addition of the underground Carrousel du Louvre—a mall with upscale shops selling clothing, records, and other decidedly non-Louvre-related merchandise—there is even a massive fast-food court. Now you can get a Universal Burger and check out David's *Coronation of Napoléon I* all in the same building. For more soigné dining, be sure to check out the museum's well-reviewed Café Marly.

The Louvre's extraordinary collections encompass paintings, drawings, antiquities, sculpture, furniture, coins, and jewelry—the quality and the sheer variety are overwhelming. The number one attraction is Leonardo da Vinci's enigmatic *Mona Lisa*. While Leonardo's portrait may need some tracking down, this is not a bad thing: along the way, you'll find the Louvre packed with legendary collections, divided into seven areas: Asian antiquities, Egyptian antiquities, Greek and Roman antiquities, sculpture, objets d'art, paintings, and prints and drawings. What follows is no more than a selection of favorites, chosen to act as key points for your exploration.

RICHELIEU WING

Below Ground and Ground Floor: As you enter the Richelieu Wing from the Pyramide, on the left and up a flight of stairs is a gallery that displays temporary exhibits that comprise the Louvre's most recent acquisitions in French sculpture. Straight ahead is **Salle 20** ("salle" is French for room) filled with more French sculpture, including frilly busts of members of the court of Louis XIV, but most people pass through this room to get to the dramatic Cour Marly to the west or Cour Puget to the east. The **Cour Marly** is filled with sculptures, many from the park at Marly commissioned by Louis XIV at the end of the 17th century to provide a lighthearted contrast to the pompous statuary at neighboring Versailles; you can just imagine all these Greco-Roman gods set into the bushes of the Sun King's garden, their clothes falling away from their perfect bodies for all eternity. The Cour Puget is named for the artist who created the sculpture at place des Victoires, now mostly reassembled in the lower court. Back to the southeast corner of Cour Marly, you will find **Salle 1** of French sculpture. In **Salle 2** are fragments of Romanesque chapels from Cluny, the powerful abbey in Burgundy that dominated French Catholicism in the 11th century. In **Salles 4–6** you can see the refinement of sculpture encouraged by the wealthy communities in the Ile-de-France. The funerary art of **Salles 7–10** ranges from spooky to risible. The late-15th-century tomb of Philippe Pot in **Salle 10** is especially eerie: You see Philippe stretched out in eternal prayer, held aloft by eight black-robed pallbearers. Walking through **Salles 11–19**, you can see how the piety and stiffness of medieval French sculpture began to give way to the more natural style of the Italian Renaissance. Many local artists were traveling to Italy during the 16th and 17th centuries, and the French nobility were importing noted Italian sculptors. Bronze, out of favor since Roman times, was being cast again, and the subject matter, which had rarely strayed from Madonnas or saints, could now be mythological, allegorical, or classical.

To the north of the Cour Puget are **Salles 25–33,** filled with the products of the Académie Royale, the art school of 18th-century France. The smaller works in **Salle 25** are all qualification pieces for the Académie—once admitted into the school based on previous works, the student was asked to produce a sculpture as proof of continuing worth. To the east of the Cour Puget is the start of the Louvre's **Oriental Antiquities** collection. Within the glass case of **Salle 1** are many ancient Mesopotamian carvings, including a 2-inch neolithic figure dating from the 6th millennium BC. Facing the case are the pieced-together fragments of the 3rd millennium BC Stela of the Vultures, containing the oldest written history known to humankind, including images of King Eannatum catching his enemies in a net. Farther along, **Salle 1b** has countless examples of the wide-eyed alabaster statues produced by the Sumerians during the 3rd millennium BC. **Salle 2** is filled with statues and fragments of Gudea, a prince who supported a neo-Sumerian artistic culture in his 23rd-century BC kingdom of Lagash. The centerpiece of **Salle 3** is the "Codex of Hammurabi," an 18th-century BC diorite stela that contains the oldest written laws known to humanity. Near the top of the text you can see Hammurabi, king of the first Babylonian dynasty, meeting a seated Shamash, the god of justice. On the east side of Salle 3 is a lion glazed onto a piece of a terra-cotta–tile wall—just one of hundreds of similar beasts that decorated the multistory 6th-century BC Gates of Babylon.

Salle 4 is the Cour Khorsabad, a re-creation of the temple erected by the Assyrian king Sargon II in the 8th century BC at the palace of Dur-Sharrukin. Walking among the temple's five massive, winged bulls known as lamassu, or benign demigods, is one of the most spectacular experiences in the Louvre, even though only three of the bulls and almost none of the reerected reliefs are authentic. The originals were lost on a frigate that sank.

First Floor: The restored rooms from the royal apartments of Napoléon III fill the southwestern portion of the first floor of the Richelieu Wing. Salle 79 is the most spectacular; the corner reception room, decorated for Napoléon III's secretary of state, gives you a good idea of the eye-popping luxury of the Second Empire. These are the sort of rooms that the great 19th-century courtesan Violette—the real-life "Dame aux Camelias," immortalized as the heroine of Verdi's *La Traviata*—would have been familiar with. The gallery running between the Cour Marly and the Cour Puget is filled with French medieval artifacts saved from the Revolution's zeal to destroy all things Christian and Roman.

Second Floor: Just to the east of the escalators is **Salle 1,** which begins the section devoted to French and Northern School paintings. At the entrance to this room is a single 14th-century gold-backed painting of John the Good—the oldest known individual portrait from north of Italy. In **Salle 4** is *The Madonna and Chancellor Rolin,* by the 15th-century Dutch master Jan van Eyck. The first artist to extensively use oil paints, van Eyck defined what became known as the "northern style," characterized by a light source illuminating one area on an otherwise dark background. You almost need a microscope to drink in all the detail in this painting, which ranks as one of the top ten paintings in the Louvre collection. One of the first self-portraits ever painted—a disheveled offering by Albrecht Dürer (1471–1528)—hangs in **Salle 8.** Walking through **Salles 9–17,** you can see how the Dutch developed a fluid and comfortable representation of the body while playing with the shiny, dark palette of oil paints.

The most dramatic gallery in this section is **Salle 18,** where a cycle of giant matching canvases by Peter Paul Rubens (1577–1640) recounts the journey Maria de' Medici made from Florence to Paris—an over-bearing immortalization of a relatively cushy trip. The swirling Baroque paintings were commissioned by Maria herself and originally hung in the Palais du Luxembourg (just a few miles from the Louvre). The riveting *Disembarkation of Maria de' Medici at the Port of Marseille* memorably portrays an artificially slimmed-down Maria about to skip over the roly-poly daughters of Poseidon as a personified France beckons her to shore.

Though the still-life genre may seem dull today, it was loaded with meaning for the Dutch. Ambriosius Bosschaert's (1573–1621) *Bouquet of Flowers in an Arch* (1620) in **Salle 27** is meant to represent the power of the colonially minded Dutch merchants: The flowers brought together in the vase in this painting couldn't have been gathered at any one moment in real life because of their diverse and exotic origins. In **Salle 31** are several paintings by Rembrandt van Rijn (1606–69), including a late self-portrait in which he goes nuts with the chiaroscuro. In his 1648 *Supper at Emmaus,* he challenges many painting conventions, such as centering the subject and delineating objects with bold brush strokes. The masterpiece of the Dutch collection is *The Lace-maker,* by Jan Vermeer (1632–75), in **Salle 38.** Obsessed with optical accuracy, Vermeer painted the red thread in the foreground as a slightly blurred jumble, just as one would actually see it if focusing on the girl.

SULLY WING

The entrance into the Sully Wing is more impressive than the entrances to the other wings—you get to walk around and through the foundations and moat of the castle built by Philippe Auguste in the 12th century and expanded by Charles V in the 14th with a series of Cinderella-like towers and moats.

Ground Floor: The northern galleries of the Sully are a continuation of the ancient **Iranian collection** started on the ground floor of the Richelieu Wing. Conflicting styles emerged as the Greco-Roman art exported by the Roman and Byzantine empires influenced the work of indigenous artisans. Adjacent to the Egyptian galleries—renovated in 1997—is **Salle 12,** housing the Greek, Etruscan, and Roman collections and the famous 2nd-century BC *Venus de Milo.* The armless statue, one of the most reproduced and recognizable works of art in the world, is actually as beautiful as they say—it is worth your trouble to push past the lecturing curators and tourist groups to get a closer look at the incredible skill with which the Greeks turned cold marble into something vibrant and graceful. Oddly enough, her face is strikingly like the *Mona Lisa*'s, with an additional mystery being the original form of her missing arms—were they holding a mirror or a net? In the 19th century, the Venus was dug up on the Greek island of Milos, then sold for 6,000 francs to the French ambassador in Constantinople, who presented her to King Louis XVIII. **Salles 13–17** are filled with all kinds of statuary: funerary stelae, body fragments, architectural details.

First Floor: The northern galleries of the first floor continue with the **objets d'art collection** started in the Richelieu Wing, picking up at the 17th century and continuing through the Revolution to the Restoration. Running alongside the Egyptian galleries to the south are works from the early period of the **Greek collection**—a smattering of coins, pottery, and other everyday objects from the 7th to 3rd centuries BC.

Second Floor: Sully picks up French painting where the Richelieu Wing leaves off, somewhere around the 17th century. At this point, a

conscious battle was under way in French art between the northern
style (epitomized by magical, candlelit canvases of Georges de La Tour
and the more stolid Le Nain brothers and centered on the work of the
Dutch) and the southern one (headed by Poussin, and coming from Florence, Venice, and Rome). The result was a blending of northern style
and technology (darkly painted interiors and oil paints) with southern
subjects and technique (ruined landscapes and one-point perspective).
Charles Le Brun (1619–90), Louis XIV's principal adviser on the arts
and the man who designed many of the greatest salons at Versailles,
painted massive "History Paintings," jam-packed with excruciating details from biblical, historical, or mythological stories. Displayed in **Salle
32** are the four colossal canvases of his late-17th-century *Story of
Alexander,* with a powerful view of the trials of the emperor (and no
small reference to Louis XIV).

An academic painter of a different genre was Antoine Watteau (1684–
1721), long considered the greatest French painter of the 18th century.
In scenes such as his 1717 *Pilgrimage to the Island of Cythera* in **Salle
36,** he depicted in wispy pastel brush strokes the bucolic and often
frivolous lifestyle of the Baroque-age court set, here depicted arriving
(or are they departing?) on Cythera, the mythological isle of love.
Here he concentrates on creating an equally poetic mood, but there is
an extra layer of emotion: the gallant gentlemen and courtly women
seem drugged by the pleasures about to be enjoyed but disturbingly
aware of their transitory nature, too. In the same room is Watteau's
enigmatic, melancholic 1718 *Pierrot* (once called Gilles), a portrait of
a boyish-looking actor whose costume and surroundings reflect the popularity of Italian commedia dell'arte at the time; this priceless painting was originally a theater sign. Maurice Quentin de La Tour (1704–
88) was another favorite court painter; his 1755 *Marquise de Pompadour* in **Salle 45** captures the leading fashion plate of Louis XV's
court. Madame de Pompadour, mistress to the king, is shown with everything a good courtesan should have: books, music manuscripts, engravings, fine clothing, and, of course, pale skin.

One revolution and two republics after the court painters of the 17th
and 18th centuries, the Académie continued to define Good Taste. In
Salle 60 you can see the paintings of Jean-Auguste Ingres (1780–1867),
which depict the exotic themes popular in the Age of Empires. His 1862
Turkish Bath portrays an orgy of steamy women who look anything
but Turkish. One of these ladies was the subject of his *La Grande Odal-
isque*; here, exoticism and the French classical tradition gel to produce
a strikingly elegant image (we dare you to find a single bone in this
woman's body).

DENON WING

Below Ground: To the south and east from the Pyramide entrance are
galleries displaying Italian sculpture from the early Renaissance, including
a 15th-century *Madonna and Child* by the Florentine Donatello (1386–
1466).

Ground Level: In the former imperial stables (**Salle 4**) you can see the
1513–15 *Slaves* of Michelangelo. After carefully selecting his slab of
marble, Michelangelo (1475–1564) would spend days envisioning the
form of the sculpture within the uncut stone. The sculptures that finally emerged openly eroticized the male body. The fact that many were
left "unfinished" (i.e., parts of the marble were left rough, making it
look as if the sculptures were trying to free themselves from the stone
blocks) was controversial at first, but the style was to inspire Rodin
and other modern artists. Nearby is the 1793 *Eros and Psyche* by the

great Italian neoclassicist Antonio Canova (1757–1822), whose delicate and precise touch made him the darling of European royalty.

To the east of the Italian sculpture collection are the galleries containing the sculptures of the **Greek, Etruscan,** and **Roman periods.** In **Salle 18** is the 6th-century BC *Etruscan Sarcophagus* from Cerveteri, showing a married couple pieced together from thousands of clay fragments.

First Floor: Stretching out from a tiny entry next to the Sully Wing is the **Galerie d'Apollon,** a 17th-century hall decorated by the painter Charles Le Brun (who immortalized himself in one of the portraits on the wall) that now holds what remains of France's **Crown Jewels.** Around the corner from the jewels, the sublime *Winged Victory of Samothrace* stands regally, if headless, at the top landing of the grand **Escalier Daru.** The spectacular 3rd-century BC statue was found on a tiny Greek island in the northern Aegean. Depicted in the act of descending from Olympus, the Winged Victory, or *Nike,* to use the ancient Greek name, originally came from the isle of Samothrace and was carved by an unknown master in 305 BC to commemorate the naval victory of Demetrius Poliorcetes over the Turks. She had a more recent moment of glory when she served as a model for Audrey Hepburn and a red Givenchy gown in *Funny Face.* Instinct with motion, "invested with an atmosphere that holds all the significance of fall and destiny," to quote one archaeologist, the Nike is represented alighting on the prow of a ship.

The **Italian painting** collection begins at the western end of the Denon Wing. The paintings in **Salle 6** (also known as the Salle des États) are large-scale canvases from the 16th-century Venetian School. Dominating the room is the massive 1562 *Feast at Cana* by Veronese (1528–88), a sumptuous scene (restored in the 1980s) centered on Jesus turning water into wine. Spread across the canvas are hundreds of still lifes and portraits, all little masterpieces within this huge painting; it is said that the great painters of the Venetian School—Titian, Bassano, Tintoretto, and even Veronese—are depicted as the musicians. When painted, it was considered scandalous to adorn the holy story with so much contemporary dress and fashionable 16th-century detail, so the painter was forced by the authority to rename the painting *Feast in the House of Levi.* In the same room is the 1525 *Entombment* by the quintessential Venetian painter, Titian (1488–1576), who used the translucent shine of the oil paints characteristic of Venetian art while contrasting dark colors against extreme whites to create a sense of light.

And now for the Most Famous Painting in the World: the *Mona Lisa* (officially known as *La Gioconda,* or *La Joconde* to the French), painted by Leonardo da Vinci (1452–1519) in 1503–06. As the portrait of the wife of one Francesco del Giocondo, a 15th-century Florentine millionaire, Leonardo's masterpiece is now believed by some historians to have been painted as a memorial after the lady's death. To those who recall Théophile Gautier's words "a sphinx of beauty," the portrait is a bit of a disappointment. The picture is smaller than you might expect and kept behind protective glass; it is invariably surrounded by a crowd of worshipers who are intent on studying her enigmatic expression (or is it she who is studying them?). Once you get in front of the videotaping tourists, you, too, may find yourself asking "Is this it?" when you are faced with this 2½- by 1¼-ft painting of an eyebrow-less woman with yellowing skin and an annoyingly smug smile. In fact, most art historians award the beauty prize instead to Leonardo's *Virgin and St. Anne,* hanging nearby. Here in this room, famously known as the Salon Carré, you find other legendary works of the High Renaissance, including Raphael's *La Belle Jardiniére.*

The 1458 *Calvary* in **Salle 8,** painted by Andrea Mantegna (1431–1506), a follower of the Florentine architect Brunelleschi's treatises on perspective, is one of the first paintings ever with a vanishing point. Although equally renowned during his lifetime as an anatomist and inventor, Leonardo da Vinci was originally trained as a painter. His breathtaking 1483 *Virgin of the Rocks* has an interesting sense of spatial relationships—the four figures create the four corners of a pyramid, while their glances and gestures keep all activity contained within this form.

Behind the *Feast at Cana* are two passages leading to **Salles 75–77,** home of the great epic-scale canvases produced in Paris during the 19th century. When official court painter Louis David (1748–1825) produced the *Coronation of Napoléon* on December 2, 1804, now hanging in Salle 75, he wisely decided not to capture the moment when Napoléon snatched the crown from the hands of Pope Pius VII to place it upon his own head—choosing instead to paint the new emperor turning to crown Josephine.

Also in Salle 75 hang two of the most famous works in the history of French painting: the 1819 *Raft of the Medusa* by Théodore Géricault (1791–1824) and the 1830 *Liberty Leading the People* by Eugène Delacroix (1798–1863). Géricault's epic work conveys a gloomily Romantic view of the human state, nightmarish despite its heroism and grand scale. Painted when Géricault was only 27 years old, it was inspired by the real-life story of the wreck of a French merchant ship: The captain lost control, the ship was without lifeboats or supplies, and ultimately the survivors resorted to cannibalism. The painting caused a stir with the government, which took offense at the stab made at the inefficiency of authority. The Académie was aghast for formal reasons: The painting had no central subject, no hero, no resolution. The survivors are a mess of living and dead bodies jumbled in and out of ominous, sickly green shadows.

Even though Delacroix wasn't directly involved in the "Trois Glorieuses"—a three-day revolution in 1830 that ousted Charles X's autocracy and brought in a parliamentary monarchy with Louis-Philippe as king—he was compelled to paint *Liberty* to commemorate the Parisians who attempted to restore the Republic. Once again, it is an unorthodox subject for a painting: Poorly armed bourgeoisie and pugnacious street urchins step over the dead bodies of comrades and slay other French folk in the name of an ultimately short-lived government. The allegorical figure of Liberty is quite a character: She is shown walking barefoot over barricades, her peasant dress falling away from her breasts, the Tricolore (French flag) held aloft with one well-muscled limb while the other grips a rifle. The painting was immediately bought by an appreciative Louis-Philippe, who hid it to keep from inciting his enemies.

The above highlights of the Louvre collection are simply the merest tip of the iceberg. You'll also find walls virtually wallpapered with masterpieces by Fra Angelico, Botticelli, Holbein, Hals, Brueghel, El Greco, Murillo, Boucher, Goya, and Caravaggio—whose *Death of the Virgin* towers over La Grand Galerie—just to mention a few of the famous names, along with one-hit wonders like Enguerrand Quarton's magnificent 15th-century *Pietà*. Other collections here will delight connoisseurs, such as the examples of French furniture—the grandiose 17th- and 18th-century productions of Boulle and Riesener, marvels of intricate craftsmanship and elegant luxury, are prized by those with a fondess for opulent decoration. In addition, temporary photography shows, exhibits of new acquisitions and donations, and events honoring individual painters or subjects usually take place in either the Salle Napoléon, the basement galleries of the Richelieu and Sully Wing, the second-floor galleries of the Denon Wing, or the showrooms of the Carrousel du Louvre. Your Louvre ticket may give you free access, or you may have to shell out an additional sum, depending on the exhibit. Admission is often charged for a wide array of other art-related events at the museum. Lectures take place in the Louvre Auditorium; the films there showcase everything from silent works to the history of art in Paris. A smattering of films, lectures, concerts, and exhibits are included in what's called Les Midis du Louvre. For recorded information in five languages (French, English, Spanish, German, and Italian), call 01–40–21–51–51 (press 2 for English). Be sure to pick up the free three-month schedule of events called Louvre at the information desk under the Pyramide, or look at the TV monitors behind the desk.

If you have time for only one visit, these selections give you an idea of the riches of the museum. But try to make repeat visits—the Louvre is about half price on Sunday (free the first Sunday of each month) and after 3 PM on other days. (Unless you plan to go to a number of museums every day, the one-, three-, and five-day tourist museum passes probably aren't worth your money, since you could easily spend a whole day at the Louvre alone.) Study the plans at the entrance to get your bearings and pick up a map to take with you. ⊠ *Palais du Louvre (it's faster to enter through the Carrousel du Louvre mall on rue de Rivoli than through the pyramid),* ☎ *01–40–20–51–51 information,* WEB *www.louvre.fr.* ⊡ *46 frs/€8, 30 frs/€4.68 after 3 pm and all day Sun., free 1st Sun. of month.* ☉ *Thurs.–Sun. 9–6, Mon. and Wed. 9 am–9:45 pm. Some sections open limited days. Métro: Palais-Royal.*

⑭ Musée du Jeu de Paume. Renovations transformed this museum, at the entrance to the Tuileries Gardens, into an ultramodern, white-walled showcase for excellent temporary exhibits of bold contemporary art. The building was once the spot of *jeu de paume* games (literally, "palm game"—a forerunner of tennis). ⊠ *1 pl. de la Concorde,* ☎ *01–42–60–69–69.* ⊡ *38 frs/€5.80.* ☉ *Tues. noon–9:30, Wed.–Fri. noon–7, weekends 10–7. Métro: Concorde.*

⑮ Musée de l'Orangerie. Currently closed for renovation (and slated to reopen in late 2002), this museum is most famous as home of several of Claude Monet's largest *Water Lilies* murals. Set in the Tuileries Gardens, the museum also has an array of early 20th-century paintings, with works by Renoir, Cézanne, Matisse, and Marie Laurencin, among other masters. ⊠ *Pl. de la Concorde,* ☎ *01–42–97–48–16.* ⊡ *30 frs/ €4.60.* ☉ *Wed.–Mon. 9:45–5:15. Métro: Concorde.*

★ **❶ Notre-Dame.** Looming above the place du Parvis on the Ile de la Cité is the Cathédrale de Notre-Dame, the most enduring symbol of Paris. Begun in 1163, completed in 1345, badly damaged during the Revolution, and restored by Viollet-le-Duc in the 19th century, Notre-Dame may not be France's oldest or largest cathedral, but in terms of beauty and architectural harmony, it has few peers—as you can see by studying the facade from the open square. The doorways seem like hands joined in prayer and the sculpted kings form a noble procession, while the rose window gleams, to wax poetic, like the eye of divinity. Above, the gallery breaks the guipure of the stone vaults and, between the two high towers, the spire soars from the cross of the transept. Seen from the front, the cathedral gives an impression of strength, dignity, and majestic serenity; seen from the Pont de l'Archevêché, it has all the proud grace of a seagoing vessel, the cross on its steeple borne like the flag on a tall mast.

An army of stonemasons, carpenters, and sculptors arrived in 1163, working on a site that had previously seen a Roman temple, an early Christian basilica, and a Romanesque church. The chancel and altar were consecrated in 1182, but the magnificent sculptures surrounding the main doors were not put into position until 1240. The north tower was finished 10 years later. If both towers seem to some a bit top-heavy, that's because two needlelike spires were originally conceived to top them but were never built. If you look carefully, you will see that the tower on the left is wider than the one on the right.

Despite various changes in the 17th century, the cathedral remained substantially unaltered until the French Revolution, when it was transformed into a Temple of Reason—busts of Voltaire and Rousseau replaced those of saints. The statues of the kings of Israel were hacked down by the mob, chiefly because they were thought to represent the despised royal line of France, and everything inside and out that was deemed "anti-Republican" was stripped away. An interesting postscript to this destruction occurred in 1977, when some of the heads of these statues were discovered salted away in a bank vault on boulevard Haussmann. They'd apparently been hidden there by an ardent royalist who owned the small mansion that now forms part of the bank. (The restored heads are now on display in the Musée National du Moyen-Age.)

By the early 19th century, the excesses of the Revolution were over, and the cathedral went back to fulfilling its religious functions again. Napoléon crowned himself emperor here in May 1804 (David's heroic painting of the lavish ceremony can be seen in the Louvre)—you can stand on the step where he stood when he crowned Josephine. Full-scale restoration started in the middle of the century, the most conspicuous result of which was the reconstruction of the spire. It was then, too, that Haussmann demolished the warren of little buildings in front of the cathedral, creating the place du Parvis.

The facade divides neatly into three levels. At the first-floor level are the three main entrances, or portals: the Portal of the Virgin on the left, the Portal of the Last Judgment in the center, and the Portal of St. Anne on the right. All three are surmounted by magnificent carvings—most of them 19th-century copies of the originals—of figures, foliage, and biblical scenes. Above these are the restored statues of the kings of Israel, the Galerie des Rois. Above the gallery is the great rose window and, above that, the Grand Galerie, at the base of the twin towers. The south tower houses the great bell of Notre-Dame, as tolled by Quasimodo, Victor Hugo's fictional hunchback. The 387-step climb to the top of the towers is worth the effort for a close-up of the famous gargoyles—most of them added in the 19th century—and the expansive view of the city.

As you enter by the Portal of the Virgin, the faith of the early builders permeates all, and the miracle of the quiet, persuasive interior provides an apt contrast to the triumphant glory of the exterior, with the soft glow of the stained-glass windows replacing the statues of saints, virgins, prophets, and apostles. The best time to visit is early in the morning, when the cathedral is at its lightest and least crowded. At the entrance are the massive 12th-century columns supporting the twin towers. Look down the nave to the transepts—the arms of the church—where, at the south (right) entrance to the chancel, you'll glimpse the haunting 12th-century statue of Notre-Dame de Paris, *Our Lady of Paris*. The chancel itself owes parts of its decoration to a vow taken by Louis XIII in 1638. Still without an heir after 23 years of marriage, he promised to dedicate the entire country to the Virgin Mary if his queen produced a son. When this miraculous event came to pass, Louis set about redecorating the chancel and choir. On the south side of the chancel is the **Trésor** (treasury), with a collection of garments, reliquaries, and silver and gold plate.

Under the square in front of the cathedral is the **Crypte Archéologique,** Notre-Dame's archaeological museum. It contains remains of previous churches on the site, scale models charting the district's development, and relics and artifacts dating from the Parisii, who lived here 2000 years ago, unearthed during excavations here in the 1960s. Slides and models detail the history of the Ile de la Cité. The foundations of the 3rd-century Gallo-Roman rampart and of the 6th-century Merovingian church can also be seen.

❷ If your interest in the cathedral is not yet sated, duck into the **Musée de Notre-Dame** (✉ 10 rue du Cloître-Notre-Dame), across the street opposite the North Door. The museum's paintings, engravings, medallions, and other objects and documents chart the history of the Cathedral of Notre-Dame. ✉ *Pl. du Parvis,* ☎ *01–44–32–16–72.* 🎫 *Towers 35 frs/€5.34, crypt 33 frs/€5, treasury 15 frs/€2.30, museum 15 frs/€2.30.* ☉ *Cathedral daily 8–7. Towers Apr.–Sept., daily 9:30–7:30; Oct.–Mar., daily 10–5. Treasury Mon.–Sat. 9:30–11:30 and 1–5:30. Crypt Tues.–Sun. 10–6. Museum Wed. and weekends 2:30–6. Métro: Cité.*

❹ **Palais de Justice** (Law Courts). The city's courts were built by Baron Haussmann in his characteristically weighty neoclassic style in about 1860. You can wander around the buildings, watch the bustle of the lawyers, or attend a court hearing. The solidity of Haussmann's buildings seems to emphasize the finesse of two important sights enclosed within the complex spared by Haussmann: La Conciergerie and Ste-Chapelle. ✉ *Bd. du Palais. Métro: Cité.*

🐾 **⓳** **Palais de la Découverte** (Palace of Discovery). A planetarium, working models, and scientific and technological exhibits on such topics as optics, biology, nuclear physics, and electricity make up this science museum behind the Grand Palais. ✉ *Av. Franklin-D.-Roosevelt,* ☎ *01– 56–43–20–21,* WEB *www.palais-decouverte.fr.* 🎫 *30 frs/€4.60, 15 frs/€2.30 extra for planetarium.* ☉ *Tues.–Sat. 9:30–6, Sun. 10–7. Métro: Champs-Élysées–Clemenceau.*

⓱ **Petit Palais.** The smaller counterpart to the Grand Palais, just off the Champs-Élysées, beautifully presents a permanent collection of French painting and furniture, with splendid canvases by Courbet and Bouguereau. Temporary exhibits are often held here, too. The sprawling entrance gallery contains several enormous turn-of-the-20th-century paintings on its walls and ceilings. Outside, take time to admire two fine statues near each corner of the building: French World War I hero Georges Clemenceau, facing the Champs-Élysées, was joined in 1998 by Jean Cardot's resolute image of Winston Churchill, facing the Seine. ✉ *Av. Winston-Churchill,* ☎ *01–42–65–12–73.* 🎫 *27 frs/€4,* ☉ *Tues.–Sun. 10–5:40. Métro: Champs-Élysées–Clemenceau.*

⓰ **Place de la Concorde.** This majestic square at the foot of the Champs-Élysées is undoubtedly one of the most balanced and harmoniously beautiful spaces in the world. Originally consecrated to the glory of Louis XV, it was laid out in the 1770s, but there was nothing in the way of peace or concord about its early years, for it was here that his successor, Louis XVI, and Marie-Antoinette were guillotined, along with more than 2,000 other people between 1793 and 1795. And here it was that Madame Roland cried, "Liberty, what crimes are committed in thy name." When the blood of the victims had been washed away and the yells of the *sans culottes* political extremists had died down, the square was renamed Concorde and, in place of a statue of Louis XV, another monument, freer of political significance, was erected in 1833: a 107-ft obelisk, originally built in the 8th century BC, and a present from the viceroy of Egypt (it received its gilded cap in 1998). A giant Ferris wheel, the *Rose de Paris,* was installed in front of the Tuileries gates in December 1999 for the millennium festivities; Parisians hoped it would become an annual feature and, at press time, were urging the government not to remove it during 2001 as scheduled. Among the handsome, symmetrical 18th-century buildings facing the square is the deluxe Hôtel Crillon, originally built by Gabriel—architect of the Petit Trianon—as an 18th-century home for three of France's wealthiest families. At the near end of high-walled rue Royale is the legendary Maxim's restaurant, but unless you choose to eat here, you won't be able to see the riot of crimson velvets and florid Art Nouveau furniture inside. *Métro: Concorde.*

❼ Place Dauphine. The Surrealists loved place Dauphine, which they called "le sexe de Paris" because of its location—at the tail western end of the Ile de la Cité—and suggestive V-shape. Its origins were much more proper: built by Henri IV, the king named the place in homage to his successor, the dauphin, who grew up to become Louis XIII. The triangular place is lined with some 17th-century houses which the writer André Maurois felt represented the very quintessence of Paris and France. Take a seat on the park bench, enjoy a picnic, and see if you agree. *Métro: Cité.*

⓴ Pont Alexandre-III. No other bridge over the Seine epitomizes the fin-de-siècle frivolity of the Belle Epoque (or Paris itself) like the exuberant, bronze lamp–lined Pont Alexandre-III. A urban masterstroke that seems as much created of cake-frosting and sugar sculptures as stone and iron, it makes an alluring backdrop for fashion shoots and the surrounding Parisian landmarks. The bridge was built, like the Grand and Petit Palais nearby, for the 1900 world's fair; it was inaugurated by the visiting Russian czar, the ill-fated Nicholas II, and ingratiatingly named in honor of his father. *Métro: Invalides.*

❾ Pont Neuf (New Bridge). Crossing the Ile de la Cité, just behind square du Vert-Galant, is the oldest bridge in Paris, confusingly called the New Bridge. It was completed in 1607 and was the first bridge in the city to be built without houses lining either side because, so some historians believe, Henri IV wanted a clear view of Notre-Dame from his windows at the Louvre. *Métro: Pont-Neuf.*

★ **❺ Sainte-Chapelle** (Holy Chapel). One of the supremely dazzling achievements of the Middle Ages, a Gothic jewel, and home to the most ancient stained-glass windows in Paris, this chapel was built by the pious Louis IX (1226–70), whose good works ensured his subsequent canonization. Constructed in less than three years, it was conceived as an enormous reliquary—as a home for what Louis believed to be the crown of thorns from Christ's crucifixion and fragments of the true cross, acquired from the impoverished Emperor Baldwin of Constantinople at phenomenal expense.

The building is actually two chapels in one. The plainer, first-floor chapel, made gloomy by insensitive mid-19th-century restorations (which could do with restoration themselves), was for servants and lowly members of the court. The infinitely more spectacular upper chapel, up a dark spiral staircase, was for the king and important members of the court. The chapel walls (if you can call them that) consist mainly of stained glass and constitute a technical tour de force. Here, again, some clumsy 19th-century work has added a deadening touch, but the glory of the chapel—the stained glass—is magically intact. The chapel is airy and diaphanous, the walls glowing and sparkling as light plays on the windows. Notice how the walls, in fact, consist of at least twice as much glass as masonry: the entire aim of the architects was to provide the maximum amount of window space.

Architecturally, for all its delicate and ornate exterior decoration—notice the open latticework of the pencil-like *flèche*, or spire, on the roof—the design of the building is simplicity itself. In essence, it's no more than a thin, rectangular box, much taller than it is wide. But think of it first and foremost as an enormous magic lantern, illuminating 1,130 figures from the Bible, to create—as one writer poetically put it—"the most marvelous colored and moving air ever held within four walls." Come early in the day to avoid the dutiful crowds that trudge around it—better still, try to attend one of the regular, candlelit concerts. ⊠ *4 bd. du Palais,* ☎ *01–43–54–30–09 concert information.* ☎ *35 frs/€5.34, joint ticket with Conciergerie 50 frs/€7.63.* ☉ *Apr.–Sept., daily 9:30–6:30; Oct.–Mar., daily 10–5. Métro: Cité.*

❸ Square Jean-XXIII. When it comes to views of Notre-Dame, no visit to the great cathedral is complete without a riverside walk past the cathedral through Square Jean-XXIII. If offers a breathtaking sight of the east end of the cathedral, ringed by flying buttresses, surmounted by the spire. From here, the building seems to float above the Seine like some vast, stone ship. *Métro: Cité.*

❽ Square du Vert-Galant. The equine statue of the Vert Galant himself—amorous adventurer Henri IV—surveys this leafy square at the western end of the Ile de la Cité. Henri, king of France from 1589 until his assassination in 1610, was something of a dashing figure, by turns ruthless and charming, a stern upholder of the absolute rights of monarchy, and a notorious womanizer. He is probably best remembered for his cynical remark that *"Paris vaut bien une messe"* ("Paris is worth a mass"), a reference to his readiness to renounce Protestantism to gain the throne of predominantly Catholic France and, indeed, be allowed to enter the city (for a riveting depiction of the king and his role in the St. Bartholomew's Day Massacre, see the French film *Queen Margot,* which stars Isabelle Adjani as his ill-fated consort). To ease his conscience he issued the Edict of Nantes in 1598, according French Protestants (almost) equal rights with their Catholic counterparts. It was Louis XIV's renunciation of the edict nearly 100 years later that led to the massive Huguenot exodus from France—an economic catastrophe for the country. The square itself is a fine spot to linger on a sunny afternoon and is the departure point for the glass-topped Vedette tour boats on the Seine (at the bottom of the steps to the right). *Métro: Pont-Neuf.*

FROM THE EIFFEL TOWER TO THE ARC DE TRIOMPHE

The Eiffel Tower lords over southwest Paris, and from nearly wherever you are on this walk, you can see it looming. For years many Parisians felt the Tour Eiffel was an iron eyesore and compared it to a giraffe, a giraffe that weighed 15 million pounds and whose head rose 1,000 ft high. Then, gradually, the tower became part of the Parisian landscape and entered the hearts and souls of Parisians and visitors alike. Thanks to its stunning nighttime illumination (in celebration of the new millennium, the Tower lit up like a giant sparkler every hour on the hour in 2000, for 10 glittering minutes, from dusk

From the Eiffel Tower to the Arc de Triomphe

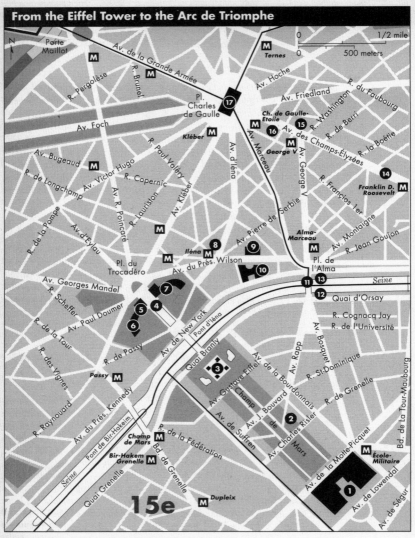

15e

till 1 AM), it continues to make Paris live up to its moniker, *La Ville Lumière*—the City of Light.

Water is the second theme of this walk: fountains playing beneath the place du Trocadéro; tours along the Seine on the Bateaux Mouches; and an underground prowl through the city's sewers, if you can stand it. Museums are the third; the area around Trocadéro is full of them. Military grandeur is the fourth; the Arc de Triomphe is Napoléon's most eye-popping legacy to Paris (the young general often surveyed his troops on the Champ de Mars, near the start of this walk). The arch stands foursquare at the top of the city's most famous avenue: the Champs-Élysées. Site of most French national celebrations, the Champs-Élysées is the last leg of the Tour de France bicycle race on the third or fourth Sunday in July and the site of vast ceremonies on Bastille Day (July 14) and Armistice Day (November 11). Its trees are often decked with the French tricolor and foreign flags to mark visits from heads of state.

Explore its commercial upper half (its verdant lower section, sloping down gracefully to the place de la Concorde, the Tuileries Gardens, and the Louvre is covered in the first walking tour. Local charm is not a feature of this grand sector of western Paris. The French moan that it's losing its character, and, as you notice the number of fast-food joints along the Champs-Élysées, you'll know what they mean—though renovation has gone some way to restoring the avenue's legendary elegance. For a real dose of high style, head to nearby avenue Montaigne, home to some of the top names in world fashion.

Numbers in the text correspond to numbers in the margin and on the Eiffel Tower to Arc de Triomphe map.

A Good Walk

Graced by the stately facade of the **École Militaire** ①, the verdant expanse of the **Champ de Mars** ②, once used as a parade ground and then as site of the World Exhibitions, provides a thrilling approach to the iron symbol of Paris, the **Tour Eiffel** ③. As you get nearer, the Eiffel Tower's colossal bulk (it's far bigger and sturdier than pictures suggest) becomes spectacularly evident. (If you want to skip this walk through the parade grounds, just take the RER directly to Champs-de-Mars for the Eiffel Tower.)

Across the Seine from the Eiffel Tower, above stylish gardens and fountains on the heights of the Trocadéro, is the Art Deco **Palais de Chaillot** ④, a cultural center containing three museums. Pause on the piazza, lined by gold statues, to admire the view of the Eiffel Tower. The south wing of the Palais, to your left as you arrive from the Seine, houses the **Musée de l'Homme** ⑤, an anthropology museum, and the **Musée de la Marine** ⑥, a maritime museum. The right wing was badly damaged by fire in 1997, and its **Musée des Monuments Français** ⑦, with copies of statues, columns, and archways from throughout France, is undergoing renovation and won't reopen until 2003.

From the Palais head right down the avenue du Président-Wilson, with its street lamps designed by Frank Lloyd Wright. Next block down on your right, surrounded most days by no fewer than nine French tricolors, is another Art Deco building, fronted by a rotunda lined with mosaics and alternating pinkish beige and pebble-dash concrete: the Conseil Economique et Social (Economic and Social Council). Echoing it across the place d'Iéna is another, slightly older rotunda, topped by a pineapple—the **Musée Guimet** ⑧, whose extensive collection of Indo-Chinese and Far Eastern art reopened early 2001 after a major renovation. Farther down the avenue du Président-Wilson, the equally pompous architecture of the **Palais Galliéra** ⑨, home to exhibits on clothing design and fashion, squares up to the cool gray outlines of the 1930s **Musée d'Art Moderne de la Ville de Paris** ⑩, a venue for temporary exhibits as well as the city's high-powered collection of modern art.

Continue down to the place de l'Alma, where a giant golden torch appears to be saluting the memory of Diana, Princess of Wales, who died in a car crash in the tunnel below in August 1997. Across the **Pont de l'Alma** ⑪ (to the left) is the entrance to **Les Égouts** ⑫, Paris's sewers. If you prefer a less malodorous tour of the city, stay on the Right Bank and head down the sloping side road to the left of the bridge to the embarkation point of the **Bateaux Mouches** ⑬ (motorboats) and their tours of Paris by water.

From the place de l'Alma head up the grand thoroughfare of avenue Montaigne, one of the leading showcases for the great haute couture houses, such as Dior, Chanel, Nina Ricci, Valentino, Prada, and Dolce & Gabbana. After some world-class window-shopping, continue on to the Rond-Point des Champs-Élysées, the main traffic nexus of Paris's most famous avenue, and turn left up the **Champs-Élysées** ⑭. At 116 bis is the famous **Lido** ⑮ nightclub, opposite the venerable Le Fouquet's restaurant-café, once frequented by Orson Welles and James Joyce. Stop in at the **Office de Tourisme de la Ville de Paris** ⑯ (the main city tourist office) at No. 127, on the left-hand side of the avenue. Continue up to the top of the avenue and place Charles-de-Gaulle, known to Parisians as L'Étoile, or The Star—a reference to the streets that fan out from it—and home to the colossal, 164-ft **Arc de Triomphe** ⑰. L'Étoile is Europe's most chaotic traffic circle: short of attempting a death-defying dash, your only way of getting to the Arc de Triomphe in the middle is to take an underground passage from the top right of the avenue des Champs-Élysées. The view from the top of the Arc de Triomphe illustrates the star effect of the 12 radiating avenues and enables you to admire the vista down the Champs-Élysées, toward the place de la Concorde and the distant Louvre. West of the Champs-Élysées, and visible from the Arc de Triomphe, are the verdant Bois de Boulogne; the posh suburb of Neuilly; and the towering office buildings and ultramodern arch of La Défense. (The Charles de Gaulle–Étoile métro and RER station, which sprawls underground beneath L'Étoile, provides quick access to the western suburbs, if you want to make the excursion now.)

TIMING

You can probably cover this 5½-km (3½-mi) walk in about four hours, but if you wish to ascend the Eiffel Tower, take a trip along the Seine, or visit any of the plethora of museums along the way, you'd be best off allowing most of the day.

Sights to See

★ ⑰ **Arc de Triomphe.** Inspired by Rome's Arch of Titus, this colossal, 164-ft triumphal arch was planned by Napoléon—who believed himself to be the direct heir to the Roman emperors—to celebrate his military successes. Unfortunately, Napoléon's strategic and architectural visions were not entirely on the same plane, and the Arc de Triomphe proved something of an embarrassment. Although the emperor wanted the monument completed in time for an 1810 parade in honor of his new bride, Marie-Louise, the arch was still only a few feet high, and a dummy arch of painted canvas was strung up to save face.

Empires come and go, and Napoléon's had been gone for more than 20 years before the Arc de Triomphe was finally finished, in 1836. It has some magnificent sculpture by François Rude, such as *The Departure of the Volunteers,* better known as *La Marseillaise,* to the right of the arch when viewed from the Champs-Élysées. Names of Napoléon's generals are inscribed on the stone facades—those underlined are the hallowed figures who fell on the fields of battle. After showing alarming signs of decay, the structure received a thorough overhaul in 1989 and is once again neo-Napoleonic in its splendor. There is a small museum halfway up the arch devoted to its history. France's Unknown Soldier is buried beneath the archway; the flame is rekindled every evening at 6:30. ⊠ *Pl. Charles-de-Gaulle,* ☎ *01–55–37–73–77,* WEB *www. monuments-france.fr.* 🎫 *40 frs/€6.10.* ☉ *Apr.–Sept., daily 9:30–11; Oct.–Mar., daily 10–10:30. Métro or RER: Étoile.*

🖐 ⑬ **Bateaux Mouches.** If you want to view Paris in slow motion, hop on one of these famous motorboats, which set off on their hour-long tours of the city waters regularly (every half hour in summer) from the place de l'Alma. Their route heads east to the Ile St-Louis and then back west, past the Eiffel Tower, as far as the Allée des Cygnes and its miniature version of the Statue of Liberty. Believe it or not, these were once used as regular ferries on a daily basis by Parisians up until the 1930s. As they bounced from bank to bank on the river, they gave rise, some say, to the name *Bateaux Mouches* (which translates as "fly boats"); more sober historians say the name "mouche" actually refers to a district of Lyon, where the boats were originally manufactured. ⊠ *Pl. de l'Alma,* ☎ *01–40–76–99–99.* WEB *www.bateaux-mouches.fr.* 🎫 *45 frs/€6.87. Métro: Alma-Marceau.*

🖐 ❷ **Champ de Mars.** This long, formal garden, landscaped at the start of the 20th century, lies between the Eiffel Tower and École Militaire. It was previously used as a parade ground and was the site of the World Exhibitions of 1867, 1889 (date of the construction of the Eiffel Tower), and 1900. *Métro: École Militaire; RER: Champ-de-Mars.*

⑭ **Champs-Élysées.** The world's most famous avenue, the Champs-Élysées was once best captured by Marcel Proust who lovingly described the *recherché* elegance of the Champs's Belle Epoque heyday, when its cobblestones resounded to the clatter of horse-and-carriage rather than the screech of tires. Although there's a certain thrill to strutting here, the abundance of bland shops and restaurants chains (and the lack of actual Parisians) makes the experience feel suspiciously like a trip to the mall. Originally an expanse of green frequented by cattle, the 2-km (1-mi) Champs-Élysées was laid out in the 1660s by the landscape gardener André Le Nôtre as a park sweeping away from the Tuileries. Today, in a losing battle against all those airline offices, car showrooms, and movie theaters, the city has planted extra trees, broadened sidewalks, installed coordinated designer street-furnishings (everything from benches and lighting to traffic lights, telephone booths, and trash cans), refurbished (i.e., Disneyfied) Art Nouveau newsstands, built underground parking to alleviate congestion, and clamped down on garish storefronts. To find the beauteous avenue of yore, look for the elegant 19th-century park pavilions along the lower half of the avenue, one of which houses the historic restaurant Ledoyen. ⊠ *Métro: Champs-Élysées–Clemenceau, Franklin-D.-Roosevelt, George-V, Étoile.*

❶ **École Militaire** (Military Academy). Napoléon was one of the more famous graduates of this military academy, whose harmonious 18th-century building, facing the Eiffel Tower across the Champ de Mars, is still in use for army training (and, consequently, not open to the public). ⊠ *Pl. du Maréchal-Joffre. Métro: École Militaire.*

⑫ **Les Égouts** (The Sewers). Brave the unpleasant—though tolerable—smell of the Paris sewers to follow an underground city of banks, passages, and footbridges. Signs indicate the streets above you, and detailed panels and displays illuminate the history of waste disposal in Paris, whose sewer system is the largest in the world after Chicago's. The tour takes about an hour. ⊠ *Opposite 93 quai d'Orsay,* ☎ *01–53–68–27–81.* 🎟 *25 frs/€3.81.* ☉ *Feb.–Dec., Sat.–Wed. 11–5. Métro: Alma-Marceau; RER: Pont de l'Alma.*

OFF THE
BEATEN PATH

AMERICAN CHURCH – This Left Bank neo-Gothic church, built 1927–31, offers help and advice to English-speaking foreigners. ⊠ *65 quai d'Orsay,* ☎ *01–47–05–07–99. Métro: Alma-Marceau; RER: Pont de l'Alma.*

---

⑮ Lido. Free-flowing champagne, foot-stomping melodies in French and English, and topless razzmatazz pack in the crowds (mostly tourists) every night for the show at this famous nightclub, which has been around since 1946. ⊠ *116 av. des Champs-Élysées,* 🌐 *www.lido.fr. Métro: George-V.*

⑩ Musée d'Art Moderne de la Ville de Paris (Paris Museum of Modern Art). Both temporary exhibits and a permanent collection of top-quality 20th-century art can be found at this modern art museum. It takes over, chronologically speaking, where the Musée d'Orsay leaves off: among the earliest works are Fauve paintings by Vlaminck and Derain, followed by Picasso's early experiments in Cubism. Its vast, unobtrusive, white-walled galleries provide an ideal backdrop for the bold statements of 20th-century art. Loudest and largest are the canvases of Robert Delaunay. Other highlights include works by Braque, Rouault, Gleizes, Da Silva, Gromaire, and Modigliani. There is also a large room devoted to Art Deco furniture and screens, where Jean Dunand's gilt and lacquered panels consume oceans of wall space. There is a pleasant, if expensive, museum café and an excellent bookshop specializing in 19th- and 20th-century art and architecture, with many books in English. ⊠ *11 av. du Président-Wilson,* ☎ *01–53–67–40–00,* 🌐 *www.paris-france.org/musees.* 🎟 *30 frs/€4.60.* ☉ *Tues.–Fri. 10–5:30, weekends 10–6:45. Métro: Iéna.*

⑧ Musée Guimet. One of the most refined and cherished of Paris museums, this Belle Epoque treasure was founded by Lyonnais industrialist Émile Guimet, who traveled around the world in the late 19th century amassing priceless Indo-Chinese and Far Eastern objets d'art. A highlight is the largest collection of Cambodian art this side of Cambodia, with celebrated works from the Angkor culture. The museum reopened early 2001 after a major renovation. ⊠ *6 pl. d'Iéna,* ☎ *01–45–05–00–98,* 🌐 *www.museeguimet.fr.* 🎟 *35 frs/€5.34. Métro: Iéna.*

⑤ Musée de l'Homme (Museum of Mankind). Picasso, it is said, discovered the bold lines of African masks and sculpture here and promptly went off to paint his *Desmoiselles d'Avignon* and create Cubism. You, too, may be inspired by the impressive artifacts, costumes, and domestic tools from around the world here, the earliest dating from prehistoric times. This earnest anthropological museum is in the south wing of the Palais de Chaillot—to find the entrance, just look for the giant totem pole from British Colombia. ⊠ *17 pl. du Trocadéro,* ☎ *01–44–05–72–72,* 🌐 *www.mnhn.fr.* 🎟 *30 frs/€4.60.* ☉ *Wed.–Mon. 9:45–5:15. Métro: Trocadéro.*

NEED A
BREAK?

Get a tremendous view of the Eiffel Tower and the Invalides dome with your ice cream, cocktail, or 21-euro lunch at **Le Totem** (☎ 01–44–05–90–00), an elegant bar and restaurant in the south wing of the Palais de Chaillot.

HOW TO
USE THIS GUIDE

Great trips begin with great planning, and this guide makes planning easy. It's packed with everything you need—insider advice on hotels and restaurants, cool tools, practical tips, essential maps, and much more.

COOL TOOLS

Fodor's Choice Top picks are marked throughout with a star.

Great Itineraries These tours, planned by Fodor's experts, give you the skinny on what you can see and do in the time you have.

Smart Travel Tips A to Z This special section is packed with important contacts and advice on everything from how to get around to what to pack.

Good Walks You won't miss a thing if you follow the numbered bullets on our maps.

Need a Break? Looking for a quick bite to eat or a spot to rest? These sure bets are along the way.

Off the Beaten Path Some lesser-known sights are worth a detour. We've marked those you should make time for.

POST-IT® FLAGS
Dog-ear no more!

"Post-it" is a registered trademark of 3M.

ICONS AND SYMBOLS

Watch for these symbols throughout:

★   Our special recommendations

✕   Restaurant

▥   Lodging establishment

✕▥   Lodging establishment whose restaurant warrants a special trip

◔   Good for kids

☞   Sends you to another section of the guide for more information

✉   Address

☏   Telephone number

FAX   Fax number

WEB   Web site

🎟   Admission price

☉   Opening hours

$-$$$$ Lodging and dining price categories, keyed to strategically sited price charts. Check the index for locations.

① ❶   Numbers in white and black circles on the maps, in the margins, and within tours correspond to one another.

ON THE WEB

Continue your planning with these useful tools found at **www.fodors.com**, the Web's best source for travel information.

"Rich with resources." —*New York Times*

"Navigation is a cinch." —*Forbes* "Best of the Web" list

"Put together by people bursting with know-how."
                    —*Sunday Times* (London)

Create a Miniguide Pinpoint hotels, restaurants, and attractions that have what you want at the price you want to pay.

Rants and Raves Find out what readers say about Fodor's picks—or write your own reviews of hotels and restaurants you've just visited.

Travel Talk Post your questions and get answers from fellow travelers, or share your own experiences.

On-Line Booking Find the best prices on airline tickets, rental cars, cruises, or vacations, and book them on the spot.

About our Books Learn about other Fodor's guides to your destination and many others.

Expert Advice and Trip Ideas From what to tip to how to take great photos, from the national parks to Nepal, Fodors.com has suggestions that'll make your trip a breeze. Log on and get informed and inspired.

Smart Resources Check the weather in your destination or convert your currency. Learn the local language or link to the latest event listings. Or consult hundreds of detailed maps—all in one place.

6 **Musée de la Marine** (Maritime Museum). In the west wing of the Palais de Chaillot, this museum contains ship models and seafaring paraphernalia illustrating French naval history up to the age of the nuclear submarine. ⊠ *17 pl. du Trocadéro,* ☎ *01–53–65–69–69.* 🎟 *38 frs/ €5.84.* ☉ *Wed.–Mon. 10–6. Métro: Trocadéro.*

7 **Musée des Monuments Français** (French Monuments Museum). One of the most fascinating museums in Paris, this place is now closed due to a 1997 fire and, unfortunately, won't reopen until 2003. Founded in 1879 by architect-restorer Viollet-le-Duc (the man mainly responsible for the extensive renovation of Notre-Dame and countless other Gothic cathedrals), it is a vast repository of copies of statues, columns, archways, and frescoes from the Romanesque and Gothic periods (roughly 1000–1500) and forms an excellent (if somewhat bogus) introduction to French medieval architecture. ⊠ *1 pl. du Trocadéro,* ☎ *01–44–05–39–10. Métro: Trocadéro.*

16 **Office de Tourisme de la Ville de Paris** (Paris Tourist Office). The modern, spacious Paris Tourist Office, near the Arc de Triomphe, is worth a visit at the start of your stay to pick up free maps, leaflets, and information on upcoming events. Most of the staff speak English and can also help book accommodations or tickets for shows. You can also exchange money here and buy métro tickets and souvenirs. ⊠ *127 av. des Champs-Élysées,* ☎ *01–49–52–53–54; 01–49–52–53–56 recorded information in English,* WEB *www.paris-touristoffice.com.* ☉ *Daily 9– 8. Métro: Charles-de-Gaulle–Étoile.*

4 **Palais de Chaillot** (Chaillot Palace). This honey-color Art Deco cultural center was built in the 1930s to replace a Moorish-style building constructed for the World Exhibition of 1878. It contains three large museums: the **Musée de l'Homme,** the **Musée de la Marine,** and the **Musée des Monuments Français.** The tumbling gardens leading to the Seine contain sculptures, dramatic fountains, and a large aquarium currently undergoing renovation. The palace terrace, flanked by gilded statuettes (and often invaded by roller skaters and skateboarders), offers a wonderful, picture-postcard view of the Eiffel Tower and is a favorite spot for fashion photographers. ⊠ *Pl. du Trocadéro. Métro: Trocadéro.*

9 **Palais Galliera.** This luxurious mansion, built in 1888 for the Duchesse de Galliera, houses rotating exhibits on costumery and clothing design. ⊠ *10 av. Pierre-1er-de-Serbie,* ☎ *01–56–52–86–00.* 🎟 *45 frs/€6.90.* ☉ *Tues.–Sun. 10–6. Métro: Iéna.*

11 **Pont de l'Alma** (Alma Bridge). This bridge is best known for the chunky stone "Zouave" statue carved into one of the pillars. Zouaves were Algerian infantrymen recruited into the French army who were famous for their bravura and colorful uniforms. There is nothing quite so glamorous, or colorful, about the Alma Zouave, however, whose hour of glory comes in times of watery distress: Parisians use him to judge the level of the Seine during heavy rains. *Métro: Alma-Marceau.*

★ ☺ **3** **Tour Eiffel** (Eiffel Tower). If the Statue of Liberty is New York, if Big Ben is London, if the Kremlin is Moscow, then the Eiffel Tower is Paris. For two years French engineer Gustave Eiffel—already famous for building viaducts and bridges—worked to erect this monument, which was designed to exalt the technical era that had begun to shine in the lamp of Edison and to stammer in the first telephone of Bell. It was created for the World Exhibition of 1889, inaugurated by Edward VII, then Prince of Wales, and was still in good shape to celebrate its own 100th birthday. Such was Eiffel's engineering wizardry that even in the strongest winds his tower never sways more than 4½ inches.

Since its colossal bulk exudes a feeling of mighty permanence, you may have trouble believing that it nearly became 7,000 tons of scrap iron when its concession expired in 1909. Many Parisians first hated the structure and agreed with designer William Morris, who arrived at its site one day to exclaim, "Why on earth have I come here? Because it's the only place I can't see it from." Only its potential use as a radio antenna saved the day (it still bristles with a forest of radio and television transmitters). By the days of the German occupation, however, Paris trembled when it was suggested that the 12,000 pieces of metal and its 2,500,000 rivets should be "requisitioned." The shimmering nocturnal illumination, installed for the millennium celebrations at the start of 2000, is breathtaking—every girder highlighted in glorious detail. If you're full of energy, stride up the stairs as far as the third deck. If you want to go to the top, you'll have to take the elevator. The view at 1,000 ft may not beat that from the Tour Montparnasse, but the setting makes it considerably more romantic. In celebration of the new century, the tower has been equipped to light up like a giant sparkler every night—ever hour on the hour, for 10 glittering minutes, from dusk to 1 AM. ⊠ *Quai Branly,* ☎ *01–44–11–23–23,* WEB *www. tour-eiffel.fr.* ⌛ *By elevator: 2nd floor, 22 frs/€3.35; 3rd floor, 44 frs/€6.70; 4th floor, 62 frs/€9.50. By foot: 2nd and 3rd floors only, 18 frs/€2.7.* ☉ *July–Aug., daily 9 am–midnight; Sept.–June, daily 9 am–11 pm. Métro: Bir-Hakeim; RER: Champ-de-Mars.*

THE FAUBOURG ST-HONORÉ

Fashions change, but the Faubourg St-Honoré—the area just north of the Champs-Élysées and the Tuileries—firmly maintains its tradition of high style. As you progress from the President's Palace, past a wealth of art galleries and the Neoclassic Madeleine Church to the stately place Vendôme, you will see that all is luxury and refinement here. On the ritzy square, famous boutiques sit side by side with famous banks—after all, elegance and finance have never been an unusual combination. It is not surprising to learn that one of the main arteries of the area, the rue de Castiglione, was named after one of its former residents—the glamorous fashion-plate Countess de Castiglione, sent to plead the cause of Italian unity with Napoléon III. The emperor was persuaded (he was easily susceptible to feminine charms), and the area became a Kingdom of Woman: famous dressmakers, renowned jewelers, exclusive perfume shops, and the most chic hotel in Paris, the Ritz, made this *faubourg* (district) a symbol of luxury throughout the world.

Today, the tradition continues, with leading names in fashion found farther east on the place des Victoires, close to what was, for centuries, the gastronomic heart of Paris: Les Halles (pronounced "lay-*al*"), once the city's main market. These giant glass-and-iron market halls were closed in 1969 and replaced by a park and a modern shopping mall, the Forum des Halles. The surrounding streets underwent a transformation and are now filled with shops, cafés, restaurants, and chic apartment buildings. The brash modernity of the mall stands in contrast to the august church of St-Eustache nearby. Similarly, the incongruous black-and-white columns in the classical courtyard of Richelieu's neighboring Palais-Royal present a further case of daring modernity—or architectural vandalism, depending on your point of view.

Numbers in the text correspond to numbers in the margin and on the Faubourg St-Honoré map.

A Good Walk

Start your walk in front of the most important home in France: the **Palais de l'Élysée** ①, the Presidential Palace; barriers and gold-braided guards keep visitors at bay. There's more to see in the plethora of art galleries and luxury fashion boutiques lining rue du Faubourg St-Honoré, where you will also see Sotheby's auction house and the British embassy. From rue du Faubourg St-Honoré, turn left onto rue Boissy-d'Anglas and cut right through an archway into Cité Berryer, a smart courtyard with several trendy shops. It leads to rue Royale, a classy street lined with jewelry stores. Looming to the left is the sturdy **Église de la Madeleine** ②.

Cross boulevard de la Madeleine and take rue Duphot down to rue St-Honoré, where you'll find **Notre-Dame de l'Assomption** ③, noted for its huge dome and solemn interior. Continue to rue de Castiglione; then head left to one of the world's most opulent squares, the **place Vendôme** ④, ringed with jewelers. That's Napoléon standing at the top of the square's bronze central column—and that's the Ritz, fronted by those Rolls-Royces, halfway down on the left. Return to rue St-Honoré and continue to the mighty church of **St-Roch** ⑤. It's worth having a look inside to see the bombastically Baroque altarpiece in the circular Lady Chapel at the far end.

Take the next right onto rue des Pyramides and cross the place des Pyramides, with its gilded statue of Joan of Arc on horseback, to the northwest wing of the Louvre, home to the **Union Centrale des Arts Décoratifs** ⑥, with three separate museums dedicated to fashion, publicity, and the decorative arts. Stay on arcaded rue de Rivoli to the place du Palais-Royal. On the far side of the square is the **Louvre des Antiquaires** ⑦, a chic shopping mall housing upscale antiques stores. Opposite, beyond the exuberant fountains of the place André-Malraux, Garnier's 19th-century Opéra beckons at the far end of the avenue of the same name.

Just beyond Jean-Michel Othaniel's aluminum and psychedelic glass entrance canopy to the Palais-Royal Métro station, erected in 2000, is the **Comédie Française** ⑧, the time-honored setting for performances of classical French drama. To the right of the theater is the unobtrusive entrance to the **Palais-Royal** ⑨; its courtyard is a surprising oasis in the heart of the city and a study in both classical and contemporary French landscape architecture. Walk down to the far end of the garden and peek into the glossy 19th-century interior of Le Grand Véfour, one of the swankiest restaurants in the city.

One block north of here, on rue de Richelieu, stands what used to be France's main national library, the **Bibliothèque Nationale Richelieu** ⑩. Rue des Petits-Champs heads east to the circular **place des Victoires** ⑪: that's Louis XIV riding the plunging steed in the center of the square. You'll find some of the city's most upscale fashion shops here and on the surrounding streets, along with the 17th-century church of **Notre-Dame des Victoires** ⑫. Head south down rue Croix-des-Petits-Champs, past the nondescript Banque de France on your right, and take the second street on the left to the circular **Bourse du Commerce** ⑬, the Commercial Exchange. Alongside it is a 100-ft-high fluted column, the **Colonne de Ruggieri.**

Today most of the market area that once sat alongside is occupied by the **Jardin des Halles** ⑭, dominated on the left by the bulky outline of the church of **St-Eustache** ⑮, a curious architectural hybrid of Gothic and classical styles. Take bustling rue de Montorgeuil beyond the church, and then turn right on rue Étienne-Marcel to admire the **Tour**

The Faubourg St-Honoré

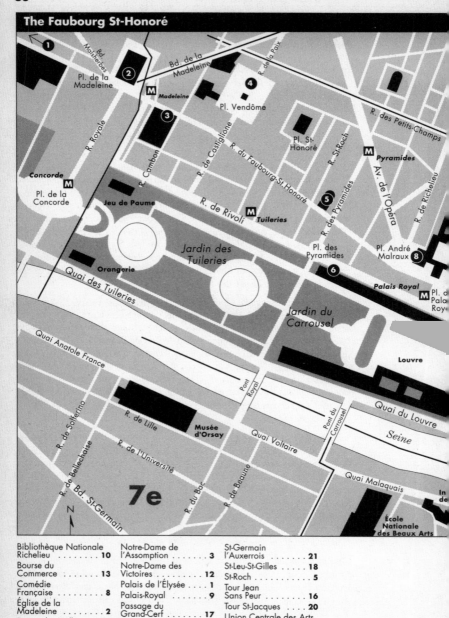

Bourse **M** La Bourse

220 yards
200 meters

10

R. Vivienne

R. N. D. des Victoires

12

R. du Mail

R. de Cléry

M

R. d'Aboukir

R. Montmartre

2e

R. Montorgueil

Rue Réaumur

R. St-Sauveur

Reaumur Sébastopol **M**

11

R. Greneta

R. Dussoubs

R. St-Denis

Banque de France

R. M. Stuart

9

R. Tiquetonne

17

R. Coquillère

R. Etienne Marcel

16

R. de Turbigo

R. Croix des Petits-Champs

15

Etienne Marcel **M**

Bd. de Sébastopol

7

13

R. Pierre Lescot

R. St-Denis

18

3e

14

M Les Halles

R. du Louvre

1er

19

R. Berger

R. Rambuteau

R. du Faubourg-St-Honoré

R. des Halles

Châtelet– Les Halles **M**

Sq. des Innocents

Centre Pompidou

Louvre **M**

R. de Rivoli

R. de l'Amiral de Coligny

21

R. de Prêtres

R. de l'Arbre-Sec

R. du Pont Neuf

R. St-Denis

Pl. Igor Stravinsky

R. St-Martin

M

Châtelet

R. St-Martin

R. du Renard

Pont des Arts

tut France

Pont Neuf

Pont Neuf

Av. Victoria

Quai de la Mégisserie

20

R. de Rivoli

4e

M

Hôtel de Ville

M

Châtelet

Conciergerie

Pont au Change

Pl. du Châtelet

Jean Sans Peur ⑯, a tower built into the old city walls in 1409. Backtrack a few yards and turn right onto rue Française, right again along quaint rue Tiquetonne, and then take your first left into rue Dussoubs. Just to your right is the entrance to one of the city's most elegant covered galleries, the **Passage du Grand-Cerf** ⑰. Turn right at the end of the gallery and go down rue St-Denis to the cozy medieval church of **St-Leu–St-Gilles** ⑱.

Stay on rue St-Denis and take a third right, along rue des Prêcheurs, to reach the **Forum des Halles** ⑲, a modern, multilevel shopping mall. Turn left on rue Pierre-Lescot to reach the square des Innocents, with its handsome 16th-century Renaissance fountain. Farther east you can see the futuristic funnels of the Centre Pompidou jutting above the surrounding buildings.

From the far end of the square des Innocents, rue St-Denis leads to place du Châtelet, with its theaters, fountain, and the **Tour St-Jacques** ⑳ looming up to your left—all that remains of a church that once stood here. Turning right on the quai de la Mégisserie, you can divide your attention between the exotic array of caged birds for sale along the sidewalk and the view across the Seine toward the turreted Conciergerie. As you cross rue du Pont-Neuf, the birds give way to the Art Deco Samaritaine department store with its panoramic rooftop café. Turn right on rue de l'Arbre-Sec, and then take the first left onto rue des Prêtres to reach **St-Germain l'Auxerrois** ㉑, once the French royal family's parish church. Opposite is the colonnaded eastern facade of the Louvre.

TIMING

With brief visits to churches and monuments, this 5½-km (3½-mi) walk should take about three to four hours. On a nice day, linger in the gardens of the Palais-Royal; on a cold day, indulge in an unbelievably thick hot chocolate at the Angélina tearoom on rue de Rivoli.

Sights to See

⑩ **Bibliothèque Nationale Richelieu** (Richelieu National Library). France's longtime national library used to contain more than 7 million printed volumes; many have been removed to the giant new Bibliothèque Nationale François-Mitterrand, though original manuscripts and prints are still here. You can admire Robert de Cotte's 18th-century courtyard, and peep into the magnificent 19th-century reading room, but you cannot enter (it's only open to researchers). The collections are on exhibit from time to time in the library's galleries. ⊠ *58 rue de Richelieu.* ⊙ *Daily 9–8. Métro: Bourse.*

⑬ **Bourse du Commerce** (Commercial Exchange). The circular, shallow-domed 18th-century Commercial Exchange building near Les Halles began life as the Corn Exchange; Victor Hugo waggishly likened it to a jockey's cap without the peak. ⊠ *Rue de Viarmes. Métro or RER: Les Halles.*

Colonne de Ruggieri (Ruggieri's Column). The 100-ft-high fluted column, behind the Bourse du Commerce, is all that remains of a mansion built here in 1572 for Catherine de' Medici. The column is said to have been used as a platform for stargazing by her astrologer, Ruggieri. *Métro: Les Halles.*

⑧ **Comédie Française.** This theater is the setting for performances of classical French drama, with tragedies by Racine and Corneille and comedies by Molière regularly on the bill. The building itself dates from 1790, but the Comédie Française company was created by that most theatrical of French monarchs, Louis XIV, back in 1680. If you understand French and have a taste for the mannered, declamatory style of French acting—it's a far cry from method acting—you'll appreciate an evening here. ⊠ *2 rue de Richelieu,* ☎ *01–44–58–15–15. Métro: Palais-Royal.*

② Église de la Madeleine. With its rows of uncompromising columns, this sturdy neoclassical edifice—designed in 1814 but not consecrated until 1842—looks more like a proudly inflated, though unfaithful, version of a Greek temple than a Christian church. The loose interpretation was intentional: The overproportioned porticoes, the interior barrel vaults-cum-domes, and the opulent versions of the Ionic and Corinthian orders were meant to be Parisian one-uppings of anything Athens had to offer. Changing political moods continued to alter the building's purpose—a Greek basilica one day, a temple to Napoléon's glory another, a National Assembly hall the next. At one point, in fact, La Madeleine, as it is known, was nearly selected as Paris's first train station. Inside, the only natural light comes from three shallow domes. The walls are richly and harmoniously decorated; gold glints through the murk (which was the result of one architect filling in the stained-glass windows of another). Nowadays the opulent interior is the site of lots of expensive concerts as well as daily masses. And if sitting in the cool interior of a Catholic church is not enough to make you reflect upon your sins, try viewing the huge fresco of the Last Judgment above you. A simpler crypt offers intimate weekday masses. ⊠ *Pl. de la Madeleine.* ⊗ *Mon.–Sat. 7:30–7, Sun. 8–7. Métro: Madeleine.*

NEED A BREAK?   **L'Écluse** (⊠ 15 pl. de la Madeleine), a cozy wine bar on the square to the west of the Église de la Madeleine, serves stylish snacks, such as foie gras and carpaccio, and a range of Bordeaux wines.

⑲ Forum des Halles. Les Halles, the iron-and-glass halls of the central Paris food market, were closed in 1969 and replaced in the late '70s by the Forum des Halles, a characterless, modern shopping mall. Nothing remains of either the market or the rambunctious atmosphere that led 19th-century novelist Émile Zola to dub Les Halles *le ventre de Paris* ("the belly of Paris"), although rue Montorgueil, behind St-Eustache, retains something of its original bustle. Unfortunately, much of the plastic, concrete, glass, and mock-marble facade of the multi-level shopping mall is already showing signs of wear and tear. This state of affairs is not much helped by the hordes of teenagers and down-and-outs who invade it toward dusk. Nonetheless, if you are a serious shopper, you might want to check out the French chain stores, the few small boutiques, and the weekly fashion shows by up-and-coming young designers held here. ⊠ *Main entrance: rue Pierre-Lescot. Métro: Les Halles; RER: Châtelet–Les Halles.*

⑭ Jardin des Halles (Les Halles Garden). This garden, crisscrossed with paths and alleyways flanked by bushes, flower beds, and trim little lawns, takes up much of the site once occupied by Les Halles, the city's central market. Children love the bush shaped like a rhinoceros. *Métro: Les Halles; RER: Châtelet–Les Halles.*

⑦ Louvre des Antiquaires. This "shopping mall" of superelegant antiques dealers, off the place du Palais-Royal opposite the Louvre, is a minimuseum in itself. Its stylish, glass-walled corridors—lined with Louis XVI *boiseries* (antique wood paneling), Charles Dix bureaux, and the pretty sort of bibelots that would have gladdened the heart of Marie-Antoinette—deserve a browse whether you intend to buy or not. ⊠ *Main entrance: Pl. du Palais-Royal.* ⊗ *Tues.–Sun. 11–7. Métro: Palais-Royal.*

NEED A
BREAK? Founded in 1903, **Angélina** (✉ 226 rue de Rivoli, ☎ 01–42–60–82–
00) is an elegant, time-worn *salon de thé* (tearoom), lined with seaside
frescoes and huge mirrors, famous for its irresistible 36-franc *chocolat
africain*, a cup of hot, thick chocolate served with whipped cream.

③ Notre-Dame de l'Assomption. This 1670 church, with its huge dome
and solemn interior, was the scene of Lafayette's funeral in 1834. It is
now a chapel for Paris's Polish community. ✉ *Rue Cambon. Métro:
Concorde.*

⑫ Notre-Dame des Victoires. Visit this central Paris church, built from
1666 to 1740, to see the 30,000 ex-voto tablets that adorn its walls.
✉ *Pl. des Petits-Pères. Métro: Sentier.*

① Palais de l'Élysée. Madame de Pompadour, Napoléon, Joséphine, the
Duke of Wellington, and Queen Victoria all stayed at this "palace,"
today the official home of the French president. Originally constructed
as a private mansion in 1718, the Élysée—incidentally, when Parisians
talk about "L'Élysée," they mean the president's palace, whereas the
Champs-Élysées is known simply as "Les Champs"—has housed pres-
idents only since 1873. President Félix Faure died here in 1899 in the
arms of his mistress, so it is said. Although you can catch a glimpse of
the palace forecourt and facade through the Faubourg St-Honoré gateway, it is difficult to get much idea of the building's size, or of the extensive gardens that stretch back to the Champs-Élysées, because it is
closed to the public. ✉ *55 rue du Faubourg-St-Honoré. Métro: Miromesnil.*

★ **⑨ Palais-Royal** (Royal Palace). One of the most Parisian sights in all of
Paris, the Palais-Royal is especially loved for its gardens, where children play, lovers whisper, and senior citizens crumble bread for the spar-
rows, seemingly oblivious to the ghosts of history that haunt this place.
Originally dating from the 1630s, this *palais* is *royal* only in that all-
powerful Cardinal Richelieu (1585–1642) magnanimously bequeathed
it to Louis XIII. In his early days as king, Louis XIV preferred the relative intimacy of this place to the intimidating splendor of the nearby
Louvre (of course, he soon decided that his own intimidating splendor warranted a more majestic setting; hence, Versailles). During the
French Revolution, it became Le Palais Egalité (the Palace of Equal-
ity) because its owner, Louis Philippe d'Orléans, the king's cousin, pro-
fessed revolutionary ideas, one of which was to convert the arcades of
the palace into boutiques and cafés (Louis XVI reputedly quipped, "My
cousin, now that you are going to keep shop I suppose we shall only
see you on Sundays"). Before one of these shops Camille Desmoulins
gave the first speech calling for the French Revolution in 1789.

Today, the Palais-Royal is home to a block of apartments and the French
Ministry of Culture, and its buildings are not open to the public (unless you are lucky enough to live here—former residents have included
André Malraux, Jean Cocteau, and Colette). They overlook a colonnaded courtyard with black-and-white-striped half-columns and re-
volving silver spheres that slither around in two fountains, the
controversial work of architect Daniel Buren. The splendid gardens beyond are bordered by arcades harboring discreet boutiques and divided
by rows of perfectly trimmed little trees. Back in the early 19th century, this was the haunt of prostitutes and gamblers: a veritable sink
of vice. These days it's hard to imagine anywhere more hoity-toity. ✉
Pl. du Palais-Royal. Métro: Palais-Royal.

⑰ Passage du Grand-Cerf. This pretty, glass-roofed *passage* (gallery) is
filled with crafts shops offering an innovative selection of jewelry,

paintings, and ceramics. ✉ *Entrances on rue Dussoubs, rue St-Denis. Métro: Étienne-Marcel.*

❹ **Place Vendôme.** Snobbish and self-important, this famous square is also gorgeous; property laws have kept away cafés and other such banal establishments, leaving the plaza stately and refined, the perfect home for the rich and famous (Chopin lived and died at No. 12; today's celebs camp out at the Hotel Ritz at No. 15, while a lucky few, including the family of the Sultan of Brunei, actually own houses here). With its granite pavement and Second Empire street lamps, Jules-Hardouin Mansart's rhythmic, perfectly proportioned example of 17th-century urban architecture shines in all its golden-stoned splendor. The square is a fitting showcase for the cluster of jewelry display windows found here. Interestingly, when the square was first built, only the facades of the hôtels particuliers were constructed, to maintain a uniform appearance— the lots behind the facades were then sold to buyers who custom-tailored their palaces to individual taste. Napoléon had the square's central column made from the melted bronze of 1,200 cannons captured at the battle of Austerlitz in 1805, and stands vigilantly on the top. Painter Gustave Courbet headed the Revolutionary hooligans who, in 1871, toppled the column (into a pile of manure, no less) and shattered it into thousands of metallic pieces. The Third Republic stuck them together again and sent him the bill. To raise a glass of champagne to honor the place's famous ghosts, repair to Hemingway's Bar at the Ritz (☞ *Close-Up Box, Hemingway's Paris, below*). *Métro: Opéra.*

⓫ **Place des Victoires.** This circular square, now home to many of the city's top fashion boutiques, was laid out in 1685 by Jules-Hardouin Mansart in honor of the military victories of Louis XIV, that indefatigable warrior whose nearly continuous battles may have brought much prestige to his country but came perilously close to bringing it to bankruptcy, too. Louis is shown galloping along on a bronze horse in the middle; his statue dates from 1822 and replaced one destroyed during the Revolution. Louis was so taken with this plaza that he commissioned the architect, who also designed much of Versailles, to built another, the place Vendôme, on the other side of the avenue de l'Opéra. *Métro: Sentier.*

⓯ **St-Eustache.** Since the demolition of the 19th-century iron-and-glass market halls at the beginning of the '70s, St-Eustache has reemerged as a dominant element on the central Paris skyline. It is a huge church, the "cathedral" of Les Halles, built as the market people's Right Bank reply to Notre-Dame on the Ile de la Cité. St-Eustache dates from a couple of hundred years later than Notre-Dame. With the exception of the feeble west front, added between 1754 and 1788, construction lasted from 1532 to 1637, spanning the decline of the Gothic style and the emergence of the Renaissance. As a consequence, the church is a curious architectural hybrid. Its exterior flying buttresses are Gothic, but its column orders, rounded arches, and thick, comparatively simple window tracery are unmistakably classical. Few buildings bear such eloquent witness to stylistic transition. St-Eustache also hosts occasional organ concerts. ✉ *2 rue du Jour,* ☎ *01–46–27–89–21 concert information.* ☉ *Daily 8–7. Métro: Les Halles; RER: Châtelet–Les Halles.*

㉑ **St-Germain l'Auxerrois.** Until 1789, this church was used by the French royal family as its Paris parish church, in the days when the adjacent Louvre was a palace rather than a museum. The fluid stonework of the facade reveals the influence of 15th-century Flamboyant Gothic style, enjoying its final shrieks before the classical takeover of the Renais-

HEMINGWAY'S PARIS

THERE IS AN OLD FAMILIAR SAYING: "Everyone has two countries, his or her own—and France." For the "Lost Generation" after World War I, these words rang particularly true. Disillusioned by America's Depression and Prohibition, lured by favorable exchange rates and a booming artistic scene, many American writers, composers, and painters moved to Paris in the 1920s and 1930s. F. Scott Fitzgerald, Gertrude Stein, Ezra Pound, e.e. cummings, Janet Flanner, and John dos Passos are just a few of the famous figures, with Ernest Hemingway heading the list. "Papa" found Paris a veritable Land of Cockaigne, where every man does what he pleases, where all could allow their personal idiosyncracies full play and apologize for them with the simple remark, Je suis comme ça. "I am like that." It is this freedom that, back then, made Paris the cultural—and hoopla—capital of the world. And the best witnesses to that amazing era were the many expatriates who came to admire, and remained to praise.

Hemingway arrived in Paris with his first wife, Hadley, in December, 1921, and made for the Left Bank—the Hôtel Jacob et d'Angleterre, to be exact (still operating at 44 rue Jacob). To celebrate their arrival, the couple went to the Café de la Paix for a meal they nearly couldn't afford. In 1922 the couple moved to 74 rue du Cardinal-Lemoine (his writing studio was around the corner on the top floor of 39 rue Descartes), then in early 1924 the couple and their baby son settled at 113 rue Notre-Dame des Champs. Nearby, he settled in at La Closerie des Lilas café to write much of *The Sun Also Rises*. It was a time "when we were very young and very happy" as he wrote in *A Moveable Feast*.

Not happy long. In 1926 Hemingway left Hadley and next year wedded his mistress Pauline Pfeiffer across town at St Honoré-d'Eylau, then moved to 6 rue Férou, near the Musée du Luxembourg, whose collection of Cézanne landscapes (now in the Musée d'Orsay) he revered. Hemingway once declared that "unless you have geography, background, you have nothing." You can follow the steps of Jake and Bill in *The Sun Also Rises* as they "circle" the Ile St-Louis before the "steep walking . . . all the way up to the place de la Contrescarpe," then right along rue du Pot-de-Fer to the "rigid north and south" of rue St-Jacques and on to boulevard du Montparnasse.

For gossip and books, Papa would visit Shakespeare and Company at 12 rue de l'Odéon, owned by Sylvia Beach, an early buddy (the bookstore can now be found at 37 rue de la Bûcherie). For cash and cocktails, Hemingway usually headed to the upscale Right Bank. The first was found at the Guaranty Trust Company, at 1 rue des Italiens. The second, when he was flush, at the bar of the Hotel Crillon, or, when poor, at the Caves Mura, at 19 rue d'Antin, or Harry's Bar, still in brisk business at 5 rue Daunou, with photos of Papa gazing down from the walls. Hemingway's legendary association with the Hotel Ritz, where he now has his own bar named for him, dates from the Liberation in 1944, when he strode in at the head of his platoon and "liberated" the joint by ordering 73 Dry Martinis. Here, Hemingway asked Mary Welsh to become his fourth wife, and also righted the world with Jean-Paul Sartre, George Orwell, and Marlene Dietrich. Paris loves naming streets after adopted sons and it is only fitting that Hemingway has a plaque of his own, heralding short Rue Ernest-Hemingway in the 15th arrondissement. This, after all, was the man who wrote: "There is never any ending to Paris."

sance. Notice the unusually wide windows in the nave and the equally unusual double aisles. The triumph of classicism is evident, however, in the fluted columns around the choir, the area surrounding the altar. These were added in the 18th century and are characteristic of the desire of 18th-century clerics to dress up medieval buildings in the architectural raiment of their own day. ⊠ *Pl. du Louvre. Métro: Louvre-Rivoli.*

⑱ St-Leu–St-Gilles. Near the Centre Pompidou, this intimate church presents a stylistic contrast between its large-windowed, 14th-century nave and the raised, 17th-century Renaissance choir. ⊠ *Rue St-Denis. Métro: Étienne-Marcel.*

❺ St-Roch. Designed by Lemercier in 1653 but completed only in the 1730s, this huge church is almost as long (138 yards) as Notre-Dame, thanks to Hardouin-Mansart's domed Lady Chapel at the far end, with its elaborate Baroque altarpiece. Classical playwright Pierre Corneille (1606–84) is buried here; a commemorative plaque honors him at the left of the entrance. ⊠ *Rue St-Honoré. Métro: Tuileries.*

⑯ Tour Jean Sans Peur. This sturdy medieval tower was built by Jean Sans Peur (John the Fearless), Duke of Burgundy, in 1409 to defend his long-since–vanished Paris mansion. You can explore the spiral staircase and admire the magnificent vaulting with its intertwined array of sculpted vines, hops, and hawthorn flowers. Ask for an English translation for all the banners detailing Paris's medieval architecture. ⊠ *20 rue Étienne-Marcel,* ☎ *01–40–26–20–28.* 🎫 *30 frs/€4.60.* ☉ *Sept.– June, Wed. and weekends 1:30–6; July–Aug., Tues.–Sun. 1:30–6. Métro: Étienne-Marcel.*

⑳ Tour St-Jacques. Now used for meteorological purposes and not open to the public, this ornate 170-ft stump tower belonged to a 16th-century church destroyed in 1797. It sits forlornly, swallowed up by surrounding traffic. ⊠ *Pl. du Châtelet. Métro: Châtelet.*

NEED A BREAK?   Twenty different international beers are available on draft, and more than 180 in bottles, at **Le Trappiste** (⊠ 4 rue St-Denis, ☎ 01–42–33–08–50), just north of the place du Châtelet. Mussels and french fries are the traditional accompaniment, although various other snacks (hot dogs, sandwiches) are also available.

★ ❻ Union Centrale des Arts Décoratifs (Decorative Arts Center). A must for lovers of fashion and the decorative arts, this northwestern wing of the Louvre building houses three famously chic museums: the **Musée de la Mode,** devoted to costumes and accessories dating back to the 18th century, usually displayed in temporary exhibitions devoted to a single theme or designer—needless to say, the place is a second home to Paris's enormous fashion community; the **Musée des Arts Décoratifs,** with furniture, tapestries, glassware, paintings and other necessities of life from the Middle Ages through Napoléon's time and beyond—a highlight here are the sumptuous period-style rooms (note the ostentatious number of chairs in the salon); and the **Musée de la Publicité,** opened in 1999, perhaps less of interest for its temporary exhibits of advertisements and posters than for Jean Nouvel's brash decor—described by one Paris critic as "hi-tec miserabalism"—combining metal-plaqued walls with exposed brickwork and faded gilding, as well as black-lacquered parquet floors, leopard-skin pillars, and a battery of TV monitors over the bar. ⊠ *107 rue de Rivoli,* ☎ *01–44–55–57–50,* 🌐 *www.ucad.fr.* 🎫 *35 frs/€5.34.* ☉ *Tues.–Sun. 11–6. Métro: Palais-Royal.*

THE GRANDS BOULEVARDS

The Grands Boulevards are the long chain of avenues that join the Madeleine to the Opéra, then, to the ancient gates of St-Denis and St-Martin, the last to the place de la République, and the République to the Bastille. Together they constitute the longest, most commercial, most representative artery of Paris, and also the most diverse. Parisians have always loved to promenade down their great avenues to feel the pulse of the city throbbing at its strongest. The focal point of this walk is the avenue that runs west to east from St-Augustin, the city's grandest Second Empire church, to place de la République, whose very name symbolizes the ultimate downfall of the imperial regime. The avenue's name changes six times along the way, which is why Parisians refer to it, in plural, as "Les Grands Boulevards."

This walk starts at the Parc Monceau, heart of one of the most fashionable residential neighborhoods, but the makeup of the neighborhoods along the Grands Boulevards changes steadily as you head from the posh 8ᵉ *arrondissement* (district) toward working-class east Paris. The *Grands Magasins* (department stores) at the start of the walk epitomize upscale Paris shopping. They stand on boulevard Haussmann, named in honor of the regional prefect who oversaw the reconstruction of the city in the 1850s and 1860s. The opulent Opéra Garnier, just past the Grands Magasins, is the architectural showpiece of the period (often termed the Second Empire and corresponding to the rule of Napoléon III).

Haussmann's concept of urban planning proved grand enough to ward off the postwar skyscrapers and property sharks that bedevil so many other European cities (Paris's urban planners have relegated them to the outskirts). Though lined with the seven-story blocks typical of Haussmann's time, the boulevards date from the 1670s, when they were created on the site of the city's medieval fortifications. These were razed when Louis XIV's military triumphs appeared to render their raison d'être obsolete, and were replaced by leafy promenades known from the outset as "boulevards."

This walk takes in some of the older sights on both sides of the boulevard, including the city's traditional auction house, the colonnaded stock exchange, and the Sentier district with its busy fabric traders. It ends on the tranquil banks of the little-known Canal St-Martin.

Numbers in the text correspond to numbers in the margin and on The Grand Boulevards map.

A Good Walk

Take the métro to Monceau in the tony 8ᵉ arrondissement and step through gold-topped iron gates to enter the **Parc Monceau** ①—the heart of an elegant residential neighborhood once called home by the likes of Paderewski, Rostand, and Sarah Bernhardt. Past the sculpted busts of Gounod, Chopin, and Bizet, near the middle of the park, head left to avenue Velasquez, which is ornamented with spectacular gates and mansions, one of which is the **Musée Cernuschi** ②—home to Chinese art from Neolithic pottery to contemporary paintings. Continue on to boulevard Malesherbes and turn right, then right again onto rue de Monceau, to reach the **Musée Nissim de Camondo** ③, whose aristocratic interiors sumptuously bring to life the days of the ancien régime.

More splendor awaits at the **Musée Jacquemart-André** ④. Continue down rue de Monceau and turn left onto rue de Courcelles, then left

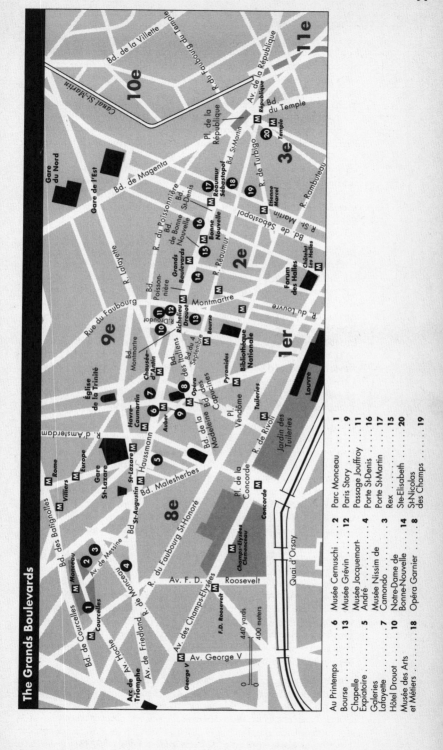

The Grands Boulevards

again onto boulevard Haussmann to find this imposing 19th-century marble palace, filled with lacquered antiques and great old master paintings amassed by a Parisian millionaire. Continue eastward along the boulevard and cross the square in front of the church of St-Augustin. Stay on boulevard Haussmann then turn right down rue d'Anjou to enter the leafy, intimate square Louis XVI with its **Chapelle Expiatoire** ⑤, dedicated to Louis XVI and Marie-Antoinette. Be sure to take a look at the amusing stone carvings on the gleaming 1930s-style facade of the bank at the corner of rue Pasquier and rue Mathurins. Some 300 yards farther down boulevard Haussmann are the Grands Magasins, Paris's most renowned department stores. First comes **Au Printemps** ⑥, then **Galeries Lafayette** ⑦. Marks & Spencer, across the street, provides an outpost for British goods like ginger biscuits and bacon rashers. Opposite Galeries Lafayette is the massive bulk of the **Opéra Garnier** ⑧. Before venturing around to inspect its extravagant facade, colorfully restored in 2000, you might like to take in a multiscreen overview of Paris and its history at the **Paris Story** ⑨ movie venue at No. 11 bis rue Scribe.

Boulevard des Capucines, lined with cinemas and restaurants, heads left from in front of the Opéra, becoming boulevard des Italiens. Look left up rue Laffitte for a startling view of the Sacré-Coeur, looming above the porticoed church of Notre-Dame-de-Lorette. Just after the intersection of boulevard Haussmann with boulevard des Italiens, turn left down rue Drouot to the **Hôtel Drouot** ⑩, Paris's central auction house. Rue Rossini leads from Drouot, as it is known, to rue de la Grange-Batelière. Halfway along on the right is the **Passage Jouffroy** ⑪, one of the many covered galleries that honeycomb the center of Paris. At the far end of the passage is the **Musée Grévin** ⑫, a waxworks museum. Cross boulevard Montmartre to the passage des Panoramas, leading to rue St-Marc. Turn right, then left down rue Vivienne, to find the foursquare, colonnaded **Bourse** ⑬, the Paris Stock Exchange.

If you wish, you can continue down rue Vivienne from the Bourse and join the Faubourg St-Honoré walk at the Bibliothèque Nationale. If you're feeling adventurous, head east along rue Réaumur, whose huge-windowed buildings once formed the heart of the French newspaper industry—stationery shops still abound—and cross rue Montmartre. You can catch sight of the St-Eustache church to your right; the distant spires of St-Ambroise emerge on the horizon. Take the second left up rue de Cléry, a narrow street that is the exclusive domain of fabric wholesalers and often crammed with vans, pallets, and delivery people creating colorful chaos. The lopsided building at the corner of rue Poissonnière looks as if it is struggling to stay upright on the district's drunken slopes. Continue up rue de Cléry as far as rue des Degrés—not a street at all but a 14-step stairway—then look for the clock and crooked turnip tower of **Notre-Dame de Bonne-Nouvelle** ⑭, hemmed in by rickety housing that looks straight out of Balzac. You can enter via No. 19 bis and cross through the church to emerge beneath the front portico on rue de la Lune. Head left as far as rue Poissonnière, and then turn right to return to the Grands Boulevards, by now going under the name of boulevard de Bonne-Nouvelle.

On the near corner of the boulevard stands the **Rex** ⑮, an Art Deco movie theater where you can take a backstage tour. Cross the boulevard for a view of its wedding-cake tower; then head up boulevard de Bonne-Nouvelle to the **Porte St-Denis** ⑯, a newly cleaned triumphal arch dating from the reign of Louis XIV. A little farther on is the smaller but similar **Porte St-Martin** ⑰. From here take rue St-Martin south to the Conservatoire National des Techniques, home to the **Musée des**

Arts et Métiers ⑱, an industrial museum, housed partly in the former church of St-Martin, which reopened in early 2000 after lengthy restoration. In the leafy square opposite, admire the red marble-pillared facade of the derelict Théâtre de la Gaîté Lyrique, a music hall designed by Jacques Hittorff in 1862; Offenbach conducted here from 1873 to 1875, and Diaghilev's Russian ballets set the stage alight from 1911 to 1913.

Farther down rue St-Martin is the high, narrow, late-Gothic church of **St-Nicolas des Champs** ⑲. Continue past the cloister ruins and Renaissance gateway that embellish the far side of St-Nicolas, and head left on rue Turbigo for 400 yards until you meet the rear end of the Baroque church of **Ste-Elisabeth** ⑳ on your right. Shortly after you will reach place de la République.

TIMING

The distance between Parc Monceau and place de la République is about 7 km (4½ mi), which will probably require at least four hours to walk, including taking coffee breaks and window-shopping.

Sights to See

❻ **Au Printemps.** Founded in 1865 by Jules Jaluzot—former employee of Au Bon Marché, which opened 13 years earlier on the Left Bank—Au Printemps swiftly became the mecca of Right Bank shoppers, enabling the current opulent Belle Epoque buildings, with their domes and gold-and-green mosaic signs, to be erected by the turn of the 20th century. The glass cupola in Café Flo dates from 1923; and the rooftop cafeteria has a splendid view of the Paris skyline. ⊠ *64 bd. Haussmann. Métro: Havre-Caumartin.*

OFF THE
BEATEN PATH

ÉGLISE DE LA TRINITÉ – This church, a worthy 1860s essay in neo-Renaissance, is fronted by a lawn and fountains and crowned by a central wedding-cake tower of dubious aesthetic merit that has nonetheless emerged as a landmark feature of the Right Bank skyline. It's at the far end of rue Mogador, opposite the back of the Opéra. ⊠ *Pl. d'Estienne-d'Orves. Métro: Trinité.*

ATELIER DE GUSTAVE MOREAU – A visit to this town house and studio of painter Gustave Moreau (1826–98), doyen of the Symbolist movement, is one of the most distinctive artistic experiences in Paris. The Symbolists strove to convey ideas through images, but many of the ideas Moreau was trying to express were so obscure that the artist had to provide explanatory texts, which rather confuses the point. But it's easy to admire his extravagant colors and flights of fantasy, influenced by Persian and Indian miniatures. From the Trinité church, take rue Blanche to the right, and then turn right on rue de la Tour-des-Dames; the museum is at the far end of rue de la Rochefoucauld. ⊠ *14 rue de la Rochefoucauld,* ☎ *01-48-74-38-50.* ▦ *22 frs/€3.35.* ☉ *Thurs.–Sun. 10–12:45 and 2–5:15, Mon. and Wed. 11–5:15. Métro: Trinité.*

⓭ **Bourse** (Stock Exchange). The Paris Stock Exchange, a serene, colonnaded 19th-century building, is a far cry from Wall Street. Bring your passport if you want to tour it. ⊠ *Rue Vivienne.* ▦ *30 frs. Guided tours only (in French), weekdays every ½ hr 1:15–4. Métro: Bourse.*

❺ **Chapelle Expiatoire.** This unkempt mausoleum emerges defiantly from the lush undergrowth of verdant square Louis-XVI off boulevard Haussmann, marking the initial burial site of Louis XVI and Marie-Antoinette after their turns at the guillotine on place de la Concorde. Two stone tablets are inscribed with the last missives of the doomed royals: touching pleas for their revolutionary enemies to be forgiven.

When compared to the pomp and glory of Napoléon's memorial at the Invalides, this tribute to royalty (France was ruled by kings until 1792 and again from 1815 to 1848) seems halfhearted and trite. ✉ *29 rue Pasquier,* ☎ *01–44–32–18–00.* ✆ *15 frs/€2.30.* ☉ *Thurs.–Sat. 1–5. Métro: St-Augustin.*

❼ Galeries Lafayette. This turn-of-the-20th-century department store has a vast, shimmering Belle Epoque glass dome that can only be seen if you venture inside. ✉ *40 bd. Haussmann. Métro: Chaussée d'Antin; RER: Auber.*

❿ Hôtel Drouot. Hidden away in a grid of narrow streets not far from the Opéra is Paris's central auction house, where everything from stamps and toy soldiers to Renoirs and 18th-century commodes is sold. The 16 salesrooms make for fascinating browsing, and there's no obligation to bid. The mix of ladies in fur coats with money to burn, penniless art lovers desperate to unearth an unidentified masterpiece, and scruffy dealers trying to look anonymous makes up Drouot's unusually rich social fabric. Sales are held most weekdays, with viewings in the morning; anyone can attend. For centuries, the French government has artificially restricted the auction trade to residents, but now that those laws have been revamped, the Drouot is abuzz with the news that Sotheby's, Christie's, and Phillips are setting up shop in Paris and aim to blow the town open. ✉ *9 rue Drouot,* ☎ *01–48–00–20–00.* ☉ *Viewings mid-Sept.–mid-July, Mon.–Sat. 11–noon and 2–6, with auctions starting at 2. Métro: Richelieu-Drouot.*

⓲ Musée des Arts et Métiers (National Technical Museum). The former church and priory of St-Martin des Champs was built between the 11th and 13th centuries. Confiscated during the Revolution, it was used first as an educational institution, then as an arms factory, before becoming, in 1799, the Conservatoire des Arts et Métiers. Today the church and the splendid 13th-century refectory, a large hall supported by central columns, form part of the National Technical Museum, an industrial museum with a varied collection of models (locomotives, vehicles, and agricultural machinery), astronomical instruments, looms, and glass, together with displays on printing, photography, and the history of television. ✉ *Sq. du Général-Morin,* ☎ *01–53–01–82–00.* ☉ *Tues.–Sun. 10–6.* ✆ *35 frs/€5.34. Métro: Arts-et-Métiers.*

❷ Musée Cernuschi. Set within an aristocratic town house, this collection includes Chinese art from Neolithic pottery (3rd century BC) to funeral statuary, painted 8th-century silks, and contemporary paintings, as well as ancient Persian bronze objects. ✉ *7 av. Velasquez,* ☎ *01–45–63–50–75.* ✆ *17 frs/€2.60.* ☉ *Tues.–Sun. 10–5:40. Métro: Monceau.*

⚘ ⓬ Musée Grévin. Founded in 1882, and granted a $7-million face-lift in 2001, this waxworks museum, around the corner from the Hôtel Drouot, ranks in scope and ingenuity with Madame Tussaud's in London. Dozens of wax renderings of historical and contemporary celebrities are on display; your ticket also allows entry to a 1900 Palace of Illusion. ✉ *10 bd. Montmartre,* ☎ *01–47–70–85–05.* ✆ *65 frs/€10.* ☉ *Sept.–June, daily 1–6:30; July–Aug. 10–7. Métro: Grands Boulevards.*

★ ❹ Musée Jacquemart-André. Often compared to New York City's Frick Collection, this was one of the grandest private residences of 19th-century Paris. Built built between 1869 and 1875, it found Hollywood fame when used as Gaston Lachaille's mansion in the 1958 musical *Gigi,* as a great stand-in for the floridly opulent home of a sugar millionaire played by Louis Jourdan. Edouard André and his painter-wife, Nélie Jacquemart, the house's actual owners, were rich and cultured, so art from the Italian Renaissance and 18th-century France compete for attention here. Note the freshly restored Tiepolo frescoes in the staircase and on the dining-room ceiling, while salons done in the fashionable "Louis XVI–Empress" style (favored by Empress Eugénie) are hung with great paintings, including Uccello's *Saint George Slaying the Dragon*, Rembrandt's *Pilgrims of Emmaus*, Jean-Marc Nattier's *Mathilde de Canisy*, and Jacques-Louis David's *Comte Antoine-Français de Nantes*. You can tour the house with a handy English audio-guide. ⊠ *158 bd. Haussmann,* ☎ *01–42–89–04–91.* 🎫 *48 frs/€7.32.* ☉ *Daily 10–6. Métro: St-Philippe-du-Roule.*

★ ❸ **Musée Nissim de Camondo.** Molière made fun of the *bourgeois gentilhomme*, the middle-class man who aspired to the class of his royal betters, but the playwright would have been in awe of Monsieur Moïse de Camondo, whose enormous sense of style, grace, and refinement could have taught the courtiers at Versailles a thing or two. After making a fortune in the late 19th century, the businessman built this grand hôtel particulier in the style of the Petit Trianon and proceeded to furnish it with some of the most exquisite furniture, *boiseries* (carved wood panels), and bibelots of the mid- to late-18th century. His wife and children (the museum is named after his son, who died in combat during World War I) then moved in and lent the house enormous warmth and charm. From ancien régime splendor, however, the family descended to the worst horrors of World War II: after the death of Count Moïse in 1935, the estate left the family's house and treasures to the government while shortly thereafter, family descendants were packed off to Auschwitz by the Nazis, where several of them were murdered. Today, the wealthy matrons of Paris have made this museum their own, and it shines anew with the beauty of the 18th century. If you want to see these enchanting salons in all their candlelit glory, view a video of *Valmont*, Milos Forman's much-overlooked 1989 filmed version of *Les Liasons Dangereuses*. ⊠ *63 rue de Monceau,* ☎ *01–53–89–06–40,* [WEB] *www.ucad.fr.* 🎫 *30 frs/€4.60.* ☉ *Wed.–Sun. 10–5. Métro: Villiers.*

❶④ **Notre-Dame de Bonne-Nouvelle.** This wide, soberly neoclassical church is tucked away off the Grands Boulevards. The previous church (the second) on the spot was ransacked during the Revolution, and the current one, built 1823–29 after the restoration of the French monarchy, was ransacked by Communard hooligans in May 1871. The highlight is the semicircular apse behind the altar, featuring some fine 17th-century paintings beneath a three-dimensional, 19th-century grisaille composition by Abel de Pujol. A wide variety of pictures, statues, and works of religious art can be found in the side chapels. ⊠ *Rue de la Lune. Métro: Bonne-Nouvelle.*

★ ❽ **Opéra Garnier.** Haunt of the "Phantom of the Opera," the setting for Degas's famous ballet paintings, and still the most opulent theater in the world, the Paris Opéra was begun in 1862 by Charles Garnier at the behest of Napoléon III. Due to its lavishness, it was not completed until 1875, five years after the emperor's abdication. Awash with Algerian colored marbles and gilded putti, it is said to typify Second Empire architecture: a pompous hodgepodge of styles with about as much subtlety as a Wagnerian cymbal crash. The composer Debussy famously compared it to a Turkish bathhouse, but lovers of pomp and splendor will adore it (Hitler called it the most beautiful building in the world)—especially now that the facade was restored to its original smash-hit glory in 2000.

To see the theater and lobby, you don't actually have to attend a performance: after paying an entry fee, you can stroll around at leisure and view the foyer and have a peek into the auditorium. The monumental Grand Foyer is nearly as big as the auditorium (together they fill 3 acres) and reminds us that this was a theater for Parisians who came to the opera primarily to be seen; on opening nights, you can still see Rothschilds and rock stars preen and prance on the grand staircase. If the lavishly upholstered auditorium seems small, it is only because the stage is the largest in the world—more than 11,000 square yards, with room for up to 450 performers. Marc Chagall painted the ceiling in 1964. The **Opera Museum,** containing a few paintings and theatrical mementos, is unremarkable. Still, if you want a full burst of Parisian grandeur, make sure you catch a performance here—while technically the official home of the Paris Ballet, this auditorium usually mounts one or two full-scale operas a season (most operas are presented at the drearily modern Opéra de la Bastille). ⊠ *Pl. de l'Opéra,* ☎ *01–40–01–22–63,* W̅E̅B̅ *www.opera-de-paris.fr.* ⌨ *30 frs/€4.60.* ☉ *Daily 10–5. Guided tours in English at 3 pm (60 frs/€9.16). Métro: Opéra.*

NEED A
BREAK?

Few cafés are as grand as the Belle Epoque **Café de la Paix** (⊠ 5 pl. de l'Opéra, ☎ 01–40–07–30–10). Once described as "the center of the civilized world," it was a regular meeting place for the glitterati of 19th- and 20th-century Paris; the prices are as grand as the setting. Today, probably only the waiters speak French.

🕊 **❶ Parc Monceau.** The most picturesque gardens on the Right Bank were laid out as a private park in 1778 and retain some of the fanciful elements then in vogue, including mock ruins and a faux pyramid. In 1797 André Garnerin, the world's first-recorded parachutist, staged a landing in the park. The rotunda—known as the Chartres Pavilion—is surely the city's grandest public rest room; it started life as a tollhouse. All in all, this remains one of the snobbiest parks in Paris and certainly one of the prettiest—no wonder director Vincente Minnelli used it as a setting in his film *Gigi.* ⊠ *Entrances on bd. de Courcelles, av. Velasquez, av. Ruysdaël, av. van Dyck. Métro: Monceau.*

❾ Paris Story. This 40-minute split-screen presentation of Paris and its history is pricey and sometimes hard to follow, but the spectacular photography and tasteful musical accompaniment, with St-Saëns's Organ Symphony employed to majestic effect, are enjoyable. Be sure to get headphones to hear the English translation. ⊠ *11 bis rue Scribe,* ☎ *01–42–66–62–06,* W̅E̅B̅ *www.paris-story.com.* ⌨ *50 frs/€7.63.* ☉ *Apr.–Oct., daily 9–8, Nov.–Mar., daily 9–6; screenings on the hr. Métro: Opéra.*

⓫ Passage Jouffroy. Built in 1846, as its giant clock will tell you, this shops-filled *passage* (gallery) was one of the first precursors to the modern-day shopping mall. ⊠ *Entrances on bd. Montmartre, rue de la Grange-Batelière. Métro: Richelieu-Drouot.*

⓰ Porte St-Denis. This 76-ft triumphal arch, which is slightly larger and older than the neighboring Porte St-Martin, was erected by François Blondel in 1672 to celebrate the victories of *Ludovico Magno* (as Louis XIV is here styled) on the Rhine. The bas-reliefs by François Girardon include campaign scenes and military attributes stacked on shallow, slender pyramids. The arch, superbly cleaned in 1998, faces rue St-Denis—formerly the royal processional route into Paris from the north (last so used by Queen Victoria in 1855) but now better known for activity along the sidewalk. ⊠ *Bd. St-Denis. Métro: Strasbourg–St-Denis.*

⓱ Porte St-Martin. This 56-ft triumphal arch, which is slightly smaller and younger than the neighboring Porte St-Denis, was designed by Blondel's pupil Pierre Bullet in 1674 and also cleaned in 1998. Louis XIV's victories at Limburg (in Flanders) and Besançon in Franche-Comté get bas-relief coverage from Martin Desjardins. ⊠ *Bd. St-Denis. Métro: Strasbourg–St-Denis.*

☝ ⑮ **Rex.** If you're a movie buff, you may want to inspect Europe's self-styled "Grandest Cinema," built in 1932—although the 50-minute backscreen tour, full of special effects and loudspeaker commentary (available in English), gives only a tantalizing glimpse of the 2,700-seat auditorium, with its star-spangled roof and onstage fountains. You're surreptitiously filmed as you go around, with an individualized souvenir video (40 francs/€6) available as you leave. If you still want more, see a movie here. ⊠ *1 bd. Poissonnière,* ☎ *08–36–68–05–93.* 🖃 *40 frs/€6.* ⊙ *Wed.–Sun. 11–7. Métro: Bonne-Nouvelle.*

⑳ **Ste-Elisabeth.** This studied essay in Baroque (built 1628–46) is pleasantly unpretentious; there's no soaring bombast here. The church has brightly restored wall paintings and a wide, semicircular apse around the choir, where biblical scenes are carved into stupendous 17th-century wood paneling transferred from an abbey in Arras in northern France. ⊠ *Rue du Temple. Métro: Temple.*

⑲ **St-Nicolas des Champs.** The rounded-arch, fluted Doric capitals in the chancel of this church date from 1560 to 1587, a full century later than the pointed-arch nave (1420–80). There is a majestic mid-17th-century organ and a fine *Assumption of the Virgin* (1629) by Simon Vouet above the high altar. The south door (1576) on rue au Maire is gloriously carved and surrounded by a small but unexpectedly well-tended lawn complete with rosebushes. ⊠ *Rue St-Martin. Métro: Arts-et-Métiers.*

FROM RÉPUBLIQUE TO LA VILLETTE

Place de la République is the gateway to northeast Paris, a largely residential area that is often underestimated by tourists. The Canal St-Martin forms the focal point of this walk. Today its barges transport mainly tourists and pleasure boats, but it was once a busy thoroughfare linking the Seine to the city's central slaughterhouse at La Villette. The Mitterrand era saw La Villette landscaped beyond recognition, with science and music museums and a concert hall built amid a wittily designed postmodern park. Nearby, 19th-century city planner Baron Haussmann let his hair down at the tumbling Buttes-Chaumont Park, going to town with a lake, a waterfall, a grotto, and phony cliffs.

Numbers in the text correspond to numbers in the margin and on the place de la République to La Villette map.

A Good Walk

Begin your walk at **place de la République** ①. Cross the square and take rue du Faubourg-du-Temple to the **Canal St-Martin** ②, whose locks and pale-green footbridges conjure up an unexpected flavor of Amsterdam. At this point, the canal emerges from a 2½-km (1½-mi) tunnel that starts beyond the Bastille. Follow it left; then take the second right up avenue Richerand to the **Hôpital St-Louis** ③, Paris's oldest hospital, with its serene courtyard and chapel still intact. Leave the hospital on rue de la Grange-aux-Belles, and turn left, then right down rue Bichat, to find the Canal St-Martin bending beneath the unassuming white facade of the **Hôtel du Nord** ④, made famous by the film of the same name. The canal continues north to the circular **Rotonde de La Villette** ⑤. It surveys both the elevated métro line and the unruffled sheen of the Bassin de La Villette, where boats leave on a mile-long trip to the **Parc de La Villette** ⑥, with its postmodern science and music mu-

84

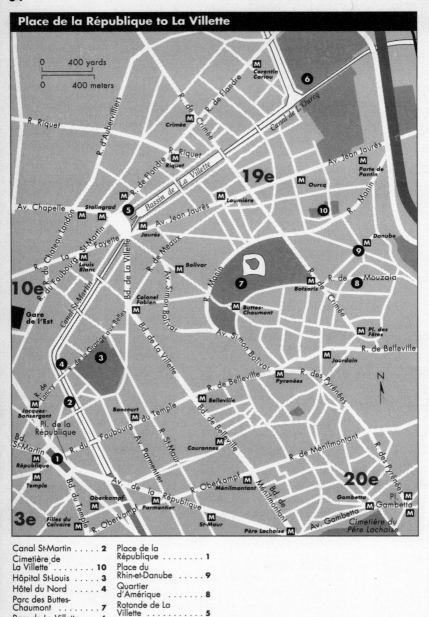

seums. If you prefer the 30-minute walk along the canal to the park, take the left bank of the quai de la Seine, past the tiny, 18th-century Portuguese Jewish cemetery at No. 44. Cross over the canal on the Pont de Crimée, near the church of St-Jacques–St-Christophe, before continuing up the quai de la Marne. Yet another option is to follow avenue Secrétan southeast from the Rotonde to the picturesque **Parc des Buttes-Chaumont** ⑦. Wend your way left around this tumbling park— once a quarry—and skirt the lake before climbing to the top of the man-made cliff for a panoramic view of the city.

Leave the park from the eastern corner. Turn left on rue Botzaris, and then right up rue de Crimée. Take the first left up a flight of stairs to the dowdy little street called villa Albert-Robida. You're now on the fringe of the **Quartier d'Amérique** ⑧, so called because the stone quarried in the Buttes-Chaumont is said to have been used to build the White House. All the two- and three-story houses around here—originally quarriers' cottages—are a far cry from the seven-story buildings dominating the rest of Paris. Turn left down rue Arthur-Rozier and continue to rue de Mouzaïa. These days these small houses are very desirable: some of the prettiest are found in the villas or mews, leading off of rue de Mouzaïa. Venture up quaint, cobbled villa Émile-Lobet on the right—the five gray skyscrapers looming at the far end are a chilling architectural contrast to the colorful paintwork and ivy-covered railings of the houses. Turn left and left again down flagstone-paved villa de Bellevue and cross to villa du Progrès. Take a left at the bottom of the street and then a right down rue de la Fraternité to reach the **place du Rhin-et-Danube** ⑨.

More mewsy alleyways can be found on either side of rue Miguel-Hidalgo, with a cute view of the foursquare brick tower of the church of St-Francis d'Assisi at the far end of villa des Boërs. From here, take a right on rue Compans and head up to the **Cimetière de La Villette** ⑩. The entrance is flanked by a grim stone cube that once served as the local morgue. Admire the extrovert windows and roofline of the new school opposite; then take allée Darius-Milhaud along the side of the cemetery. This promenade curves through the heart of this district, which was totally rebuilt in the 1990s; cross rue Petit and continue to the flight of stairs leading up to the bulky silhouette of the Cité de la Musique, a modern music academy. The entry to the Parc de La Villette is down to the left.

TIMING

The stretch along the Canal St-Martin from place de la République to the Bassin de La Villette, via the Hôpital St-Louis, is approximately 2 km (1 mi). You may want to allot a whole morning or afternoon to exploring the Parc des Buttes-Chaumont or the Parc de La Villette. Or you might want to return to one of these on another day.

Sights to See

❷ **Canal St-Martin.** The canal was built, at the behest of Napoléon, from 1802 to 1825, with the aim of providing the city with drinking water. It was not assigned to navigable traffic until the 1850s and was partly covered (between Bastille and République) by Haussmann in 1862. With its quiet banks, locks, and footbridges, the canal is much loved by novelists and film directors; Simenon's famous inspector, Maigret, solved many a mystery along its deceptively sleepy banks. Major development has transformed the northern end of the canal, around place de Stalingrad and its 18th-century rotunda, and there are 10-franc boat trips (✉ Embarkation at 13 quai de la Loire) along the once industrial Bassin de La Villette to the nearby Parc de La Villette. *Métro: Jacques-Bonsergent, Jaurès.*

⑩ Cimetière de La Villette (La Villette Cemetery). One of Paris's smallest cemeteries, it is reserved for residents of the 19th arrondissement. ✉ *Entrance on rue d'Hautpoul. Métro: Ourcq.*

❸ Hôpital St-Louis (St. Louis Hospital). Though it's not, technically speaking, a tourist sight, no one will begrudge you a discreet visit to Paris's first hospital, erected in 1607–10, at the same time as the place des Vosges. The main courtyard, known as the Quadrilatère Historique, with its steep roofs and corner pavilions, has been remarkably preserved. The chapel, tucked away along rue de la Grange-aux-Belles, was the first building in Paris to be lit by gaslight and shelters *Suffer Little Children to Come unto Me,* a painting by Charles de La Fosse (1636–1716), and a handsome wood balcony carved with trumpeting angels and the monograms of hospital founders Henri IV and Maria de' Medici. ✉ *Entrances on av. Richerand, rue de la Grange-aux-Belles, av. Claude-Vellefaux. ☉ Daily 5 am–9 pm; chapel weekday afternoons.*

❹ Hôtel du Nord (North Hotel). Despite its unassuming white facade, this hotel is famous in France for its starring role in director Marcel Carné's 1938 movie of the same name. Plans to demolish it provoked a public outcry and it was restored to its former glory (as a café-restaurant) in 1995. ✉ *102 quai de Jemmappes,* ☎ *01–40–40–78–78. Métro: Jacques-Bonsergent.*

❼ Parc des Buttes-Chaumont. This picturesque, steep-sloped park in northeast Paris has a lake, waterfall, and cliff-top folly. Until town planner Baron Haussmann got his hands on it in the 1860s, the area was a garbage dump and quarry—legend has it that the local gypsum was used in the foundation of the White House. ✉ *Rue Botzaris. Métro: Buttes-Chaumont, Botzaris.*

❻ Parc de La Villette. Until the 1970s this 130-acre site, in an unfashionable corner of northeast Paris commonly known as "La Villette," was home to a cattle market and slaughterhouse (*abattoir*). Only the slaughterhouse, known as **La Grande Halle** (Great Hall), remains: a magnificent iron-and-glass structure ingeniously transformed into an exhibition-cum-concert center. But everything else here—from the science museum and spherical cinema to the music academy, each interconnected by designer gardens with canopied walkways and red cubical follies—is futuristic.

Although La Villette breathes the architectural panache of the Mitterrand era, the late president only oversaw one project himself: the **Cité de la Musique,** a giant postmodern music academy with a state-of-the-art concert hall. Designed by architect Christian de Portzamparc, it was completed in 1997 with the opening of the spectacular **Musée de la Musique** (Music Museum). The museum contains a mind-tingling array of 900 instruments; their story is told with wireless headphones (ask for English commentary).

The **park** itself, laid out in the 1980s to the design of Bernard Tschumi—a heavyweight of the postmodern movement—links the academy to the science museum half a mile away. Water and the Grande Halle are the park's focal elements. Two new bridges cross the Canal de l'Ourcq, which bisects the park; one becomes a covered walkway, running parallel to the Canal St-Denis, and continues up to the science museum—itself surrounded by the unruffled sheen of a broad moat, reflecting the spherical outline of **La Géode.** This looks like a huge silver golf ball but is actually a cinema made of polished steel, with an enormous, 180-degree curved screen.

The pompously styled **Cité des Sciences et de l'Industrie** (Industry and Science Museum) tries to do for science and industry what the Centre Pompidou does for modern art. Adrien Fainsilber's rectangular building, also conceived in the 1970s, even looks like the Centre Pompidou, minus the gaudy piping. Inside, displays are bright and thought-provoking, though most are in French only. The brave attempt to render technology fun and easy involves 60 do-it-yourself contraptions that make you feel more participant than onlooker. Lines (especially during school holidays) can be intimidating. ⊠ *Science Museum: 30 av. Corentin-Cariou; Music Museum: 221 av. Jean-Jaurès,* ☎ *01–40–05–80–00 Science Museum; 01–44–84–44–84 Music Museum,* WEB *www.cite-sciences.fr.* ⊠ *Science 50 frs/€7.63 (inc. planetarium), Music 40 frs/€6.* ☉ *Science Tues.–Sun. 10–6; Music Tues.–Thurs. noon–6, Fri. and Sat. noon–7:30, Sun. 10–6. Métro: Porte de La Villette, Porte de Pantin.*

❶ **Place de la République.** This large, oblong square, laid out by Haussmann in 1856–65, is dominated by a matronly, Stalin-size statue symbolizing *The Republic* (1883). The square is often used as a rallying point for demonstrations. République has more métro lines than any other station in Paris. *Métro: République.*

❾ **Place du Rhin-et-Danube.** Although seven streets intersect at this square in the Quartier d'Amérique, it retains a rural, unhurried feel. The small white statue of a young girl clutching a sheaf of wheat recalls the area's pastoral origins, before it was absorbed into Paris in the 19th century. The métro station underneath was built in a former quarry. *Métro: Danube.*

❽ **Quartier d'Amérique** (America Quarter). This neighborhood is so named because the gypsum that was once quarried here (mostly on the site that was transformed into the Parc des Buttes-Chaumont in the 1860s) was shipped to America and used, so the story goes, in building the White House. The quartier is made up of a grid of streets and narrow mews (known as "villas") lined with modest two- and three-story houses and once inhabited by quarriers—now some of the most sought-after homes in the city. *Métro: Botzaris.*

❺ **Rotonde de La Villette.** This strange circular building was one of the tollhouses built around the edge of Paris by Nicolas Ledoux in the 1780s. Most of these austere, daunting buildings, symbols, to the populace, of taxes and oppression, were promptly dismantled during the Revolution. Luckily, the Rotunda survived to remind us of Ledoux's thrilling architecture. Like Mitterrand, Ledoux was fascinated by masonic symbols such as spheres and pyramids. Although the Rotunda is partly obscured by the aboveground métro as you approach from the south, its clean-cut outlines and honey-color stonework can be admired from the north, where a paved courtyard overlooks the Bassin de La Villette and the barges lining up at the lock to reach the Canal St-Martin. ⊠ *Pl. de Stalingrad. Métro: Stalingrad.*

FROM BASTILLE TO NATION

At the center of the Bastille neighborhood is place de la Bastille, site of the infamous prison stormed on July 14, 1789—an event that came to symbolize the beginning of the French Revolution. Largely in commemoration of the bicentennial of the Revolution, the Bastille area was renovated and soon became one of the liveliest areas in Paris. Galleries, shops, theaters, cafés, restaurants, and bars now fill formerly decrepit buildings and alleys. Southeast of the Bastille are the imposing place de la Nation and the up-and-coming Bercy neighborhood. Other high-

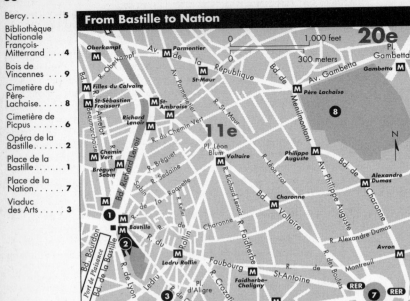

lights of this tour include the verdant Bois de Vincennes, the new and spectacular Bibliothèque Nationale François-Mitterrand, and the evocative Père Lachaise cemetery, final resting place of Balzac, Proust, Wilde, and many other famous figures.

Numbers in the text correspond to numbers in the margin and on the From Bastille to Nation map.

A Good Walk

Start your walk at **place de la Bastille** ①, which is easily accessible by métro. Today the square is dominated by the Colonne de Juillet and the curving glass facade of the modern **Opéra de la Bastille** ②. Leading away from the square is rue de la Roquette, a street alive with shops and cafés, which in turn leads first to vibrant rue de Lappe, lined with bars, clubs, and restaurants; then to rue des Taillandiers and rue Keller, with their bookshops and music stores. All these streets are worth exploring—and rue de Lappe is especially hopping at night. Turn right at the end of rue de Lappe onto rue de Charonne to reach rue du Faubourg-St-Antoine, famous for its cabinetmakers. You'll see why if you take the unevenly cobbled passage du Chantier, just opposite. Its boutiques sell furniture and nothing else. (Peek into other *passages* as well for more glimpses of the behind-the-scenes life of the Bastille.)

Continue along rue du Faubourg-St-Antoine, and then take a right down avenue Ledru-Rollin, crossing rue Charenton and passing the modern church of St-Antoine, to reach avenue Daumesnil. The disused railroad viaduct has been tastefully transformed into a series of designer boutiques with a walkway on top—restyled the **Viaduc des Arts** ③.

Saunter down as far as rue Hector-Malot; then turn right across avenue Daumesnil and head down boulevard Diderot to Gare de Lyon métro station. If you'd like to visit the large, new national library, the **Bibliothèque Nationale François-Mitterrand** ④, take line 14 from Gare de Lyon for three stops to the Bibliothèque station. Or get off one stop earlier at Cour St-Emilion and explore the revamped **Bercy** ⑤ neighborhood, with its restored wine warehouses and innovative park. The four L-shape towers of the national library loom across the Seine as you head west toward the grass-covered walls of the Palais Omnisports stadium. Follow rue de Bercy, under the elephantine Ministère des Finances, and then turn right through the tunnel, up to rue de Rambouillet. Here rejoin avenue de Daumesnil and the Viaduc des Arts. Head up the steps to see what's on top of the viaduct: gone are the tracks, ousted by the Promenade Plantée, a walkway lined with trees and flowers. The walkway continues for another 2½ km (1½ mi). But you might just want to stay on it for about 1 km (½ mi) before turning left on rue de Picpus. Some 350 yards up on the right is the entry to the **Cimetière de Picpus** ⑥, where General Lafayette is buried.

Continue on rue de Picpus for about 250 yards, and then cross rue Fabre-d'Eglantine to reach the majestic **place de la Nation** ⑦, flanked to the right by two towering columns that once marked the eastern entry to Paris. From here it's a short métro ride to the city's most famous cemetery, the **Cimetière du Père-Lachaise** ⑧, or to the **Bois de Vincennes** ⑨, a large park with lakes, castle, and a zoo.

TIMING
The walk from place de la Bastille to place de la Nation, including an excursion to the Bercy neighborhood, is about 7 km (4½ mi) long and takes about four hours to complete. Count on more time if you also visit the new national library.

Sights to See

❺ **Bercy.** Bercy is a testament to the French genius for urban renewal. Tucked away on the Right Bank of the Seine, south of the Gare de Lyon in the 12e arrondissement, this colorful district was for decades filled with warehouses storing wine from the provinces. Now sport and finance set the tone. The first thing you'll see as you emerge from the Bercy métro station is the mighty glass wall of the **Ministère des Finances** (Finance Ministry), which moved—grudgingly—to these new quayside offices from the Louvre. To the left is the ingeniously sloping, grass-walled **Palais Omnisports,** a weird-looking stadium that hosts sports and music events and seats 17,000, approached on all sides by gleaming white steps. Across the Seine, dominating the city's southeast skyline, are the four glass towers of architect Dominique Perrault's new national library, the Bibliothèque Nationale François-Mitterrand. A hundred yards from the Palais Omnisports is a quirky, Cubist building designed by Frank Gehry, who described it as "a dancing figure in the park." It opened as the American Center in 1994 but closed in 1996 due to lack of funds and at press time was slated to reopen by 2002 as a French movie museum, or **Maison du Cinéma.** The **jardin** (garden) opposite is a witty, state-of-the-art designer park with trim lawns, vines, rose-strewn arbors, and cobbled alleys lined by centurion trees providing a ghostly map of the former wineries. At the **Maison du Jardin** (Garden Center; ⊠ rue Paul-Belmondo) you can get gardening advice and see displays of seasonal vegetables. Curved walkways fly over rue de Dijon to land by a Chinese lily pond near the Cour St-Emilion, where two rows of wine warehouses have been preserved, and transformed into boutiques and cafés. *Métro: Bercy, Cour St-Emilion.*

❹ **Bibliothèque Nationale François-Mitterrand** (National Library). As the last of former president François Mitterrand's *grands travaux* (grand building projects) before he left office, the *Très Grande Bibliothèque*

(Very Big Library, as some facetiously call it) opened in early 1997. The new library subsumes the majority of the collections in the old Bibliothèque Nationale and, with some 11 million volumes between its walls, surpasses the Library of Congress as the largest library in the world. Architect Dominique Perrault's controversial design features four soaring 24-story towers that house most of the books. The design is thought-provoking—the four towers imitate four open volumes—but criticism was heaped on the project since books are housed in the towers (whose windows need to be covered to protect the stacks), while library goers are relegated to underground reading rooms. A stunning interior courtyard—sunk beneath ground level and invisible as you approach, despite its thicket of full-size evergreens—provides breathing space. You can visit part of the library for free or pay to inspect one of the temporary exhibits or to consult some of the more than 300,000 books (millions more are available to qualified researchers). The library is fronted by a giant flight of wooden steps overlooking the Seine (note the red *Batofar* lightship, now used for techno concerts), but be warned—the library's two entrances are tucked away almost secretively at either end. ✉ *11 quai François-Mauriac,* ☎ *01–53–79–59–59,* [WEB] *www.bnf.fr.* ✉ *Library 20 frs/€3, exhibitions 35 frs/€5.34.* ☉ *Mid-Sept.– Aug., Tues.–Sat. 10–7, Sun. noon–6. Métro or RER: Bibliothèque.*

👆 ❾ **Bois de Vincennes** (Vincennes Woods). Sandwiched between the unexciting suburb of Charenton and the working-class district of Fontenay-sous-Bois, to the southeast of Paris, the Bois de Vincennes is often considered a poor man's Bois de Boulogne. But the comparison is unfair: the Bois de Vincennes is no more difficult to get to (✉ métro to Porte Dorée; Bus 46) and has equally illustrious origins. It, too, was landscaped under Napoléon III, although a park had already been created here by Louis XV in 1731. The park has several lakes, notably **Lac Daumesnil,** with two islands, and **Lac des Minimes,** with three; rowboats can be hired at both. In addition, the park is home to a zoo, a tribal art museum, the **Hippodrome de Vincennes** (a cinder-track racecourse), a castle, a flower garden, and several cafés. In the spring there's an amusement park, the **Foire du Trône.** Bikes can be rented from the Château de Vincennes métro station for 25 francs/€3.81 an hour or 100 francs/€15.38 a day. Note that the Bois suffered severe damage in the hurricane that lashed Paris during Christmas 1999.

Some 600 mammals and 200 species of birds can be seen at the Bois de Vincennes's 33-acre **Parc Zoologique,** the largest zoo in France. Most striking feature is the 210-ft steel and concrete **Grand Rocher,,** an artificial rock inhabited by wild mountain sheep and penguins. The rock, built in 1934 of reinforced concrete, reopened in 1996 after a large-scale restoration program that added a new elevator to the top. ✉ *53 av. de St-Maurice,* ☎ *01–44–75–20–10.* ✉ *40 frs/€6.* ☉ *Apr.–Oct., daily 9–6; Nov.–Mar., daily 9–5. Métro: Porte Dorée.*

The **Musée des Arts d'Afrique et d'Océanie** (Museum of the Arts of Africa and Oceania) is at the Porte Dorée entrance to the Bois de Vincennes. It's housed in an Art Deco building whose awesome facade is covered with a sculpted frieze depicting sites and attractions of France's erstwhile overseas empire. Inside, headdresses, bronzes, jewelry, masks, statues, and pottery from former French colonies are spaciously displayed under subtle spotlighting. Look out for the ominous Hakenkreuz set in the patterned mosaic floor of the huge reception hall; the sinister overtones it was soon to acquire, as the Nazi swastika emblem, were unsuspected when the building opened for the Colonial Exhibition in 1931. There is also a tropical aquarium (open from 10 AM weekends) in the basement, with rows of tanks filled with colorful tropical fish. ✉ 293 av. Daumesnil, ☎ 01–44–74–85–01. 🖭 30 frs/€4.6. ☺ Wed.–Mon. 10–5:30. Métro: Porte Dorée.

The historic **Château de Vincennes** is on the northern edge of the Bois de Vincennes. Built in the 15th century by various French kings, the castle is France's medieval Versailles, an imposing, high-walled castle surrounded by a dry moat and dominated by a 170-ft keep. The sprawling castle grounds also contain a modest replica (built 1379–1552) of the Sainte-Chapelle on the Ile de la Cité and two elegant, classical wings designed by Louis Le Vau in the mid-17th century, now used for naval-military administration and closed to the public. ✉ Av. de Paris, ☎ 01–48–08–31–20. 🖭 32 frs/€4.90. ☺ Apr.–Sept., daily 10–6; Oct.–Mar., daily 10–5. Métro: Château de Vincennes.

The **Parc Floral de Paris** (Paris Floral Park) is the Bois de Vincennes's 70-acre flower garden. It includes a lake and water garden and is renowned for its seasonal displays of blooms. It also contains a miniature train, a game area, and an "exotarium" with tropical fish and reptiles. ✉ Rte. de la Pyramide, ☎ 01–43–43–92–95. 🖭 10 frs/€1.52. ☺ Apr.–Sept., daily 9:30–8; Oct.–Mar., daily 9:30–5. Métro: Château de Vincennes.

★ ⑧ **Cimetière du Père-Lachaise** (Father Lachaise Cemetery). The largest, most interesting, and most prestigious of Paris's cemeteries dates from the start of the 19th century. On the eastern fringe of Paris, it is a veritable necropolis whose tombs compete in grandiosity, originality, and often, alas, dilapidation. Cobbled avenues, steep slopes, and lush vegetation create a powerful atmosphere. Named after the Jesuit father—Louis XIV's confessor—who led the reconstruction of the Jesuit Rest House completed here in 1682, the cemetery houses the tombs of the composer Chopin; the playwright Molière; the writers Honoré Balzac, Marcel Proust, Paul Eluard, Oscar Wilde, and Gertrude Stein and Alice B. Toklas (buried in the same grave); the popular French actress Simone Signoret and her husband, singer-actor Yves Montand; and Edith Piaf. Perhaps the most popular shrine is to rock star Jim Morrison, where dozens of faithful fans, following the trail of spray-painted graffiti, come to pay homage to the songwriter. (Now, along with the fans, there's a guard who makes sure you don't stay too long.) Of less dubious taste is the sculpted tomb of Romantic artist Théodore Géricault, shown brush in hand above a bronze relief plaque replicating his Raft of the Medusa. The cemetery was the site of the Paris Commune's final battle, on May 28, 1871, when the rebel troops were rounded up, lined against the Mur des Fédérés (Federalists' Wall) in the southeast corner, and shot. Get hold of a map at the entrance—Père Lachaise is an easy place to get lost in. ✉ Entrances on rue des Rondeaux, bd. de Ménilmontant, and rue de la Réunion. ☺ Easter–Sept., daily 8–6; Oct.–Easter, daily 8 am–dusk. Métro: Gambetta, Philippe-Auguste, Père-Lachaise.

⑥ **Cimetière de Picpus.** Most of those 1,300 executed at the guillotine on place de la Nation in 1794 were buried in a mass grave at the nearby Picpus Cemetery. Also buried here is General Lafayette, whose grave site can be identified by its U.S. flag. ✉ Entrance at 35 rue Picpus (once inside, ring bell of caretaker's home for access to cemetery), ☎ 01–43–44–18–54. 🖭 15 frs/€2.30. ☺ Oct.–Easter, Tues.–Sat. 2–4; Easter–Sept., Tues.–Sat. 2–6. Guided visits Tues.–Sun. at 2:30 and 4. Métro or RER: Nation.

② **Opéra de la Bastille** (Bastille Opera). Designed by Argentine-born architect Carlos Ott, the state-of-the-art Bastille Opera, on the south side of place de la Bastille, opened July 14, 1989, in commemoration of the bicentennial of the French Revolution and in hope of making Paris once more the center of European opera. The steeply sloping auditorium seats more than 3,000 and has earned more plaudits than the curving glass facade, which strikes Parisians as depressingly like that of yet another modern office building, if not sports arena. ⊠ *Pl. de la Bastille,* ☏ *01-40-01-19-70.* ▨ *Guided tours 60 frs/€9.20 (call ahead to book). Métro: Bastille.*

❶ **Place de la Bastille.** Nothing remains of the infamous Bastille prison destroyed at the beginning of the French Revolution. Until 1988, there was little more to see here than a huge traffic circle and the **Colonne de Juillet** (July Column). As part of the countrywide celebrations for July 1989, the bicentennial of the French Revolution, the Opéra de la Bastille was erected, inspiring substantial redevelopment on the surrounding streets, especially along rue de Lappe—once a haunt of Edith Piaf—and rue de la Roquette. What was formerly a humdrum neighborhood rapidly became one of the most sparkling and attractive in the city. Streamlined art galleries, funky jazz clubs, and Spanish-style tapas bars set the tone.

The Bastille, or, more properly, the Bastille St-Antoine, was a massive building, protected by eight immense towers and a wide moat (its ground plan is marked by paving stones set into the modern square). It was built by Charles V in the late 14th century. He intended it not as a prison but as a fortress to guard the eastern entrance to the city. By the reign of Louis XIII (1610–43), however, the Bastille was used almost exclusively to house political prisoners. Voltaire, the Marquis de Sade, and the mysterious Man in the Iron Mask were all incarcerated here, along with many other unfortunates. It was this obviously political role—specifically, the fact that the prisoners were nearly always held by order of the king—that led the "furious mob" (in all probability no more than a largely unarmed rabble) to break into the prison on July 14, 1789, kill the governor, steal what firearms they could find, and free the seven remaining prisoners.

Later in 1789, the prison was knocked down. A number of the original stones were carved into facsimiles of the Bastille and sent to each of the provinces as a memento of royal oppression. The key to the prison was given by Lafayette to George Washington, and it has remained at Mount Vernon ever since. The power of legend being what it is, what soon became known as the Storming of the Bastille was elevated to the status of a pivotal event in the course of the French Revolution, demonstrating the newfound power of a long-suffering population. Thus it was that July 14 became the French national day, an event now celebrated with patriotic fervor throughout the country. *Métro: Bastille.*

❼ **Place de la Nation.** The towering early 19th-century, statue-topped columns on majestic place de la Nation stand sentinel at the Gates of Paris—the eastern sector's equivalent of the Arc de Triomphe, with the bustling but unpretentious Cours de Vincennes providing a down-to-earth echo of the Champs-Élysées. Place de la Nation (known as place du Trône—Throne Square—until the Revolution) was the scene of 1,300 executions at the guillotine in 1794. Most were buried in a mass grave at the nearby Cimetière de Picpus. *Métro or RER: Nation.*

❸ **Viaduc des Arts** (Arts Viaduct). With typical panache, Paris planners have converted this redbrick viaduct—originally the last mile of the suburban railroad that led to place de la Bastille (the site of the Bastille Opéra was once a station)—into a stylish promenade. Upscale art, crafts, and furniture shops occupy the archways below, and a walkway, with shrubs, flowers, and benches, has replaced the tracks up above. ⊠ *Av. Daumesnil. Métro: Gare de Lyon, Daumesnil, Bel-Air.*

VANISHED REVOLUTION

ON THE MORNING of July 14, 1789, six hundred rioters attacked the grim fortress of the Bastille. Its prisoners then included four forgers, two lunatics, a young nobleman imprisoned at the request of his father, and not one political prisoner. History, however, had decreed that the Bastille represented tyranny and the rioters considered it a symbol of arbitrary power. It was taken by assault by the people of Paris in the name of liberty; on that fateful morning, they came to dance in front of the gutted Bastille—a custom repeated each year throughout the streets of the city on Bastille Day.

But Parisians had a rebellious reputation long before the French Revolution. Such was Louis XIV's disdain for the Paris mob that he moved his court out to Versailles, which remained the capital of France until 1789.

But the writing was on Louis's garden wall. On June 20, 1789, the Third Estate met in Versailles and swore to end absolute monarchy at the **Jeu de Paume** (which still stands). Then, three months later, a horde of half-starved citizens stomped 16 km (10 mi) from Paris to force the royal family to return to the city.

That was after the storming of the Bastille. Nothing remains of the fortress-cum-prison whose name is synonymous with the outbreak of the Revolution—the huge pillar in the middle of today's **place de la Bastille** hails the rebels who ousted Charles X in 1830.

Louis XVI and Marie-Antoinette were ensconced in the **Tuileries Palace,** which blocked off the west wing of the Louvre (facing the Tuileries Gardens) until revolutionaries burnt it down during the Paris Commune of 1871. It was from the Tuileries that the royal family made their ill-fated flight on June 20, 1791. But they were hauled back and jailed in the **Prison du Temple,** on the site of the Carreau de Temple on rue Perrée, just south of what

is now place de la République. The prison was razed in 1808 to put an end to royalist pilgrimages.

Louis XVI went to the scaffold in the northwest corner of **place de la Concorde,** near today's Hôtel Crillon, on January 21, 1793. The guillotine was later moved to the Tuileries gates and another 1,342 people subjected to it over the next two years. Marie-Antoinette, who spent the last two months of her life in **La Conciergerie** on the Ile de la Cité, was slain on October 16, 1793. Danton (April 5, 1794) and Robespierre (July 28, 1794) followed her; their cells can still be seen.

Meanwhile, on July 13, 1793, revolutionary firebrand Jean-Paul Marat was stabbed to death in his bath by Charlotte Corday at his home on **rue des Cordeliers.** Marat's journal L'Ami du Peuple, a vociferous advocate of the death penalty, was printed in the nearby **cour de Commerce St-André** (at No. 8)—just opposite the house (No. 9) where Dr. Joseph Guillotin is said to have dreamt up his penal machine.

Perhaps the most poignant epitaph to all the bloodshed is the little mausoleum erected in **square Louis-XVI,** the garden just off boulevard Haussmann, where the bones of Louis XVI and Marie-Antoinette sojourned for 20 years before joining those of their ancestors at St-Denis.

By then, the Revolution had joined them in the trash-can of history, its republican ideals buried when Napoléon crowned himself emperor of the French on December 2, 1804, in the erstwhile Temple of Reason—henceforth known once more as **Notre-Dame Cathedral.**

A giant painting of that ceremony by artist Louis David, who orchestrated the revolutionary pageants on the **Champ de Mars,** can be seen in the **Louvre,** along with his famous icon to bathtub victim Marat. Period mementos can be admired in the **Musée Carnavalet** in the Marais.

THE MARAIS

The Marais is one of Paris's oldest, most picturesque, and most sought-after residential districts. Renovation is the keynote; well into the '70s this was one of the poorest areas, filled with dilapidated tenements and squalid courtyards. The area's regeneration was sparked by the building of the Centre Pompidou (known to Parisians as Beaubourg)—until Frank Gehry's Guggenheim Museum opened in Bilbao, Spain, in 1997, it was unquestionably Europe's most architecturally whimsical museum. The gracious architecture of the 17th and early 18th centuries, however, sets the tone for the rest of the Marais. Today, most of the Marais's *hôtels particuliers*—loosely, "mansions," onetime residences of aristocratic families—have been restored by rich, with-it couples, and many of the buildings are now museums, the grandest of them being the Musée Carnavalet and the most visited of them the Musée Picasso. There are trendy boutiques and cafés among the kosher shops of the traditionally Jewish neighborhood around rue des Rosiers.

The history of the Marais—the word, incidentally, means marsh or swamp—goes back to when Charles V, king of France in the 14th century, moved his court here from the Ile de la Cité. However, it wasn't until Henri IV laid out place Royale, today place des Vosges, in the early 17th century, that the Marais became *the* place to live. Aristocratic dwellings began to dot the neighborhood, and their salons filled with the beau monde. But following the French Revolution, the Marais rapidly became one of the most deprived, dissolute areas in Paris.

It was spared the attentions of Baron Haussmann, the man who rebuilt so much of Paris in the mid-19th century—so, though crumbling, the Marais's ancient, golden-hued buildings and squares remained intact. You won't be able to get into many of the historic homes that spangle the neighborhood but this shouldn't stop you from admiring their handsome facades or trying to glimpse through the formal portals (*portes cochères*) to study the discreet courtyards that lurk behind them.

Jewish heritage is also an important part of the Marais's history. Jewish immigrants began settling in this area in the 13th century, though the main wave of immigrants (from Russia and Central Europe) came in the 19th century. Another wave—of Sephardic Jews from North Africa—arrived here in the 1960s following Algerian independence. Today there are still many kosher shops and restaurants among the trendy, newer arrivals.

Numbers in the text correspond to numbers in the margin and on the Marais map.

A Good Walk

Begin this walk in front of the **Hôtel de Ville** ①. You can't inspect the lavish interior, but head left to the traffic-free square, with its fountains and forest of street lamps, to admire the exuberant facade. Turn left along the quai de l'Hôtel de Ville; *bouquinistes* (booksellers) line the Seine, and you may catch a glimpse of the towers of Notre-Dame through the trees. Take the next left up picturesque rue des Barres to the church of **St-Gervais–St-Protais** ②, one of the last Gothic constructions in the country and a newly cleaned riot of Flamboyant decoration. From the church, head up to rue de Rivoli and take a left to get to rue du Temple. On your way, you'll pass one of the city's most popular department stores, the Bazar de l'Hôtel de Ville, or BHV, as it's known. Take rue de la Verrerie, the first street on your left, and pause as you cross rue du Renard to take in an impressive clash of architectural styles: to your left, the medieval silhouette of Notre-Dame; to the right, the gaudy colored pipes of the Centre Pompidou.

Cross rue du Renard and take the second right to the ornate 16th-century church of **St-Merri** ③. Rue St-Martin, full of stores, restaurants, and galleries, leads past the designer Café Beaubourg. Turn right to reach **Square Igor-Stravinsky** ④ with its unusual fountain; on one side of the square is IRCAM, where you can hear performances of contemporary classical music. Up ahead looms the newly renovated **Centre Pompidou** ⑤, overlooking a sloping piazza that is often aswarm with musicians, mimes, dancers, and fire-eaters. On the far side you can visit the **Atelier Brancusi** ⑥ before crossing rue Rambuteau to the Quartier de l'Horloge; take pedestrian rue de Brantôme and turn left onto rue Bernard-de-Clairvaux to admire *Le Défenseur du Temps,* a modern mechanical clock that whirs into action on the hour as St. George defends Time against a dragon, an eagle, or a crab (symbols of fire, air, and water). At noon, 6 PM, and 10 PM he takes on all three at once.

Return to rue Rambuteau, turn left, and cross rue Beaubourg. If you're with children, duck into impasse Berthaud to visit the **Musée de la Poupée** ⑦. Otherwise, stay on rue Rambuteau and turn left onto rue du Temple, where the **Musée d'Art et d'Histoire du Judaïsme** ⑧ is in the stately Hôtel de St-Aignan at No. 71. The **Hôtel de Montmor** ⑨ at No. 79 is another splendid 17th-century mansion. Take a right onto rue des Haudriettes; just off to the left at the next corner is the **Musée de la Chasse et de la Nature** ⑩, the Museum of Hunting and Nature, housed in one of the Marais's grandest mansions. Head right on rue des Archives, crossing rue des Haudriettes, and admire the medieval gateway with two fairy-tale towers, now part of the **Archives Nationales** ⑪, the archives museum entered from rue des Francs-Bourgeois around to the left.

Continue past the Crédit Municipal (the city's grandiose pawnbroking concern), the Dôme du Marais restaurant (housed in a circular 18th-century chamber originally used for auctions), and the church of **Notre-Dame des Blancs-Manteaux** ⑫, with its superb inlaid pulpit. A corner-turret signals rue Vieille-du-Temple; turn left past the palatial Hôtel de Rohan (now part of the Archives Nationales), then right onto rue de la Perle to the **Musée Bricard** ⑬, occupying a mansion as impressive as the assembly of locks and keys within. From here it is a step down rue de Thorigny (opposite) to the palatial 17th-century Hôtel Salé, now the **Musée Picasso** ⑭. Church lovers may wish to detour up rue de Thorigny and along rue du Roi-Doré to admire the severe neoclassic portico of **St-Denis-du-St-Sacrement** ⑮ and the *Deposition* by Delacroix inside.

Backtrack along rue de Thorigny and turn left onto rue du Parc-Royal. Halfway down rue Elzévir is the **Musée Cognacq-Jay** ⑯, a must if you are interested in 18th-century furniture, porcelain, and paintings. If you can't face another museum, take the next right, rue Payenne, instead, and tarry in the sunken garden at square Georges-Cain, opposite the 16th-century Hôtel de Marle, now used as a Swedish culture center. Next door you can enjoy a rear view of the steep-roofed Cognacq-Jay building. Rue Payenne becomes rue Pavée as you pass beneath a lookout turret. Peek into the next courtyard on the left at the cheerfully askew facade of the Bibliothèque Historique de la Ville de Paris. Continuing on rue Pavée takes you to rue des Rosiers, with its excellent Jewish bakeries and falafel shops. Back on rue des Francs-Bourgeois is the **Musée Carnavalet** ⑰, the Paris History Museum, in perhaps the swankiest edifice in the Marais, and famous for its period rooms and collection of the decorative arts. A short walk along rue des Francs-

The Marais

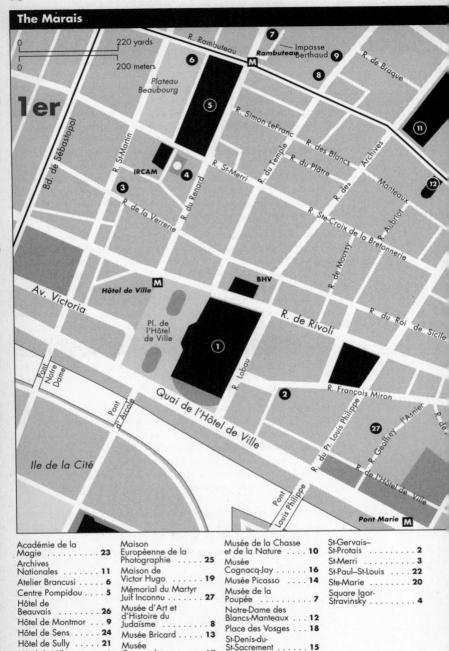

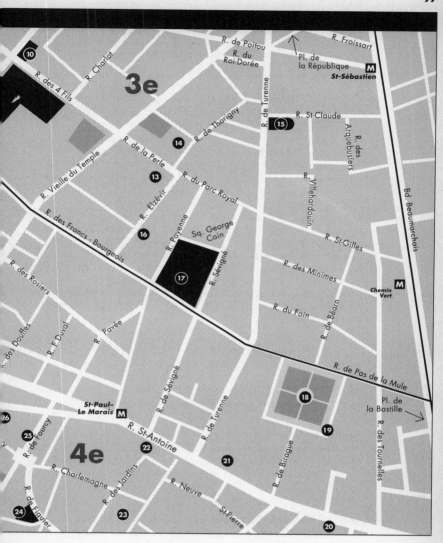

Bourgeois takes you to large, pink-brick **place des Vosges** ⑱, lined with covered arcades, and the most beautiful legacy of the French Renaissance still extant in Paris. At No. 6, you can visit the **Maison de Victor Hugo** ⑲, where the workaholic French author once lived.

Exit the square by rue de Birague to reach rue St-Antoine: to the left is the church of **Ste-Marie** ⑳; to the right is the **Hôtel de Sully** ㉑, home to the Caisse Nationale des Monuments Historiques (Historic Monuments Trust) at No. 62 and a textbook example of 17th-century architecture. Across rue St-Antoine, pause to admire the mighty Baroque church of **St-Paul–St-Louis** ㉒. Take the left-hand side door out of the church into narrow passage St-Paul, and then turn right onto rue St-Paul, past the grid of courtyards that make up the Village St-Paul antiques-shops complex. Children enjoy the **Académie de la Magie** ㉓ farther down at No. 11. At rue de l'Ave-Maria, turn right to reach the painstakingly restored **Hôtel de Sens** ㉔, a strange mixture of defensive stronghold and fairy-tale château. If you are a photography fan, head up rue Figuier, then down rue de Fourcy to the **Maison Européenne de la Photographie** ㉕. Head left on rue François-Miron past the 17th-century **Hôtel de Beauvais** ㉖. Note the two half-timber houses, among the oldest in Paris, across the street at numbers 11 and 13, and the Belle Epoque bakery, Au Petit Versailles, at the corner of Rue Tiron. The next left, rue Geoffroy-l'Asnier, leads past the stark **Mémorial du Martyr Juif Inconnu** ㉗, a huge bronze memorial to those who died in Nazi concentration camps.

TIMING

At just over 5 km (3 mi) long, this walk will comfortably take a whole morning or afternoon. If you choose to spend an hour or two in any of the museums along the way, allow a full day. Be prepared to wait in line at the Picasso Museum. Note that some of the museums don't open until the afternoon and that many shops in the Marais don't open until late morning.

Sights to See

🐾 ㉓ **Académie de la Magie** (Museum of Magic). Housed in a 16th-century cellar, this museum contains antique magic paraphernalia, including some from Houdini's bag of tricks. There's a magic show every hour. ✉ *11 rue St-Paul,* ☎ *01–42–72–13–26.* 🎟 *45 frs/€6.90.* ☉ *Wed. and weekends 2–7. Métro: St-Paul.*

★ ⑪ **Archives Nationales** (National Archives). Palatially housed in a mansion that showcases the earliest flowering of the elegant Louis XV style—the Hôtel de Soubise—the Archives Nationales will tempt serious history buffs, who will be fascinated by the thousands of intricate historical documents, dating from the Merovingian period to the 20th century. The highlights are the Edict of Nantes (1598), the Treaty of Westphalia (1648), the wills of Louis XIV and Napoléon, and the Declaration of Human Rights (1789). Louis XVI's diary is also in the collection, containing his sadly ignorant entry for July 14, 1789, the day the Bastille was stormed and, for all intents and purposes, the French Revolution began: "*Rien*" ("Nothing").

The buildings housing the Archives have their own attractions, too: the **Hôtel de Soubise** and the **Hôtel de Rohan** (originally built for the archbishop of Strasbourg), across the lawn facing rue Vieille-du-Temple, both display the cool, column-fronted elegance of the mid-18th century; the Porte de Clisson, a turreted gateway on rue des Archives, was erected in 1380 for the Hôtel de Clisson, the Paris base of the Duke of Bedford (regent of France during the English occupation from 1420 to 1435). The Hôtel de Soubise was one of the grandest houses in Paris when built. Connoisseurs of the decorative arts flock to this museum to see the apartments of the prince and princess de Soubise; their rooms were among the first examples of the rococo—the lighter, more dainty style that followed the heavier Baroque opulence favored by the age of Louis XIV. ⊠ *60 rue des Francs-Bourgeois,* ☎ *01–40–27–60–96.* ⊡ *20 frs/€3.* ⊙ *Mon. and Wed.–Fri. 10–5:45, weekends 1:45–5:45. Métro: Rambuteau.*

❻ Atelier Brancusi (Brancusi Studio). Romanian-born sculptor Constantin Brancusi settled in Paris in 1898 at age 22. This light, airy museum in front of the Centre Pompidou, designed by Renzo Piano, contains four glass-fronted rooms that reconstitute Brancusi's working studios, crammed with smooth, stylized works from all periods of his career. ⊠ *11 rue St-Paul,* ☎ *01–44–78–12–33.* ⊡ *30 frs/€4.60.* ⊙ *Wed.–Mon. noon–10. Métro: Rambuteau.*

❺ Centre Pompidou (Pompidou Center). The Centre National d'Art et de Culture Georges-Pompidou is its full name, although it is known to Parisians simply as Beaubourg (for the neighborhood). Georges Pompidou (1911–74) was the president of France who launched the project. Unveiled in 1977, three years after his death, the Centre Pompidou was soon attracting more than 8 million visitors a year—five times more than intended. Hardly surprising, then, that it was soon showing signs of fatigue: the much-vaunted, gaudily painted service pipes snaking up the exterior (painted the same colors that were used to identify them on the architects' plans) needed continual repainting, while the plastic tubing enclosing the exterior escalators was cracked and grimy. In 1996 the government stepped in and took drastic action, shutting the center until the end of 1999 and embarking on top-to-bottom renovation.

Place Georges-Pompidou, a gently sloping piazza with a giant gold flowerpot in one corner and the Atelier Brancusi in the other, leads to the center's sprawling, stationlike, concrete-floored entrance hall, with huge, psychedelically colorful signs, ticket counters on the back left, and an extensive art shop to your right, topped by a café. Head left for the famous escalators (since 2000, access is no longer free) that climb the length of the building, offering fine views of Paris, ranging from the Tour Montparnasse to the left, around to the Sacré-Coeur on its hill to the right. Since the recent renovations, the **Musée National d'Art Moderne** (Modern Art Museum, entrance on Level 4) has doubled in size to occupy most of the center's top two stories: one devoted to modern art, largely French; the other to a more international array of abstract work since the '60s. Also look for rotating exhibits of contemporary art. In addition, there's a public reference library, a language laboratory, an industrial design center, two cinemas, and a new rooftop restaurant, Georges, which features a great view of the skyline and Eiffel Tower. ⊠ *Pl. Georges-Pompidou,* ☎ *01–44–78–12–33,* WEB *www. centrepompidou.fr.* ⊡ *30 frs/€4.60, including Atelier Brancusi; free 1st Sun. of month.* ⊙ *Wed.–Mon. 11–9. Métro: Rambuteau.*

NEED A BREAK? The view at night of the Eiffel Tower from **Georges** (⊠ Pl. Georges-Pompidou, ☎ 01–44–78–47–99), the new Costes brothers' restaurant on the roof of the Centre Pompidou, is a marvel. The Costes are behind some of Paris's most chic restaurants and hotels and the buzz about this place draws a fun crowd. The food is not up to the decor, but the crowd and view are wonderful.

㉖ Hôtel de Beauvais. Dating from 1655, this newly renovated mansion is one of the finest in the Marais. It was built for Pierre de Beauvais with surprisingly generous funding from the normally parsimonious Louis XIV. The reason for the Sun King's unwonted largesse: a reward for de Beauvais's willingness to turn a blind eye to the activities of his wife, Catherine-Henriette Bellier, in educating the young monarch in matters sexual. Louis, who came to the throne in 1643 at the age of 4, was 14 when de Beauvais's wife first gave him the benefit of her expertise; she was 40. ⊠ *68 rue François-Miron. Métro: St-Paul.*

❾ Hôtel de Montmor. This 17th-century mansion was once home to M. Montmor, Louis XIII's financial adviser. His son ran a salon here frequented by such luminaries as philosopher and mathematician Pierre Gassend, physicist Gilles de Roberval, writer and professor of medicine Gui Patin, and Dutch astronomer Christian Huygens. This informal gathering of the "Boffins" prompted the creation of the Académie des Sciences in 1666. Note the huge windows and intricate ironwork on the second-floor balcony. ⊠ *79 rue de Temple. Métro: Rambuteau.*

㉔ Hôtel de Sens. One of a handful of civil buildings in Paris to have survived from the Middle Ages—witness the pointed corner towers, Gothic porch, and richly carved decorative details—this sumptuous Marais mansion was built in 1474 for the archbishop of Sens. Its best-known occupants were Henri IV and his queen, Marguérite, philanderers both. While Henri dallied with his mistresses—he is said to have had 56—at a series of royal palaces, Marguérite entertained her almost equally large number of lovers here. Today the building houses occasional exhibits and a fine-arts library, the **Bibliothèque Forney**. ⊠ *1 rue du Figuier,* ☎ *01–42–78–14–60.* ⊡ *Exhibitions 20 frs/€3.* ☉ *Tues.–Sat. 1:30–8. Métro: Pont-Marie.*

㉑ Hôtel de Sully. A major monument of the French Renaissance style, this mansion, begun in 1624, has a stately garden and a majestic courtyard with statues, richly carved pediments, and dormer windows. It is the headquarters of the **Caisse Nationale des Monuments Historiques,** responsible for administering France's historic monuments. Guided visits to Paris sites and buildings begin here, though all are conducted in French. The excellent bookshop, just inside the gate, has a wide range of publications on Paris, many of them in English. The bookshop is open daily 10–12:45 and 1:45–6. ⊠ *62 rue St-Antoine,* ☎ *01–44–61–20–00. Métro: St-Paul.*

❶ Hôtel de Ville (City Hall). Overlooking the Seine, the City Hall is something of a symbol for the regeneration of the surrounding Marais district, since much of the finance and direction for the restoration of the area has been provided by municipal authorities. As the area has been successfully redeveloped, the prestige of the mayor of Paris has grown. In fact, until 1977, Paris was the only city in France without a mayor; with the creation of the post and the election of Jacques Chirac (elected president of France in 1995), leader of the right-of-center Gaullist party, the position became pivotal in both Parisian and French politics. It comes as no surprise, therefore, that Chirac oversaw a thorough restoration of the Hôtel de Ville, both inside and out.

The square in front of the Hôtel de Ville was relaid in the 1980s and adorned with fancy lamps and fountains; an open-air ice rink is installed from December through February. Back in the Middle Ages this was the site of public executions. Most victims were hanged, drawn, and quartered; the lucky ones were burned at the stake. Following the short-lived restoration of the Bourbon monarchy in 1830, the building became the seat of the French government, a role that came to a sudden end with the uprisings in 1848. During the Commune of 1871, the Hôtel de Ville was burned to the ground. Today's exuberant building, based closely on the 16th-century Renaissance original, went up between 1874 and 1884. In 1944, following the liberation of Paris from Nazi rule, General de Gaulle took over the leadership of France from here. ⊠ *Pl. de l'Hôtel-de-Ville.* ◐ *For special exhibitions only. Métro: Hôtel-de-Ville.*

㉕ Maison Européenne de la Photographie (European Photography Center). This museum, unveiled in 1996, combines spacious modern galleries with the original stonework of a venerable hôtel particulier. Despite its name, the museum has an impressive collection of both European and American photography and stages up to four different exhibitions every three months. ⊠ *5 rue de Fourcy,* ☎ *01–44–78–75–00,* WEB *www.mep-fr.org.* ⊡ *30 frs/€4.60, free Wed. after 5 pm.* ◐ *Wed.–Sun. 11–8. Métro: St-Paul.*

⑲ Maison de Victor Hugo (Victor Hugo's Home). The workaholic French author, famed for *Les Misérables* and the *Hunchback of Notre-Dame,* lived in a corner of beautiful place des Vosges between 1832 and 1848. The memorabilia here include several of his atmospheric, Gothic-horror-movie ink sketches, tribute to Hugo's unsuspected talent as an artist, along with illustrations for his writings by other artists, including Bayard's rendition of Cosette (from "Les Miz," which has graced countless T-shirts). The rooms upstairs represent Hugo's living style in several of his many homes; the central room of the floor, for instance, is decorated with Chinese-theme panels and woodworks he created for his mistress's home outside Paris. ⊠ *6 pl. des Vosges,* ☎ *01–42–72–10–16.* ⊡ *22 frs/€3.35.* ◐ *Tues.–Sun. 10–5:45. Métro: St-Paul.*

㉗ Mémorial du Martyr Juif Inconnu (Memorial of the Unknown Jewish Martyr). In March 1992, this memorial was erected at the **Centre de Documentation Juive Contemporaine** (Center for Contemporary Jewish Documentation)—50 years after the first French Jews were deported from France—to honor the memory of the 6 million Jews who died "without graves" at the hands of the Nazis. The basement crypt has a dramatic black marble Star of David containing the ashes of victims from Nazi death camps in Poland and Austria. The center has archives, a library, and a gallery that hosts temporary exhibitions. ⊠ *17 rue Geoffroy-l'Asnier,* ☎ *01–42–77–44–72.* ⊡ *15 frs/€2.30.* ◐ *Sun.–Fri. 10–1 and 2–5:30. Métro: Pont-Marie.*

⑧ Musée d'Art et d'Histoire du Judaïsme (Museum of Jewish Art and History). With its clifflike courtyard ringed by giant pilasters, the Hôtel St-Aignan, completed in 1650 to the design of Pierre le Muet, is one of the most awesome sights in the Marais. It opened as the city's Jewish museum in late 1998 after a 20-year restoration. The interior has been renovated to the point of blandness, but the exhibits have good explanatory English texts on Jewish history and practice, and you can ask for a free audioguide in English. Highlights include an array of 13th-century tombstones excavated in Paris; wooden models of destroyed East European synagogues; a roomful of early Chagalls; and Christian Boltanski's stark, two-part tribute to Shoah victims, in the form of plaques on an outer wall naming the (mainly Jewish) inhabitants of the Hôtel St-Aignan in 1939, and canvas hangings with the personal data of the 13 residents who were deported and died in concentration camps. Jewish people settled in France in the Rhône Valley as early as the 1st century BC; a synagogue existed in Paris by 582; an expulsion order was issued by Charles VI in 1394 but fitfully enforced; and 40,000 French Jews were granted full citizenship by the Revolution in 1791. France's Jewish population went from 300,000 to 180,000 with the deportation and departure during World War II but has since grown to around 700,000. ✉ *71 rue du Temple,* ☎ *01–53–01–86–60.* ✉ *40 frs/€6.* ⊘ *Sun.–Fri. 11–6. Métro: Rambuteau, Hôtel-de-Ville.*

⑬ Musée Bricard. Also called the Musée de la Serrure (Lock Museum), this museum is housed in a exquisitely elegant Baroque mansion designed in 1685 by the architect of Les Invalides, Libéral Bruand, for himself. Anyone with a taste for fine craftsmanship will appreciate the intricacy and ingenuity of many of the older locks displayed here. One represents an early security system—it would shoot anyone who tried to open it with the wrong key. Another was made in the 17th century by a master locksmith who was himself held under lock and key while he labored over it—the task took him four years. ✉ *1 rue de la Perle,* ☎ *01–42–77–79–62.* ✉ *30 frs/€4.60.* ⊘ *Weekdays 2–5. Métro: St-Paul.*

★ ⑰ Musée Carnavalet. To get a picture of the eternal yet ever-changing face of Paris throughout the ages, head to these two adjacent mansions in the heart of the Marais. Devoted to Parisian history, they include many salons filled with antiques and historic artifacts. Material dating from the city's origins until 1789 is in the Hôtel Carnavalet, and material from 1789 to the present is in the Hôtel Peletier St-Fargeau. In the late 17th century, the Hôtel Carnavalet was home to the most brilliant salon in Paris, presided over by Madame de Sévigné, best known for the hundreds of letters she wrote to her daughter; they've become one of the most enduring chronicles of French high society in the 17th century. The Hôtel Carnavalet, transformed into a museum in 1880, is full of maps and plans, furniture, and busts and portraits of Parisian worthies down the ages. The section on the Revolution includes riveting models of guillotines and objects associated with the royal family's final days, including the king's razor, and the chess set used by the royal prisoners at the approach of their own endgame. Lovers of the decorative arts will enjoy the period rooms here, especially those devoted to that most French of French styles, the 18th-century Rococo. Most entertaining, however, are the recreations of Marcel Proust's cork-lined bedroom, the late 19th-century Fouquet jewelry shop, and a room from that Art Nouveau monument, the Café de Paris. ✉ *23 rue de Sévigné,* ☎ *01–44–59–58–58.* ✉ *30 frs/€4.60.* ⊘ *Tues.–Sun. 10–5:40. Métro: St-Paul.*

NEED A
BREAK?

Marais Plus (✉ 20 rue des Francs-Bourgeois, ☎ 01–48–87–01–40), on the corner of rue Elzévir and rue des Francs-Bourgeois, is a delightful, artsy gift shop with a cozy salon de thé in the back.

---

⑩ Musée de la Chasse et de la Nature (Museum of Hunting and Nature). This museum is housed in the Hôtel de Guénégaud, designed around 1650 by François Mansart and one of the Marais's most stately mansions. There's an extensive collection of hunting paraphernalia, including a series of immense 17th- and 18th-century still lifes (notably by Desportes and Oudry) of dead animals and a wide variety of swords, guns, muskets, and taxidermy. ✉ *60 rue des Archives,* ☎ *01–42–72–86–42.* ✉ *30 frs/€4.60.* ⊘ *Wed.–Mon. 11–6. Métro: Rambuteau.*

⑯ Musée Cognacq-Jay. Another rare opportunity to see how cultured and rich Parisians once lived, this mansion is devoted to the arts of the 18th century and contains an outstanding collection of furniture, porcelain, and paintings (notably by Watteau, Boucher, and Tiepolo) amassed by Ernest Cognacq and his wife, Louise Jay, founder of La Samaritaine, the city's largest department store. ✉ *8 rue Elzévir,* ☎ *01–40–27–07–21.* ✉ *22 frs/€3.35.* ⊘ *Tues.–Sun. 10–5:40. Métro: St-Paul.*

★ ⑭ Musée Picasso. The Picasso Museum opened in the fall of 1985 and shows no signs of losing its immense popularity. The building itself, put up between 1656 and 1660 for financier Aubert de Fontenay, quickly became known as the Hôtel Salé—*salé* meaning, literally, "salted"—as a result of the enormous profits made by de Fontenay as the sole appointed collector of the salt tax. The mansion was luxuriously restored by the French government as a permanent home for the pictures, sculptures, drawings, prints, ceramics, and assorted works of art given to the government by Picasso's heirs after the painter's death in 1973 in lieu of death duties. It's the largest collection of works by Picasso in the world—no masterpieces, but "Picasso's Picassos," all works kept and sentimentally valued by Picasso himself. There are pictures from every period of his life: a grand total of 230 paintings, 1,500 drawings, and nearly 1,700 prints, as well as works by Cézanne, Miró, Renoir, Braque, Degas, and Matisse. The palatial surroundings of the Hôtel Salé add to the pleasures of a visit. ⊠ *5 rue de Thorigny,* ☎ *01–42–71–25–21.* ⊠ *30 frs/€4.60, Sun. 20 frs/€3.* ☉ *Thurs.–Mon. 9:30–5:30. Métro: St-Sébastien.*

🦢 ❼ **Musée de la Poupée** (Doll Museum). If you love dolls, make a detour to this quaint, low-ceilinged house in a cul-de-sac behind the Centre Pompidou to admire the rarefied collection of 300 French dolls dating back to the 1850s—many wearing their original costumes. Bisque-head dolls with enamel eyes were the Paris specialty, with Steiner, Bru, and Jumeau among the leading makers represented here. Two of the museum's six rooms are devoted to temporary exhibits, and there's a well-stocked gift shop. ⊠ *Impasse Berthaud,* ☎ *01–42–72–73–11.* ⊠ *35 frs/€5.34.* ☉ *Tues.–Sun. 10–6. Métro: Rambuteau.*

⑫ **Notre-Dame des Blancs-Manteaux.** The Blancs Manteaux were white-robed 13th-century mendicant monks whose monastery once stood on this spot. For the last 100 years, this late-17th-century church has had an imposing 18th-century façade that belonged to a now-destroyed church on the Ile de la Cité. Unfortunately, the narrow streets of the Marais leave little room to step back and admire it. The inside has fine woodwork and a Flemish-style rococo pulpit whose marquetry panels are inlaid with pewter and ivory. ⊠ *Rue des Blancs-Manteaux. Métro: Rambuteau.*

★ ⑱ **Place des Vosges.** The oldest monumental square in Paris—and probably still its most nobly proportioned—the place des Vosges was laid out by Henri IV at the start of the 17th century. Originally known as place Royale, it has kept its Renaissance beauty nearly intact, although its buildings have been softened by time, their pale pink brick crumbling slightly in the harsh Parisian air and the darker stone facings pitted with age. It stands on the site of a former royal palace, the Palais des Tournelles, which was abandoned by the Italian-born queen of France, Catherine de' Medici, when her husband, Henri II, was killed in a tournament here in 1559. It was always a highly desirable address, reaching a peak of glamour in the early years of Louis XIV's reign, when the nobility were falling over themselves for the privilege of living here. The two larger buildings on either side of the square were originally the king's and queen's pavilions. The statue in the center is of Louis XIII. It's not the original; that was melted down in the Revolution, the same period when the square's name was changed in honor of the French département of the Vosges, the first in the country to pay the new revolutionary taxes. With its arcades, symmetrical pink-brick town houses, and trim green garden, bisected in the center by gravel paths and edged with plane trees, the square achieves harmony and balance: it's a pleasant place to tarry on a sultry summer afternoon. To actually enter one of the square's imposing town houses, visit the **Maison de Victor Hugo** at No. 6. *Métro: Chemin-Vert.*

⑮ St-Denis-du-St-Sacrement. This severely neoclassical edifice dates from the 1830s. It is a formidable example of architectural discipline, oozing restraint and monumental dignity (or banality, according to taste). The grisaille frieze and gilt fresco above the semicircular apse have clout if not subtlety; the Delacroix *Deposition* (1844), in the front right-hand chapel as you enter, has both. ⊠ *Rue de Turenne. Métro: St-Sébastien.*

❷ St-Gervais–St-Protais. This imposing church near the Hôtel de Ville is named after two Roman soldiers martyred by the emperor Nero in the 1st century AD. The original church—no trace remains of it now—was built in the 7th century. The present church, a riot of Flamboyant-style decoration, went up between 1494 and 1598, making it one of the last Gothic constructions in the country. Pause to look at the facade, constructed between 1616 and 1621. It's an early example of French architects' use of the classical orders of decoration on the capitals (topmost sections) of the columns. Those on the first floor are plain and sturdy Doric; the more elaborate Ionic is used on the second floor; and the most ornate of all—Corinthian—is used on the third floor. The church hosts occasional organ and choral concerts. ⊠ *Pl. St-Gervais,* ☎ *01–47–26–78–38 concert information.* ⊙ *Tues.–Sun. 6:30 am–8 pm. Métro: Hôtel de Ville.*

❸ St-Merri. This church near the Centre Pompidou, completed in 1552, has a turret containing the oldest bell in Paris (cast in 1331) and an 18th-century pulpit supported on carved palm trees. ⊠ *Rue de la Verrerie. Métro: Hôtel de Ville.*

㉒ St-Paul–St-Louis. The leading Baroque church in the Marais, with its elegant dome rising 180 ft above the crossing, was begun in 1627 by the Jesuits and partly modeled on their Gesu church in Rome. Look for Delacroix's dramatic *Christ on the Mount of Olives* high up in the transept, and the two huge shells, used as fonts, presented by Victor Hugo when he lived on nearby place des Vosges. ⊠ *Rue St-Antoine. Métro: St-Paul.*

⑳ Ste-Marie. Constructed 1632–34 by François Mansart as the chapel of the Convent of the Visitation, this is now a Protestant "reformed" church. The large dome above the distinctive nave rotunda is one of the earliest in Paris. ⊠ *Rue St-Antoine. Métro: Bastille.*

❹ Square Igor-Stravinsky. The café-lined square, next to the Centre Pompidou and backed by the church of St-Merri, has a fountain animated by the colorful and imaginative sculptures of French artist Niki de St-Phalle, together with the aquatic mechanisms of her Swiss partner, Jean Tinguely. The fountain (sculptures and all) was erected in 1980. It is not part of the Centre Pompidou, but it fits right in. *Métro: Rambuteau.*

THE LATIN QUARTER AND THE ILE ST-LOUIS

South of Ile de la Cité on the Left Bank of the Seine is the bohemian Quartier Latin, with its warren of steep sloping streets, populated largely by Sorbonne students and academics who fill the air of the cafés with their ideas—and tobacco smoke. The name Latin Quarter comes from the university tradition of studying and speaking in Latin, a tradition that disappeared during the Revolution. The university began as a theological school in the Middle Ages and later became the headquarters of the University of Paris; in 1968, the student revolution here had an explosive effect on French politics, resulting in major reforms in the education system.

The Latin Quarter and the Ile St-Louis

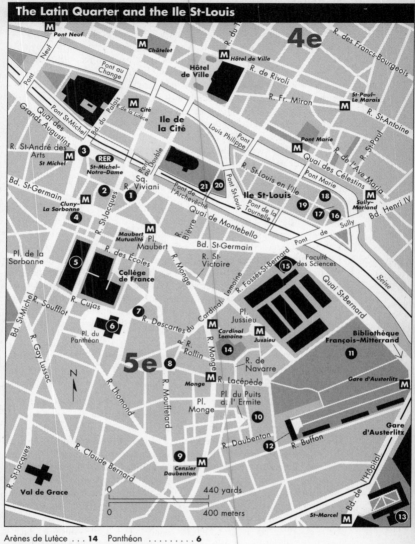

In fact, since ancient times, this quartier has detested the *bourgeoisie,* for here the ghost of Villon walks, that great poet and rapscallion who died sordidly in a tavern brawl. And here Verlaine, among the students and the shopkeepers of the rue Mouffetard, drank his eternal absinthe and wrote his poems. Today, however, the area is becoming increasingly upscale, with dozens of Right Bank luxury boutiques and antiques stores rubbing elbows with the bookstores. A grim modern skyscraper at the Jussieu campus, the science division of the University of Paris, reiterates the area's yen for learning yet fails to outgun the mighty dome of the Panthéon in its challenge for skyline supremacy. Most of the district's appeal is less emphatic: Roman ruins, tumbling street markets, the two oldest trees in Paris, and chance glimpses of Notre-Dame all await your discovery.

As does the Ile St-Louis. Of the two islands in the Seine—the Ile de la Cité is located just to the west—it is the Ile St-Louis that best retains the romance and loveliness of *le Paris traditionnel*. It has remained in the heart of Parisians as it has remained in the heart of every tourist who came upon it by accident, and without warning—a tiny universe unto itself, shaded by trees, bordered by Seine-side quais, and overhung with ancient stone houses. These have long comprised some of the most prized addresses in Paris—Voltaire, Daumier, Cézanne, Baudelaire, Chagall, Helena Rubenstein, and the Rothschilds are just some of the lucky people who have called the Ile St-Louis home. Up until the 1800s it was reputed that some island residents never crossed the bridges to get to Paris proper—and once you discover the island's quiet charm, you may understand why.

Numbers in the text correspond to numbers in the margin and on the Latin Quarter and the Ile St.-Louis map.

A Good Walk

Start at the Seine along the Pont au Double and head to square René-Viviani, where you'll find a battered acacia—which vies with a specimen in the Jardin des Plantes for the title of oldest tree in Paris—and a spectacular view of Notre-Dame. Behind the square lies the church of **St-Julien-le-Pauvre** ①, built at the same time as Notre-Dame, and the tiny, elegant streets of the Maubert district. Turn left out of the church and cross rue St-Jacques to the elegantly proportioned church of **St-Séverin** ②. The surrounding streets are for pedestrians only and crammed with cheap restaurants fronted by suave waiters touting customers at most hours of the day and night. Take rue St-Séverin, a right on rue Xavier-Privas, and a left on rue de la Huchette—home to Paris's smallest theater and oldest jazz club—to reach **place St-Michel** ③. The grandiose fountain, depicting St. Michael slaying the dragon, is a popular meeting spot at the nerve center of the Left Bank.

Turn left up boulevard St-Michel and cross boulevard St-Germain. To your left, behind some forbidding railings, lurks a garden with ruins that date from Roman times. These belong to the Hôtel de Cluny, home to the **Musée National du Moyen-Age** ④, the National Museum of the Middle Ages. The entrance is down rue Sommerard, the next street on the left. Cross place Paul-Painlevé, in front of the museum, up toward the **Sorbonne** ⑤ university, fronted by a small plaza where the Left Bank's student population congregates after classes. Continue uphill until you are confronted, up rue Soufflot on your left, by the menacing domed bulk of the **Panthéon** ⑥, originally built as a church but now a monument to France's most glorious historical figures. On the far left corner of place du Panthéon stands **St-Étienne-du-Mont** ⑦, a church whose facade is a mishmash of architectural styles. Explore the top of quaint rue de la Montagne-Ste-Geneviève alongside; then turn right onto rue

Descartes to reach **place de la Contrescarpe** ⑧. This square looks almost provincial during the day as Parisians flock to the daily market on rue Mouffetard.

Duck into the old church of **St-Médard** ⑨ at the foot of rue Mouffetard; then head left for 250 yards along rue Censier and turn left again into rue du Gril to discover the beautiful white **Mosquée** ⑩, complete with minaret. Blink twice and you'll be convinced you've left Paris behind. On the far side of the mosque extends the **Jardin des Plantes** ⑪, spacious botanical gardens; the first building you'll come to is the **Grande Galerie de l'Evolution** ⑫, a museum with a startling collection of taxidermy, many of extinct or endangered animals. The museums of entomology, paleontology, and mineralogy are on the south side of the park along rue Buffon; an old-fashioned zoo is on the other.

Although it's a bit out of the way, **St-Louis de la Salpêtrière** ⑬, the church of the Salpêtrière Hospital, is within walking distance from the Jardin des Plantes: take boulevard de l'Hôpital, at the far end of the park; the church is in the grounds of the hospital beyond Gare d'Austerlitz. Farther upriver, via the quai d'Austerlitz and the quai de la Gare, is the new Bibliothèque Nationale François-Mitterrand, the French National Library, with its four huge, shiny glass towers.

If you forgo the distant pleasures of southeast Paris, take the northwest exit from the Jardin des Plantes up rue Lacépède then rue de Navarre to the **Arènes de Lutèce** ⑭, the remains of a Roman amphitheater. Rue des Arènes and rue Limé lead to place Jussieu and its hideous 1960s concrete campus; there's greater refinement around the corner down rue des Fossés-St-Bernard at the glass-facaded **Institut du Monde Arabe** ⑮, a center devoted to Arab culture.

Cross the Seine on Pont de Sully to the **Ile St-Louis** ⑯, the smaller of the city's two islands; it's a time capsule of old Paris and a tranquil place for taking a stroll back to the 17th and 18th centuries. The **Hôtel Lambert** ⑰ and the **Hôtel de Lauzun** ⑱, set near the eastern prow of the island, are two of the most majestic mansions on the island. Rue St-Louis-en-l'Ile runs the length of the island, dividing it in two. Walk down the street and admire the strange, pierced spire of **St-Louis-en-l'Ile** ⑲; stop off for an ice cream at Berthillon at No. 31. Then head down to the Pont St-Louis at the island's western tip to admire the celebrated views of Notre-Dame, and the Hôtel de Ville and St-Gervais church on the Right Bank. Just across the bridge on Ile de la Cité lies the **Mémorial de la Déportation** ⑳, a starkly moving modern crypt dedicated to the French Jews who died in Nazi concentration camps. You may wish to linger in the quiet garden above before savoring the view of Notre-Dame from the **Pont de l'Archevêché** ㉑, which links the island to the Left Bank.

TIMING

At just under 6 km (about 3½ mi), this walk can be done in a morning or afternoon, or serve as the basis for a leisurely day's exploring—given that several sites, notably the Musée de Cluny, deserve a lengthy visit. Note that the Grande Galerie d'Évolution stays open until 10 PM on Thursday. You can easily make a brief excursion to St-Louis de la Salpêtrière as well as the Bibliothèque Nationale François-Mitterrand.

Sights to See

⑭ **Arènes de Lutèce** (Lutetia Amphitheater). This Roman arena was only discovered in 1869 and has since been excavated and landscaped to reveal parts of the original amphitheater. Designed as a theater and circus, the arena was almost totally destroyed by the barbarians in AD 280, though you can still see part of the stage and tiered seating. Along with the remains of the baths at the Cluny, this constitutes rare evidence of the powerful Roman city of Lutetia that flourished on the Left Bank in the 3rd century. ⊠ *Entrance at rue Monge or rue de Navarre.* ⊙ *Daily 8–sunset. Métro: Monge.*

⑫ **Grande Galerie de l'Evolution** (Great Hall of Evolution). This vast, handsome glass-and-iron structure in the Jardin des Plantes was built, like the Eiffel Tower, in 1889 but abandoned in the 1960s. It reopened amid popular acclaim in 1994 and now contains one of the world's finest collections of taxidermy, including a section devoted to extinct and endangered species. There's a reconstituted dodo—only a foot actually remains of this clumsy, flightless bird from Mauritius—and a miniature South African zebra, the quagga, which disappeared early in the 20th century. Stunning lighting effects include push-button spotlighting and a ceiling that changes color to suggest storms, twilight, or hot savannah sun. ⊠ *36 rue Geoffroy-St-Hilaire,* ☎ *01–40–79–39–39,* WEB *www.mnhn.fr/evolution.* 🎟 *40 frs/€6.* ⊙ *Wed. and Fri.–Mon. 10–6, Thurs. 10–10. Métro: Monge.*

⑰ **Hôtel Lambert.** Without this house—one of the most famous in Paris— Versailles probably wouldn't exist as we know it. Sitting on the eastern end of the Ile St-Louis, it was created by the three great "Le"'s of the French Baroque: architect Louis Le Vau (1612–70), decorator Charles Le Brun, and painter Eustache Le Sieur. Built by the banker Lambert "le riche," the mansion was so impressive Nicolas Fouquet ordered the team to build his chateau of Vaux-le-Vicomte, which, in turn, inspired Louis XIV to commission them to create Versailles. Voltaire was the most famous occupant of the Lambert, then owned by his lover, the Marquise du Châtelet. Here, in the Galerie d'Hercule, many of Paris's most famous costume balls were held; guests included everyone from Chopin to Empress Eugénie. Today, as through all of its privileged history, the house is private and has been lovingly restored by the Barons Rothschild. If you go around to the neighboring quai and bridge you can see part of the garden and, just possibly, the Galerie illuminated at night. ⊠ *2 rue St-Louis-en-l'Ile. Métro: Pont-Marie.*

★ ⑱ **Hôtel de Lauzun.** Gilded and mirrored to within an inch of their lives, the salons here are some of the most important examples of the Baroque style in Paris and are a must-see for art historians—others will be curious to visit this Ile St-Louis mansion because of the house's fascinating history. It was built in about 1650 and designed in part by Charles Le Brun for Charles Gruyn, a supplier of goods to the French army who accumulated an immense fortune, then landed in jail before the house was even completed. In the 19th century, the revolutionary critic and visionary poet Charles Baudelaire (1821–67) had an apartment here, where he kept a cache of stuffed snakes and crocodiles, and wrote a large chunk of *Les Fleurs du Mal* (The Flowers of Evil), his masterpiece. In 1848, the poet Théophile Gautier (1811–72) moved in, making it the meeting place of the Club des Haschischines (Hashish Eaters' Club); novelist Alexandre Dumas and painter Eugène Delacroix were both members. The club came to represent more than just a den of drug takers and gossips, for these men believed passionately in the purity of art and the crucial role of the artist as sole interpreter of the chaos of life. Art for Art's Sake—the more refined and exotic the better— was their creed. Anything that helped the artist reach heightened states of perception was applauded. Now the building is used for more decorous receptions by the mayor of Paris and is open to the public on weekends from Easter to October. ⊠ *17 quai d'Anjou,* ☎ *01–43–54–27–*

14. ⚄ *25 frs/€3.81.* ☉ *Easter–Oct., weekends 10–5:30. Métro: Pont-Marie.*

⑯ Ile St-Louis. The smaller of the two Paris islands is linked to the Ile de la Cité by Pont St-Louis. The contrast between the islands is striking: whereas the Ile de la Cité is steeped in history and dotted with dignified public buildings, the Ile St-Louis is a discreet residential district. The island's most striking feature is its architectural unity, which stems from the efforts of a group of early 17th-century property speculators. At that time, there were two islands here, the Ile Notre-Dame and Ile aux Vaches—Cow Island, a reference to its use as grazing land. The speculators, led by an energetic engineer named Christophe Marie (after whom the Pont Marie was named), bought the two islands, joined them together, and divided the newly formed Ile St-Louis into building plots. Baroque architect Louis Le Vau was commissioned to erect a series of imposing town houses, and by 1664 the project was largely complete. People still talk about the quaint, village-street feel of rue St-Louis-en-l'Ile, which runs the length of the island, dividing it neatly in two. From the quai de Bourbon at the western end, facing the Ile de la Cité, there are attractive views of Notre-Dame, the Hôtel de Ville, and the church of St-Gervais. In summer, rows of baking bodies attest to the quai's enduring popularity as the city's favorite sunbathing spot, while crowds line up for a scoop from Berthillon's shop, the mecca of Parisian ice cream. You can savor your cone of *glace de Grande Marnier* by strolling along the isle's Seine-side streets—as Brässai and other photographers proved, they are among Paris's most romantic sights. *Métro: Pont-Marie.*

⑮ Institut du Monde Arabe (Institute of the Arab World). Jean Nouvel's striking glass-and-steel edifice adroitly fuses Arabic and European styles and was greeted with enthusiasm when it opened in 1988. Note the 240 shutterlike apertures that open and close to regulate light exposure. Inside, the institute tries to do for Arab culture what the Centre Pompidou does for modern art, with the help of a sound-and-image center; a vast library and documentation center; and an art museum containing an array of Arab-Islamic art, textiles, and ceramics, plus exhibits on Arabic mathematics, astronomy, and medicine. Glass elevators whisk you to the ninth floor, where you can sip mint tea at the rooftop café and enjoy a memorable view of the Seine and Notre-Dame. ✉ *1 rue des Fossés-St-Bernard,* ☎ *01–40–51–38–38.* ⚄ *40 frs/€6.* ☉ *Tues.–Sun. 10–6. Métro: Cardinal-Lemoine.*

👆 ⑪ Jardin des Plantes (Botanical Gardens). Bordered by the Seine, the drab Gare d'Austerlitz, and the utilitarian Jussieu campus (a branch of the Paris University system), this enormous swath of greenery contains botanical gardens, the Grande Galerie de l'Evolution, and three other natural history museums, which celebrated their centenary with a six-month renovation program in 1998. The **Grande Galerie de l'Evolution** is devoted to stuffed animals; the **Musée Entomologique** to insects; the **Musée Paléontologique** to fossils and skeletons dating back to prehistoric times; and the **Musée Minéralogique** to rocks and minerals. The stock of plants in the botanical gardens, dating from the first collections from the 17th century, has been enhanced by subsequent generations of devoted French botanists. The garden shelters what is claimed to be Paris's oldest tree, an *acacia robinia,* planted in 1636. There is also an alpine garden, an aquarium, a maze, a number of hothouses, and one of the world's oldest zoos, the Ménagerie, started by Napoléon. ✉ *Entrances on rue Geoffroy-St-Hilaire, rue Civier, and rue Buffon.* ⚄ *Museums and zoo 30 frs/€4.60.* ☉ *Museums Wed.–Mon. 10–5. Zoo*

June–Aug., daily 9–6; Sept.–May, daily 9–6. Garden daily 7:30 am–sunset. Métro: Monge.

㉔ Mémorial de la Déportation (Memorial of the Deportation). On the eastern tip of the Ile de la Cité, in what was once the city morgue, lies a starkly moving modern crypt, dedicated to all the French men, women, and children who died in Nazi concentration camps. ✉ *Free.* ☉ *Apr.–Sept., daily 9–6; Oct.–Mar., daily 9 am–dusk. Métro: Maubert-Mutualité.*

⑩ Mosquée (Mosque). This beautiful white mosque was built from 1922 to 1925, complete with arcades and minaret, and decorated in the style of Moorish Spain. Students from the nearby Jussieu and Censier universities pack themselves into the tea salon, for cups of sweet mint tea at the café and for copious quantities of couscous at the restaurant. The sunken garden and tiled patios are also open to the public (the prayer rooms are not), as are the *hammams,* or Turkish baths. ✉ *2 pl. du Puits-de-l'Ermite,* ☎ *01–45–35–97–33.* ✉ *Guided tour 15 frs/€2.30, Turkish baths 85 frs/€13.* ☉ *Baths daily 10–9 (Tues. and Sun. men only, Mon. and Wed.–Sat. women only). Guided tours of mosque Sat.–Thurs. 9–noon and 2–6. Métro: Monge.*

OFF THE BEATEN PATH	**CHINATOWN –** If China, rather than Arabia, is your cup of tea, take the métro at nearby Censier-Daubenton to Paris's Chinatown. Although not as ornamental as San Francisco's or New York's, Paris's Chinatown nevertheless has myriad electronics and clothing stores and dozens of restaurants with an exciting array of Chinese *comestibles* (foods). **Tang-Frères Chinese supermarket** (✉ 48 av. d'Ivry) packs in a serious crowd of shoppers. The **Temple de l'Association des Résidents d'Origine Chinoise** (✉ 37 rue du Disque) is a small Buddhist temple that looks like a cross between a school cafeteria and an exotic Asian enclave filled with Buddha figures, fruit, and incense. For a more upscale version of Chinese culture, head out to **Chinagora** in the eastern suburbs. *Métro: Tolbiac.*

★ ④ Musée National du Moyen-Age (National Museum of the Middle Ages). Devoted to the arts of the Middle Ages, this museum—often referred to as the Museé de Cluny—is housed in that celebrated relic of the 15th-century, the **Hôtel de Cluny.** The mansion has an intricately vaulted chapel and a cloistered courtyard with mullioned windows that originally belonged to monks of the Cluny Abbey in Burgundy. A stunning array of tapestries heads its vast exhibition of medieval decorative arts; don't miss the world-famous *Dame à la Licorne* (Lady and the Unicorn) series, woven in the 15th or 16th century, probably in the southern Netherlands. Alongside the mansion are a reconstituted medieval garden, with 58 species of flora and fauna depicted in the *Dame à la Licorne* tapestries, and remnants of the city's Roman baths—both hot (*Caldarium*) and cold (*Frigidarium*), the latter containing the *Boatmen's Pillar,* Paris's oldest sculpture. ✉ *6 pl. Paul-Painlevé,* ☎ *01–53–73–78–00,* 🌐 *www.museemoyenage.fr.* ✉ *30 frs/€4.60, Sun. 20 frs/€3.* ☉ *Wed.–Mon. 9:15–5:45. Métro: Cluny–La Sorbonne.*

⑥ Panthéon. Originally commissioned by Louis XV to mark his recovery from illness in 1744, Germain Soufflot's mighty domed church was not begun until 1764, or completed until 1790—whereupon the godless philosophers of the Revolution had its windows blocked and ordered it transformed into a national shrine. Puvis de Chavannes's giant frescoes in the nave, retracing the life of St. Genevieve, warrant appraisal, along with a model of Foucault's pendulum, first hoisted in 1851 to prove the earth's rotation on its axis. Today the Panthéon is a monument to France's most glorious historical figures; the crypt holds the remains of Voltaire, Zola, Rousseau, and dozens of other national heroes. Nobel Prize–winning scientist Marie Curie became the first woman to join their ranks, in 1995. ⊠ *Pl. du Panthéon,* ☎ *01–44–32–18–00.* ⌨ *35 frs/€5.34.* ☉ *Apr.–Sept., daily 9:30–6:30; Oct.–Mar., daily 10–6:15. Métro: Cardinal-Lemoine; RER: Luxembourg.*

OFF THE
BEATEN PATH

LYCÉE LOUIS-LE-GRAND – Molière, Voltaire, and Robespierre studied at this venerable school, founded in 1530 by François I as the College of Three Languages. Students learned High Latin, Greek, and Hebrew as well as many other subjects eschewed by academics at the Sorbonne. Today's buildings, dating from the 17th century, are still part of a school. From the Panthéon, follow rue Soufflot, and then take the first right onto rue St-Jacques. ⊠ *123 rue St-Jacques. RER: Luxembourg.*

❽ Place de la Contrescarpe. This intimate square behind the Panthéon doesn't start to swing until after dusk, when its cafés and bars fill up. During the day, the square looks almost provincial as Parisians flock to the daily market at the bottom of rue Mouffetard, a steeply sloping street that retains much of its bygone charm. *Métro: Monge.*

❸ Place St-Michel. This square on the Seine was named for Gabriel Davioud's grandiose 1860 fountain, depicting St. Michael slaying the dragon. *Métro, RER: St-Michel.*

㉑ Pont de l'Archevêché (Archbishop's Bridge). This bridge, built in 1828, links Ile St-Louis to the Left Bank. The bridge offers a breathtaking view of the east end of the cathedral, ringed by flying buttresses, floating above the Seine like some vast stone ship. *Métro: Maubert-Mutualité.*

❼ St-Étienne-du-Mont. The ornate facade of this mainly 16th-century church combines Gothic, Baroque, and Renaissance elements. Inside, the curly, carved rood screen (1525–35), separating nave and chancel, is the only one of its kind in Paris. Note the uneven-floored chapel behind the choir, which can be reached via a cloister containing exquisite 17th-century stained glass. ⊠ *Pl. de l'Abbé-Basset. Métro: Cardinal-Lemoine.*

❶ St-Julien-le-Pauvre. This tiny church was built at the same time as Notre-Dame (1165–1220), on a site where a succession of chapels once stood. The church belongs to a Greek Orthodox order today but was originally named for St. Julian, bishop of Le Mans, who was nicknamed Le Pauvre (The Poor) after he gave all his money away. ⊠ *Rue St-Julien-le-Pauvre. Métro: St-Michel.*

⓭ St-Louis de la Salpêtrière. The church of the Salpêtrière Hospital stands next to the Gare d'Austerlitz, which it dominates with its unmistakable, lantern-topped octagonal dome. The church was built (1670–77) in the shape of a Greek cross from the designs of Libéral Bruant. ⊠ *Bd. de l'Hôpital. Métro: Gare d'Austerlitz.*

⓳ St-Louis-en-l'Ile. The only church on the Ile St-Louis, built from 1664 to 1726 to the Baroque designs of architect Louis Le Vau, is lavishly furnished and has two unusual exterior features: its original pierced spire, holy in every sense, and an iron clock, added in 1741. ⊠ *Rue St-Louis-en-l'Ile. Métro: Pont-Marie.*

NEED A
BREAK?

Cafés all over sell the haute couture of ice cream, but **Berthillon** (⊠ 31 rue St-Louis-en-l'Ile, ☎ 01–43–54–31–61) itself is the place to come. More than 30 flavors are served; expect to wait in line. The shop is open Wednesday–Sunday.

9 **St-Médard.** This church at the bottom of rue Mouffetard contains the painting *St. Joseph with the Christ Child* by Spanish master Zurbarán. The nave and facade, with its large late-Gothic window, date from the late 15th century. The 17th-century choir is in contrasting classical style. ⊠ *Rue Mouffetard. Métro: Censier-Daubenton.*

OFF THE   **MANUFACTURE DES GOBELINS** – Tapestries have been woven on this spot
BEATEN PATH   in southeastern Paris, on the banks of the long-covered Bièvre River, which once flowed into the Seine, since 1662. Guided tours—in French only—combine historical explanation with the chance to admire both old tapestries and today's weavers at work in their airy workshops. ⊠ *42 av. des Gobelins,* ☎ *01–44–08–52–00.* ☞ *50 frs/€7.63.* ☉ *Tues.–Thurs., guided tours only at 2 and 2:45. Métro: Gobelins.*

2 **St-Séverin.** This unusually wide Flamboyant Gothic church dominates the Left Bank neighborhood filled with squares and pedestrian streets. In the 11th century, the church that stood here was the parish church for the entire Left Bank. Louis XIV's cousin, a capricious woman known simply as the Grande Mademoiselle, adopted St-Séverin when she tired of St-Sulpice; she then spent vast sums getting court decorator Le Brun to modernize the chancel in the 17th century. Note the splendidly deviant spiraling column in the forest of pillars behind the altar. ⊠ *Rue des Prêtres-St-Séverin.* ☉ *Weekdays 11–5:30, Sat. 11–10. Métro: St-Michel.*

5 **Sorbonne.** Named after Robert de Sorbon, a medieval canon who founded a theological college here in 1253 for 16 students, the Sorbonne is one of the oldest universities in Europe. For centuries it has been one of France's principal institutions of higher learning, as well as the hub of the Latin Quarter and nerve center of Paris's student population. The church and university buildings were restored by Cardinal Richelieu in the 17th century, and the maze of amphitheaters, lecture rooms, and laboratories, and the surrounding courtyards and narrow streets, retains a hallowed air. You can visit the main courtyard on rue de la Sorbonne and peek into the main lecture hall, a major meeting point during the tumultuous student upheavals of 1968 and also of interest for a giant mural by Puvis de Chavannes, the *Sacred Wood* (1880–89). The square is dominated by the university church, the noble **Église de la Sorbonne,** whose outstanding exterior features are its cupola and Corinthian columns. Inside is the white marble tomb of that ultimate crafty cleric, Cardinal Richelieu himself. ⊠ *Rue de la Sorbonne. Métro: Cluny–La Sorbonne.*

OFF THE   **CENTRE DE LA MER ET DES EAUX** – A spell of fish-gazing is a soothing,
BEATEN PATH   mesmerizing experience for young and old. The Center of Sea and Waters is one of the principal aquariums in Paris. From the Sorbonne, go up rue de la Sorbonne, and then take the first left on rue Cujas, and a right on rue St-Jacques. ⊠ *195 rue St-Jacques,* ☎ *01–44–32–10–90,* WEB*www.oceano.org.* ☞ *30 frs/€4.60.* ☉ *Tues.–Fri. 10–12:30 and 1:15–5:30, weekends 10–5:30. RER: Luxembourg.*

FROM ORSAY TO ST-GERMAIN

This walk covers the western half of the Left Bank, from the Musée d'Orsay in the stately 7e arrondissement, to the Faubourg St-Germain, a lively and colorful area in the 6e arrondissement. The headliner here is the Musée d'Orsay, which houses a superb array of Impressionist paintings in a spectacularly converted Belle Epoque rail station on the Seine. Farther along the river, the 18th-century Palais Bourbon, home

Orsay to St-Germain

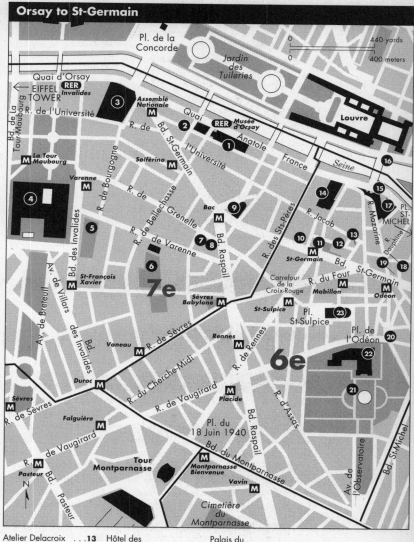

to the National Assembly, sets the tone. This is Edith Wharton territory—select, discreet *vieille France,* where all the aristocrats live in gorgeous, sprawling, old-fashioned apartments or *maisons particulières*
(town houses). Luxurious ministries and embassies—including the
Hôtel Matignon, residence of the French prime minister—line the surrounding streets, their majestic scale completely in keeping with the
Hôtel des Invalides, whose gold-leafed dome climbs heavenward above
the regal tomb of Napoléon. The splendid Rodin Museum—one of the
few houses here where you can explore the grand interior—is only a
short walk away.

To the east, boulevard St-Michel slices the Left Bank in two: on one
side, the Latin Quarter; on the other, the Faubourg St-Germain, named
for St-Germain-des-Prés, the oldest church in Paris. The venerable
church tower has long acted as a beacon for intellectuals, most famously
during the 1950s, when Albert Camus, Jean-Paul Sartre, and Simone
de Beauvoir ate and drank existentialism in the neighborhood cafés.
Today most of the philosophizing is done by tourists, yet a wealth of
bookshops, art stores, and antiques galleries ensure that St-Germain,
as the area is known, retains its highbrow appeal. A highlight of St-
Germain is the Jardin du Luxembourg, the city's most famous and colorful park. The 17th-century palace overlooking the gardens houses
the French Senate.

*Numbers in the text correspond to numbers in the margin and on the
Orsay to St-Germain map.*

A Good Walk

Arrive at the **Musée d'Orsay** ① early to avoid the crowds that flock to
see the museum's outstanding works of art, including many of the most
beloved Impressionist paintings in France. A good meeting point is the
pedestrian square outside the museum, where huge bronze statues of
an elephant and a rhinoceros disprove the notion that the French take
their art too seriously. Across the square stands the **Musée de la Légion d'Honneur** ②, where you can find an array of French and foreign
decorations. A stylish two-tiered footbridge, opened in 2000, crosses
the Seine to the Tuileries. But we suggest you either cut south down
rue de Bellechasse (if you're short of time) to the Hôtel Matignon or
head west along rue de Lille to the **Palais Bourbon** ③, home of the Assemblée Nationale (the French Parliament). There's a fine view across
the Seine to place de la Concorde and the church of the Madeleine.

Rue de l'Université leads from the Assemblée to the grassy Esplanade
des Invalides and an encounter with the **Hôtel des Invalides** ④, founded
by Louis XIV to house wounded (*invalid*) veterans. The most impressive dome in Paris towers over the church at the back of the Invalides—
the Église du Dôme. From the church, turn left, then left again onto
boulevard des Invalides, then right on rue de Varenne to reach the elegant Hôtel Biron, better known as the **Musée Rodin** ⑤. Here you can
see a fine collection of Auguste Rodin's emotionally charged statues
and some wonderful gardens. The quiet, distinguished 18th-century
streets between the Rodin Museum and the Parliament are filled with
embassies and ministries. The most famous, farther along rue de
Varenne, is the **Hôtel Matignon** ⑥, residence of the French prime minister. Just before, at No. 51, is one of Paris's handful of private cul-de-
sacs. Next door at No. 53 you can pay your respects to American novelist
Edith Wharton, who lived and worked here from 1910 to 1920. Take
the next left onto rue du Bac, then right onto rue de Grenelle, past the
Musée Maillol ⑦, dedicated to the work of sculptor Aristide Maillol,
and Bouchardon's monumental **Fontaine des Quatre Saisons** ⑧.

Turn left down boulevard Raspail and cross to rue de Luynes. Carry on across boulevard St-Germain to inspect the stately 17th-century church of **St-Thomas d'Aquin** ⑨; then double back and head east along boulevard St-Germain for 400 yards to the **Café de Flore** ⑩, one of the principal haunts of the intelligentsia after World War II. Another popular café, two doors down, is **Les Deux Magots** ⑪; politicians and showbiz types still wine and dine at the pricey Brasserie Lipp across the street. Looming above cobbled place St-Germain-des-Prés stands **St-Germain-des-Prés** ⑫, Paris's oldest church.

Follow rue de l'Abbaye, along the far side of the church, to rue de Furstenberg. The street opens out into place Furstenberg, a picturesque square bedecked with white globe lamps and catalpa trees, where you'll find Eugène Delacroix's studio, the **Atelier Delacroix** ⑬. Take a left on rue Jacob and turn right down rue Bonaparte to the **École Nationale des Beaux-Arts** ⑭, whose students can often be seen painting and sketching on the nearby quays and bridges. Wander into the courtyard and galleries of the school to see the casts and copies of the statues stored here for safekeeping during the Revolution.

Continue down to the Seine and turn right along the quai, past the **Institut de France** ⑮. With its distinctive dome and commanding position overlooking the **Pont des Arts** ⑯—a footbridge affording delightful views of the Louvre and Ile de la Cité—the institute is one of the city's most impressive waterside sights. Farther along, on the quai de Conti, you pass the **Hôtel des Monnaies** ⑰, the old national mint.

Head up rue Dauphine, the street that singer Juliet Greco put on the map when she opened the erstwhile Tabou jazz club here in the '50s. It's linked 150 yards up by the open-air passage Dauphine to rue Mazarine, which leads left to the **Carrefour de Buci** ⑱, a busy crossroad. Fanning out from the Carrefour are lively rue de Buci, with one of the best food markets in Paris; rue de l'Ancienne-Comédie, so named because it was the first home of the legendary Comédie Française, cutting through to busy place de l'Odéon; and rue St-André des Arts, which leads swiftly to the historic **Cour du Commerce St-André** (opposite No. 66), a cobbled pedestrian street. Halfway down on the left—opposite the oldest café in Paris, **Le Procope** ⑲—stands one of the few remaining towers of the 12th-century fortress wall built by Philippe-Auguste, overlooking a tiny courtyard, the **Cour de Rohan.** (From here it's a short walk to place St-Michel.)

Head to the end of cour du Commerce St-André, cross boulevard St-Germain, and climb rue de l'Odéon to the colonnaded **Théâtre de l'Odéon** ⑳. Behind the theater, across rue de Vaugirard, lies the spacious **Jardin du Luxembourg** ㉑, one of the most stylish parks in the city. The large pond, usually animated by an armada of toy boats that can be hired alongside, enjoys the scenic backdrop of the rusticated 17th-century **Palais du Luxembourg** ㉒. Today the palace houses the French Senate and is not open to the public.

Return to rue de Vaugirard and head west before turning right down pretty rue Férou to place St-Sulpice, a spacious square ringed with cafés; Yves Saint Laurent's famous Rive Gauche store is at No. 6. Looming over the square is the enormous church of **St-Sulpice** ㉓. If you wish to now explore Montparnasse, walk west down rue du Vieux-Colombier and take the métro three stops to Vavin.

TIMING

Depending on how long you spend in the plethora of museums and shops along the way, this 6½-km (4-mi) walk could take four hours to a couple of days. Aim for an early start—that way you can hit the Musée d'Orsay early, when crowds are smaller, then get to the rue de Buci street market in full swing, in the late afternoon (the stalls are generally closed for lunch until 3 PM). Note that the Hôtel des Invalides is open daily, but Orsay is closed Monday. You might consider returning to one or more museums on another day or night—Orsay is open late on Thursday evenings.

Sights to See

⓭ Atelier Delacroix. The studio of artist Eugène Delacroix (1798–1863) contains only a small collection of his sketches and drawings, but if you want to pay homage to France's foremost Romantic painter, it's a good place to visit. Another reason to pay a call: the atelier is set on place Furstenberg, one of the tiniest, most romantic squares in Paris. ⊠ *6 rue Furstenberg,* ☏ *01–44–41–86–50,* WEB *www.musee.delacroix.fr.* ☞ *23 frs/€3.51.* ☺ *Wed.–Mon. 9:30–5. Métro: St-Germain-des-Prés.*

⓾ Café de Flore. In the postwar years, Jean-Paul Sartre and Simone de Beauvoir would meet their friends and followers at this popular café. These days it's mostly filled with tourists. ⊠ *172 bd. St-Germain. Métro: St-Germain-des-Prés.*

⓲ Carrefour de Buci. This crossroads was once a notorious Left Bank landmark: during the 18th century, it contained a gallows, an execution stake, and an iron collar for punishing troublemakers. In September 1792 the revolutionary army used this daunting site to enroll its first volunteers, and many Royalists and priests lost their heads here during the bloody course of the Revolution. There's nothing sinister, however, about the carrefour today, as brightly colored flowers spill onto the sidewalk at the flower shop on the corner of rue Grégoire-de-Tours. A couple of the small streets fanning out from the carrefour are of interest. **Rue de Buci** has a good outdoor food market, open Tuesday–Saturday 8–1 and 4–7, Sunday 9–1. **Rue de l'Ancienne-Comédie** got its name because it was the first home of the Comédie Française. *Métro: Mabillon.*

NEED A BREAK?   If you happen to arrive when the market on rue de Buci is closed, **La Vieille France** (⊠ 14 rue de Buci, ☏ 01–43–26–55–13) pâtisserie may help fill the gap.

Cour du Commerce St-André. Revolutionary Jean-Paul Marat printed his newspaper, *L'Ami du Peuple,* at No. 8; and at No. 9, Dr. Guillotin conceived the idea for a new, "humane" method of execution—it was rumored that he practiced it on sheep first—that remained in force for murderers until 1981. *Métro: Odéon.*

Cour de Rohan (Rohan Courtyard). This series of cloistered courtyards and passageways was once part of the home of the archbishops of Rouen (over the years the name was transformed into Rohan.) It's now lined with cafés and shops. ⊠ *Entrance on cour du Commerce St-André. Métro: Odéon.*

⓫ Les Deux Magots. This old-fashioned St-Germain café, named after the two Chinese figures, or *magots,* inside, still thrives on its post–World War II reputation as one of the Left Bank's prime meeting places for the intelligentsia. It remains crowded day and night, but these days you're more likely to rub shoulders with tourists than with philosophers. Still, if you are in search of the mysterious glamour of the Left Bank, you can do no better than to station yourself at one of the sidewalk tables—or at a window table on a wintry day—to watch the passing parade. ⊠ *6 pl. St-Germain-des-Prés,* ☏ *01–45–48–55–25. Métro: St-Germain-des-Prés.*

⑭ **École Nationale des Beaux-Arts** (National Fine Arts College). Occupying three large mansions near the Seine, this school—today the breeding ground for painters, sculptors, and architects—was once the site of a convent, founded in 1608 by Marguerite de Valois, the first wife of Henri IV. During the Revolution, the convent was turned into a depot for works of art salvaged from the monuments that were under threat of destruction by impassioned mobs. Only the church and cloister remained by the time the Beaux-Arts school was established in 1816. ⊠ *14 rue Bonaparte.* ☉ *Daily 1–7. Métro: St-Germain-des-Prés.*

NEED A BREAK? The popular **La Palette** café (⊠ 43 rue de Seine, ☎ 01–43–26–68–15), on the corner of rue de Seine and rue Callot, has long been a favorite haunt of Beaux-Arts students. One of them painted the ungainly portrait of the patron François that presides with mock authority.

❽ **Fontaine des Quatre Saisons** (Four Seasons Fountain). This allegorical fountain, designed by Edme Bouchardon in 1739 to help boost the district's water supply, has a wealth of sculpted detail. Flanked by a majestic curved screen, the seated figure of Paris, framed by Ionic columns, surveys the rivers Seine and Marne, while bas-reliefs peopled by industrious cupids represent the seasons. ⊠ *57–59 rue de Grenelle. Métro: Rue du Bac.*

❹ **Hôtel des Invalides.** Les Invalides, as it is widely known, is an outstanding monumental Baroque ensemble, designed by architect Libéral Bruand in the 1670s at the behest of Louis XIV to house wounded (*invalid*) soldiers. Although no more than a handful of old soldiers live at the Invalides today, the military link remains in the form of the **Musée de l'Armée** (Army Museum), one of the world's foremost military museums, with a vast, albeit musty, collection of arms, armor, uniforms, banners, and military pictures down through the ages. Up in the attic in the same space is the **Musée des Plans-Reliefs** (Model Town Museum), with its fascinating collection of old scale models of French towns; the largest and most impressive is Strasbourg, which takes up an entire room. The main, cobbled courtyard is a fitting scene for the parades and ceremonies still occasionally held at the Invalides.

The 17th-century **Église St-Louis des Invalides,** the Invalides's original church, was the site of the first performance of Berlioz's *Requiem,* in 1837. The most impressive dome in Paris towers over Jules Hardouin-Mansart's **Église du Dôme** (Dome Church), built onto the end of Église St-Louis but blocked off from it in 1793—no great pity, perhaps, as the two buildings are vastly different in style and scale. Fittingly, for ★ this military complex, **Napoléon's Tomb** is found here—his remains are kept in a series of no fewer than six coffins, one inside the next, within a bombastic memorial of red porphyry, ringed by low reliefs and a dozen statues symbolizing his campaigns. Among others commemorated in the church are French World War I hero Marshal Foch; Napoléon's brother Joseph, erstwhile king of Spain; and military architect Sébastien de Vauban.

Some 200 display cabinets in the west wing of the Invalides, at the **Musée de l'Ordre de la Libération** (Order of Liberation Museum), evoke various episodes of World War II: de Gaulle's Free France organization, the Resistance, the Deportation, and the 1944 Liberation. The Order of the Liberation was created by General de Gaulle after the fall of France in 1940 to honor those who made outstanding contributions to the Allied victory in World War II (Churchill and Eisenhower figure among the rare foreign recipients). ⊠ *Pl. des Invalides; Liberation Museum* *entrance: 51 bis bd. de La Tour-Maubourg,* ☎ *01–44–42–37–72 Army and Model museums; 01–47–05–04–10 Liberation Museum,* WEB *www. invalides.org.* 🎫 *Joint ticket 38 frs/€5.80.* ☉ *Dome Church, Army and Model museums, Apr.–Sept., daily 10–5:45; Oct.–Mar., daily 10–4:45; Liberation Museum Mon.–Sat. 10–5. Métro: La Tour–Maubourg.*

❻ Hôtel Matignon. The residence of the French prime minister, built in 1721, is the Left Bank counterpart to the president's Élysée Palace. From 1888 to 1914, it was the embassy of the Austro-Hungarian Empire; only since 1958 has it housed heads of government. ⊠ *57 rue de Varenne. Not open to the public. Métro: Varenne.*

⓱ Hôtel des Monnaies (Royal Mint). Louis XVI transferred the Royal Mint to this imposing mansion in the late 18th century. Although the mint was moved again, to Pessac, near Bordeaux, in 1973, weights and measures, medals, and limited-edition coins are still made here. The **Musée de la Monnaie** (Coin Museum) has an extensive collection of coins, documents, engravings, and paintings. On Tuesday and Friday at 2 PM you can catch the coin metal craftsmen at work in their ateliers overlooking the Seine. ⊠ *11 quai de Conti,* ☎ *01–40–46–55–35.* 🎫 *20 frs/€3.* ☉ *Tues.–Fri. 11–5:30, weekends noon–5:30. Métro: Pont-Neuf.*

⓯ Institut de France (French Institute). The Institute is one of France's most revered cultural institutions, and its curved, dome-topped facade is one of the Left Bank's most impressive waterside sights. The Tour de Nesle, which formed part of Philippe-Auguste's wall fortifications along the Seine, used to stand here and, in its time, had many royal occupants, including Henry V of England. The French novelist Alexandre Dumas (1824–95) featured the stormy history of the Tour de Nesle—during which the lovers of a number of French queens were tossed from its windows—in a melodrama of the same name. In 1661 the wealthy Cardinal Mazarin left 2 million French *livres* (pounds) in his will for construction of a college that would be dedicated to educating students from Piedmont, Alsace, Artois, and Roussillon, provinces that had been annexed to France during the years of his ministry. Mazarin's coat of arms is sculpted on the dome, and the library in the east wing, which holds more than 350,000 volumes, still bears his name.

At the beginning of the 19th century, Napoléon stipulated that the Institute be transferred here from the Louvre. The Académie Française, the oldest of the five academies that compose the institute, was created by Cardinal Richelieu in 1635. Its first major task was to edit the definitive French dictionary (which still isn't finished); it is also charged with safeguarding the purity of the French language. Election to its ranks, subject to approval by the French head of state, is the highest literary honor in the land—there can only be 40 "immortal" lifelong members at any one time. The appointment of historian and author Marguerite Yourcenar to the Académie in 1986 broke its centuries-old tradition as a male bastion. The Institute also embraces the Académie des Beaux-Arts, the Académie des Sciences, the Académie des Inscriptions et Belles Lettres, and the Académie des Sciences Morales et Politiques. ⊠ *Pl. de l'Institut.* ☉ *Guided visits reserved for cultural associations only. Métro: Pont-Neuf.*

⓴ Jardin du Luxembourg (Luxembourg Gardens). Immortalized in countless paintings, the Jardin du Luxembourg possesses all that is unique and befuddling about Parisian parks: swarms of pigeons, cookie-cutter trees, ironed-and-pressed dirt walkways, and immaculate lawns meant for admiring, not touching. The tree- and bench-lined paths offer a reprieve from the incessant bustle of the Quartier Latin, as well as an opportunity to discover the dotty old women and smooching university students who once found their way into Doisneau photographs. Somewhat austere during the colder months, the garden becomes intoxicating as spring fills the flower beds with daffodils, tulips, and hyacinths; the pools teem with boats nudged along by children, and the paths with Parisians thrusting their noses toward the sun. The park's northern boundary is dominated by the Palais du Luxembourg, surrounded by a handful of well-armed guards; they are protecting the senators who have been deliberating in the palace since 1958. Feel free to move the green chairs around to create your own picnic area or people-watching site.

Although the garden may seem purely French, the original 17th-century planning took its inspiration from Italy. When Maria de' Medici acquired the estate of the deceased Duke of Luxembourg in 1612, she decided to turn his mansion into a version of the Florentine Medici home, the Palazzo Pitti. She ended up with something more Franco-Italian than strictly Florentine. The land behind the palace was loosely modeled on the Boboli Gardens. The landscapers, like the architects, didn't design a true version of the Florentine garden, opting for the emerging style of heavy-handed human manipulation of nature—linear vistas, box-trimmed trees, and color-coordinated flower beds—thereby further defining the "French" garden. A tiny corner of the park still possesses that nature-on-the-brink-of-overwhelming-civilization look that was the trademark of the Renaissance Italian garden—namely, the intentionally overgrown cluster of trees and bushes lining the 1624 Fontaine de Médicis. The park captured the hearts of Parisians when it became public after the Revolution; thousands turned out in the mid-1860s to prevent a Haussmann-directed boulevard from being built through its middle.

One of the great attractions of the park is the Théâtre des Marionnettes, where on Wednesday, Saturday, and Sunday at 3 and 4:15 PM you can catch one of the classic guignols (marionette shows) for a small admission charge. The wide-mouthed kiddies, though, are the real attraction; their expressions of utter surprise, despair, or glee have fascinated the likes of Henri Cartier-Bresson and François Truffaut. And finally, for those eager to burn off their pastry breakfasts: The Jardin de Luxembourg has a well-maintained trail around the perimeter, and it is one of the few public places the French will be seen in athletic clothes. It takes an average jogger 20 minutes to get all the way around, and water fountains are strategically placed along the way. Men of all ages are also strategically placed; their comments to female runners are irritating, but otherwise this is a great escape. ⊠ *Bordered by blvd. St-Michel and rues de Vaugirard, de Médicis, Guynemer, and Auguste-Comte. Métro: Odéon; RER: Luxembourg.*

❷ Musée de la Légion d'Honneur (Legion of Honor Museum). French and foreign decorations are displayed in this mansion by the Seine, linked to the Tuileries opposite by an elegant, two-tiered footbridge since 2000. The original building, constructed in 1786, was one of the largest and grandest mansions in town. The Hôtel de Salm—as it is officially known—was burned down during the Commune in 1871, and rebuilt in 1878 in glittering neoclassical style. ⊠ *2 rue de Bellechasse,* ☎ *01–40–62–84–25.* 🖃 *25 frs/€3.81.* ☉ *Tues.–Sun. 11–5. Métro: Solférino; RER: Musée d'Orsay.*

❼ Musée Maillol. Bronzes by Art Deco sculptor Aristide Maillol (1861–1944), whose sleek, stylized nudes adorn the Tuileries Gardens, can be admired at this handsome town house lovingly restored by his former muse, Dina Vierny. Maillol's drawings, paintings, and tapestries are also on show. Works by other artists include a roomful of Poliakoff abstractions and two sensuous Zitman nudes in the barrel-vaulted cellar café. ✉ *61 rue de Grenelle,* ☎ *01–42–22–59–58.* 🎫 *40 frs/€6.* ☉ *Wed.–Mon. 11–6. Métro: Rue du Bac.*

★ ❶ **Musée d'Orsay.** Setting out to form a bridge between the classical collections of the Louvre and the modern collections of the Centre Pompidou, the collection of the Musée d'Orsay includes many of the most famous Impressionist and Postimpressionist paintings in the world. On top of that, its building—a spectacularly renovated Belle Epoque train station—is a work of art in itself. Beginning in 1900, the building was used as a depot for routes between Paris and the southwest of France. By 1939, the Gare d'Orsay had become too small for mainline travel, and intercity trains were transferred to the Gare d'Austerlitz, with the d'Orsay becoming a suburban terminus until it closed in the 1960s. The building was temporarily used as a theater, an auction house, and a setting for Orson Welles's movie *The Trial,* based on Kafka's novel, before it was finally slated for demolition. However, the destruction of the 19th-century Les Halles (market halls) across the Seine provoked a furor among conservationists, and in the late 1970s, former president Giscard d'Estaing ordered the d'Orsay to be transformed into a museum. Architects Pierre Colboc, Renaud Bardou, and Jean-Paul Philippon were commissioned to remodel the building; Gae Aulenti, known for her renovation of the Palazzo Grassi in Venice, was hired to reshape the interior. Aulenti's modern design in a building almost a century old provoked much controversy, but the museum's attributes soon outweighed any criticism shortly after its opening in December 1986.

The collection is devoted to the arts (mainly French) spanning the period 1848–1914. Exhibits take up three floors, but the immediate impression is of a single, vast, stationlike hall. While the chief artistic attraction is the Impressionists, whose works are displayed under the roof, the museum also prominently features lesser-ranked academic and salon painters, many of whose names will be unfamiliar to most. Renoir, Sisley, Pissarro, and Monet do not, in other words, compose the entire history of French 19th-century art. Still, the highlights include Monet's *Les Coquelicots* (*Poppy Fields*) and Renoir's *Le Moulin de la Galette* (*Wafer Windmill*), which differs from many other Impressionist paintings in that Renoir worked from numerous studies and completed it in his studio rather than painting it in the open air. Nonetheless, its focus on the activities of a group of ordinary Parisians amusing themselves in the sun on a Montmartre afternoon is typical of the spontaneity and fleeting sense of moment that are the essence of Impressionism. Whereas Monet, the only one of the group to adhere faithfully to the tenets of Impressionism throughout his career, strove to catch the effects of light—for more of this great master, remember to also visit the Musée Marmottan—Renoir was more interested in the human figure.

The Postimpressionists—Cézanne, van Gogh, Gauguin, and Toulouse-Lautrec—are also represented on the top floor. You may find the intense, almost classical serenity of Cézanne the dominant presence here; witness his magnificent Mont Ste-Victoire series, in which he paints and repaints the same subject, in the process dissolving form until the step to Cubism and abstract painting seems an inevitability. Or you may be drawn by the vivid simplicity and passion of van Gogh or by the psychedelic, pagan rhythms of Gauguin.

On the first floor are the works of Manet and the delicate nuances of Degas. Be sure to see Manet's *Déjeuner sur l'Herbe* (*Lunch on the Grass*), the painting that scandalized Paris in 1863 at the Salon des Refusés, an exhibit organized by artists refused permission to show their work at the academy's official annual salon. The painting shows a nude woman and two clothed men picnicking in a park. In the background, another girl bathes in a stream. Manet took the subject, poses and all, from a little-known Renaissance print in the Louvre but updated the clothing to mid-19th-century France. What would otherwise have been thought a respectable "academic" painting thus became deeply shocking: two clothed men with a naked woman in 19th-century France! The loose, bold brushwork, a far cry from the polished styles of the Renaissance, added insult to artistic injury. Another reworking by Manet of a classical motif is his reclining nude, *Olympia*. Gazing boldly out from the canvas, she was more than respectable 19th-century Parisian proprieties could stand, with her unfinished hands (they were described as monkey paws) and black cat (a symbol of female sexuality). These two Manet works all but ushered in the age of modern painting. American works are also on view, one of which, Whistler's iconic portrait of his mother, *Arrangement in Black and White,* might seem to be merely a dose of American spartan puritanism; its minimalist palette and striking sense of design, however, were almost as revolutionary as Manet's achievements.

If you prefer more academic paintings, look at Puvis de Chavannes's larger-than-life classical canvases. The pale, limpid beauty of his figures is enjoying renewed attention after years of neglect. For sheer spectacle, lose yourself in Thomas Couture's *Romans of the Decadence*, a Cinerama-screen-size depiction of ancient excess. If you are more excited by more modern developments, look for the early 20th-century Fauves (meaning "wild beasts," the name given them by an outraged critic in 1905)—particularly Matisse, Derain, and Vlaminck. Thought-provoking sculptures also litter the museum at every turn. Two further highlights are the faithfully restored Belle Epoque restaurant and the model of the entire Opéra quarter, displayed beneath a glass floor, along with an extensive display of drawings and models given over to that 19th-century masterwork, the Opéra Garnier. ⊠ *1 rue de la Légion d'Honneur,* ☎ *01-40-49-48-14,* WEB *www.musee-orsay.fr.* 🎟 *40 frs/€6, Sun. 30 frs/€4.60.* ☉ *Tues.–Wed. and Fri.–Sat. 10–6, Thurs. 10–9:45, Sun. 9–6. Métro: Solférino; RER: Musée d'Orsay.*

NEED A BREAK? Find respite from the overwhelming collection of art in the gorgeous **Musée d'Orsay Café,** in the Musée d'Orsay behind one of the giant station clocks, close to the Impressionist galleries on the top floor. From the rooftop terrace alongside there is a panoramic view across the Seine toward Montmartre and the Sacré-Coeur.

★ ❺ **Musée Rodin.** The splendid Hôtel Biron, with its spacious vestibule, broad staircase, and patrician salons lined with boiseries, retains much of its 18th-century atmosphere and makes a somewhat startling setting for the sculpture of Auguste Rodin (1840–1917). His funeral, at the height of World War I, drew the largest nonmilitary crowd of the time (26,000); while alive, however, Rodin was stalked by controversy. His career took off in 1876 with *L'Age d'Airain* (The Bronze Age), inspired by a pilgrimage to Italy and the sculptures of Michelangelo. Because the work was so realistic, some critics accused Rodin of having stuck a live boy in plaster, while others blasted him for what was seen as a sloppy sculpting and casting technique. His seeming messiness, though, was intentional; Rodin sought to capture the sculpting process through the imprints of fingers, rags used to keep the clay moist, and tools he left on his works.

Four years later, Rodin was commissioned to create the doors for the newly proposed Musée des Arts Décoratifs (Museum of Decorative Arts). He set out to sculpt a pair of monumental bronze doors in the tradition of Italian Renaissance churches, calling his proposal *La Porte de l'Enfer* (The Gate of Hell). The Gate, a visual representation of stories from Dante's Divine Comedy, became his obsession: He spent the last 37 years of his life working on it. Possibly Rodin's most celebrated work is *Le Penseur* (The Thinker, ca. 1880), the muscular man caught in a moment of deep thought and flex. The version here in the garden is the original—the city of Paris, its intended owner, refused to accept it. Before installing the permanent bronze statue on the steps of the Panthéon, Rodin set up a full-scale plaster cast. Its physicality horrified the public; crowds gathered around the statue, debates ensued, and Rodin was ridiculed in the press. A sad footnote in the collection is evidenced by works by Rodin's mistress Camille Claudel (1864–1943), a remarkable sculptor in her own right. Her torturous relationship with Rodin drove her out of his studio—and out of her mind. In 1913 she was packed off to an asylum, where she remained, barred from any artistic activities, until her death in 1943. As much as a work of art as the sculptures on view, the gardens of the Musée Rodin are justly famous for their rosebushes (more than 2,000 of them, representing 100 varieties). Here, you'll find some prime Rodin pieces, such as the powerful *Balzac* and the mythic *Burghers of Calais,* along with a new pavilion that sometimes hosts temporary exhibitions (when not the scene for some of Paris's biggest charity parties). ⊠ *77 rue de Varenne,* ☎ *01–44–18–61–10,* WEB *www.musee-rodin.fr.* 🎟 *28 frs/€4.30, Sun. 18 frs/€2.74, gardens only 5 frs/€.70.* ☉ *Easter–Oct., Tues.–Sun. 9:30–5:45; Nov.–Easter, Tues.–Sun. 9:30–4:45. Métro: Varenne.*

❸ Palais Bourbon. The most prominent feature of the Palais Bourbon—home of the Assemblée Nationale, the French Parliament since 1798—is its colonnaded facade, commissioned by Napoléon to match that of the Madeleine across the Seine. Cortot's sculpted pediment portrays France holding the tablets of law, flanked by Force and Justice. ⊠ *Pl. du Palais-Bourbon.* ☉ *During temporary exhibits only. Métro: Assemblée Nationale.*

OFF THE
BEATEN PATH

STE-CLOTILDE – Once the most fashionable church in 19th-century Paris, this neo-Gothic church (built 1846–58) is notable for its imposing twin spires, visible from across the Seine. French classical composer César Franck was organist here from 1858 to 1890. From the Palais Bourbon, take rue Bourgogne south; then take a left on rue Las-Cases. ⊠ *Rue Las-Cases. Métro: Solférino.*

㉒ Palais du Luxembourg (Luxembourg Palace). The gray, imposing, rusticated Luxembourg Palace was built, like the surrounding Luxembourg Gardens, for Maria de' Medici, widow of Henri IV, at the beginning of the 17th century. Maria was born and raised in Florence's Pitti Palace, and, having languished in the Louvre after the death of her husband, she was eager to build herself a new palace, where she could recapture something of the lively, carefree atmosphere of her childhood. In 1612, she bought the Paris mansion of the Duke of Luxembourg, tore it down, and built her palace. It was not completed until 1627, and Maria was to live there for just five years (the grand series of canvases Rubens painted to decorate the palace are now in the Louvre). In 1632, Cardinal Richelieu had her expelled from France, and she saw out her declining years in Cologne, Germany, dying there almost penniless in 1642.

The palace remained royal property until the Revolution, when the state took it over and used it as a prison. Danton, the painter David, and Thomas Paine were all detained here. Today the French Senate meets here, so the building is not open to the public. ⊠ *15 rue de Vaugirard. Métro: Odéon; RER: Luxembourg.*

🔟 **Pont des Arts** (Arts Footbridge). Immortalized in paintings by Renoir and Pissarro, this iron-and-wood footbridge linking the Louvre to the Institut de France is a favorite with painters, art students, and misty-eyed romantics moved by the delightful views of the Ile de la Cité. The bridge got its name because the Louvre was once called the Palais des Arts (Arts Palace). *Métro: Pont-Neuf.*

🔟 **Le Procope.** The oldest café in Paris was opened in 1686 by an Italian named Francesco Procopio. Many of Paris's most famous literary sons and daughters have imbibed here through the centuries, ranging from erudite academics like Denis Diderot to debauchees like Oscar Wilde, as well as Voltaire, Balzac, George Sand, Victor Hugo, and even Benjamin Franklin, who popped in whenever business brought him to Paris. The fomenters of the French Revolution met at the Procope, too, so old Ben may have rubbed shoulders with Marat, Danton, Robespierre, and company. In 1988 a large restaurant group bought the Procope, aiming to give it a "new lease on life and a renewed literary and cultural vocation." They have succeeded in resuscitating it as a restaurant, but it's now filled with tourists, not writers. ⊠ *13 rue de l'Ancienne-Comédie,* ☎ *01–43–26–99–20. Métro: Odéon.*

🔟 **St-Germain-des-Prés.** Paris's oldest church was first built to shelter a relic of the true cross, brought back from Spain in AD 542. The chancel was enlarged and the church then consecrated by Pope Alexander III in 1163; the tall, sturdy tower—a Left Bank landmark—dates from this period. The colorful 19th-century frescoes in the nave by Hippolyte Flandrin, a pupil of the classical painter Ingres, depict vivid scenes from the Old Testament. The church stages superb organ concerts and recitals. ⊠ *Pl. St-Germain-des-Prés.* ☉ *Weekdays 8–7:30, weekends 8 am–9 pm. Métro: St-Germain-des-Prés.*

🔟 **St-Sulpice.** Dubbed the Cathedral of the Left Bank, this enormous 17th-century church has entertained some unlikely christenings—the Marquis de Sade's and Charles Baudelaire's, for instance—and the nuptials of irreverent wordsmith Victor Hugo. The 18th-century facade was never finished, and its unequal towers add a playful touch to an otherwise sober design. The interior is baldly impersonal, despite the magnificent Delacroix frescoes—notably *Jacob Luttant avec l'Ange* (*Jacob Wrestling with the Angel*)—in the first chapel on your right. ⊠ *Pl. St-Sulpice. Métro: St-Sulpice.*

🔟 **St-Thomas d'Aquin.** This elegant, domed church, designed by Pierre Bulet in 1683, was originally dedicated to St. Dominique and flanked by a convent—whose buildings now belong to the army. The east-end chapel was added in 1722 and the two-tiered facade in 1768. Pope Pius VII popped in during his trip to Paris for Napoléon's coronation in December 1804. ⊠ *Pl. St-Thomas-d'Aquin. Métro: Rue du Bac.*

🔟 **Théâtre de l'Odéon.** At the north end of the Luxembourg Gardens, on place de l'Odéon, sits the colonnaded Odéon Theater—a masterpiece of the neoclassical style. It was established in 1792 to house the Comédie Française troupe; the original building was destroyed by fire in 1807. Since World War II it has specialized in 20th-century productions and was the base for Jean-Louis Barrault's and Madeleine Renaud's theater company, the Théâtre de France, until they fell out of favor with the authorities for their alleged role in spurring on student revolutionaries in May 1968. Today, the theater is the French home of the Theater of Europe and stages excellent productions by major foreign companies, sometimes in English. ⊠ *1 pl. de l'Odéon,* ☎ *01–44–41–36–36. Métro: Odéon.*

MONTPARNASSE

About 15 blocks south of the Seine lies the Montparnasse district, named after Mount Parnassus, the Greek mountain associated with the worship of Apollo and the Muses. Montparnasse's cultural heyday came in the first four decades of the 20th century, when it replaced Montmartre as *the* place for painters and poets to live. Pablo Picasso, Amedeo Modigliani, Ernest Hemingway, Jean Cocteau, and Leon Trotsky were among the luminaries who spawned an intellectual café society—later to be found at St-Germain—and prompted the launch of a string of arty brasseries along the district's main thoroughfare, the broad boulevard du Montparnasse.

The boulevard may lack poetic charm these days, but nightlife stays the pace as bars, clubs, restaurants, and cinemas crackle with energy beneath continental Europe's tallest high-rise, the 59-story Tour Montparnasse. Although the tower itself is a typically bland product of the early 1970s, of note only for the view from the top, several more adventurous buildings have risen in its wake. Ricardo Bofill's semicircular Amphithéâtre housing complex, with its whimsical postmodernist quotations of classical detail, is the most famous. The glass-cubed Cartier center for contemporary art and the Montparnasse train station, with its giant glass facade and designer garden above the tracks, are other outstanding examples.

If you have a deeper feel for history, you may prefer the sumptuous Baroque church of Val-de-Grâce or the quiet earth of Montparnasse cemetery, where Baudelaire, Sartre, Bartholdi (who designed the Statue of Liberty), and actress Jean Seberg slumber. The Paris underground had its headquarters nearby—in the Roman catacombs—during the Nazi occupation. After ignoring Hitler's orders to blow up the city, Governor von Choltitz signed the German surrender in Montparnasse in August 1944.

Numbers in the text correspond to numbers in the margin and on the Montparnasse map.

A Good Walk

Take the métro or walk to the Vavin station (only three stops from St-Sulpice), beneath Rodin's 10-ft statue of Balzac and alongside the café La Rotonde at the corner of boulevards Raspail and Montparnasse. Three other cafés, famous since Montparnasse's interwar heyday, are all within a stone's throw on boulevard du Montparnasse: Le Sélect at No. 99 and, across the street, the Café du Dôme (No. 108) and **La Coupole** ①, with its painted columns and restored Art Deco interior (No. 102). Head west along boulevard du Montparnasse to **place du 18-Juin-1940** ②. Towering above the square is the **Tour Montparnasse** ③. Behind the building is the huge, gleaming glass facade of Gare Montparnasse, the train station that is home to the 200-mph *TGV Atlantique,* serving western France.

Cross place Bienvenüe, to the right of Tour Montparnasse; then take avenue Maine, then your first left onto rue Antoine-Bourdelle. The sharp brick outlines of the **Musée Bourdelle** ④, full of the powerful sculpture of Antoine Bourdelle, loom halfway along. Continue to the end of the street and turn left onto rue Armand-Moissant; note the elegant beige

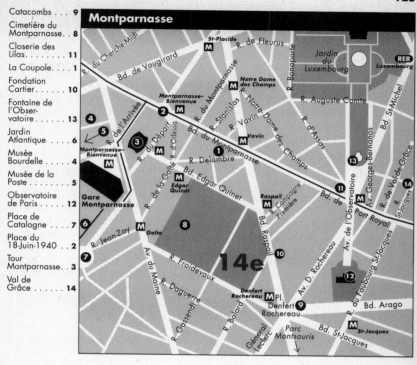

and green brick facade of the École Commerciale on your left before turning right onto boulevard de Vaugirard. There's a fine view from here of Tour Montparnasse away to your left. A short way along the boulevard is the **Musée de la Poste** ⑤, a must if you're a stamp collector. Cross the boulevard and take the elevator by No. 25 to reach the **Jardin Atlantique** ⑥, a modern park laid over the rail tracks of Montparnasse station. Memories of World War II—notably the French Resistance and the Liberation of Paris—are evoked in a modern museum at the park entrance.

Cross the Jardin Atlantique at the far end and turn left down to **place de Catalogne** ⑦, dominated by the monumental curves of the postmodern Amphithéâtre housing complex. Explore its arcades and circular forecourts, and compare its impersonal grandeur with the cozy charm of the small church of Notre-Dame du Travail behind. Rue Jean-Zay leads from place de Catalogne to the corner of the high-walled **Cimetière du Montparnasse** ⑧. Enter the cemetery down rue Froidevaux if you wish to pay homage to local and foreign worthies. Rue Froidevaux continues to place Denfert-Rochereau, where you can admire the huge bronze *Lion of Belfort* by Frédéric-Auguste Bartholdi, the sculptor of the Statue of Liberty (he, too, is buried in Montparnasse cemetery), and visit the extensive underground labyrinth of the **catacombs** ⑨, which tunnel under much of the Left Bank and the suburbs.

Walk up boulevard Raspail, past the eye-catching glass cube that houses the **Fondation Cartier** ⑩. Take the third right onto rue Campagne-Première, a handsome street once inhabited by Picasso, Miró, Kandinsky, and Modigliani. Note the tiled facade on the artists' residence at No. 31. Turn right at the bottom of the street onto boulevard du Montparnasse. At avenue de l'Observatoire stands perhaps the most famous bastion of Left Bank café culture, the **Closerie des Lilas** ⑪. Up avenue de l'Observatoire is the **Observatoire de Paris** ⑫, Louis XIV's astronomical observatory. In the other direction, the tree-lined avenue sweeps past the **Fontaine de l'Observatoire** ⑬. To the right of the fountain, at the bottom of rue du Val-de-Grâce, is the imposing Baroque dome of **Val de Grâce** ⑭. Straight ahead is the Jardin du Luxembourg.

TIMING

This walk around Montparnasse is just under 5-km (3-mi) long and should comfortably take a morning or an afternoon if you choose to check out one of the historic cafés, the cemetery, and the catacombs along the way.

Sights to See

❾ **Catacombs.** *"Arrête! C'est ici l'Empire de la Mort"* ("Stop! This is the Empire of Death"). This message scrawled at the entrance was enough to convince German troops in World War II to leave promptly before they guessed that Resistance fighters used the tunnels in the catacombs as a base. This dire warning now welcomes you after a winding descent through dark, clammy passages to Paris's principal ossuary and most disturbing collection of human remains. Bones from the notorious Cimetière des Innocents were the first to be transplanted here in 1786, when decomposing bodies started seeping into neighboring cellars, bringing swarms of ravenous rats with them. The legions of bones dumped here are arranged not by owner but by type—witness the rows of skulls, stacks of tibias, and piles of spinal disks. There are also some bizarre attempts at bone art, like skulls arranged in the shape of hearts. It's macabre and makes you feel quite . . . mortal. Among the bones in here are those of Mirabeau (1749–91), the Revolutionary leader; sixteenth-century satirist and writer Rabelais (1490–1553) was transplanted from the former cemetery at the Église St-Paul–St-Louis; and famous courtesan Madame de Pompadour (1721–64) is mixed in with the rabble after a lifetime spent as the mistress to Louis XV. Be prepared to walk long distances when you come here—the tunnels stretch for miles, and the only light comes from the flashlight that you bring yourself. ⊠ *1 pl. Denfert-Rochereau,* ☎ *01–43–22–47–63,* WEB *www. paris-france.org/musees.* ☎ *33 frs/€5.* ☉ *Tues.–Fri. 2–4, weekends 9– 11 and 2–4. Guided tours Wed. at 2:45; 20 frs extra. Métro and RER: Denfert-Rochereau.*

❽ **Cimetière du Montparnasse** (Montparnasse Cemetery). High walls encircle this cemetery, a haven of peace in one of Paris's busiest shopping and business areas. It is not picturesque (with the exception of the towered rump of an old windmill that used to be a student tavern) but contains many of the quarter's most illustrious residents, buried only a stone's throw away from where they lived and loved: Charles Baudelaire, Bartholdi (who designed the Statue of Liberty), Alfred Dreyfus, Guy de Maupassant, Camille Saint-Saëns, Jean-Paul Sartre, Tristan Tzara, and, more recently, photographer Man Ray, playwright Samuel Beckett, actress Jean Seberg, and singer-songwriter Serge Gainsbourg. ⊠ *Entrances on rue Froidevaux, bd. Edgar-Quinet. Métro: Raspail, Gaîté.*

⓫ **Closerie des Lilas.** Now a pricey bar-restaurant, the Closerie remains a staple of all literary tours of Paris. Commemorative plaques fastened to the bar mark the places where literati like Baudelaire, Verlaine, Hemingway, and Apollinaire used to station themselves. Although the lilacs (*lilas*) have gone from the terrace, it still opens onto a garden wall of luxuriant evergreen foliage and is as crowded in the summer as it ever was in the '30s. ⊠ *171 bd. du Montparnasse,* ☎ *01–43–26–70–50. Métro: Vavin; RER: Port-Royal.*

MUSÉE ZADKINE – Russian-born sculptor Ossip Zadkine (1890–1967) trained in London before setting up in Paris in 1909. The works on exhibit at this museum, in Zadkine's former house and studio, reveal the influences of Rodin, African art, and Cubism. ⊠ *100 bis rue d'Assas,* ☎ *01–43–26–91–90.* 🎟 *22 frs/€3.35.* 🕙 *Tues.–Sun. 10–4:30. Métro: Vavin.*

❶ **La Coupole.** One of Montparnasse's most famous brasseries, La Coupole opened in 1927 as a bar–restaurant–dance hall and soon became a home-away-from-home for Apollinaire, Max Jacob, Cocteau, Satie, Stravinsky, and Hemingway. It may not be quite the same mecca these days, but it still pulls in a classy crowd. The columns painted by a host of Parisian artists, including Chagall and Brancusi, which lend La Coupole its Art Deco panache, were restored in the late '80s, along with the mosaic floor and original citronwood furniture. ⊠ *102 bd. du Montparnasse,* ☎ *01–43–20–14–20.* 🕙 *Daily 7:30 am–2 am. Métro: Vavin.*

❿ **Fondation Cartier** (Cartier Foundation). Architect Jean Nouvel's eye-catching giant glass cube is a suitable setting for the temporary, thought-provoking shows of contemporary art organized here by jewelry giant Cartier. ⊠ *261 bd. Raspail,* ☎ *01–42–18–56–50.* 🎟 *30 frs/€4.60.* 🕙 *Tues.–Sun. noon–8. Métro: Raspail.*

⓭ **Fontaine de l'Observatoire** (Observatory Fountain). Gabriel Davioud's fountain, built in 1873, is topped by Jean-Baptiste Carpeaux's four bronze statues of female nudes holding a globe, representing Les Quatre Parties du Monde (The Four Continents). ⊠ *Av. de l'Observatoire. RER: Port-Royal.*

❻ **Jardin Atlantique** (Atlantic Garden). Built over the tracks of Gare Montparnasse, this smart designer park, opened in 1994, features an assortment of trees and plants found in coastal regions near the Atlantic Ocean—thus the name. A museum building at the station end of the garden houses souvenirs and video coverage of World War II inside the **Mémorial du Maréchal-Leclerc,** commemorating the liberator of Paris, and the **Musée Jean-Moulin,** devoted to the leader of the French Resistance. In the center of the park, what looks like a quirky piece of metallic sculpture is actually a meteorological center, with a battery of flickering lights reflecting temperature, wind speed, and monthly rainfall. ⊠ *Pont des Cinq-Martyrs-du-Lycée-Buffon,* ☎ *01–40–64–39–44.* 🎟 *Musée 22 frs/€3.35,* 🕙 *Musée Tues.–Sun. 10–5:40. Métro: Montparnasse-Bienvenüe.*

❹ **Musée Bourdelle** (Bourdelle Museum). Opened in 1949 in the studios and gardens where Rodin's pupil Antoine Bourdelle (1861–1929) lived and worked, and extended by Christian de Portzamparc in 1992, this spacious brick museum houses 500 works in plaster, marble, and bronze, including castings of Bourdelle's landmark works, *Heracles the Archer* and the *Dying Centaur.* ⊠ *18 rue Antoine-Bourdelle,* ☎ *01–49–54–73–73.* 🎟 *22 frs/€3.35.* 🕙 *Tues.–Sun. 10–5:40. Métro: Falguière.*

❺ **Musée de la Poste** (Postal Museum). On display at this multistory museum of postal history are international and French stamps (dating as far back as 1849), postal carriers' uniforms and mailboxes, sorting and stamp-printing machines, and one of the balloons used to send mail out of Paris during the Prussian siege of 1870. Top-to-bottom renovation was expected to be finished during 2001–2002. ⊠ *34 bd. de Vaugirard,* ☎ *01–42–79–23–45.* 🎟 *30 frs/€4.60.* 🕙 *Mon.–Sat. 10–6. Métro: Montparnasse-Bienvenüe.*

⓬ **Observatoire de Paris** (Paris Observatory). The observatory was constructed in 1667 for Louis XIV by architect Claude Perrault. Its four

ARTISTS, WRITERS, AND EXILES

FOR THREE-QUARTERS of a century—roughly from the 1880s to the 1950s—Paris enjoyed a reputation as Europe's most creative and bohemian capital, acting as a magnet for the international avant-garde.

The decades before World War I saw the slopes of **Montmartre,** in north Paris, alive with the sound of Belle Epoque music. Whirling windmills and swirling petticoats set the tone, no more so than at the Moulin Rouge cabaret, whose dancers doing the cancan were immortalized in posters and paintings by Toulouse-Lautrec. Femmes fatales? Lautrec drank and drugged himself to premature death.

Artists had moved into the district as early as the 1860s, when Monet and Manet pursued their interest in steam and rail at the Gare St-Lazare. New boulevards meant easier access to nearby Montmartre: cheap and pretty, with an abundance of shady nightlife, the area was an artist's dream. Van Gogh, Cézanne, Seurat, Signac, Degas, Vuillard, and Dufy all followed. Renoir painted his *Moulin de la Galette*; Picasso and Braque sighted Cubism in the Bateau-Lavoir on place Émile-Goudeau.

Montmartre lost its luster after World War I; Utrillo remained, his repetitive street scenes a weak postscript to the powerful austerity of his youthful "White Period."

The Roaring '20s saw the Paris art scene shift south to another hill: **Montparnasse.** Picasso and Modigliani decamped to rue Campagne-Première, joined by Miró and Kandinsky; Braque worked nearby in rue du Douanier-Rousseau.

Belle Epoque cabarets lost out to Art Deco bars and brasseries, a whole string of them along boulevard du Montparnasse: the Coupole, Dôme, Select, Rotonde, and the Closerie des Lilas, most of them assiduously frequented by Ernest Hemingway. Gertrude Stein held court for her "Lost Generation" near the Luxembourg Gardens, hosting Picasso and writers like Ezra Pound, Henry Miller, and Zelda and F. Scott Fitzgerald. Redevelopment, epitomized by the Tour Montparnasse, has long since exiled aesthetes.

After World War II the literati went north to **St-Germain-des-Prés,** whose own cluster of cafés—Flore (where Sartre and de Beauvoir preached existentialism), Lipp, Les Deux Magots (once favored by Rimbaud and Gide)—became the beacon for left-wing intellectuals in the 1950s and 1960s.

Picture and antiques dealers crowd the streets of St-Germain, rubbing shoulders with the publishing houses that have been here since before Joyce first published *Ulysses* at Shakespeare & Company on rue de l'Odéon in 1922. Baudelaire, Voltaire, and Oscar Wilde (as well as Delacroix, Sibelius, and Wagner) all lived in the area; Voltaire died there in 1788, and Wilde expired around the corner at **13 rue des Beaux-Arts**—a plaque on the building commemorates the spot and the street is still home to a fine-arts school.

These days, however, once they finish school, few art students stick around: Paris is no longer the thriving center for contemporary art that it once was. But intellectual ghosts still haunt the Left Bank: at the bouquinistes by the Seine, along the creaking floorboards of Shakespeare & Co. on rue de la Bûcherie, or in the tiny Théâtre de la Huchette nearby, where Ionesco's *bald soprano* sings nightly for her supper to full houses.

facades are aligned with the four cardinal points—north, south, east, and west—and its southern wall is the determining point for Paris's official latitude, 48° 50′11″N. French time was based on this Paris meridian until 1911, when the country decided to adopt the international Greenwich Meridian. The interior is not open to the general public. ⊠ *Av. de l'Observatoire. RER: Port-Royal.*

❼ Place de Catalogne (Catalonia Square). This circular square is dominated by the monumental **Amphithéâtre,** a housing complex built in the 1980s by architect Ricardo Bofill. Its chunky reinvention of classical detail may strike you as witty—or as overkill. Behind is the turn-of-the-20th-century **Notre-Dame du Travail** church, which made a powerful statement when it was built: its riveted iron-and-steel framework was meant to symbolize the work ethos enshrouded in the church's name. The Sebastopol Bell above the facade is a trophy from the Crimean War. ⊠ *Pl. de Catalogne. Métro: Gaîté.*

❷ Place du 18-Juin-1940. This square beneath the Tour Montparnasse is named for the date of the radio speech Charles de Gaulle broadcast from London, urging the French to resist the Germans after the Nazi invasion of May 1940. It was here that German military governor Dietrich von Choltitz surrendered to the Allies in August 1944, ignoring Hitler's orders to destroy the city as he withdrew. A plaque on the wall of what is now a shopping center—originally the Montparnasse train station extended this far—commemorates the event. *Métro: Montparnasse-Bienvenüe.*

❸ Tour Montparnasse (Montparnasse Tower). Continental Europe's tallest skyscraper, completed in 1973, this 685-ft building offers a stupendous view of Paris from its open-air roof terrace. It attracts 800,000 visitors each year; on a clear day, you can see for 40 km (25 mi). A glossy brochure, "Paris Vu d'en Haut" ("Paris Seen from on High") explains just what to look for. It is also supposed to have the fastest elevator in Europe. Fifty-two of the 59 stories are taken up by offices, and a vast commercial complex, including a Galeries Lafayette department store, spreads over the first floor. Banal by day, the tower becomes Montparnasse's neon-lit beacon at night. ⊠ *Rue de l'Arrivée,* ☎ *01–45–38–52–56,* WEB *www.tourmontparnasse56.com.* 🎫 *48 frs/€7.32.* ☉ *Apr.–Sept., daily 9:30 am–11:30 pm; Oct.–Mar., daily 9:30 am–10:30 pm. Métro: Montparnasse-Bienvenüe.*

❿ Val de Grâce. This imposing 17th-century Left Bank church, extensively restored in the early 1990s, was commissioned by Anne of Austria and designed by François Mansart. Its powerfully rhythmic two-story facade rivals the Dôme Church at the Invalides as the city's most striking example of Italianate Baroque. Pierre Mignard's 1663 cupola fresco features more than 200 sky-climbing figures. The church's original abbey buildings are now a military army hospital, with a small museum of army medical history. ⊠ *1 pl. Alphonse-Laveran,* ☎ *01–40–51–51–94.* 🎫 *Museum 30 frs/€4.60.* ☉ *Museum Tues.–Wed. noon–6, weekends 1:30–5. RER: Port-Royal.*

MONTMARTRE

Topped by its "sculpted cloud"—the famous Sacré-Coeur Basilica—and set on a dramatic rise above the city, Montmartre is the picturesque quartier once the haunt of Toulouse-Lautrec, Utrillo, and van Gogh. Although the fabled nightlife of old Montmartre has fizzled down to some glitzy nightclubs and porn shows, Montmartre still exudes a sense of history, a timeless quality infused with that hard-to-define Gallic charm.

Windmills once dotted Montmartre (often referred to by Parisians as *La Butte,* meaning "the mound"). They were set up here not just because the hill was a good place to catch the wind—at more than 300 ft, it's the highest point in the city—but because Montmartre was covered with wheat fields and quarries right up to the end of the 19th century. Today, only two of the original twenty windmills remain.

Visiting Montmartre means negotiating a lot of steep streets and flights of steps. The crown atop this urban peak, Sacré-Coeur, is something of an architectural oddity. It has been called everything from grotesque to sublime; its silhouette, viewed from afar at dusk or sunrise, looks more like a mosque than a cathedral.

There is a disputed story of how Montmartre got its name. Some say the name comes from the Roman temple to Mercury that was once here, called the Mound of Mercury, or *Mons Mercurii.* Others contend that it was an adaptation of *Mons Martyrum,* a name inspired by the burial here of Paris's first bishop, St. Denis. The popular version of his martyrdom is that he was beheaded by the Romans in AD 250 but arose to carry his severed head from rue Yvonne-Le-Tac to a place 6½ km (4 mi) to the north, an area now known as St-Denis. A final twist on the name controversy is that Montmartre briefly came to be known as Mont-Marat during the French Revolution. Marat was a leading revolutionary figure who was stabbed to death in his bath.

Numbers in the text correspond to numbers in the margin and on the Montmartre map.

A Good Walk

Take the métro to the Blanche stop and start your tour at one of Paris's least-known but most atmospheric cemeteries, the tumbling **Cimetière de Montmartre** ① at the end of avenue Rachel (off boulevard de Clichy). Return to **place Blanche,** home to the famous **Moulin Rouge** ②, the windmill turned dance hall immortalized by Toulouse-Lautrec. The Café Cyrano, next door to the Moulin Rouge, was once the haunt of Salvador Dalí and his fellow Surrealists. A few steps along the boulevard is the **Musée de l'Erotisme** ③, whose collection of erotic artifacts from around the world pays fulsome tribute to Montmartre's Sin City image.

Walk up lively rue Lepic from place Blanche. The tiny Lux Bar at No. 12 has a 1910 mosaic showing place Blanche at the beginning of the 20th century. Wind your way up to the **Moulin de la Galette** ④, on your left, atop its leafy hillock opposite rue Tholozé, once a path over the hill. Then turn right down rue Tholozé, past **Studio 28** ⑤, the first cinema built expressly for experimental films.

Continue down rue Tholozé to rue des Abbesses, and turn left toward the triangular **place des Abbesses** ⑥. Note the austere, redbrick facade of **St-Jean l'Evangéliste** ⑦. Tiny rue André-Antoine, to the right of the popular Café St-Jean, leads to what was originally the **Théâtre Libre** ⑧, or Free Theater, at No. 37. Return to the square and take rue Yvonne-Le-Tac, off to the right. Paris's first bishop, St. Denis, is commemorated by the 19th-century **Chapelle du Martyre** ⑨ at No. 9, built on the spot where he is said to have been beheaded.

Return to the square and follow rue Ravignan as it climbs, via place Émile-Goudeau, an enchanting little cobbled square, to the **Bateau-Lavoir** ⑩, or Boat Wash House, at its northern edge. Painters Picasso and Braque had studios in the original building; this drab concrete building was built in its place. Continue up the hill via rue de la Mire to **place Jean-Baptiste-Clément** ⑪, where Modigliani had a studio.

Montmartre

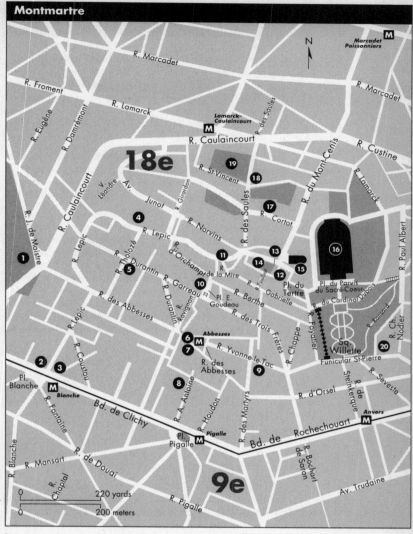

The upper reaches of rue Lepic lead to rue Norvins, formerly rue des Moulins (Windmill Street). At the end of the street, to the left, is stylish avenue Junot, site of the Cité Internationale des Arts (International Residence of the Arts), where the city authorities rent out studios to artists from all over the world. Continue right past the bars and tourist shops until you reach famous **place du Tertre** ⑫. Check out the restaurant **La Mère Catherine** ⑬, a favorite with the Russian Cossacks when they occupied Paris in 1814. Fight your way through to the southern end of the square for a breathtaking view of the city. Around the corner on rue Poulbot, the **Espace Salvador-Dalí** ⑭ houses works by Salvador Dalí, who once had a studio in the area.

Return to place du Tertre. Just off the square is the tiny church of **St-Pierre de Montmartre** ⑮. Looming menacingly behind is the scaly white dome of the **Sacré-Coeur basilica** ⑯. The cavernous interior is worth visiting for its golden mosaics; climb to the top of the dome for the view of Paris.

Walk back toward place du Tertre. Turn right onto rue du Mont-Cenis and left onto rue Cortot, site of the **Musée de Montmartre** ⑰, which, like the Bateau-Lavoir, once sheltered an illustrious group of painters, writers, and assorted cabaret artists. One of the best things about the museum, however, is its view of the tiny vineyard on neighboring rue des Saules. Another famous Montmartre landmark is at No. 22: the bar-cabaret **Lapin Agile** ⑱, originally one of the raunchiest haunts in Montmartre and the subject of one of Picasso's most famous paintings. Opposite the Lapin Agile is the tiny **Cimetière St-Vincent** ⑲.

Return to Sacré-Coeur and head down the cascading staircases to place St-Pierre. On the corner to the left is the **Halle St-Pierre** ⑳, site of the Museum of Naive Art. The neighboring streets teem with fabric shops, which are good places to find inexpensive materials. From the top of rue de Steinkerque, one of the busiest shopping streets, you can take in the archetypal view of Sacré-Coeur soaring skyward atop its grassy mound, with the funicular railway to the left. Turn right at the bottom of rue de Steinkerque and head toward place Pigalle, notorious as a center of sleazy nightlife, although recently classier bars and nightclubs have been springing up.

If, after you've walked around Montmartre, you still have the energy to see another illustrious church, make the excursion to the Gothic **Basilique de St-Denis** in the nearby suburb of St-Denis. Take the métro at place de Clichy to St-Denis–Basilique. Or get on at Anvers (near the Halle St-Pierre) and transfer at place de Clichy.

TIMING

Reserve four to five hours for this 4-km (2½-mi) walk: many of the streets are steep and slow going. Include half an hour each at Sacré-Coeur and the museums (the Dalí museum is open daily, but the Montmartre museum is closed Monday). Leave about two hours for the excursion to St-Denis, including the métro ride there. From Easter through September, Montmartre is besieged by tourists. Two hints to avoid the worst of the rush: come on a gray day, when Montmartre's sullen-tone facades suffer less than most in the city; or during the afternoon, and return to place du Tertre (maybe via the funicular) by the early evening, once the tourist buses have departed. More festive times of the year are June 24, when fireworks and street concerts are staged around Montmartre, and the first weekend of October, when revelry accompanies the wine harvest at the vineyard on rue des Saules.

Sights to See

⑩ Bateau-Lavoir (Boat Wash House). Montmartre poet Max Jacob coined the name for the original building on this site, which burned down in 1970. He said it resembled a boat and that the warren of artists' studios within was perpetually paint-splattered and in need of a good hosing down. It was in the original Bateau-Lavoir that, early in the 20th century, Pablo Picasso and Georges Braque made their first bold stabs at Cubism—a move that paved the way for abstract painting. The poet Guillaume Apollinaire also had a studio here; his book *The Painters of Cubism* (1913) set the seal on the movement's historical acceptance. The new building also contains art studios, but, if you didn't know its history, you'd probably walk right past it; it is the epitome of poured-concrete drabness. ⊠ *13 pl. Émile-Goudeau. Métro: Abbesses.*

➒ Chapelle du Martyre (Martyr's Chapel). It was in the crypt of the original chapel—built over the spot where St. Denis is said to have been martyred around AD 250—that Ignatius of Loyola, Francis Xavier, and five other companions swore an oath of poverty, chastity, and service to the Church in 1534. This led to the founding of the Society of Jesus (the Jesuits) in Rome six years later—a decisive step in the efforts of the Catholic Church to reassert its authority in the face of the Protestant Reformation. ⊠ *9 rue Yvonne-Le-Tac. Métro: Abbesses.*

➊ Cimetière de Montmartre (Montmartre Cemetery). Although not as large as the better-known Père Lachaise, this leafy split-level cemetery is just as moving and evocative. Incumbents include painters Jean-Baptiste Greuze, Jean-Honoré Fragonard, and Edgar Degas; Adolphe Sax, inventor of the saxophone; composers Hector Berlioz and Jacques Offenbach; and La Goulue, the Belle Epoque cabaret dancer who devised the French cancan. The florid Art Nouveau tomb of novelist Émile Zola (1840–1902), who died in nearby rue de Clichy, lords over a lawn near the entrance—though Zola's mortal remains were removed to the Panthéon in 1908. ⊠ *Av. Rachel. Métro: Blanche.*

⑲ Cimetière St-Vincent (St. Vincent Cemetery). It's a small graveyard, but if you're a serious student of Montmartre you may want to visit painter Maurice Utrillo's burial place. ⊠ *Entrance on rue Lucien-Gaulard (via rue St-Vincent), behind the Lapin Agile. Métro: Lamarck-Caulaincourt.*

⑭ Espace Salvador-Dalí (Dalí Center). Some of Salvador Dalí's less familiar works are among the 25 sculptures and 300 prints housed in this museum. The atmosphere is meant to approximate the surreal experience, with black walls, low lighting, and a New Agey musical score—punctuated by recordings of Dalí's own voice. ⊠ *11 rue Poulbot,* ☎ *01-42-64-40-10.* 🎫 *40 frs/€6.* ☉ *Daily 10–6:30. Métro: Abbesses.*

👣 ⑳ Halle St-Pierre (St. Peter's Market Hall). This elegant iron-and-glass 19th-century market hall, at the foot of Sacré-Coeur, houses a children's play area, a café, and the **Musée de l'Art Naïf Max-Fourny** (Max Fourny Museum of Naive Art), with its psychedelic collection of contemporary international Naive painters. ⊠ *2 rue Ronsard,* ☎ *01-42-58-72-89.* 🎫 *Museum 40 frs/€6.* ☉ *Daily 10–6. Métro: Anvers.*

★ ⑱ Lapin Agile. This bar-cabaret is still one of the most picturesque spots in Montmartre. It got its curious name—the Nimble Rabbit—when the owner, André Gill, hung up a sign (now in the Musée du Vieux Montmartre) of a laughing rabbit jumping out of a saucepan clutching a bottle of wine. In those days, the place was still tamely called *La Campagne* (The Countryside). Once the sign went up, locals rechristened it the Lapin à Gill, meaning Gill's Rabbit. When, in 1886, it was sold to cabaret

singer Jules Jouy, he called it the *Lapin Agile,* which has the same pro-
nunciation in French as *Lapin à Gill.* In 1903, the premises were
bought by the most celebrated cabaret entrepreneur of them all, Aristide Bruand, portrayed by Toulouse-Lautrec in a series of famous
posters, and soon thereafter Picasso painted his famous *Au Lapin
Agile* (sold at auction in the 1980s for nearly $50 million and on view
at New York City's Metropolitan Museum). Today, the Lapin Agile
manages to preserve at least something of its earlier flavor, unlike the
Moulin Rouge. ⊠ *22 rue des Saules,* ☏ *01–46–06–85–87.* 🎫 *130
frs/€20.* ☉ *Tues.–Sun. 9 pm–2 am. Métro: Lamarck-Caulaincourt.*

🔟 **La Mère Catherine.** This restaurant was a favorite with the Russian Cossacks who occupied Paris in 1814. Little did they know that when they
banged on the tables and shouted "*bistro,*" the Russian word for
"quickly," they were inventing a new breed of French restaurant. ⊠
6 pl. du Tertre. Métro: Abbesses.

④ **Moulin de la Galette** (Wafer Windmill). This windmill, on a hillock
shrouded by shrubbery, is one of the remaining two in Montmartre.
It was once the focal point of an open-air cabaret (made famous in a
painting by Renoir, now part of the collection of the Musée d'Orsay),
and rumor has it that the miller, Debray, was strung up on its sails and
spun to death after striving vainly to defend it against invading Cossacks in 1814. Unfortunately, it is now privately owned and can only
be admired from the street below. ⊠ *Rue Tholozé. Métro: Abbesses.*

② **Moulin Rouge** (Red Windmill). Built in 1885 as a windmill, this world-
famous cabaret was transformed into a dance hall in 1900. Those wild,
early days were immortalized by Toulouse-Lautrec in his posters and
paintings. It still trades shamelessly on the notion of Paris as a city of
sin: if you fancy a Vegas-style night out, with computerized light shows
and troupes of bare-breasted women sporting feather headdresses,
this is the place to go. The cancan, by the way—still a regular feature
here—was considerably raunchier when Toulouse-Lautrec was around.
⊠ *82 bd. de Clichy,* ☏ *01–53–09–82–82. Métro: Blanche.*

③ **Musée de l'Erotisme** (Museum of Eroticism). Opened in 1997, this seven-
story museum at the foot of Montmartre claims to provide "a prestigious showcase for every kind of erotic fantasy." Its 2,000 works of
art—you may find that this term is used rather loosely—include Pe-
ruvian potteries, African carvings, Indian miniatures, Nepalese bronzes,
Chinese ivories, and Japanese prints. Three floors are devoted to temporary exhibitions of painting and photography. ⊠ *72 bd. de Clichy,*
☏ *01–42–58–28–73.* 🎫 *40 frs/€6.* ☉ *Daily 10 am–2 am. Métro:
Blanche.*

🔷 **Musée de Montmartre** (Montmartre Museum). In its turn-of-the-20th-
century heyday, Montmartre's historical museum was home to an illustrious group of painters, writers, and assorted cabaret artists.
Foremost among them were Renoir—he painted the *Moulin de la
Galette,* an archetypal Parisian scene of sun-drenched revelers, while
he lived here—and Maurice Utrillo, Montmartre painter par excellence.
Utrillo was encouraged to paint by his mother, Suzanne Valadon, a model
of Renoir's and a major painter in her own right. Utrillo's life was anything but happy, despite the considerable success his paintings enjoyed. He was an alcoholic continually in trouble with the police and
spent most of his declining years in hospitals. He took the gray, crumbling streets of Montmartre as his subject matter, working more ef-
fectively from postcards than from the streets themselves. For all that,
almost all his best works—from his "White Period"—were produced
before 1916 (he died in 1955). They evoke the atmosphere of old

Montmartre hauntingly: to help convey the decaying buildings of the area, he mixed plaster and sand with his paints. The museum also provides a view of the tiny **vineyard**—the only one in Paris—on neighboring rue des Saules. A token 125 gallons of wine are still produced every year. It's hardly *grand cru* stuff, but there are predictably bacchanalian celebrations during the harvest on the first weekend of October. ✉ *12 rue Cortot,* ☎ *01–46–06–61–11.* 🖾 *25 frs/€3.81.* ⊙ *Tues.–Sun. 11–6. Métro: Lamarck-Caulaincourt.*

❻ **Place des Abbesses.** This triangular square is typical of the picturesque, slightly countrified style that has made Montmartre famous. The entrance to the Abbesses métro station, designed by the great Hector Guimard as a curving, sensuous mass of delicate iron, is one of the two original Art Nouveau entrance canopies left in Paris. *Métro: Abbesses.*

Place Blanche. The name place Blanche—White Square—comes from the clouds of chalky dust that used to be churned up by the carts that carried wheat and crushed flour from the nearby windmills, including the Moulin Rouge. *Métro: Blanche.*

OFF THE BEATEN PATH

MUSÉE DE LA VIE ROMANTIQUE – The very quintessence of 19th-century Paris, this tranquil, countrified town house, set in a little park at the foot of Montmartre, was for years the site of Friday-evening salons hosted by the Dutch-born painter Ary Scheffer and including the likes of Ingres, Delacroix, Turgenev, Chopin, and Sand. The memory of author George Sand (1804–76)—real name Aurore Dudevant—haunts the museum. Portraits, furniture, and household possessions, right down to her cigarette box, have been moved here from her house in Nohant in the Loire Valley. There's also a selection of Scheffer's competent artistic output on the first floor. The salons are newly asparkle, thanks to the eye of Jacques Garcia, France's most fashionable interior decorator. Take a moment to enjoy a cup of tea in the garden café. Head down rue Blanche from place Blanche; the third left is rue Chaptal. ✉ *16 rue Chaptal,* ☎ *01–48–74–95–38.* 🖾 *30 frs/€4.60.* ⊙ *Tues.–Sun. 10– 5:40. Métro: St-Georges.*

⓫ **Place Jean-Baptiste-Clément.** Painter Amedeo Modigliani (1884–1920) had a studio here at No. 7. Some say he was the greatest Italian artist of the 20th century, fusing the genius of the Renaissance with the modernity of Cézanne and Picasso. He claimed that he would drink himself to death—he eventually did—and chose the right part of town to do it in. Look for the octagonal tower at the north end of the square; it's all that's left of Montmartre's first water tower, built around 1840 to boost the area's feeble water supply. ✉ *Pl. Jean-Baptiste-Clément. Métro: Abbesses.*

⓬ **Place du Tertre** (Mound Square). This tumbling square (*tertre* means hillock) regains its village atmosphere only in the winter, when the branches of the plane trees sketch traceries against the sky. At any other time of year you'll be confronted by a swarm of artists clamoring to do your portrait and crowds of tourists. If one produces a picture of you without your permission, you're under no obligation to buy. *Métro: Abbesses.*

NEED A BREAK?

Patachou (✉ 9 pl. du Tertre, ☎ 01–42–51–06–06) sounds the one classy note on place du Tertre, serving exquisite, if expensive, cakes and teas.

★ ⓰ **Sacré-Coeur** (Sacred Heart Basilica). The white domes of this basilica patrol the Paris skyline from the top of Montmartre. The French government decided to erect Sacré-Coeur in 1873, as a sort of national guilt-offering in expiation for the blood shed during the Commune and Franco-Prussian War in 1870–71. It was to symbolize the return of self-confidence to late-19th-century Paris. Even so, the building was to some extent a reflection of political divisions within the country: it was largely financed by French Catholics fearful of an anticlerical backlash and determined to make a grandiloquent statement on behalf of the Church. Construction lasted until World War I; the basilica was not consecrated until 1919. Stylistically, the Sacré-Coeur borrows elements from Romanesque and Byzantine models. Built on a grand scale, the church is strangely disjointed and unsettling; architect Paul Abadie (who died in 1884, long before the church was finished) had made his name by sticking similar scaly, pointed domes onto the medieval cathedrals of Angoulême and Périgueux in southwest France. The gloomy, cavernous interior is worth visiting for its golden mosaics; climb to the top of the dome for the view of Paris. ⊠ *Pl. du Parvis-du-Sacré-Coeur. Métro: Anvers.*

❼ St-Jean l'Evangéliste. This redbrick church, built in 1904, was one of the first concrete buildings in France; despite its sinuous Art Nouveau curves, the bricks had to be added later to soothe offended locals. ⊠ *Pl. des Abbesses. Métro: Abbesses.*

NEED A BREAK?   **Le St-Jean** (⊠ 23 rue des Abbesses) is an intimate, large-windowed café, popular with locals on account of its authentic 1950s decor—neon lighting, vast bar, and mosaic-tile floor. The tables outside offer a good vantage point over busy place des Abbesses.

⓯ St-Pierre de Montmartre. Sitting awkwardly beneath the brooding silhouette of Sacré-Coeur, just off place du Tertre, is this church—one of the oldest in Paris. Built in the 12th century as the abbey church of a substantial Benedictine monastery, it has been remodeled on a number of occasions through the years; thus the 18th-century facade, built under Louis XIV, clashes with the mostly medieval interior. ⊠ *Off pl. du Tertre. Métro: Anvers.*

❺ Studio 28. What looks like no more than a generic little movie theater has a distinguished dramatic history: when it opened in 1928, it was the first one purposely built for *art et essai,* or experimental theater, in the world. Over the years, the movies of directors like Jean Cocteau, François Truffaut, and Orson Welles have been shown here before their official premieres. ⊠ *10 rue Tholozé,* ☎ *01–46–06–36–07. Métro: Abbesses.*

❽ Théâtre Libre (Free Theater). Founded in 1887 by director André Antoine (1858–1943), this theater was immensely influential in popularizing the work of iconoclastic young playwrights such as Ibsen and Strindberg. Antoine later became the director of the Odéon Theater in 1906. ⊠ *37 rue André-Antoine. Métro: Abbesses.*

PASSY, AUTEUIL, AND THE BOIS DE BOULOGNE

Passy and Auteuil were independent villages until Baron Haussmann soldered them together in 1860 and annexed them to Paris under the mundane title of the 16e arrondissement. Tumbling alleys and countrified cul-de-sacs recall those bygone days, colliding with some of the city's finest 20th-century architecture, by Guimard, Perret, Le Corbusier, and Mallet-Stevens. One of the city's most overlooked museums is here— the Musée Marmottan, with its enormous Monet collection.

Not far away from those Monets is the sprawling Bois de Boulogne— an enormous park that also assumed its present form during the days of Haussmann and Napoléon III, when it became Parisians' favorite day trip. The 16ᵉ is the largest arrondissement in Paris, and Le Bois, as it is known, is almost of equal size. Public transportation to the Bois is poor, and few Parisians ever get to know all its glades and pathways— but all know and love the Bois's Pré Catalan and Bagatelle gardens, two of Paris's prettiest nooks. The photogenic Lac Supérieur, however, which anchors the Bois's eastern sector, is easy to reach by foot and métro.

Numbers in the text correspond to numbers in the margin and on the Passy, Auteuil, and the Bois de Boulogne map.

A Good Walk

Start at the **Cimetière de Passy** ①, above place du Trocadéro. A map to the left of the entrance charts the tombs of the famous buried here. Leaving the cemetery, cross avenue Paul-Doumer, and veer left to a small garden (Square Yorktown) where there is a statue of Benjamin Franklin. Turn right down rue Benjamin-Franklin. Verdant gardens flank the curved wing of the Palais de Chaillot to your left. On the right, at No. 25 bis, note the huge-windowed Immeuble Perret—an innovative building for its time (1903), with a reinforced-concrete facade clad in floral-patterned ceramic tiles. Auguste Perret, then just 29, was to become one of the century's leading architects.

Cross place Costa-Rica, with its plummeting view of the aboveground métro as it shoots across the Seine, and take rue Raynouard. Opposite No. 12, turn left down rue des Eaux, a sinister-looking stone staircase flanked by barbed wire: the nearest Paris gets to urban hell, straight out of Dickens, and duly depositing you on rue Charles-Dickens at the bottom. You reemerge into daylight to be confronted by a templelike town house with huge Greek columns and, to your left, the quaint **Musée du Vin** ②, with exhibits on wine in its medieval cellars. After an excursion through pastures bacchanalian, big-city reality hits again as you retrace your steps along rue Charles-Dickens and venture through a metal grille toward a vast building site. Turn right to reach avenue Marcel-Proust, in search of the time when the fortresslike walls on the right supported some of the fanciest flats in Paris, and the majestic double-staircase halfway along once led down to the grand entrance of the Ministry of Public Works (relocated to La Défense) rather than the emerging Parc de Passy housing complex.

A policeman generally lurks a hundred yards on, barring the leafy driveway to the Turkish embassy. You might have to consult him for advice as you search for rue Bertin, a cobbled, ivy-clad alley that sneaks off right, undisturbed by traffic, to a flight of stairs that leads back to rue Raynouard and the **Maison de Balzac** ③, a dachalike bungalow with trim lawns, once home to France's own Dickens. Rue Benjamin-Franklin returns at the corner of rues Raynouard and Singer where— says a tall, tapering plaque—the great man invented the lightning conductor between 1777 and 1785. Rue Raynouard tumbles down past the circular bulk of **Maison de Radio France** ④, the headquarters of state radio and television. If you'd like to see a miniversion of the **Statue of Liberty** ⑤, head left toward the Seine; it's at the end of the Allée des Cygnes, a striplike artificial island backed by the skyscrapers of the

Passy, Auteuil, and the Bois de Boulogne

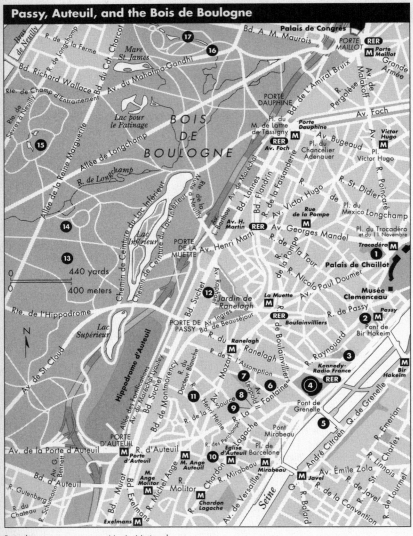

1970s Front de Seine complex that cynical Parisians dub their mini-Manhattan.

Continue on rue Raynouard, which becomes rue La Fontaine, to inspect the **Castel-Béranger** ⑥ at No. 14, one of the city's earliest Art Nouveau buildings. If you're a fan of sculptor Auguste Rodin you may want to make a detour next right up avenue du Recteur-Poincaré to **place Rodin** ⑦ to see a small bronze casting of his male nude, *The Bronze Age*. Otherwise stay on rue La Fontaine, pass the **Orphelins d'Auteuil** ⑧—a still-functioning orphanage. Pause at No. 60, the **Hôtel Mezzara** ⑨, another fine Guimard mansion. Some 150 yards along, turn left onto rue des Perchamps. Note the bay-windowed, striped-tile Studio Building at No. 20—it looks contemporary but was built by Henri Sauvage in 1927. Also note the funky white mansion at the corner of rue Leconte-de-l'Isle, with its heavy, outsized triglyphs. Some beefy Baroque caryatids on loan from Vienna are visible across the street at No. 33, incongruously supporting a row of wafer-thin balconies.

Continue along rue des Perchamps to **rue d'Auteuil** ⑩. To the left is the elongated dome of the Église d'Auteuil, modeled on the papal tiara. Head right along this old, crooked shopping street to sloping place Jean-Lorrain, home to a crowded market on Wednesday and Saturday mornings; then turn right down rue La Fontaine toward the chunky Crédit Lyonnais bank. Veer left up avenue Mozart and pause at No. 122; the elongated doorway and sinuous window frames again pay tribute to Guimard. Around the corner in Villa Flore, a tiny cul-de-sac, you can see the odd-shape site Guimard had to contend with: the building ends in a narrow point, with jagged brickwork vainly beckoning an addition.

Take the next left up rue Henri-Heine, with its row of elegant town houses; then turn left onto rue du Dr-Blanche, and left again to get to square du Dr-Blanche, a leafy cul-de-sac. At the far end is the **Fondation Le Corbusier** ⑪. If you like such spartan interwar architecture and want to see more, backtrack along rue du Dr-Blanche and explore rue Mallet-Stevens, a mews lined with sturdy evergreens and elegant houses from the late 1920s. Turn left at the end of rue du Dr-Blanche onto rue de l'Assomption, then right, and, opposite the end of rue du Ranelagh, cross the disused St-Lazare-Auteuil rail line. Take a right on avenue Raphaël, which overlooks the elegant Jardin du Ranelagh—site of the world's first hot-air balloon launch, in 1783. At the corner of rue Louis-Boilly is the **Musée Marmottan–Claude Monet** ⑫, famed for its collection of Impressionist pictures and illuminated manuscripts.

Continue on avenue Raphaël and cross boulevard Suchet to sprawling place de Colombie. Turn left down avenue de St-Cloud to reach the large **Bois de Boulogne** ⑬. Straight ahead is the bigger of the park's two lakes, the Lac Inférieur; you can cross to the island in the middle on a little ferry for a picnic or café lunch. When you're done, skirt south around the lake to check out the less picturesque Lac Supérieur; then take the chemin de Ceinture, then route de la Grande-Cascade to the **Pré Catalan** ⑭, home to the Shakespeare Garden, trim lawns, stately trees, and a historic restaurant. Cross the Pré Catalan and exit from its north side. If you're short on time or energy, head right via the Lac Inférieur and return to civilization at Porte Dauphine; otherwise head left along route des Lacs à Bagatelle to the **Parc de Bagatelle** ⑮, with its magnificent flower garden and 18th-century château. A good walk east from here will take you along avenue du Mahatma-Gandhi, past the **Musée National des Arts et Traditions Populaires** ⑯ and the children's amusement park, the **Jardin d'Acclimatation** ⑰, to Porte Maillot, where you can get a métro back to central Paris.

TIMING

This walk, which divides neatly into two—town (Paris) and country (Bois de Boulogne)—will probably take you a full day. (You may want to save the Bois de Boulogne for another day.) The Lac Inférieur is a good midway spot to stop for lunch. By then you'll have covered 5–6 km (3–3½ mi), depending on whether you detour to the Statue of Liberty and place Rodin. The second half of the tour covers just under 4 km (2½ mi) if you return from the Pré Catalan to **Porte Dauphine,** or just under 6 km (3½ mi) if you take in the Parc de Bagatelle and return to Porte Maillot. Sturdy, comfortable footwear is a must to negotiate the slopes and steps of the Paris sector and the gravelly pathways of the Bois de Boulogne.

Sights to See

Bois de Boulogne. Class and style have been associated with this 2,200-acre wood—known to Parisians simply as *Le Bois*—ever since it was landscaped into an upper-class playground by Baron Haussmann in the 1850s. Emphasizing that onetime glamour is Haussmann's approach road from the Arc de Triomphe: avenue Foch, Paris's widest boulevard (120 yards across), originally named avenue de l'Impératrice in honor of Empress Eugénie (wife of Napoléon III). The Porte Dauphine métro station at the bottom of avenue Foch retains its original Art Nouveau iron-and-glass entrance canopy, designed by Hector Guimard.

The wood, which lost thousands of trees during the 100-mph wind storms over Christmas 1999, is crisscrossed by broad, leafy roads, home to rowers, joggers, strollers, riders, *pétanque* (a sort of bowling game) players, picnickers, and lovers. Meetings at **Longchamp** and **Auteuil** racetracks are high up the social calendar and re-create something of a Belle Epoque atmosphere. The French Open tennis tournament at the beautiful **Roland Garros** stadium in late May is another occasion when Parisian style and elegance are on full display.

The manifold attractions of Le Bois include cafés, restaurants, lakes, waterfalls, gardens, and museums. Rowboats can be rented at both **Lac Inférieur** and **Lac Supérieur.** A cheap and frequent ferry crosses to the idyllic island in the middle of Lac Inférieur. The **Fête à Neu-Neu,** a giant carnival, takes place every September and October around the two lakes. Buses traverse the Bois de Boulogne during the day (take Bus 244 from Porte Maillot), but Le Bois becomes a distinctly adult playground after dark, when prostitutes of various genders come prowling for clients. Instead, explore it in full daylight, when it looks much the same as it did when it was caught on film in *Gigi* and proved a memorable backdrop to Maurice Chevalier warbling "Thank Heaven for Little Girls." *Main entrance at bottom of av. Foch. Métro: Porte Maillot, Porte Dauphine, Porte d'Auteuil; Bus 244.*

Castel-Béranger. Dreamt up in 1895 by Hector Guimard (of métro fame) when he was 28, this building is considered the city's first Art Nouveau structure. The apartment building once housed Postimpressionist Paul Signac as well as Guimard himself. Today, the place looks a little dowdy and its occupants are less illustrious—though this hasn't stopped them from posting a menacing sign on the asymmetrical iron doorway warning you to keep out. Rust-streaked pale green paintwork, however, fails to detract from the florid appeal of the iron doors and balconies, or from the eccentric use of colored brick. Cross the street to admire the mask-fronted iron balconies and quilt-patterned brown, red, and turquoise brickwork; then venture around the side into Hameau Béranger to see rampant ivy obliterating the original fancy iron fencing, beneath the dismayed gaze of stylized sea horses halfway up the walls. There's a cleaner, subtler display of Art Nouveau at the corner of rue Lafontaine and rue Gros, where a finely carved stone apartment building segues into the dainty rue Agar. Tucked away at the corner of rue Gros is a tiny café-bar with Art Nouveau glass front and furnishings. ⊠ *14 rue la Fontaine. Métro: Ranelagh; RER: Maison de Radio-France.*

NEED A BREAK? It seats just 15, but the **Café-Bar Antoine** (⊠ 17 rue la Fontaine, ☎ 01–40–50–14–30) warrants a visit for its Art Nouveau facade, floor tiles, and carved wooden bar. Count on 200 francs/€30 for a meal or stick to a snack and coffee.

❶ **Cimetière de Passy** (Passy Cemetery). Perched on a spur above place du Trocadéro in the shadow of the Eiffel Tower and Palais de Chaillot, this cemetery was opened in 1820 when Passy was a country village. Its handsome entrance—two sturdy pavilions linked by a colonnade—is a 1930s Art Deco cousin to the nearby Palais de Chaillot. Precocious painter-poetess Marie Baskirtseff's tomb, with its pinnacles and stone Byzantine dome, dominates the cemetery; a Pietà behind Plexiglas mourns Hungarian peer Pierre Perenyi nearby. Just left of the main crossroads is a weathered bust of Impressionist Edouard Manet, buried with his wife, Berthe Morisot, next to the poignant figure of a girl in a hat—calling to mind Zola's novel *A Page of Love*, which ends with the burial of the young heroine Jeanne in Passy Cemetery, "alone, facing Paris, forever." Claude Debussy is also among the incumbents. ⊠ *Rue du Commandant-Schloesing.* ⊙ *Daily 9–8 or dusk. Métro: Trocadéro.*

⑪ **Fondation Le Corbusier** (Le Corbusier Foundation). The Villa Laroche is less of a museum in honor of Swiss architect Charles-Edouard Jeanneret, better known as Le Corbusier (1887–1965), than a well-preserved 1923 example of his innovative construction techniques, based on geometric forms, recherché color schemes, and unblushing recourse to iron and concrete. The sloping ramp that replaces the traditional staircase is one of the most eye-catching features. ⊠ *10 sq. du Dr-Blanche,* ☎ *01–42–88–41–53.* ⊡ *15 frs/€2.30.* ⊙ *Weekdays 10–12:30 and 1:30–6. Métro: Jasmin.*

❾ **Hôtel Mezzara.** With its sumptuous wrought-iron staircase, Art Nouveau windows, and plaster molding, this Hector Guimard mansion, built in 1911 as a workshop for textile designer Paul Mezzara, has one of the finest interiors in Paris. Unfortunately, it is only open during exhibitions, though a bit of curiosity and perseverance might get you through the door. ⊠ *60 rue la Fontaine,* ☎ *01–45–27–02–29. Métro: Jasmin.*

✆ ⑰ **Jardin d'Acclimatation** (Amusement Park). At this children's zoo and amusement park on the northern edge of the Bois de Boulogne (*above*), you can see a mix of exotic and familiar animals, take a boat trip along an "enchanted river," ride a miniature railway, and enjoy various fairground booths that keep young and old entertained. The zoo and amusement park can be reached via the miniature railway—a surefire hit with children—that runs from Porte Maillot on Wednesday and weekends, beginning at 1:30; tickets cost 6.5 francs/€1. Many of the attractions have separate entry fees (except the zoo, which is spread throughout the park), notably the child-oriented art museum and workshop center, the **Musée en Herbe** (literally, "museum in the grass"); admission is 26 francs/€4. ⊠ *Bd. des Sablons,* ☎ *01–40–67–97–66.* ⊡ *14 frs/€2.* ⊙ *Daily 10–6. Métro: Les Sablons.*

❸ **Maison de Balzac** (Balzac's House). The Paris home of the great French 19th-century novelist Honoré de Balzac (1799–1850) contains a wide range of exhibits charting his tempestuous life. ✉ *47 rue Raynouard,* ☎ *01–55–74–41–80.* ✉ *30 frs/€4.60.* ◷ *Feb.–Dec., Tues.–Sun. 10–5:40. Métro: Passy.*

④ Maison de Radio France (Radio France Building). The home to state radio, completed in 1962, is a monstrous circular building—more than 500 yards in circumference and said to be the largest in France in terms of floor space—with a 200-ft tower overlooking the Seine. You can explore the foyer, obtain tickets to attend recordings, or join a guided tour (in French) of the studios and the museum, with its notable array of old radios. ✉ *116 av. du Président-Kennedy,* ☎ *01–56–40–15–16.* ✉ *Guided tours (at half past the hour) 25 frs/€3.81.* ◷ *Mon.–Sat. 10:30–4:30. Métro: Ranelagh; RER: Maison de Radio-France.*

★ **⑫ Musée Marmottan–Claude Monet.** One of the most underestimated museums in town, the Marmottan is Paris's "other" Impressionist museum (after the Musée d'Orsay). A few years ago this museum, in an elegant 19th-century mansion, tacked "Claude Monet" onto its official name—and justly so, as this may be the best collection of the artist's works anywhere. Monet occupies a specially built basement gallery, where you'll find such spectacular works as the *Cathédrale à Rouen* (1892–96) series and *Impression: Soleil Levant* (Impression–Sunrise, 1872), the work that helped give the Impressionist movement its name. Other exhibits include letters exchanged by Impressionist painters Berthe Morisot and Mary Cassatt. There's a roomful of priceless illuminated medieval manuscripts on the ground floor, and impressive Empire furniture from Napoléon's time makes you feel as if you're at an actual salon, with comfortable couches and grand windows overlooking the Jardin de Ranelagh on one side and the hotel's private yard on the other. ✉ *2 rue Louis-Boilly,* ☎ *01–42–24–07–02,* ⟦WEB⟧ *www.marmottan.com.* ✉ *40 frs/€6.* ◷ *Tues.–Sun. 10–5. Métro: La Muette.*

⑯ Musée National des Arts et Traditions Populaires (National Museum of Folk Arts and Traditions). In a nondescript modern building next to the Jardin d'Acclimatation, this museum contains an impressive variety of artifacts related principally to preindustrial rural life. Many exhibits have buttons to press and knobs to twirl; however, there are no descriptions in English. The museum is a favorite destination for school field trips, so avoid weekday afternoons. ✉ *6 av. du Mahatma-Gandhi,* ☎ *01–44–17–60–00.* ✉ *22 frs/€3.35.* ◷ *Wed.–Mon. 9:30–5:15. Métro: Les Sablons.*

② Musée du Vin (Wine Museum). In the vaulted cellars of a former 13th-century abbey, this small museum is devoted to traditional wine-making artifacts. The premises double as a wine bar and the visit includes a wine-tasting. ✉ *5 sq. Charles-Dickens,* ☎ *01–45–25–63–26.* ✉ *35 frs/€5.34.* ◷ *Tues.–Sun. 10–6. Métro: Passy.*

⑧ Orphelins d'Auteuil (Auteuil Orphanage). This still-functioning orphanage, founded in 1866 by Abbé Roussel, has pretty sloping gardens, a redbrick cloister, a crafts shop, and a tasteful neo-Gothic chapel (built 1927). ✉ *40 rue La Fontaine,* ☎ *01–44–14–75–20. Métro: Jasmin.*

⑮ Parc de Bagatelle. This beautiful floral garden counts irises, roses, tulips, and water lilies among its showstoppers; it is at its most colorful between April and June. The velvet green lawns and the bijou château (only open when hosting exhibitions) are fronted by a terrace with attractive views of the Seine. The white-walled château was built by the Comte d'Artois in 1777 on a bet with Marie-Antoinette that it could be finished within two months; 900 construction workers toiled day and, by torchlight, at night, to make it happen. ✉ *Rte. de Sèvres-à-*

Neuilly or rte. des Lacs-à-Bagatelle, ☎ 01–40–67–97–00. ✉ Gardens 10 frs/€1.52, château entrance according to exhibition. ⊙ Daily 9–8 or dusk. Métro: Pont de Neuilly.

⑦ Place Rodin. A half-sized bronze casting of Rodin's virile *L'Age d'Airain* (*The Bronze Age*) nude, created in 1874, emerges unblushingly from rosebushes at the heart of this minor roundabout. *Métro: Ranelagh.*

⑭ Pré Catalan. This garden in the Bois de Boulogne contains one of Paris's largest trees: a copper beech more than 200 years old. The **Jardin Shakespeare** (Shakespeare Garden) on the west side has flowers, herbs, and trees mentioned in Shakespeare's plays. Nearby still stands the restaurant Le Pré Catalan, where *le tout Paris* in the early 20th century used to dine on its beautiful garden terrace. ✉ *Rte. de la Grande-Cascade.* ✉ *Pré Catalan free, Shakespeare Garden 5 frs/€.7.* ⊙ *Pré Catalan, daily 8–dusk; Shakespeare Garden, daily 3–3:30 and 4:30–5. Métro: Porte Dauphine.*

⑩ Rue d'Auteuil. This narrow, crooked shopping street escaped the attentions of Baron Haussmann and retains a country feel. Molière once lived on the site of No. 2; Racine was on nearby rue du Buis; the pair met up to clink glasses and exchange drama notes at the Mouton Blanc Inn, now a brasserie at No. 40. Note some genuinely old buildings dating from the 17th and 18th centuries at Nos. 19, 21, 25, and 29; the elegant courtyard of the school at No. 11 bis; and the scaly dome of the **Église d'Auteuil** (built in the 1880s), an unmistakable small-time cousin of the Sacré-Coeur. Rue d'Auteuil is at its liveliest on Wednesday and Saturday mornings, when a much-loved street market crams onto place Jean-Barraud. *Métro: Michel-Ange–Auteuil, Église d'Auteuil.*

OFF THE
BEATEN PATH

MUSÉE NATIONAL DE LA CÉRAMIQUE – Hundreds of the finest creations of the world-famous Sèvres porcelain works are displayed at the National Ceramics Museum, at the southern end of the tumbling, wooded Parc de St-Cloud, a short métro ride from the Michel-Ange–Auteuil stop. ✉ *Pl. de la Manufacture, Sèvres*, ☎ 01–41–14–04–20. ✉ 22 frs/€3.35. ⊙ *Wed.–Mon. 10–5:15. Métro: Pont de Sèvres; Tramway: Musée de Sèvres.*

SERRES D'AUTEUIL – Tropical and exotic plants sweat it out in mighty hothouses just off place de la Porte-d'Auteuil, on the southern fringe of the Bois de Boulogne. A bewildering variety of plants and flowers are grown here for use in Paris's municipal parks and for displays on official occasions. The surrounding gardens' leafy paths and well-tended lawns offer cooler places to admire floral virtuosity. ✉ *3 av. de la Porte-d'Auteuil*, ☎ 01–40–71–76–07. ✉ 5 frs/€.7. ⊙ *Daily 10–6. Métro: Porte d'Auteuil.*

⑤ Statue of Liberty. Just in case you'd forgotten that the enduring symbol of the American dream is actually French, a reduced version of Frédéric-Auguste Bartholdi's matriarch brandishes her torch at the southern tip of the Allée des Cygnes. To Bartholdi's dismay, she originally faced the city and was only turned around to gaze across the waters of the Seine in 1937. The best view of her can be had during a Bateaux-Mouche river tour: boats usually make an obliging U-turn right in front. The original statue—the one in New York City—is known in French as *La Liberté Éclairant le Monde* (Liberty Lighting Up the World); it was made in Paris in 1886 with the help of a giant steel framework designed by Gustave Eiffel. ✉ *Allée des Cygnes. Métro: Javel; RER: Maison de Radio-France.*

OFF THE BEATEN TRACK

If you're in search of wide-open green spaces, skyscrapers, the church where Gothic architecture made its first appearance, or great Art Deco architecture, make a brief excursion to the city's peripheries.

Sights to See

★ **Basilique de St-Denis.** Built between 1136 and 1286, St. Denis Cathedral is in some ways the most important Gothic church in the Paris region. It was here, under dynamic prelate Abbé Suger, that Gothic architecture (typified by pointed arches and rib vaults) arguably made its first appearance. Suger's writings also show the medieval fascination with the bright, shiny colors that appear in stained glass. The kings of France soon chose St-Denis as their final resting place, and their richly sculpted tombs—along with what remains of Suger's church—can be seen in the choir area at the east end of the church. The vast 13th-century nave is a brilliant example of structural logic; its columns, capitals, and vault are a model of architectural harmony. The facade, retaining the rounded arches of the Romanesque style that preceded the Gothic style, is set off by a small rose window, reputedly the earliest in France. ⊠ *1 rue de la Légion d'Honneur,* ☎ *01–48–09–83–54.* ⊠ *Choir and tombs 32 frs/€4.9.* ☉ *Easter–Sept., Mon.–Sat. 10–7, Sun. noon–7; Oct.–Easter, Mon.–Sat. 10–5, Sun. noon–5. Guided tours daily at 1:15 and 3. Métro: St-Denis–Basilique.*

La Défense. You may be pleasantly surprised by the absence of high-rise buildings and concrete towers in central Paris; one of the reasons for this is that French planners, with their usual desire to rationalize, ordained that modern high-rise development be expelled to the outskirts. Over the last 20 years, La Défense, just west of Paris across the Seine from Neuilly, has been transformed into a futuristic showcase for state-of-the-art engineering and architectural design. A few people actually live amid all this glass and concrete; most just come to work. The soaring high-rises are mainly taken up by offices—often the French headquarters of multinational companies—with no expense spared in the pursuit of visual ingenuity. Highlights include the **Musée de l'Automobile** for car fans, and, crowning the plaza, the **Grande Arche de La Défense,** an enormous open cube aligned with avenue de la Grande-Armée, the Arc de Triomphe, the Champs-Élysées, and the Louvre. Tubular glass elevators whisk you 360 ft to the top. ⊠ *Parvis de La Défense,* ☎ *01–49–07–27–57,* WEB *www.grandearche.com.* ⊠ *Arch 46 frs/€7, auto museum 35 frs/€5.34.* ☉ *Arch daily 10–7, auto museum daily 12:15–7. Métro, RER: Grande Arche de La Défense.*

☺ **Parc Andre-Citroën** (Andre-Citroën Park). This innovative and lovely park in southwest Paris was built on the site of the former Citroën automobile factory. Now it has lawns, Japanese rock gardens, rambling wildflowers, and elegant greenhouses full of exotic plants and flowers. There's also a delightful, computer-programmed "dancing fountain" that you can play in. On a sunny day, it's a great place to take a break from sightseeing. ⊠ *Entrances on rue St-Charles and rue de la Montagne de l'Esperou. Métro, RER: Javel.*

☺ **Parc Montsouris and Cité Universitaire** (Montsouris Park and University City). The picturesque, English-style Montsouris Park and the University "City," or campus, are in the residential 14ᵉ arrondissement, south of Montparnasse. Parc Montsouris has cascades, a lake, and a meteorological observatory disguised as a Tunisian Palace. The Cité Universitaire, opposite Parc Montsouris and next to the futuristic Stade Charléty athletics stadium, houses 5,000 international students in buildings that date mainly from the 1930s and reflect the architecture of different countries. Le Corbusier designed the Swiss and Brazilian houses; John D. Rockefeller funded the Maison Internationale; and the Sacré-Coeur church recalls the simple, muscular confidence of buildings erected in Mussolini's Italy. ✉ *Parc Montsouris: entrances on av. Reille, bd. Jourdan, and rue Gazan; Cité Universitaire: entrance at 19 bd. Jourdan,* ☎ *01–44–16–64–00 Cité Universitaire information. RER: Cité Universitaire.*

Parcours des Années Trente and Musée des Années 30 (1930s Trail and 1930s Museum). For a look at outstanding Art Deco buildings by such architects as Le Corbusier, Auguste Perret, Raymond Fisher, and Robert Mallet-Stevens, follow the 1930s Trail in the suburb of Boulogne-Billancourt. The route is outlined in an illustrated booklet available at the magnificent Hôtel de Ville (✉ av. André-Morizet), built by Tony Garnier in 1934. More Art Deco is to be found at the 1930s Museum, next to the Hôtel de Ville. This museum has a wealth of beautifully presented paintings and sculpture produced in France during the interwar period. There's also an intriguing section on "colonial art," which borders between the naive and the patronizing. The collection of furniture and objects is disappointingly sparse. ✉ *28 av. André-Morizet, Boulogne-Billancourt,* ☎ *01–55–18–46–42.* 🖾 *30 frs/€4.60.* ☉ *Tues.– Sun. 11–6. Métro: Marcel-Sembat.*

2 DINING

Forget the Louvre, the Tour Eiffel, and the Bateaux Mouches—the real reason for a visit to Paris is to dine at its famous temples of gastronomy. Whether you get knee-deep in white truffles at Alain Ducasse or merely encounter pistachioed sausage (the poor man's caviar) at a classic corner bistro, you'll discover that food here is an obsession, an art, a subject of endless debate. And if the lobster soufflé is delicious, the historic ambience in which it is presented is often more so. Just request Empress Josephine's table at Le Grand Véfour and find out.

Revised and
updated by
Rosa Jackson

PARIS HAS WORKS OF ART OF VARIED KINDS: some hang on the walls of the Louvre and some smile up at you from a table. Clearly anyone who has ordered a dessert at Taillevent and received a concoction that looks like a Lacroix hat out of the pages of French *Vogue* knows that in Paris food is not just something to fill you up. To the French, gastronomy is a fine art, and it is always regarded as the larger art of living, the art of transforming the gross and humdrum sides of existence into something witty, charming, and gracious. Parisians, above all, feel that every meal is—if not a way of life—certainly an event that demands undivided attention. Happily, the city's chefs exist principally to please demanding residents on that score, so it is no surprise that Paris is also a place where visitors expect to experience full gastronomic rapture.

Even though a dramatic and widely heralded improvement in the restaurants of other cities from Boston to Brisbane has closed the gap that once made the French capital nonpareil, no other metropolis in the world has a food culture that is as refined, reasoned, and deeply rooted as that of Paris. From the edible genius of haute cuisine wizard Alain Ducasse—whose turbot with "marmalade" of asparagus will make you purr—to brilliant bistro chef Yves Camdeborde's red mullet with chestnuts and cèpes, dining in Paris can easily leave you in a pleasurable stupor. And when it all seems a bit overwhelming, you can slip away to a casual little place for an earthy, bubbling cassoulet; make a midnight feast of the world's silkiest oysters; or even opt out of Gaul altogether for superb pasta, couscous, or an herb-bright Vietnamese stir-fry. Once you know where to go, Paris is a city where perfection awaits at all levels of the food chain.

These days, Paris is undergoing a modest culinary transformation—one that will, however, likely prove to be more influential and enduring than the showier revolutions occurring elsewhere. Call it the French Evolution. "Fusion often leads to confusion," says chef Alain Ducasse, whose Paris and Monte Carlo restaurants offer excellent examples of the imaginative but prudent innovations taking place in the best kitchens in France. "If you go much beyond the measured use of two or three ingredients, what you often find on your plate is incoherent," Ducasse says, and most French chefs would agree with him. Not for them the wild encounters between, say, Thai and French food that team foie gras with lemongrass, mangoes, and goat cheese that you find in newer-than-nouvelle circles. What they're after is a subtler, lighter, and discreetly unexpected cuisine.

The French Evolution is being even more strongly felt in the new bistros opened by ambitious young chefs during the last 10 years. The much-loved red-check-tablecloth venues serving boeuf bourguignon have hardly disappeared, but alongside them a new field of delicious possibilities has sprung up (often in set-price menus that are real bargains). Helping to reinvent the classic formulas, these modern bistros generally offer the same cozy, relaxed settings and conviviality as the sepia-toned originals. What has changed is that their menus are inventively colorful, with young chefs transforming regional classics with judiciously borrowed preparations from foreign kitchens. Take the salad of crunchy baby squid and langoustine in a thatch of finely grated carrot and celery with a gingery Oriental dressing served by chef Pierre Jay at his popular new bistro, L'Ardoise, in the 1ᵉʳ arrondissement; or the stylish updates of classic Toulouse food that have made chef Hélène Darroze's eponymous Left Bank restaurant a roaring success. Today, there's almost no part of the city that doesn't have a modern bistro so good that it pulls crowds from all over town, from the Le Clos du Gourmet in the sedate 7ᵉ arrondissement to Chez Michel in the busy 10ᵉ or Le Repaire de Cartouche in the increasingly trendy 11ᵉ.

Biologique is the word du jour. Following the recent food scares in England, Belgium, and France, a growing number of restaurants are featuring organic produce, and we're not just talking tofu and sprouts. At Le Safran, an excellent bistro in the heart of town, chef Caroll Sinclair proudly announces that she uses as much *biologique,* or organic produce, as possible, including lamb, dairy produce, and vegetables, and this trend looks set to remain for the next few years. You may also be surprised to discover that Parisians are *fou*—crazy—for egg foo yung, tacos, paella, and sushi. If ethnic restaurants in Paris formerly ran to pizzerias, couscous parlors, and the odd Vietnamese place, the city now has a choice of international tables that is bettered only by London in Europe—and Parisians will rightly insist that their North African food is easily the best in the world, a legacy, of course, of France's former colonial empire.

For the many people who come to Paris looking for a dose of elegance in an increasingly Gap-dressed world, the revival of the dining rooms in the city's grande dame hotels provides an ideal opportunity to show off their new Givenchys and Balmains. Many of the best young chefs in the city are now cooking at hotels, including Eric Frechon at the Bristol and Alain Solivères at Les Élysées in the Hotel Vernet. These sanctuaries of gilt moldings, crystal chandeliers, and muted champagne corks are often also citadels of classic French luxury food—think caviar sorbets, lobster with black truffles, and *pâtisseries* crafted as delicately as precious jewelry. To taste all this grandeur, partake of the lavish *carte* (menu) served by chef Dominique Bouchet in the Hotel Crillon's Les Ambassadeurs restaurant—just don't bat an eyelash when the *addition* (bill) is presented. On the flip side of the coin, decor-wise, is the fact that some of the best bistros in Paris look downright simple—it's a kind of reverse *snobbisme*. No matter where you head, try to enjoy a taste of the grape along the way, whether *vin ordinaire* (table wine) or a Romanée-Conti. As the French say, a day without wine is like a day without sun.

Included in this listing are a variety of restaurants and price ranges. More than half are in the 1ᵉʳ–8ᵉ arrondissements, within easy reach of hotels and sights; many others are in the 14ᵉ and 16ᵉ, also popular visitor areas; and some are in the 11ᵉ–20ᵉ, outlying, often residential neighborhoods where the rents are cheaper and young chefs can afford to strike out on their own. Recognizing that even in Paris you may not want to eat French food at every meal, several ethnic restaurants are also listed. (One area worth exploring—especially at lunchtime—is Paris's Chinatown in the 13ᵉ arrondissement; the main streets are avenue d'Ivry and avenue du Choisy.)

Mealtimes

Generally, Paris restaurants are open from noon to about 2 and from 7:30 or 8 to 10 or 10:30. Brasseries have longer hours and often serve all day and late into the evening; some are open 24 hours. The iconoclastic wine bars do as they want, frequently serving hot food only through lunch and cold assortments of charcuterie and cheese until a late-afternoon or early evening close. Assume a restaurant is open every day unless otherwise indicated. Surprisingly, many restaurants close on Saturday as well as Sunday. July and August are the most common months for annual closings, but Paris in August is no longer the total culinary wasteland it used to be.

Menus

All establishments must post their menus outside, so study them carefully before deciding to enter. Most restaurants have two basic types of menu: à la carte and fixed price (prix fixe, or *un menu*). The prix-fixe menu is usually the best value, though choices are more limited. Most menus begin with a first course (*une entrée*), often subdivided into cold and hot starters, followed by fish and poultry, then meat; it's rare today that anyone orders something from all three. However, outside brasseries, wine bars, and other simple places, it's inappropriate to order just one dish, as you'll understand when you see the waiter's expression. In recent years, the *menu dégustation* (tasting menu) has become popular; consisting of numerous small courses, it allows for a wide sampling of the chef's offerings. In general, consider the season when ordering; daily specials are usually based on what's freshest in the market that day.

See the Menu Guide in Chapter 8 for guidance with menu items that appear frequently on French menus and throughout the reviews that follow.

Prices

Although prices can be steep at luxury restaurants, we have made an effort to include a number of lower-priced establishments. By French law, prices must include tax and tip (*service compris* or *prix nets*), but pocket change left on the table in basic places, or an additional 5% in better restaurants, is always appreciated. Beware of bills stamped "Service Not Included" in English or restaurants slyly using American-style credit-card slips, hoping that you'll be confused and add the habitual 15% tip. In neither case should you tip beyond the guidelines suggested above.

CATEGORY	COST*
$$$$	over 250 frs/€38
$$$	150 frs–250 frs/€23–€38
$$	80 frs–150 frs/€12–€23
$	under 80 frs/€12

* *per person for a main course, including tax (19.6%); note that if a restaurant only offers prix-fixe (set price) meals, it has been given the price category that reflects the full prix-fixe price.*

Reservations

In the reviews below, we have only indicated where reservations are essential (and when booking weeks or months in advance is necessary) and where reservations are not accepted. Because restaurants are open for only a few hours for lunch and dinner, and because meals are long affairs here, we urge you to make reservations. To help you translate some of the needed phrases—"Hello/Good evening. I'd like to make a reservation for X people for today/tomorrow/day-of-week at X-time. The last name is . . . Thank you"—here are a few sentences to help out if needed: "*Bonjour (Bonsoir* after 6 PM). *Je voudrais faire une réservation pour X* (1, *un/une;* 2, *deux;* 4, *quatre;* 6, *six) personnes pour le dîner* (evening)/ *le déjeuner* (lunch) *aujourd'hui à X heures* (today at X o'clock)/*demain à X heures* (tomorrow at X o'clock)/*lundi* (Monday), *mardi* (Tuesday), *mercredi* (Wednesday), *jeudi* (Thursday), *vendredi* (Friday), *samedi* (Saturday), *dimanche* (Sunday) *à X heures. Le nom est* (your own name). *Merci bien.*" Note that most wine bars do not take reservations; reservations are also unnecessary for brasserie and café meals at odd hours.

Restaurant Types

What's the difference between a bistro and a brasserie? Can you order food at a café? Can you go to a restaurant just for a snack? The following definitions should help.

A **restaurant** traditionally serves a three-course meal (first, main, and dessert) at both lunch and dinner. Although this category includes the most formal, three-star establishments, it also applies to humble neighborhood spots. Don't expect to grab a quick snack. In general, restaurants are what you choose when you want a complete meal and when you have the time to linger over it. Wine is typical with restaurant meals. Hours are fairly consistent.

Many say that **bistros** served the world's first fast food. After the fall of Napoléon, the Russian soldiers who occupied Paris were known to bang on zinc-topped café bars, crying "*bistro*"—"quickly" in Russian. In the past, bistros were simple places with minimal decor and service. Although many nowadays are quite upscale, with beautiful interiors and chic clientele, most remain cozy establishments serving straightforward, frequently gutsy cooking; a wide variety of meats; and long-simmered dishes such as pot-au-feu and veal blanquette.

Brasseries—ideal places for quick, one-dish meals—originated when Alsatians fleeing German occupiers after the Franco-Prussian War came to Paris and opened restaurants serving specialties from home. Pork-based dishes, *choucroute* (sauerkraut), and beer (*brasserie* also means brewery) were—and still are—mainstays here. The typical brasserie is convivial and keeps late hours. Some are open 24 hours a day—a good thing to know, since many restaurants stop serving at 10:30 PM.

Like bistros and brasseries, **cafés** come in a confusing variety. Often informal neighborhood hangouts, cafés may also be veritable showplaces attracting chic, well-heeled crowds. At most cafés, regulars congregate at the bar, where coffee and drinks are cheaper than at tables. At lunch, tables are set and a limited menu is served. Sandwiches, usually with *jambon* (ham), *fromage* (cheese, often Gruyère or Camembert), or *mixte* (ham and cheese), are served throughout the day. Cafés are for lingering, for people-watching, and for daydreaming; they are listed separately below.

Wine bars, or *bistros à vins,* are a newer phenomenon. These informal places often serve very limited menus, perhaps no more than open-face sandwiches (*tartines*) and selections of cheeses and cold cuts (*charcuterie*). Owners concentrate on their wine lists, which often include less well-known, regional selections, many of them available by the glass. Like today's bistros and brasseries, some wine bars are very upscale indeed, with full menus and costly wine lists. Still, most remain friendly and unassuming places for sampling wines you might otherwise never try.

Smoking

You can count on it: Parisians smoke before, during, and after meals. Restaurants are supposed to have no-smoking sections—if you want to sit in one, make this very clear—though these areas are often limited to a very few tables and are generally not strictly enforced.

What to Wear

Casual dress is acceptable at all but the fanciest restaurants. Be aware that in Paris, however, casual usually means stylish sportswear, which is often more dressed up than you may be used to. When in doubt, leave the blue jeans and sneakers behind. Most of all, use your judgment.

In the reviews below, we have indicated where a jacket and/or tie are required.

Wine

The wine that suits your meal is the wine you like. The traditional rule of white with fish and red with meat no longer applies. If the restaurant has a sommelier, let him (yes, it's usually a man) help you. Most sommeliers are knowledgeable about their lists and will suggest what is appropriate after you've made your tastes and budget known. In addition to the wine list, informal restaurants will have a *vin maison* (house wine) that is less expensive. Simpler spots will have wines *en carafe* (in a carafe) or *en pichet* (in a pitcher). Except for wine bars and brasseries, most restaurants do not sell wine by the glass. If you'd like something before the meal, consider ordering your wine for the meal ahead of time, or sample a typical French *apéritif*, such as a *kir*, chilled white wine with black-currant liqueur.

Restaurants by Arrondissement

1er Arrondissement (Louvre/Les Halles)
See Right Bank Dining map.

FRENCH

$$$$ ✗ **Gérard Besson.** With decor a bit like that of your French maiden aunt's house (if you had one)—a collection of ceramic and metallic roosters in lit glass cases, pale pink fabrics, and carved wood paneling—this is an old-fashioned but intimate Parisian favorite. Chef Besson has mastered a superb classical repertoire, subtly enlivened by creative touches, such as his terrine of Bresse chicken with foie gras and oyster flan. In winter, his game menu is probably the best in town: try the perfectly executed *lièvre à la royale*, braised hare in a luscious truffled sauce. For dessert, sample the distinctive confit of fennel with vanilla ice cream. Other pluses include an excellent wine cellar and a good-value 280-franc/€43 lunch menu. ⊠ *5 rue du Coq-Héron*, ☎ *01–42–33–14–74. AE, DC, MC, V. Closed Sun. No lunch Sat. Jan.–Sept. Métro: Les Halles.*

$$$$ ✗ **Le Grand Véfour.** Victor Hugo could stride in and still recognize this
★   place—in his day, as now, a contender for the prize as the most beautiful restaurant in Paris. Originally built in 1784, set in the arcades of the Palais-Royal, it has welcomed everyone from Napoléon to Colette to Jean Cocteau—nearly every seat bears a plaque commemorating a famous patron, and you can request to be seated at your idol's table. The mirrored ceiling and Restauration-era glass paintings of goddesses and muses create a beguiling atmosphere of restrained seduction—it is all terribly romantic, but think more in terms of stroking your beloved's wrist than pouncing, since this place is also ever so well mannered. Foodies as well as fashionable folk gather here to enjoy chef Guy Martin's unique blend of sophistication and rusticity. He hails from Savoie, so you'll find lake fish and mountain cheeses on the menu alongside such luxurious dishes as foie gras–stuffed ravioli and truffled veal sweetbreads. For dessert, try the house specialty, *palet aux noisettes* (meringue cake with milk chocolate mousse, hazelnuts, and caramel ice cream)—or just drink in the glittering salons. If you can't spring for an extravagant feast, try the lunchtime prix-fixe for a mere 390 francs/ €60. ⊠ *17 rue Beaujolais*, ☎ *01–42–96–56–27. Reservations essential at least a week in advance. Jacket and tie. AE, DC, MC, V. Closed weekends and Aug. No dinner Fri. Métro: Palais-Royal.*

$$$ ✗ **Le Meurice.** A dining room custom-tailored for Proust's Princess de
★   Guermantes, this is one of the most opulently beautiful salons in Europe: a cake-frosted fantasy in dazzling white, complete with Louis-

Right Bank Dining

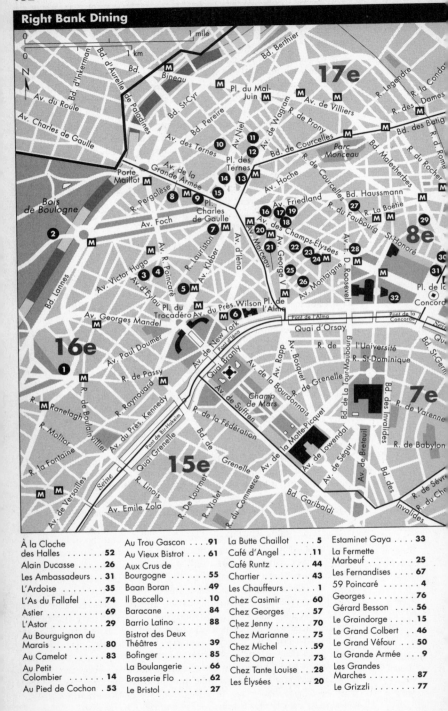

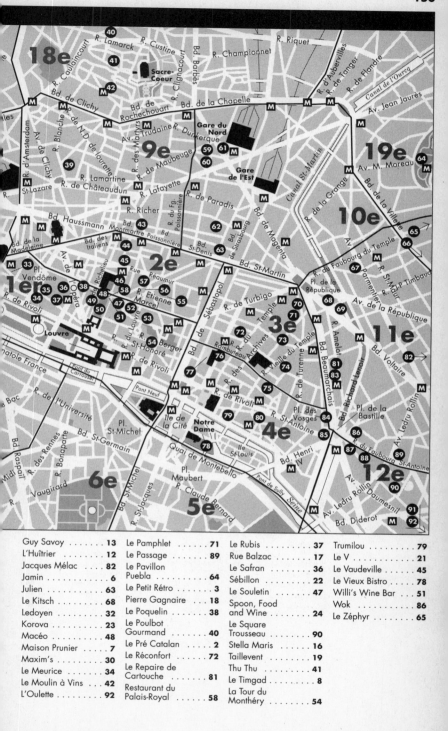

Left Bank Dining

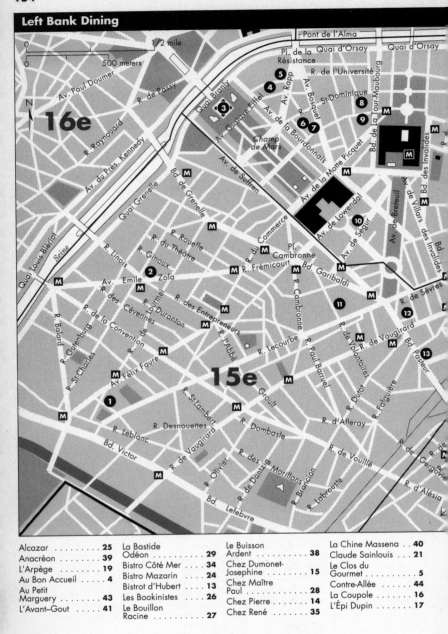

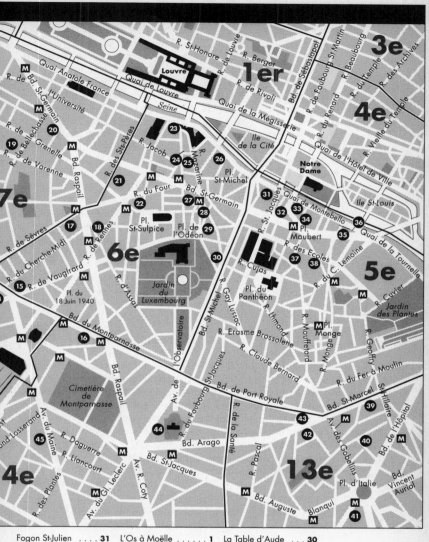

VXI-Impèratrice boseries, gilded corniced ceilings, Edwardian-era murals, glittering chandeliers, and hand-carved bergère armchairs. While this grande dame of a restaurant saw its luster dim over the decades, it has now been given a spectacular refurbishment thanks to its owner, the Sultan of Brunei. If the decor is blissfully old-fashioned the usually superlative menu is not—the kitchen here can be nouvelle, if not eccentric (turbot cooked in seaweed accompanied by a rhubarb fondue and peanut sauce). A full dinner here is an orgyization of richness—no matter that your liver may be screaming, you'll want to savor every bite of your dessert: roast figs in raspberry and fig pastry, drizzled with raspberry sauce and sorbet. To cap it all off, the wait staff here is Proustian in its refinement. ⊠ *Hôtel Meurice, 228 rue de Rivoli,* ☎ *01–44–58–10–10. Jacket and tie. AE, DC, MC, V. Métro: Tuileries.*

$$$ ✕ **Restaurant du Palais-Royal.** Tucked away in the northeast corner of the magnificent Palais-Royal garden, this pleasant bistro offers traditional cuisine with a few contemporary touches and—very prime real estate—a lovely terrace. Sole and scallops are beautifully prepared, but juicy steak with fat, symmetrically stacked *frites* is also a favorite of the expense-account lunchers who love this place. Finish up with an airy puff pastry-and-cream *mille-feuille* that changes with the seasons—mango or berries in summer, hazelnut in winter. Since this is a wonderful spot for a romantic tête-à-tête, be sure to book in advance, especially during the summer, when the terrace tables are hotly sought after. ⊠ *Jardins du Palais-Royal, 110 Galerie Valois,* ☎ *01–40–20–00–27. AE, MC, V. Closed Sun. No lunch Sat. Oct.–Apr. Métro: Palais-Royal.*

$$–$$$ ✕ **Macéo.** If you want to enjoy classic French food with a modern spin, ★   then Macéo delivers in have-your-*gateau*-and-eat-it-too fashion. Run by the owner of Willi's Wine Bar, the restaurant is bathed in natural light streaming in from both sides; a broad, curved staircase leads to a spacious upstairs room. Metallic leaves adorn the bar at the front, where you can sink into brightly colored armchairs, while bold contemporary lamps add an original touch to the otherwise classic dining room, painted brick red and cream. With its reasonably priced set menus (220 francs/€34 at lunch and 250 francs/€38 in the evening), this is an ideal spot for an elegant yet relaxed meal after a day at the Louvre and Palais-Royal gardens. The subtly modernized cooking reflects the decor and might include such dishes as foie gras with chutney, duck breast with spices and chicory, and almond cake on a bed of mango "marmalade." The wine list is extensive and user-friendly but on the pricey side. ⊠ *15 rue des Petits-Champs,* ☎ *01–42–97–53–85. MC, V. Closed Sun. No lunch Sat. Métro: Palais-Royal.*

$$ ✕ **L'Ardoise.** This minuscule storefront, painted white and decorated with enlargements of old sepia postcards of Paris, is the very model of the new contemporary bistros making waves in Paris. This one's claim to fame is chef Pierre Jay, who trained at La Tour d'Argent. His first-rate, prix-fixe three-course menu (180 francs/€28) features dishes that are often original, from starters like a flan of crab in creamy emulsion of parsley to entrées like fresh cod with grilled chips of chorizo, served on a tempting bed of mashed potatoes. Just as enticing are the desserts, such as a superb *feuillantine au citron*—sugar-glazed, cinnamon-sprinkled pastry leaves filled with lemon cream and lemon segments. If you don't feel up to a three-course extravaganza it's also possible to order à la carte at no extra cost. With friendly service and a small but well-chosen wine list (a pleasant Coteaux d'Aix at 125 francs/€19), the only drawback is that L'Ardoise is often crowded and noisy. ⊠ *28 rue du Mont Thabor,* ☎ *01–42–96–28–18. Reservations essential. MC, V. Closed Mon.–Tues. Métro: Concorde.*

$$ ✕ **Au Pied de Cochon.** Recently acquired by the Frères Blanc, who expanded the terrace, this 24-hour classic retains its trademark dishes of breaded pig's trotters with béarnaise and cheesy onion soup—the latter said to cancel out the effects of a boisterous night on the town. The decor is Busby Berkleyesque—wall sconces are adorned with giant bunches of frosted-glass grapes. Though tourists make up the bulk of the clientele, Au Pied de Cochon also attracts a frisky crowd of night owls—club kids, off-duty cops, couples coming up for air, earnest business travelers from the provinces avoiding a lonesome hotel room— and the terrace is a good spot for people-watching. ✉ *6 rue Coquillière,* ☎ *01–40–13–77–00. AE, DC, MC, V. Métro: Les Halles.*

$$ ✕ **Le Poquelin.** The theater-like scenery gives this welcoming little restaurant an atmosphere that's both elegant and relaxed. Owners Maggie and Michel Guillaumin proudly serve classic French cooking with a twist, such as duck breast topped with foie gras. The popular, regularly changing *menu Molière* is excellent value at 195 francs/€30, offering a choice of six starters, six mains, and six desserts. Wines are well chosen and fairly priced. ✉ *17 rue Molière,* ☎ *01–42–96–22–19. AE, DC, MC, V. Closed Sun. No lunch Sat. or Mon. Métro: Palais-Royal.*

$$ ✕ **Le Safran.** *La bone chère,* in the classic sense, means more than just good cooking: it is relaxation, good companionship, conversation, and enjoyment of what life has to offer. All of that is on tap at this bistro, masterminded by passionate chef Caroll Sinclair, who previously had several other popular restaurants in Paris. The little room is pretty, intimate, and painted in the sunny color that explains the name of the place. It makes a fine setting for a relaxed meal, since service is friendly and Sinclair's cooking has an appealing, homey touch. She works almost exclusively with organic produce, and her small menu changes according to what she finds in the market—creamy shellfish and spinach soup brightened by fresh coriander, red mullet stuffed with cèpe mushrooms, and *gigot de sept heures* (leg of lamb cooked for seven hours) are some signature dishes. Cool it all off with dessert such as black grapes with caramelized pineapple or a saffron crème brûlée. The wines on her short list come from Les Caves Taillevent, one of the best wine merchants in Paris. ✉ *29 rue d'Argenteuil,* ☎ *01–42–61–25–30. MC, V. Closed Sun. Métro: Tuileries, Pyramides.*

$$ ✕ **La Tour du Montlhéry.** When the centuries-old Les Halles marketplace became a soulless shopping mall, many neighborhood bistros closed or went upscale. The Montlhéry managed to hang on to the old-market feel, with its sagging wood-beam ceilings, red-check tablecloths, and exposed brick walls lined with imaginative portraits. If you don't mind passing under hanging samples of your future meal (sausages, etc.) on your way into the dining room, then you can enjoy the simple grilled food served by jovial waiters. Go for the *côte de boeuf* (prime rib) or grilled lamb and wash it down with a good Beaujolais. ✉ *5 rue des Prouvaires,* ☎ *01–42–36–21–82. Reservations essential. MC, V. Closed weekends and July 14–Aug. 15. Métro: Les Halles.*

$$ ✕ **Willi's Wine Bar.** Don't be fooled by the name—this English-owned spot is no modest watering hole but a stylish haunt for Parisian and foreign gourmets. The often original menu changes daily to reflect the market's offerings and might include chicken liver terrine, cod with pesto and eggplant, and crème brûlée or a bitter chocolate *terrine* (pudding). Owner Mark Williamson—who also runs the classy restaurant Macéo in the same area—has a passion for Rhône Valley wines, reflected in the extensive list, and for Spanish sherries. Service can be leisurely, so come with time on your hands. ✉ *13 rue des Petits-Champs,* ☎ *01– 42–61–05–09. MC, V. Closed Sun. Métro: Bourse.*

$–$$ ✕ **Aux Crus de Bourgogne.** This delightfully old-fashioned bistro, with its bright lights and red-check tablecloths, attracts a happy, lively crowd. Open since 1905, it has been run by the same family since 1932. They made it popular by serving two luxury items—foie gras and cold lobster with homemade mayonnaise—at surprisingly low prices, a tradition that happily continues. Among the bistro classics on the menu, which changes seasonally, you'll find soul-warming winter dishes such as *boeuf au gros sel* (beef boiled in bouillon with vegetables and garnished with rock salt) and *confit de canard* (duck confit). ✉ *3 rue Bachaumont,* ☎ *01–42–33–48–24. AE, MC, V. Closed weekends. Métro: Sentier.*

$ ✕ **À la Cloche des Halles.** Forgive the tacky decor and enjoy quiches, *oeufs au plat* (eggs baked in a flat pan) with ham and cheese, and assortments of high-quality cheeses and charcuterie at this small, popular, crowded wine bar. Served by the glass or bottle, wines include some good Beaujolais. Get here by 12:30 PM for lunch; the simple menu is served until 10 PM. ✉ *28 rue Coquillière,* ☎ *01–42–36–93–89. No credit cards. Closed Sun. No dinner Sat. Métro: Les Halles.*

$ ✕ **Le Rubis.** This humble neighborhood wine bar enjoys tremendous popularity with everyone from executives to construction workers who come at lunch for hearty plats du jour such as *petit salé* (slow-cooked salt pork) with lentils and *boudin noir* (blood sausage). Evening fare is less warming—canapés and other bite-size snacks. There's an eclectic selection of adequate wines by the glass or bottle, poured with a certain nonchalance. ✉ *10 rue du Marché St-Honoré,* ☎ *01–42–61–03–34. Reservations not accepted. No credit cards. Closed Sun. and mid-Aug. No dinner Sat. Métro: Tuileries.*

SEAFOOD

$$$ ✕ **Estaminet Gaya.** Come here for affordable seafood in all its guises, from marinated anchovies to Basque tuna to bouillabaisse. The colorful Portuguese tiles on the ground floor are delightful; the upstairs dining room, decorated with photos, seems plain in comparison. Given the often exorbitant prices at fish restaurants in Paris, the prix-fixe menu at 172 francs/€26 is excellent value. Other prices vary with the day's catch. ✉ *17 rue Duphot,* ☎ *01–42–60–43–03. AE, MC, V. Closed weekends. Métro: Madeleine.*

THAI

$–$$ ✕ **Baan Boran.** A recent addition to the genteel streets around the Palais-Royal, Baan Boran steers clear of Thai kitsch with its sunny yellow dining room and contemporary plastic chairs. The home-style cooking, concocted by two women from central and northern Thailand, is just as original. Instead of the Royal cuisine favored at most Thai restaurants in Paris, here you'll find such regional dishes as *gaeng mussaman,* beef in a rich, peanuty sauce scented with cinnamon and cardamom. Dishes with no added fat are listed separately: why not try the *yam som-o,* tangy chunks of pomelo in a creamy coconut sauce? ✉ *17 rue Duphot,* ☎ *01–40–15–90–45. AE, DC, MC, V. Closed Sun. Métro: Palais-Royal.*

2ᵉ Arrondissement (La Bourse)

See Right Bank Dining map.

FRENCH

$$–$$$ ✕ **Chez Georges.** When you ask sophisticated Parisians—think bankers, aristocrats, or antiques dealers—to name their favorite bistro, many would choose Georges. The traditional bistro fare is good—herring, sole, kidneys, steaks, and *frites* (fries)—and the atmosphere is better. A wood-paneled entry leads you to an elegant and unpretentious dining room where one long, white-clothed stretch of tables lines the mirrored walls and attentive waiters sweep efficiently along the entire length. ✉ *1 rue du Mail*, ☎ *01–42–60–07–11. AE, DC, MC, V. Closed Sun. and 3 weeks in Aug. Métro: Sentier.*

$$ ✕ **Café Runtz.** Next to the noted theater of Salle Favart, in a neighborhood once filled with theaters, this friendly bistro has been given an overhaul by star decorator Jacques Garcia. Old brass gas lamps on each table and rich *boiseries* (woodwork) create a cozy and Flaubertian atmosphere. Tasty, hearty Alsatian dishes include Gruyère salad, onion tart, choucroute, and fresh fruit tarts. Order a pitcher of Riesling or other Alsatian wine to go along. The two prix-fixe menus are a good value; one of them, the *"Salé-Sucré,"* includes quiche with green salad, a fruit tart, and a glass of wine or mineral water and is served all afternoon. ✉ *16 rue Favart*, ☎ *01–42–96–69–86. AE, MC, V. Closed Sun. and Aug. No lunch Sat. Métro: Richelieu-Drouot.*

$$ ✕ **Le Grand Colbert.** One of the few independently owned brasseries left in Paris, Le Grand Colbert feels grand, with its globe lamps and ceiling moldings, but not overpolished—old theater posters still line the walls. The high-ceilinged dining room attracts a wonderfully Parisian mix of elderly lone diners, business lunchers, tourists, and couples, who come for hearty nourishment in the form of steak with *frites*, robust stews, and well-prepared fish. It's best to stick to classics, though, as this is what the kitchen does best: finish with profiteroles or a fluffy chocolate mousse. To aid digestion, stroll through the gorgeous Galerie Vivienne next door, which houses tempting clothing and gift shops. ✉ *2–4 rue Vivienne*, ☎ *01–42–86–87–88. AE, DC, MC, V. Métro: Bourse.*

$$ ✕ **Le Vaudeville.** One of Jean-Paul Bucher's seven Parisian brasseries, Le Vaudeville is filled with well-dressed Parisians (many of them from the Stock Exchange across the street) and is a good value, thanks to its assortment of prix-fixe menus. Shellfish, house-smoked salmon, and desserts such as profiteroles are particularly good. Enjoy the handsome 1930s decor—almost the entire interior of this intimate dining room is done in real or faux marble—and lively dining until 2 AM daily. ✉ *29 rue Vivienne*, ☎ *01–40–20–04–62. AE, DC, MC, V. Métro: Bourse.*

$–$$ ✕ **Le Souletin.** Sandwiched between the fashion and financial districts on either side of place des Victoires, this polished bistro attracts a potentially intimidating crowd of designer suits, but the atmosphere is jovial and the food reassuringly rustic. Specializing in the gutsy cuisine of the Basque country, Le Souletin serves such regional dishes as *axua*—a veal, tomato, and pepper stew spiced with dried Espelette pepper—and smooth white bean soup with nibbles of panfried foie gras. Sorbets, often an afterthought, are exceptionally fruity here—proof that this restaurant doesn't neglect the details. ✉ *6 rue La Vrillière*, ☎ *01–42–61–43–78. MC, V. Closed Sun. and Aug. No lunch Sat. Métro: Bourse.*

3e Arrondissement (Beaubourg/Marais)
See Right Bank Dining map.

FRENCH

$$$ ✕ **Le Pamphlet.** Chef Alain Carrere's modern and very affordable take on the hearty cooking of the Basque country and Béarn region of southwestern France has made this Marais bistro popular with an artsy local crowd. Beyond the delicious, homey food, what many Parisians love is the provincial feel, with beamed ceiling, old-fashioned lamps, generously spaced tables, polite service, and faience that seems to have been borrowed from *grandmère*. The menu is market-fresh and runs from first courses like sea bream and salmon tartare with oyster sauce to a juicy pork chop with béarnaise and hand-cut *frites*. Finish up with a slice of sheep's cheese or the fine homemade desserts, such as banana cake with banana ice cream. ⊠ *38 rue Debelleyme,* ☎ *01–42–72–39–24. Reservations essential. MC, V. Closed Sun., first 2 wks of Jan., and Aug. 8–23. No lunch Sat. Métro: St-Sébastien–Froissart.*

\$\$–\$\$\$ ✕ **Chez Jenny.** Taken over by the Frères Blanc group in 1999, this classic two-story brasserie retains its infectious buzz and outstanding choucroute, delivered weekly by a private supplier in Alsace and served with a variety of charcuterie and a big grilled ham knuckle. To finish, the perfectly aged Muenster cheese and homemade blueberry tart are fine choices. Staff in regional dress add authentic Alsatian atmosphere. ⊠ *39 bd. du Temple,* ☎ *01–44–54–39–00. AE, DC, MC, V. Métro: République.*

\$\$ ✕ **Le Réconfort.** This bistro on the northern edge of the Marais scores big with the fashion crowd, giving the place a definite buzz. No matter, that male fashion buyer with the ponytail may be laughing too loud or that female editor may be cooing on her portable phone—you can still enjoy the traditional French food, which arrives with North African and Italian touches. A typical meal might start with a *compôte de légumes* (vegetable and chickpea cake with Moroccan spices) and continue with confit de canard with crispy potatoes. The brief wine list has several good buys, like the house Côtes du Rhône. ⊠ *37 rue Poitou,* ☎ *01–49–96–09–60. Reservations essential. MC, V. Closed Sun. Métro: St-Sébastien–Froissart.*

NORTH AFRICAN

\$\$ ✕ **Chez Omar.** Popular with a high-voltage fashion crowd—yes, that is Vivienne Westwood having dinner with Alexander McQueen—this is the place to come for couscous, whether you're a die-hard fan or have yet to taste this signature North African dish in all its glory. Order it with grilled skewered lamb, spicy *merguez* sausage, a lamb shank, or chicken—portions are generous—and wash it down with robust Algerian or Moroccan wine (98 francs/€15 a bottle). The restaurant, in a former 1910 bistro, is overseen by proprietor Omar Guerida, who speaks English and is famously friendly. Since he doesn't take reservations, arrive early or be prepared for a mouthwatering wait. ⊠ *47 rue de Bretagne,* ☎ *01–42–72–36–26. Reservations not accepted. No credit cards. No lunch Sun. Métro: Filles du Calvaire.*

4ᵉ Arrondissement (Marais/Ile St-Louis)

See Right Bank Dining map.

CONTEMPORARY

\$\$–\$\$\$ ✕ **Georges.** It's hard to keep track of all the Costes brothers' new brasseries, but the one to have made the biggest recent splash is Georges, on the top floor of the tubular Centre Pompidou. Starkly decorated in white and gray, with angular chairs and giant metallic shells, it sets off its graceful view of Paris, dominated by Notre-Dame just across the river. Staff are as sleek as the furniture, and at night the terrace has distinct snob appeal: come snappily dressed or suffer the consequences (you may be relegated to something resembling a dentist's waiting room). The menu features predictable Costes comfort food such as macaroni with morel mushrooms, steak tartare, and raw tuna with a sesame crust, but, sadly, the food is considerably less dazzling than the view—with the exception of desserts by star pâtissier Stéphane Secco, whose YSL (as in Yves St-Laurent, darling) bitter chocolate cake is an event. ⊠ *Centre Pompidou, 6th floor, rue Rambuteau,* ☎ *01–44–78–47–99. AE, DC, MC, V. Closed Tues. Métro: Rambuteau.*

FRENCH

\$\$–\$\$\$ ✕ **Bofinger.** One of the oldest, most beautiful, and most popular brasseries in Paris has generally improved since brasserie maestro Jean-

Paul Bucher took over. Settle in to one of the tables dressed in crisp white linen under the gorgeous Art Nouveau glass cupola, and enjoy classic brasserie fare, such as oysters, grilled sole, or lamb fillet. The house Muscadet is a good white wine, the Fleurie a pleasant red. Note that the no-smoking section here is not only patrolled but is also in the prettiest part of the restaurant. ⊠ *5–7 rue de la Bastille,* ☎ *01–42–72–87–82. AE, DC, MC, V. Métro: Bastille.*

$$ ✕ **Au Bourguignon du Marais.** The handsome, contemporary look of
★ this Marais bistro and wine bar is the perfect backdrop for the good traditional fare and excellent Burgundies served by the glass and bottle. Always on the menu are Burgundian classics such as *jambon persillé* (ham in parsleyed aspic jelly), escargots, and *oeufs en meurette* (eggs poached in a red wine sauce); another favorite is the steak, served grilled or chopped and nicely seasoned in a tartare. ⊠ *19 rue de Jouy,* ☎ *01–48–87–15–40. MC, V. Closed weekends and July 14–Aug. 10. Métro: St-Paul.*

$$ ✕ **Baracane.** Come to this small, plain place for the food, not the atmosphere, which is scant. The menu is robust, with specialties from the owner's native southwestern France—roast lamb with thyme, cassoulet, and madeleine cakes with stewed rhubarb are three delights. The reasonable dinner menu and the even cheaper lunch menu keep Baracane solidly affordable and one of the best values in the Marais. ⊠ *38 rue des Tournelles,* ☎ *01–42–71–43–33. MC, V. Closed Sun. No lunch Sat. Métro: Bastille.*

$$ ✕ **Le Grizzli.** It's said that this 19th-century bistro used to have danc-
★ ing bears out front—thus the name. A real charmer, this is one of the last of the unselfconsciously old-fashioned bistros left in Paris (right down to the creaky spiral staircase leading up to the rest room). The solicitous, soft-spoken owner gets many of his ingredients—especially the wonderful ham and cheeses—from his native Pyrénées. Several dishes are cooked on a hot slate, including the salmon and the lamb. There's an interesting selection of wines from southwestern France. ⊠ *7 rue St-Martin,* ☎ *01–48–87–77–56. AE, DC, MC, V. Closed Sun. No lunch Mon. or Sat. Métro: Châtelet.*

$$ ✕ **Trumilou.** Crowds of students, artist types, and others on a budget come here to eat bistro cuisine, such as leg of lamb and apple tarts. The nondecor is somehow homey, the staff is friendly, and the location facing the Seine and the Ile St-Louis is especially pleasant in nice weather, when you can sit on the narrow though noisy terrace under the trees. ⊠ *84 quai de l'Hôtel de Ville,* ☎ *01–42–77–63–98. MC, V. Métro: Pont Marie.*

$$ ✕ **Le Vieux Bistro.** Despite the obvious location next to Notre-Dame and the dull name, "The Old Bistro" still pulls a worldly crowd of Parisians, including the likes of Leslie Caron, for home-style Paris comfort food such as the sublime, slow-simmered boeuf bourguignon. After 35 years under the same owner, this restaurant recently changed hands, but the menu of bistro classics remains untouched: beef fillet with marrow, éclairs, and tart Tatin. Though the decor is nondescript, the frequently fancy crowd doesn't seem to notice. ⊠ *14 rue du Cloître-Notre-Dame,* ☎ *01–43–54–18–95. MC, V. Métro: Hôtel-de-Ville.*

MIDDLE EASTERN

$ ✕ **L'As du Fallafel.** The long line of hungry folks waiting for their falafel fix here reminds us that the chic Marais area is home to an array of kosher restaurants, delis, and Middle Eastern bakeries. Indeed, look no farther than the fantastic falafel stands on rue de Rosiers for some of the cheapest and tastiest meals in Paris, with the laurel crown usually awarded to this place. Lenny Kravitz paid homage to this standing-room-only restaurant-grocery-deli in a *Rolling Stone* interview; now, it pays homage to him—the wall is adorned with pictures of Lenny and his former girlfriend, the sexy French sugarpop singer Vanessa Paradis. A falafel costs around 30 francs/€4.58, but shell out some extra money for the deluxe with grilled eggplant, cabbage, hummus, tahini, and hot sauce. ⊠ *34 rue des Rosiers,* ☎ *01–48–87–63–60. No credit cards. Closed Sat. Métro: St-Paul.*

$ ✕ **Chez Marianne.** You'll know you've found Marianne's place when you see the line of people reading the bits of wisdom and poetry painted across her windows. The restaurant-deli serves excellent Middle Eastern specialties like hummus and *babaganoush* (eggplant dip) and couscous weekdays for 55 francs/€8. The sampler platter lets you try four, five, or six items. If you don't want to wait, make reservations, grab something to go from the deli, or get a fabulous 25-franc/€4 Israeli-style falafel (with beets and cabbage) from the window outside. ⊠ *2 rue des Hospitalières-St-Gervais,* ☎ *01–42–72–18–86. MC, V. Métro: St-Paul.*

5ᵉ Arrondissement (Latin Quarter)
See Left Bank Dining map.

CHINESE

$ ✕ **Mirama.** Regulars at this popular and rather chaotic Chinese restaurant order the soup, a rich broth with a nest of thick noodles garnished with dumplings, barbecued pork, or smoked duck. Main courses are generous—the best are made with shellfish; the Peking duck is also excellent. Service is brisk, so plan on coffee in a nearby café. For dining alone, it's quick and easy. ⊠ *17 rue St-Jacques,* ☎ *01–43–29–66–58. MC, V. Métro: St-Michel.*

FRENCH

$$$$ ✕ **La Tour d'Argent.** A meal at La Tour d'Argent has always been a giddy experience—now, under chef Jean Locussol, the food is once again as scintillating as the view across the Seine. Many of the restaurant's classic dishes are available on the excellent-value 350 franc/€54 lunchtime prix-fixe, including the famous pressed duck (*caneton*), prepared with great ceremony in the dining room. Each serving of duck comes with a numbered card—the restaurant started counting in 1919 and is approaching its millionth mallard. Start with the pike dumplings (*quenelles*), as fluffy as clouds. If the wine list—more of a Bible, really—seems too daunting, put your faith in one of the 15 sommeliers or go with the relatively affordable suggestions on the day's menu. The lunch crowd is remarkably relaxed and casually dressed, while evenings are a more formal affair, attracting a mix of suited tycoons and smoochy couples. ⊠ *15 quai de la Tournelle,* ☎ *01–43–54–23–31. Reservations essential. Jacket and tie at dinner. AE, DC, MC, V. Closed Mon. Métro: Cardinal Lemoine.*

$$–$$$ ✕ **Bistrot Côte Mer.** Run by celebrated chef Michel Rostang's daughter Caroline, this reasonably priced fish house has become a local hit for the professionalism of its staff, warm decor, and very delicious food. Best bets include a celery and apple remoulade with fresh scallops, shrimps cooked *à la plancha,* and grilled sea bass with black-olive polenta. Though it's not called "Sea Side" for nothing, this bistro does offer two daily meat specials such as saddle of lamb. End it all with crepes flamed in Grand Marnier—which gives the waiters a chance to ham it up a bit—or the first-rate cocoa soufflé. The dining room can get a bit noisy when full, so if you're out for a peaceful tête-à-tête, request a table on the terrace. ⊠ *16 bd. St-Germain,* ☎ *01–43–54–59–10. AE, MC, V. Métro: Maubert-Mutualité.*

$$–$$$ ✕ **Chez René.** Cozy and appealingly shabby, this reliable address at the eastern end of boulevard St-Germain has satisfied three generations of

Parisians, who count on finding dishes from Burgundy, such as boeuf bourguignon and coq au vin. As you sit on the red leatherette banquettes, be sure to enjoy some of the wines of the Mâconnais and Beaujolais available here. ⊠ *14 bd. St-Germain,* ☎ *01–43–54–30–23. MC, V. Closed Sun.–Mon., Aug., and late Dec.–early Jan. Métro: Cardinal Lemoine.*

$$ ✕ **Le Buisson Ardent.** Just across the street from the ugly Jussieu campus of the University of Paris, this cozy spot is a good example of how the modern bistro genre is thriving in Paris. The airy front room is a pleasant place for a meal with a solicitous proprietor, good waiters, and scrumptious food from chef Philippe Duclos, a student of Alain Senderens and Jacques Cagna. Note his style in such dishes as the rolled country ham filled with cucumber remoulade, the creamy tomato gratin of aubergine, or the pork chop with lentils garnished with foie gras. ⊠ *25 rue Jussieu,* ☎ *01–43–54–93–02. AE, MC, V. Closed Sun.–Mon. and Aug. Métro: Jussieu.*

$$ ✕ **Le Reminet.** Chandeliers and mirrors add an unexpected note of el-
★ egance at this relaxed and unusually good bistro, set in a narrow salon with stone walls. The menu changes regularly and displays the young chef's talent with dishes like a salad of scallops, greens, and sesame seeds, and roasted guinea hen with buttered Savoy cabbage. If it's available, try the luscious caramelized pears with cream. A prix-fixe dinner menu for 110 francs/€17 is served on Wednesday and Thursday only. ⊠ *3 rue des Grands-Degrés,* ☎ *01–44–07–04–24. MC, V. Closed Mon.–Tues., 2 wks in Aug., and 3 wks in Jan. Métro: Maubert-Mutualité.*

$–$$ ✕ **Les Pipos.** The tourist-trap restaurants along romantic rue de la Mon-
★ tagne Ste-Geneviève are enough to make you despair—and then you stumble across this corner bistro, bursting with chatter and laughter. Slang for students of the famous École Polytechnique nearby, Les Pipos is everything you could ask of a Latin Quarter bistro: the space is cramped, the food is substantial (the cheese comes from the Lyon market), and conversation flows as freely as the wine. ⊠ *2 rue de L'École Polytechnique,* ☎ *01–43–54–11–40. No credit cards. Closed Sun. Métro: Maubert-Mutualité.*

SPANISH

$$ ✕ **Fogon St-Julien.** On one of Paris's oldest streets, this intimate, sunny yellow restaurant serves outstanding Spanish food. Begin, of course, with some tasty tapas selections; then make a beeline for one of the six superb paellas, such as saffron with seafood, inky squid or Valencia-style with rabbit, chicken, snails, and vegetables. Finish up with the custardy crème Catalan, accompanied by a glass of Muscatel, or splurge on one of the excellent Riojas. ⊠ *10 rue St-Julien-le-Pauvre,* ☎ *01–43–54–31–33. Reservations essential. MC, V. No lunch weekdays. Métro: St-Michel.*

6e Arrondissement (St-Germain-des-Prés)
See Left Bank Dining map.

FRENCH

$$$ ✕ **La Bastide Odéon.** Just a few steps from the Luxembourg Gardens
★ you can find this little corner of Provence in Paris—a bright and cheerful restaurant with old oak tables and chairs, and a fine, loving hand with Mediterranean cuisine in the kitchen. Chef Gilles Ajuelos cooks good fish dishes; wonderful pastas, such as tagliatelle in *pistou* (basil and pine nuts) with wild mushrooms; and heartwarming main courses, like roast suckling pig and cod with capers. ⊠ *7 rue Corneille,* ☎ *01–43–26–03–65. AE, MC, V. Closed Sun.–Mon., 1st week in Jan., 1 wk in Apr., and 3 wks in Aug. Métro: Odéon; RER: Luxembourg.*

$$$ ✕ **L'Épi Dupin.** Half-timber walls, sisal carpeting, and crisp white table linens are the backdrop for this pocket-size bistro, which draws a loyal business crowd at noon, a mix of Gaultier-clad locals and food-loving tourists at night. The menu of delicious, updated French classics is revised regularly and might include an upside-down tart of caramelized Belgian endive and goat's cheese, curried saddle of rabbit with sweet potato chutney, and crisp, pyramid-shape pastry filled with apples and candied fennel for dessert. Service is efficient if occasionally brusque: the cramped quarters, with no space for customers to wait, make the waiters' job a challenge. The menu is prix-fixe only. ⊠ *11 rue Dupin,* ☎ *01–42–22–64–56. Reservations essential. AE, MC, V. Closed weekends. No lunch Mon. Métro: Sèvres-Babylone.*

$$$ ✕ **Hélène Darroze.** Hélène Darroze has been crowned the newest fe-
★ male culinary star in Paris, thanks to the creative flair she has given the tried-and-true classics of southwestern French cooking, from the lands around Albi and Toulouse. You know it's not going to be *la même chanson,* or the same old thing, from the moment you see the resolutely contemporary Tse & Tse tableware and red-and-purple color scheme. The intriguingly modern kitchen offers a sublime duck foie-gras confit served with chutney of exotic fruits, a scallop and squid salad jeweled with tiny stuffed clams and piquillo peppers, and a blowout of roast wild duck stuffed with foie gras and truffles. Few can resist the *île flottante* meringue in a rose water–flavored sauce anglaise. After a fine southwestern wine such as Madiran, Cahors, or Gaillac, enjoy your coffee with madeleines and three types of homemade jam. Detracting from the quality of the food, though, are the high prices, dainty servings, and often unprofessional service. Recently made over, the downstairs bistro offers the same dishes as the restaurant upstairs in even smaller, tapas-style portions, but you can still expect to pay 400–600 francs/€62–92 per person with wine. ⊠ *4 rue d'Assas,* ☎ *01–42–22–00–11. AE, DC, MC, V. Closed Sun. No lunch Sat. Métro: Sèvres-Babylone.*

$$–$$$ ✕ **Alcazar.** Englishman Sir Terence Conran conquered his hometown
★ by creating enormous scene-arena restaurants such as Bluebird in London. Now, he's headed over the Channel to transform this former legendary cabaret into one of the most chic spots in Paris. To take in the scene—and quite a scene it is, as this place seats 300 under a skylight roof, with a dramatic hanging vase—opt for a table on the mezzanine, where a long, brushed-steel bar gives you a bird's-eye view. Recently revamped to satisfy cool Parisians' evolving tastes, the menu now features "so British" fish-and-chips and such contemporary dishes as scallops with caramelized Belgian endives. Chef Guillaume Lutard trained at Taillevent and Prunier, which shows in the quality of the predictably pricey food. Roasted pears in caramel are a divinely sweet send-off. For 115 francs/€18 you can snack on a main dish with a glass of wine at the funky bar. ⊠ *62 rue Mazarine,* ☎ *01–53–10–19–99. AE, DC, MC, V. Métro: Odéon.*

$$–$$$ ✕ **Chez Dumonet-Josephine.** Stylish and convivial, this venerable bistro with amber walls, moleskin banquettes, and frosted glass lamps is popular with theater people and politicians. Generous portions of classic French cuisine are served; typical are the very good boeuf bour-guignon and the roasted saddle of lamb with artichokes. The wine list is excellent but expensive. ⊠ *117 rue du Cherche-Midi,* ☎ *01–45–48–52–40. AE, MC, V. Closed weekends and Aug. Métro: Duroc.*

$$–$$$ ✕ **Claude Sainlouis.** This cheerful spot has served the same dependable food for a very long time: steak with *frites,* lamb knuckle, pork with lentils, salad. There's not much variety, but all those in the know—professionals, tourists, lovers—crowd boisterously into the discreetly lit red dining room. This bistro recently changed owners after 41 years, but new *patron* Denis Wagner, who was on staff for 25 years, has made only the subtlest of changes. ⊠ *27 rue du Dragon,* ☎ *01–45–48–29–68. MC, V. Closed Sun.–Mon. and Aug. Métro: St-Germain-des-Prés.*

$$–$$$ ✕ **Le Montagnard.** This rustic little spot—"The Mountaineer"—has a hip, festive crowd that comes to dine on fondue and *raclette* (cheese melted on potatoes) before hitting the many local bars. Split an *assiette montagnard,* an appetizing assortment of Savoyard cold cuts such as *viande de Grisons* (air-dried beef), and then go for the cheese or beef fondue. End your meal with runny vacherin cheese, available only in winter, or a regional dessert such as blueberry tart. And bear in mind a little tip from the mountains: fresh black pepper makes a cheese meal much more digestible. ⊠ *24 rue des Canettes,* ☎ *01–43–26–47–15. AE, MC, V. Métro: Mabillon.*

$$ ✕ **Les Bookinistes.** Run by inventive chef William Ledeuil, this is the most popular of Guy Savoy's "baby bistros." You can expect to hear more English than French in the cheery dining room, looking out on to the Seine, but the food—such as mussel and pumpkin soup or baby chicken roasted in a casserole with root vegetables—is as authentic as you could hope for. Only the vegetarian option disappoint: unimaginative steamed vegetables drizzled with olive oil. The rather expensive wine list contrasts with the reasonable food prices. Service is friendly but erratic and occasionally overfamiliar. ⊠ *53 quai des Grands-Augustins,* ☎ *01–43–25–45–94. AE, DC, MC, V. Closed Sun. No lunch Sat. Métro: St-Michel.*

$$ ✕ **Le Bouillon Racine.** Originally a *bouillon*—a Parisian soup kitchen popular at the turn of the 20th century—this two-story restaurant is now a lushly renovated Belle Epoque oasis featuring a sophisticated Belgian menu. The leek terrine and the ham mousse are fine starters; *waterzooi* (Belgian stewed chicken and vegetables) and roast cod with white beans are excellent main dishes. For a finale, opt for the mocha-beer mousse with malt sauce. In honor of Belgium's some 400 different brews, the beer selection is vast: 6 on tap and about 50 by the bottle. ⊠ *3 rue Racine,* ☎ *01–44–32–15–60. Reservations essential. AE, MC, V. Métro: Odéon.*

$$ ✕ **Chez Maître Paul.** Just a few steps from the Odéon, this calm, comfortable little restaurant is a great place to discover the little-known cooking of the Jura and Franche-Comté regions of eastern France. Though sturdy, this cuisine appeals to modern palates, too, as you'll discover with the *montbéliard,* a smoked sausage served with potato salad ample enough for two. Also try one of the succulent free-range chicken dishes, either in a sauce of *vin jaune*—a dry wine from the region that resembles sherry—or baked in cream and cheese. The walnut meringue is wonderfully sinful, and the regional Arbois wines are not the usual selection. ⊠ *12 rue Monsieur-le-Prince,* ☎ *01–43–54–74–59. AE, DC, MC, V. Closed weekends July–Aug. Metro: Odéon.*

$$ ✕ **La Table d'Aude.** Rive Gauche students, senators, and book editors who dine here are on to a good thing, since this jolly restaurant serves some of the best *cuisine régionale* in Paris. Owner Bernard Patou and his wife, Véronique, take a contagious pleasure in serving up the best of their home turf—the Aude, that long, narrow region in Languedoc-Roussillon that includes Carcassonne and Castelnaudry, which is famed for its cassoulet and some of the most rapidly ascending vineyards in France. Almost everyone orders the cassoulet, bubbling hot in a small, high-sided ceramic dish and filled to the brim with white beans, sausage, and preserved duck. Of the house wines, go with the rich, cherry-color Corbières. Good-value prix-fixe menus are also available for 160 francs/€24 and 190 francs/€29. ⊠ *8 rue de Vaugirard,* ☎ *01–43–26–36–36. MC, V. Closed Sun. No lunch Sat., no dinner Mon. Métro: Odéon.*

$–$$ ✕ **Bistro Mazarin.** Leave the tourists on boulevard St-Germain and join local gallery owners and students at this casual bistro for bags of atmosphere and sturdy, satisfying food made to order with fresh ingredients. Lentil salad, steak with Roquefort sauce or one of two daily fish specials, and a pitcher of the house wine make for a decent meal. In good weather, the terrace offers great people-watching potential. ✉ *42 rue Mazarine,* ☎ *01–43–29–99–01. AE, MC, V. Métro: Mabillon.*

7ᵉ Arrondissement (Invalides)
See Left Bank Dining map.

FRENCH

$$$$ ✕ **L'Arpège.** Alain Passard, one of the most respected chefs in Paris, shocked the French culinary world in late 2000 by eliminating most meat and fish from his menu at L'Arpège in reaction to a series of food scares, the scariest of which is "mad cow" disease (though this is still quite rare in France). He now offers lobster and sea bass when he is sure of the source, and very occasionally meat; otherwise, he relies on vegetables supplied by his own producer. This might sound radical for a French chef—and it is—but if anyone can pull it off it should be Passard: his trademark dish, after all, is the "twelve-flavor" tomato stuffed with fruits and spices. It only remains to be seen whether Parisians will be willing to forgo their meat fix at a luxury restaurant. ✉ *84 rue de Varenne,* ☎ *01–45–51–47–33. AE, DC, MC, V. Closed weekends and Aug. Métro: Varenne.*

$$$$ ✕ **Jules Verne.** Top-ranked chef Alain Reix's cuisine—not to mention a location at 400 ft up, on the second level of the Eiffel Tower—makes a table at the Jules Verne one of the hardest dinner reservations to get in Paris. Sautéed baby squid with duck foie gras and veal filet mignon cooked with preserved lemon and dried fruits are examples of Reix's cooking, which, like the restaurant's private elevator, has its ups and downs. Come for lunch—a table is easier to snag—arrive early for a prime seat near the window, and be prepared for the distinctive all-black decor, a rather strange and tired hybrid of *Star Trek* and '70s disco. Though service has been variable in the past, on our last visit the waiters showed exceptional good humor and patience. ✉ *Eiffel Tower,* ☎ *01–45–55–61–44. Reservations essential. Jacket and tie. AE, DC, MC, V. Métro: Bir-Hakeim.*

$$$–$$$$ ✕ **Le Violon d'Ingres.** Christian Constant, former head of the Hôtel Crillon's kitchens and mentor to many a successful bistro chef, runs his own dressed-up bistro in one of the quieter but elegant parts of the city. A suit-clad crowd comes to sample the regularly revised menu, which may include such dishes as cream of pumpkin soup with sheep's cheese, risotto with boned chicken wings, and guinea hen on a bed of diced turnips. ✉ *135 rue St-Dominique,* ☎ *01–45–55–15–05. Reservations essential. AE, DC, MC, V. Closed Sun. Métro: École Militaire.*

$$$ ✕ **Le Clos du Gourmet.** Talented chef Arnaud Pitrois and his charming wife, Christel, preside over a big hit at this bistro, set in a quiet part of town but usually packed with local couples who like the set-price menu and the pretty butter-yellow and robin's-egg-blue Regence dining room. Pitrois trained with Guy Savoy among other chefs but has developed a wonderfully deft style of his own, seen in such delicacies as risotto with deboned chicken wings and tiny mousseron mushrooms and asparagus, fresh cod with aioli (garlic mayonnaise), and a sea bream with fennel. Choose the perfectly ripened Brie de Meaux, or a delicious and imaginative dessert like the preserved fennel with lemon sorbet and fresh basil. If you're lucky in the summer, you'll land a table on the small, pleasant terrace. The menu is prix-fixe only. ✉ *16 av. Rapp,* ☎ *01–45–51–75–61. AE, MC, V. Closed Sun.–Mon. and Aug. Métro: Alma-Marceau.*

$$$ ✕ **Lapérouse.** Feeling like a place where Voltaire might have dined, this historic warren of intimate salons in a 17th-century Seine-side town house is still struggling to establish its identity after too many changes of owners and chefs. The latest chef at the helm is Alain Hacquard, whose intriguing menu features such dishes as foie gras terrine with Spanish paprika, roasted Dublin Bay prawns with avocado cream, and the timeless Lapérouse classic, bitter chocolate soufflé. Dinner is an investment at 600 to 700 francs/€92 to 108 a head (for 690 francs/€106 each, you will be served a set menu in a salon for two), but it would be hard to go wrong with the lunch menu at 195 francs/€30. Food aside, this remains one of the most romantic spots in Paris, from the seductive bar to the private dining rooms, where the delights have not always been only of the culinary kind. ⊠ *51 quai des Grands Augustins,* ☎ *01–43–26–68–04. Reservations essential. AE, DC, MC, V. Closed Sun. No lunch Sat. Métro: St-Michel.*

$$$ ✕ **Le Petit Troquet.** In the shadow of the Eiffel Tower is this tiny, pleasant bistro filled with homey antiques like old tin signs for clocks and soda siphons. The prix-fixe-only menu changes daily but may include such dishes as goat's cheese mousse with smoked salmon, roast chicken, and fruit crumble for dessert. It's popular with locals, so book ahead. ⊠ *28 rue de l'Exposition,* ☎ *01–47–05–80–39. MC, V. Reservations essential. Closed Sun.–Mon. Métro: École Militaire.*

$$–$$$ ✕ **Au Bon Accueil.** To see what well-heeled Parisians like to eat these
★ days, book a table at this extremely popular bistro as soon as you get to town. The excellent, reasonably priced *cuisine du marché* (daily menu based on what's in the markets) has made it a hit: typical of the winter fare is roast suckling pig with thyme and endives. Desserts are homemade and delicious, from the fruit tarts to the superb *pistache,* a pastry curl filled with homemade pistachio ice cream. ⊠ *14 rue de Montessuy,* ☎ *01–47–05–46–11. Reservations essential. MC, V. Closed weekends. Métro, RER: Pont de l'Alma.*

$$ ✕ **L'Oeillade.** The food—such as shrimp tempura, and calves' liver in a raspberry vinegar sauce—is generally very good and the prices are unbeatable. Watch out for the wines, however—they will intoxicate your bill. The blond-wood paneling and interesting 20th-century paintings are unpretentious—the same cannot always be said about the clientele or the owner. ⊠ *10 rue de St-Simon,* ☎ *01–42–22–01–60. MC, V. Closed Sun. Métro: Rue du Bac.*

$$ ✕ **Les Olivades.** Excellent Provençal cuisine by Florence Mikula—one of the up-and-coming female chefs in Paris and a native of Avignon—is served by a cheerful staff in this brightly decorated former storefront café. Winners include the ravioli stuffed with goat's cheese, scallops with vegetables, and, of course, the melting chocolate cake with lavender ice cream. The three-course dinner and two-course lunch menus are a good value. ⊠ *41 av. Ségur,* ☎ *01–47–83–70–09. Reservations essential. MC, V. Closed Sun. and 2 wks in Aug. No lunch Mon. or Sat. Métro: Ségur, École Militaire.*

$$ ✕ **Thoumieux.** Delightfully Parisian, this place charms with red velour banquettes, yellow walls, and bustling waiters in white aprons. Budget prices for rillettes, duck confit, and cassoulet make Thoumieux—owned by the same family for three generations—popular. Don't come with gourmet expectations but for a solid, gently priced meal. ⊠ *79 rue St-Dominique,* ☎ *01–47–05–49–75. AE, MC, V. Métro: Invalides.*

SEAFOOD

$$$–$$$$ ✕ **Paul Minchelli.** Minchelli is a minimalist who believes that seasonings should not distract from the taste of his impeccably fresh—and very expensive—catch of the day. The baby clams with garlic and fiery Espelette peppers as well as the sea bass drizzled with lemon and olive

oil are just two of his wonderful dishes. The dressy dining room with gentle lighting and witty trompe l'oeil "views" out of "portholes" is the backdrop for a very stylish crowd, often sprinkled with celebrities like Catherine Deneuve. ⊠ *54 bd. de La Tour-Maubourg,* ☎ *01–47–05–89–86. MC, V. Closed Sun.–Mon. Métro: École Militaire.*

8e Arrondissement (Champs-Élysées)
See Right Bank Dining map.

CONTEMPORARY

$$–$$$ ✕ **Korova.** Named after the Milk Bar in the film *Clockwork Orange* (*korova* is Russian for "cow"), this funky new "diner" is about as cool as it gets in Paris these days. (And just how cool is that? You be the judge.) Four curvy rooms are done up in white, pearl gray, and watery green: groovy music and soft lighting complete the space-age picture. Run by personalities Jean-Claude Delarue (a television presenter) and Hubert Boukobza (who is behind many of the city's most happening nightclubs), Korova has a jet-set menu that hops from hot dogs (with lobster and mayonnaise) to chicken (with Coca-Cola sauce) to vintage canned sardines. Desserts are by none other than master *pâtissier* Pierre Hermé. A meal will set you back at least 300 francs/€46 a head, but you could always drop in from 8 AM for breakfast or after 11 PM for a drink in the lounge to watch the city's fashion victims in action. ⊠ *33 rue Marbeuf,* ☎ *01–53–89–93–93. AE, DC, MC, V. No lunch May 1. Métro: Franklin-D.-Roosevelt.*

$$–$$$ ✕ **Spoon, Food and Wine.** Star chef Alain Ducasse's bistro for the 21st century has been packed ever since it opened in late 1998. What draws the trendy crowd is the playful, Asian- and American-inspired menu; the *Wallpaper*-y decor (at night, the large white linen shades on the walls are rolled up to reveal plum upholstery); and the fact that it's so hard to get a reservation. The idea here was to democratize and internationalize the Paris dining scene by introducing a do-it-yourself fusion-food menu, meaning that here you can mix and match dishes that are diversely American, Asian, and Italian in origin. Try the Thai soup, the pasta with three-tomato marmalade, and the pan-seared tuna with satay sauce and wok-sautéed vegetables. Parisians can't get over the fact that 90% of the wines are foreign and more than half are American. Sign of the future? There are many salads and vegetable and grain dishes on the menu, helping to make this a headliner for high-style vegetarians everywhere. Reservations are as coveted as Sharon Stone's Burberry shoes—call a month ahead—but you can drop in for a snack at the bar. Come late for the models and movie stars. ⊠ *14 rue de Marignan,* ☎ *01–40–76–34–44. Reservations essential. AE, MC, V. Métro: Franklin-D.-Roosevelt.*

FRENCH

$$$$ ✕ **Alain Ducasse.** Megastar chef Alain Ducasse recently took over the
★   restaurant of the Hotel Plaza-Athénée (beloved of Yankee glitterati). You may need to set a steel trap outside his door actually to catch him in this kitchen—Ducasse now has restaurants around the globe (and never cooks on weekends)—but it would probably be worth the wait. The rosy rococo salons have been updated by decorator Patrick Jouin, who draped metallic organza over the chandeliers and, in a symbolic move, made time stand still by stopping the clock. Overlooking the prettiest courtyard in Paris, this makes for a setting as delicious as Ducasse's roast lamb garnished with "crumbs" of dried fruit or duckling roasted with fig leaves. The most daring dish on the menu, lobster with curried risotto (for a stratospheric 558 francs/€85), has been criticized for tasting, well, like a curry. Still, when you sample the *bisque de homard* (lobster bisque) or the pork belly, you know you are getting the real

thing—each is made from as many elements (shell, skin, juice, pan drippings) as possible and offers the absolute essence of the ingredients. At these prices, the presentation *sur la table*—there are few sauce "paintings," orchid blossoms, or other visual adornments to garnish Ducasse's creations—could be enhanced. Service is slick but overly stiff. Incidentally, Ducasse has now transformed his old haunt, set in a suite of Belle Epoque salons, into a new luxe bistro, 59 Poincaré. ⊠ *Hotel Plaza-Athénée, 27 av. Montaigne,* ☎ *01-53-67-66-65. Reservations essential weeks in advance. AE, DC, MC, V. Closed weekends. No lunch Mon.–Wed. Métro: Alma-Marceau.*

$$$$ ✕ **Les Élysées.** Chef Alain Solivères is a passionate cook whose repu-
★ tation continues to grow in Paris gourmet circles. Come here when you want to treat yourself, since not only is the food exquisite, but service is also impeccable and the intimate dining room, under a beautiful turn-of-the-20th-century *verrière* (glass ceiling), is the kind of place where you want to linger. Solivères's menu changes seasonally and draws inspiration from southern France—the Basque country, Bordeaux, and Languedoc. Dishes include a risotto of wheat grains cooked in squid's ink, and a roasted duck liver served with baby artichokes and arugula. There's also superb wine service from a rosy-cheeked young man who was formerly the personal sommelier of President Jacques Chirac. ⊠ *Hôtel Vernet, 25 rue Vernet,* ☎ *01-44-31-98-98. AE, DC, MC, V. Reservations essential. Closed weekends and Aug. Métro: George V.*

$$$$ ✕ **Ledoyen.** This elegant restaurant tucked away in the quiet gardens flanking the Champs-Élysées is a study in the grandiose style of Napoléon III, as revisited a few years ago by decorator Jacques Grange, with gilded ceilings and walls, plush armchairs, and tables with candelabra (head for the historic rooms upstairs; avoid downstairs). Unfortunately, this aging beauty needs a face-lift, at least from the looks of the upholstery and even some rather lackluster dishes served up by the kitchen. Still, whether you want to eat light or hearty, young chef Christian Le Squer's elegant, beautifully realized menu is usually a treat. He uses superb produce, as seen in *les coquillages* (shellfish), a delicious dish of risotto made bright green by herbs and topped with lobster, langoustine, scallops, and grilled ham. The turbot with truffled mashed potatoes is excellent, too, and don't skip the first-rate cheese trolley. Ledoyen is near place de la Concorde. ⊠ *1 av. Dutuit, on the Carré des Champs-Élysées,* ☎ *01-53-05-10-01. Reservations essential. AE, DC, MC, V. Closed weekends. Métro: Place de la Concorde, Champs-Élysées–Clemenceau.*

$$$$ ✕ **Maxim's.** Count Danilo sang "I'm going to Maxim's" in Lehar's *The Merry Widow,* Leslie Caron was kleig-lit here by Cecil Beaton for *Gigi,* and Audrey Hepburn adorned one of its banquettes with Peter O'Toole in *How to Steal a Million:* no wonder it's long been the dream of every millionaire (and nearly everyone else) to spend at least one evening dancing and dining *chez Maxim's.* The reality is that a meal at Maxim's might not have the glamour it once did—the restaurant had its heyday 100 years ago during the wicked, joyous days of La Belle Epoque, when *le tout Paris* swarmed here for hedonistic pleasures—but this exuberant Art Nouveau sanctuary still offers a taste of the good life under its breathtaking painted ceiling. Opened in 1893 by Maxime Gaillard—who anglicized his name to make it sound more chic—this former ice cream shop soon began to attract the *crème de la crème* of Paris society. Designer Pierre Cardin has owned Maxim's since 1981 and, while he could be accused of over-commercializing the name (there are Maxim's around the world, and even in Charles de Gaulle airport), at least he has not toyed with the original, other than countless changes of chef. Current chef Bruno Stril has breathed new life into the formerly tired food with such dishes as poached eggs with truffle

and ravioli with clams, but for traditionalists the Edward VII lamb fillet and sole with vermouth are still on the menu. And, when the orchestra plays every night, you can't help but feel that life is indeed rosy. ⊠ *3 rue Royale,* ☎ *01–42–65–30–26. Reservations essential. AE, DC, MC, V. Closed Sun. Métro: Concorde.*

$$$$ ✕ **Pierre Gagnaire.** Legendary chef Pierre Gagnaire's cooking is at once
★ intellectual and poetic—in a single dish at least three or four often unexpected tastes and textures are brought together in a sensational experience. Two intriguing dishes from a recent menu—it changes seasonally—included roast Asian-spiced duck served with a grapefruit and mango crumble, and a sauté of rabbit and squid. The *"Grand Dessert,"* a seven-dessert marathon, is not to be missed—Gagnaire's soufflés may be showmanlike but they can hardly compete. The businesslike gray-and-wood dining room feels refreshingly informal, but uneven service and a scanty wine list are unfortunate drawbacks at this price. ⊠ *6 rue de Balzac,* ☎ *01–44–35–18–25. Reservations essential. AE, DC, MC, V. Closed Sat. and mid-July–mid-Aug. No lunch Sun. Métro: Charles-de-Gaulle–Étoile.*

$$$$ ✕ **Le V.** The massive flower arrangement at the entrance proclaims the no-holds-barred luxury that is on offer here. Painted powder blue, with stuccoed medallions worked into the ceiling trim, this beautiful (though staid) room overlooks the freshly renovated hotel's atrium and makes a fitting stage set for chef Philippe Legendre. Formerly at Taillevent, he is clearly thriving in his new kitchens, where he has apparently been given carte blanche with caviar, lobster, and foie gras. ⊠ *Hotel Four Seasons George V, 31 av. George V,* ☎ *01–49–52–70–00. Reservations essential. Jacket and tie. AE, DC, MC, V. Métro: George V.*

$$$–$$$$ ✕ **Les Ambassadeurs.** Looking as if Madame de Pompadour might stroll
★ in the door at any moment, Les Ambassadeurs offers a setting of ancien régime splendor. With its dramatic floor of black-and-white diamonds and honey-color marble walls, the place is polished and furnished to such a degree it would make Louis XV (who had it built in 1758) proud. Originally the formal foyer of the opulent Hôtel Crillon, once a grand private residence, the space was meant to be overpowering and hardly a restaurant—but it's now one of the best in Paris, thanks to chef Dominique Bouchet. He likes to mix luxe with more down-to-earth flavors: potato pancakes topped with smoked salmon, caviar-flecked scallops wrapped in bacon with tomato and basil, duck with rutabaga, turbot with cauliflower. It's also difficult to fault the view of place de la Concorde, the distinguished service, or the memorable wine list. Lunch is more affordable, though still expensive; there is even a breakfast—talk about luxury—served from 7 to 10:30 AM. ⊠ *10 pl. de la Concorde,* ☎ *01–44–71–16–16. Reservations essential. Jacket and tie at dinner. AE, DC, MC, V. Métro: Concorde.*

$$$–$$$$ ✕ **Le Bristol.** After a rapid ascent at his own place that led to his
★ renown as one of the more inventive young chefs in Paris, Eric Frechon has become head chef at the Bristol. By choosing him, this elegant hotel made a savvy choice that underlines the Bristol's importance as a showcase in the world of Paris haute cuisine. Frechon uses one of the grandest pantries in Paris to create masterworks—ravioli of foie gras in mushroom cream with truffles, or scallops on a bed of diced celery root in truffle juice. Courtly service and two beautiful dining rooms—an oval oak-paneled one for fall and winter and a marble-floored pavilion overlooking the courtyard garden for spring and summer—make this a top destination for a memorable meal. ⊠ *Hotel Bristol, 112 rue du Faubourg-St-Honoré,* ☎ *01–53–43–43–00. Reservations essential. Jacket and tie. AE, DC, MC, V. Métro: Miromesnil.*

$$$–$$$$ ✕ **Stella Maris.** A pretty Art Deco front window is the calling card for this spot near the Arc de Triomphe. An expense-account crowd mixes with serious French gourmets to dine on the very subtle cuisine of Japanese chef Taderu Yoshino, who trained with Joël Robuchon and rewrites his menu four times a year. You'll find nuances of Japan in delicious dishes—made with organic ingredients—such as eel *blanquette* (stew) with grilled cucumber, and rice pudding with white truffle. ⊠ *4 rue Arsène-Houssaye,* ☎ *01–42–89–16–22. Reservations essential. AE, DC, MC, V. Closed Sun. No lunch Sat. or Mon. Métro: Étoile.*

$$$–$$$$ ✕ **Taillevent.** Perhaps the most traditional—for many diners this is only
★ high praise—of all Paris luxury restaurants, this grande dame was recently the object of a certain uncharacteristic buzz, since the arrival of chef Michel Del Burgo. Del Burgo formerly cooked at Le Bristol, where he won a reputation for food that is at once earthy yet refined. Now he has judiciously revised the traditional (nay, conservative) menu here, adding creations that sometimes eerily resemble dishes served in modern bistros. Classics like the *boudin de homard*—an airy sausage-shaped lobster soufflé—offer continuity with the fabled past. Service is exceptional, the setting—19th-century paneled salons now accented (sacré bleu!) with abstract paintings—is *luxe,* the well-priced wine list probably one of the top 10 in the world: all in all, a meal here comes as close to the classic haute cuisine experience as you can find in Paris today. Not surprisingly, you must reserve your table for dinner three or four weeks in advance—lunch is more accessible. ⊠ *15 rue Lamennais,* ☎ *01–44–95–15–01. Reservations essential. Jacket and tie. AE, DC, MC, V. Closed weekends and Aug. Métro: Charles-de-Gaulle–Étoile.*

$$$ ✕ **L'Astor.** Chef Eric Lecerf pays homage to his mentor, Joël Robuchon, by offering some classic Robuchon dishes like cauliflower cream with caviar and spiced roasted lobster. But he also shows his own talent with sophisticated offerings like sole with baby squid and artichokes. The service and wine list are superb. Trendy interior designer Frédérique Méchiche is responsible for the spacious and attractive dining room, which takes a cue from the '30s with star appliqués on the walls and a checkerboard carpet. The 298-franc/€46 prix-fixe lunch menu is great value. ⊠ *Hôtel Astor, 11 rue d'Astorg,* ☎ *01–53–05–05–20. AE, DC, MC, V. Métro: Madeleine.*

$$–$$$ ✕ **La Fermette Marbeuf.** Graced with one of the most magically beautiful Belle Epoque rooms in town—accidentally rediscovered during renovations in the 1970s—this is a favorite haunt of French TV and movie stars who adore the Art Nouveau mosaic and stained-glass mise-en-scène. The menu features solid, updated classic cuisine. Try the snails in puff pastry, saddle of lamb with *choron* (a tomato-spiked béarnaise sauce), and bitter chocolate fondant—but ignore the prix-fixe unless you are on a budget, as the chef seems to have cut corners on ingredients. Popular with tourists and businesspeople at lunch, La Fermette becomes truly animated around 9 PM. ⊠ *5 rue Marbeuf,* ☎ *01–53–23–08–00. AE, DC, MC, V. Métro: Franklin-D.-Roosevelt.*

$$–$$$ ✕ **Rue Balzac.** Opened by haute cuisine chef Michel Rostang and flamboyant French rock star Johnny Hallyday, this fashionable new restaurant has won an inordinate amount of praise from starry-eyed French critics. True, the menu is original: you can order anything from a truffle sandwich to roast lamb with shallots caramelized in aged vinegar, and the pineapple crème brûlée, served in the fruit's shell, is an improvement on the original. But prices are steep, service is snooty—the more you actually look like Johnny and his young wife, Laetitia, the better you will be treated—and some dishes miss the mark, such as a ham-and-cheese French take on risotto. The scene makes entertaining theater, though, and the high-ceilinged room is pleasant with its ceiling moldings, pastel colors, Miro-esque murals, and modern light fixtures. ⊠ *3–5 rue Balzac,* ☎ *01–53–89–90–91. AE, DC, MC, V. Closed Aug. Métro: Franklin-D.-Roosevelt.*

$$ ✕ **Chez Tante Louise.** Chef Bernard Loiseau's three Paris outposts—his original eponymous restaurant is in Saulieu in Burgundy—are appealing bastions of traditional Burgundian cooking. Here, he has wisely left the vintage '30s decor almost completely untouched. The food is pleasantly old-fashioned and hearty—like *oeufs en meurette à la bourguignonne* (poached eggs in red wine sauce with bacon) and sole "Tante Louise," in which a fillet is served on a bed of *duxelles* (finely chopped mushrooms). Of course, there's a nice selection of Burgundies, and service is prompt and professional for the well-dressed crowd. ✉ *41 rue Boissy d'Anglas,* ☎ *01–42–65–06–85. Reservations essential. AE, DC, MC, V. Closed weekends and Aug. Métro: Madeleine.*

$$ ✕ **Sebillon.** The original Sebillon has nurtured chic residents of the fashionable suburb of Neuilly for generations; this elegant, polished branch off the Champs-Élysées continues the tradition. The menu includes lobster salad, lots of shellfish, and—the specialty—roast leg of lamb sliced table-side and served until you beg the waiter to stop. Service is notably friendly. ✉ *66 rue Pierre-Charron,* ☎ *01–43–59–28–15. AE, DC, MC, V. Métro: Franklin-D.-Roosevelt.*

9ᵉ Arrondissement (Opéra/Pigalle-Clichy)
See Right Bank Dining map.

FRENCH

$$$ ✕ **Bistrot des Deux Théâtres.** Quality is high and prices are low at this well-run restaurant in the Pigalle-Clichy area. The prix-fixe menu includes apéritif, first and main dishes, a cheese or dessert course, half a bottle of wine, and coffee. The food—such as foie gras salad, steak with morels, and apple tart flambéed with Calvados—is far from banal. ✉ *18 rue Blanche,* ☎ *01–45–26–41–43. AE, DC, MC, V. Métro: Trinité.*

$ ✕ **Chartier.** People come here more for the bonhomie than the food, which is often stunningly ordinary. This cavernous 1896 restaurant enjoys a huge following among budget-minded students, solitary bachelors, and tourists. You may find yourself sharing a table with strangers as you study the long, old-fashioned menu of such favorites as hard-boiled eggs with mayonnaise, steak tartare, and roast chicken with fries. ✉ *7 rue du Faubourg-Montmartre,* ☎ *01–47–70–86–29. Reservations not accepted. AE, DC, MC, V. Métro: Montmartre.*

10ᵉ Arrondissement (République/Gare du Nord)
See Right Bank Dining map.

FRENCH

$$$ ✕ **Chez Michel.** Enthusiastic young chef Thierry Breton pulls in a
★ stylish crowd of Parisians and tourists with his wonderful market-inspired cooking, despite the out-of-the-way location in a pretty neighborhood near Gare du Nord. The menu changes constantly, but you'll almost invariably find the Breton specialties *kig ha farz* (a robust pork stew with a bread stuffing) and *kouing aman* (the butteriest cake imaginable). In winter, don't miss Breton's succulent game dishes (for a 50-franc/€8 supplement) such as the surprisingly mild-tasting boar chops, served in a cast-iron pot with tiny potatoes and roasted garlic, and deep red venison fillet with a pumpkin gratin. The cheese course, served on a slate from Breton's farm in Brittany, is outstanding. Chez Michel's formerly fusty decor has recently been brightened up, and there is a long, convivial table in the vaulted cellar. ✉ *10 rue Belzunce,* ☎ *01–44–53–06–20. Reservations essential. MC, V. Closed Sun.–Mon. and Aug. Métro: Gare du Nord.*

$$ ✕ **Brasserie Flo.** The first of brasserie king Jean-Paul Bucher's many Paris addresses is hard to find down its passageway near the Gare de

l'Est, but it's worth the effort, as much for the decor and atmosphere as the food. The rich wood and stained glass are typically Alsatian, and brasserie standards such as shellfish, steak tartare, and choucroute are savory. Order a carafe of Alsatian wine to go with your meal. It's open until 1:30 AM, with a special late-night menu for 138 francs/€21 from 10 PM. ⊠ *7 cour des Petites-Écuries,* ☎ *01–47–70–13–59. AE, DC, MC, V. Métro: Château d'Eau.*

$$ ✕ **Julien.** Famed for its 1879 decor—think Majorelle bar, Art Nouveau stained glass, *La-Bohème*-ish street lamps hung with vintage hats—this Belle Epoque dazzler certainly lives up to its oft-quoted moniker, "the poor man's Maxim's." Fare includes smoked salmon, foie gras, stuffed roast lamb, cassoulet, and its famous *profiteroles* (puff-pastry smothered in chocolate). Diners are ebullient and lots of fun; this place has a strong following with the fashion crowd, so it's mobbed during the biannual fashion and fabric shows. The downside? Letters from readers have complained about some lackluster dishes and even worse service (not to mention the market shops along the street). The wait for your entrée might be long, but at least your eyes can fill up on those luscious plaster moldings. There's service until 1:30 AM, with a special late-night menu for 138 francs/€21 from 10 PM. ⊠ *16 rue du Faubourg St-Denis,* ☎ *01–47–70–12–06. AE, DC, MC, V. Métro: Strasbourg–St-Denis.*

$–$$ ✕ **Chez Casimir.** Another project of chef Thierry Breton of Chez Michel, this easygoing bistro is equally popular with stylish Parisian professionals for whom it serves as a sort of canteen—why cook when you can eat this well for so little money? The menu shows Breton's cooking style with dishes like lentil soup with fresh croutons, braised endive and andouille sausage salad, and roast lamb on a bed of Paimpol beans. Good desserts include *pain perdu,* a version of French toast, eaten for dessert—here it's topped with a roasted pear or whole cherries. The café-style nondecor is inoffensive but the lighting is just that little bit too bright. ⊠ *6 rue de Belzunce,* ☎ *01–48–78–28–80. No credit cards. Closed weekends. Métro: Gare du Nord.*

$ ✕ **Au Vieux Bistrot.** If you're staying near the Gare du Nord or looking for a meal in the area before taking the train, this pleasant, old-fashioned neighborhood bistro is a good bet. From the big zinc bar to the steak with mushroom sauce and veal in cream, this place delivers a traditional bistro experience. Finish up with the fruit tart. Service is friendly. ⊠ *30 rue Dunkerque,* ☎ *01–48–78–48–01. MC, V. Closed Sun. No dinner Sat. Métro: Gare du Nord.*

11ᵉ Arrondissement (Bastille/République)
See Right Bank Dining map.

CHINESE

$$ ✕ **Wok.** Design-it-yourself Asian stir-fry in a slick, minimalist setting has made this spot a hit with the penny-wise hipsters who hang out in the clubs around party-hearty Bastille. You select the type of noodle you want, the waiter brings you a bowl, and you load up at a buffet with bins of chicken, white fish, shrimp, salmon, beef, and vegetables; then join the line to discuss your preferred seasoning with the chefs who man the woks in the open kitchen. The all-you-can-eat single-price tariff lets you walk the wok as many times as you want. Otherwise, there are deep-fried spring rolls as starters and a signature dessert of caramelized fruit salad. Mobbed on weekends but unfortunately closed at lunch, this place is fun, nourishing, and cheap. ⊠ *23 rue des Taillandiers,* ☎ *01–55–28–88–77. MC, V. Closed Sun. No lunch Mon.– Sat. Métro: Bréguet-Sabin, Bastille, Ledru-Rollin.*

FRENCH

$$$ ✕ **Au Camelot.** This minuscule bistro with a single five-course fixed-
★ price menu brings in the crowds, who come for the excellent home-
style cooking, some of the best in Paris today. A meal here usually begins
with a generous serving of soup, followed by a fish course, a main dish,
cheese, and dessert. Chef Didier Varnier trained with guru Christian
Constant at the Crillon and it shows in such creative dishes as pump-
kin soup with goat's-cheese ravioli, squid-ink risotto with Dublin Bay
prawns, sweet-and-sour duck with dried-fruit tabouleh, and spice
bread pudding with lemon cream. Though the place is noisy and very
crowded, service is friendly, and the house Bordeaux is a treat. ✉ *50
rue Amelot,* ☎ *01–43–55–54–04. Reservations essential. MC, V.
Closed Sun.–Mon. Métro: République.*

$$ ✕ **Astier.** The prix-fixe menu (there's no à la carte) at this popular though
★ plainly decorated restaurant must be one of the best values in town.
Among the beautifully prepared seasonal dishes are baked eggs topped
with truffled foie gras, fricassee of *joue de boeuf* (beef cheeks), rabbit
in mustard sauce with fresh tagliatelle, and plum *clafoutis* (a fruit
flan). This is a great place to come if you're feeling cheesy, since it's
locally famous for having one of the best *plateaux de fromages* (cheese
plates) in Paris—a giant wicker tray lands on the table and you help
yourself. Service can be rushed, but the enthusiastic horde does not seem
to mind. The lengthy, well-priced wine list is a connoisseur's dream.
✉ *44 rue Jean-Pierre Timbaud,* ☎ *01–43–57–16–35. Reservations essential. MC, V. Closed weekends, Aug., and Christmas week. Métro:
Parmentier.*

$$ ✕ **Le Repaire de Cartouche.** Between Bastille and République, this
★ split-level, '50s-style bistro with dark-wood decor offers excellent food
for good-value prices. Young chef Rodolphe Paquin is a creative and
impeccably trained cook who does a stylish take on earthy French re-
gional dishes. The menu changes regularly, but typical are a salad of
haricots verts (string beans) topped with tender slices of squid, scal-
lops on a bed of diced pumpkin, and old-fashioned desserts like cus-
tard with tiny madeleine cakes. The wine list is very good, too, with
bargains like a Pernand-Vergelesses (red Burgundy) for $20. ✉ *99 rue
Amelot,* ☎ *01–47–00–25–86. Reservations essential. MC, V. Closed
Sun.–Mon. and Aug. Métro: Filles du Calvaire.*

$–$$ ✕ **Les Fernandises.** The chef-owner of this neighborhood spot near place
de la République is more concerned with his Normandy-inspired cui-
sine than with his restaurant's inconsequential decor. Fresh foie gras
sautéed in cider and scallops in cream sauce are examples of his varied style. Choose from at least six Camemberts at any given time, including one doused in Calvados and another coated in hay. ✉ *17 rue
Fontaine-au-Roi,* ☎ *01–43–57–46–25. MC, V. Closed Sun.–Mon. and
Aug. Métro: République.*

$–$$ ✕ **Le Passage.** Not far from place de la Bastille, in the obscure pas-
sage de la Bonne Graine, is this friendly spot with a homey ambience.
Though it bills itself as a wine bar, it has a full menu, including nine
kinds of *andouillette* (chitterling sausage). The initials AAAAA, by the
way, mean the sausage has the stamp of approval from the French andouillette aficionados' association. Since the andouillette's pungent aroma
is, er, an acquired taste, other, less fragrant dishes are available. Le Passage is also a delight for wine lovers, with many unusual bottles. ✉
18 passage de la Bonne Graine (enter by 108 av. Ledru-Rollin), ☎ *01–
47–00–73–30. AE, MC, V. Closed weekends. Métro: Ledru-Rollin.*

$ ✕ **Jacques Mélac.** Robust cuisine matches noisy camaraderie at this
popular wine bar–restaurant, owned by mustachioed Jacques Mélac.
The charcuterie, salad of preserved duck gizzards, braised beef, and
cheeses from central France are all good choices. Monsieur Mélac, who

has a miniature vineyard out front, hosts a jolly party at harvesttime. There is an actual no-smoking section, reached by crossing the minimalist kitchen. ✉ *42 rue Léon Frot,* ☎ *01–43–70–59–27. MC, V. Closed Sun., Aug., and Christmas week. No dinner Mon. Métro: Charonne.*

$ ✕ **Le Kitsch.** Fighting the good fight against ennui, this whimsically casual place attracts graphic designers, couturiers-in-training, and other denizens of its arty neighborhood. There's more than a touch of Pee-Wee's Playhouse here—faux-stucco walls, plastic children's furniture, and naif paintings of cats make this a cute boutique restaurant. Happily, once you taste the dishes here, you won't need to call the chef The Mad Batter: the food here is snappy, if not stylish, and tasty enough to give a satisfied buzz to the room. ✉ *10 rue Oberkampf,* ☎ *01–40–21–94–14. No credit cards. Métro: Oberkampf.*

12ᵉ Arrondissement (Bastille/Gare de Lyon)

See Right Bank Dining map.

FRENCH

$$$ ✕ **Au Trou Gascon.** This winsome Belle Epoque establishment off place
★ Daumesnil is run by Alain Dutournier, who is chef at the high-class restaurant Le Carré des Feuillants. Here, you'll find a slightly more affordable take on the cuisine of Gascony—a region of outstanding ham, foie gras, lamb, and poultry—plus his classic white chocolate mousse. Both lunch and dinner are prix-fixe, with the lunch for 200 francs/€3 an excellent value. ✉ *40 rue Taine,* ☎ *01–43–44–34–26. AE, MC, V. Closed Sun. and Aug. No lunch Sat. Métro: Daumesnil.*

$$$ ✕ **L'Oulette.** Chef-owner Marcel Baudis's take on the cuisine of his na-
★ tive southwestern France is original and delicious, and service here is effusive—qualities that will help you overlook the out-of-the-way location and out-of-date design. The menu changes with the seasons, but you'll always find his trademark dishes: marinated squid, braised oxtail with foie gras and a mousseline of Puy lentils, and *pain d'épices* (spice cake). The restaurant, in the rebuilt Bercy district, is a bit hard to find, so start out with your map. There is a prix-fixe menu only. ✉ *15 pl. Lachambeaudie,* ☎ *01–40–02–02–12. AE, DC, MC, V. Closed weekends. Métro: Dugommier.*

$$ ✕ **Les Grandes Marches.** After restoring many of the city's most legendary brasseries—Brasserie Flo, Julien, Bofinger, La Coupole, to name a few—the Flo group appears to be taking on the Costes brothers (of Café Marly and Hôtel Costes fame) with this foray into the 21st century. Following a $2.2 million renovation designed by Elisabeth and Christian de Portzamparc, who have also worked for the Costes, this formerly anonymous café has become a cool modern space, with a sweeping metallic staircase and high-backed asymmetrical chairs. Gray is the predominant color, making the dining room feel a little cold, but service is warm and efficient and the food more original than in most brasseries—no surprise, as former Crillon chef Christian Constant helped write the menu. Prices are as steep as the Opéra Bastille's steps next door, but the 195 franc/€30 menu is reasonable value, featuring such dishes as a jellied artichoke and crab terrine, lamb chops with white beans, and a bitter coffee, cream, and chocolate *gelée.* ✉ *6 pl. de la Bastille,* ☎ *01–43–42–90–32. AE, DC, MC, V. Métro: Bastille.*

$$ ✕ **Le Square Trousseau.** Since fashion designer Jean-Paul Gaultier moved his headquarters nearby, this beautiful Belle Epoque bistro has become fashionable. You might see a supermodel—Claudia Schiffer often comes in when in town—while dining on the homemade foie gras and the tender baby chicken with mustard and bread-crumb crust. Some dishes are more successful than others, but atmosphere is never lacking and staff are cheerful. Wines from small producers are good value, especially the Morgon, a fruity red. ✉ *1 rue Antoine Vollon,* ☎ *01–*

43–43–06–00. *MC, V. Closed Sun.–Mon., 2 weeks in Feb., Aug., and Christmas wk. Métro: Ledru-Rollin.*

\$–\$\$ ✕ **Barrio Latino.** The latest mega-seater fashion restaurant in Paris has a rather speciously New York–goes–Puerto Rican theme, so don't come here expecting *West Side Story*—the place pulls a rather self-consciously trendy crowd to its theater-like atrium (it used to be a furniture showroom). The food's passable—just—but the raison d'être for this place is to make the scene and hang out over rather watery tropical cocktails. As long as you don't mind being sized up by bouncers and know what you're getting into, it can be a fun time. ✉ *46–48 rue du Faubourg St-Antoine,* ☎ *01–55–78–84–75. AE, DC, MC, V. Métro: Bastille.*

13ᵉ Arrondissement (Les Gobelins)
See Left Bank Dining map.

CHINESE

\$ ✕ **La Chine Massena.** With a wonderfully overwrought decor that includes what looks like a whole restaurant-supply catalog's worth of Asiana, plus four monitors showing the very latest in Hong Kong music videos, this is a fun place to come hungry with friends. Not only is the Chinese-Vietnamese-Thai food good and moderately priced, but the setting itself has a lot of entertainment value—wedding parties often provide a free floor show, and, on weekends, variety shows followed by Asian disco come as part of your meal. Steamed dumplings and lacquered duck are specialties, but for the best value come at noon for the bargain lunch menus. ✉ *Centre Commercial Massena, 13 pl. de Venetie,* ☎ *01–45–83–98–88. MC, V. Métro: Porte de Choisy.*

FRENCH

\$\$\$–\$\$\$\$ ✕ **Au Petit Marguery.** So authentic is this bistro that a French film was made about the three brothers who run it—*les frères Cousin.* The French classics here are more than reliable, but if you're hunting for game this is the place to catch it (in late fall), in such dishes as the deeply flavored *lièvre à la royale* (hare in a carnivorous wine-and-blood sauce). ✉ *9 bd. de Port Royal,* ☎ *01–43–31–58–59. AE, DC, MC, V. Closed weekends, Christmas wk, and Aug. Métro: Les Gobelins.*

\$\$–\$\$\$ ✕ **Anacréon.** André le Letty, who polished his cooking technique at La Tour d'Argent, has transformed a neighborhood café into a pleasant new-wave bistro. Inventive dishes such as pressed duck with red peppercorns and fresh cod with spices have been highlights on the regularly changing menu. Desserts are always good, too, and the St-Joseph is a perfect choice from the wine list. The menu is prix-fixe. ✉ *53 bd. St-Marcel,* ☎ *01–43–31–71–18. Reservations essential. AE, DC, MC, V. Closed Sun.–Mon. and Aug. Métro: Les Gobelins.*

\$\$ ✕ **L'Avant-Gout.** For excellent contemporary French cooking at very reasonable prices, it's worth seeking out this tiny, off-the-beaten-path bistro in a residential part of the city. Though "The Foretaste" can get crowded and noisy, you won't be disappointed by young chef Christophe Beaufront's appealing and unusual daily prix-fixe chalkboard menu, which might include dishes like sea bass with creamy celery root and almonds, and steak with roasted shallots. Delicious homemade desserts and a good wine list with a good selection of lower-priced bottles round off the meal. ✉ *26 rue Bobillot,* ☎ *01–53–80–24–00. Reservations essential. MC, V. Closed Sun.–Mon., 1st wk in Jan., 1st wk in May, 3 wks in Aug. Métro: Place d'Italie.*

\$\$ ✕ **Le Terroir.** A jolly crowd of regulars makes this little bistro festive. Based on first-rate ingredients from all over France, the menu is solidly classical—salads with chicken livers or fresh marinated anchovies, calves' liver or monkfish with saffron, and pears marinated in wine for dessert, for instance. There's also a well-balanced wine list. ✉ *11 bd. Arago,* ☎ *01–47–07–36–99. AE, MC, V. Closed weekends. Métro: Les Gobelins.*

14ᵉ Arrondissement (Montparnasse)
See Left Bank Dining map.

FRENCH

$$$ ✕ **La Régalade.** To satisfy the hungry hordes who trek to the edge of
★ town for his inspired seasonal cooking, Yves Camdeborde does three dinner sittings—and you still have to book at least two weeks ahead. The crowded, no-frills setting evokes the provinces, but the food is worthy of a luxury restaurant: tempting dishes on a recent winter menu were paper-thin Dublin Bay prawn carpaccio, juicy roast capon with chestnuts, fresh duck foie gras panfried in spice-bread crumbs, and a bitter, adult dessert of grapefruit in Campari jelly. Portions are small, but the country pâté that begins each meal will take the edge off your appetite. Camdeborde was one of the first chefs to introduce a limited-choice, prix-fixe menu in Paris and still sets the standard by which his many imitators must be judged. ✉ *49 av. Jean-Moulin,* ☎ *01–45–45–68–58. Reservations essential 2 wks in advance. MC, V. Closed Sun.–Mon. and Aug. Métro: Alésia.*

$$ ✕ **Contre-Allée.** Left Bank students and professors crowd this large restaurant, simply decorated with bullfighting posters. The menu has original selections such as squid salad with mussels and roast cod with Parmesan; homemade fresh pasta accompanies many dishes. A sidewalk terrace enlivens shady avenue Denfert-Rochereau in summer. The restaurant serves until 11:30 PM. ✉ *83 av. Denfert-Rochereau,* ☎ *01–43–54–99–86. AE, DC, MC, V. No lunch Sat. Métro: Denfert-Rochereau.*

$$ ✕ **La Coupole.** This world-renowned, cavernous spot in Montparnasse practically defines the term brasserie (it's owned by restaurant kingpin Jean-Paul Bucher)—and its Art Deco murals are famous, too. It might have lost its intellectual aura since the Flo group's restoration—that giant rotating sculpture was one of the "improvements"—but La Coupole has been popular since the days when Jean-Paul Sartre and Simone de Beauvoir were regulars and is still great fun. Today it attracts a mix of bourgeois families, tourists, and elderly lone diners treating themselves to a dozen oysters. Expect the usual brasserie menu—including perhaps the largest shellfish platter in Paris—choucroute, and a wide range of over-the-top desserts. ✉ *102 bd. du Montparnasse,* ☎ *01–43–20–14–20. AE, DC, MC, V. Métro: Vavin.*

SEAFOOD

$$ ✕ **Vin & Marée.** The third, lower-priced annex of the fancy Right Bank fish house La Luna is a welcome addition to Montparnasse. Begin with a tasty bowl of baby clams in a creamy lemon-butter sauce, offered as an hors d'oeuvre; then have a generous plate of fresh red shrimp sautéed in thyme, followed by white tuna in shallot sauce or sautéed red mullets, if available—the menu changes depending on what's in the market that day. Nicely chosen wines come by the bottle, carafe, or glass. ✉ *108 av. du Maine,* ☎ *01–43–20–29–50. AE, MC, V. Métro: Montparnasse, Gaité.*

15ᵉ Arrondissement (Motte-Picquet/Balard)
See Left Bank Dining map.

FRENCH

$$$ ✕ **Bistrot d'Hubert.** In a studied environment that might have sprung from the pages of *Elle Decor,* this popular bistro draws a stylish crowd and serves food that perfectly expresses the counter-currents of the

Parisian culinary landscape. The prix-fixe menu is split into two: "tradition" and "innovation." You might have the crab in a garlic mayonnaise with a pickled cactus garnish, followed by a tuna steak in a "caramel" of balsamic vinegar, or go for the more classic roast lamb. Don't skip the superb tiramisu with chicory ice cream. Service is very friendly, the short, well-chosen wine list offers chef Alain Senderens' (of Lucas Carton) Cahors and a lovely Domaine de Mont Redon rosé, and the menu is prix-fixe only. ⊠ *41 bd. Pasteur,* ☎ *01–47–34–15–50. Reservations essential. AE, DC, MC, V. No lunch Sat. Métro: Pasteur.*

$$$ ✕ **L'Os à Moelle.** This small, popular bistro has a very good-value six-★ course dinner menu (there's no à la carte) that changes daily; portions are generous. A sample meal might include white-bean soup, sautéed foie gras, *rouget* (red mullet fish), lamb with potato puree, cheese with a small salad, and a delicious roasted pear with cinnamon ice cream. At lunchtime, there's a short à la carte menu that's as good. With an excellent list of fairly priced wines, your bill can stay comfortably low—but, if you're feeling broke, the restaurant's casual wine bar across the street is a tempting option. ⊠ *3 rue Vasco-de-Gama,* ☎ *01–45–57–27–27. Reservations essential. MC, V. Closed Sun.–Mon. and Aug. Métro: Balard.*

$$$ ✕ **Philippe Detourbe.** With its black-lacquer trim, mirrors, and Burgundy velvet upholstery, this place is unexpectedly glamorous. Detourbe, a self-taught chef, is gifted and very ambitious—his menu of contemporary French cooking changes with every meal. Dishes may include smoked salmon filled with cabbage remoulade or John Dory with baby leeks, fresh almonds, and country ham. He has perhaps spread himself too thin with the opening of annexes, though, as the overall quality of his cooking has slipped and service can be annoyingly erratic. The wine list is brief but well chosen; the menu is prix-fixe. ⊠ *8 rue Nicolas Charlet,* ☎ *01–42–19–08–59. Reservations essential. AE, MC, V. Closed Sun. No lunch Mon. Métro: Pasteur.*

$$$ ✕ **Le Troquet.** Tucked away on a quiet street in a residential neighborhood ★ near the UNESCO headquarters, this contemporary modern bistro feeds a crowd of regulars. They come for chef Christian Etchebest's tasty, constantly changing prix-fixe menu of dishes from the Basque and Béarn regions of southwestern France. A typical meal might include vegetable soup with foie gras and cream, hot scallops on a bed of mixed vegetables, pan-roasted dove, sheep's cheese with cherry preserves, and a chocolate macaroon. The Béarn red wine makes for good drinking at a good price. Though the dining room looks a little fusty—Etchebest took over this bistro from his uncle in 1998—the atmosphere is relaxed and the staff eager to please. ⊠ *21 rue François-Bonvin,* ☎ *01–45–66–89–00. MC, V. Closed Sun.–Mon., 3 wks in Aug., and Christmas wk. Métro: Ségur.*

$–$$ ✕ **Chez Pierre.** Specializing in Burgundian cooking, this small, old-fashioned restaurant has the ambience of a Doisneau photo, replete with friendly waiters ready with a wry remark. For 175 francs/€27 you can feast on three courses plus an apéritif, coffee, and half-bottle of wine: the prix-fixe includes such classic starters as *oeufs en meurette* (poached eggs in red wine sauce) and *jambon persillé* (parsleyed ham), and main dishes like beef bourguignon and coq au vin. Finish off with a homemade plum tart or a chocolate Bavarois. The short wine list features a good selection of reasonably priced Burgundies. ⊠ *117 rue de Vaugirard,* ☎ *01–47–34–96–12. MC, V. Closed Sun. No lunch Sat. Métro: Falguière.*

THAI

$ ✕ **Sawadee.** Once you've tried the delicious Thai food here, you'll understand why this off-the-beaten-path spot is full every night. Statues and wood carvings dress up the warm dining room, while a casual atmosphere and friendly service add to the charm. Start with the unusual fried-rice salad, or the delicate shrimp and pork ravioli, and then try the shrimp sautéed with salt and pepper or the chopped beef with basil. ✉ *53 av. Émile-Zola,* ☎ *01–45–77–68–90. AE, MC, V. Closed Sun. Métro: Charles-Michel.*

16ᵉ Arrondissement (Trocadéro/Bois de Boulogne)
See Right Bank Dining map.

FRENCH

$$$$ ✕ **Le Pré Catalan.** Dining beneath the chestnut trees on the terrace of this fanciful *pavillon* in the Bois de Boulogne is a Belle Epoque fantasy. Chef Frédéric Anton has brought new life to the cuisine of this venerable establishment, and you can find winners such as spit-roasted baby pigeon in a caramelized sauce, sweetbreads with morels and asparagus tips, and roast pear on a caramelized waffle with bergamot ice cream. Unfortunately, other dishes are decidedly lackluster. Still and all, the opulent surroundings may make you quickly forget that limp turbot, especially during the more reasonably priced lunch menu. ✉ *Bois de Boulogne, rte. de Surèsnes,* ☎ *01–44–14–41–14. Reservations essential. Jacket and tie. AE, DC, MC, V. Closed Mon. and mid-Feb. No dinner Sun. Métro: Porte Dauphine.*

$$$–$$$$ ✕ **Jamin.** At this intimate, elegant restaurant, where Joël Robuchon
★ made his name, you can find excellent haute cuisine at almost half the price of other restaurants of its kind: there is a lunch prix-fixe at just 280 francs/€43 and a 410-franc/€63 menu at lunch and dinner. Benoît Guichard, Robuchon's second for many years, is a subtle and accomplished chef and a particularly brilliant *saucier* (sauce maker). The menu changes regularly, but Guichard favors such dishes as sea bass with pistachios in fennel sauce and braised beef with cumin-scented carrots. The seasonal gratin of rhubarb with a red-fruit sauce makes an excellent dessert. ✉ *32 rue de Longchamp,* ☎ *01–45–53–00–07. Reservations essential. AE, DC, MC, V. Closed weekends, Feb. 10–18, and 3 wks in Aug. Métro: Iéna.*

$$$ ✕ **59 Poincaré.** After moving his haute cuisine restaurant to the Plaza Athenée hotel, Alain Ducasse has closed Le Relais du Parc in the Sofitel Victor Hugo and opened this dressed-up bistro in the splendiferous premises of his former Restaurant Alain Ducasse. Ducasse had originally intended to create a variation on his stylish Monaco restaurant Bar et Boeuf ("Sea Bass and Beef")—but, always the businessman, he quickly adapted to the "mad cow" scare with a menu featuring vegetables, lamb, lobster, and fruit. Downstairs is a sleek modern brasserie where you can drop in for a quick meal, while the upstairs Belle Epoque dining rooms—portraits, trompe l'oeil library shelves, and "stockbroker" wood paneling—have been transformed with the addition of giant color photos of farmers, gadgets (chopsticks, notepads, high-tech ashtrays) on the tables, cream-linen-draped chairs, and a hip sound track. An army of rather over-attentive waiters ensures a seamless meal, while the food itself ranges from the delectable (Canadian lobster with caramelized endives and a fruity curry sauce) to the disappointing (ho-hum shoulder of lamb with a soulless *jus*). Desserts of panfried mango with tropical sorbet and a shortbread tart Tatin were excellent, fortifying you for the sight of an alarming bill—expect to spend at least 500 francs/€77 a head. ✉ *59 av. Raymond-Poincaré,* ☎ *01–44–05–66–10. Reservations essential. AE, DC, MC, V. Closed Sun.–Mon. Métro: Victor-Hugo.*

$$ ✕ **La Butte Chaillot.** A dramatic iron staircase connects two levels in turquoise and earth tones at one of the most popular of chef Guy Savoy's fashionable bistros. Dining here is part theater, as the à la mode clientele demonstrate, but it's not all show: the very good food includes tasty ravioli from the town of Royans, roast free-range chicken with mashed potatoes, and stuffed veal breast with rosemary. Renovations in spring 2001 expanded the dining room, making it feel more harmonious. A wide sidewalk terrace fronts tree-shaded avenue Kléber. ⊠ *112 av. Kléber,* ☎ *01–47–27–88–88. AE, DC, MC, V. Métro: Trocadéro.*

$$ × **La Grande Armée.** The Costes brothers, who own the most stylish
★ hotel in Paris (the Costes), are perpetually in the forefront of whatever's trendy in town. Their brasserie near the Arc de Triomphe is a great spot to check out their gig, since it's open daily, serves nonstop, and has knockout decor designed by Jacques Garcia, whose super-opulent re-creations of historic salons have won the hearts of the super-rich everywhere. Here he's unleashed an exotic Napoléon III bordello decor—think black lacquered tables, leopard upholstery, Bordeaux velvet, and a carefully tousled clientele picking at those dishes that chic Parisians like best these days—such as a salad of lamb's lettuce and fresh truffles for 180 francs/€28, and yogurt for dessert. ⊠ *3 av. de la Grande Armée,* ☎ *01–45–00–24–77. AE, DC, MC, V. Métro: Charles-de-Gaulle-Étoile.*

$$ × **Le Petit Rétro.** Two different clienteles—men in expensive suits at noon and well-dressed locals in the evening—frequent this little bistro with Art Nouveau tiles and bentwood furniture. You can't go wrong with the daily special, which is written on a chalkboard presented by one of the friendly waitresses. Come in some night when you want a good solid meal, like the perfect *pavé de boeuf* (thick steak) in a ruddy red-wine and stock sauce, accompanied by potatoes au gratin and caramelized braised endive. ⊠ *5 rue Mesnil,* ☎ *01–44–05–06–05. AE, MC, V. Closed Sun. No lunch Sat. Métro: Victor Hugo.*

$ × **Les Chauffeurs.** Not only is this tranquil bistro in an expensive part of town a favorite address of well-dressed regulars, but it's also the night-off hangout for some of the capital's best-known chefs, including the now-retired Joël Robuchon. What attracts the discerning is the moderately priced, reliably good classic cooking and the pleasant, relaxed ambience. Try the airy fish terrine or an Alsatian *cervelas* (pork sausage) salad, and then, depending on what's on the menu, go for the sole meunière, roast chicken, or choucroute. Good Beaujolais wines are served by the carafe. More than one reader has found this place to be disappointing, however. ⊠ *8 chaussée de la Muette,* ☎ *01–42–88–50–05. MC, V. Closed Christmas day, New Year's day, 2 wks in Aug. Métro: La Muette.*

SEAFOOD

$$–$$$ × **Maison Prunier.** Founded in 1925, this seafood restaurant is one of
★ the best, and surely the prettiest, in Paris—even more so following renovations completed in May 2001. Hemingway loved to come here when he won at the races. The famous Art Deco mosaics glitter and the white marble counters overflow with the impeccably fresh shellfish displayed like precious jewels. At press-time (summer 2001) there are plans afoot to transform this into a caviar house. ⊠ *16 av. Victor-Hugo,* ☎ *01–44–17–35–85. Jacket and tie. AE, DC, MC, V. Closed Sun.–Mon. Métro: Étoile.*

17ᵉ Arrondissement (Monceau/Clichy/Arc de Triomphe)

See Right Bank Dining map.

FRENCH

$$$$ × **Guy Savoy.** Redecorated by Jean-Michel Wilmotte, who dressed up
★ the space with dark African wood, rich leather (like the inside of a Rolls-Royce), and cream-color marble, Guy Savoy's luxury restaurant near

the Arc de Triomphe has stepped gracefully into the 21st century. Come here for a perfectly measured, contemporary haute cuisine experience, since Savoy's several bistros have not lured him away from his kitchen. The artichoke soup with black truffles, sea bass with spices, and veal kidneys in mustard-spiked jus reveal the magnitude of his talent, and his mille-feuille is a contemporary classic. Half-portions allow you to graze your way through the menu, and reasonably priced wines are available. Best of all, the atmosphere is joyful—Savoy senses that having fun is just as important as eating well. ⊠ *18 rue Troyon,* ☎ *01–43–80–40–61. AE, MC, V. Closed Sun. No lunch Sat. Métro: Charles-de-Gaulle–Étoile.*

$$$ ✕ **Au Petit Colombier.** This is a perennial favorite among Parisians, who come to eat comforting *cuisine bourgeoise* (traditional cuisine) in the warm dining rooms accented with wood and bright copper. Seasonal specialties include milk-fed lamb chop *en cocotte* (in a small, enameled casserole), game in all its guises, and truffles. Service is friendly and unpretentious. ⊠ *42 rue des Acacias,* ☎ *01–43–80–28–54. AE, MC, V. Closed Sun. and Aug. No lunch Sat. Métro: Charles-de-Gaulle–Étoile.*

$$ **Café d'Angel.** A trend-conscious yuppie crowd frequents this relaxed little bistro near the Arc de Triomphe, whose name is echoed in its angel-print tablecloths. The menu changes regularly but offers interesting modern bistro dishes and good value for the money. Try the haddock with green cabbage and horseradish, rabbit compote with radish salad, carpaccio of tuna, delicious venison with wheat risotto and chestnuts, and mille-feuille of oranges and pineapple. ⊠ *16 rue Brey,* ☎ *01–47–54–03–33. MC, V. Closed weekends and 3 wks in Aug. Métro: Charles-de-Gaulle–Étoile.*

$$ ✕ **Le Graindorge.** Formerly at the justly popular Au Trou Gascon, chef-owner Bernard Broux has thrived since he opened his own establishment. He prepares an original mix of the cuisines of southwestern France and his native Flanders: experience the succulent eel terrine in a delicious herb aspic (seasonal) and red mullet with endives in beer sauce, followed by a small but judicious selection of potent northern cheeses. Madame Broux oversees the pleasant dining rooms, which have a decidedly provincial feel, and can help you select one of the many fine beers. ⊠ *15 rue de l'Arc-de-Triomphe,* ☎ *01–47–54–00–28. AE, MC, V. Closed Sun. and 2 wks in Aug. Métro: Charles-de-Gaulle–Étoile.*

ITALIAN

$$–$$$ ✕ **Il Baccello.** Young chef Raphael Bembaron's talent is pulling crowds to this outpost for first-rate contemporary Italian food. Bembaron trained at Lucas Carton in Paris, Enoteca Pinchiorri in Florence, and Joia, the gourmet vegetarian restaurant in Milan, and his background comes through in every dish. Appetizers like whole-wheat pappardelle with wild mushrooms and a chickpea soup garnished with pancetta-wrapped langoustines are first rate. Main courses like risotto cooked with Barolo wine and garnished with duck breast and aged Mimolette cheese as well as langoustines on toothpicks with almond-stuffed green olives on a bed of spelt and broccoli in a pumpkin coulis are memorable. Finish up with the almond-flavored panna cotta in prune sauce or the fruit brandy aspics. This is also a good address for vegetarians. The dining room is done in sleek (if noisy) minimalist style. ⊠ *33 rue Cardinet,* ☎ *01–43–80–63–60. AE, DC, MC, V. Closed Sun.–Mon., Christmas wk, and 3 wks in Aug. Reservations essential. Métro: Wagram.*

NORTH AFRICAN

$$$ ✕ **Le Timgad.** For a stylish evening out and a night off from French food, head to this elegant, beautifully decorated North African restau-

rant. Start with a savory *brick* (crispy parchment pastry filled with meat, eggs, or seafood), followed by tasty couscous or succulent *tagine* (meat or poultry that's slowly braised inside a domed pottery casserole). The lamb tagine with artichokes is especially good. ⊠ *21 rue de Brunel,* ☎ *01–45–74–23–70. AE, DC, MC, V. Métro: Argentine.*

SEAFOOD

\$\$–\$\$\$ ✕ **L'Huîtrier.** If you share the Parisians' craving for oysters, this is the place for you. The friendly owner will describe the different kinds available; you can follow these with any of several daily fish specials. The excellent cheeses are from the outstanding shop of Roger Alléosse. Blond wood and cream colors prevail. Should you have trouble getting a table, L'Huîtrier also runs the Presqu'île next door. ⊠ *16 rue Saussier-Leroy,* ☎ *01–40–54–83–44. AE, MC, V. Closed Mon. and Aug. Métro: Ternes.*

18ᵉ Arrondissement (Montmartre)

See Right Bank Dining map.

FRENCH

\$\$ ✕ **Le Poulbot Gourmand.** Engravings of old Montmartre and discreet lighting create a relaxed, comfortable atmosphere at this tiny, popular neighborhood restaurant named after the chef and owner's favorite painter, Francisque Poulbout. Working in a mostly traditional register, Jean-Paul Langevin creates dishes like escargots on artichoke hearts and roast duckling with turnips. The *sablé* (a shortbread pastry) with raspberries is a treat. There's a well-chosen wine list and several good-buy prix-fixe menus. ⊠ *39 rue Lamarck,* ☎ *01–46–06–86–00. MC, V. No dinner Sun. Métro: Lamarck-Caulaincourt.*

\$ ✕ **Le Moulin à Vins.** The atmosphere at this popular wine bar–bistro is sepia-toned, since both the place itself and surrounding neighborhood evoke premodern Paris. It's perfect for a lunch of salad or a cold-meat-and-cheese plate while touring Montmartre. In the evening it's much livelier, when devoted regulars—a great mix that runs from bikers to bankers—come for the daily short list of hot dishes. Opt for the delicious rabbit in mustard sauce with tagliatelle if it's available, or one of the southwestern dishes. Standards like the country terrine and quiche Lorraine are excellent, too, and the wine list is outstanding, especially the Côtes du Rhône. ⊠ *6 rue Burq,* ☎ *01–45–52–81–27. AE, MC, V. Closed Sun.–Mon. and 3 wks in Aug. No lunch Tues., Fri., or Sat. Métro: Abbesses.*

VIETNAMESE

\$ ✕ **Thu Thu.** Just across the street from the town hall of the 18th arrondissement, this little spot is a great address for thrifty fans of Vietnamese cooking. The engaging owner, Julia Le Phuong, serves up first-rate *pho* (Vietnamese noodle soup); *nems* (deep-fried spring rolls); duck with ginger; and great pork spareribs simply roasted with salt and pepper. There's also a good choice of vegetarian dishes here, and the lunch menu, at 45 francs/€7, is a real bargain. ⊠ *51 bis rue Hermel,* ☎ *01–42–54–70–30. MC, V. Closed Mon. and 2 wks in Aug. Métro: Simplon.*

19ᵉ Arrondissement (Buttes-Chaumont/La Villette)

See Right Bank Dining map.

FRENCH

\$\$–\$\$\$ ✕ **Le Pavillon Puebla.** A bucolic setting and original, flavorful cuisine, such as squid sautéed in saffron and boned pigeon with chorizo-stuffed cabbage, are the draw at this 1900s building in the spectacular Parc des Buttes-Chaumont. The elegant dining rooms are a romantic cold-weather setting, and the large terrace is extremely popular in summer.

The restaurant feels wonderfully removed from the bustle of the city, but it's a bit hard to find. Seduction comes (relatively) cheaply here if you opt for the prix-fixe menus at 190 francs/€29 or 260 francs/€40. ✉ *In the Parc Buttes-Chaumont (entrance on rue Botzaris),* ☎ *01–42–08–92–62. AE, MC, V. Closed Sun.–Mon. Métro: Buttes-Chaumont.*

20ᵉ Arrondissement (Père Lachaise)
See Right Bank Dining map.

FRENCH

$$ ✕ **Le Zéphyr.** Don't let the obscure location put you off—this restau-
★ rant is easy to get to from central Paris and well worth the small ef-
fort for its buzzy Art Deco dining room and inventive bistro food. The
menu changes often, but you might find such creations as a northern-
inspired soup of endives and potent Maroilles cheese, roast duck with
lavender honey, spiced polenta and quince, and banana mousse lay-
ered with coconut and chocolate. Edith Piaf grew up near here, and
you can still feel her spirit in this part of the neighborhood—Le Zé-
phyr's popular terrace allows you to take in the atmosphere. ✉ *1 rue
du Jourdain,* ☎ *01–46–36–65–81. AE, DC, MC, V. Closed Sun. and
Aug. No lunch Sat. Métro: Jourdain.*

$ ✕ **La Boulangerie.** This friendly, incredibly good-value bistro—three
courses cost 112 francs/€18—is a great bet if you're planning on a night
out in the increasingly trendy Ménilmontant neighborhood or maybe
are hoping to bring yourself back to life after a visit to Père-Lachaise
Cemetery. Occupying an old bakery, this place attracts a relaxed,
young local crowd, which comes for the sincere and satisfying bistro
specials offered on the chalkboard menu. The menu changes daily but
runs to dishes like tuna tartare, grilled red mullet on a bed of spinach,
pot au feu, and excellent desserts like the rhubarb-filled mille-feuille.
✉ *15 rue des Panoyaux,* ☎ *01–43–58–45–45. MC, V. Closed 2 wks
in Aug. No lunch Sat. Métro: Père-Lachaise.*

Cafés and Salons de Thé

Along with air, water, and wine (Parisians eat fewer and fewer three-
course meals), the café remains one of the basic necessities of life in
Paris. Though they continue to close in the face of changing work and
eating habits, cafés can still be found on almost every corner. Many of
them look alike—the unfortunate result of '60s and '70s renovations—
and only if you stick around long enough and become a regular (or
write entire books, as Simone de Beauvoir did) will you discover their
true intrigue. The more modest establishments (look for nonchalant
locals) will give you a cheaper cup of coffee and a feeling of what real
French café life is like. Cafés are required to post a *tarif des consom-
mations,* a list that includes prices for the basics ranging from *café*
(espresso) to *vin rouge* (red wine) and list two prices, *au comptoir* (at
the counter) and *à terrasse* or *à salle* (seated at a table). If you just need
a quick cup of coffee, have it at the counter and save yourself money.
If you have a rendezvous, take a table: remember you're paying rent
on that little piece of wood, and hang out as long as you like.

1ᵉʳ and 2ᵉ Arrondissements (Les Halles/Palais-Royal)
A Priori Thé. Stop in for tea while browsing through the lovely Galerie
Vivienne shopping arcade. ✉ *35–37 Galerie Vivienne, at 66 rue Vivi-
enne,* ☎ *01–42–97–48–75. Métro: Bourse.*
Au Père Tranquille. One of the best places in Paris for people-watch-
ing, this café also offers free entertainment from street artists and local
performers. ✉ *16 rue Pierre Lescot,* ☎ *01–45–08–00–34. Métro: Les
Halles.*

LUNCH BOX

IF YOU'RE A BUDGET-WISE GOURMET, the chimes of noon should be music to your ears. Many of Paris's best restaurants have prix-fixe lunch menus that are dramatically more affordable than dinner from their à la carte menus. At elegant Ledoyen, for example, the 320-franc (€49) lunch menu is less than half of what an average à la carte meal would cost (875 francs, or about €135, per person). To be sure to enjoy these midday feasts, it is essential that you make reservations.

Keep in mind that you may have to ask for the lunch menu, for obvious reasons—most restaurants would prefer that you order à la carte. Also note that the prix-fixe lunch menus often have a more limited selection—you usually get a choice of only a few appetizers, main courses, and desserts. These menus are more often than not designed to have broad appeal, but you might see scrumptious-looking dishes from the à la carte menu en route to other tables—this is one possible drawback to the prix-fixe lunch, and, unfortunately, substitutions are rarely allowed.

To keep a lid on costs, skip the cocktail before your meal, ask for a carafe of water instead of bottled water (even if you do get some nasty stares from waiters), go with the house wine, and be aware that coffee is often extra and can run 30 francs–35 francs/€5 for an espresso (find a nice café nearby instead). Note, too, that many more modest restaurants have excellent-value prix-fixe menus at midday, such as the 135-franc/€22 lunch at L'Épi Dupin and Le Grizzli bistros. Also look out for chalkboards announcing the modestly priced plat du jour at restaurants and cafés.

Following is a list of outstanding noontime buys from the restaurants listed in this chapter: Les Ambassadeurs, 380 francs/€58; L'Arpège, 490 francs/€75; L'Astor, 298 francs/€46; Au Bon Accueil, 145 francs/€22; Au Trou Gascon, 200 francs/€31; Chez René, 175 francs/€27; Les Élysées, 420 francs/€65; L'Épi Dupin, 115 francs/€18; Gérard Besson, 280 francs/€43; Jamin, 280 francs/€43; Jules Verne, 290 francs/€45; Les Olivades, 135 francs/€21; Pierre Gagnaire, 550 francs/€85; La Tour d'Argent, 350 francs/€54. And to put things in final perspective, if 550 francs/€85 per person at Pierre Gagnaire sounds stiff, keep in mind that the average price for an à la carte meal there is 1,000 francs/€154.

Another option is to put your own meal together. Paris has many open-air markets as well as a medley of specialty shops—including *boulangeries* (bakeries, which also sell premade sandwiches), *fromageries* (cheese shops), *pâtisseries* (pastry shops), and *supermarchés* (supermarkets). Also look out for *épiceries* (food shops) or *charcuteries* (French delis); the pâtés and meat products that once filled the shelves have moved over to make room for prepared salads, quiches, breads, and desserts. Choose what appeals to you most and take it to one of the city's parks for your own *déjeuner sur l'herbe* (picnic or, literally, "lunch on the grass").

Three sandwich shops are worth looking out for if you have too much sightseeing to do and want to eat in a hurry. **Au Pain Quotidien** (⊠ 18 pl. du Marché-St-Honoré, 1ᵉʳ) is a Belgian chain serving sandwiches and salads, as well as good breakfasts, at long wooden tables. **Cosi** (⊠ 54 rue de Seine, 6ᵉ) is a cozy spot for hearty Italian sandwiches, served on focaccia. At **Lina's** (⊠ 7 av. de l'Opéra, 1ᵉʳ; 50 rue Étienne Marcel, 2ᵉ; 30 bd. des Italiens, 9ᵉ; 23 av. de Wagram, 17ᵉ), you can get American-style sandwiches with such fillings as roast beef and smoked salmon, and excellent brownies.

Bernardaud. Decorated by interior-design star Olivier Gagnère, this quiet spot in a covered atrium serves good snacks on the company's own china. ⊠ *11 rue Royale*, ☎ *01–42–66–22–55. Métro: Concorde.*

Café Marly. Run by the Costes brothers, this café overlooking the main courtyard of the Louvre and I. M. Pei's glass pyramid is one of the most chic places in Paris to meet for a drink or a coffee. Note that ordinary café service shuts down during meal hours, when overpriced, mediocre food is served. Still, the spectacular decor is a feast for the eyes at any hour. ⊠ *Cour Napoléon du Louvre (enter from the Louvre courtyard), 93 rue de Rivoli,* ☎ *01–49–26–06–60. Métro: Palais-Royal.*

Café Verlet. Many Parisians think this compact spot serves the best coffee in town. You can also get sandwiches and delicious tarts. ⊠ *256 rue St-Honoré,* ☎ *01–42–60–67–39. Métro: Tuileries.*

Le Fumoir. From the same team that made the China Club one of the more enduringly hip addresses in Paris, this new café-restaurant has just passed over the curve of red-hot chic to become permanent and useful. Its location just across from the Louvre helps, but ultimately what makes it work is that the fashionable folks—press attachés with cell phones, sulky tatooed model-artists, and so on—actually like this place, with its decor that seems variously inspired by Vienna, Edward Hopper, and Scandinavia. The most intimate room is the book-lined library, thoughtfully stocked with an international selection of magazines and papers, at the head of the dining room. The food's expensive and indifferent, so come play for the price of a coffee or a glass of wine. ⊠ *Pl. du Louvre, 6 rue de l'Amiral-Coligny,* ☎ *01–42–92–00–24. Métro: Louvre.*

Le Ruc Univers. Actors from the Comédie Française and young hipsters hang out at this sleekly modern café near the Louvre. ⊠ *1 pl. André-Malraux,* ☎ *01–42–60–31–57. Métro: Palais-Royal.*

Salon de Thé du Palais-Royal. Have tea here on the terrace overlooking the gardens of the Palais-Royal. ⊠ *Jardins du Palais-Royal, 110 Galérie de Valois,* ☎ *01–40–20–00–27. Métro: Palais-Royal.*

4ᵉ Arrondissement (Marais/Beaubourg/Ile St-Louis)

Brasserie de l'Ile St-Louis. In one of the most picturesque parts of the city, this brasserie serves good food on a great terrace. ⊠ *55 quai de Bourbon,* ☎ *01–43–54–02–59. Métro: Pont Marie.*

Café Beaubourg. Near the Centre Pompidou, this slick, modern café, designed by architect Christian de Portzamparc, is one of the trendiest spots to rendezvous for fashion and art types. Omelets and decent salads are served if you've missed lunch or want a light dinner. ⊠ *43 rue St-Merri,* ☎ *01–48–87–63–96. Métro: Hôtel-de-Ville.*

L'Etoile Manquante. Owned by Xavier Denamur, who runs several stylish cafés in this street, the "Missing Star" is a great spot for people-watching, but the real attraction is the rest rooms: an electric train is just one of the surprises in store. ⊠ *34 rue Vieille-du-Temple,* ☎ *01–42–72–48–34. Métro: Hôtel-de-Ville, St-Paul.*

Le Flore en l'Ile. At this café on the Ile St-Louis you can find renowned Berthillon ice cream and a magnificent view of the Seine. ⊠ *42 quai d'Orléans,* ☎ *01–43–29–88–27. Métro: Pont Marie.*

Le Loir dans la Théière. This wonderful tea shop in the heart of the Marais has comfortable armchairs and delicious pâtisseries. ⊠ *3 rue des Rosiers,* ☎ *01–42–72–90–61. Métro: St-Paul.*

Ma Bourgogne. On the exquisite place des Vosges, this is a calm oasis for a coffee or a light lunch away from the noisy streets. ✉ *19 pl. des Vosges,* ☎ *01–42–78–44–64. Métro: St-Paul.*

Mariage Frères. This elegant salon de thé serves 500 kinds of tea, along with delicious tarts. ✉ *30 rue du Bourg-Tibourg,* ☎ *01–42–72–28–11. Métro: Hôtel-de-Ville.*

Petit Fer à Cheval. Great coffee is served in the perfect setting for watching the fashionable Marais locals saunter by. ✉ *30 rue Vieille-du-Temple,* ☎ *01–42–72–47–47. Métro: St-Paul.*

6ᵉ Arrondissement (St-Germain/Montparnasse)

Brasserie Lipp. This brasserie, with its turn-of-the-20th-century decor, was a favorite spot of Hemingway's; today television celebrities, journalists, and politicians come here for coffee on the small glassed-in terrace off the main restaurant. ✉ *151 bd. St-Germain,* ☎ *01–45–48–53–91. Métro: St-Germain-des-Prés.*

Café de Flore. Picasso, Chagall, Sartre, and de Beauvoir, attracted by the luxury of a heated café, worked and wrote here in the early 20th century. Today you'll find more tourists than intellectuals, but its outdoor terrace is still popular. ✉ *172 bd. St-Germain,* ☎ *01–45–48–55–26. Métro: St-Germain-des-Prés.*

Café de la Mairie. Preferred by Henry Miller and Saul Bellow to those on noisy boulevard St-Germain, this place still retains the quiet and unpretentious air of a local café—although Catherine Deneuve could easily be a passerby here. ✉ *8 pl. St-Sulpice,* ☎ *01–43–26–67–82. Métro: St-Sulpice.*

Café Orbital. Have a snack while you access your e-mail or the Internet. ✉ *13 rue de Médicis,* ☎ *01–43–25–76–77. RER: Luxembourg.*

Les Deux Magots. Dubbed the second home of the *élite intellectuelle,* this café counted Rimbaud, Verlaine, Mallarmé, Wilde, and the Surrealists among its regulars. These days it's overpriced and mostly filled with tourists. ✉ *170 bd. St-Germain,* ☎ *01–45–48–55–25. Métro: St-Germain-des-Prés.*

La Palette. In good weather, the terrace is as popular with local art students and gallery owners as it is with tourists. On a rainy afternoon, the interior, too, is cozy—it's decorated with works of art by its habitués. ✉ *43 rue de Seine,* ☎ *01–43–26–68–15. Métro: Odéon.*

La Rotonde. The café, a second home to foreign artists and political exiles in the '20s and '30s, has a less exotic clientele today. But it's still a pleasant place to have a coffee on the sunny terrace. ✉ *105 bd. Montparnasse,* ☎ *01–43–26–68–84. Métro: Montparnasse.*

Le Sélect. Isadora Duncan and Hart Crane used to hang out here; now it's a popular spot for a post-cinema beer. ✉ *99 bd. Montparnasse,* ☎ *01–45–48–38–24. Métro: Vavin.*

Le Vieux Colombier. Take a seat on the lovely wicker furniture in front of one of the big windows in this café just around the corner from St-Sulpice and the Vieux Colombier theater. ✉ *65 rue de Rennes,* ☎ *01–45–48–53–81. Métro: St-Sulpice.*

8ᵉ Arrondissement (Champs-Élysées)

Ladurée. Pretty enough to bring a tear to Proust's eye, this ravishing and famous salon de thé looks barely changed from 1862. Grandmother's grandmother, antiques dealers, and lovers of beauty make up the clientele, which dotes on the lemon and caramel signature macaroons, little tea sandwiches, and a slew of teas that will make you want to stick out your little pinky. A new branch—one that also boasts a time-burnished ambience—is at 75 avenue des Champs-Élysées. ⊠ *16 rue Royale,* ☎ *01–42–60–21–79. Métro: Madeleine.*

Le Paris. This buzzy little café with a hip crowd and decor is the latest outpost of the Costes brothers, local trendsetters and high-style mavens, and it reflects the fact that the famous avenue is coming back into fashion. Service can be chilly, but it's worth putting up with for the interesting crowd and good, light food. ⊠ *93 av. des Champs-Elysées,* ☎ *01–47–23–54–37. Métro: George V.*

11e Arrondissement (Bastille)

Café de l'Industrie. Have a late-afternoon coffee or beer in the warm yellow rooms of this Bastille hangout, where the walls are covered with photos of movie stars. ⊠ *16 rue St-Sabin,* ☎ *01–47–00–13–53. Métro: Bastille.*

Pause Cafe. This hip Bastille spot attracts a chic, artsy crowd for coffee, cheap beer, and tasty, inexpensive chili and quiche at its red-and-yellow Formica tables. ⊠ *41 rue de Charonne,* ☎ *01–48–06–80–33. Métro: Ledru-Rollin.*

14e Arrondissement (Montparnasse)

Café du Dôme. Now a fancy brasserie—though you can still just have a cup of coffee or a drink here—this place began as a dingy meeting place for exiled artists and intellectuals such as Lenin, Picasso, and Chaim Soutine. ⊠ *108 bd. Montparnasse,* ☎ *01–43–35–25–81. Métro: Vavin.*

Café de la Place. This café is a charming wood-paneled spot that is perfect for watching the activity inside and out. ⊠ *23 rue d'Odessa,* ☎ *01–42–18–01–55. Métro: Montparnasse.*

18e Arrondissement (Montmartre)

La Crémaillère. Alphonse Mucha frescoes decorate the walls at this veritable monument to 19th-century fin-de-siècle art in Montmartre. ⊠ *15 pl. du Tertre,* ☎ *01–46–06–58–59. Métro: Anvers.*

Le Sancerre. Sit on the terrace sipping a coffee or a beer and watch the artists, hipsters, and tourists all pass by on their way through Montmartre. ⊠ *35 rue des Abbesses,* ☎ *01–45–58–08–20. Métro: Abbesses.*

19e Arrondissement (Buttes-Chaumont/La Villette)

Café de la Musique. This vast, stylishly postmodern café is adjacent to the Cité de la Musique in the Parc de La Villette. In the evenings it's primarily filled with people attending concerts, but the free jazz on Wednesday night and the interesting crowd make it worth the excursion. ⊠ *214 av. Jean-Jaurès,* ☎ *01–48–03–15–91. Métro: Porte de Pantin.*

Wine Bars

Paris wine bars are the perfect place to enjoy a glass (or bottle) of wine with a plate of cheese, charcuterie, or a simple but delicious hot meal. Bar owners are often true wine enthusiasts ready to dispense expert advice. Hours vary widely, so it's best to check ahead if your heart is set on a particular place; many, however, close around 10 PM.

Au Sauvignon. A stylish but jolly Left Bank crowd frequents this homey, friendly spot with an ideally placed terrace. Delicious *tartines* (open-face sandwiches) are served. ⊠ *80 rue des Sts-Pères, 7e,* ☎ *01–45–48–49–02. Métro: Sèvres-Babylone.*

Aux Bons Crus. This cramped, narrow venue has an authentic Parisian feel (it dates from 1905). ⊠ *7 rue des Petits-Champs, 1er,* ☎ *01–42–60–06–45. Métro: Bourse.*

Le Baron Bouge. Known as Le Baron Rouge for 20 years, this red bar near the boisterous place d'Aligre market had never registered the name so recently was forced to change it. Thankfully, the neighborhood atmosphere remains intact. ⊠ *1 rue Théopile-Roussel, 12e,* ☎ *01–43–43–14–32. Métro: Ledru-Rollin.*

Le Comptoir. Glasses of Burgundy and Bordeaux, as well as more unusual selections such as wines from Corsica, are served. ⊠ *5 rue Monsieur-Le-Prince, 6e,* ☎ *01–43–29–12–05. Métro: Odéon.*

Jacques Mélac. This wine bar is named after the jolly owner who harvests grapes from the vine outside and bottles several of his own wines. ⊠ *42 rue Léon-Frot, 11e,* ☎ *01–43–70–59–27. Métro: Charonne.*

Le Moulin à Vins. Wines from the southwest and the Rhône Valley and sturdy bistro cuisine are served. Stop by and elbow your way in among the locals at the bar. ⊠ *6 rue Burq, 18e,* ☎ *01–42–52–81–27. Métro: Abbesses.*

La Robe et le Palais. Come here for the more than 120 wines from all over France, served *au compteur* (according to the amount consumed), as well as a daily selection of good bistro-style dishes for lunch and dinner. ⊠ *13 rue des Lavandières-Ste-Opportune, 1er,* ☎ *01–45–08–07–41. Métro: Châtelet-les- Halles.*

Le Rouge Gorge. This sophisticated Marais wine bar attracts discriminating locals, who come for unusual wines by the glass and the hearty food. ⊠ *8 rue St-Paul, 4e,* ☎ *01–48–04–75–89. Métro: Bourse.*

Le Rubis. This resolutely old-time bar specializes in Burgundies. It's most crowded during the day; from 7 to 9:30 PM it's best to be smoke-resistant. ⊠ *10 rue du Marché St-Honoré, 1er,* ☎ *01–42–61–03–34. Métro: Tuileries.*

La Tartine. Inexpensive wine and tartines in a tatty, almost seedy, late 19th-century bar have given this place antihero status among the rebel cognoscenti. ⊠ *24 rue de Rivoli, 4e,* ☎ *01–42–72–76–85. Métro: St-Paul.*

3 LODGING

Hemingway had it right: Paris is indeed a moveable feast. But even he had to occasionally push himself away from the table, lay his head upon a pillow, and call it a night. But where? For Papa, it was usually the Ritz. You, however, might be more at home in a clean, well-lit room off a garden courtyard in Montmartre, or a Starck-designed suite near the shops of St-Honoré, or perhaps the Duke and Duchess of Windsor's favorite apartment at the Meurice. Whether you're an heiress, a CEO, or just someone out for a budget lark, you'll find most of our options deliciously combine charm and tradition.

Revised and
updated by
Christopher
Mooney

A RIGHT BANK HOTEL SUITE—late-morning sunshine streams through the brocade curtains on the gilded windows framing a Monet-worthy view of plane trees in the Tuileries just outside; beyond, the violet-hued Seine flows past quay-side dwellings lining the embankment. You're two sips of *petit crème* and half a croissant into your day—almost awake but still lolling under crisp sheets, a down duvet, and a shot-silk bed canopy, circa 1925. A Belle Epoque silver service sits on the Napoléon III–style bedside table, next to a leather-bound Pléiade edition of Stendhal, borrowed from the hotel's oak-paneled library. You've slept in and missed housekeeping, but they'll be by again—twice—to clean your room, pick up your laundry, lay out fresh towels and robes, and restock the two marble-and-onyx bathrooms with Hermès toiletries. Your eyes lift from the rim of the Limoges cup to the painted ceiling above the canopied bed and take in the gossamer clouds and the azure-blue sky, then drift outside to the needle-sharp spire of Sainte-Chapelle. Freeze frame. Slow fade to bliss.

Typical? Sure, if you're paying 50,000 francs/€7,692 a night. Drop two zeros and, more often than not, you get "Paris Hotel Room, Take 2": sound up on a dripping faucet as we track along peeling chintz wallpaper to the rusting bed where you lie, U-shaped and shivering, under thin blankets and dun-color sheets. Someone is coughing on the other side of the paper-thin wall. A diesel truck rumbles past the mud-streaked window. Freeze frame. Slow fade to bleak.

This doesn't have to be your lot. As part of a general upgrade of the city's hotels in recent years, scores of lackluster, shabby Paris lodgings have been replaced by good-value establishments in the lower to middle price ranges. Whatever price range you're looking for, compared to most other cities Paris is a hotel paradise for the weary traveler tired of dreary, cookie-cutter rooms. If you're out for luxury, Paris has places so luxe they make Versailles look like a Zen teahouse—and the bar keeps getting raised higher and higher: just last year the Sultan of Brunei sank a fortune into the refurbishment of the beloved Meurice, while the grande dame Georges V underwent a $100 million face-lift. In the middle range, there are those wonderful *hôtels de charme*—set in 19th-century town houses, with an air of elegance just slightly gone to seed and with large windows to catch the elusive Paris sun. Even if you're lucky enough to find yourself in a snug room with a lumpy mattress, pipes that gurgle in the night, a defective heating system, and cooing pigeons parked on the window ledge, just tell yourself that it's atmosphere! After all, this is Paris.

Our criteria when selecting the hotels reviewed below were quality, location, and character. Few chain hotels are listed, since most (with some notable exceptions) lack the charm and authenticity found in typical Parisian lodgings. Similarly, fewer hotels are in outlying arrondissements (the 10ᵉ to the 20ᵉ) because these are farther from the major sights. Generally, there are more hotels on the Right Bank offering luxury—at any rate, formality—than on the Left Bank, where the hotels are frequently smaller and richer in old-fashioned ambience. The Right Bank's 1ᵉʳ and 8ᵉ arrondissements are still the most exclusive, and prices here reflect this. Less-expensive alternatives on the Right Bank may be found in the fashionable Marais quarter (3ᵉ and 4ᵉ arrondissements) and the 11ᵉ and 12ᵉ, near the Opéra Bastille.

Despite widespread improvement, many Paris hotels (especially budget-level accommodations) still have idiosyncrasies—some endearing, others less so. Hotel rooms in Paris's oldest quarters are generally much smaller than their American counterparts. The French double bed is slightly smaller than the American standard. Although air-conditioning has become de rigueur in mid- to higher-priced hotels, it is generally not a prerequisite for comfort except during the hottest summer days, nor is it always available (ask, if you want to be absolutely sure). Reviews indicate the number of rooms with private baths (which may include a shower or a tub, but not necessarily both). It's rare to find moderately priced places that expect guests to share toilets or bathrooms, but be sure you know what you are getting when you book a budget hotel.

Always reserve well in advance, especially if you're determined to stay in a specific place. You can do this by telephoning or faxing ahead, and asking for written or faxed confirmation. As you will probably be asked to send a deposit, be sure to discuss refund policies before releasing your credit card number or mailing a check or money order. During peak seasons, some hotels require total prepayment. Always demand written confirmation of your reservation, detailing the duration of your stay, the price, the location and type of room desired (single or double, twin beds or double), and the bathroom: shower (*douche*) or bath (*baignoire*), private or shared.

Almost all Paris hotels charge extra for breakfast, with prices ranging from 30 francs to more than 200 francs/€30 per person in luxury establishments. Though hotels may not automatically add the breakfast charge to your bill, it's wise to inform the desk staff if you plan to have breakfast away from the hotel (you may want to find the nearest café instead). For anything more than the standard Continental breakfast of café au lait and baguette or croissants, the price will be higher. Some hotels have especially pleasant breakfast areas, and we have noted this where applicable. Luxury hotels often have restaurants, but finding a place to eat in Paris is rarely a problem.

We list hotels by price. Over the past few years luxury hotel prices have risen faster than their more moderate counterparts. Often a hotel in a certain price category will have a few rooms that are less expensive; it's worth asking about. Rates must be posted in all rooms (usually on the back of the door), with all extra charges clearly shown. There is a nominal *taxe de séjour* of 7 francs/€1 per person, per night.

Unless otherwise stated, the hotels reviewed below have elevators; rooms have TVs (many with cable, including CNN), minibars, and telephones; and English is spoken. Additional facilities, such as restaurants and health clubs, are listed at the end of each review.

CATEGORY	COST*
$$$$	over 1,750 frs/€269
$$$	1,000 frs–1,750/€153 frs–€269
$$	600 frs–1,000 frs/€92–€153
$	under 600 frs/€92

All prices are for a standard double room, including tax and service.

1er Arrondissement (Louvre)

See Right Bank Lodging map.

$$$$ 🏨 **Costes.** Baron de Rothschild hasn't invited you to drop in this time?
★ No matter—if you stay here, at Paris's most stylishly sumptuous hotel, you'll quickly get over it. Five years after opening its doors onto the city's most expensive shopping street, Jean-Louis and Gilbert Costes's eponymous hotel remains the darling of decorating magazines and a magnet for supermodels and off-duty celebrities. Once an intimate, 19th-

Right Bank Lodging

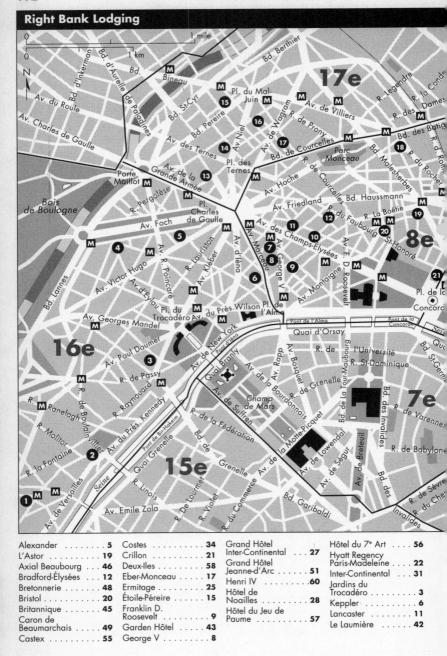

Left Bank Lodging

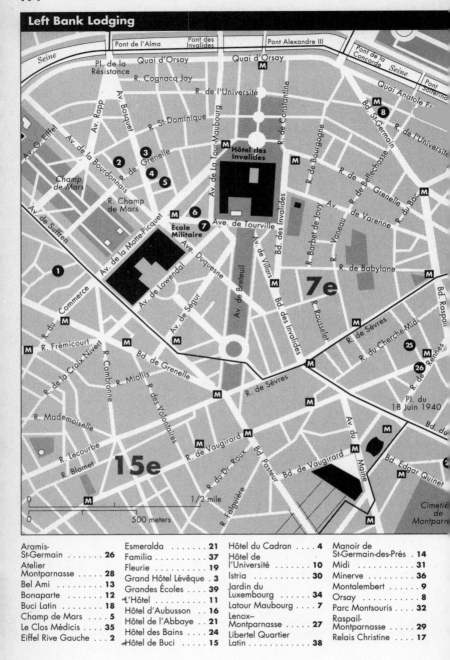

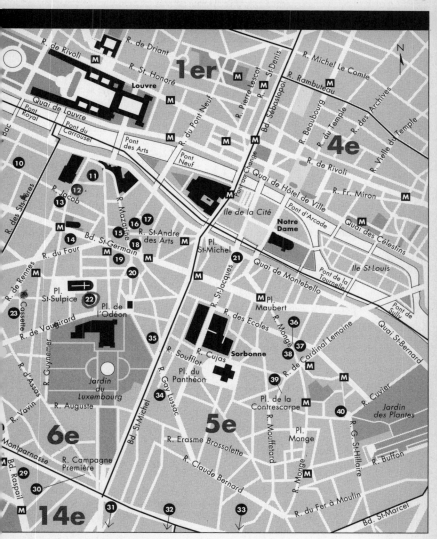

century town house, the Costes now conjures up the palaces of Napoléon III, thanks to the genius of Jacques Garcia, France's leading decorator. Nearly every room is swathed in enough rich garnet, patterned $400-a-yard fabrics, heavy swags, and enough *passementerie* (decorative fringe) to blanket the Champs-Élysées. The bathrooms are truly marvelous affairs, and a seductive, go-for-baroque bar, with its labyrinth of little rooms and secluded nooks, is *the* place in Paris to be seen trying not to be seen. For taste, in every sense of the word, this is the top Paris hotel. ⊠ *239 rue St-Honoré, 75001,* ☎ *01–42–44–50–50,* 𝔽𝔸𝕏 *01–42–44–50–01,* ᴡᴇʙ *www.hotelcostes.com. 77 rooms, 5 suites, with bath. Restaurant, bar, air-conditioning, in-room data ports, in-room safes, room service, indoor pool, sauna, gym, laundry service. AE, DC, MC, V. Métro: Tuileries.*

$$$$ ⊞ **Inter-Continental.** Stravinsky not only stayed here, he gave concerts in several of the hotel's magnificent salons. This exquisite, late-19th-century hotel, with period details sumptuously restored, was designed by the architect of the Paris Opéra, Charles Garnier. The music theme continues on the guest list, which is studded with famous names, such as Jessye Norman. Three of its gilt-and-stuccoed Napoléon III and Imperial public rooms are official historic monuments. Guest rooms, though more sedate than the public spaces, have Empire-style furnishings and rich period fabrics. The most coveted and spacious guest rooms overlook quiet inner courtyards. In summer, breakfast on the patio is a delicious experience. *Naturellement,* service is always impeccable. ⊠ *3 rue de Castiglione, 75001,* ☎ *01–44–77–11–11; 800/327–0200 in the U.S.,* 𝔽𝔸𝕏 *01–44–77–14–60,* ᴡᴇʙ *www.interconti.com. 375 rooms, 70 suites, with bath. Restaurant, bar, air-conditioning, in-room safes, no-smoking floor, room service, baby-sitting, laundry service, concierge, meeting room. AE, DC, MC, V. Métro: Concorde.*

$$$$ ⊞ **Meurice.** One of the finest hotels in the world is now even finer. Thanks to the millions of the Sultan of Brunei, the fabled restaurant and the elaborately gilded 18th-century rococo salons have been entirely restored, and the rooms—furnished with Persian carpets, marble mantelpieces, and ormolu clocks—are now more soigné than ever, if that's possible (book well in advance for a room or a suite overlooking the Tuileries Gardens). The bathrooms, redone in red and ocher marble from the Pyrénées and white and gray marbles from Italy, are truly elaborate affairs. The 230-square-ft Suite 628, decorated in the style of a Napoléonic tent, is next to impossible to land, unless you're an off-duty celebrity. By no means miss a chance to dine in the restaurant, which has reigned for nearly a century as one of Paris's most stunningly opulent salons. ⊠ *228 rue de Rivoli, 75001,* ☎ *01–44–58–10–10,* 𝔽𝔸𝕏 *01–44–58–10–15,* ᴡᴇʙ *www.meuricehotel.com. 161 rooms, 35 suites, with bath. 2 restaurants, bar, air-conditioning, in-room data ports, in-room safes, minibars, no-smoking room, room service, sauna, laundry service, concierge, business services. AE, DC, MC, V. Métro: Tuileries, Concorde.*

$$$$ ⊞ **Régina.** On handsome place des Pyramides, this 100-year-old Art Nouveau gem oozes old-fashioned grandeur in both its public spaces and guest rooms, where fine antiques abound. There's also a sublime Belle Epoque lounge. Request a room on rue de Rivoli, facing the Louvre and the Tuileries Gardens. ⊠ *2 rue des Pyramides, 75001,* ☎ *01–42–60–31–10,* 𝔽𝔸𝕏 *01–40–15–95–16,* ᴡᴇʙ *www.regina-hotel.com. 130 rooms, 14 suites, with bath. Restaurant, bar, air-conditioning, in-room safes, no-smoking room, room service, laundry service, meeting room. AE, DC, MC, V. Métro: Tuileries.*

$$$$ ⊞ **Ritz.** Surrounded by the city's finest jewelers, the Ritz is the crown-
★   ing gem on sparking place Vendôme. Festooned with Napoléonic gilt and ormolu, sparkling with crystal chandeliers, and adorned with

qualité de Louvre antiques, it was founded in 1896 as a temple of luxury by Cesar Ritz. This legendary haven of the flamboyantly wealthy has been regilded at a cost of $150 million by owner Mohammed al-Fayed. Be warned, however, that there really are two Ritz spheres. The first is the gilded place Vendôme wing—this is where Gary Cooper serenaded Audrey Hepburn in *Love in the Afternoon* and features the suites named after former residents, such as Marcel Proust and Coco Chanel. The newer wing, off the back of the building, remains surprisingly (disappointingly?) intimate. Still, every room is highly comfortable and endowed with all the latest gimmickry (many have a control panel hidden in the nightstand), and everyone is served by a staff that is ubiquitous, discreet, and multilingual. The lack of lobby discourages paparazzi and sightseers, so you'll have to hang out in the wood-paneled bars, including one that Papa Hemingway "liberated" in 1944. The hotel's Espadon restaurant's warm-weather terrace patio, with tables and chairs covered in elegant fabrics, is almost too pretty for words. Lucky guests can also repair to the basement health club and pool—a splendid spa that looks like a Louis XIV temple of sweat. ⊠ *15 pl. Vendôme, 75001,* ☎ *01–43–16–30–30,* FAX *01–43–16–36–68,* WEB *www.ritz.com. 135 rooms, 40 suites, with bath. 3 restaurants, 2 bars, air-conditioning, in-room data ports, in-room safes, room service, indoor pool, hair salon, health club, shops, laundry service, meeting room, parking (fee). AE, DC, MC, V. Métro: Opéra.*

$$$–$$$$ 🏨 **Vendôme.** This hotel has the highest staff-to-guest ratio in Paris and
★ offers every luxury imaginable. Rooms are handsomely done in Second Empire style, with walls and furnishings in muted earth tones and hand-carved wood detailing throughout. Bathrooms are over the top: brass, marble and silver bathtubs, waterproof telephones, and toiletries from Guerlain. Best of all, besides a videophone for checking out visitors at the door, is the fully automated bedside console that controls the lights, curtains, and electronic do-not-disturb sign. ⊠ *1 pl. Vendôme, 75001,* ☎ *01–42–60–32–84,* FAX *01–49–27–97–89. 19 rooms, 7 suites, with bath. Restaurant, bar, air-conditioning, room service, in-room safes, in-room data ports, laundry service. AE, DC, MC, V. Métro: Concorde, Opéra.*

$$$ 🏨 **Paris Hôtel des Tuileries.** This remarkably quiet hotel, tucked away in an 18th-century town house on a small side street, is within walking distance of the Louvre, Tuileries Gardens, and place Vendôme. Everything, from the creaky cage elevator and wide French windows to the sturdy wooden armoires and gilt mirrors, is quaintly old-fashioned. A tiny lobby lounge and tapestry-covered breakfast room are the only public areas. ⊠ *10 rue Ste-Hyacinthe, 75001,* ☎ *01–42–61–04–17,* FAX *01–49–27–91–56. 21 rooms, 5 suites, with bath. Bar, air-conditioning, in-room safes, room service, laundry service. AE, DC, MC, V. Métro: Tuileries, Concorde.*

$$ 🏨 **Britannique.** Open since 1870, the Britannique blends courteous English service with old-fashioned French elegance. It has a handsome winding staircase and soundproof rooms appointed in mahogany and warm tones. During World War I, the hotel served as headquarters for a Quaker mission. ⊠ *20 av. Victoria, 75001,* ☎ *01–42–33–74–59,* FAX *01–42–33–82–65. 40 rooms, 31 with bath, 9 with shower. Bar, in-room data ports, in-room safes, no-smoking room. AE, DC, MC, V. Métro: Châtelet.*

$$ 🏨 **Londres St-Honoré.** An appealing combination of character and comfort distinguishes this small, inexpensive hotel, a five-minute walk from the Louvre. Exposed oak beams, statues in niches, and rustic stone walls give this place old-fashioned charm, while modern pluses include satellite TV. Though rooms have floral bedspreads and standard hotel furniture, they are pleasant and the price is right. Note that the elevator only starts on the second floor. ⊠ *13 rue St-Roch, 75001,* ☎ *01–42–60–15–62,* FAX *01–42–60–16–00. 29 rooms with bath. AE, DC, MC, V. Métro: Pyramides.*

$$ 🖪 **Régence Opéra.** This location is almost *too* convenient—right in the heart of Paris and within a stone's throw of the Opéra Garnier, Palais-Royal, Louvre, and the throbbing Grands Boulevards. Rooms are more spacious than you'd expect for the price, though they are furnished somewhat generically, with pastel hues, floral bedspreads, and standard-issue wooden furnishings. ⊠ *5 rue Thérèse, 75001,* ☎ *01–42–96–10–01,* FAX *01–42–96–15–22. 43 rooms with bath. Bar, no-smoking floor, room service, baby-sitting, laundry service. AE, DC, MC, V. Métro: Pyramides.*

$ 🖪 **Henri IV.** The Surrealists loved place Dauphine, which they called *le sexe de Paris* because of its location—on the Ile de la Cité, at the very center of Paris—and suggestive V-shape. Today, it is loved for its tony restaurants and wine bars and for this old-fashioned hotel, one of the city's cheapest deals and worst-kept "secrets." The lobby is drab, the narrow staircase (five floors, no elevator) creaks, and the rooms, though spacious enough, are shabby. But the price and the super location—on Paris's celebrated island and just a short walk from Notre-Dame—have made it one of the toughest reservations in the city. Bathrooms are in the hallway; pay a little extra and get one of the three rooms with shower. ⊠ *25 pl. Dauphine, 75001,* ☎ *01–43–54–44–53, 21 rooms without bath, 3 with shower. No credit cards. Métro: Cité, St-Michel.*

$ 🖪 **Louvre Forum.** This hotel is a find: smack in the center of Paris, it has extremely reasonably priced, clean, comfortable, well-equipped rooms and a friendly feel. What it lacks in old-world appeal it makes up for in location, amenities, and price. Breakfast is served in a homey vaulted cellar. ⊠ *25 rue du Bouloi, 75001,* ☎ *01–42–36–54–19,* FAX *01–42–33–66–31. 27 rooms with bath. Bar. AE, DC, MC, V. Métro: Louvre.*

$ 🖪 **Tiquetonne.** Just off marché Montorgueil and a short hoof from Les Halles, this is one of the least expensive hotels in the city center. The rooms aren't much to look at but they're always clean and some are downright spacious. Book on one of the top two floors facing the quiet, pedestrian rue Tiquetonne, not the loud, car-strangled rue Turbigo. ⊠ *6 rue Tiquetonne, 75002,* ☎ *01–42–36–94–58,* FAX *01–42–36–02–94. 47 rooms with bath or shower. AE, MC, V. Métro: Étienne-Marcel, Châtelet.*

2ᵉ Arrondissement (La Bourse)

See Right Bank Lodging map.

$$$$ 🖪 **Westminster.** This former private mansion on an elegant street between the Opéra and place Vendôme was built in the mid-19th century. It maintains a gracious atmosphere with marble fireplaces, crystal chandeliers, and parquet floors. The pleasant piano bar is a popular rendezvous spot, and the hotel's restaurant, Le Céladon, serves outstanding French cuisine. ⊠ *13 rue de la Paix, 75002,* ☎ *01–42–61–57–46; 800/203–3232 in the U.S.,* FAX *01–42–60–30–66,* WEB *www.warwickhotels.com. 83 rooms, 18 suites, with bath. Restaurant, bar, air-conditioning, in-room safes, no-smoking room, room service, baby-sitting, laundry service, meeting room, parking (fee). AE, DC, MC, V. Métro: Opéra.*

$$$ 🖪 **Victoire Opéra.** This terrific hotel on a bustling, pedestrian-only market street near Les Halles, the Centre Pompidou, and the Marais, has a new name and a new look. Formerly the Besançon, this terrific hotel has rooms that are now more spacious and decorated in a tastefully restrained modern style. ⊠ *56 rue Montorgueil, 75002,* ☎ *01–42–36–41–08,* FAX *01–45–08–08–79. 20 rooms with bath. In-room data ports, in-room safes, room service, baby-sitting, laundry service. AE, DC, MC, V. Métro: Étienne Marcel, Les Halles.*

$$ ⊞ **Hôtel de Noailles.** With a nod to the work of postmodern designers like Puttman and Starck, this nouveau-wave inn (part of the Tulip Inn group) is a star among Paris's new crop of well-priced, style-driven boutique hotels. Though not to everyone's taste, rooms are imaginatively decorated with funky furnishings and contemporary details, such as rubbery curtains; the look is fun and very hip. A young, cosmopolitan clientele has made this one its own. ⊠ *9 rue de Michodière, 75002,* ☎ *01–47–42–92–90,* FAX *01–49–24–92–71. 58 rooms with bath. Bar, air-conditioning, sauna, health club, laundry service, meeting room. AE, DC, MC, V. Métro: Opéra.*

3ᵉ Arrondissement (Marais)

See Right Bank Lodging map.

$$$$ ⊞ **Pavillon de la Reine.** On 17th-century place des Vosges, this mag-
★   nificent mansion was reconstructed from original plans. It's filled with Louis XIII–style antiques, rich-toned fabrics, and fireplaces. For an absolutely royal feeling, ask for a duplex with French windows overlooking the first of two flower-filled courtyards behind the historic Queen's Pavilion. Breakfast is served in the vaulted cellar, apéritifs in front of the salon's gargantuan fireplace. ⊠ *28 pl. des Vosges, 75003,* ☎ *01–40–29–19–19; 800/447–7462 in the U.S.,* FAX *01–40–29–19–20. 30 rooms, 25 suites, with bath. Bar, breakfast room, air-conditioning, room service, laundry service, free parking. AE, DC, MC, V. Métro: Bastille, St-Paul.*

4ᵉ Arrondissement (Marais/Ile St-Louis)

See Right Bank Lodging map.

$$$ ⊞ **Hôtel du Jeu de Paume.** The showpiece of this lovely 17th-century hotel on the Ile St-Louis is the stone-walled, vaulted lobby–cum–breakfast room. It stands on an erstwhile court where French aristocrats once played *jeu de paume,* an early version of tennis using palm fronds. The bright rooms are nicely done up in butter yellow, with rustic antiques, tasteful objets and bric-a-brac, beamed ceilings, and damask upholstery. The little garden is a haven of sun-drenched tranquillity. ⊠ *54 rue St-Louis-en-l'Ile, 75004,* ☎ *01–43–26–14–18,* FAX *01–40–46–02–76,* WEB *www.jeudepaumehotel.com. 30 rooms, 1 junior suite, with bath. Bar, sauna, baby-sitting, laundry service, health club, meeting room. AE, DC, MC, V. Métro: Pont Marie.*

$$ ⊞ **Axial Beaubourg.** A solid bet in the Marais, this hotel in a 16th-century building has beamed ceilings in the lobby and in the six first-floor rooms. Most have pleasant if functional decor, and all have satellite TV. The Centre Pompidou and the Picasso Museum are five minutes away. ⊠ *11 rue du Temple, 75004,* ☎ *01–42–72–72–22,* FAX *01–42–72–03–53. 39 rooms with bath. Air-conditioning, in-room data ports, in-room safes, no-smoking room. AE, DC, MC, V. Métro: Hôtel-de-Ville.*

$$ ⊞ **Bretonnerie.** This small hotel is in a 17th-century *hôtel particulier* (town house) on a tiny street in the Marais, a few minutes' walk from the Centre Pompidou. The Louis XIII–style rooms come complete with upholstered walls, antiques, beamed ceilings, four-poster beds, and marble-clad bathrooms, or some combination thereof. Their size varies considerably from spacious to cramped; the larger ones are pricier. Breakfast is served in the vaulted cellar. ⊠ *22 rue Ste-Croix-*

de-la-Bretonnerie, 75004, ☎ *01–48–87–77–63,* FAX *01–42–77–26–78,* WEB *www.labretonnerie.com. 24 rooms, 6 suites, with bath. In-room safes, parking (fee). MC, V. Métro: Hôtel-de-Ville.*

$$ ★ 🖫 **Caron de Beaumarchais.** The theme of this intimate hotel is the work of Caron de Beaumarchais, who wrote *The Marriage of Figaro* in 1778. First-edition copies of his books adorn the public spaces, while one suite features possibly the prettiest bed in Paris—a grand Louis XV four-poster recently photographed in *Travel & Leisure.* Rooms faithfully reflect the taste of 18th-century French nobility, right down to the reproduction wallpapers and upholsteries. Fresh flowers and fluffy bathrobes are a bonus for the price. Bathrooms feature heavy antique mirrors and hand-painted tiles. Streetside rooms on the second through fifth floors are the largest, while the slightly smaller sixth-floor garrets under the mansard roof have beguiling views across Right Bank rooftops. ✉ *12 rue Vieille-du-Temple, 75004,* ☎ *01–42–72–34–12,* FAX *01–42–72–34–63. 19 rooms with bath. Air-conditioning, laundry service. AE, DC, MC, V. Métro: Hôtel-de-Ville.*

$$ 🖫 **Deux-Iles.** This converted 17th-century mansion on the Ile St-Louis has long won plaudits for charm and comfort. Flowers and plants are scattered throughout the stunning main hall, and tapestries cover the exposed stone walls. The delightfully old-fashioned rooms, blessed with exposed beams, are small but airy and sunny. Ask for one overlooking the little garden courtyard. In winter, a roaring fire warms the lounge. ✉ *59 rue St-Louis-en-l'Ile, 75004,* ☎ *01–43–26–13–35,* FAX *01–43–29–60–25. 17 rooms with bath. Air-conditioning, in-room safes, baby-sitting. AE, MC, V. Métro: Pont Marie.*

$$ 🖫 **Hôtel du 7ᵉ Art.** The theme of this hip Marais hotel fits its name ("The Seventh Art" is what the French call filmmaking): Hollywood from the '40s to the '60s. Posters of James Cagney, Marilyn Monroe, Charlie Chaplin, and other stars decorate the walls throughout. Rooms are small and spartan but clean, quiet, and equipped with cable TV. There is no elevator. Breakfast is served in the handsome wood-paneled lounge; there's also an invitingly kitschy bar, and a brand-new gym in the rustic cellar room. The clientele is young, trendy, and *très* American. ✉ *20 rue St-Paul, 75004,* ☎ *01–44–54–85–00,* FAX *01–42–77–69–10. 23 rooms with bath. Bar, in-room safes. AE, DC, MC, V. Métro: St-Paul.*

$$ 🖫 **Place des Vosges.** A loyal, eclectic clientele swears by this small, historic Marais hotel on a delightful street just off place des Vosges. The Louis XIII–style reception area and rooms with oak-beamed ceilings, rough-hewn stone, and a mix of rustic finds from secondhand shops evoke the old Marais. Ask for the top-floor room, the hotel's largest, for its view over Right Bank rooftops; others can be the size of walk-in closets and are less expensive. ✉ *12 rue de Birague, 75004,* ☎ *01–42–72–60–46,* FAX *01–42–72–02–64. 16 rooms with bath. Breakfast room. AE, DC, MC, V. Métro: Bastille.*

$$ 🖫 **St-Louis.** Louis XIII–style furniture and oil paintings set the tone in the public areas in this 17th-century town house on the Ile St-Louis. Guest rooms are much simpler and more standard, but exposed beams and stone walls make them appealing. Breakfast is served in the atmospheric cellar. ✉ *75 rue St-Louis-en-l'Ile, 75004,* ☎ *01–46–34–04–80,* FAX *01–46–34–02–13. 21 rooms with bath. In-room data ports, in-room safes. MC, V. Métro: Pont Marie.*

$$ 🖫 **Vieux Marais.** This pleasingly old-fashioned hotel with a turn-of-the-20th-century facade is on a quiet street in the heart of the Marais. Rooms are bright, impeccably clean, and equipped with satellite TV; try to get one overlooking the just-renovated courtyard. Recently, they've made the bathrooms much bigger and brighter. Breakfast is served in a pretty lounge. The staff is exceptionally courteous. ✉ *8 rue du*

Plâtre, 75004, ☎ *01–42–78–47–22,* FAX *01–42–78–34–32. 30 rooms with bath. Air-conditioning, in-room safes. MC, V. Métro: Hôtel-de-Ville.*

$ ▣ **Castex.** This Marais hotel in a Revolution-era building is a bargain hunter's dream. Rooms are low on frills but squeaky clean. The owners are extremely friendly, and the prices are rock-bottom, which ensures that the hotel is often booked months ahead by a largely young, largely American clientele. There is no elevator, and only one room has a TV (another one graces the ground-floor salon). ✉ *5 rue Castex, 75004,* ☎ *01–42–72–31–52,* FAX *01–42–72–57–91,* WEB *www.castexhotel.com. 29 rooms with bath. In-room data ports. MC, V. Métro: Bastille.*

$ ▣ **Grand Hôtel Jeanne-d'Arc.** If you're on a budget, you're sure to get your money's worth at this hotel near place des Vosges in the Marais. Though rooms are on the spartan side, they are clean, well maintained, and fairly spacious (some have a couch). The staff is welcoming and friendly. ✉ *3 rue de Jarente, 75004,* ☎ *01–48–87–62–11,* FAX *01–48–87–37–31. 36 rooms with bath. MC, V. Métro: St-Paul.*

5ᵉ Arrondissement (Latin Quarter)

See Left Bank Lodging map.

$$$ ▣ **Libertel Quartier Latin.** The new flagship of the Libertel chain combines sleek design with intellectual rigor. Interior decorator Didier Gomez took his cues from the nearby Sorbonne university, turning the downstairs lounge into an elegant reading room and lining the walls with photos and portraits of celebrated writers. Rooms, furnished with ebony furniture and quilted bedcovers, emphasize sculpted lines and quiet comfort. Ask for one on the sixth floor, preferably No. 602 or 603, which have beautiful views of Notre-Dame from their balconies. If this doesn't inspire you finally to write that novel, maybe the carpets will: they're inscribed with quotations from Balzac and Baudelaire. ✉ *9 rue des Écoles, 75005,* ☎ *01–44–27–06–45,* FAX *01–43–25–36–70. 23 rooms, 6 suites, with bath. Air-conditioning, in-room safes, room service. AE, DC, MC, V. Métro: Cardinal Lemoine.*

$$ ▣ **Esméralda.** Once any *Vogue* editor's best-kept secret, this place
★ used to be the ultimate Left Bank *hôtel de charme.* Set in a fusty 17th-century building across from Notre-Dame, it has long been cherished for its cozy, eccentric charm. Some closet-size rooms are nearly overpowered by gaudy imitation antiques or 1970s fabrics, while others could be cleaner; for the best and largest rooms, book those in *l'annexe* (there are even some triples, or rooms with three beds). On the street side, there are several rooms with views of the cathedral that would have reduced Delacroix to sobs of joy. The tiny lobby—adorned with silk flowers, daub and wood moldings, Grandmother's sofa, snoozing cats—is right out of a Flaubert novel. ✉ *4 rue St-Julien-le-Pauvre, 75005,* ☎ *01–43–54–19–20,* FAX *01–40–51–00–68. 19 rooms, 15 with bath. No credit cards. Métro: St-Michel.*

$$ ▣ **Jardin du Luxembourg.** Blessed with a personable staff and a smart,
★ stylish look, this hotel, on a calm side street just a block from the Luxembourg Gardens, is one of the most sought-after in the Latin Quarter, especially among psychoanalysts—Freud slept here. Rooms are small (common for this locale) but cleverly furnished, to optimize space; the rustic pieces and warm ocher, rust, and indigo tones give them a Provençal feel. Ask for one with a balcony overlooking the street; the best room, No. 25, has dormer windows revealing a peekaboo view of the Eiffel Tower. ✉ *5 impasse Royer-Collard, 75005,* ☎ *01–40–46–08–88,* FAX *01–40–46–02–28. 27 rooms with bath. Air-conditioning, in-room safes, no-smoking room, sauna. AE, DC, MC, V. Métro: Luxembourg.*

$$ ⊡ **Timhotel Jardin des Plantes.** Across the street from the lovely Jardin des Plantes, this pleasant, modern hotel—part of the Timhotel chain—has very reasonable prices and perfectly suitable rooms with blond-wood furnishings and floral upholsteries. There's a fifth-floor terrace where you can breakfast or sunbathe in summer, and a sauna in the cellar. ⊠ *5 rue Linné, 75005,* ☎ *01–47–07–06–20,* FAX *01–47–07–62–74. 33 rooms with bath. Sauna. AE, DC, MC, V. Métro: Jussieu.*

$ ⊡ **Familia.** It's hard to beat the price or this level of homespun com-
★   fort—the hospitable Gaucheron family, the hotel's owners, bend over backward for you. More than half the rooms have sepia frescoes of celebrated Paris scenes painted by an artist from the Beaux Arts school; some are appointed with exquisite Louis XV–style furnishings, while others have nice mahogany or cherrywood pieces. Those overlooking the animated Latin Quarter street have double-glazed windows, and those on the second and fifth floors have their own walk-out balcony with breakfast table and chairs. Book at least a month in advance. ⊠ *11 rue des Écoles, 75005,* ☎ *01–43–54–55–27,* FAX *01–43–29–61–77. 30 rooms with bath. AE, MC, V. Métro: Cardinal Lemoine.*

$ ⊡ **Grandes Écoles.** This delightfully intimate hotel looks and feels like a country cottage dropped smack in the middle of the Latin Quarter. It is off the street and occupies three buildings on a beautiful, leafy garden, where breakfast is served in summer. Parquet floors, Louis-Philippe furnishings, lace bedspreads, and the absence of TV all add to the rustic ambience. ⊠ *75 rue du Cardinal Lemoine, 75005,* ☎ *01–43–26–79–23,* FAX *01–43–25–28–15. 51 rooms with bath. Parking (fee). MC, V. Métro: Cardinal Lemoine.*

$ ⊡ **Minerve.** Fans of the Gaucheron family—and they are legion—will
★   be delighted to learn that the Minerve is now part of the Familia fold. Just next door to the Familia, and twice as big, the hotel has been completely refurbished in the inimitable Gaucheron style: flowers and breakfast tables on the balconies, frescoes in the rooms and the spacious lobby, tapestries on the walls, and cherrywood furniture in the rooms. The Minerve is less intimate than the Familia but just as charming, and the Gaucherons hope their new acquisition will take some of the pressure off—with 54 more rooms on offer here, maybe they won't have to turn away so many guests. ⊠ *13 rue des Écoles, 75005,* ☎ *01–43–26–26–04,* FAX *01–44–07–01–96. 54 rooms with bath. Breakfast room, in-room data ports. AE, MC, V. Métro: Cardinal Lemoine.*

6ᵉ Arrondissement (St-Germain/Montparnasse)

See Left Bank Lodging map.

$$$$ ⊡ **Bel Ami.** After the huge success of the Montalembert and the Lancaster, design diva Grace Leo-Andrieu has opened yet another feng shui-friendly hotel, this time in stylish St-Germain-des-Prés. "Affordable chic" is the business concept behind the hotel, and it works: situated around the corner from Café Flore and Deux Magots, not to mention numerous bookstores and designer boutiques galore, the Bel Ami attracts a young, fashionable clientele who want a hip address but don't want to dish out $2,000 a night for a suite at the Lancaster. The hotel's sleek yet casual decor is in the Christian Liagre mold; a coffee-to-chocolate brown, cream, and olive-green palette and a minimalist Japanese touch in the hotel's reception; copper and glass-mosaic bar and multilingual Internet café; and a fireplace lounge and breakfast room. Rooms continue in the same hiply elegant aesthetic and are equipped with marble, glass and chrome bathrooms, and cotton bathrobes of such heft you'll never want to take yours off. ⊠ *7–11 rue St-Benoît, 75006,* ☎ *01–42–61–53–53,* FAX *01–49–27–09–33,* WEB *www.hotel-bel-ami.com. 113 rooms, 2 suites. Bar, air-conditioning, in-room data ports, room* *service, baby-sitting, laundry service, concierge. AE, DC, MC, V. Métro: St-Germain-des-Prés.*

$$$$ 🏨 **Relais Christine.** On a quiet street between the Seine and boulevard St-Germain, this luxurious and popular hotel, occupying 16th-century abbey cloisters, oozes romantic ambience. Rooms are spacious (particularly the duplexes on the upper floors) and well appointed in the old Parisian style (rich upholsteries, mahogany pieces); the best have exposed ceiling beams and overlook the garden. The breakfast room is an erstwhile stone chapel. ✉ *3 rue Christine, 75006,* ☎ *01–40–51–60–80; 800/447–7462 in the U.S.,* FAX *01–40–51–60–81. 31 rooms, 18 suites, with bath. Bar, air-conditioning, no-smoking room, room service, baby-sitting, laundry service, meeting room, free parking. AE, DC, MC, V. Métro: Odéon.*

$$$–$$$$ 🏨 **L'Hôtel.** Rock idols and movie stars adore this eccentric Left Bank
★ hotel. In fact, how can you resist a place that calls itself L'Hôtel (as if someone called her cat "Cat")? Or one with such an intriguing history? Originally an 18th-century *pavilion d'amour* (inn for trysts), it had become the Hôtel d'Alsace by the time Oscar Wilde checked in, and then died, in Room 16 (for 2,800 frs/€431, you can spend a night in his death bed). Wilde's last words about his room's wallpaper—"One of us will have to go"—must have come back to haunt today's owners, who gutted the building and spent a fortune to make it into a decorator's dream. One small double is decorated entirely in leopard-skin motifs; another handsome suite features the mirrored, Art Deco boudoir furniture of vaudeville star Mistinguett. The downside? Many rooms are snug. Still, you can always hang out in the hotel bar, still popular with an international crowd. The hotel has just received another decor refurbishment by the celebrated style king, Jacques Garcia, so call even further ahead than usual to book. ✉ *13 rue des Beaux-Arts, 75006,* ☎ *01–44–41–99–00,* FAX *01–43–25–64–81. 25 rooms, 2 suites, with bath. Bar, air-conditioning, in-room safes, baby-sitting. AE, DC, MC, V. Métro: St-Germain-des-Prés.*

$$$–$$$$ 🏨 **Hôtel d'Aubusson.** This 17th-century mansion, once home to Paris's
★ first literary salon, is now one of the finest *petites hôtels de luxe* in the city, with original Aubusson tapestries, Versailles-style parquet floors, a chiseled stone fireplace, and restored antiques. Even the smallest rooms are good-sized by Paris standards, and all are decked out in rich burgundies, greens, or blues. The 10 best rooms have canopied beds and ceiling beams. In summer, you can have your breakfast or predinner drink in the paved courtyard. ✉ *33 rue Dauphine, 75006,* ☎ *01–43–29–43–43,* FAX *01–43–29–12–62,* WEB *www.hoteldaubusson.com. 49 rooms with bath. Bar, air-conditioning, in-room data ports, in-room safes, room service, baby-sitting, laundry service. AE, MC, V. Métro: Odéon.*

$$$ 🏨 **Buci Latin.** Modern artwork on the walls and zebra-upholstered chairs
★ in the lobby set the tone at this funky, upscale hotel. Each room's door is inspired by the work of a famous artist—Magritte, Léger, Monet, or Basquiat—done by local painters. Rooms are small, but the Santa Fe decor, ocher walls, exposed beams, and arty contoured tables give them a quirky feel. The more spacious duplex suite on the top floor, right under the roof, has a small bathroom loft with a shower, makeup table, and freestanding bathtub. ✉ *34 rue de Buci, 75006,* ☎ *01–43–29–07–20,* FAX *01–43–29–67–44. 25 rooms, 2 suites, with bath. Air-conditioning, in-room data ports, minibars, room service, laundry service. AE, DC, MC, V. Métro: Mabillon.*

$$$ 🏨 **Hôtel de Buci.** The eager-to-please staff adds to the luxurious feeling of this small hotel on the lively rue de Buci market street. Rooms, which vary in size from cozy to spacious, have armoires and reproductions of 18th-century fabrics in warm, regal patterns; bathrooms are done in marble. Ask for a room overlooking the rear for a quieter night's sleep, or one in front for a glimpse of Paris. The lobby, filled with club chairs and fresh flowers, and the cellar breakfast room are good spots to rendezvous. ✉ *22 rue de Buci, 75006,* ☎ *01–55–42–74–74,* FAX *01–55–42–74–44,* WEB *www.hotelbuci.fr. 24 rooms with bath. Breakfast room, in-room data ports, minibars, business services, meeting room. AE, DC, MC, V. Métro: Odéon.*

$$$ 🏨 **Hôtel de l'Abbaye.** Once a convent, this delightful hotel near St-Sulpice features a stone-vaulted entrance and a lovely flower-filled back garden with a stone fountain. The blend of stylishly rustic antiques and earthy apricot and ocher tones makes for a calm, cozy atmosphere. The first-floor rooms open onto the garden; most of those on the upper floors have oak beams and sitting alcoves. The four duplexes with private terraces are more expensive. Breakfast is included. ✉ *10 rue Cassette, 75006,* ☎ *01–45–44–38–11,* FAX *01–45–48–07–86. 42 rooms, 4 suites, with bath. Bar, air-conditioning, room service, baby-sitting, laundry service. AE, MC, V. Métro: St-Sulpice.*

$$$ 🏨 **Manoir de St-Germain-des-Prés.** This stylish hotel is right next to the Brasserie Lipp and across from the Café de Flore. Rooms are done up in traditional 18th-century luxe, with wainscoting and rich upholsteries. Amenities promote genuine R&R, from hot tubs and soundproof rooms to thirsty terry robes and well-stocked minibars; and breakfast is included. ✉ *153 bd. St-Germain-des-Prés, 75006,* ☎ *01–42–22–21–65,* FAX *01–45–48–22–25. 32 rooms with bath. Bar, air-conditioning, in-room data ports, in-room safes, hot tub, laundry service. AE, DC, MC, V. Métro: St-Germain-des-Prés.*

$$$ 🏨 **Relais St-Germain.** The interior-designer owners of this outstanding hotel in the heart of St-Germain-des-Prés have exquisite taste and a superb respect for tradition and detail. Moreover, rooms are at least twice the size of what you find at other hotels in the area for the same price. Much of the furniture was selected with a knowledgeable eye from the city's *brocantes* (secondhand dealers), and every room has its own unique treasures. Doubles have separate sitting areas; four have kitchenettes. Breakfast is included. ✉ *9 carrefour de l'Odéon, 75006,* ☎ *01–43–29–12–05,* FAX *01–46–33–45–30. 21 rooms, 1 suite, with bath. Bar, air-conditioning, in-room data ports, in-room safes, minibars, room service, baby-sitting, laundry service. AE, DC, MC, V. Métro: Odéon.*

$$–$$$ 🏨 **Le Clos Médicis.** Contemporary style meets Provençal tradition at this classy little hotel in St-Germain-des-Prés. Warm colors and a mix of modern pieces, painted country furnishings, and wrought-iron items set the tone. Rooms are small (except for the duplex) but laden with comforts, such as minibars and crisp terry robes. ✉ *56 rue Monsieur-le-Prince, 75006,* ☎ *01–43–29–10–80,* FAX *01–43–54–26–90. 38 rooms with bath. Bar, air-conditioning, in-room data ports, no-smoking room. AE, DC, MC, V. Métro: Luxembourg.*

$$–$$$ 🏨 **Fleurie.** On a quiet side street near place de l'Odéon, this spiffy, family-run hotel has pretty, pastel-color rooms and many modern luxury amenities, including beautifully tiled bathrooms with heated towel racks. Antiques, Oriental rugs, and rich upholsteries fill the 18th-century building. The staff is helpful. ✉ *32–34 rue Grégoire-de-Tours, 75006,* ☎ *01–53–73–70–00,* FAX *01–53–73–70–20. 29 rooms with bath. Bar, air-conditioning, in-room data ports, in-room safes, baby-sitting, laundry service. AE, DC, MC, V. Métro: Odéon.*

➔ $$–$$$ 🏨 **Relais St-Sulpice.** A savvy clientele with discerning taste frequents this fashionable little hotel. It's a stylish blend of various periods and regions—African artwork lines the hallways; Provençal tiles adorn the bathrooms; Chinese engravings wink to Parisians' penchant for the Orient in the 1930s; heavy fabrics drape the windows; and thick, cottonpiqué downy comforters envelop wrought-iron beds. There's a sauna downstairs, right off the atrium breakfast salon. Room 11 has a terrific view of St-Sulpice. ⊠ *3 rue Garancière, 75006,* ☎ *01–46–33–99–00,* FAX *01–46–33–00–10. 26 rooms with bath. Air-conditioning, in-room safes, no-smoking room, sauna, baby-sitting, laundry service, meeting room, parking (fee). AE, DC, MC, V. Métro: St-Germain-des-Prés, St-Sulpice.*

$$–$$$ ⊡ **St-Grégoire.** On a calm street off bustling rue de Rennes, this dis-
★ creet little hotel offers quiet and comfortable refuge from the hectic pace of Paris. Rooms, done in muted pinks, yellows, and beiges, have simple antique furnishings and bucolic prints on the walls. The sitting room–lobby is especially cozy, with its rustic fireplace and flowery wallpaper. Particularly romantic are Rooms 14 and 16, which have enclosed, ivy-covered terraces. ⊠ *43 rue de l'Abbé-Grégoire, 75006,* ☎ *01–45–48–23–23,* FAX *01–45–48–33–95. 19 rooms, 1 suite, with bath. Air-conditioning, baby-sitting. AE, DC, MC, V. Métro: St-Placide.*

$$ ⊡ **Aramis-St-Germain.** You get great value for your money at this hotel, which, surprisingly, is part of the Best Western chain. It is understated yet classically French. Rooms have damask bedspreads and sturdy cherrywood armoires. All are soundproof and equipped with cable TV; about half have air-conditioning, and nine have whirlpool baths. Harvey's Piano Bar, on the ground floor, is popular with the smart business set. ⊠ *124 rue de Rennes, 75006,* ☎ *01–45–48–03–75; 800/ 528–1234 in the U.S.,* FAX *01–45–44–99–29. 42 rooms with bath. Bar, minibars, laundry service. AE, DC, MC, V. Métro: St-Placide.*

$$ ⊡ **Atelier Montparnasse.** This Art Deco–inspired gem was designed with style and comfort in mind. Rooms are tastefully done, and all the bathrooms feature unique mosaic reproductions of famous French paintings. The hotel is across the street from the famous brasseries Le Sélect and La Coupole and within walking distance of the Luxembourg Gardens and St-Germain-des-Prés. Art lovers, take note: the hotel hosts monthly exhibits of the works of local painters. Families will want to book the room with three beds. ⊠ *49 rue Vavin, 75006,* ☎ *01–46–33–60–00,* FAX *01–40–51–04–21. 17 rooms with bath. Bar, room service, baby-sitting, laundry service. AE, DC, MC, V. Métro: Vavin.*

→ $$ ⊡ **Bonaparte.** The congeniality of the staff only makes a stay in this intimate place more of a treat. Old-fashioned upholsteries, 19th-century furnishings, and paintings create a quaint feel in the relatively spacious rooms. And the location in the heart of St-Germain is nothing short of fabulous. ⊠ *61 rue Bonaparte, 75006,* ☎ *01–43–26–97–37,* FAX *01–46–33–57–67. 29 rooms with bath. Air-conditioning, in-room safes, refrigerator, laundry service. MC, V. Métro: St-Germain-des-Prés.*

7e Arrondissement (Invalides/École Militaire)

See Left Bank Lodging map.

$$$$ ⊡ **Montalembert.** Created by hotel goddess Grace Leo-Andrieu, this
★ is one of Paris's most originally voguish boutique accommodations. Refurbished yet again, the rooms have been stripped of Christian Liagre's dark wood, causing many in the fashion world, who view the hotel as a shrine to modern design, to gasp in horror. They needn't worry: whether appointed with traditional or contemporary furnishings, the rooms are still all about simple lines and chic luxury. The Frette linens and fabrics remain in place, as are the Cascais marble bathrooms and cast-bronze door fittings. Ask about special package deals if you're staying for more than three nights. ⊠ *3 rue de Montalembert, 75007,* ☎ *01–45–49–68–68; 800/628–8929 in the U.S.,* FAX *01–45–49–69–49,* WEB *www.montalembert.fr. 48 rooms, 8 suites, with bath. Restaurant, bar, air-conditioning, in-room data ports, in-room safes, in-room VCRs,*

room service, massage, baby-sitting, concierge, meeting room. AE, DC, MC, V. Métro: Rue-du-Bac.

$$–$$$ ⊞ **Le Tourville.** Here is a rare find: a cozy, upscale hotel that doesn't
★ cost a fortune. Each room has crisp, virgin-white damask upholstery
set against pastel or ocher walls, a smattering of antique bureaus and
lamps, original artwork, and fabulous old mirrors. The hotel attracts
a young, fashionable crowd, especially in the dishy Art Deco bar. The
junior suites have hot tubs. The staff couldn't be more helpful. ⊠ *16
av. de Tourville, 75007,* ☎ *01–47–05–62–62; 800/528–3549 in the U.S.,*
[FAX] *01–47–05–43–90,* [WEB] *www.hoteltourville.com. 27 rooms, 3 junior
suites, with bath. Bar, breakfast room, air-conditioning, laundry service. AE, DC, MC, V. Métro: École Militaire.*

$$ ⊞ **Hôtel du Cadran.** Colorful window boxes lend a welcoming touch
to this cheerful hotel in a handsome corner building near the market
on rue Cler. The charming Madame Chaine and her gracious staff go
out of their way to ensure that you enjoy your stay, from recom-
mending a bistro to booking theater tickets. Rooms have coordinat-
ing drapes and bedspreads in cheery colors and are very comfortable.
Ask about special weekend rates. ⊠ *10 rue du Champ de Mars, 75007,*
☎ *01–40–62–67–00,* [FAX] *01–40–62–67–13. 42 rooms with bath. Bar,
air-conditioning, in-room data ports, in-room safes, no-smoking room,
baby-sitting, laundry service, concierge, meeting room, travel services.
AE, DC, MC, V. Métro: École Militaire.*

$$ ⊞ **Hôtel de l'Université.** Staying at this hotel in a 17th-century town
house between boulevard St-Germain and the Seine feels like going back
in time. Guest rooms have English and French antiques and original
fireplaces. Ask for one with a terrace on the fifth floor. Note that the
cheapest guest rooms have showers—no tubs—in the bathrooms. ⊠
22 rue de l'Université, 75007, ☎ *01–42–61–09–39,* [FAX] *01–42–60–40–
84. 27 rooms with bath. Air-conditioning, in-room data ports, in-
room safes, room service. AE, MC, V. Métro: Rue-du-Bac.*

$$ ⊞ **Latour Maubourg.** In the heart of the elegant 7e arrondissement, a
stone's throw from the Invalides and the prime minister's residence, is
this small hotel where personalized service is emphasized. The place
is homey and unpretentious, from its very helpful staff to its simply
furnished rooms with their mix of appealingly mismatched finds. ⊠
150 rue de Grenelle, 75007, ☎ *01–47–05–16–16,* [FAX] *01–47–05–16–
14,* [WEB] *www.latour-maubourg.fr. 9 rooms, 1 suite, with bath. Air-con-
ditioning. MC, V. Métro: La Tour-Maubourg.*

$$ ⊞ **Orsay.** Across the street from the Musée d'Orsay, the Orsay (formerly the Solférino) is a cheerful little hotel, with spacious, comfort-
able rooms and attentive service. The look is upbeat, with bright color
schemes and flower-filled window boxes; rooms have satellite TV. The
skylighted breakfast room is a pleasant place to greet the day. ⊠ *93
rue de Lille, 75007,* ☎ *01–47–05–85–54,* [FAX] *01–45–55–51–16. 41
rooms with bath. AE, DC, MC, V. Métro: Solférino.*

$ ⊞ **Champ de Mars.** Françoise and Stéphane Gourdal's comfortable hotel
★ has an appealing blue-and-yellow French country-house style. Rooms are
equipped with satellite TV and CNN; the two on the ground floor open
onto a leafy courtyard. The location—near the Eiffel Tower and Invalides—is difficult to beat. ⊠ *7 rue du Champ de Mars, 75007,* ☎ *01–
45–51–52–30,* [FAX] *01–45–51–64–36,* [WEB] *www.hotel-du-champ-de-mars.
com. 25 rooms with bath. In-room data ports. MC, V. Métro: École Militaire.*

$ ⊞ **Eiffel Rive Gauche.** On a quiet side street just a couple of blocks from
the Eiffel Tower, this modern hotel with a leafy patio is a great budget find. The look is functional, but rooms are spacious and comfortable. The owner, Monsieur Chicheportiche, is a multilingual, walking
encyclopedia of Paris. One caveat: a steep phone surcharge is added if

you make a collect call. ⊠ *6 rue du Gros Caillou, 75007,* ☎ *01–45–51–24–56,* FAX *01–45–51–11–77. 30 rooms with bath. AE, MC, V. Métro: École Militaire.*

$ ⊞ **Grand Hôtel Lévêque.** The Eiffel Tower is just around the corner, but the real draw here is the picturesque street market just outside the hotel's front door. Recently renovated, this immaculate hotel has an eager-to-please staff, comfortable rooms, satellite TV, and a bistro-style breakfast room. Make sure to get a room facing the street and reserve early—this is a very popular address among French and American foodies. ⊠ *29 rue Cler, 75007,* ☎ *01–47–05–49–15,* FAX *01–45–50–49–36. 50 rooms, 45 with bath. AE, MC, V. Métro: École Militaire.*

8e Arrondissement (Champs-Élysées)

See Right Bank Lodging map.

$$$$ ⊞ **L'Astor.** Part of the Sofitel hotel group, L'Astor is a bastion of highly stylized, civilized chic. The Art Deco lobby is decked out in boldly patterned armchairs, huge mirrors, and clever ceiling frescoes. There's also a cozy bar; a small, neoclassic-inspired library; and a stunning trompe l'oeil dining room. Guest rooms are testimonials to the sober Regency style, with weighty marble fireplaces and mahogany furnishings. Several suites have walk-out balconies with superb vistas. The hotel's restaurant is supervised by the celebrated chef Joël Robuchon. ⊠ *11 rue d'Astorg, 75008,* ☎ *01–53–05–05–05; 800/763–4385 in the U.S.,* FAX *01–53–05–05–30,* WEB *www.hotel-astor.net. 129 rooms, 5 suites, with bath. Restaurant, bar, air-conditioning, in-room data ports, in-room safes, no-smoking room, room service, massage, health club, baby-sitting, laundry service. AE, DC, MC, V. Métro: Miromesnil, St-Augustin.*

$$$$ ⊞ **Bristol.** Money and power don't shout at the Bristol—they whisper.
★ The understated facade on rue du Faubourg St-Honoré might mislead the unknowing, but the Bristol ranks among Paris's top four hotels and has the prices to prove it. Many billionaires and celebrities refuse to stay anywhere else, attracted by the tasteful luxe and the staff's finishing-school discretion (put to a rigorous test several years ago when a Rothschild magnate committed suicide in one of the rooms here). Some of the spaciously elegant rooms have authentic Louis XV and Louis XVI furniture and magnificent marble bathrooms in pure 1920s Art Deco; others have a more relaxed 19th-century style. The public salons are palatially stocked with old master paintings, sculptures, sumptuous carpets, and tapestries. ⊠ *112 rue du Faubourg St-Honoré, 75008,* ☎ *01–53–43–43–00,* FAX *01–53–43–43–01. 154 rooms, 41 suites, with bath. Restaurant, bar, air-conditioning, in-room data ports, in-room safes, room service, indoor pool, sauna, health club, laundry service, meeting room, free parking. AE, DC, MC, V. Métro: Miromesnil.*

$$$$ ⊞ **Crillon.** To anyone with a taste for history, the name Crillon chimes
★ a whole carillon of bells. In 1758, Louis XV commissioned the architect Jacques-Ange Gabriel to build two facades of the mansion, which would complete the imposing north side of one of Paris's most celebrated landmarks, place de la Concorde. As the comte de Crillon's palace, it welcomed royal guests, including Marie-Antoinette, who took singing lessons here (one of the original *grands appartements,* now protected as national treasures, has been named after her), then lost her life on the guillotine on the square outside. In 1909 it became a hotel and not long after was the site of the signing of the League of Nations charter by Woodrow Wilson. Since then it has played host to generations of diplomats, politicians, and refined travelers (movie stars prefer the rooms that face the square, which come with double-glazed windows). Most

rooms are lavishly decorated with rococo and Directoire antiques, crystal and gilt wall sconces, and gold-leaf fittings. The sheer quantity of marble in the highly praised Les Ambassadeurs restaurant is staggering—you can almost imagine you are dining in one of the ballrooms at Versailles. ⊠ *10 pl. de la Concorde, 75008,* ☎ *01–44–71–15–00; 800/888–4747 in the U.S,* FAX *01–44–71–15–02,* WEB *www.crillon-paris. com. 117 rooms, 43 suites, with bath. 2 restaurants, 2 bars, tea shop, air-conditioning, in-room data ports, in-room safes, no-smoking room, room service, gym, baby-sitting, laundry service, meeting room. AE, DC, MC, V. Métro: Concorde.*

$$$$ 🏨 **George V.** Two years and $125 million in renovations later, the George
★ V has finally reopened its glittering gold doors. General Eisenhower's headquarters during the Liberation of Paris is now owned by a Saudi prince (who gets first dibs on the $8,500-a-night Royal Suite) and managed by the Four Seasons group. The palace hotel is as bright and shiny as the day it opened in 1928: the original Art Deco detailings and 17th-century tapestries have been restored; the bas-reliefs releafed in gold; the marble-floor mosaics rebuilt tile by tile. New additions include private health-club facilities for couples, a gourmet Hédiard boutique next to the lobby, and, most impressively, Le V—one of Paris's latest and greatest outposts of haute cuisine, now presided over by the legendary Philippe Legendre of Taillevent fame and Europe's top sommelier, Eric Beaumont, stewarding the wine list. If the Saudi prince shows up, don't worry about getting bumped from your bed: there are five other suites priced in more or less the same stratosphere. ⊠ *31 av. George V, 75008,* ☎ *01–49–52–70–00,* FAX *01–49–52–70–10,* WEB *www.fourseasons.com. 185 rooms, 60 suites, with bath. Restaurant, bar, air-conditioning, in-room data ports, in-room safes, no-smoking room, room service, indoor pool, hair salon, sauna, health club, laundry service, business services, meeting room. AE, DC, MC, V. Métro: George V.*

$$$$ 🏨 **Hyatt Regency Paris-Madeleine.** This Haussmannesque building near the Opéra Garnier feels more like a boutique hotel than an international chain, thanks to stylized details like cherry paneling and mismatched bedside tables. You can also expect the usual plush carpeting and luxurious upholsteries. Book a room on the seventh or eighth floor facing boulevard Malesherbes for a view of the Eiffel Tower. ⊠ *24 bd. Malesherbes, 75008,* ☎ *01–55–27–12–34; 800/223–1234 in the U.S.,* FAX *01–55–27–12–35. 81 rooms, 5 suites, with bath. Restaurant, bar, air-conditioning, in-room data ports, in-room safes, no-smoking floor, room service, sauna, gym, laundry service, business services, meeting room. AE, DC, MC, V. Métro: St-Augustin.*

$$$$ 🏨 **Lancaster.** Another jewel in Grace Leo-Andrieu's crown, the Lan-
★ caster, one of Paris's most venerable institutions, has been transformed by her legion of star designers into a stellar and modish luxury hotel. The overall feel—a seamless blend of traditional with contemporary— is one of timeless elegance. Every detail speaks of quality, from the hotel's own line of bath products to the Porthault linens. Many of the suites pay homage to the hotel's colorful regulars, from Garbo to John Huston to Sir Alec Guinness. Marlene Dietrich's is decorated in lilac (her favorite color) and features a superb Louis XV desk. ⊠ *7 rue de Berri, 75008,* ☎ *01–40–76–40–76; 877/757–2747 in the U.S.,* FAX *01–40– 76–40–00,* WEB *www.hotel-lancaster.com. 50 rooms, 10 suites, with bath. Restaurant, bar, air-conditioning, in-room data ports, in-room safes, in-room VCRs, room service, sauna, gym, baby-sitting, laundry service, meeting room, parking (fee). AE, DC, MC, V. Métro: George V.*

$$$$ 🏨 **Paris Marriott Champs-Élysées.** Take a ground-zero locale, a stylish atrium lobby, and a chic, 19th-century style, and you've got the Paris Marriott. Ebony furnishings and antique prints are some of the nice touches that make you forget this is a chain, and state-of-the-art sound-proofing shuts out the cacophonic Champs. The hotel restaurant specializes in high-end *cuisine americaine.* ✉ *70 av. des Champs-Élysées, 75008,* ☎ *01–53–93–55–00; 800/228–9290 in the U.S.,* FAX *01–53–93–55–01. 174 rooms, 18 suites, with bath. Restaurant, 2 bars, air-conditioning, in-room data ports, in-room safes, no-smoking floor, room service, sauna, gym, baby-sitting, laundry service, business services, meeting room. AE, DC, MC, V. Métro: George V.*

$$$$ 🖭 **Prince de Galles.** Another splendid Art Deco edifice, the recently refurbished Prince de Galles is the kinder, gentler brother of its next-door neighbor, the George V. Here, where the legendary discretion and attentiveness of the staff so aptly recall the days of yesteryear, the 1920s don't so much roar as purr. The restaurant, with its summer patio of Moorish blue and gold mosaics, is an oasis of calm amid the frenzied interplay of boulevards and business just outside the hotel's front door. Le Regency, a cigar-friendly, club-style bar boasting a wall of single malts and a special luncheon for those with temporal (rather than financial) restrictions, is the perfect *entent cordial* between English sobriety and French culinary expertise. Rooms and suites are spacious and bright, with crystal chandeliers in every room except the marbled bathrooms. A new business center and high-tech conference rooms are discreetly hidden below the elegant lobby. ✉ *33 av. George V, 75008,* ☎ *01–53–23–77–77,* FAX *01–53–23–78–78,* WEB *www.luxurycollection.com. 138 rooms, 30 suites, with bath. Restaurant, bar, air-conditioning, in-room data ports, in-room safes, minibars, room service, hair salon, health club, baby-sitting, laundry service, concierge, business services, meeting room. AE, DC, MC, V.*

$$$–$$$$ 🖭 **Franklin D. Roosevelt.** One of the last family-run boutique hotels in the Champs-Élysées area, this true *hôtel de charme* is an intimate alternative to grander establishments in the same price category. Entirely renovated last year, the hotel has the look and feel of a London club, with hunting scenes on the walls and a fire crackling in the smoking salon. French fashion magazines have done photo spreads on the cozy bar and the three colonial-style lounges, but it is just as stylish upstairs—rooms and suites have mahogany doors and antiques, Oriental carpets and ceramics, cashmere draperies and printed calico wall coverings. Book a room on the fifth floor if you want to breakfast on a balcony. ✉ *18 rue Clément Marot, 75008,* ☎ *01–53–57–49–50,* FAX *01–47–20–44–30,* WEB *www.Franklin-Roosevelt.com. 42 rooms, 3 suites, with bath. Breakfast room, air-conditioning, in-room data ports, in-room safes, minibars, meeting room. AE, DC, MC, V. Métro: Marbeuf.*

$$$ 🖭 **Bradford-Élysées.** This turn-of-the-20th-century hotel conserves its old-fashioned feel while providing modern amenities. An old wooden elevator carries you from the flower-filled lobby to the spacious, luxurious rooms equipped with Louis XVI–style furniture, brass beds, and marble fireplaces. ✉ *10 rue St-Philippe-du-Roule, 75008,* ☎ *01–45–63–20–20,* FAX *01–45–63–20–07. 50 rooms with bath. Air-conditioning, in-room data ports, in-room safes, minibars, no-smoking room, baby-sitting, laundry service. AE, DC, MC, V. Métro: St-Philippe-du-Roule.*

$$ 🖭 **Résidence Monceau.** Within a stone's throw of the elegant Parc Monceau, this friendly and fashionable hotel is an oasis of refined tranquillity. Warm tones make rooms cozy; the efficient and professional staff makes your stay easy. The breakfast garden, surrounded by ivy-covered trellises, is a lovely place to start the day. ✉ *85 rue du Rocher, 75008,* ☎ *01–45–22–75–11,* FAX *01–45–22–30–88. 50 rooms, 1 suite, with bath. Bar, no-smoking room, travel services. AE, DC, MC, V. Métro: Villiers.*

9ᵉ Arrondissement (Opéra)

See Right Bank Lodging map.

$$$$ ▥ **Grand Hôtel Inter-Continental.** Opened by Napoléon III and his
empress Eugénie in 1862, Paris's biggest luxury hotel has a facade that
seems as long as the Louvre's. The hotel got a latter-day Art Deco
makeover, and the grand salon's dome and the restaurant's splendidly
painted ceilings are registered landmarks. Even the guest rooms are Art
Deco and are spacious and light. As in the days of the Impressionists,
the hotel's famed Café de la Paix is one of the city's great people-watching spots. ⊠ *2 rue Scribe, 75009,* ☎ *01–40–07–32–32; 800/327–
0200 in the U.S.,* ℻ *01–42–66–12–51,* ☒ *www.interconti.com. 492
rooms, 22 suites, with bath. 3 restaurants, 2 bars, air-conditioning, in-
room data ports, in-room safes, in-room VCRs, no-smoking room, room
service, sauna, health club, laundry service, business services, meeting
room. AE, DC, MC, V. Métro: Opéra.*

$$$$ ▥ **Millennium Opéra.** The grande dame of boulevard Haussmann is
back: built in 1927, this Art Deco edifice has been restored and renamed
(formerly the Commodore) and is now the best-equipped luxury hotel
in the quarter, with fiber-optic PC links in the rooms and a regal oyster bar in the brand-new brasserie. The glass Belle Epoque elevator still
sweeps guests from their floors to the spacious lobby below, but those
wanting to cut a rug will have to hoof it elsewhere, as the basement
cabaret has been converted into a seven-room conference center. ⊠ *12
bd. Haussmann, 75009,* ☎ *01–49–49–16–00,* ℻ *01–49–49–17–00,*
☒ *www.mill-cop.com. 152 rooms, 11 suites, with bath. Restaurant,
bar, air-conditioning, in-room data ports, in-room safes, room service,
baby-sitting, laundry service, concierge, meeting room. AE, DC, MC,
V. Métro: Le Peletier.*

11ᵉ Arrondissement (Bastille)

See Right Bank Lodging map.

$ ▥ **Garden Hôtel.** This family-run hotel is on a pretty garden square in
a quiet residential neighborhood 10 minutes from Père-Lachaise Cemetery. Rooms are functional but spotless; those in front have lovely views
of the verdant square, and all have double-glazed windows to ensure
quiet. The staff speaks little English. Bathtubs are half size. Triples (rooms
with three beds) go for 450 francs/€69. ⊠ *1 rue du Général-Blaise,
75011,* ☎ *01–47–00–57–93,* ℻ *01–47–00–45–29. 42 rooms with
bath. AE, MC, V. Métro: St-Ambroise.*

$ ▥ **Résidence Alhambra.** The white facade, back garden, and flower-
filled window boxes brighten an otherwise lackluster neighborhood.
Inside, the look is more spartan, with smallish, modernly appointed
rooms; all have satellite TV. The best reason to stay here is that prices
are rock-bottom and the hotel is near the Marais and accessible to five
métro lines at place de la République. ⊠ *13 rue de Malte, 75011,* ☎
01–47–00–35–52, ℻ *01–43–57–98–75. 58 rooms with bath. MC, V.
Métro: Oberkampf.*

12ᵉ Arrondissement (Bastille/Gare de Lyon)

See Right Bank Lodging map.

$$–$$$ ▥ **Le Pavillon Bastille.** Here's a smart address (across from the Opéra
Bastille) for savvy travelers who appreciate getting perks for less. The
transformation of this 19th-century hôtel particulier into a colorful,
high-design hotel garnered architectural awards. A fiercely loyal, hip
clientele loves its bright blue and yellow interior and whimsical touches.
Every detail is pitch-perfect, from the friendly staff right down to the

17th-century fountain in the garden. ✉ *65 rue de Lyon, 75012,* ☎ *01–43–43–65–65; 800/233–2552 in the U.S.,* 𝙵𝙰𝚇 *01–43–43–96–52. 24 rooms, 1 suite, with bath. Bar, air-conditioning, in-room safes, mini-bars, room service. AE, DC, MC, V. Métro: Bastille.*

$$ 🖭 **Modern Hôtel-Lyon.** Just a block from the Gare de Lyon is this cozy, congenial, family-run hotel, open since 1903. Rooms done up in blues and lavenders give the place a French country feel. ✉ *3 rue Parrot, 75012,* ☎ *01–43–43–41–52,* 𝙵𝙰𝚇 *01–43–43–81–16. 47 rooms, 1 suite, with bath. In-room safes. AE, DC, MC, V. Métro: Gare-de-Lyon.*

13ᵉ Arrondissement (Gobelins)

See Left Bank Lodging map.

$ 🖭 **Résidence les Gobelins.** Wicker furniture and warm colors create a cozy feel at this small, simple hotel on a quiet side street between place d'Italie and the Latin Quarter. Some rooms overlook a small, flower-filled garden, as does the lounge where breakfast is served. ✉ *9 rue des Gobelins, 75013,* ☎ *01–47–07–26–90,* 𝙵𝙰𝚇 *01–43–31–44–05. 32 rooms with bath. In-room data ports. AE, DC, MC, V. Métro: Gobelins.*

14ᵉ Arrondissement (Montparnasse)

See Left Bank Lodging map.

$$–$$$ 🖭 **Raspail-Montparnasse.** Guest rooms here are named after the artists who made Montparnasse the art capital of the world in the '20s and '30s—Picasso, Chagall, and Modigliani, to name a few. Instead of their raw, fauve colors, pastels are the dominant shades here, complemented by contemporary blond-wood furniture and crisp cotton upholsteries. Most rooms are at the low end of this price category; five have spectacular panoramic views of Montparnasse and the Eiffel Tower. All are soundproofed. Contemporary art exhibitions are held in the main hall. ✉ *203 bd. Raspail, 75014,* ☎ *01–43–20–62–86; 800/448–8355 in the U.S.,* 𝙵𝙰𝚇 *01–43–20–50–79,* 𝚆𝙴𝙱 *www.globe-market.com. /h75014raspail.htm. 38 rooms with bath. Bar, air-conditioning, in-room safes. AE, DC, MC, V. Métro: Vavin.*

$–$$ 🖭 **Istria.** This small, family-run hotel on a quiet side street was a Montparnasse artists' hangout in the '20s and '30s. It has a flower-filled courtyard and simple, clean, comfortable rooms with soft, pastel-toned Japanese wallpaper and light-wood furnishings. Breakfast is served in a pretty, vaulted cellar. ✉ *29 rue Campagne-Première, 75014,* ☎ *01–43–20–91–82,* 𝙵𝙰𝚇 *01–43–22–48–45. 26 rooms with bath. In-room safes. AE, DC, MC, V. Métro: Raspail.*

$–$$ 🖭 **Lenox-Montparnasse.** The hotel may be modern, '60s-era, but it's in the heart of Montparnasse, just around the corner from the famous Dôme and Coupole brasseries, and close to the Luxembourg Garden. The best rooms have fireplaces, old mirrors, and exposed beams; others follow a more functional, contemporary style. ✉ *15 rue Delambre, 75014,* ☎ *01–43–35–34–50,* 𝙵𝙰𝚇 *01–43–20–46–64. 52 rooms, 6 suites, with bath. Bar, no-smoking room, in-room data ports, room service, laundry service, parking (fee). AE, DC, MC, V. Métro: Vavin.*

$ 🖭 **Hôtel des Bains.** A charming neighborhood, tastefully decorated rooms, satellite TV, friendly staff: can anyone explain why this hotel has only one government-ranked star? The price can't be beat, especially for the family-friendly two-room suites (564 frs/€88–747 frs/€115) in a separate building off the courtyard garden. ✉ *33 rue Delambre, 75014,* ☎ *01–46–56–26–27,* 𝙵𝙰𝚇 *01–42–79–82–78. 40 rooms with bath. MC, V. Métro: Vavin or Edgar-Quinet.*

$ 🏨 **Midi.** Don't be put off by the facade and the reception area, which might make you think you're in a chain hotel. Rooms are French-provincial style—rich colors, stenciled furniture, and lots of wrought iron—and have large floor-to-ceiling windows. Some have air-conditioning, others have whirlpool baths, and those facing the street are quite spacious. ⊠ 4 av. Réné-Coty, 75014, ☎ 01–43–27–23–25, FAX 01–43–21–24–58. 46 rooms with bath. Parking (fee). AE, DC, MC, V. Métro and RER: Denfert-Rochereau.

$ 🏨 **Parc Montsouris.** This modest hotel in a 1930s villa is on a quiet residential street next to the city's nicest park, Parc Montsouris. Recently renovated, the small but clean rooms are embellished with attractive oak pieces and high-quality French fabrics; satellite TV is another plus. Those with showers are very inexpensive; suites sleep four. Adjoining double rooms are available. Ask for a room at the front; the views onto the park are lovely. ⊠ 4 rue du Parc-Montsouris, 75014, ☎ 01–45–89–09–72, FAX 01–45–80–92–72. 28 rooms, 7 suites, with bath. Air-conditioning, in-room data ports, no-smoking room, laundry service. AE, MC, V. Métro: Montparnasse-Bienvenüe.

15ᵉ Arrondissement (Champ de Mars)

See Left Bank Lodging map.

$ 🏨 **Timhotel Tour Eiffel.** Inside this '70s-era hotel, within walking distance of the Eiffel Tower, are inexpensive, comfortable rooms with modern bathrooms, cable TV with CNN, and double-glazed windows that block out street noise. The light-wood furniture and crisp damask give rooms a clean if simple feel; some of them have great views of the Eiffel Tower. The buffet breakfast is one of the city's least expensive. ⊠ 11 rue Juge, 75015, ☎ 01–45–78–29–29, FAX 01–45–78–60–00. 40 rooms with bath. No-smoking floor, laundry service, travel services, parking (fee). AE, DC, MC, V. Métro: Dupleix.

16ᵉ Arrondissement (Trocadéro/Bois de Boulogne)

See Right Bank Lodging map.

$$$$ 🏨 **Saint James Paris.** Called the "only château-hôtel in Paris," this gracious, late-19th-century (viz., neo-faux-echt Second Empire) mansion is surrounded by a lush private park. Ten rooms—done in the neoclassic mode—on the third floor open onto a winter garden; the poshest option is booking one of the two duplex gatehouses. The magnificent bar-library is lined with floor-to-ceiling oak bookcases. The restaurant is reserved for guests; in warm weather, meals are served in the garden. ⊠ 43 av. Bugeaud, 75116, ☎ 01–44–05–81–81; 800/447–7462 in the U.S., FAX 01–44–05–81–82. 20 rooms, 28 suites, with bath. Restaurant, bar, air-conditioning, in-room data ports, in-room safes, no-smoking room, room service, sauna, health club, baby-sitting, laundry service, meeting room, free parking. AE, DC, MC, V. Métro: Porte Dauphine.

$$$$ 🏨 **Trocadéro's Dokhan's.** Though part of the Sofitel chain, this newly opened town-house hotel has an idiosyncratic style entirely its own. Already a hit among fashionistas, Trocadéro's Dokhan's attention to detail sets it apart from other posh flophouses in this very upscale neighborhood: a Louis Vuitton steamer trunk elevator; an elegant bar stocked with 50 varieties of bubbly; a tea salon; and, in every room and suite, over-equipped marble bathrooms with Roger et Gallet toiletries. The best rooms are the deluxe doubles; only the suites have views of the Eiffel Tower. ⊠ 111 rue Lauriston, 75116, ☎ 01–53–65–66–99, FAX 01–53–65–66–88. 41 rooms, 4 suites, with bath. Bar, air-conditioning, in-room data ports, in-room safes, no-smoking rooms, room service. AE, DC, MC, V. Métro: Porte Dauphine.

$$$ ⊞ **Alexander.** Everything about this hotel smacks of Old Europe, from the old-fashioned cage elevator to the 20-ft corniced ceilings and period wall sconces (which bathe all in warm, rosy hues). It's also on one of Paris's finest shopping avenues. Note that air-conditioning is available on the sixth floor only. ⊠ *102 av. Victor Hugo, 75116,* ☏ *01–45–53–64–65; 800/843–3311 in the U.S.,* ℻ *01–45–53–12–51. 60 rooms, 2 suites, with bath. Laundry service. AE, DC, MC, V. Métro: Victor Hugo.*

$$–$$$ ⊞ **Jardins du Trocadéro.** This good-value hotel near the Trocadéro and the Eiffel Tower seamlessly blends old-style French elegance (period antiques, Napoléon draperies) with modern conveniences (soundproofing, satellite TV, VCRs, modem lines). Marble bathrooms feature terry robes and whirlpool baths. ⊠ *35 rue Benjamin-Franklin, 75116,* ☏ *01–53–70–17–70; 800/246–0041 in the U.S.,* ℻ *01–53–70–17–80. 18 rooms, 5 suites, with bath. Bar, air-conditioning, in-room data ports, in-room safes, no-smoking room, room service, hot tub, laundry service, meeting room, parking (fee). AE, DC, MC, V. Métro: Trocadéro.*

$$$ ⊞ **Square.** There's little that's "square" about this very hip boutique hotel. Owned by restaurateur Patrick Derderian, it's also home to his trendy Zebra Square café. Rooms are bright and spacious by Paris standards and decorated in what is best described as extravagant minimalism. Curved doors, walls, and furniture break up a hard-edged design dominated by stripes and squares, while flowers, designer lamps, and enormous beds help soften the Zen aesthetic. Large desks, plus three phone lines and a fax-answering machine in each room, make it ideal for business travelers. But the reading room, art gallery, and very sleek bar make it a good choice for pleasure seekers as well. ⊠ *3 rue de Boulainvilliers, 75001,* ☏ *01–44–14–91–90,* ℻ *01–44–14–91–99,* 🕸 *www.hotelsquare.com. 16 rooms, 6 suites, with bath. Restaurant, bar, air-conditioning, in-room data ports, in-room safes, minibars, room service, laundry service, meeting room, parking (fee). AE, DC, MC, V. Métro: Passy.*

$ ⊞ **Keppler.** On the border of the 8e and 16e arrondissements, near the Champs-Élysées, is this small hotel in a 19th-century building. The spacious, airy rooms have simple teak furnishings and floral upholsteries and some nice amenities (like satellite TV and room service) for the price. ⊠ *12 rue Keppler, 75016,* ☏ *01–47–20–65–05,* ℻ *01–47–23–02–29. 49 rooms with bath. Bar, in-room safes, no-smoking room, room service. AE, MC, V. Métro: Georg V.*

$ ⊞ **Queen's Hotel.** One of only a handful of hotels in the tony residen-
★   tial district near the Bois de Boulogne, Queen's is a small, comfortable, old-fashioned hotel with a high standard of service. Each room focuses on a different 20th-century French artist. The newly renovated rooms with baths have hot tubs and brand-new beds. ⊠ *4 rue Bastien-Lepage, 75016,* ☏ *01–42–88–89–85,* ℻ *01–40–50–67–52,* 🕸 *www.queens-hotel. fr. 22 rooms with bath. Air-conditioning, in-room safes, minibars, no-smoking room. AE, DC, MC, V. Métro: Michel-Ange-Auteuil.*

17e Arrondissement (Monceau/Clichy)

See Right Bank Lodging map.

$$–$$$ ⊞ **Eber-Monceau.** This small hotel—part of the Relais du Silence group—is just one block from the Parc Monceau. It attracts a stylish media and fashion set, though the engaging owner, Jean-Marc Eber, delights in welcoming all first-time guests. Rooms are tastefully done in bright, cheerful colors; ask for one overlooking the courtyard. ⊠ *18 rue Léon-Jost, 75017,* ☏ *01–46–22–60–70,* ℻ *01–47–63–01–01.*

18 rooms, 13 with bath, 5 with shower. Bar, air-conditioning, laundry service, parking (fee). AE, DC, MC, V. Métro: Courcelles.

$$ ⌂ **Étoile-Péreire.** The extremely congenial owner has created a unique,
★ intimate hotel, behind a quiet, leafy courtyard in a chic residential district. It consists of two parts: a fin-de-siècle building on the street and a 1920s annex overlooking an interior courtyard. Rooms and duplexes—in deep shades of roses or blues with crisp, white damask upholstery—have a very tailored, very finished look. Only the duplex suites have air-conditioning. The copious breakfast is legendary, featuring 40 assorted jams and jellies. ⌧ *146 bd. Péreire, 75017,* ☎ *01–42–67–60–00,* ℻ *01–42–67–02–90. 21 rooms, 5 suites, with bath. Bar, in-room safes, no-smoking room, laundry service. AE, DC, MC, V. Métro: Péreire.*

$$ ⌂ **Regent's Garden.** Built in the mid-19th century by Napoléon III for his doctor, this Best Western hotel near the Arc de Triomphe is adorned, as you might imagine, with marble fireplaces, mirrors, gilt furniture, and cornicing. Ask for a room overlooking the gorgeous garden, where breakfast is served in summer. ⌧ *6 rue Pierre-Demours, 75017,* ☎ *01–45–74–07–30,* ℻ *01–40–55–01–42. 39 rooms with bath. Air-conditioning, lobby lounge, parking (fee). AE, DC, MC, V. Métro: Charles-de-Gaulle–Étoile, Ternes.*

$$ ⌂ **Excelsior.** Only a five-minute walk from Montmartre and near more than a dozen bus and métro lines is this tiny, endearing place. Rustic antiques and heavy armoires in the small, spotless rooms exude a warm, cozy feel. Request one overlooking the little garden. ⌧ *16 rue Caroline, 75017,* ☎ *01–45–22–50–95,* ℻ *01–45–22–59–88. 22 rooms with bath. Laundry service. AE, DC, MC, V. Métro: Place de Clichy.*

$ ⌂ **Palma.** This modest hotel in a small 19th-century building between the Arc de Triomphe and Porte Maillot is one of the best deals in the city. Cheerful and homey, if not luxurious, rooms have basic wood furnishings and bright floral wallpaper; ask for one on the top floor with a view across Right Bank rooftops. There's air-conditioning on the sixth (top) floor only. ⌧ *46 rue Brunel, 75017,* ☎ *01–45–74–74–51,* ℻ *01–45–74–40–90. 37 rooms with bath. AE, MC, V. Métro: Argentine.*

18ᵉ Arrondissement (Montmartre)

See Right Bank Lodging map.

$ ⌂ **Ermitage.** This elfin, family-run hotel dates from Napoléon III's time and is filled with antiques of the period. Rooms have a feeling of old-fashioned elegance. The building is only two stories high, but the hilly Montmartre neighborhood ensures that some rooms have a nice view of Paris. ⌧ *24 rue Lamarck, 75018,* ☎ *01–42–64–79–22,* ℻ *01–42–64–10–33. 12 rooms with bath. No credit cards. Métro: Lamarck-Caulaincourt.*

$ ⌂ **Regyn's Montmartre.** Despite the small rooms, this owner-run hotel on Montmartre's evocative place des Abbesses provides comfortable accommodations. Each floor is dedicated to a Montmartre artist; poetic homages by local writers are featured in the hallways; and reproductions of works hang in rooms. Otherwise, rooms are spotless but functional. Ask to stay on one of the two top floors for great views of either the Eiffel Tower or Sacré-Coeur; those on the lower floors are darker and less inviting. Overall, courteous service and a relaxed atmosphere make this an attractive choice. ⌧ *18 pl. des Abbesses, 75018,* ☎ *01–42–54–45–21,* ℻ *01–42–23–76–69. 22 rooms with bath. In-room safes. AE, MC, V. Métro: Abbesses.*

$ ⌂ **Utrillo.** This very likable hotel is on a quiet side street at the foot of Montmartre, near colorful rue Lepic. Reproduction prints and marble-top breakfast tables in every room make them feel charmingly old-fashioned, while the white-and-pastel color scheme makes them feel brighter and more spacious than they actually are. Two rooms (Nos. 61 and 63) have views of the Eiffel Tower. ⊠ *7 rue Aristide-Bruant, 75018,* ☎ *01–42–58–13–44,* FAX *01–42–23–93–88. 30 rooms with bath. Sauna. AE, DC, MC, V. Métro: Abbesses, Blanche.*

19ᵉ Arrondissement (Buttes-Chaumont)

See Right Bank Lodging map.

$ ⊞ **Le Laumière.** Though it's some distance from the city center, the rock-bottom rates of this family-run hotel near the rambling Buttes-Chaumont park make it hard to resist. The staff, too, is exceptionally helpful. Unfortunately, the modern, modular furniture is less inspiring, though some of the larger rooms overlook a garden. Ask about special rates. ⊠ *4 rue Petit, 75019,* ☎ *01–42–06–10–77,* FAX *01–42–06–72–50. 54 rooms with bath. MC, V. Métro: Laumière.*

Apartment Rentals

If you will be staying longer than a week, want to do your own cooking, or need a base large enough for a family, consider a furnished rental. Policies differ from company to company, but you can generally expect a minimum required stay of one week; a refundable deposit (expect to pay $200–$500), payable on arrival; and weekly or biweekly maid service.

Following is a list of good-value residence hotels, each with multiple properties in Paris. **Citadines Résidences Hôtelières** (⊠ 18 rue Favart, 75002, ☎ 01–41–05–79–04, FAX 01–44–50–23–50). **Mercure** (⊠ 20 esplanade Charles-de-Gaulle, 92000 Nanterre, ☎ 01–46–69–79–00, FAX 01–47–25–46–48). **Orion** (⊠ 30 pl. d'Italie, 75013, ☎ 01–40–78–54–54; 212/688–9538; 800/546–4777 in the U.S.; FAX 01–40–78–54–55; 212/688–9467 in the U.S.). **Paris Appartements Services** (⊠ 69 rue d'Argout, 75002, ☎ 01–40–28–01–28, FAX 01–40–28–92–01).

The **Rothray** agency (⊠ 10 rue Nicolas Flamel, 74004, ☎ 01–48–87–13–37 or 01–40–28–91–84, FAX 01–42–78–17–72 or 01–40–26–34–33) has pretty apartments for short- or long-term rental in stylish neighborhoods like the Marais. U.S.-based agencies also rent apartments in Paris; for information about these, *see* Lodging *in* Smart Travel Tips A to Z.

4 NIGHTLIFE AND THE ARTS

With a heritage that includes the cancan, the Folies-Bergère, Mistinguett, and Josephine Baker, Paris is one city where no one has ever had to ask "Is there any place exciting to go tonight?" Today, the city's nightlife and arts scenes are still filled with pleasures: hear a *chansonnier* belt out Piaf, take in a Victor/Victoria show, catch a Molière play at the Comédie Française, commune with the Phantom's spirit at the Opéra Garnier, or perhaps spot Madonna at the Buddha Bar. When midnight strikes, remember that Paris is one of the greatest jazz cities in the world.

NIGHTLIFE

Revised and
updated by
Ian Phillips

The City of Light truly lights up after dark. So, if you want to paint
the town *rouge* after dutifully pounding the parquet in museums all
day, there's a dazzling array of options to discover. The hottest night
spots are near Menilmontant and Parmentier, the Bastille, and the
Marais. The Left Bank is definitely a lot less happening. The Champs-
Élysées is making a comeback, especially with yuppie singles bars on
its side streets, though the clientele on the main drag itself remains
predominantly foreign. On weeknights, people are usually home after
closing hours at 2 AM, but weekends mean late-night partying. Take
note: the last métro runs between 12:30 and 1 AM (you can take a cab,
though they can be hard to find between midnight and 2 AM on weekends); you may just have to stay out until the métro starts running
again at 5:30 AM.

Bars

The best of the bars in Paris have character, witty waiters, local color,
and inventive cocktails at prices that permit consuming without count-
ing. The variety of bars is also impressive—bars serving light food, moody
late-night bars, bars with DJs, and bars with live music. Other options
include cafés, many of which turn into bars at night, and wine bars.

BASTILLE AND THE EASTERN RIGHT BANK

Barrio Latino (✉ 46–48 rue du Faubourg St-Antoine, 12ᵉ, ☎ 01–55–
78–84–75, métro Bastille) is one of the latest additions to the Bastille
party district, and it's a better bet for a drink than a meal. The decor
is a lush cross of casbah, Old Havana, and SoHo loft that pulls a very
mixed crowd of hipsters, including everyone from threadbare art students to ambitious young lawyers. Though pricey, and the drinks could
be better, it can be a fun scene.

Café Charbon (✉ 109 rue Oberkampf, 11ᵉ, ☎ 01–43–57–55–13,
métro St-Maur, Parmentier) is a beautifully restored 19th-century café
whose trendsetting clientele converses to jazz in the background. The
atmosphere gets livelier after 10 PM, when a DJ takes over.

Café de la Musique (✉ 213 av. Jean Jaurès, in the Parc de La Villette,
19ᵉ, ☎ 01–48–03–15–91, métro Porte de Pantin) has a large selection
of cocktails and limited brasserie offerings in a comfortable setting inspired by the '40s. DJs take to the turntables from Wednesday to Saturday and serve up a menu of laid-back, jazzy sounds.

Chez Prune (✉ 36 rue Beaurepaire, 10ᵉ, ☎ 01–42–41–30–47, métro
Jacques Bonsergent) is a lively bar with a terrace overlooking one of
the footbridges crossing the Canal St-Martin. The area has recently become one of the hottest in Paris, yet, while you're more than likely to
spot some hip fashion designer, celebrity photographer Mario Testino,
and lots of beautiful people, the neighborhood atmosphere is refreshingly more relaxed that poseur-y.

China Club (✉ 50 rue de Charenton, 12ᵉ, ☎ 01–43–43–82–02, métro
Ledru-Rollin) has three floors of bars and a restaurant with lacquered
furnishings and a colonial Asia theme. During happy hour (7–9), all
cocktails are 35 francs/€5.3. There are also jazz concerts at 10 PM in
the basement club on Friday and Saturday.

La Fabrique (✉ 53 rue du Faubourg St-Antoine, 11ᵉ, ☎ 01–43–07–
67–07, métro Bastille) is a bar and restaurant that brews its own beer
(look out for the huge copper vats by the entrance). It really gets going
every evening after 9 PM, when a DJ hits the turntables.

La Favela Chic (⊠ 18 rue du Faubourg du Temple, 11ᵉ, ☎ 01–40–21–38–14, métro République) was originally one of the bars that made Oberkampf into the hippest area in Paris a few years ago. A couple of years ago, however, it decamped to this new, large space, hidden in a courtyard behind iron gates. There is an organic juice bar, caipirnhas, and mojitos, guest DJs, and an almost nonstop Latino party atmosphere.

La Flèche d'Or (⊠ 102 bis rue de Bagnolet, 20ᵉ, ☎ 01–43–72–04–23, métro Alexandre Dumas), housed in a former railway station, is one of the best places in Paris to take in some live music. There are concerts at 9 PM Monday to Saturday and at 5 PM on Sunday. The music runs the gamut from reggae to rock to world music, plus an open stage on Tuesday for any budding stars.

Le Gast (⊠ 5 rue Crespin-du-Gast, 11ᵉ, ☎ 01–43–55–53–34, métro Ménilmontant) is a rarity—a quiet, friendly neighborhood bar in the bustling Oberkampf district. There is a curvaceous wooden counter, cocktails such as Ti punch and piña colada, and Polaroids of regulars stuck on the walls.

Le Piston Pélican (⊠ 15 rue de Bagnolet, 20ᵉ, ☎ 01–43–70–35–00, métro Alexandre Dumas), with its pewter bar and Belle Epoque decor, is one of those quintessential Parisian places. Often packed with a vibrant crowd, it plays host to DJs and live music on Friday and Saturday.

Sanz Sans (⊠ 49 rue du Faubourg St-Antoine, 11ᵉ, ☎ 01–44–75–78–78, métro Bastille) has added a new twist to bar life—the "actors" on the upstairs lounge's gilt-framed video screen are really the habitués of the downstairs bar.

Wax (⊠ 15 rue Daval, 11ᵉ, ☎ 01–40–21–16–16, métro Bastille) would be worth a visit simply for its Psychedelic Moderne decor—check out the orange and pink walls, multicolored squiggles on the columns, and moulded plastic banquettes by the window. It is also one of the most happening places in the city music-wise, with DJs spinning techno and house every evening.

CHAMPS-ÉLYSÉES/OPÉRA/LOUVRE

Barramundi (⊠ 3 rue Taitbout, 9ᵉ, ☎ 01–47–70–21–21, métro Richelieu-Drouot) is one of Paris's hubs of nouveau-riche chic. The lighting is dim, the copper bar long, and the walls artfully textured. During the week, chill-out and world music is piped through to the bar. By the weekend, however, things get moving with a program of regular *soirées*, with names like "Super Nature," "Reelax," and "Corpus Noctem."

Buddha Bar (⊠ 8 rue Boissy d'Anglas, 8ᵉ, ☎ 01–53–05–90–00, métro Concorde) offers one of the most glittery settings in Paris, with its towering gold-painted Buddha contemplating enough Dragon Empress screens and colorful chinoiserie for five MGM movies. The crowd ranges from camera-friendly faces—*Vogue* did a big fashion spread here—to suburban trendsetters, with groups of office ladies out on the town now making the scene. A spacious mezzanine bar overlooks the dining room, where cuisines East and West meet somewhere between Blandsville and California.

Le Fumoir (⊠ 6 rue Amiral-de-Coligny, 1ᵉʳ, ☎ 01–42–92–00–24, métro Louvre) is a fashionable spot for a late-afternoon beer or early evening cocktail (dinner is also served). There's a large bar in front, a library with shelves of books in back, and leather couches throughout.

Harry's New York Bar (⊠ 5 rue Daunou, 2ᵉ, ☎ 01–42–61–71–14, métro Opéra), a cozy, wood-paneled hangout decorated with dusty college pennants and popular with expatriates, is haunted by the ghosts of Ernest Hemingway and F. Scott Fitzgerald. This place claims to have invented the Bloody Mary, and one way or another, the bartenders here do mix a mean one.

Man Ray (✉ 34 rue Marbeuf, 8ᵉ, ☎ 01–56–88–36–36, métro Franklin-D.-Roosevelt) is one of the hottest places in town, which is not surprising given that it is owned by Johnny Depp, Sean Penn, and Simply Red's Mick Hucknall. The Asian–Art Deco style is reminiscent of a slightly Disneyesque 1930s supper club in Chinatown. The bar is open until 2 AM and serves cocktails, tapas, and sushi.

Polo Room (✉ 3 rue Lord Byron, 8ᵉ, ☎ 01–40–74–07–78, métro George V), situated on the first floor of a building in a sleepy street off the Champs-Élysées, is the very first martini bar in Paris. The American's owner's target clientele is the world of business (35- to 45-year-olds), and his aim to give this space a very New York feel. There are polo photos on the wall, a 36-ft bar, and a selection of 28 different martini cocktails (who can resist the Martini Chocolat?). There are also regular live jazz concerts and DJs every Friday and Saturday night.

LATIN QUARTER

Alcazar (✉ 62 rue Mazarine, 6ᵉ, ☎ 01–53–10–19–99, métro Odéon), Sir Terence Conran's first Parisian restaurant, has a stylish bar on the first floor, where you can sip a glass of wine under the huge glass roof. From Wednesday to Saturday, a live DJ spins either lounge or Latin music.

Le Comptoir (✉ 5 rue Monsieur-Le-Prince, 6ᵉ, ☎ 01–43–29–12–05, métro Odéon) is a wine bar serving Burgundies and Bordeaux by the glass, as well as more unusual wines, such as ones from Corsica.

Les Etages (✉ 5 rue de Buci, 6ᵉ, ☎ 01–46–34–26–26, métro Odéon) is a laid-back, student-y type of place occupying three floors of a building near St-Germain-des-Prés. The walls are rustic red and ocher, the decor is simple, while the terrace the perfect place to sit out in the summer.

Oya (✉ 25 rue de la Reine Blanche, 13ᵉ, ☎ 01–47–07–59–59, métro Gobelins) is a haven for fans of board games. The owners have assembled more than 200 from around the world, which you can play for 30 francs/€4.6 a game.

MARAIS

Le Café du Trésor (✉ 5 rue Trésor, 4ᵉ, ☎ 01–44–78–06–60, métro St-Paul) is a lively, sophisticated bar, where every night except Sunday DJs spin a mixture of house and funk. There's also a restaurant adjacent.

La Chaise au Plafond (✉ 10 rue du Trésor, 4ᵉ, ☎ 01–42–76–03–22, métro St-Paul) has the feel of a traditional bistro with a few offbeat contemporary touches. Never overcrowded, it's the perfect place for an excellent glass of wine.

La Perla (✉ 26 rue François Miron, 4ᵉ, ☎ 01–42–77–59–40, métro Hôtel-de-Ville, Saint-Paul) is one of the chicest spots in town for Latin lovers. Sit back, sip a margarita, munch on a few tapas, and take in a few of the beautiful people.

La Tartine (✉ 24 rue de Rivoli, 4ᵉ, ☎ 01–42–72–76–85, métro St-Paul) serves inexpensive glasses of wine and *tartines* (open-face sandwiches) in a tatty, almost seedy turn-of-the-20th-century bar that has earned antihero status among the cognoscenti.

Le Web Bar (✉ 32 rue de Picardie, 3ᵉ, ☎ 01–42–72–66–55, métro Temple) is an lively, eclectic place, where you can surf in free salsa classes on Monday, or take in a photo exhibition or short film. There are also musical brunches on Sunday and whole host of soirées. For detailed information of events, check out the Web site at www.webbar.fr.

MONTMARTRE

Café Carmen (✉ 22 rue de Douai, 9ᵉ, ☎ 01–45–26–21–17, métro Pigalle) bears a name that is homage to Georges Bizet, whose opera set

Paris ablaze in the early 20th century. The building once belong to his composer's widow, then became a soup kitchen, then a high-class brothel. Today, it maintains the magnificent Napoléon III decor (think moulded ceilings, chandeliers, and gilt mirrors). In the basement is a cozy bar, where there are regular operetta concerts given by a distant relative of Toulouse-Lautrec and evenings dominated by deep lounge music.

Le Jungle Montmartre (✉ 32 rue Gabrielle, 18ᵉ, ☎ 01–46–06–75–69, métro Abbesses) is a gem of a place in a very sleepy, off-the-beat street in Montmartre. Upstairs is an African restaurant; downstairs is a small bar with Senegalese sculptures and tiger and leopard designs on the tabletops. There is a DJ every evening from 9 PM (music ranges from reggae and funk to techno and drum and bass), who is often joined by traditional African musicians.

Moloko (✉ 26 rue Fontaine, 9ᵉ, ☎ 01–48–74–50–26, métro Blanche), a smoky late-night bar with several rooms, a mezzanine, a jukebox, and a small dance floor, is a popular spot with a trendy, fun-loving crowd.

Le Sancerre (✉ 35 rue des Abbesses, 18ᵉ, ☎ 01–42–58–08–20, métro Abbesses), a café by day, turns into a lively watering hole for jovial Montmartrois and artist types.

Hotel Bars

Elegant and upscale, with a classic Parisian feel, the city's hotel bars are quiet spots to meet for a drink. Following are some of the best: **Bristol** (✉ 112 rue du Faubourg St-Honoré, 8ᵉ, ☎ 01–53–43–43–42, métro Miromesnil). **Crillon** (✉ 10 pl. de la Concorde, 8ᵉ, ☎ 01–44–71–15–39, métro Concorde). **L'Hôtel** (✉ 10 rue des Beaux-Arts, 6ᵉ, ☎ 01–44–41–99–00, métro St-Germain-des-Prés). **Inter-Continental** (✉ 3 rue Castiglione, 1ᵉʳ, ☎ 01–44–77–10–47, métro Tuileries). **Lutétia** (✉ 45 bd. Raspail, 6ᵉ, ☎ 01–49–54–46–09, métro Sèvres-Babylone), which is popular with female French legends Catherine Deneuve and Juliette Gréco. **Le Meurice** (✉ 228 rue de Rivoli, 1ᵉʳ, ☎ 01–44–58–10–66, métro Tuileries). **Ritz Hemingway Bar** (✉ 15 pl. Vendôme, 1ᵉʳ, ☎ 01–43–16–33–65, métro Opéra), where the writer drank to the liberation of Paris.

Le Dokhan's (✉ 117 rue Lauriston, 16ᵉ, ☎ 01–53–65–66–99, métro Trocadéro) has a bar, decorated by top Parisian designer Frédéic Méchiche, which serves nothing but champagne. Every week, there is a different champagne by the glass, as well as special musical evenings once a month.

Cabarets

Paris's cabarets range from boîtes once haunted by Picasso and Piaf to those sinful showplaces where tableaux vivants offer acres of bare female flesh (so much so that one critic recently exclaimed, "I'm not going to look anymore unless somebody has three of them"). These extravaganzas are often shunned by Parisians but loved by tourists. You can dine at many of them, but come with tempered expectations, since the food is more about mass-catering than gaining gourmet pleasure: prices range from 200 francs/€30 (simple admission plus one drink) to more than 750 francs/€115 (dinner plus show). For 400–500 francs/€61–77, you get a seat plus half a bottle of champagne.

L'Âne Rouge (✉ 3 rue Laugier, 17ᵉ, ☎ 01–43–80–79–97, métro Ternes) is a typical French cabaret playing to a mixed Parisian and foreign crowd, where the emphasis is on laughs and entertainment, with a host of singers, magicians, comedians, and ventriloquists.

Au Lapin Agile (✉ 22 rue des Saules, 18ᵉ, ☎ 01–46–06–85–87, métro Lamarck-Caulaincourt), in Montmartre, considers itself the doyen of cabarets and is a miraculous survivor from the 19th century. Founded in 1860, it is still housed in a fetchingly picturesque maison-cottage, once a favorite subject of painter Maurice Utrillo. At one point owned by Aristide Bruant (immortalized in manyToulouse-Lautrec posters), it became the home-away-from-home for Braque, Modigliani, Apollinaire, and Vlaminck. The most famous habitué, however, was Picasso, who once paid for a meal with one of his paintings, then promptly went out and painted another, which he named after this place—today, after being purchased for nearly $50 million, it hangs in New York's Metropolitan Museum. Happily, this glamour hasn't entirely affected the Nimble Rabbit—prices are lower than elsewhere, as it is more of a large bar than a full-blown cabaret. If you want to commune with the spirit of the past (and any visiting ghosts), the best time to come is during the early morning hours.

Au Pied de la Butte (✉ 62 bd. Rochechouart, 18ᵉ, ☎ 01–46–06–02–86, métro Anvers) played host in the past to Edith Piaf, Jacques Brel, and Maurice Chevalier. Today, it has three shows per evening with modern-day songsters interpreting the traditional French repertoire and magicians performing tricks.

Le Caveau de la Bolée (✉ 25 rue de l'Hirondelle, 6ᵉ, ☎ 01–43–54–62–20, métro St-Michel) was a prison in the 14th century, but these days you are free to sing along to Edith Piaf melodies or be entertained by magicians, comics, and mind readers.

Crazy Horse (✉ 12 av. George V, 8ᵉ, ☎ 01–47–23–32–32, métro Alma-Marceau) is one of the best-known clubs, which celebrated its 50th anniversary last year. It is renowned for pretty dancers and raunchy routines with lots of humor and few clothes.

Éléphant Bleu (✉ 49 rue de Ponthieu, 8ᵉ, ☎ 01–42–25–17–61, métro Franklin-D.-Roosevelt) is a cabaret-cum-restaurant with an exotic (often Asian) touch to most of its shows.

Lido (✉ 116 bis av. des Champs-Élysées, 8ᵉ, ☎ 01–40–76–56–10, métro George V) stars the famous Bluebell Girls; the owners claim no show this side of Las Vegas can rival it for special effects.

Le Limonaire (✉ 21 rue Bergère, 9ᵉ, ☎ 01–45–23–33–33, métro Grands-Boulevards) is a small restaurant that simply oozes with Parisian charm. This is the kind of place where you could imagine Edith Piaf belting out "*Je ne regrette rien,*" and, in fact, imagination is often not required at 10 PM, Tuesday to Sunday, when the service stops and a singer takes to the floor. The house specialty is *la chanson française,* and one of its finest guest artists is the modern-day Little Sparrow, Kalifa. There are also traditional *bals musettes* (popular dances with accordion music) at 6 PM the first Sunday of every month and silent-film screening the third Sunday.

Madame Arthur (✉ 75 bis rue des Martyrs, 18ᵉ, ☎ 01–42–54–40–21, métro Pigalle) stages a wacky burlesque drag show—men dressed as famous French female vocalists—that's not for the faint-hearted.

Michou (✉ 80 rue des Martyrs, 18ᵉ, ☎ 01–46–06–16–04, métro Pigalle) is owned by the always blue-clad Michou, famous in Paris circles. The men on stage wear extravagant drag—high camp and parody are the order of the day.

Moulin Rouge (✉ 82 bd. de Clichy, 18ᵉ, ☎ 01–53–09–82–82, métro Blanche), that old favorite at the foot of Montmartre, mingles the Doriss Girls, the cancan, and a horse in an extravagant spectacle.

Paradis Latin (✉ 28 rue du Cardinal Lemoine, 5ᵉ, ☎ 01–43–25–28–28, métro Cardinal-Lemoine) is perhaps the liveliest, busiest, and trendiest cabaret on the Left Bank.

Clubs

Paris's *boîtes de nuit* (nightclubs) tend to be both expensive and exclusive—if you know someone who is a regular or who knows the ropes, you'll have an easier time getting through the door. Many clubs are closed Monday and some on Tuesday. The best soirées tend to take place on Thursday and are generally more intimate and elitist than at the weekend. Nowadays, specific soirées are hosted at many different venues, so the party-hearty crowd is no longer faithful to just one club; on Mondays, they may go to Disco Night at the Queen, on Fridays to "Automatik" at the Rex, on Saturdays to "Scream" at the Elysée Montmartre. Many of these, such as "Scream" and "TGV," take place either just once or twice a month. For information about dates, look out for flyers in bars.

BASTILLE AND THE EASTERN RIGHT BANK

Les Bains (⊠ 7 rue du Bourg-l'Abbé, 3ᵉ, ☎ 01–48–87–01–80, métro Étienne Marcel), opened in 1978 and often—back in the disco era—featured in the pages of French *Vogue,* is very much a Parisian institution. The upstairs bar and restaurant is generally packed wall-to-wall with stars, while downstairs house music rules on the dance floors. First, however, you have to get past the particularly selective door policy: if you don't look like Claudia Schiffer or Brad Pitt's double, this could prove more difficult than you might imagine.

Le Balajo (⊠ 9 rue de Lappe, 11ᵉ, ☎ 01–47–00–07–87, métro Bastille), in an old Java ballroom, offers a bit of everything: salsa, techno, and retro. On Thursdays and Sunday afternoon, there are even *bals musettes*, which feature the accordion music so evocative of Montmartre street balls.

Batofar (⊠ 11 quai François Mauriac, 11ᵉ, ☎ 01–56–29–10–00, métro Bibliothèque) is an old Port of Paris lighthouse tug, now refitted to include a bar, a club, and a concert venue that's become one of the hippest spots in town. Star DJs from other European capitals often arrive to animate the dance floor.

Les Étoiles (⊠ 61 rue Château d'Eau, 10ᵉ, ☎ 01–47–70–60–56, métro Château d'Eau), open Thursday–Saturday, is the place for salsa (with a live band). Dinner, featuring South American specialties, is served 9–11.

Le Gibus (⊠ 18 rue du Faubourg-du-Temple, 11ᵉ, ☎ 01–47–00–78–88, métro République) is one of Paris's most famous music venues. In more than 30 years, there have been 6,500 concerts and more than 3,000 performers (including Police, Deep Purple, and Billy Idol). Today, the Gibus's cellars are *the* place for trance, techno, and jungle. There are also regular Latino House parties on Saturday.

La Java (⊠ 105 rue du Faubourg du Temple, 10ᵉ, ☎ 01–42–02–20–52, métro Belleville), where Edith Piaf and Maurice Chevalier made their names, has live Latin music and Cuban jam sessions on Thursday, Friday, and Saturday night. Before the party proper gets under way, there are also salsa lessons.

CHAMPS-ÉLYSÉES AND GRANDS-BOULEVARDS

Le Cabaret (⊠ 68 rue Pierre-Charron, 8ᵉ, ☎ 01–42–89–44–14, métro Franklin-D.-Roosevelt), once just that, still has the original red velvet and flock-wallpaper decor. Nowadays it's a hip, chic club. Princess Caroline of Monaco, Liza Minnelli, and Naomi Campbell have all been spotted here.

Maxim's (⊠ 3 rue Royale, 8ᵉ, ☎ 01–42–65–27–94, métro Concorde) used to be the most stylish restaurant in the city. Today, the restaurant may still be legendary, but its worn-out Belle Epoque decor tends to attract only tourists. Or rather, it did until recently. Now, party organizer Leo Chabot has turned it into the hottest spot in the city on Friday evenings. Young designers, models, and lots of beautiful people, dressed head-to-toe in designer clobber, flock there to groove to the trip-hop and trance in the bar or the funk, salsa, and rock in the blue-lit Jardin d'Hiver.

Niel's (⊠ 27 av. Ternes, 17ᵉ, ☏ 01–47–66–45–00, métro Ternes) attracts a well-off set of regulars, as well as top models and showbiz glitterati. Music runs the gamut from salsa to house.

Le Rex (⊠ 5 blvd. Poissonnière, 2ᵉ, ☏ 01–42–36–10–96, métro Grands-Boulevards), open Thursday through Saturday, is the Paris temple of techno and house. On Thursday, you'll often find France's most famous DJ, Laurent Garnier, at the turntables. The techno "Automatik" soirées on Fridays are particularly popular.once just that, still has the original red-velvet-and-flock-wallpaper.

Le VIP Room (⊠ 76 av. des Champs-Élysées, 8ᵉ, ☏ 01–56–69–16–66, métro Franklin-D.-Roosevelt), located under Planet Hollywood, is owned by Jean Roch, the ringleader of nightlife in St-Tropez. If you like spending your evenings with young women dressed in micro-mini dresses and men sporting shades (even in the dark), then this is the place for you. You may even spot a few stars. Leonardo DiCaprio, George Michael, and French rocker Johnny Hallyday have all put in appearances. Beware: the club is frequently booked for private parties and film premieres (call ahead to check availability).

MONTPARNASSE

Dancing La Coupole (⊠ 100 bd. du Montparnasse, 14ᵉ, ☏ 01–43–27–56–00, métro Vavin) has retro disco on Friday and Saturday night; and on Tuesday, salsa, preceded at 8:30 by an optional refresher course—an idea that seems to have breathed new life into this monument. There are also popular tea dances at 3 PM on Sunday.

L'Enfer (⊠ 34 rue du Départ, 14ᵉ, ☏ 01–42–71–79–19, métro Montparnasse-Bienvenüe) has been given a second lease on life in recent years, with the organization of a number of regular, predominantly gay soirées. There is "Scandal" every Thursday, the monthly "House of Legend," as well as the after-party "Discotek" on the same evenings as "Scream" at the Élysée Montmartre.

MONTMARTRE

Bus Palladium (⊠ 6 rue Fontaine, 9ᵉ, ☏ 01–53–21–07–33, métro Blanche) invites women free on Tuesday; on other nights it caters to a fashionable but relaxed crowd. Fear no techno; it serves up a mixture of rock, funk, and disco.

L'Élysée Montmartre (⊠ 72 bd. de Rochechouart, 18ᵉ, ☏ 01–55–07–06–00, métro Pigalle) holds extremely popular *bals* (balls) every other Saturday, where the music runs the gamut of hits from the '40s to the '80s and the DJ is backed up by a 10-piece orchestra. Its regular "Scream" parties (with a predominately gay crowd) are on top of every serious clubber's list.

Les Folies Pigalle (⊠ 11 pl. Pigalle, 9ᵉ, ☏ 01–48–78–55–25, métro Pigalle) is a former cabaret decorated like a '30s bordello. The ambience is decadent; the music varies according to the day of the week (hip-hop on Wednesday and Sunday, a mixture of house and techno at other times); and on Saturday from 9 to 11 PM there's a male strip show (for women only).

Gay and Lesbian Bars and Clubs

Gay and lesbian bars and clubs are mostly concentrated in the Marais and include some of the hippest addresses in the city. Keep in mind, however, that clubs fall in and out of favor at lightning speed. The best way to find out what's hot is by picking up a copy of the free weekly *e.m@le* in one of the bars listed below.

For Men and Women

Amnésia Café (⌧ 42 rue Vieille-du-Temple, 4ᵉ, ☎ 01–42–72–16–94, métro Rambuteau, St-Paul) has an underlit bar and Art Deco ceiling paintings that attract a young, professional gay and lesbian crowd.

Banana Café (⌧ 13 rue de la Ferronnerie, 1ᵉʳ, ☎ 01–42–33–35–31, métro Châtelet-les-Halles) has a trendy, energetic, and scantily clad mixed crowd; dancing on the tables is the norm.

Le Dépôt (⌧ 10 rue aux Ours, 3ᵉ, ☎ 01–44–54–96–96, métro Étienne Marcel) is a bar, club, and back room. The ever-popular Gay Tea Dance on Sunday (from 5 PM) is held here.

Queen (⌧ 102 av. des Champs-Élysées, 8ᵉ, ☎ 01–53–89–08–90, métro George V) is one of the most talked-about nightclubs in Paris: everyone lines up to get in. Monday is disco night. On Sunday, there is the "Overkitsch" party, with a mix of hits from the '80s. On other days, expect to dance to house and techno; the "Break" evening on Wednesday is particularly popular and quite mixed.

Mostly Men

Bar d'Art/Le Duplex (⌧ 25 rue Michel-Le-Comte, 3ᵉ, ☎ 01–42–72–80–86, métro Rambuteau) is frequented by young, tortured-artist types who enjoy the frequent art exhibitions, alternative music, and dim lighting.

Café Cox (⌧ 15 rue des Archives, 4ᵉ, ☎ 01–42–72–08–00, métro Hôtel-de-Ville) is a prime gay pickup joint. Behind the smoked-glass windows, men line the walls and check out the talent.

L'Open Café (⌧ 17 rue des Archives, 4ᵉ, ☎ 01–42–72–26–18, métro Hôtel-de-Ville) is more convivial than neighboring Café Cox, with sunny yellow walls. In summer, the crowd spills out onto the street.

Le Scorp (⌧ 25 bd. Poissonnière, 9ᵉ, ☎ 01–40–26–01–50, métro Rue Montmartre) is one of Paris's longest-standing gay nightclubs. Wednesday is disco night, Thursday is devoted to French pop, Friday to house, Saturday to techno, and Sunday to New Wave.

Mostly Women

Alcantara Café (⌧ 30 rue du Roi de Sicile, 4ᵉ, ☎ 01–42–74–45–00, métro St-Paul) is a cool and friendly bar in the heart of the Marais. There is happy hour every evening from 6 to 8 PM, regular events (flamenco, tap, or salsa dancers), and a DJ in the tiny bar in the basement on Friday and Saturday evenings. Men are allowed in small numbers on weekdays.

Champmeslé (⌧ 4 rue Chabanais, 2ᵉ, ☎ 01–42–96–85–20, métro Bourse) is the hub of lesbian nightlife (open until dawn). Thursday night (starting at 10) is a cabaret of traditional French songs. There are also regular painting exhibitions and a *voyante* (fortune-teller) on hand the last Friday and Saturday of every month.

Le Pulp (⌧ 25 bd. Poissonnière, 2ᵉ, ☎ 01–40–26–01–93, métro Grands Boulevards), one of the rare lesbian clubs in Paris, is housed in a space which hosts tea dances for retirees in the afternoon. On Thursday, the music is house and guys are admitted in small numbers. On Friday and Saturday, it's strictly women-only.

Les Scandaleuses (⌧ 8 rue des Écouffes, 4ᵉ, ☎ 01–48–87–39–26, métro St-Paul) is probably Paris's hippest lesbian hangout. Men are also allowed in (in small numbers), as long as they are accompanied by "scandalous women."

Jazz Clubs

Paris is the celebrated home of *le jazz hot,* and its performing calendar offers plenty of variety, including some fine, distinctive local talent. Most jazz clubs are in the Latin Quarter or around Les Halles. For nightly schedules, consult the specialty magazines, *Jazz Hot, Jazzman,* or *Jazz Magazine.* Note that nothing gets going until 10 or 11 PM and that entry prices vary widely from about 40 francs/€6 to more than 100 francs/€15. Also look out for the annual Villette Jazz Festival (☎ 01–40–03–75–75), held at La Villette at the end of June. The A Fleur de Jazz Festival also offers free concerts at 4:30 PM on Saturday and Sunday at the Parc Floral in the Bois de Vincennes from early March to the end of July.

CHAMPS-ÉLYSÉES

Lionel Hampton Jazz Club (⊠ Méridien Hotel, 81 bd. Gouvion–St-Cyr, 17ᵉ, ☎ 01–40–68–30–42, métro Porte Maillot), named for the zingy vibraphonist loved by Parisians, hosts a roster of international jazz musicians in a spacious, comfortable atmosphere.

LATIN QUARTER/ST-GERMAIN/MONTPARNASSE

Le Bilboquet (⊠ 13 rue St-Benoît, 6ᵉ, ☎ 01–45–48–81–84, métro St-Germain-des-Prés) is the place to find primarily French musicians playing mainstream jazz in a faded Belle Epoque decor.

Le Petit Journal (⊠ 71 bd. St-Michel, 5ᵉ, ☎ 01–43–26–28–59, métro Cluny-La Sorbonne; ⊠ 13 rue du Commandant-Mouchotte, 14ᵉ, ☎ 01–43–21–56–70, métro Montparnasse-Bienvenüe), with two locations, has long attracted the greatest names in French and international jazz. It now specializes in Dixieland jazz and also serves dinner 8:30–midnight.

LES HALLES/GARE DU NORD

Au Duc des Lombards (⊠ 42 rue des Lombards, 1ᵉʳ, ☎ 01–42–33–22–88, métro Châtelet-les-Halles) has modern contemporary jazz in an ill-lit, romantic bebop venue with decor inspired by the Paris métro.

Le Baiser Salé (⊠ 58 rue des Lombards, 1ᵉʳ, ☎ 01–42–33–37–71, métro Châtelet-les-Halles) attracts a younger crowd with salsa, rhythm and blues, fusion, and funk.

New Morning (⊠ 7 rue des Petites-Écuries, 10ᵉ, ☎ 01–45–23–51–41, métro Château d'Eau) is a premier spot for serious fans of avant-garde jazz, folk, and world music; decor is spartan, the mood reverential.

Le Petit Opportun (⊠ 15 rue des Lavandières–Ste-Opportune, 1ᵉʳ, ☎ 01–42–36–01–36, métro Châtelet-les-Halles), in a converted bistro, always has French artists and sometimes features top-flight American soloists with French backup.

Le Sunset (⊠ 60 rue des Lombards, 1ᵉʳ, ☎ 01–40–26–46–60, métro Châtelet-les-Halles) delivers jazz from both French and American musicians, with an accent on jazz fusion and groove. Concerts start at 10 PM.

Le Sunside (⊠ 60 rue des Lombards, 1ᵉʳ, ☎ 01–40–26–21–25, métro Châtelet-les-halles) is at the same address at Le Sunset. It specializes in more classic, traditional jazz and swing. There is also a featured vocalist on Monday night. Concerts start at 9 PM.

Pubs

Pubs wooing English-speaking clients with a selection of beers are becoming increasingly popular with Parisians. They are also good places to find reasonably priced food at off-hours.

The Auld Alliance (⊠ 80 rue François Miron, 4ᵉ, ☎ 01–48–04–30–40, métro St-Paul) has walls adorned with Scottish shields and the bar staff dressed in kilts. There are more than 120 malt whiskies to choose from, true Scottish beers, darts and pool competitions, and the odd evening of bagpipe music.

Connolly's Corner (⊠ 12 rue Mirbel, 5ᵉ, ☎ 01–43–31–94–22, métro Place Monge) is a convivial Irish pub with Guinness on tap and traditional Irish music on Tuesday, Thursday, Saturday, and Sunday. Just make sure you don't wear a tie—it will be snipped off and stuck on the wall (though you'll be compensated with a free pint).

The Cricketer (⊠ 41 rue des Mathurins, 8ᵉ, ☎ 01–40–07–01–45, métro St-Augustin) replies to the virtual Irish monopoly on Paris pubs with Newcastle Brown Ale on tap. Cricket memorabilia adorns the walls.

Finnegan's Wake (⊠ 9 rue des Boulangers, 5ᵉ, ☎ 01–46–34–23–65, métro Jussieu) is a wonderfully quiet and charming Irish pub situated on a steep cobbled street. There is Guinness, Kilkenny, and Murphys on tap, Breton lessons on Monday at 7 PM, and concerts of Irish music on Friday. Happy Hour runs from 6 to 8 PM every evening.

The **Frog and Rosbif** (⊠ 116 rue St-Denis, 2ᵉ, ☎ 01–42–36–34–73, métro Étienne Marcel) has everything you could want from an English "local." Beers are brewed on premises, and rugby and football matches are shown on the giant-screen TV.

Rock, Pop, and World Music Venues

Unlike jazz, French rock is generally not considered to be on a par with its American and British cousins. Even so, Paris is a great place to catch some of your favorite groups, because concert halls tend to be smaller and tickets can be less expensive. It's also a good spot to see all kinds of world music. Most places charge about 90–120 francs/€14–18 and get going around 11 PM. The best way to find out about upcoming concerts is to consult the bulletin boards in FNAC stores.

Le Bataclan (⊠ 50 bd. Voltaire, 11ᵉ, ☎ 01–43–14–35–35, métro Oberkampf) is a legendary venue for live rock, rap, and reggae in an intimate setting.

Casino de Paris (⊠ 16 rue de Clichy, 9ᵉ, ☎ 01–49–95–99–99, métro Trinité), once a favorite with Serge Gainsbourg, has a horseshoe balcony and a cramped, cozy, music-hall feel.

La Cigale (⊠ 120 bd. Rochechouart, 18ᵉ, ☎ 01–49–25–89–99, métro Pigalle) often plays host to up-and-coming French rock bands.

Divan du Monde (⊠ 75 rue des Martyrs, 18ᵉ, ☎ 01–44–92–77–66, métro Pigalle) attracts a varied crowd, depending on the music of the evening: reggae, soul, funk, or salsa. Most nights after the concert, a DJ takes over.

L'Élysée Montmartre (⊠ 72 bd. Rochechouart, 18ᵉ, ☎ 01–55–07–06–00, métro Anvers) dates from Gustave Eiffel, its builder, who, it is hoped, liked a good concert. It's one of the prime venues for emerging French and international rock groups.

Olympia (⊠ 18 rue Caumartin, 9ᵉ, ☎ 01–47–42–25–49, métro Madeleine), a legendary venue once favored by Jacques Brel and Edith Piaf, still hosts leading French singers. Rather strangely, the original hall was demolished a few years ago to make way for an underground carpark and an identical theater constructed in the same building.

L'Opus Café (⊠ 167 quai de Valmy, 10ᵉ, ☎ 01–40–34–70–00, métro Louis Blanc), on the picturesque Canal St-Martin, has jazz and soul concerts.

Palais Omnisports de Paris-Bercy (⊠ 8 bd. de Bercy, 12ᵉ, ☎ 08–25–03–00–31, métro Bercy) is the largest venue in Paris and is where English and American pop stars perform.

Zenith (⊠ Parc de La Villette, 211 av. Jean-Jaurès, 19ᵉ, ☎ 01–42–08–60–00, métro Porte de Pantin) is a large concert hall that primarily stages rock shows; check posters and listings for details. The neighboring Grande Halle de La Villette organizes lively world music festivals in June.

After-Hours Dining

Chances are that some of your nocturnal forays will have you looking for sustenance at an unlikely hour. If so, you might find it handy to know that there are restaurants open round the clock.

L'Alsace (⊠ 39 av. des Champs-Élysées, 8ᵉ, ☎ 01–53–93–97–00, métro Franklin-D.-Roosevelt) is a smart, if characterless, brasserie-restaurant, serving seafood and sauerkraut around the clock.

Au Chien Qui Fume (⊠ 33 rue du Pont-Neuf, 1ᵉʳ, ☎ 01–42–36–07–42, métro Les Halles), open until 2 AM, is filled with paintings (in the style of old masters) of smoking dogs. Traditional French cuisine and seafood platters are served.

Au Pied de Cochon (⊠ 6 rue Coquillière, 1ᵉʳ, ☎ 01–40–13–77–00, métro Les Halles), near St-Eustache church, once catered to the all-night workers at the adjacent Paris food market. Its Second Empire decor has been restored, and traditional dishes like pig's trotters and chitterling sausage still grace the menu.

Le Bienvenu (⊠ 42 rue d'Argout, 2ᵉ, ☎ 01–42–33–31–08, métro Louvre) certainly doesn't look like much (check out the slightly kitsch mural on the back wall), but it serves up a welcome couscous in the early hours of the morning. Open until 7 AM, it also offers simple French food, such as pâté and Niçoise salad.

La Cloche d'Or (⊠ 3 rue Mansart, 9ᵉ, ☎ 01–48–74–48–88, métro Place de Clichy) is a Paris institution where the likes of the late François Mitterrand, Depêche Mode, and the dancers from the Moulin Rouge have all dined on its traditional French cuisine. It's open until 4 AM every day except Sunday, when it closes at 1 AM.

Les Coulisses (⊠ 5 rue du Mont-Cenis, 18ᵉ, ☎ 01–42–62–89–99, métro Lamarck-Caulaincourt), in Montmartre, near picturesque place du Tertre, has the most character of all the late-night restaurants: its red banquettes and 18th-century Venetian mirrors make it look like an Italian theater. The food—traditional French—is served until 4 AM. In the basement is a club, open Thursday–Saturday.

Grand Café des Capucines (⊠ 4 bd. des Capucines, 9ᵉ, ☎ 01–43–12–19–00, métro Opéra), whose exuberant pseudo–Belle Epoque dining room matches the mood of the neighboring Opéra, serves excellent oysters, fish, and meat dishes at hefty prices. It's open around the clock.

Le Tambour (⊠ 41 rue Montmartre, 2ᵉ, ☎ 01–42–33–06–90, métro Étienne Marcel, Les Halles) is full of old-fashioned charm. The owner has one of those quintessential Parisian moustaches, there is an old métro map on the wall, and advertising signs from yesteryear catch the eye. Le Tambour calls itself a "*bistrot de l'urbain bucolique*" (a "bistrot for the bucolic city dweller") and serves up traditional French fare (onion soup, foie gras, steak tartare, confit de canard—what else?). It's open around the clock.

THE ARTS

Without a doubt, Paris has been one of the 20th century's greatest capitals of the arts. In 1909, Serge Diaghilev arrived in the city with his Ballets Russes. In the '20s, Josephine Baker charmed audiences at the Théâtre des Champs-Élysées. And in the '40s, Jean-Paul Sartre and Simone de Beauvoir wrote masterpieces at the Café de Flore. Nowadays, despite lavish government subsidies, the city's artistic life doesn't have the avant-garde edge it once did, but Parisians are still proud of being intellectual and passionate about all things cultural. The city has an impressive number of venues and regularly attracts international theater, dance, and opera companies. In addition, the phenomenal number of movie theaters makes Paris a cinephile's heaven.

The music and theater season runs September to June; in summer, most productions are found at festivals elsewhere in France. There is, however, an excellent festival in Paris during July and August called Paris–Quartier d'Eté, which attracts international stars of dance, classical music, and jazz. Detailed entertainment listings can be found in the weekly magazines *Pariscope* (which has an English-language section), *L'Officiel des Spectacles, Zurban,* and *Figaroscope* (a supplement to *Le Figaro* newspaper). The **Paris Tourist Office's 24-hour hot line** in English (☎ 08–36–68–31–12) and its Web site (WEB www.paris-touristoffice.com) are other good sources of information about activities in the city.

Tickets can be purchased at the theater itself (try to get them in advance, as many of the more popular performances sell out quickly). Your hotel or a travel agency such as **Opéra Théâtre** (⊠ 7 rue de Clichy, 9ᵉ, ☎ 01–40–06–01–00, métro Trinité) may also be able to help you. They take a 20% commission on each ticket and also have a Web site: WEB www.operatheatre.com. Tickets can also be purchased at **FNAC** stores, especially the one in the Forum des Halles (⊠ 1–5 rue Pierre Lescot, 3rd level down, 1ᵉ, ☎ 01–49–87–50–50, métro Châtelet-les-halles). **Virgin Megastore** (⊠ 52 av. des Champs-Élysées, 8ᵉ, ☎ 08–03–02–30–24, métro Franklin-D.-Roosevelt) also sells theater and concert tickets. Half-price tickets for same-day theater performances are available at the **Kiosques Théâtre** (⊠ across from 15 pl. de la Madeleine, métro Montparnasse-Bienvenüe; outside the Gare Montparnasse, pl. Raoul Dautry, 15ᵉ, métro Montparnasse-Bienvenüe), open Tuesday–Saturday 12:30–8 and Sunday 12:30–4. Expect to pay a 16-franc/€2.44 commission per ticket and stand in line. Half-price tickets are also available in numerous private theaters during the first week of each new show. Check the weekly guides for details.

Circus

You don't need to know French to enjoy the circus. Venues change frequently, so it is best to check one of the weekly guides; tickets range 40–180 francs/€6–27. **Cirque Alexis Gruss** (⊠ Pelouse de Madrid, Allée de la Reine, Bois de Boulogne, ☎ 01–44–17–96–22, métro Porte Maillot, then bus 244 to the Route des Lacs stop) is in Paris five months of the year and remains an avowedly old-fashioned production with showy horsemen. **Cirque Alexandra Bouglione** (⊠ Jardin d'Acclimatation, Bois de Boulogne, ☎ 01–44–17–96–22, métro Sablons) has acrobats, jugglers, clowns, contortionists, trapeze artists, snakes, doves, and a show inspired by Greek mythology. From tigers to yaks, dogs, and clowns, **Cirque Diana Moreno Bormann** (⊠ 9 bd. du Bois Leprêtre, 17ᵉ, ☎ 01–64–05–36–25, métro Porte de St-Ouen) is good for all ages; performances are on Saturday, Sunday, and Wednesday at 3 PM. **Cirque d'Hiver** (⊠ 110 rue Amelot, 11ᵉ, ☎ 01–47–00–12–25, métro Filles du Calvaire), constructed in 1852 as a circus hall, is now only occasionally home to the circus; more often fashion shows and parties are held here. **Cirque de Paris** (⊠ 115 bd. Charles-de-Gaulle, Villeneuve-la-Garenne, ☎ 01–47–99–40–40, métro Porte de Clignancourt, then Bus 137) offers "A Day at the Circus": a peek behind the scenes in the morning, lunch with the artists, and a performance in the afternoon.

Classical Music

Cité de la Musique (✉ in the Parc de La Villette, 221 av. Jean-Jaurès, 19ᵉ, ☎ 01–44–84–44–84, métro Porte de Pantin) presents a varied program of classical, experimental, and world music concerts in a postmodern setting.

IRCAM (✉ 1 pl. Igor-Stravinsky, 4ᵉ, ☎ 01–44–78–48– 16, métro Châtelet-les-Halles, Hôtel-de-Ville) organizes concerts of contemporary classical music on the premises, at the Centre Pompidou next door, or at the Cité de la Musique.

Maison de Radio France (✉ 116 av. du Président-Kennedy, 16ᵉ, ☎ 01–56–40–15–16, RER Maison de Radio-France), the base for countless radio and TV stations, is also home to the Orchestre National de France. The Orchestre Philharmonique de Radio France often performs in the smallish, modern Salle Olivier Messiaen.

L'Opéra Royal (✉ Château de Versailles, ☎ 01–30–83–78–88, RER Versailles-Rive Gauche) was built in 20 months for the marriage of the future Louis XVI and Marie-Antoinette. In the 18th century, both *Castor et Pollux* by Rameau and *Iphigénie* by Glück were given there. Today, it plays host to a season of chamber and orchestral concerts, vocal recitals, dance, and theater called "Les Nouveaux Plaisirs" (March–September).

Salle Cortot (✉ 78 rue Cardinet, 17ᵉ, ☎ 01–47–63–85–72, métro Malesherbes) is an acoustic gem, built by Auguste Perret in 1918. At the time, he promised to construct a "hall that sounds like a violin." Today, it plays host to jazz and classical concerts. There are also free recitals at 12:30 PM on Tuesday and Thursday by the students of the adjoining École Normale de Musique.

Salle Gaveau (✉ 45 rue de la Boétie, 8ᵉ, ☎ 01–49–53–05–07, métro Miromesnil) is a small hall of only 1,200 seats with an old-world atmosphere and fantastic acoustics. Its original gold and white decoration was restored during recent renovation work. It plays host to chamber music, piano, and vocal recitals.

Salle Pleyel (✉ 252 rue du Faubourg St-Honoré, 8ᵉ, ☎ 08–25–00–02–52, métro Ternes) is Paris's principal home of classical music. The Orchestre de Paris and other leading international orchestras play here regularly, and there's a fine series of recitals by international stars. Note that the hall will close for extensive renovation work at the end of July 2002.

Théâtre des Champs-Élysées (✉ 15 av. Montaigne, 8ᵉ, ☎ 01–49–52–50–50, métro Alma-Marceau) was the scene of the famous Battle of the Rite of Spring in 1913, when police had to be called in after the audience started ripping up the seats in outrage at Stravinsky's *Le Sacre du Printemps* music and Nijinsky's choreography. Today, this elegantly restored, plush Art Deco temple is worthy of a visit based solely on architectural merit and ambience. It also hosts top-quality concerts and ballet.

Théâtre du Palais-Royal (✉ 38 rue Montpensier, 1ᵉʳ, ☎ 01–48–24–16–97, métro Palais-Royal) is a sparkling 750-seat Italian theater bedecked in gold and purple. From January until June, it plays host to "*Les Concerts du Palais-Royal*": a series of performances of Baroque music, vocal recitals, and opera bouffe.

Church and Museum Concerts

Paris has a never-ending stream of free or inexpensive lunchtime and evening church concerts, ranging from organ recitals to choral music and orchestral works. Some are scheduled as part of the **Festival d'Art Sacré** (☎ 01–44–70–64–10 information) between mid-November and Christmas. Check the weekly listings for information; telephone numbers for most church concerts vary with the organizer.

Sainte-Chapelle (⊠ 4 bd. du Palais, 1ᵉʳ, ☎ 01–42–77–65–65, métro Cité) holds memorable candlelit concerts April through mid-October; make reservations well in advance. Other churches with concerts include the following: **Notre-Dame** (⊠ Ile de la Cité, 4ᵉ, métro Cité); **St-Eustache** (⊠ Rue du Jour, 1ᵉʳ, métro Les Halles); **St-Germain-des-Prés** (⊠ Pl. St-Germain-des-Prés, 6ᵉ, métro St-Germain-des-Prés); **St-Julien-Le-Pauvre** (⊠ 23 quai de Montebello, 5ᵉ, métro St-Michel); **St-Louis-en-l'Ile** (⊠ 19 bis rue St-Louis-en-l'Ile, 4ᵉ, métro Pont Marie); and **St-Roch** (⊠ 296 rue St-Honoré, 1ᵉʳ, métro Tuileries).

Museums are another good place to find classical concerts. Some of the best are held in the **Auditorium du Louvre** (⊠ Palais du Louvre, ☎ 01–40–20–84–00, métro Palais-Royal–Musée du Louvre) on Wednesday evening and Thursday lunchtime. The **Musée d'Orsay** (⊠ 1 rue de Bellechasse, 7ᵉ, ☎ 01–40–49–47–57, RER Musée d'Orsay) regularly holds small-scale concerts (song cycles, piano recitals, or chamber music) at lunchtime or in the early evening. The **Musée du Moyen Age** (⊠ 6 pl. Paul Painlevé, 5ᵉ, ☎ 01–53–73–78–16, métro Cluny–La Sorbonne) stages early music concerts between March and October.

There is also a fine Chopin Festival at the delightfully picturesque **Orangerie de Bagatelle** (⊠ Parc de Bagatelle, av. de Longchamp, Bois de Boulogne, ☎ 01–45–00–22–19, métro Sablons) in late June and early July. In August and September, there are also free classical concerts in the Parc Floral of the Bois de Boulogne on Saturday and Sunday at 4:30 PM.

Dance

As a rule, more avant-garde or up-and-coming choreographers show their works in the smaller performance spaces in the Bastille and the Marais and in theaters in nearby suburbs. Classical ballet is found in places as varied as the opera house and the sports stadium. Check the weekly guides for listings.

Maison des Arts et de la Culture (1 pl. Salvador Allende, 94000 Créteil, ☎ 01–45–13–19–19, métro Créteil-Préfecture), situated just outside Paris, is a fine venue for dance, which often attracts top-flight international and French companies, such as Blanca Li, Mikhail Baryshnikov's White Oak Project, and Philippe Decouflé.

Opéra Garnier (⊠ Pl. de l'Opéra, 9ᵉ, ☎ 08–36–69–78–68, métro Opéra) is the sumptuous Napoléon-III home of the well-reputed Ballet de l'Opéra National de Paris and almost never hosts other dance companies. When performing, it offers the same program—a full-length ballet like *Sylvia* or *La Sylphide* or an evening of shorter works— for six or so consecutive performances. Seat prices range 30–395 francs/€4.60–60; many of the cheaper seats have obstructed views.

Théâtre de la Bastille (⊠ 76 rue de la Roquette, 11ᵉ, ☎ 01–43–57–42–14, métro Bastille) merits mention as an example of the innovative activity in the Bastille area; it has an enviable record as a launching pad for tomorrow's modern dance stars.

Théâtre de la Cité Internationale (⊠ 21 bd. Jourdan, 14ᵉ, ☎ 01–43–13–50–50, métro Cité-Universitaire) is a complex of three theaters at the heart of the international student residence, the Cité Universitaire. It often plays host to young, avant-garde companies and is also the main venue for the Presqu'Iles de Danse festival in February.

Théâtre de la Ville (⊠ 2 pl. du Châtelet, 4ᵉ, métro Châtelet; 31 rue des Abbesses, 18ᵉ, métro Abbesses; ☎ 01–42–74–22–77 for both) is *the* place for contemporary dance. Troupes like La La La Human Steps and Anne-Teresa de Keersmaeker's Rosas company are presented here.

The queen of modern European dance, Pina Bausch, also comes every June (getting tickets for her shows, however, often proves more difficult than finding a needle in the proverbial haystack).

Film

Paris has hundreds of cinemas showing contemporary and classic French and American movies, as well as an array of independent, international, and documentary films. A number of theaters, especially in principal tourist areas such as the Champs-Élysées, boulevard des Italiens near the Opéra, St-Germain-des-Prés, and Les Halles, run English-language films. Check the weekly guides for a movie of your choice. The initials "v.o." mean *version originale,* or not dubbed; films that are dubbed are indicated by the initials "v.f." (*version française*). Cinema admission runs 35–55 francs/€5.34–8.40; some cinemas have reduced rates on certain days (normally Monday, sometimes Wednesday) or for early shows; others offer reductions with the purchase of a multiple-entry card. Most theaters post two show times: the *séance,* when the commercials, previews, and, sometimes, short films begin; and the feature presentation, which usually starts 10–25 minutes later.

Paris has a number of big-screen cinemas: **Gaumont Grand Écran** (⊠ 30 pl. d'Italie, 13ᵉ, ☎ 01–45–80–77–00, métro Place d'Italie) boasts the biggest screen in Paris; **Grand Rex** (⊠ 1 bd. Poissonnière, 2ᵉ, ☎ 01–42–36–83–93, métro Bonne-Nouvelle) opened in 1932—with its capacity of 2,800, it actually attracted more people than the Louvre back in 1960; **Kinopanorama** (⊠ 60 av. de la Motte-Piquet, 15ᵉ, ☎ 01–43–06–50–50, métro La Motte Picquet–Grenelle) is a small theater of just 520 seats, so get there early for screenings; **Max Linder Panorama** (⊠ 24 bd. Poissonnière, 9ᵉ, ☎ 01–48–24–00–47, métro Grands-Boulevards) opened in 1932 and was named after French burlesque actor Max Linder; check out the marble floors and Florentine stucco on the walls; **MK2 Quai de Seine** (⊠ 14 quai de Seine, 19ᵉ, ☎ 01–53–26–41–77, métro Stalingrad), a relatively new complex showing major releases, is well worth a visit for its location on the Bassin de la Villette. **UGC Ciné Cité Les Halles** (⊠ Pl. de la Rotonde, Forum des Halles, Level 3, access by the Porte du Jour near St-Eustache church, 1ᵉʳ, ☎ 01–40–26–40–45, métro Les Halles) is a huge complex of 19 theaters in the underground Les Halles shopping complex.

Unique in all the world is **La Pagode** (⊠ 57 bis rue de Babylone, 7ᵉ, ☎ 01–45–55–48–48, métro St-François Xavier)—where else but in Paris would you find movies screened in an antique pagoda? A Chinese fantasy, this structure was built in 1896 for the wife of the owner of the Au Bon Marché department store, whose salon attracted notable writers and painters here. By the 1970s, it had become a cinema slated for demolition (and then was saved by director Louis Malle). Though the fare is standard, the decor is enchanting—who can resist seeing a flick in the silk-and-gilt Salle Japonaise?

For the *cinéaste* (movie lover) who was brought up on Fellini, Bergman, and Resnais, the main mecca is the famed **Cinémathèque Française** (⊠ 42 bd. de Bonne-Nouvelle, 10ᵉ, ☎ 01–56–26–01–01, métro Bonne-Nouvelle and **Palais de Chaillot** (⊠ 7 av. Albert-de-Mun, 16ᵉ, ☎ 01–56–26–01–01, métro Trocadéro). This venerable institution pioneered the preservation of early films. Today, its schedules often pay homage to major film directors, with the main programs scheduled for the Palais de Chaillot venue Wednesday–Sunday.

Other than the Cinémathèque Française, Paris has many other theaters showing classic and independent films, often found in the Latin Quarter (with some notable exceptions). Showings are often organized around retrospectives (check "Festivals" in weekly guides). Following is a list of some of the noteworthy independent cinemas: **Accatone** (✉ 20 rue Cujax, 5ᵉ, ☏ 01–46–33–86–86, métro Cluny-La Sorbonne, Luxembourg) shows mainly European art films; **Action Écoles** (✉ 23 rue des Écoles, 5ᵉ, ☏ 01–43–29–79–89, métro Maubert-Mutualité) specializes in old American classics; **Champo** (✉ 51 rue des Écoles, 5ᵉ, ☏ 01–43–54–51–60, métro Cluny–La Sorbonne) often programs Hitchcock films; **Grande Action** (✉ 5 rue des Écoles, 5ᵉ, ☏ 01–43–29–44–40, métro Cardinal-Lemoine, Jussieu) usually features American classics; **Quartier Latin** (✉ 9 rue Champollion, 5ᵉ, ☏ 01–43–26–84–65, métro Cluny–La Sorbonne) is one of a number of cinemas near the Sorbonne; and **St-André-des-Arts** (✉ 30 rue St-André-des-Arts, 6ᵉ, ☏ 01–43–26–48–18, métro St-Michel) is one of the best cinemas in Paris, and generally has a festival devoted to one director, such as Bergman or Tarkovski.

Cinéma des Cinéastes (✉ 7 av. de Clichy, 17ᵉ, ☏ 01–53–42–40–20, métro Place de Clichy) shows previews of feature films, as well as documentaries, short subjects, and rarely shown movies; it's in an old cabaret transformed into a movie theater and wine bar. **L'Entrepôt** (✉ 7 rue Francis-de-Pressensé, 14ᵉ, ☏ 01–45–40–78–38, métro Pernety) screens films and has a café, bar, restaurant, and bookstore. **Balzac** (✉ 1 rue Balzac, 8ᵉ, ☏ 01–45–61–10–60, métro George V) often holds talks by directors before screenings. **Le Forum des Images** (✉ Forum des Halles, Porte St-Eustache entrance, 1ᵉʳ, ☏ 01–44–76–62–00, métro Les Halles) organizes thematic viewings of its archives of films and videos on the city of Paris. For 30 francs/€4.60 you can watch up to four films, two hours of video, and surf the Web for 30 minutes. The **Centre Pompidou** also hosts regular themed film festivals, and the **Maison Européenne de la Photo** is a fine place to take in documentaries on photography. **Dôme Imax** (✉ La Défense, ☏ 08–36–67–06–06, RER La Défense) shows 3-D flicks. **La Géode** (✉ At the Cité des Sciences et de l'Industrie, Parc de La Villette, 26 av. Corentin-Cariou, 19ᵉ, ☏ 01–40–05–12–12, métro Porte de la Villette) screens wide-angle Omnimax films—usually documentaries—on a gigantic spherical surface. In summer at the **Parc de La Villette** (métro Porte de Pantin, Porte de La Villette) movies are shown outdoors on a large screen. Most people take along a picnic. You can also rent deck chairs by the entrance; check the weekly guides for films.

Galleries

Art galleries are scattered throughout the city, but those focusing on the same period are often clustered in one neighborhood. There are many contemporary art galleries, for instance, near the Centre Pompidou, the Picasso Museum, and the Bastille Opéra. More recently, several avant-garde galleries have moved to rue Louise Weiss near the Bibliothèque François-Mitterrand in the 13ᵉ. (Note that it's not uncommon for galleries to be hidden away in courtyards, with the only sign of their presence a small plaque on the front of the buildings; take these as invitations to push through the doors.) Around St-Germain, the galleries are generally more traditional, and works by old masters and established modern artists dominate the galleries around rue du Faubourg St-Honoré and avenue Matignon. To help you plot your gallery course, get a free copy of the map published by the Association des Galeries; it's available at many of the galleries listed below.

These days the Parisian art world is abuzz because, after many years' delay, the main French auctioneers, most based at the **Hôtel Drouot** (✉ 9 rue Drouot, 9ᵉ, ☏ 01–48–00–20–00, métro Richelieu-Drouot), have lost their monopoly on art auctions in Paris. **Christie's** (✉ 9 av. Matignon, 8ᵉ, ☏ 01–40–76–85–85) opened shop in 2001 with lavish new showrooms and a calendar of auctions. **Sotheby's** (✉ 76 rue du Faubourg St-Honoré, 8ᵉ, ☎ 01–53–05–53–05, métro St-Phillipe du Roule), Christie's arch-rival, has an ambitious calendar of sales scheduled. New-kid-on-the-block, **Phillips, de Pury, and Luxembourg,** are due to open Paris offices in either 2001 or 2002.

Agathe Gaillard (✉ 3 rue Pont Louis-Philippe, 4ᵉ, ☎ 01–42–77–38–24, métro Hôtel-de-Ville) was the first person to open a photo gallery in Paris way back in 1975. Since, she has exhibited many of the great names of the genre, from Kertesz and Cartier-Bresson to Edouard Boubat. Today, she also represents a stable of up-and-coming stars.

Artcurial (✉ 61 av. Montaigne, 8ᵉ, ☎ 01–42–99–16–16, métro Franklin-D.-Roosevelt) has the feel of a museum shop. It sells artist-designed decorative objects and exhibits works by such artists as Bram van Velde and Zao Wou-Ki.

Carré Rive Gauche (métro St-Germain-des-Prés, Rue du Bac) is an area sheltering dozens of art and antiques galleries on its narrow lanes.

Galerie 213 (✉ 213 bd. Raspail, 14ᵉ, ☎ 01–43–22–83–23, métro Raspail) is owned by Marion de Beaupré, former agent of top photographers like Peter Lindbergh and Paolo Roversi. Today, she runs this space, which has a bookstore on the ground floor, in a magnificent early Art Nouveau decor. On the first floor is a white gallery space, where she exhibits work by the likes of Elger Esser, Gueorgui Pinkhassov, and Guido Mocafico.

Galerie Arnoux (✉ 27 rue Guénégaud, 6ᵉ, ☎ 01–46–33–04–66, métro Odéon), one of many galleries on this street, specializes in abstract painting of the '50s, as well as in the works of young painters and sculptors.

Galerie Camera Obscura (✉ 12 rue Ernest Cresson, 14ᵉ, ☎ 01–45–45–67–08, métro Mouton-Duvernet) is a small photography gallery with a very Zen-like atmosphere. The work on show is top quality, and the photographers represented include Lucien Hervé, Willy Ronis, and Yasuhiro Ishimoto.

Galerie Claude Bernard (✉ 5 rue des Beaux-Arts, 6ᵉ, ☎ 01–43–26–97–07, métro St-Germain-des-Prés) is very well established in the domain of traditional figurative work.

Galerie Dina Vierny (✉ 36 rue Jacob, 6ᵉ, ☎ 01–42–60–23–18, métro St-Germain-des-Prés) was set up after the war by the former muse of sculptor Aristide Maillol. Since, she has discovered artists such as Serge Poliakoff, Vladimir Yankelevsky, and Ilya Kabakov.

Galerie Laage-Salomon (✉ 57 rue du Temple, 4ᵉ, ☎ 01–42–78–11–71, métro Hôtel-de-Ville) shows a well-known, very international group of artists, such as Per Kirkeby, Georg Baselitz, and Candida Höfer.

Galerie Lelong (✉ 13 rue de Téhéran, 8ᵉ, ☎ 01–45–63–13–19, métro Miromesnil), which also has galleries in New York and Zurich, represents a mix of contemporary artists.

Galerie Louis Carré (✉ 10 av. de Messine, 8ᵉ, ☎ 01–45–62–57–07, métro Miromesnil) has a long history of promoting French artists, including Bazaine, but it is not lost in the past.

Galerie Maeght (✉ 42 rue du Bac, 7ᵉ, ☎ 01–45–48–45–15, métro Rue du Bac) is the Paris branch of the Fondation Maeght in St-Paul-de-Vence. You can find paintings as well as books, prints, and reasonably priced posters.

Galerie Templon (⊠ in courtyard of 30 rue Beaubourg, 3ᵉ, ☎ 01–42–72–14–10, métro Rambuteau) was the first to bring American artists to Paris in the '60s; now it represents many artists, including French star Jean-Pierre Raynaud.

Galerie Yvon Lambert (⊠ 108 rue Vieille-du-Temple, 3ᵉ, ☎ 01–42–71–09–33, métro St-Sébastien Froissart) is run by the man known to the French as "the discoverer of minimalism and Conceptual Art"—indeed, one of his more famous exploits was his sale of a painting to a blind man. Over the years, he has exhibited everyone from Daniel Buren and Christo to Sol Lewitt and Julian Schnabel. Today, he exhibits artists like Jenny Holzer, Douglas Gordon, and Christian Boltanski.

Joyce (⊠ Palais-Royal, 9 rue de Valois, 1ᵉʳ, ☎ 01–40–15–03–72, métro Palais-Royal) is a gallery and boutique set up by successful Asian retailer Joyce Ma, who regularly invites Asian artists to show their work.

Louvre des Antiquaires (⊠ 2 pl. du Palais-Royal, 1ᵉʳ, ☎ 01–42–97–27–00, métro Palais-Royal) is an elegant multifloor complex where 250 of Paris's leading dealers showcase their rarest objects, including Louis XV furniture, tapestries, and antique jewelry. The center is open Tuesday–Sunday 11 AM–7 PM; it's closed Sunday in July and August.

Opera

Paris is a mecca for world-class opera. Consequently, getting tickets to the two main venues, the **Opéra de la Bastille** and the **Opéra Garnier**, can be difficult on short notice, so it is a good idea to plan ahead. Get a list of performances by getting a copy of the Paris Tourist Office's "*Saison de Paris*" booklet or by writing to the **Opéra de la Bastille** (⊠ 120 rue de Lyon, 75576, Paris Cedex 12) well in advance. Make your selection and send back the booking form, giving several choices of nights and performances. If the response is affirmative, just pick up and pay for your tickets before the performance (you can also pay for them by credit card in advance). A word of caution: buying from a scalper is not recommended, as there have been reports of people selling counterfeit tickets.

Opéra de la Bastille (⊠ Pl. de la Bastille, 12ᵉ, ☎ 08–36–69–78–68, WEB www.opera-de-paris.fr, métro Bastille), the ultramodern facility built in 1989 and designed by architect Carlos Ott, has taken over the role as Paris's main opera house from the Opéra Garnier; tickets for the Opéra de Paris productions range 45–670 francs/€7–103 and go on sale at the box office two weeks before any given show or a month ahead by phone. The opera season usually runs September to June and the box office is open Monday to Saturday 11–6:30.

Opéra Comique (⊠ 5 rue Favart, 2ᵉ, ☎ 01–42–44–45–46, métro Richelieu-Drouot) is a lofty old hall that has been given a new lease on life ever since Jérôme Savary—one of France's *enfants terribles* of theater—took over as director in 2000. As well as staging operettas, the hall also plays host to modern dance, classical concerts, and vocal recitals.

Former haunt of the Phantom, the painter Edgar Degas, and any number of legendary opera stars, the magnificent and magical **Opéra Garnier** (⊠ Pl. de l'Opéra, 9ᵉ, ☎ 08–36–69–78–68, WEB www.opera-de-paris. fr, métro Opéra) still hosts occasional performances of the Opéra de Paris, along with a fuller calendar of dance performances, as the auditorium is the official home of the Ballet de l'Opéra National de Paris. The grandest opera productions are usually mounted at the Opéra de la Bastille, while the Garnier now presents smaller-scale opera, such as Mozart's *La Clemenza di Tito* and *Cosi fan Tutte*. Gorgeous though the Garnier is, its tiara-shape theater means that many seats have limited sight lines, so it's best to ask specifically what the sight lines are like when booking (partial-view in French is *visibilité partielle*). Needless to say, the cheaper seats are often those with partial views. Budget-minded American and British opera-goers will be shocked to learn there is no standing room at either opera house. Ticket prices for opera range 30–670 francs/€4.60–103. Seats go on sale at the box office two weeks before any given show or a month ahead by phone; you must go in person to buy the 30-franc/€4.60 and 60-franc/€9.20 tickets. Sometimes rush tickets, if available, are offered 15 minutes before a performance. The box office is open 11 to 6:30 daily. **Théâtre Musical de Paris** (⊠ Pl. du Châtelet, 1ᵉʳ, ☎ 01–40–28–28–40, métro Châtelet), better known as the Théâtre du Châtelet, puts on some of the finest opera productions in the city and regularly attracts international divas like Cecilia Bartoli and Anne-Sofie von Otter. It also plays host to classical concerts, dance performances, and the occasional play.

Puppet Shows

On most Wednesday, Saturday, and Sunday afternoons, the Guignol—the French equivalent of Punch and Judy—can be seen going through their ritualistic battles in a number of Paris's parks, including the **Champ de Mars** (☎ 01–48–56–01–44, métro École Militaire) and the **Jardins du Ranelagh** (☎ 01–45–83–51–75, métro La Muette). The **Jardin du Luxembourg** (☎ 01–43–26–46–47, métro Vavin) and the **Jardin d'Acclimatation** (in the Bois de Boulogne, ☎ 01–45–01–53–52, métro Sablons) both have year-round, weatherproof performance spaces.

Theater

A number of theaters line the Grands Boulevards between the Opéra and République, but there is no Paris equivalent to Broadway or the West End. Shows are mostly in French, with a few notable exceptions. Information about performances can be obtained on the site www. theatreonline.fr, which lists 170 different theaters, offers critiques, and provides an on-line reservation service. A genre that has recently become particularly popular in France is the "Broadway musical." Up until 1999, Parisians had shunned most all-singing-and-dancing shows, but then came the smash-hit *Notre-Dame-de-Paris,* which launched the fashion for Broadway-style musicals (and went on to be produced in Las Vegas and London's West End); for years, the French weren't into musicals at all, but they have now become crazy about them. Numerous other Gallic musicals have since debuted; most are staged at either the Palais des Sports or the Palais des Congrès.

Bouffes du Nord (⊠ 37 bis bd. de la Chapelle, 10ᵉ, ☎ 01–46–07–34–50, métro La Chapelle) is the wonderfully atmospheric, slightly decrepit home of English director Peter Brook, who regularly delights with his wonderful experimental productions.
Café de la Gare (⊠ 41 rue du Temple, 4ᵉ, ☎ 01–42–78–52–51, métro Hôtel-de-Ville) is a fun spot to experience a particularly Parisian form of theater, the *café-théâtre*—a mixture of satirical sketches and variety show riddled with slapstick humor, performed in a café setting. You need a good grasp of French.
La Cartoucherie (⊠ In the Bois de Vincennes, ☎ 01–43–74–24–08 or 01–43–28–36–36, métro Château de Vincennes, then shuttle bus), a complex of five theaters in a former munitions factory, turns cast and spectators into an intimate theatrical world. The resident director is

the revered Ariane Mnouchkine. Go early for a simple meal; the cast often helps serve.

Comédie des Champs-Élysées (✉ 23 rue de la Huchette, 5ᵉ, ☎ 01–43–26–38–99, métro St-Michel) offers fine productions in a theater neighboring the larger Théâtre des Champs-Élysées. This is where Yasmina Reza's international hit *Art* first came to the public's attention.

Comédie Française (✉ Pl. Colette, 1ᵉʳ, ☎ 01–44–58–15–15, métro Palais-Royal) dates back to 1680 and is the most hallowed institution in French theater. It specializes in classical French plays by the likes of Racine, Molière, and Marivaux. Reserve seats in person about two weeks in advance, or turn up an hour beforehand and wait in line for cancellations.

MC93 Bobigny (✉ 1 bd. Lenine, Bobigny, ☎ 01–41–60–72–72, métro Bobigny–Pablo-Picasso), in a suburb northeast of Paris, often stages top-flight English and American productions.

Théâtre Gérard Philippe (✉ 59 bd. Jules-Guesdes, St-Denis, ☎ 01–48–13–17–00, métro St-Denis–Basilique) is run by one of France's most talented young directors, Stanislas Nardey. For only 50 francs/€7.6, you can see high-caliber, innovative theater and the occasional contemporary dance performance.

Théâtre de la Huchette (✉ 23 rue de la Huchette, 5ᵉ, ☎ 01–43–26–38–99, métro St-Michel) is a highlight for Ionesco admirers; this tiny Left Bank theater has been staging *The Bald Soprano* every night since 1950! (Note that the box office is only open 5–9 PM Monday–Saturday.)

Théâtre de Marigny (✉ Carré Marigny, 8ᵉ, ☎ 01–53–96–70–00, métro Champs-Elysées Clémenceau) is a private theater, where you're likely to find a big French star topping the bill. This is where Isabelle Adjani decided to make her stage comeback, in *La Dame aux Camélias* in 2000.

Théâtre Mogador (✉ 25 rue de Mogador, 9ᵉ, ☎ 01–53–32–32–00, métro Trinité), one of Paris's most sumptuous theaters, is the place for musicals and other productions with popular appeal.

Théâtre National de Chaillot (✉ 1 pl. du Trocadéro, 16ᵉ, ☎ 01–53–65–30–00, métro Trocadéro) is a cavernous place with two theaters dedicated to drama and dance. The program ranges from Shakespeare to cabaret shows and tango festivals. Top-flight dance companies like the Ballet Royal de Suède and William Forsythe's Ballet Frankfurt are also regular visitors.

Théâtre de l'Odéon (✉ Pl. de l'Odéon, 6ᵉ, ☎ 01–44–41–36–36, métro Odéon) has made pan-European theater its primary focus and offers some of the finest productions in Paris.

Théâtre de la Renaissance (✉ 20 bd. St-Martin, 10ᵉ, ☎ 01–42–08–18–50, métro Strasbourg–St-Denis) was once home to Belle Epoque star Sarah Bernhardt (she was manager from 1893 to 1899). Big French stars often perform in plays here.

5 OUTDOOR ACTIVITIES AND SPORTS

Parisians are often envied for their ability to stay thin despite their love of buttery foods and chocolate treats and their seeming disdain for exercise. The truth is they do actually like to be *sportif*. Nowadays, if they're not walking or bicycling, many Parisians are swimming, playing soccer, and working out at health clubs. Although facilities in the heart of the city are limited, you can find places to exercise and get outdoors. There are also a number of large stadiums in and around the city where you can see soccer, rugby, and tennis matches.

Revised and
updated by Ian
Phillips

PARISIANS MAY NOT BE AS FANATICAL about exercising as those elsewhere, but in the past few years—perhaps in anticipation of the city's bid to host the 2008 Olympics?—interest in sports has been growing. A new network of bike lanes has seen the number of cyclists boom, there has been a citywide fad for in-line skating, and the number of gyms has been steadily rising. That Olympic bid is a serious one, attested to by the city's excellent sporting facilities. The fact remains that most of them tend to be on the outskirts of the city—space for athletic activities at the heart of it remains somewhat limited. In fact, it was only in 1997 that laws were passed allowing people to sit, walk, or even play sports on the grass in parks (once strictly forbidden); these days you can enjoy (most) lawns without being reprimanded. One of the best spots for sports in Paris is the Buttes-Chaumont, a park with enough space for soccer and other games. Also good are Paris's two large parks—the Bois de Boulogne, on the western fringe of the city, and the Bois de Vincennes, on the eastern side—where wide-open spaces allow for a variety of activities.

The best starting point for finding out about athletic activities in Paris is the booklet *Le Guide du Sport à Paris,* available from the Paris Tourist Office. In French, it lists sports facilities in each arrondissement, has a map of bike lanes throughout the city, and contains a calendar of big sporting events. Further information can be obtained by calling the **Allô-Sports Service** (☎ 01–42–76–54–54), Monday–Thursday 10:30–5 and Friday 10:30–4:30; it's in French only.

PARTICIPANT SPORTS

Aerobics

From 9 to noon on Sunday, the Paris town authorities organize free aerobics and stretch classes in 11 venues dotted throughout the city (there are no classes offered in July and August). Left Bank devotees head to the Pavillon des Gardes in the **Jardin du Luxembourg** (RER Luxembourg). For the Montparnasse area, classes are offered at the the Mire de l'Observatoire in the **Parc Montsouris** (✉ Bd. Jourdan, 14ᵉ, RER Cité-Universitaire). At the **Parc des Buttes-Chaumont,** the meeting place is the music kiosk on place Armand Carrel in front of the town hall of the 19ᵉ arrondissement. Note that there are no classes during July and August.

Bicycling

Maps of Paris's main cycle paths can be found in *Le Guide du Sport à Paris*. Paris's two large parks are the best places for biking. Bike enthusiasts on the western side of Paris tend to flock to the **Bois de Boulogne** (métro Porte Maillot, Porte Dauphine, Porte d'Auteuil; Bus 244). On the east side of Paris, the most bike trails can be found in the vast **Bois de Vincennes** (métro Château de Vincennes, Porte Dorée).

The city also has more than 167 km (94 mi) of **bike lanes,** and there are plans to develop even more. Unfortunately, most bike routes are along the main axes of the city, which means that you may find yourself riding in traffic. Cars, however, have been banned altogether on Sunday from certain scenic routes, including the banks of the Seine from 9 to 5, mid-March through late autumn, and the picturesque **Canal St-Martin** from noon to 6 year-round.

The following places rent bikes, and many of these establishments also organize guided excursions. **Bike 'n Roller** (⊠ 6 rue St-Julien-le-Pauvre, 5ᵉ, ☎ 01–44–07–35–89, métro Cité, St-Michel) hires bikes for 80 francs/€12 for three hours and 110 francs/€17 for the day. **Escapade Nature** (⊠ 69 bd. Diderot, 12ᵉ, ☎ 01–53–17–03–18, métro Reuilly-Diderot) organizes daily bike tours of Paris. Their *Ballades Détentes* (leisure bike) begin at 11 AM and last for about two hours and cost 100 francs/€15.30 (including bike rental). The more comprehensive three-hour *Ballades Découvertes* at 3 PM cost 160 francs/€24 (including bike rental). There are also regular tours on Sunday of the greater Paris region (250 francs/€38, including the price of the train and bike hire), which last the whole day. **Pariscyclo** (⊠ Rond Point de Jardin d'Acclimatation, in the Bois de Boulogne, ☎ 01–47–47–76–50, métro Les Sablons) is the perfect place for bike rentals if you want to explore the Bois de Boulogne. **Paris à Vélo, C'est Sympa** (⊠ 37 bd. Bourdon, 4ᵉ, ☎ 01–48–87–60–01, métro Bastille) rents bikes for 60 francs/€9.20 for half day and 80 francs/€12.30 for full day and also organizes three-hour excursions of both the heart of Paris and lesser-known sites. Times vary according to season, so either call ahead for information or consult the organization's Web site www.parisvelosympa.com. Tours cost 185 francs/€28.24 (160 francs/€24.42 for under-26s). A security deposit of 2,000 francs/€307 is also required, so do take along a credit card. **Paris Vélo Rent a Bike** (⊠ 2 rue Fer à Moulin, 5ᵉ, ☎ 01–43–37–59–22, métro Censier-Daubenton) charges 75 francs/€11.50 for half-day and 90 francs/€13.80 for full-day bike rental (with an additional security deposit of 2,000 francs/€307).

Health Clubs

Short-term passes are available from the following health clubs.

Club Jean de Beauvais (⊠ 5 rue Jean-de-Beauvais, 5ᵉ, ☎ 01–46–33–16–80, métro Maubert-Mutualité) has an entire floor of exercise equipment and classes, as well as a sauna. A one-day pass costs 200 francs/€30.70; a week is 600 francs/€92.35. There is also the possibility of balneotherapy treatments at an additional cost. It's open Monday, Tuesday, and Thursday 7 AM–10:30 PM; Wednesday and Friday 7 AM–10 PM; Saturday 8:30–7; and Sunday 9:30–6. For more information, consult the Web site www.clubjeandebeauvais.com.
Club Quartier Latin (⊠ 19 rue de Pontoise, 5ᵉ, ☎ 01–55–42–77–88, métro Maubert-Mutualité) has a 33-m skylighted pool, squash courts, and exercise equipment. For 85 francs/€13 per day you can use the gym and pool (the pool only is 25 francs/€3.81); add another 75 francs/€11.55 per 40 minutes for squash (15-franc/€2.30 racquet rental). It's open weekdays 9 AM–midnight, weekends 9:30–7.
Espace Vit'Halles (⊠ Pl. Beaubourg, 48 rue Rambuteau, 3ᵉ, ☎ 01–42–77–21–71, métro Rambuteau) has a broad range of aerobics classes (100 francs/€15.30 per class, 900 francs/€138 for 10), exercise machines, sauna, and steam room (100 francs/€15.30 a day). It's open Monday, Wednesday, and Friday 8 AM–10 PM; Tuesday and Thursday 8 AM–11 PM; Saturday 10–7; and Sunday 10–6.
Pilates Studio (⊠ 39 rue du Temple, 4ᵉ, ☎ 01–42–72–91–74, métro Hôtel-de-Ville) is run by Philippe Taupier, who studied in New York with one of the pupils of the technique's founder, Joseph Pilates. It may be based in just a three-room apartment but it attracts numerous celebrities, such as actress Kristin Scott Thomas and former French *Vogue* editor Joan Juliet Buck. One-hour solo classes cost 380 francs/€58. Duo classes are 300 francs/€46 per person and group classes 150 francs/€23.

Hotel Health Clubs

The hotels with the best fitness facilities are generally the newer ones on the perimeter of the city center.

Ritz Health Club (⊠ Pl. Vendôme, 1er, ☎ 01–43–16–30–60, métro Opéra), as fancy as the hotel, has a swimming pool, sauna, steam room, hot tub, exercise machines, and aerobics classes (all for 600 francs/€92.30 on weekdays, 700 francs/€107 on weekends). It's open daily 7 AM–10 PM.

Sofitel Paris Vitatop Club (⊠ 8 rue Louis-Armand, 15e, ☎ 01–45–54–79–00, métro Balard) has a 15-m pool, a sauna, a steam room, and a hot tub, plus a stunning view of the Paris skyline (200 francs/€30.70 per day, free to hotel guests). It's open Monday and Wednesday–Friday 8 AM–10 PM, Tuesday 8 AM–midnight, Saturday 9–7, and Sunday 9–5.

Ice-Skating

From mid-December through the end of February, weather permitting, a small skating rink is erected on **place de l'Hôtel-de-Ville** (the square in front of the Hôtel de Ville); hours are 9 AM–10 PM daily. An RER ride away from central Paris, **Disneyland Paris's Hotel New York** (Disneyland Paris, Marne-la-Vallée, ☎ 01–60–45–75–96, RER Marne-la-Vallée/Chessy) has an outdoor skating rink complete with Disney characters (tickets to the park aren't necessary). It's open daily 2–4, 4:30–6:30, and 7–10; admission to each session is 60 francs/€9.20, including skates. In the suburb of St-Ouen is the **Patinoire de St-Ouen** (⊠ 4 rue Dr-Bauer, St-Ouen, ☎ 01–40–11–43–38, métro Mairie de St-Ouen), an indoor rink, open year-round. Admission ranges from 13 to 46 francs/€2–7, with skate rental, depending on when you go. It's open Tuesday 11:30–1 and 8:30–11; Wednesday 10–noon and 2:30–6; Thursday 11:30–1 and 6–8; Friday 11:30–1 and 8:30–11; Saturday 2:30–6 and 8:30–11; and Sunday 10–12:30 and 2:30–6.

Jogging

Running through the streets of Paris may sound romantic, but it can be quite unpleasant if you don't go early: there's just too much traffic on the narrow streets. Exceptions are quai de la Tournelle, along the Seine, and along the Canal St-Martin. The city's parks are better places to run. The **Champ de Mars** (métro École Militaire), next to the Eiffel Tower, measures 2½ km (1½ mi) around the perimeter. Many jogging fans prefer the pleasant route—though shorter and more crowded that the Champs de Mars—that is the 1½-km (1-mi) loop just inside the fence around the **Jardin du Luxembourg** (métro Odéon, RER Luxembourg). The **Jardin des Tuileries** (métro Concorde, Tuileries) measures about 1½ km (1 mi) around. The **Bois de Boulogne** has miles of trails through woods, around lakes, and across grassy meadows. There are 1,800- and 2,500-m loops. The especially bucolic **Bois de Vincennes** has a 14½-km (9-mi) circuit or a 1½-km (1-mi) loop around the Château de Vincennes itself. Maps of routes in both Bois can be found in *Le Guide du Sport à Paris*. Those who prefer track running can have access to Paris's athletics facilities during times when they have not been booked by schools or clubs. Try any of the following, but make sure to call ahead to check availability. In the 12e district, head to the **Centre Sportif Léo-Lagrange** (⊠ 68 bd. Poniatowski, ☎ 01–46–28–31–57, métro Porte de Charenton). In the 15e district, try the **Centre Sportif Suzanne-Lenglen** (⊠ 2 rue Louis-Armand, ☎ 01–45–54–72–85, métro Balard). In the 16e district, check out **Stade Porte-de-la-Muette** (⊠ 60 bd. Lannes, ☎ 01–45–04–54–85, RER Av. Henri-Martin).

There are a number of annual running races that are open to the public. The **Paris Marathon** takes place in April (subscription details from Athlétisme Organisation; ☎ 01–41–33–15–94). A lesser-known event is the **20km de Paris,** held in October (✉ Atalante, 9–11 rue Letellier, 15ᵉ, ☎ 01–45–75–67–12). **Le Cross du Figaro** is a cross-country race organized each December by the French national daily, *Le Figaro* (for information, contact the paper's Service Événements; ☎ 01–42–21–60–00).

In-line Skating

A craze for in-line skating has swept over Paris during the last five years. Where once it was rare to see people with a pair of skates on their feet, now it seems like almost every other Parisian is an adept of *le roller.* To avoid pedestrians and road crossings, they often use the city's cycle paths. You'll also see them doing their tricks on **place du Palais-Royal** and the esplanade at the **Musée d'Art Moderne de la Ville de Paris** on avenue du Président-Wilson. Another popular place to go in-line skating is along the **Promenade Plantée,** running along the former viaduct in the 12ᵉ arrondissement. On weekends, when **allée de la Reine Marguerite** in the Bois de Boulogne is closed to traffic, it becomes a blader's haven. On Sunday, when cars are banned, **quai de la Tournelle,** along the Seine (9–5), and the **Canal St-Martin** (noon–6) are also ideal in-line skating spots.

Every Friday night starting at 10, thousands of in-line skaters gather at **place de l'Italie** to take a different weekly three-hour route through Paris (roads are blocked off). The pace is pretty hairy, so novices are discouraged. For details, check the Web site www.pari-roller.com. A more leisurely three-hour route is organized on Sunday at 2:30 PM and leaves from **Roller Location Nomades** near place de la Bastille. For those who want to practice their acrobatics, there are two ramps in the **Stade Boutroux** (✉ 1 av. Boutroux, 13ᵉ, ☎ 01–45–84–08–46, métro Porte d'Ivry).

In-line skates can be rented from **Bike 'n Roller** (✉ 6 rue St-Julien-le-Pauvre, 5ᵉ, ☎ 01–44–07–35–89, métro Bastille; 137 St-Dominique, 7ᵉ, ☎ 01–44–18–30–39, métro École Militaire; and 38 rue Fabert, 7ᵉ, ☎ 01–45–50–38–27, métro La Tour-Maubourg) for 60 francs/€9.20 for three hours and 80 francs/€12.30 per day. **Rollerland** (✉ 3 bd. Bourdon, 4ᵉ, ☎ 01–40–27–96–97, métro Bastille, Quai de la Rapée; 34 rue Bayen, 17ᵉ, ☎ 01–45–72–39–59, métro Ternes) offers individual and group lessons and rents out skates. **Roller Location Nomades** (✉ 37 bd. Bourdon, 4ᵉ, ☎ 01–44–54–07–44, métro Bastille) rents skates for about 60 francs/€9.20. **Vertical Line** (✉ 60 av. Raymond Poincaré, 16ᵉ, ☎ 01–47–27–21–21) rents skates for 30–60 francs/€4.60–9.20.

The rink **La Main Jaune** (✉ Rue du Caporal-Peugeot, 17ᵉ, ☎ 01–47–63–26–47, métro Porte de Champerret) is the spot for old-fashioned roller-skating. It's open Wednesday, Saturday, and Sunday 2:30–7 and Friday and Saturday from 10 PM on for roller discos; admission is 50 francs/€7.63 with skate rental.

Swimming

Every arrondissement has its own public *piscine* (pool); the Paris Tourist Office's *Le Guide du Sport à Paris* lists addresses. One of the biggest and best is the **Piscine des Halles** (✉ Pl. de la Rotonde, Forum des Halles, 1ᵉʳ, ☎ 01–42–36–98–44, métro Châtelet-les-Halles), a 50-m pool inside the shopping mall in the center of Paris. It's open Monday 11:30–8; Wednesday 10–7; Tuesday, Thursday, and Friday 11:30–10; and weekends 9–5. Admission is 25 francs/€3.81 and you can stay as long as you like. The **Piscine St-Germain** (✉ 12 rue de Lobineau, 6ᵉ, ☎ 01–43–29–08–15, métro Mabillon), one of the nicest pools in Paris, is open Tuesday 7 AM–8 AM, 11:30 AM–1 PM, and 5 PM–7:30 PM, Wednesday 7 AM–8 AM and 11:30 AM–5:30 PM; Thursday and Friday 7 AM–8 AM and 11:30 AM–1 PM; Saturday 7 AM–5:30 PM; and Sunday 8 AM–5:30 PM. Admission is 16 francs/€2.44. Those who fancy taking in a bit of architectural heritage while they swim should try the **Piscine Butte-aux-Cailles** (✉ 5 pl. Paul-Verlaine, 13ᵉ, ☎ 01–45–89–60–05, métro Place d'Italie). Classed as a historic monument, the **Piscine des Amiraux** (✉ 6 rue Hermann-Lachapelle, 18ᵉ, ☎ 01–46–06–46–47, métro Simplon, Marcadet-Poissonniers) is also a picturesque venue. In summer, many Parisians head off to to the open-air **Piscine de la Grenouillère** (✉ Parc d'Antony, 146 bis av. du Général-de-Gaulle, Antony, ☎ 01–46–60–75–30, RER Croix-de-Berny), which is open daily 9–7 from mid-May to mid-September.

Aquaboulevard (✉ 4 rue Louis-Armand, 15ᵉ, ☎ 01–40–60–10–00, métro Balard), the best place to take kids, has an enormous indoor wave pool with water slides and a simulated outdoor beach in summer. It's open Monday–Thursday 9 AM–11 PM, Friday 7 AM–8 AM, Saturday 7 AM–8 AM, and Sunday 7 AM–8 AM. Last admissions each day is at 9 PM. Adults can stay for six hours for 120 francs/€18.40. The **Club Quartier Latin** has a very nice, skylighted, 33-m pool that you can use for 25 francs/€3.81.

Tennis

Paris has a number of municipal courts, but getting to play on them is not so easy. Normally, you must apply for a special card from the local *mairie* (town hall; each arrondissement has one), which takes one month to process, and then reserve a court in advance. You can, however, take a chance, turn up at the public courts, and, if there is one available, play (the best time to go is the middle of the day during the week); the cost is 38 francs/€5.80 an hour per court, which you pay there. The most central, and most crowded, courts are in the **Jardin du Luxembourg.**

SPECTATOR SPORTS

The French passion for sport is amazing—the daily sports paper *L'Equipe* is actually the country's best-selling national newspaper. Paris often hosts major international sporting events; in 1998 it was the site of the Soccer World Cup and is the location for the French Open every May. Information on upcoming events can be found on posters around the city or in the weekly guide *Pariscope.* You can also call the ticket agency of **FNAC** (☎ 08–03–80–88–03). **Virgin Megastore** (☎ 08–03–02–30–24) runs a popular agency with ticket for sporting events of all kinds.

A wide range of sporting events, including indoor athletics, ice-skating, horse shows, gymnastics, and stock-car racing, take place at the **Palais Omnisports de Paris-Bercy** (✉ 8 bd. de Bercy, 12ᵉ, ☎ 08–03–03–00–31, métro Bercy). Details of events are also on their Web site www.bercy.com. **Parc des Princes** (✉ 24 rue du Cdt. Guilbaud, 16ᵉ, ☎ 01–42–88–02–76, métro Porte d'Auteuil) is where the city's soccer team, Paris St-Germain, plays its home matches. **Roland-Garros** (✉ 2 av. Gordon Bennett, 16ᵉ, ☎ 01–47–43–48–00, métro Porte d'Auteuil) is the venue for the French Open tennis tournament. The **Stade de France** (✉ St-Denis, ☎ 01–55–93–00–00, RER La Plaine–Stade de France) was built for the World Cup in 1998 and is now home to the French national soccer and rugby teams.

Athletics

The annual **Paris Marathon** takes place in early April and attracts more than 20,000 participants. It sets off from the Champs-Élysées and finishes at the top of avenue Foch, near the Arc de Triomphe. Along the route, in spots like place de la Concorde and place de la République, there are groups who play live music to create a more festive atmosphere. The Paris track-and-field **Grand Prix** meeting is held at the Stade de France in June and generally attracts a host of top international stars.

Horse Racing

Paris and its suburbs are remarkably well endowed with *hippodromes* (racetracks). Admission is between 15 francs/€2.30 and 50 francs/€7.63. Details of meetings can be found in the daily newspaper **Le Parisien** or the specialist racing paper **Paris Turf.** The easiest racetrack to get to is the **Hippodrome d'Auteuil** (⊠ Bois de Boulogne, 16ᵉ, ☎ 01–40–71–47–47, métro Porte d'Auteuil) in the Bois de Boulogne. Also in the Bois de Boulogne is the city's most beautiful track, the **Hippodrome de Longchamp** (⊠ Rte. des Tribunes, Bois de Boulogne, 16ᵉ, ☎ 01–44–30–75–00, métro Porte d'Auteuil, then free shuttle), stage for the prestigious (and glamorous) Prix de l'Arc de Triomphe in October. The **Hippodrome de Vincennes** (⊠ Rte. Ferme, Bois de Vincennes, ☎ 01–49–77–17–17, RER Joinville-Le-Pont) is a cinder track used for trotting races. The French Derby (Prix du Jockey-Club) and the very chic French Oaks (Prix de Diane-Hermès) are held at the beginning of June at **Chantilly,** north of Paris; direct trains from the Gare du Nord take about 40 minutes. Other racetracks near Paris are in **Enghien-les-Bains, Évry,** and **St-Cloud.**

Rugby

The Paris Université Club plays home matches on Sunday in winter at 3 PM at the **Stade Charléty** (⊠ 99 bd. Kellermann, 13ᵉ, RER Cité-Universitaire); tickets are 30 francs/€4.60. For information and game dates, call the club directly (☎ 01–44–16–62–69). France's national rugby team plays at the **Stade de France** in St-Denis. Admissions range 50–600 francs/€7.63–92; your best bet is to get tickets from FNAC or Virgin Megastore in advance or contact the **Fédération Française de Rugby** (☎ 01–53–21–15–15). The Racing Club de France has games Saturday or Sunday afternoon at the **Stade Charléty.** For information about games, call the Racing Club directly (☎ 01–45–67–55–86). Paris's top team, Le Stade Français, were French champions in 1998. They usually play home matches on Saturday or Sunday afternoon at the **Stade Jean Bouin** (26 av. du Général Sarrail, 16ᵉ, métro Porte d'Auteuil). Call 01–46–51–51–11 or check the Web site www.stade.fr for details of dates.

Soccer

As in most other European cities, *football* (soccer) is the sport that pulls in the biggest crowds. Paris St-Germain, the city's main club, was founded in 1970 and has won various titles, including the European Cup in 1996. It plays at the **Parc des Princes** stadium in southwest Paris. Most matches are on Saturday evening at 8 PM, although times do vary. It is best to check ahead on the club's official Web site (WEB www.psg.fr). Admission is 100–350 francs/€15.30–53.80; your best bet is to get tickets from FNAC in advance.

Tennis

The highlight of the tennis season—in fact the second most important European tennis tournament after Wimbledon—is the **French Open,** held during the last week of May and the first in June at the Roland-Garros Stadium. Center-court tickets are difficult to obtain; try your hotel or turn up early in the morning (matches start at 11 AM) and buy a general ground ticket. Tickets range 90–340 francs/€13.80–52. The **Bercy Indoor Tournament** in November at the Palais Omnisports de Paris-Bercy awards one of the largest prizes in the world and attracts most of the top players. The **Open Gaz de France** at the Stade Pierre de Coubertin (⊠ 82 av. Georges-Lafont, 16ᵉ, ☎ 01–45–27–79–12, métro Porte de St-Cloud) every February is one of the official tournaments on the women's tour. Tickets for both events can be purchased at FNAC or Virgin Megastore, or at the stadium.

6 SHOPPING

In the most beautiful city in the world, it's no surprise to discover that the local greengrocer displays his tomatoes as artistically as Cartier does its rubies. The capital of style, Paris has an endless array of delights to tempt shop-till-you-droppers, from grand couturiers to the funkiest flea markets. Glamour is everywhere—even the Champs-Élysées stamp market was immortalized in the Audrey Hepburn–Cary Grant thriller, *Charade*. Happily, Paris chic is often about pairing a vintage Dior jacket with a casual crewneck T-shirt, so whether you're *fauché*—broke—or want to buy up a storm, this city can be the most rewarding of hunting grounds.

Revised and
updated by
Ian Phillips

W INDOW SHOPPING IS ONE OF PARIS'S greatest spectator sports, and the French have come up with a wonderful expression for this highly cultivated art. They call it *lèche-vitrine*—literally, "licking the windows"—which is quite fitting because many of the displays are good enough to eat. Sonia Rykiel always fills her windows with the latest literary releases, Dior has commissioned artwork for its windows, and a coffee-table book has even been dedicated to those at Hermès, whose *vitrines,* or shop windows, are sometimes like diminutive theaters, small masterpieces of fantasy. Yet, even the sight of the local *traiteur,* or delicatessen, is sure to set you drooling quite uncontrollably.

No matter where you look, tastefully displayed wares—luscious cream-filled éclairs, lacy lingerie, rare artwork, gleaming copper pots—entice the eye and awaken the imagination. And shopping is one of the city's greatest pastimes, a chance to mix with Parisians and feel the heartbeat of the country. Who can understand the magic of French cuisine until he or she has explored a Paris open-air produce market on a weekend morning? Or resist the thrill of seeing a Chanel evening gown displayed in a boutique where even the doorknobs are shaped like Chanel crystal perfume-bottle stoppers?

Happily, the shopping opportunities in Paris are endless and geared to every taste. You can price emerald earrings at Cartier, spend an afternoon browsing through bookstalls along the Seine, tour the high-gloss department stores, or haggle over the price for one of those flea-market "Souvenir de Paris" bracelets, which clank with tin Eiffel Towers and poodles. For many, however, "chic" is the thing the French do best. No matter if a waitress or a countess, all seem to share a common denominator: the Parisian woman's chic—an elusive quality that depends less on the way she chooses her clothes than on her manner of wearing them.

It is that quality that inspires the city's couturiers and tastemakers to this day and that makes half the world flock to Paris's shops. Today, every neighborhood seems to reflect a unique attitude and style: designer extravagance and haute couture characterize avenue Montaigne and rue Faubourg St-Honoré; classic sophistication pervades St-Germain; avant-garde style dresses up the Marais; while a hip feel suffuses the area around Les Halles. With trends popping up like so many *mignonettes de Paris* (little white mushrooms), even what's old is new again: the great old names of Paris style continue to welcome new designer blood, as Martin Margiela at Hermès, Marc Jacobs at Louis Vuitton, and the dazzlingly retro jewels designed by Victoire de Castellane for Dior all prove.

Credit Cards
Credit cards are widely used in France. Even the flea market is likely to honor plastic for purchases of more than 100 francs/€15.3. Visa is the most common and preferred card, followed closely by Master-Card/EuroCard. American Express, Diners Club, and Access are also accepted in the larger international stores.

Duty-Free Shopping
A value-added tax of 19.6%, known in France as the TVA or *détaxe,* is imposed on most consumer goods. Non–European Union residents, ages 15 and over, who stay in France and/or the EU for less than six months can reclaim part of this tax. To qualify, your purchases in a single shop on one day must total at least 1,200 francs/€184. The amount of the refund varies from shop to shop but usually hovers between 13%

and 16%. You may opt to be reimbursed by check, but a refund credited directly to your credit card is the easiest and fastest way to receive your money. The major department stores have simplified the process with special détaxe desks where the *bordereaux* (export sales invoices) are prepared. Most high-profile shops with international clients have détaxe forms, but stores are not required to do this paperwork. If the discount is extremely important to you, ask if it is available before making your purchase. There is no refund for food, wine, and tobacco. Invoices and bordereaux forms must be presented to French customs upon leaving the country. The items purchased should be available for inspection.

Sales and Mailing Purchases Home
When hunting for bargains, watch for the word *soldes* (sales). The two main sale seasons are January and July, when the average discount is 30%–50% off regular prices. Also look for goods marked *dégriffé*—designer labels, often from last year's collection, for sale at a deep discount.

Smaller shops are reluctant to mail purchases overseas, though department stores often will. Mailing goods oneself is quite easy—all French post offices sell self-sealing mailing boxes—although postage is costly. Remember that if you are claiming a value-added tax deduction, you must have the goods with you when you leave the country.

Shopping by Neighborhood

Avenue Montaigne and Surroundings
Shopping really doesn't come much more chic than on avenue Montaigne. This exclusive, elegant boulevard and the area around are a showcase of international haute couture houses: **Chanel, Dior, Nina Ricci, Céline, Valentino, Max Mara, Genny, Krizia, Escada, Thierry Mugler, Hanae Mori, Emanuel Ungaro, Prada,** and **Dolce & Gabbana.** You'll also find accessories by **S. T. Dupont, Loewe,** and **Louis Vuitton.** Many of the boutiques are housed in exquisite mansions with wrought-iron gates in front. On the sidewalks, you'll spy effortlessly elegant "ladies who lunch"—and more than a dash of true Parisian attitude. Neighboring rue François 1er and avenue George V are also lined with many designer boutiques: **Versace, Yves Saint Laurent,** and **Balenciaga.**

Champs-Élysées
Cafés and movie theaters keep the once-chic Champs-Élysées active 24 hours a day, but the invasion of exchange banks, car showrooms, and fast-food chains has certainly lowered the tone. Nowadays, shops like the **Virgin Megastore, Gap,** and the **Disney Store** capture most of the retail action. However, more recently, a little bit of style has returned to the avenue in the form of the cosmetic wonder store **Sephora,** as well as the new **Louis Vuitton** boutique, which sells the clothing collections designed for the house by American designer Marc Jacobs.

The Faubourg St-Honoré
This chic shopping and residential district along rue Faubourg St-Honoré is also quite a political hub. It is home to the Élysée Palace, as well as the official residences of the American and British ambassadors. The Paris branches of **Sotheby's** and **Christie's** and renowned antiques galleries such as **Didier Aaron** add artistic flavor. Boutiques include **Hermès, Lanvin, Gucci, Chloé,** and **Christian Lacroix.**

Left Bank
After decades of clustering on the Right Bank's venerable shopping avenues, the high-fashion houses have stormed the Rive Gauche. The first to arrive were **Sonia Rykiel** and **Yves Saint Laurent** in the late '60s. Some

Champs-Élysées and Avenue Montaigne Area

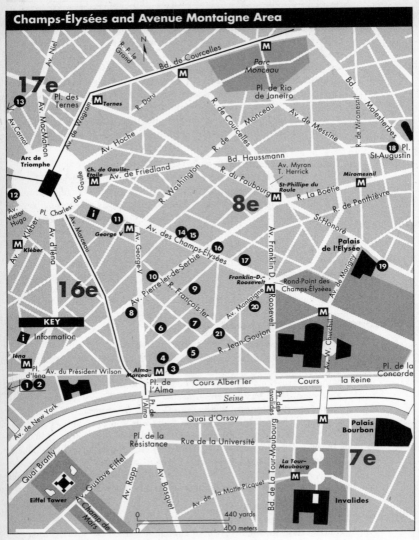

of the more recent arrivals have included **Christian Dior** and **Louis Vuitton.** Rue des St-Pères and rue de Grenelle are lined with designer names; the latter is especially known for its top-quality shoe shops, such as **Christian Louboutin, Sergio Rossi, Patrick Cox,** and **Stéphane Kélian.**

Les Halles
Most of the narrow pedestrian streets on the former site of Paris's wholesale food market are lined with fast-food joints, sex shops, jeans outlets, and garish souvenir stands. But rue du Jour is an attractive exception. Not far away, rue Tiquetonne is a mecca for retro cool. In the middle of the action is the **Forum des Halles,** a multilevel underground shopping mall, which, though it has its share of teens and chain stores, also has begun attracting higher-quality merchants and a clutch of promising designers.

Louvre–Palais-Royal
The elegant and eclectic shops clustered in the 18th-century arcades of the Palais-Royal sell such items as antiques, toy soldiers, cosmetics, jewelry, and vintage designer dresses. The glossy, marble **Carrousel du Louvre** mall, beneath the Louvre Museum, is lit by an immense inverted glass pyramid. Shops, along with a lively international food court, are open on Sunday—still a rare convenience in Paris.

Le Marais
Between the pre-Revolution mansions and tiny kosher food shops that characterize this area are scores of trendy gift and clothing stores, as well as some of the best furniture and homewares boutiques in Paris. Avant-garde designers **Azzedine Alaïa, Tsumori Chistato,** and **Christophe Lemaire** have boutiques within a few blocks of stately place des Vosges and the Picasso and Carnavalet museums. The Marais is one of the few neighborhoods where nearly all shops are open on Sunday. The streets to the north of the Marais, close to the Arts-et-Métiers métro stop, are historically linked to the cloth trade, and some shops sell garments at wholesale prices.

Opéra to Madeleine
Three major department stores—**Au Printemps, Galeries Lafayette,** and the British **Marks & Spencer**—dominate boulevard Haussmann, behind Paris's ornate 19th-century Opéra Garnier. Place de la Madeleine is home to two luxurious food stores, **Fauchon** and **Hédiard. Lalique** and **Baccarat Crystal** also have opulent showrooms near the Église de la Madeleine.

Place Vendôme and Rue de la Paix
The magnificent 17th-century place Vendôme, home of the Ritz hotel, and rue de la Paix, leading north from Vendôme, are where you can find the world's most elegant jewelers: **Cartier, Boucheron, Bulgari, Van Cleef and Arpels, Répossi, Mauboussin,** and **Chaumet.** The most exclusive, however, is the discreet **Jar's.**

Place des Victoires and Rue Étienne Marcel
The graceful, circular place des Victoires, near the Palais-Royal, is the playground of cutting-edge fashion icons such as **Kenzo** and **Victoire.** Seriously avant-garde designers like **Comme des Garçons** and **Yohji Yamamoto** line rue Étienne Marcel. In the nearby **Galerie Vivienne** shopping arcade, **Jean-Paul Gaultier** has a shop. And at 3 rue d'Argout, the hottest club-wear emporium in Paris, **Le Shop,** rents retail space to hip, up-and-coming designers.

Rue St-Honoré
A fashionable set makes its way to rue St-Honoré to shop at Paris's most trendy boutique, **Colette.** The street is lined with numerous de-

250

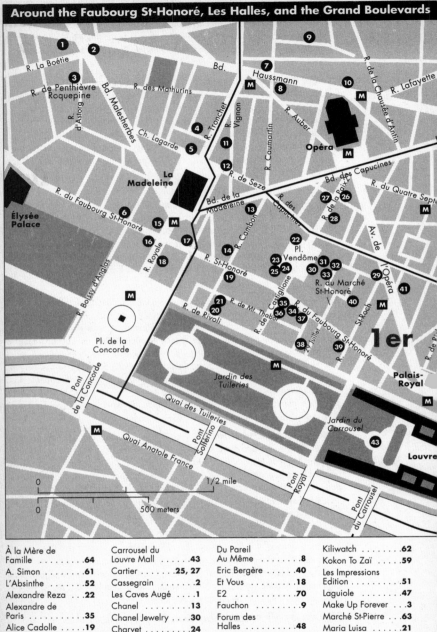

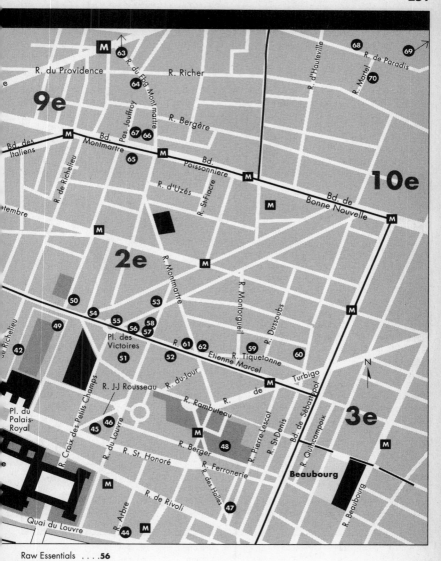

9e

R. du Providence

R. Richer

M 63

R. du Fbg. Montmartre

R. de Paradis

68

69

R. Martel

70

R. Bergère

Pas. Jouffroy

64

67 66

10e

Bd. des Italiens

M

Bd. Montmartre

65

M

Bd. Poissonniere

M

R. d'Hauteville

Bd. de Bonne Nouvelle

M

R. de Richelieu

R. d'Uzés

R. St-Fiacre

M

M

2e

R. Montmartre

M

50

53

R. Montorgueil

R. Dussoubs

54

49

55

58

56 57

N

R. Richelieu

42

51

52

R. 61 62

Etienne Marcel

R. Tiquetonne

59

60

M

R. J-J Rousseau

R. du-Jour

Turbigo

de

M

Bd. de Sébastopol

3e

Pl. des Victoires

R. Croix des Petits Champs

R. du Louvre

R. Rambuteau

R.

R. Pierre-Lescot

R. St-Denis

R. Quincampoix

M

Pl. du Palais-Royal

45

46

R. St. Honoré

R. Berger

M

48

R. Ferronerie

Beaubourg

M

R. de Rivoli

R. des Halles

47

R. Beaubourg

Quai du Louvre

R. Arbre

44

M

Around the Marais

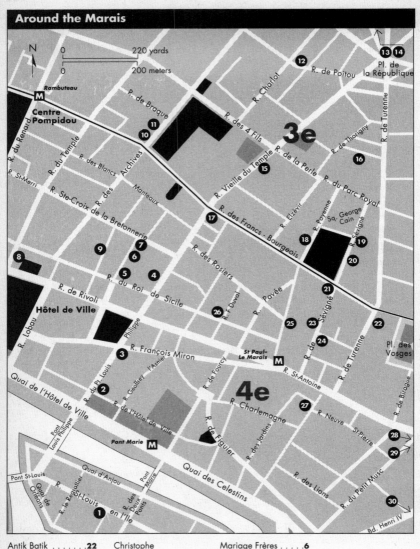

N

0 — 220 yards
0 — 200 meters

Rambuteau
Ⓜ
Centre Pompidou

R. du Renard
R. St-Merri
R. du Temple
R. des Blancs Manteaux
R. des Archives
R. de Braque
R. des 4 Fils
R. Charlot
R. de Poitou
R. de Turenne

⑪
⑩
Pl. de la République
⑬ ⑭
⑫

3e

R. de Thorigny
⑯
R. Vieille du Temple
R. de la Perle
R. du Parc Royal
⑮
R. Ste-Croix de la Bretonnerie
R. des Francs - Bourgeois
⑰
R. Elzévir
R. Payenne
Sq. George Cain
R. de Sévigné
⑱
⑲
⑨
⑦
⑥
⑧
R. des Rosiers
⑤
④
R. du Roi de Sicile
R. de Rivoli
⑳
Hôtel de Ville
R. Lobau
R. Pavée
R. F. Duval
㉑
㉖
㉕
㉓
㉒
Philippe
R. de Sévigné
㉔
Pl. des Vosges
③
R. François Miron
St Paul-Le Marais
Ⓜ
R. St-Antoine
R. de Turenne
②
R. du Pt Louis
R. Geoffroy l'Asnier
R. de Fourcy
R. de l'Hôtel de Ville
4e
R. Charlemagne
㉗
R. Neuve
St-Pierre
R. de Braque
㉘
㉙
Quai de l'Hôtel de Ville
R. du Figuier
des Jardins
Pont Louis Philippe
Pont Marie Ⓜ
Quai des Celestins
R. des Lions
R. du Petit Musc
㉚
Pont St-Louis
Quai d'Anjou
Pont Marie
Quai de Orléans
R. le Regrattier
R. St-Louis en l'Ile
R. des Deux Ponts
①
Bd. Henri IV

Left Bank Shopping

signer names, as well as the delightful vintage jewelry store **Dary's.** On nearby rue Cambon, you'll find the wonderfully elegant **Maria Luisa** and the main **Chanel** boutique. A number of hip designers, such as **Jean-Charles de Castelbajac** and **Comme des Garçons,** have also recently opened stores on place du Marché St-Honoré.

Department Stores

Paris's top department stores offer both convenience and style. Most are open Monday through Saturday from about 9:30 AM to 7 PM, and some are open until 10 PM one weekday evening. All six major stores listed below have multilingual guides, international welcome desks, détaxe offices, and restaurants. Most are on the Right Bank, near the Opéra and the Hôtel de Ville; the notable exception is Au Bon Marché, on the Left Bank.

Au Bon Marché (⊠ 24 rue de Sèvres, 7ᵉ, ☎ 01–44–39–80–00, métro Sèvres-Babylone), founded in 1852, is an excellent hunting ground on the Left Bank for linens, table settings, and high-quality furniture. In the last few years, it has undergone a complete face-lift and is now incontestably Paris's most chic department store. You often spot public figures, such as French prime minister Lionel Jospin, doing their shopping here. La Grande Épicerie is one of the largest groceries in Paris and a gourmet's mecca, and the basement is a great place for books, records, classy stationery, and arty gifts.

Au Printemps (⊠ 64 bd. Haussmann, 9ᵉ, ☎ 01–42–82–50–00, métro Havre-Caumartin, Opéra, Auber) has recently undergone quite a transformation. In doing so, this classic doyenne of department stores has taken on a hip new persona. All seven floors of the fashion shop have been renovated, and one of them is now dedicated uniquely to 15- to 25-year-olds and also offers the latest and fanciest Japanese gadgets. Watch out also for trendy exhibitions with themes like trousers and eccentricity. Free fashion shows are held on Tuesday (all year) and Friday (April–October) at 10 AM under the cupola on the seventh floor of La Mode, the building dedicated to women's and children's fashion. (**Reservations** can be made in advance by calling ☎ 01–42–82–63–17; tickets can also be obtained on the day of show at the service desk on the first floor.) The three-store complex also includes La Maison, for housewares and furniture, and Le Printemps de L'Homme, a six-floor emporium devoted to menswear. Flo Prestige, the celebrated Parisian brasserie chain, runs the in-house restaurant.

Bazar de l'Hôtel de Ville (⊠ 52–64 rue de Rivoli, 4ᵉ, ☎ 01–42–74–90–00, métro Hôtel-de-Ville), better known as BHV, houses an enormous basement hardware store that sells everything from doorknobs to cement mixers. The fashion offerings are minimal, but BHV is noteworthy for quality household goods, home decor materials, and office supplies.

Galeries Lafayette (⊠ 40 bd. Haussmann, 9ᵉ, ☎ 01–42–82–34–56, métro Chaussée-d'Antin, Opéra, Havre-Caumartin; ⊠ Centre Commercial Montparnasse, 14ᵉ, ☎ 01–45–38–52–87, métro Montparnasse-Bienvenüe) carries nearly 80,000 fashion labels under its roof. Free **fashion shows** are held every Tuesday at 11 AM and Friday (April–October) at 2:30 PM (☎ 01–48–74–02–30 reservations). Along with the world's largest perfumery, the main store has the "Espace Lafayette Maison," a huge Yves Taralon–designed emporium dedicated to the art of living *à la française.* There's also a gourmet food hall, a separate men's store, and a sports shop.

Marks & Spencer (⊠ 35 bd. Haussmann, 9ᵉ, ☎ 01–47–42–42–91, métro Havre-Caumartin, Auber, Opéra; ⊠ 88 rue de Rivoli, 4ᵉ, ☎ 01–44–61–08–00, métro Hôtel-de-Ville) is a British chain chiefly noted for its moderately priced basics (underwear, socks, sleep- and sportswear) as well as its popular English grocery store and takeout.

La Samaritaine (⊠ 19 rue de la Monnaie, 1ᵉʳ, ☎ 01–40–41–20–20, métro Pont Neuf, Châtelet), a sprawling five-store complex, has everything from designer fashions to a free climbing wall but is especially known for kitchen supplies, housewares, and furniture. Its most famous asset is the Toupary restaurant in Building 2, from which there's a marvelous view of Notre-Dame and the Left Bank.

Budget

Monoprix and **Prisunic** are French dime stores—with branches throughout the city—that stock inexpensive everyday items like toothpaste, groceries, toys, typing paper, and bath mats—a little of everything. Both chains carry inexpensive children's clothes of surprisingly fine quality and are good places to stock up on unexpectedly good wine.

Tati (⊠ 2–28 bd. Rochechouart, 18ᵉ, ☎ 01–55–29–50–00, métro Barbès) is one of Paris's most iconic stores. The ultimate haven for bargain-basement prices, it is certainly not for the faint-hearted or claustrophobic. On an average day, it is jam-packed with people of all colors, classes, and sizes, rifling through the jumbled trays in search of a great buy. One of its most famous scoops was to offer undershorts for just one franc/€.15 a pair. It is also well known for its pink and white Vichy shopping bags, ridiculously inexpensive bridal store, and chain of cheap jewelry shops, **Tati Or**.

Markets

Flea Markets

Le Marché aux Puces St-Ouen (métro Porte de Clignancourt), on Paris's northern boundary, still attracts the crowds when it opens on weekends and Monday, but its once-unbeatable prices are now a feature of the past. This century-old labyrinth of alleyways packed with antiques dealers' booths and junk stalls spreads for more than a square mile. Arrive early to pick up the most worthwhile loot (like old prints). But be warned—if there's one place in Paris where you need to know how to bargain, this is it! For lunch, stop for mussels and fries in one of the rough-and-ready cafés.

On the southern and eastern sides of the city—at **Porte de Vanves** and **Porte de Montreuil**—are other, less-impressive flea markets (although Vanves is excellent for vintage furniture). Both have an enormous amount of junk to sift through to find any real bargains.

Flower and Bird Markets

Paris's main flower market is in the heart of the city on the Ile de la Cité (métro Cité), between Notre-Dame and the Palais de Justice. It's open every day. On Sunday, it also plays host to a bird market. Other colorful flower markets are held beside the Madeleine church (métro Madeleine, open Monday–Saturday 9 AM–9 PM and alternate Sundays 9:30 AM–8:30 PM) and on place des Ternes (métro Ternes, open Tuesday–Sunday).

Food Markets

Paris's open-air food markets number more than 70 and are among the city's most colorful attractions. Fruits and vegetables are piled high in vibrant pyramids. The variety of cheeses is always astounding. The lively—and somewhat chaotic—atmosphere that reigns in most markets makes them a sight worth seeing, even if you don't want or need to buy anything. Every *quartier* (neighborhood) has at least one, although many are open only a few days each week. Sunday morning, till 1 PM, is usually a good time to go; Monday they are likely to be closed.

Many of the better-known markets are in areas you'd visit for sight-seeing; here is a list of the top bets. **Rue de Buci** (✉ 6ᵉ, métro Odéon), near St-Germain-des-Prés, is closed Sunday PM and Monday. **Rue Mouffetard** (✉ 5ᵉ, métro Monge), near the Jardin des Plantes, is best on weekends. **Rue Montorgueuil** (✉ 1ᵉʳ, métro Châtelet-les-Halles) is closed Monday. **Rue Lepic** in Montmartre (✉ 18ᵉ, métro Blanche or Abbesses) is best on weekends. **Rue Lévis** (✉ 17ᵉ, métro Villiers), near Parc Monceau, is closed Sunday PM and Monday. **Boulevard Richard Lenoir** (✉ 11ᵉ, métro Bastille). **Bir-Hakeim** (✉ 15ᵉ, métro Bir-Hakeim). The **Marché d'Aligre** (✉ Rue d'Aligre, 12ᵉ, métro Ledru-Rollin), open until 1 PM every day except Monday, is a bit farther out but is the cheapest market in Paris; on weekends a small flea market is also held here.

Stamp Market

Philatelists (and fans of the Audrey Hepburn–Cary Grant 1963 thriller, *Charade*) will want to head for Paris's unique **stamp market** at the intersection of avenue Marigny and avenue Gabriel (métro Champs-Élysées–Clemenceau) overlooking the gardens at the bottom of the Champs-Élysées. On sale are vintage postcards and stamps from all over the world. It is open Thursday, weekends, and public holidays.

Shopping Arcades

Paris's 19th-century commercial arcades, called *passages,* are the forerunners of the modern shopping mall. Glass roofs, decorative pillars, and inlaid mosaic floors make these spaces real architectural gems. In 1828, they numbered 137, of which only 24 are left. The major arcades are in the 1ᵉʳ and 2ᵉ arrondissements on the Right Bank. Shops range from the avant-garde (Gaultier and Yuki-Torii designs in the luxurious Galerie Vivienne) to the genteel (embroidery supplies and satin ribbons at Le Bonheur des Dames in the passage Jouffroy). You can find all sorts of dusty curiosity shops tucked into the arcades, with such items as rare stamps, secondhand books, and antique canes.

Galerie Véro-Dodat (✉ 19 rue Jean-Jacques Rousseau, 1ᵉʳ, métro Louvre) was built in 1826. At what is now the Café de l'Epoque, the French writer Gérard de Nerval took his last drink before heading to Châtelet to hang himself. The gallery has painted ceilings and slender copper pillars, and shops selling old-fashioned toys, contemporary art, stringed instruments, and leather goods. It is best known, however, for its antiques stores.

Galerie Vivienne (✉ 4 rue des Petits-Champs, 2ᵉ, métro Bourse), between the Stock Exchange (Bourse) and the Palais-Royal, is home to a range of interesting shops; a quite delicious tearoom, A Priori Thé; and Cave Legrand, a quality wine shop.

Passage du Grand-Cerf (✉ 145 rue St-Denis, 2ᵉ, métro Étienne Marcel) has recently been completely renovated and is now certainly the hippest of all of Paris's shopping arcades. Take a look at the design showroom, Haute Definition, at No. 4, check out the African objects and furniture at As'Art and the Zen-like furnishings at PM Style, or pop into the boutiques of milliner Jean-Louis Pinabel and jewellers Marie-Lise Goëlo, Eric & Lydie, and Didier Guillemin.

Passage Jouffroy (✉ 12 bd. Montmartre, 9ᵉ, métro Montmartre) is full of shops selling toys, antique canes, Oriental furnishings, and cinema books and posters. Try Pain d'Épices at No. 29 and Au Bonheur des Dames at No. 39.

Passage des Panoramas (✉ 11 bd. Montmartre, 2ᵉ, métro Montmartre), opened in 1800, is the oldest arcade; it's especially known for its stamp shops.

Passage Verdeau (✉ 4–6 rue de la Grange Batelière, 9ᵉ, métro Montmartre) is across the street from passage Jouffroy and has shops carrying antique cameras, comic books, and engravings.

Specialty Shops

Arts and Antiques

Antiques dealers proliferate in the **Carré Rive Gauche** (✉ Between St-Germain-des-Prés and the Musée d'Orsay, 6ᵉ, métro St-Germain-des-Prés, Rue du Bac). Several antiques dealers are around the **Drouot** auction house (✉ Corner of rue Rossini and rue Drouot, 9ᵉ, métro Richelieu-Drouot) near the Opéra. The **Louvre des Antiquaires** (✉ Pl. du Palais-Royal, 1ᵉʳ, métro Palais-Royal) is a stylish mall devoted primarily to antiques. Many big-name dealers—price tags often *start* in the five figures at these places—such as **Didier Aaron, Ariane Dandois,** and **Jacques Perrin** are on rue du Faubourg St-Honoré, place Beauvau, and place Bourbon. The **Viaduc des Arts** (✉ 9–147 av. Daumesnil, 12ᵉ, métro Ledru-Rollin) houses dozens of art galleries, artisans' boutiques, and upscale shops under the arches of a stone viaduct that once supported train tracks. **Village St-Paul** (✉ Enter from rue St-Paul, 4ᵉ, métro St-Paul) is a clutch of streets with many antiques shops.

Bags, Scarves, and Accessories

Alexandre de Paris (✉ 235 rue St-Honoré, 1ᵉʳ, ☎ 01–42–61–41–34, métro Tuileries) carries a whole array of hair accessories, named after one of the 20th?century's most famous hairdressers, whose clients included the Duchess of Windsor, Sophia Loren, Jean Cocteau, and Elizabeth Taylor.

Le Cachemirien (✉ 13 rue de Tournon, 6ᵉ, ☎ 01–43–29–93–82, métro Odéon) is exclusively dedicated to the fabrics of the Kashmir region of India. Decorated with silk rugs and Anglo-Indian armchairs, it is a veritable treasure trove of exquisitely embroidered shawls, pashminas, scarves, and elegantly, pared-down clothing made from materials like pashmina and silk.

E. Goyard (✉ 233 rue St-Honoré, 1ᵉʳ, ☎ 01–42–60–57–04, métro Tuileries) has been making the finest luggage since 1853. Clients in the past included Arthur Conan Doyle, Gregory Peck, and the Duke and Duchess of Windsor. Today, Karl Lagerfeld and Madonna are both Goyard fans. Check out the house's signature chevron monogram, which can be found on everything from polo chests and hatboxes to suitcases and wallets.

Hermès (✉ 24 rue du Faubourg St-Honoré, 8ᵉ, ☎ 01–40–17–47–17, métro Concorde) was established as a saddlery in 1837 and went on to create the famous, eternally chic Kelly bag, for Grace Kelly. The magnificent silk scarves—truly fashion icons—are legendary for their rich colors and intricate designs, which change yearly (and men, don't overlook the sumptuous ties). The pared-down women's wear collection is created by avant-garde Belgian designer Martin Margiela. During semiannual sales, in January and July, the astronomical prices are slashed by up to 50%. A coffee-table book was recently devoted to the shop's fantastical window displays.

Losco (✉ 20 rue de Sévigné, 4ᵉ, ☎ 01–48–04–39–93, métro St-Paul; ✉ 5 rue de Sèvres, 6ᵉ, ☎ 01–42–22–77–47, métro Sèvres-Babylone) allows customers to design their own high-quality, reasonably priced belts by mixing and matching buckles and straps.

Madeleine Gely (✉ 218 bd. St-Germain, 7ᵉ, ☎ 01–42–22–63–35, métro Rue du Bac) is the queen of walking sticks. Late president François Mitterrand used to buy his at this tiny shop also filled with an amazing range of umbrellas.

Peggy Huynh Kinh (⊠ 11 rue Coëtlogon, 6ᵉ, ☎ 01–42–84–83–82, métro St-Sulpice) formerly designed fashions for the prestigious Parisian houses Pierre Balmain and Céline. Nowadays, she creates bags and scarves for Cartier, as well as her own line of accessories, which she sells through this store. There are chicly pared-down totes, shoulder bags, wallets, and belts in quality leather, as well as a line of office accessories.

Renaud Pellegrino (⊠ 78 rue de Seine, 6ᵉ, ☎ 01–43–54–62–25, métro Odéon) used to design bags for Yves Saint Laurent in the late 1970s. Nowadays, he sells his creations under his own name in this discreet boutique at the back of a courtyard. Inspiration for his shoulder bags and totes comes from artists like Matisse and Braque, fans include Catherine Deneuve and model Laetitia Casta. Recently, Pellegrino has also successfully turned his hand to shoes.

DISCOUNT

Accessoires à Soie (⊠ 21 rue des Acacias, 17ᵉ, ☎ 01–42–27–78–77, métro Argentine) is where savvy Parisians buy superb silk scarves and ties in all shapes and sizes. The wide selection includes many big-name designers, and everything costs about half of what you'd pay elsewhere.

Books (English-Language)

The scenic open-air bookstalls along the Seine sell secondhand books (mostly in French), prints, and souvenirs. Numerous French-language bookshops—specializing in a wide range of topics including art, film, literature, and philosophy—are found in the scholarly Latin Quarter and the publishing district, St-Germain-des-Prés. For English-language books and magazines, try the following.

7L (⊠ 7 rue de Lille, 7ᵉ, ☎ 01–42–92–03–58, métro St-Germain-des-Prés) is a rather minimalistic space, owned by the book-addicted Karl Lagerfeld. The fashion designer has a personal library of more than 240,000 different volumes, and in this store, he chooses to display and sell a selection of his favorite new releases, as well as the books he edits himself.

The Abbey Bookstore (⊠ 29 rue Parcheminerie, 5ᵉ, ☎ 01–46–33–16–24, métro Cluny-La Sorbonne) is Paris's Canadian bookstore. It sells Canadian newspapers (*La Presse* and the *Toronto Globe & Mail*), books on Canadian history, as well as new and secondhand Québecois and English-language novels. The Canadian Club of Paris also organizes regular poetry readings and literary conferences here.

Brentano's (⊠ 37 av. de l'Opéra, 2ᵉ, ☎ 01–42–61–52–50, métro Opéra) is stocked with everything from classics to children's titles. It also has a slightly haphazardly arranged international magazine section.

La Chambre Claire (⊠ 14 rue St-Sulpice, 6ᵉ, ☎ 01–46–34–04–31, métro Odéon) is chock-a-block with photography books by everyone from Edward Weston to William Wegman. It even stocks instruction manuals and is a favorite with fashion folk, including designer Martine Sitbon.

Comptoir de l'Image (⊠ 44 rue de Sévigné, 3ᵉ, ☎ 01–42–72–03–92, métro St-Paul) is where designers John Galliano, Marc Jacobs, and Emanuel Ungaro stock up on old copies of *Vogue, Harper's Bazaar,* and *The Face*. It also sells trendy magazines like *Dutch, Purple,* and *Spoon,* designer catalogs from the past, and rare photo books.

Galignani (⊠ 224 rue de Rivoli, 1ᵉʳ, ☎ 01–42–60–76–07, métro Tuileries) stocks both French- and English-language books and is especially known for its extensive range of art books and coffee-table tomes.

La Hune (✉ 170 bd. St-Germain, 6ᵉ, ☎ 01–45–48–35–85, métro St-Germain-des-Prés), sandwiched between the Café de Flore and Les Deux Magots, is a landmark for intellectuals. French literature is downstairs, but the main attraction is the comprehensive collection of international books on art and architecture upstairs. Stay here until midnight with all the other genius-insomniacs.

Ofr (✉ 78 rue de Seine, 6ᵉ, ☎ 01–43–54–62–25, métro Odéon) provides magazines to hip stores from London to San Francisco. In this messy store, you can rub shoulders with photo and press agents and check out the latest in underground, artistic, and alternative monthlies.

Shakespeare and Company (✉ 37 rue de la Bûcherie, 5ᵉ, ☎ 01–43–26–96–50, métro St-Michel), the sentimental Left Bank favorite, is named after the publishing house, which first edited James Joyce's *Ulysses*. Nowadays, it specializes in expatriate literature. The staff tends to be rather pretentious, but the shelves of secondhand books hold real bargains. Poets give readings upstairs on Monday at 8 PM; there are also tea-party talks on Sunday at 4 PM.

Tea & Tattered Pages (✉ 24 rue Mayet, 6ᵉ, ☎ 01–40–65–94–35, métro Duroc) sells cheap secondhand paperbacks, plus new books (publishers' overstock) at low prices. Tea and brownies are served, and browsing is encouraged.

Village Voice (✉ 6 rue Princesse, 6ᵉ, ☎ 01–46–33–36–47, métro Mabillon), known for its selection of contemporary authors, hosts regular literary readings.

W. H. Smith (✉ 248 rue de Rivoli, 1ᵉʳ, ☎ 01–44–77–88–99, métro Concorde) carries an excellent range of travel and language books, cookbooks, and fiction for adults and children. It also has the best selection of foreign magazines in Paris.

Clothing (Children's)

Almost all the top designers make minicouture, but you can expect to pay upwards of 1,200 francs/€184 for each wee outfit. Following is where mere mortal Parisian parents shop to keep their kids looking chic.

L'Angelot par Gilles Neveu (✉ 28 rue Bonaparte, 6ᵉ, ☎ 01–56–24–21–22, métro St-Germain-des-Prés) has everything that even the best-born new baby could desire: clothes in white and beige, bed linen, cuddly teddy bears and rabbits, and jewelry in solid gold. Personalized embroideries and engravings are available upon request, as are deliveries to foreign destinations.

Dipaki (✉ 18 rue Vignon, 8ᵉ, ☎ 01–42–66–24–74, métro Madeleine) is a mecca for affordably priced infants' and kids' clothing in bold, primary colors.

Du Pareil Au Même (✉ 15 and 23 rue des Mathurins, 8ᵉ, ☎ 01–42–66–93–80, métro Havre-Caumartin; ✉ 14 rue St-Placide, 6ᵉ, ☎ 01–45–44–04–40, métro St-Placide) is a moderately priced chain selling well-made, adorable basics in soft, brightly colored jersey and cotton. Sizes and styles range from newborn to young teen.

Pom d'Api (✉ 28 rue du Four, 6ᵉ, ☎ 01–45–48–39–31, métro St-Germain-des-Prés) stocks footwear for babies and preteens, in quality leathers and wonderful vivid colors.

Clothing (Discount)

Cacharel Stock (✉ 114 rue d'Alésia, 14ᵉ, ☎ 01–45–42–53–04) offers impressive savings (up to 40% off) on women's, men's, and children's clothing (even bigger markdown sales are held from time to time).

L'Habilleur (✉ 44 rue Poitou, 3ᵉ, ☎ 01–48–87–77–12, métro Sébastien-Froissart) carries end-of-line clothing and accessories from designers such as Helmut Lang, John Bartlett, and Patrick Cox—all sold at half the retail price or less.

Majestic by Chevignon (⊠ 122 rue d'Alésia, 14ᵉ, ☎ 01–45–43–40–25, métro Alésia) discounts Chevignon casual wear for teens and adults at up to 50% off.

Rue d'Alésia (métro Alésia), in the 14ᵉ arrondissement, is the main place to find shops selling last season's items at a discount. Mendès, in the 2ᵉ, is a notable exception. Be forewarned: most of these shops are much more downscale than their elegant sister shops, and dressing rooms are not always provided.

SR Store (⊠ 64 rue d'Alésia, 14ᵉ, ☎ 01–43–95–06–13, métro Alésia) slices 50% off last year's prices on Sonia Rykiel women's fashions and still manages to chop up to another 40% off during the sales in January and July.

Clothing (Men's)

Charvet (⊠ 28 pl. Vendôme, 1ᵉʳ, ☎ 01–42–60–30–70, métro Opéra) is the Parisian equivalent of a Savile Row tailor: a conservative, aristocratic institution famed for made-to-measure shirts and exquisite ties and accessories.

L'Eclaireur (⊠ 12 rue Mahler, 4ᵉ, ☎ 01–44–54–22–11, métro St-Paul) has opened this loft-style menswear store, just a stone's throw from its flagship store on rue des Rosiers. At the front of the boutique is a counter selling Diptyque candles and scents; at the back, fashions by designers like Jil Sander, Helmut Lang, and Dirk Schönberger.

Le Printemps de L'Homme (⊠ Au Printemps department store, 61 rue Caumartin, 9ᵉ, ☎ 01–42–82–50–00, métro Havre-Caumartin, Opéra) has recently been renovated, and this sleek store is now Paris's menswear fashion leader: six floors of suits, sportswear, underwear, coats, ties, and accessories in all price ranges. The funkiest designers, such as Paul Smith, Comme des Garçons, and Martin Margiela, can be found on the third floor, more classic labels like Christian Dior and Burberry on the sixth floor. Make sure you check out the mega-cool Helmut Lang corner, as well as the rocking World Bar, whose walls are covered with newspapers from all over the globe.

Clothing (Resale)

Anouschka (⊠ 6 av. Coq, 9ᵉ, ☎ 01–48–74–37–00, métro St-Lazare, Trinité) has set up shop in her apartment (open Monday–Saturday noon–7) and has rack upon rack of vintage clothing, dating from as far back as the 1920s. She calls it a "designer laboratory" and teams from the top fashion houses often pop by, looking for inspiration.

Catherine Baril (⊠ 14 rue de la Tour, 16ᵉ, ☎ 01–45–20–95–21, métro Passy) has one-of-a-kind, barely worn haute couture and designer ready-to-wear; the store's specialty is old Chanel.

Didier Ludot (⊠ Jardins du Palais-Royal, 24 galerie Montpensier, 1ᵉʳ, ☎ 01–42–96–06–56, métro Palais-Royal) is one of the world's most famous vintage clothing dealers. His clientele ranges from model Stephanie Seymour to fashion designer Azzedine Alaïa. Check out the French couture from the '20s to the '70s on the racks: wonderful old Chanel suits, Balenciaga dresses, and Hermès scarves. Ludot also has his own contemporary core collection of 13 little black dresses, designed by his friend Felix Farrington. They are made-to-measure upon request.

Guerrisold (⊠ 17 bis bd. Rochechouart, 9ᵉ, ☎ 01–42–80–66–18, métro Barbès-Rochechouart) is a treasure trove of secondhand clothes. Though there's a lot of junk, if you sift through the racks carefully, you can pick up great suits, shirts, and dresses at ridiculously low prices.

Kiliwatch (⊠ 64 rue Tiquetonne, 2ᵉ, ☎ 01–42–21–17–37, métro Étienne Marcel) is Paris's hippest hand-me-down shop, with everyone from Carla Bruni to Christian Lacroix stopping by to find the next trend.

You'll find racks and racks of fabulous secondhand, vintage, and retro clothing; sexy, look-at-me party wear; and hip club wear from the in-house label.

Réciproque (✉ 88, 89, 92, 95, 101, and 123 rue de la Pompe, 16ᵉ, ☎ 01–47–04–30–28, métro Rue de la Pompe) is Paris's largest and most exclusive swap shop. Savings on designer wear—Hermès, Dior, Chanel, and Louis Vuitton—are significant, but prices are not as cheap as you might expect, and there's not much in the way of service or space. The shop at No. 89 specializes in leather goods. The store is closed Sunday and Monday.

Scarlett (✉ 78 rue de Seine, 6ᵉ, ☎ 01–43–54–62–25, métro Odéon) calls itself the "antique dealer of fashion." Situated at the heart of the famous "Golden Triangle" of luxury goods boutiques, it offers vintage couture dresses by the likes of Givenchy, Poiret, Schiaparelli, and Vionnet, as well as secondhand designer bags and accessories.

Clothing (Women's)

CHIC AND CASUAL

Chacok (✉ 18 rue de Grenelle, 7ᵉ, ☎ 01–42–22–69–99, métro Sèvres-Babylone) is *the* label for fashion-savvy Parisians, who adore the colorful, sunny, and feminine collection, especially its lightweight muslins and linens, and knits.

Et Vous (✉ 6 rue des Francs-Bourgeois, 3ᵉ, ☎ 01–42–71–75–11, métro St-Paul) is where hip Parisiennes find their stylish, contemporary women's wear—everything from little zip-up suede dresses to cotton stretch jeans. The styles reproduce designer trends at distinctly un-designer prices.

Tara Jarmon (✉ 18 rue du Four, 6ᵉ, ☎ 01–46–33–26–60, métro Mabillon) is a Canadian designer who has garnered plaudits from Paris's trend watchers. Her understated, classic knee-length coats are especially popular.

Ventilo (✉ 27 bis rue du Louvre, 2ᵉ, ☎ 01–44–76–83–00, métro Louvre) opened its first Parisian store in 1972 and has since been delighting Parisians with its ethnic-influenced fashions. On the third floor are housewares and a café serving the best chocolate cake in the world.

Zara (✉ 44 av. des Champs-Élysées, 8ᵉ, ☎ 01–45–61–52–80, métro Franklin-D.-Roosevelt; ✉ 109 rue St-Lazare, 9ᵉ, ☎ 01–53–32–82–95, métro St-Lazare) is the perfect place to pick up the latest trends without busting the bank. The styles are classic rather than outrageous, the quality more than decent for the price, and the stock changes regularly every few weeks to keep the clients coming back.

CLASSIC CHIC

No matter, say the French, that fewer and fewer of their top couture houses are still headed by compatriots. It's the chic elegance, the classic ambience, the *je ne sais quoi,* that remains undeniably Gallic. Most of the high-fashion shops are on avenue Montaigne, avenue George-V, and rue du Faubourg St-Honoré on the Right Bank, though St-Germain-des-Prés has also become a stomping ground for renowned designers. Following are just a few of Paris's haute couture highlights.

Chanel (✉ 42 av. Montaigne, 8ᵉ, ☎ 01–47–23–74–12, métro Franklin-D.-Roosevelt; ✉ 31 rue Cambon, 1ᵉʳ, ☎ 01–42–86–28–00, métro Tuileries) is helmed by Karl Lagerfeld, a master at updating Coco's signature look with fresh colors and free-spirited silhouettes.

Christian Dior (✉ 30 av. Montaigne, 8ᵉ, ☎ 01–40–73–54–44, métro Franklin-D.-Roosevelt) installed flamboyant British designer John Galliano as head designer after his triumphant run at Givenchy. His dramatic creations, however, have little to do with the Dior tradition.

Sonia Rykiel (⌧ 175 bd. St-Germain, 6ᵉ, ☏ 01–49–54–60–60, métro St-Germain-des-Prés; ⌧ 70 rue du Faubourg St-Honoré, 8ᵉ, ☏ 01–42–65–20–81, métro Concorde) is the undisputed queen of French fashion. Since the '60s she has been designing stylish knit separates and has made black her color of predilection.

Ungaro (⌧ 2 av. Montaigne, 8ᵉ, ☏ 01–43–54–62–25, métro Odéon) is a hot ticket once again with a new generation of devotees, including Britney Spears, Jennifer Lopez, and Whitney Houston. The boutique is particularly cozy, with sofas, big cushions, candles, and a few Oriental touches.

TRENDSETTERS

L'Absinthe (⌧ 74–76 rue Jean-Jacques Rousseau, 1ᵉʳ, ☏ 01–42–33–54–44, métro Les Halles) is a discreet but magical address where the likes of Peter Gabriel, Lauren Bacall, Tom Cruise, and Catherine Deneuve pick up clothing that is new but actually looks vintage. The owner, with her wavy hair and 1920s-style makeup, cultivates a decidedly retro look and sets the atmosphere by playing jazz music from a bygone era.

Antik Batik (⌧ 18 rue de Turenne, 4ᵉ, ☏ 01–48–87–95–95, métro St-Paul) is based in the former headquarters of a transport company. The two designers work with craftsmen in countries like India, China, Morocco, and Peru to produce hippie-chic, ethnic-inspired clothing, bags, and shoes, popular with supermodels and young Parisiennes.

Antoine & Lili (⌧ 95 quai de Valmy, 10ᵉ, ☏ 01–40–37–41–55, métro Jacques-Bonsergent) makes bright, young designs for fashion-forward women. Just as colorful are its storefronts—the clothing store (which also sells eclectic objects like Tibetan talc, dolls, and tribal art) is pink, the green boutique next door sells plants, while the yellow storefront houses a tea shop.

A-POC (⌧ 47 rue des Francs-Bourgeois, 4ᵉ, ☏ 01–44–54–07–05, métro St-Paul), which stands for "A Piece of Cloth," is Japanese designer Issey Miyake's latest venture. He has developed a new fabrication technique, which allows for hundreds of clothes to be cut from one piece of cloth. The very white, very gallery-like interior is by rising French design stars Erwin and Ronan Bouroullec.

Azzedine Alaïa (⌧ 7 rue de Moussy, 4ᵉ, ☏ 01–42–72–19–19, métro Hôtel-de-Ville) made his name in the '80s as the undisputed "king of cling." Then, his figure-hugging creations were often so tight that models had to be squeezed into them. Now, he's seriously back in style—with museum retrospectives, no less—with clothes that are more relaxed but no less exquisite.

Beauty by Et Vous (⌧ 25 rue Royale, 8ᵉ, ☏ 01–55–25–30–30, métro Madeleine) is one of the numerous concept stores that have sprouted up in Paris recently. Inside are the latest (and trendiest) in designer fashions, accessories, and cosmetics, along with constantly changing video installations.

Christophe Lemaire (⌧ 36 rue de Sévigné, 3ᵉ, ☏ 01–42–74–54–90, métro St-Paul) is one of France's most talked-about young designers. As well as selling his own collection, he carries CDs and vinyl records and organizes regular exhibitions of contemporary design.

Colette (⌧ 213 rue St-Honoré, 1ᵉʳ, ☏ 01–55–35–33–90, métro Tuileries) is the most fashionable, most hip, and most hyped store in Paris (and possibly in the world). The ground floor, which stocks design objects, gadgets, and makeup, is generally packed with fashion victims and the simply curious. Upstairs are handpicked fashions (only a few outfits from each designer), accessories, and magazines and books, which simply ooze trendiness and street cred. The high-tech basement café is a fashionable place to break for coffee.

E2 (✉ 15 rue Martel, 10ᵉ, ☎ 01–47–70–15–14, métro Château d'Eau) is the name designers Michèle and Olivier Châtenet came up for their new fashion concept. They buy up vintage clothing and kimonos and then customize them. Their embroidered kilts are especially popular with fans like Gwyneth Paltrow. If you want to plan a rendezvous here, remember it's strictly by appointment.

L'Éclaireur (✉ 3 rue des Rosiers, 4ᵉ, ☎ 01–48–87–10–22, métro St-Paul) has been on the cutting edge of fashion for years. It was the first to introduce Belgian designers like Martin Margiela into France and is still trying to keep one step ahead of the competition; today it stocks names like Prada, Dries Van Noten, Ann Demeulemeester, and Marni and Josephus Thimister, as well as hip sportswear and street-wear labels.

Eric Bergère (✉ 16 rue de la Sourdière, 1ᵉʳ, ☎ 01–47–03–33–19, métro Tuileries) has been one of France's top fashion names for two decades now. After heading up the design helm at both Hermès and Lanvin in the 1980s, he created his own label in 1995. This, his first boutique in Europe, was conceived by rising interiors star India Mahdavi-Hudson (whose other projects have included a new concept for the Givenchy boutiques and Ian Schrager's Empire Hotel in New York). Check out the black floors, red rugs, and medieval-style chandelier.

Isabel Marant (✉ 16 rue de Charonne, 11ᵉ, ☎ 01–49–29–71–55, métro Ledru-Rollin; ✉ 1 rue Jacob, 6ᵉ, ☎ 01–43–26–04–12, métro St-Germain-des-Prés) is one of the Paris press's favorite designers. French fashionistas flock to her Bastille boutique and new St-Germain store for her youthful and feminine designs.

Jean-Charles de Castelbajac Concept Store (✉ 26 rue Madame, 6ᵉ, ☎ 01–45–48–40–55, métro St-Sulpice; ✉ 31 pl. du Marché St-Honoré, 1ᵉʳ, ☎ 01–42–60–41–55, métro Tuileries) carries the memorably elegant yet quirky designs of the designer's own clothing collection, along with furniture, candles, blankets, and luggage. There is also jewelry by different young designers each season; cool books and magazines like *Dutch, Crash,* and *Very*; and Keith Haring–designed dominoes. There are also ace creams and toothpaste by a certain Professeur Draude.

Kokon To Zaï (✉ 48 rue Tiquetonne, 2ᵉ, ☎ 01–42–36–92–41, métro Étienne Marcel) is a Japanese expression to sum up the concept of opposing extremes (such as hot and cold, young and old). It is also a hip boutique, selling the creation of more than 40 young designers, including Jeremy Scott, Bernard Wilhelm, and Viktor & Rolf.

Lagerfeld Gallery (✉ 40 rue de Seine, 6ᵉ, ☎ 01–55–42–75–51, métro Mabillon) sells Karl's own signature Lagerfeld line, as well as the collection he designs for Italian fur house Fendi. On the first floor are accessories, perfumes, magazines, and exhibitions of Lagerfeld's own photography.

Maria Luisa (✉ 2 rue Cambon, 1ᵉʳ, ☎ 01–47–03–96–15, métro Concorde) is a boudoirlike boutique that has become a legend in its own time. It was one of the very first stores to carry Helmut Lang and John Galliano and now also stocks Martin Margiela, Jean-Paul Gaultier, Ann Demeulemeester, and Olivier Theyskens. An accessories store is at No. 4, a men's store around the corner at 38 rue du Mont-Thabor, and a funky, new unisex boutique at 19 bis rue du Mont-Thabor.

NIM (✉ 16 rue du Bourg-Tibourg, 4ᵉ, ☎ 01–42–77–19–79, métro Hôtel-de-Ville) is the name of Levi's Parisian concept store. The simple concrete boutique has 501s and customized vintage jeans hanging on hooks on the walls, as well as limited-edition accessories and an exhibition space for avant-garde art installations.

Onward (✉ 147 bd. St-Germain, 6ᵉ, ☎ 01–55–42–77–55, métro St-Germain-des-Prés), formerly known as Kashiyama, stocks fashion-forward clothes and accessories by the likes of Ann Demeulemeester, Martin Margiela, Martine Sitbon, Véronique Branquinho, and A. F. Vandevorst. It also gives over a space each season to up-and-coming labels, like Luella, Viktor & Rolf, and Alexandre Mathieu.

Raw Essentials (⊠ 46 rue Étienne-Marcel, 2ᵉ, ☎ 01–42–21–44–33, métro Louvre) is a haven for fans of raw denim. It uniquely stocks the designs of the Dutch-based label G-Star, whose highly desirable jeans have replaced those of Levi's as the ones to be seen in. There is also a range of military-inspired clothing, bags, and T-shirts.

Shine (⊠ 30 rue de Charonne, 11ᵉ, ☎ 01–48–05–80–10, métro Ledru-Rollin) travels the world to find clothes and accessories which embody the store's spirit: chic, glamorous, and rock and roll. The designers come from as far afield as Japan and Brazil but change with every season. As well as taking in the fashions, also check out the fabulous floral wallpaper and sparkly, gold wall displays.

Le Shop (⊠ 3 rue d'Argout, 2ᵉ, ☎ 01–40–28–95–94, métro Louvre) is the Parisian address for fans of street wear and techno. The industrial-style shop rocks to the beat of resident DJs and carries numerous hip designers as well as skateboards, sports shoes, and flyers for raves and parties. The whole experience is rather like shopping in a nightclub.

Le Webstore (⊠ 29 rue du Louvre, 2ᵉ, ☎ 01–40–26–92–77, métro Louvre) is the showcase for the Web site www.le-webstore.com. Created by brothers Jean-Yves and Hubert Lanvin (great-nephews of the famed couturière Jeanne), it sells everything from funky T-shirts and scented bracelets to designer radiators and miniature cameras.

Cosmetics

When it comes to *le maquillage* (makeup), many Parisian women head directly to those two beloved dime stores, **Monoprix** and **Prisunic.** Both are gold mines for inexpensive, good-quality cosmetics. Brand names to look for are Bourjois, whose products are made in the Chanel factories, and Arcancil.

Anne Sémonin (⊠ 2 rue des Petits-Champs, 2ᵉ, ☎ 01–42–60–94–66, métro Palais-Royal; ⊠ 108 rue du Faubourg St-Honoré, 8ᵉ, ☎ 01–42–66–24–22, métro Champs-Élysées–Clemenceau) sells exceptional skin-care products made out of seaweed and trace elements, as well as essential oils that are popular with fashion models.

By Terry (⊠ 21 Galerie Véro-Dodat, 1ᵉʳ, ☎ 01–44–76–00–76, métro Louvre, Palais-Royal) is the brainchild of Yves Saint Laurent's former director of makeup, Terry de Gunzberg. This small and refined jewel of a store offers her own brand of "ready-to-wear" makeup as well as personalized lipsticks, foundation, blush, and eye shadow, developed specifically for each client. The service requires a consultation, which should be booked at least three weeks in advance, and costs 3,200 francs/€492.

Make Up for Ever (⊠ 5 rue de la Boétie, 8ᵉ, ☎ 01–42–66–01–60, métro St-Augustin), at the back of a courtyard, is a must-stop for makeup artists, models (Kate Moss is a regular), and actresses (Madonna has dropped in, too). The ultrahip selection spans 100 shades of foundation, 100 different lipsticks, 125 eye shadows, 24 glittering powders, and scores of fake eyelashes.

Sephora (⊠ 70 av. des Champs-Élysées, 8ᵉ, ☎ 01–53–93–22–50, métro Franklin-D.-Roosevelt; ⊠ 1 rue Pierre Lescot, in the Forum des Halles, 1ᵉʳ, ☎ 01–40–13–72–25, métro Châtelet-les-Halles), the leading chain of perfume and cosmetics stores in France, sells its own makeup as well as all the big brands. Choose from 365 colors of lipstick, browse through the "Cultural Gallery" at the Champs-Élysées store, and even send e-mails for free from the in-store computers.

Fabrics

Les Impressions Edition (⊠ 8 rue Hérold, 1ᵉʳ, ☎ 01–42–21–32–44, métro Louvre) edits some of the most beautiful fabrics in the world. Owner Dominique Kieffer's creations are favored by some of the world's most famous interior designers, such as Christian Liaigre, Jacques Grange, and Jonathan Reed. The fabrics are only available to professionals . . . which shouldn't stop you looking. The magnificent cushions with feathers, raffia, and braiding can, however, be bought by anyone.

Manuel Canovas (⊠ 7 rue de Fürstenberg, 6ᵉ, ☎ 01–43–25–75–98, métro St-Germain-des-Prés) is one of the most famous names in French fabrics. This store stocks his extremely varied collections, which are remarkable for their wide range of colors.

Marché St-Pierre (⊠ 2 rue Charles Nodier, 18ᵉ, ☎ 01–46–06–92–25, métro Anvers), a five-floor warehouse in Montmartre, supplied designers like Kenzo in his salad days. Its inventory runs the gamut from fine brocades to fake furs, and there are often good specials on cheap end-of-bolt upholstery and fabrics. The market is open Monday 1:30 PM–6:30 PM and Tuesday–Saturday 10 AM–6:30 PM.

Pierre Frey (⊠ 2 rue de Fürstenberg, 6ᵉ, ☎ 01–43–26–82–61, métro St-Germain-des-Prés) features some of the most witty designs around and carries all sorts of fabrics as well as tablecloths and pillows.

Flowers

Au Nom de la Rose (⊠ 46 rue du Bac, 7ᵉ, ☎ 01–42–22–08–09, métro Rue du Bac; ⊠ 87 rue St-Antoine, 4ᵉ, ☎ 01–42–71–34–24, métro St-Paul), as its name suggests, specializes in roses of all different kinds.

Christian Tortu (⊠ 6 carrefour de l'Odéon, 6ᵉ, ☎ 01–43–26–02–56, métro Odéon), Paris's most fashionable florist, has made a name for himself with his very natural-looking bouquets. More recently, he has moved into homeware and has opened a store around the corner, which sells glassware, tableware, candles, and his must-have zinc vases.

Mille Feuilles (⊠ 2 rue Rambuteau, 3ᵉ, ☎ 01–42–78–32–93, métro Rambuteau, Hôtel-de-Ville) is one of the best addresses for beautiful bouquets. You'll find flowers in divine shades of red, orange, pink, and yellow, as well as vases, pots, picture frames, and lamps.

Food and Wine

À la Mère de Famille (⊠ 35 rue du Faubourg-Montmartre, 9ᵉ, ☎ 01–47–70–83–69, métro Cadet) is an enchanting shop well versed in French regional specialties and old-fashioned bonbons, sugar candy, and more.

Les Caves Augé (⊠ 116 bd. Haussmann, 8ᵉ, ☎ 01–45–22–16–97, métro St-Augustin), one of the best wine shops in Paris since 1850, is just the ticket whether you're looking for a rare vintage for an oenophile friend or a seductive Bordeaux for a tête-à-tête. English-speaking Marc Sibard is a knowledgeable and affable adviser.

Debauve & Gallais (⊠ 30 rue des Sts-Pères, 7ᵉ, ☎ 01–45–48–54–67, métro St-Germain) was founded in 1800 by two former chemists to Louis XVI who decided to start making chocolates. Today, their delectable recipes can still be found here.

L'Épicerie (⊠ 51 rue St-Louis-en-L'Ile, 4ᵉ, ☎ 01–43–25–20–14, métro Pont Marie) sells 90 types of jam (such as figs with almonds and cinnamon), 70 kinds of mustard (including one with chocolate and honey), numerous olive oils, and flavored sugars.

Fauchon (⊠ 26 pl. de la Madeleine, 8ᵉ, ☎ 01–47–42–60–11, métro Madeleine) is the most famous and iconic of all Parisian food stores. Established in 1886, it sells renowned pâté, honey, jelly, and private-label champagne. Hard-to-find foreign foods (U.S. pancake mix, British lemon curd) are also stocked, and delectable pastries and chocolates are served in the café. Prices can be eye-popping—chocolates for $70 a pound, marzipan fruits for $95 a pound—but who can naysay that soigné, top-of-the-line Fauchon chocolate box, whose cover bears an antique engraving of place de la Madeleine.

La Grande Épicerie (⊠ 38 rue de Sèvres, 7ᵉ, ☎ 01–44–39–81–00, métro Sèvres-Babylone), on the ground floor of Au Bon Marché, stocks an extensive array of fine French foodstuffs.

Hédiard (⊠ 21 pl. de la Madeleine, 8ᵉ, ☎ 01–43–12–88–88, métro Madeleine), established in 1854, was famous in the 19th century for its high-quality imported spices. These—along with rare teas and beautifully packaged house brands of jam, mustard, and cookies—are still sold.

La Maison du Chocolat (⊠ 56 rue Pierre Charron, 8ᵉ, ☎ 01–47–23–38–25, métro Franklin-D.-Roosevelt; ⊠ 8 bd. de la Madeleine, 9ᵉ, ☎ 01–47–42–86–52, métro Madeleine; ⊠ 225 rue du Faubourg St-Honoré, 8ᵉ, ☎ 01–42–27–39–44, métro Ternes) is heaven if you love chocolate: take some home or have a treat in the tearooms at the store on rue Pierre Charron or Madeleine.

Mariage Frères (⊠ 30 rue du Bourg-Tibourg, 4ᵉ, ☎ 01–42–72–28–11, métro Hôtel-de-Ville), with its colonial atmosphere and wooden counters, is the place to get tea in Paris. You can choose from more than 450 blends from 32 different countries and purchase teapots, teacups, books about tea, and tea-flavored biscuits and candies.

Verlet (⊠ 256 rue St-Honoré, 1ᵉʳ, ☎ 01–42–60–67–39, métro Palais-Royal) is *the* place in Paris to buy coffee. There are more than 20 varieties, from places as far flung as Hawaii and Papua New Guinea (you can also sample the brews on the premises). Also on sale are teas, jams from the Savoie region, and (during winter months) a stunning assortment of candied fruits.

Hats

Marie Mercié (⊠ 23 rue St-Sulpice, 6ᵉ, ☎ 01–43–26–45–83, métro Mabillon, St-Sulpice) is one of Paris's most fashionable hatmakers. Her husband, Anthony Peto, makes men's hats and has a store at 58 rue Tiquetonne.

Philippe Model (⊠ 33 pl. du Marché St-Honoré, 1ᵉʳ, ☎ 01–42–96–89–02, métro Tuileries) started off making hats favored by fashionable society ladies. More recently, he has added shoes and housewares in two adjacent and contrasting shops.

Housewares

Agatha Ruiz de la Prada (⊠ 9 rue Guénégaud, 6ᵉ, ☎ 01–43–25–86–88, métro Odéon) is nothing if not prolific. She designs clothing and accessories for the Spanish department store El Corte Inglès, watches for Swatch, and furniture for Amat. In this small store, she sells a wide range of her own creations, from bags and children's fashions to yo-yos and notebooks. All are typified by naive motifs in primary colors.

Alexandre Biaggi (⊠ 14 rue de Seine, 6ᵉ, ☎ 01–44–07–34–73, métro St-Germain-des-Prés) is one of the best addresses for 20th-century furniture. He specializes in the period 1910–1950 and also commissions the occasional design from talented contemporary designers, such as Nicolas Aubagnac and Hervé van der Straeten.

A. Simon (⊠ 48 rue Montmartre, 2ᵉ, ☎ 01–42–33–71–65, métro Étienne Marcel) is one of the places where all those wonderful Parisian chefs come to acquire everything they need in the kitchen—from plates and glasses to pans, dishes, and wooden spoons. The quality is excellent and the prices pleasantly reasonable.

Avant-Scène (⊠ 4 pl. de l'Odéon, 6ᵉ, ☎ 01–46–33–12–40, métro Odéon) has been editing original, poetic furniture for the past 15 years. Owner Elisabeth Delacarte commissions limited-edition pieces from artists like Mark Brazier-Jones, Franck Evennou, and Hubert Le Gall.

Catherine Memmi (✉ 32–34 rue St-Sulpice, 6ᵉ, ☎ 01–44–07–22–28, métro Mabillon, St-Sulpice; ✉ 43 rue Madame, 6ᵉ, ☎ 01–45–48–18–34, métro St-Sulpice) sells wonderfully chic bed linens, bath products, lamps, table settings, furniture, and cashmere sweaters—all in elegantly neutral colors and minimalist designs. Cheaper items in cotton are sold at the rue Madame address.

Christian Liaigre (✉ 42 rue du Bac, 7ᵉ, ☎ 01–53–63–33–66, métro Rue du Bac) is one of the most fashionable interior decorators at the moment. He designed the Mercer Hotel in New York and the homes of designer Kenzo and French actress Carole Bouquet. His range of fashionably simple furniture is sold in this flagship boutique.

Christofle (✉ 24 rue de la Paix, 2ᵉ, ☎ 01–42–65–62–43, métro Opéra; ✉ 9 rue Royale, 8ᵉ, ☎ 01–55–27–99–00, métro Concorde, Madeleine), founded in 1830, is *the* name to know in French silver. Come here for perfectly elegant table settings, vases, cigarette holders, jewelry boxes, and more.

Christophe Delcourt (✉ 76 bis rue Vieille-du-Temple, 3ᵉ, ☎ 01–42–78–44–97, métro Rambuteau, St-Paul) originally trained to become a farmer. In 1993, however, he started making objects out of chicken wire and soon found himself to be one of France's most sought-after interior designers. Fashion designers and film stars flock to this store to snap up his lamps based on old-fashioned drawing tools, waxed-steel furniture, and sleek, wooden tables.

Compagnie Française de l'Orient et de la Chine (✉ 163 bd. St-Germain, 6ᵉ, ☎ 01–45–48–00–18, métro St-Germain-des-Prés) imports ceramics and furniture from China and Mongolia. On the first floor are vases, teapots, and table settings; in the basement are straw hats, raffia baskets, and bamboo footstools.

The **Conran Shop** (✉ 117 rue du Bac, 7ᵉ, ☎ 01–42–84–10–01, métro Sèvres-Babylone; ✉ 30 bd. des Capucines, 9ᵉ, ☎ 01–53–43–29–00, métro Madeleine) is the brainchild of British entrepreneur Terence Conran. Here you can find expensive contemporary furniture, beautiful bed linens, glassware, kitchen utensils, vases, lamp shades, and bathroom accessories.

Diptyque (✉ 34 bd. St-Germain, 5ᵉ, ☎ 01–43–26–45–27, métro Maubert-Mutualité) sells scented candles (fashion designer Karl Lagerfeld is a fan) in natural fragrances such as rose, tea, and honeysuckle. It also has lamp oils and perfumes.

Gien (✉ 18 rue de l'Arcade, 8ᵉ, ☎ 01–42–66–52–32, métro Madeleine) has been making fine china since 1821. As well as traditional designs, you'll also find place settings especially designed by contemporary artists.

Laguiole (✉ 1 pl. Ste-Opportune, 1ᵉʳ, ☎ 01–40–28–09–42, métro Châtelet) is the name of the country's most famous knife. Today, designers like Philippe Starck and Sonia Rykiel have created special models for the company. Starck also designed this striking boutique (note the animal horn sticking out of the wall).

R & Y Augousti (✉ 103 rue du Bac, 7ᵉ, ☎ 01–42–22–22–21, métro Sèvres-Babylone) are two Paris-based designers who make furniture and objects for the home in materials like coconut, bamboo, fish skin, palm wood, and parchment. Also on sale is their relatively new line of textiles, inspired by peacock feathers. Treat yourself to one of their cushions in pashmina, raffia, leather, or printed cotton.

Sentou Galerie (✉ 24 rue du Pont Louis-Philippe, 4ᵉ, ☎ 01–42–71–00–01, métro St-Paul) specializes in contemporary design objects—lamps designed by artists, furniture by up-and-coming designers, and re-editions of seminal chairs and stools. At No. 18 is a store devoted to tableware.

Van Der Straeten (⊠ 11 rue Ferdinand Duval, 4ᵉ, ☏ 01–42–78–99–99, métro St-Paul) is the lofty gallery-cum-showroom of Paris designer Hervé van der Straeten. He started out creating jewelry for Saint Laurent and Lacroix, designed a perfume bottle for Christian Dior, and also moved into making rather baroque and often wacky furniture. On show are necklaces, rugs, chairs, and startling mirrors.

Jewelry

Most of the big names are on or near place Vendôme. Designer semiprecious and costume jewelry can generally be found in boutiques on avenue Montaigne and rue du Faubourg St-Honoré.

Alexandre Reza (⊠ 23 pl. Vendôme, 1ᵉʳ, ☏ 01–42–96–64–00, métro Opéra), one of Paris's most exclusive jewelers, is first and foremost a gemologist. He travels the world looking for the finest stones and then works them into stunning pieces, many of which are replicas of jewels of historical importance.

Arthus-Bertrand (⊠ 6 pl. St-Germain-des-Prés, 6ᵉ, ☏ 01–49–54–72–10, métro St-Germain-des-Prés) dates back to 1803 and is the official purveyor of medals and decorations to the States. It also carries a whole range of designer jewelry and numerous objects to celebrate births.

Au Vase de Delft (⊠ 19 rue Cambon, 1ᵉʳ, ☏ 01–42–60–92–49, métro Concorde) specializes in fine vintage jewelry, ivory sculptures from China and Japan, gold boxes, watches, and Russian-made silverware (some by Fabergé).

Chanel (⊠ 18 pl. Vendôme, 1ᵉʳ, ☏ 01–55–35–50–00, métro Tuileries, Opéra) spent a year renovating the building that houses its jewelry boutique. The interior is extremely refined, with beige sofas, animal sculptures, and Coromandel screens like the famous ones the designer used to have in her apartment. On sale are a selection of Chanel watches, rings, earrings, and bracelets with semiprecious stones, and some extraspecial pieces with diamonds, sapphires, and pearls. Prices range from an affordable 5,000 francs/€769 to a quite extravagant 15 million francs/€2,307,692.

Dary's (⊠ 362 rue St-Honoré, 1ᵉʳ, ☏ 01–42–60–95–23, métro Tuileries) carries antique jewelry, as well as modern secondhand jewelry; paperweights, and porcelain trinkets. Less expensive than Au Vase de Delft, it's a favored haunt of models and fashion stylists.

Christian Dior (⊠ 28 av. Montaigne, 8ᵉ, ☏ 01–47–23–52–39, métro Franklin-D.-Roosevelt; ⊠ 8 pl. Vendôme, 1ᵉʳ, métro Opéra) opened this, its first ever jewelry boutique, in 1999 on the avenue Montaigne (an additional boutique is to open on the place Vendôme in Summer 2001) and entrusted the design of the *"haute joaillerie"* collection to Victoire de Castellane, one of Paris's style makers. She has taken much inspiration from the life of Christian Dior himself and has come up with lucky charms as a nodding reference to the designer's great superstition and earrings in the form of his favorite flowers—roses and lilies of the valley. All the stones used are the real McCoy, so don't expect to get anything for cheap. Indeed, prices go up to 3 million francs/€462,538 for a necklace.

Jewels & Pashminas (⊠ 12 rue Jacob, 6ᵉ, ☏ 01–43–25–84–85, métro St-Germain-des-Prés) is composed of two stores, discreetly situated in a leafy courtyard. The jewelry store is the only outlet in Europe for the sublime creations made in the legendary Gem Palace in Jaipur. There are stunning necklaces in rubies, diamonds set in gold, and some staggering combinations of color and stones. Prices for rings vary between 3,500 francs/€538 and 60,000 francs/€9,230. In the neighboring pashmina boutique, you'll find Nepalese clothing, hand-embroidered shawls, and cushions decorated with antique pieces of pashmina.

Matière Première (✉ 12 rue de Sévigné, 4ᵉ, ☏ 01–42–78–40–87, métro St-Paul) sells everything you need to make your own necklaces and bracelets—thousands of beads, pendants, and wire. If you prefer to buy ready-made items, there's a delightful in-house jewelry collection.

Lingerie
Alice Cadolle (✉ 14 rue Cambon, 1ᵉʳ, ☏ 01–42–60–94–94, métro Concorde) has been selling the finest lingerie to Parisians since 1889. In the first-floor boutique are ready-to-wear bras, corsets, and sleepwear. Upstairs, Madame Cadolle offers a made-to-measure service, popular with couture clients from nearby Chanel.
Capucine Puerari (✉ 63 rue des Sts-Pères, 6ᵉ, ☏ 01–42–22–14–09, métro St-Germain-des-Prés) is one of those discreet addresses loved by Parisian women; it's well stocked with lingerie, swimwear, and a stylish collection of clothing.
Sabbia Rosa (✉ 73 rue des Sts-Pères, 6ᵉ, ☏ 01–45–48–88–37, métro St-Germain-des-Prés) is a discreet, boudoirlike boutique you could easily walk straight past. It is, however, probably the finest lingerie store in the world and the place where supermodels Naomi Campbell and Claudia Schiffer, and actresses Sharon Stone, Catherine Deneuve, and Isabelle Adjani buy their smalls in the finest French silk.

Miscellaneous
Kirk & Richie Rich (✉ 9 rue de La Trémoille, 8ᵉ, ☏ 01–47–23–81–00, métro Alma-Marceau) has an abundance of objects that owner Gisela Trigano brings back from her travels. Among her *coups de coeur* are shoes and Murano glass from Italy, pashminas from India, blankets from England, wooden sculptures from Nepal, and ancestor paintings from China.
Nature et Découvertes (✉ In the Carrousel du Louvre, 99 rue de Rivoli, 1ᵉʳ, ☏ 01–47–03–47–43, métro Palais-Royal) has a large selection of children's toys as well as a whole range of objects linked to nature—telescopes, birdseed, gardening equipment, hiking gear, crystals, aromatherapy diffusers, and little Zen gardens.

Music
FNAC (✉ Forum des Halles, 1ᵉʳ, ☏ 01–40–41–40–00, métro Les Halles; ✉ 74 av. des Champs-Élysées, 8ᵉ, ☏ 01–53–53–64–64, métro Franklin-D.-Roosevelt; ✉ 136 rue de Rennes, 6ᵉ, ☏ 01–49–54–30–00, métro St-Placide) is a high-profile French chain selling music and books, and photo, TV, and audio equipment at good prices, by French standards.
Fréderic Sanchez (✉ 5 rue St-Anastase, 3ᵉ, ☏ 01–44–54–89–54, métro St-Paul) is the French fashion world's favorite DJ. He often mixes the music for top catwalk shows and has now opened this small space, which offers everything he considers swank listening. The CD selection ranges from opera to Bryan Ferry, plus all the latest in electronic music. There is also a smattering of vinyl records and sophisticated electronic gadgetry.
Virgin Megastore (✉ 52 av. des Champs-Élysées, 8ᵉ, ☏ 01–49–53–50–00, métro Franklin-D.-Roosevelt; ✉ In the Carrousel du Louvre, 99 rue de Rivoli, 1ᵉʳ, ☏ 01–49–53–52–90, métro Palais-Royal) has acres of CDs and tapes; the Champs-Élysées store has a large book section and a trendy café upstairs.

Perfumes
Annick Goutal (✉ 14 rue de Castiglione, 1ᵉʳ, ☏ 01–42–60–52–82, métro Concorde) sells its own exclusive line of 18 signature scents, which come packaged in gilded gauze purses.

L'Artisanat Parfumeur (⊠ 32 rue du Bourg Tibourg, 4ᵉ, ☎ 01–48–04–72–75, métro Hôtel-de-Ville) sells its own brand of scents for the home and perfumes with names like Méchant Loup (Naughty Wolf) and Riviera Palace.

L'Atelier du Savon (⊠ 29 rue Vieille-du-Temple, 4ᵉ, ☎ 01–44–54–06–10, métro St-Paul) is a soap addict's heaven. There are blocks of chocolate and lime soap, mint and lemon soap, and others that look strangely like brownies. Fizzy balls for the bath have rose petals and sequins inside of them, and shampoos come in solid blocks.

Comme des Garçons (⊠ 23 pl. du Marché St-Honoré, 1ᵉʳ, ☎ 01–47–03–60–72, métro Tuileries) is the very first boutique in the world devoted to the trendy Japanese label's perfumes, scented candles, and body creams. The shop is worth a visit simply to admire the whiter-than-white store design with pink tinted lighting.

Creed (⊠ 38 av. Pierre 1ᵉʳ de Serbie, 8ᵉ, ☎ 01–47–20–58–02, métro George V) was founded in 1760 and was the official perfume supplier to Queen Victoria and numerous European courts. Today, it sells a selection of its own scents and makes personalized perfumes.

Guerlain (⊠ 68 av. des Champs-Élysées, 8ᵉ, ☎ 01–45–62–52–57, métro Franklin-D.-Roosevelt; ⊠ 47 rue Bonaparte, 6ᵉ, ☎ 01–43–26–71–19, métro Mabillon) boutiques are the only authorized Paris outlets for legendary perfumes like Shalimar, Jicky, Vol de Nuit, Mitsouko, Chamade, and, the latest, Champs-Élysées.

Parfums de Nicolaï (⊠ 69 av. Raymond Poincaré, 16ᵉ, ☎ 01–47–55–90–44, métro Victor-Hugo) is run by a member of the Guerlain family, Patricia de Nicolaï. It has a range of children's, women's, and men's perfumes, as well as sprays for the home and scented candles. Celebrity clients include Isabelle Adjani and Elton John.

Les Salons du Palais Royal Shiseido (⊠ Jardins du Palais-Royal, 142 Galerie de Valois, 25 rue de Valois, 1ᵉʳ, ☎ 01–49–27–09–09, métro Palais-Royal) is a magical place with marble floors and purple walls. Every year Shiseido's creative director, Serge Lutens, dreams up two new scents, which are sold exclusively in this boutique.

DISCOUNT

The airport duty-free shops are your best bet for minor purchases. But if you're going to spend more than 1,200 francs/€184, it's worthwhile to seek out the top discounters. Don't forget to claim your *détaxe*!

Les Halles Montmartre (⊠ 85 rue Montmartre, 2ᵉ, ☎ 01–42–33–11–13, métro Bourse) routinely discounts its wide range of perfumes and cosmetics by up to 20%.

Michel Swiss (⊠ 16 rue de la Paix, 2nd floor, 2ᵉ, ☎ 01–42–61–61–11, métro Opéra; ⊠ 24 av. de l'Opéra, 1ᵉʳ, ☎ 01–47–03–49–11, métro Pyramides) offers savings of up to 25% on perfumes, designer jewelry, and fashion accessories. There's no storefront window; enter the courtyard to take the elevator upstairs.

Shoes

Berluti (⊠ 26 rue Marbeuf, 8ᵉ, ☎ 01–53–93–97–97, métro Franklin-D.-Roosevelt) has been making fantastically exquisite and expensive men's shoes for more than a century. "Nothing is too beautiful for feet" is Olga Berluti's motto. She even exposes her creations to the moonlight to give them an extraspecial patina! One model is named after Andy Warhol, and other famous clients of the past have included the Duke of Windsor, Fred Astaire, and James Joyce.

Christian Louboutin (⊠ 19 rue Jean-Jacques Rousseau, 1ᵉʳ, ☎ 01–42–36–05–31, métro Palais-Royal, Sèvres-Babylone; ⊠ 38 rue de Grenelle, 7ᵉ, ☎ 01–42–22–33–07, métro Palais-Royal, Sèvres-Babylone) is famous for his wacky but elegant creations and his trademark blood-red soles; Caroline of Monaco, Catherine Deneuve, and Elizabeth Taylor are some of his clients.

Mare (✉ 23 rue des Francs-Bourgeois, 4ᵉ, ☎ 01–48–04–74–63, métro St-Paul; ✉ 4 rue du Cherche-Midi, 6ᵉ, ☎ 01–45–44–55–33, métro St-Sulpice) has stylish, trendy shoes made from fine Italian leather.

Michel Perry (✉ 4 rue des Petits-Pères, 2ᵉ, ☎ 01–42–44–10–07, métro Palais-Royal) is famous for his elegant, slender, high-heeled shoes. The rose-color boudoir-style store also stocks a range of hip labels, including Chloé, Colette Dinnigan, and Guy Laroche.

Rodolphe Menudier (✉ 14 rue de Castiglione, 1ᵉʳ, ☎ 01–42–60–86–27, métro Tuileries) is a gem of a boutique, which sells some of the most beautiful shoes in the world. As well as creating his own mules and stilettos, he also creates the footwear for Christian Dior. The interior design—think sleek black windows, metal cupboards, and a wall covered in white crocodile leather—is the creation of hip interiors star Christophe Pillet.

Shoe Bizz (✉ 42 rue Dragon, 6ᵉ, ☎ 01–45–44–91–70, métro St-Germain-des-Prés; ✉ 48 rue Beaubourg, 3ᵉ, ☎ 01–48–87–12–73, métro Rambuteau) zeroes in on the season's hottest shoe styles and replicates them at prices 30% cheaper than you'll find elsewhere in the city.

DISCOUNT

Mi-Prix (✉ 27 bd. Victor-Hugo, 15ᵉ, ☎ 01–48–28–42–48, métro Porte de Versailles) is an unruly jumble of end-of-series designer shoes and accessories from the likes of Gucci, Philippe Model, Walter Steiger, Prada, Michel Perry, and Azzedine Alaïa, priced at up to 70% below retail.

Stationery

Calligrane (✉ 4-6 rue Pont Louis Philippe, 4ᵉ, ☎ 01–48–04–31–89, métro St-Paul; ✉ 68 rue de Grenelle, 7ᵉ, ☎ 01–45–49–96–02, métro Sèvres-Babylone) has three adjacent stores in the 4ᵉ arrondissement. One uniquely sells an Italian paper called Fabriano, another designer office equipment (notebooks covered in ostrich skin; pens; and staplers), and the third features different types of paper from India, Japan, and Mexico.

Cassegrain (✉ 422 rue St-Honoré, 8ᵉ, ☎ 01–42–60–20–08, métro Sèvres-Babylone; ✉ 81 rue des Sts-Pères, 6ᵉ, ☎ 01–42–22–04–76, métro Sèvres-Babylone) is the last word on beautifully engraved cards and elegant French stationery. The desk accessories and inexpensive glass-nib writing pens make great gifts.

Marie Papier (✉ 26 rue Vavin, 6ᵉ, ☎ 01–43–26–46–44, métro Vavin) sells an extraordinary variety of colored, marbled, and Japanese writing paper and notebooks, plus every kind of stylish writing accessory. One fan is fashion designer Donna Karan, who stocks part of the range in her Madison Avenue store.

Toys

Au Nain Bleu (✉ 408 rue St-Honoré, 8ᵉ, ☎ 01–42–60–39–01, métro Concorde) is a high-priced wonderland of elaborate dollhouses, miniature sports cars, and enchanting hand-carved rocking horses.

C'est Ma Chambre (✉ 45 rue des Archives, 3ᵉ, ☎ 01–48–87–26–67, métro Rambuteau) is the place to spoil your kids; it sells beautiful wooden toys and gorgeous furniture for kids' rooms.

Marais Plus (✉ 20 rue des Francs-Bourgeois, 3ᵉ, ☎ 01–48–87–01–40, métro St-Paul) is one of the most delightful addresses in the city for children's toys and clothes. Upstairs are dolls, teddy bears, hobby horses, and mobiles; downstairs are very cute clothes made out of recycled materials and a tea shop.

7 SIDE TRIPS FROM PARIS

Visitors to Paris are undeniably lucky. With just a quick trip to the countryside, they can explore some of the most fabled sights of France's regal past. Versailles—less a monument to Louis XIV than an entire world unto itself—remains the world's most glittering palace. Nearby, *la vie du château* can be yours by calling on Chantilly, Fontainebleau, and Vaux-le-Vicomte. Just beyond, Gothic architecture reaches its pinnacle in the soaring spires of Chartres, while Claude Monet's gardens at Giverny offer a sublime day in the country. Last but not least, a newer fairy-tale city beckons to all—Disneyland Paris.

Revised and
updated by
Simon Hewitt

E VEN THOUGH PARIS ITSELF HAS SO MUCH TO SEE, you should plan on taking a short trip outside the city, for just beyond its gates lies the fabled region known as Ile-de-France, the ancient heartland of France—the core from which the French kings gradually extended their power over the rest of a rebellious, individualistic nation. Though Ile-de-France is not really an island (*île*), it is figuratively isolated from the rest of France by three rivers—the Seine, the Marne, and the Oise—that weave majestic, meandering circles around its periphery. Remarkably, this fairly confined region contains 10 million people—one-sixth of France's population. This type of statistic conjures up visions of a never-ending suburban sprawl, but nothing could be further from the truth.

Grand cathedrals and stately châteaux dot the lush, gently rolling landscape. The kings and clerics who ruled France liked to escape from the capital now and then: Châteaux went up at Versailles, Fontainebleau, and Chantilly; cathedrals soared skyward in Chartres and Senlis. The region never lost favor with the powerful, partly because its many forests—large chunks of which still stand—harbored sufficient game to ensure even the most indolent monarch an easy kill. First Fontainebleau, in humane Renaissance proportions, then Versailles, on a minion-crushing, Baroque scale, reflected the royal desire to transform hunting lodges into palatial residences.

In 1992 Disney wrought its own kind of kingdom here: Disneyland Paris. Since then, the park has emerged as France's leading tourist attraction, with 11 million visitors a year. Getting from the capital to the sights in this region is easy: almost all are within an hour of central Paris, and most are easily accessible by train.

CHARTRES

The noble, soaring spires of Chartres are one of the most famous sights in Europe. Try to catch a glimpse of them surging out of the vast, golden grain fields of the Beauce as you approach from the northeast. Although you're probably visiting Chartres chiefly for its magnificent Gothic cathedral and its world-famous stained-glass windows, the whole town is also worth leisurely exploration. Ancient streets tumble down from the cathedral to the Eure River; the view of the rooftops beneath the cathedral from rue du Pont-St-Hilaire is particularly appealing. Like the cathedral, the old part of town, studded with picturesque houses and streets, has been preserved in its cloak of mellowing old stone; other sectors have been slapped with modern apartment buildings and whizzing traffic.

The **Cathédrale de Chartres** is the sixth church to occupy the same spot. It dates mainly from the 12th and 13th centuries; the previous, 11th-century building burned down in 1194. A well-chronicled outburst of religious fervor followed the discovery that the relic kept in the church, the Virgin Mary's tunic, had miraculously survived unsinged. Reconstruction went ahead at a breathtaking pace. In only 25 years Chartres Cathedral rose again, and it has remained substantially unchanged ever since.

Worship on the site of the cathedral goes back to before the Gallo-Roman period; the crypt contains a well that was the focus of Druid ceremonies. With the arrival of Christianity, the original cult of the fertility goddess merged into that of the Virgin Mary. In the late 9th century, King Charles the Bold presented Chartres with what was believed to be the

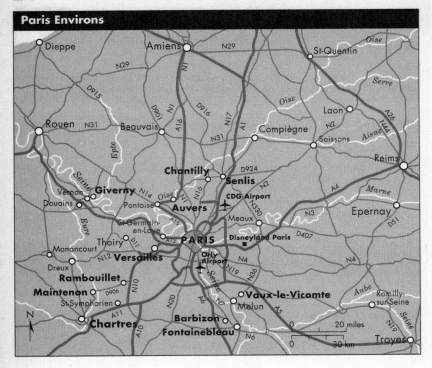

tunic of the Virgin Mary. This precious relic attracted hordes of pilgrims, and Chartres swiftly became—and has remained—a prime destination for the faithful. To this day, pilgrims trek to Chartres from Paris on foot.

The lower half of the facade is all that survives from the 11th-century Romanesque church. (The Romanesque style is evident in the use of round, rather than pointed, arches.) The main door—the **Portail Royal** (Royal Portal)—is richly sculpted with scenes from the life of Christ. The flanking towers are also Romanesque, though the upper part of the taller of the two **spires** (380 ft versus 350 ft) dates from the start of the 16th century, and its fanciful flamboyance contrasts with the stumpy solemnity of its Romanesque counterpart. The **rose window** above the main portal dates from the 13th century. The three windows below it contain some of the finest examples of 12th-century stained glass in France.

The interior is somber, so you'll need time to adjust to the dark. Your reward will be a view of the gemlike richness of the stained glass, dominated by the famous deep "Chartres blue." The oldest window, and perhaps the most stunning, is **Notre-Dame de la Belle Verrière** (Our Lady of the Lovely Window), in the south choir. It is well worth taking binoculars, if you have a pair, to pick out the details. If you wish to know more about stained-glass techniques and the motifs used, visit the small exhibit in the gallery opposite the north porch. The vast black-and-white medieval pattern on the floor of the nave is one of the few to have survived from the Middle Ages. The faithful were expected to crawl along its entire length (some 300 yards) on their knees. A longtime Chartres aficionado, Malcolm Miller knows more than most art historians and gives fabulous tours in English daily at noon and 2:45 PM, providing information on the narrative stained glass and his own travels for a fee. Otherwise, you can head out the cathedral's south

Chartres

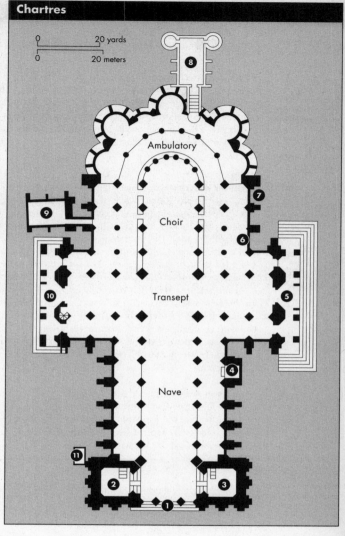

0   20 yards
0   20 meters

Ambulatory

Choir

Transept

Nave

door to the crypt across the street and rent a Walkman and a (vastly
inferior) tape-recorded tour in English.

Guided tours of the crypt start from the **Maison de la Crypte** (Crypt
House) opposite the south porch. The Romanesque and Gothic chapels
running around the crypt have recently been stripped of the 19th-cen-
tury paintings that used to disfigure them. You will also be shown a
4th-century Gallo-Roman wall and some 12th-century wall paintings.
⊠ *16 cloître Notre-Dame,* ☎ *02–37–21–56–33,* WEB *www.chartres.com.*
🎟 *Towers 10 frs/€1.52, English guided tour 30 frs/€4.60.* ☙ *Guided
tours of crypt Easter–Oct., daily at 11, 2:15, 3:30, 4:30, and 5:15; Nov.–
Easter, daily at 11 and 4.*

The **Musée des Beaux-Arts** (Fine Arts Museum) is a handsome 18th-
century building just behind the cathedral—it used to serve as the
bishop's palace. Its varied collection includes Renaissance enamels, a
portrait of Erasmus by Holbein, tapestries, armor, and some fine,
mainly French paintings of the 17th, 18th, and 19th centuries. There

is also a room devoted to the forceful 20th-century works of painter Maurice de Vlaminck, who lived in the region. ⊠ *29 cloître Notre-Dame,* ☎ *02–37–36–41–39.* ⊡ *10 frs/€1.52 (20 frs/€3 for special exhibitions).* ☉ *Apr.–Oct., Wed.–Mon. 10–6; Nov.–Mar., Wed.–Mon. 10–noon and 2–5.*

The Gothic **Église St-Pierre** (⊠ Rue St-Pierre) near the Eure River has magnificent medieval windows from a period (circa 1300) not represented at the cathedral. The oldest stained glass here, portraying Old Testament worthies, is to the right of the choir and dates from the late 13th century. There is more fine stained glass (17th century) to admire at the **Église St-Aignan** (⊠ Rue des Grenets), around the corner from St-Pierre.

Dining

$$$ ✕ **Château d'Esclimont.** This magnificently restored Renaissance château, part of the Relais & Châteaux group, is frequented by high-profile Parisian businesspeople. Lamb with asparagus, hare fricassee (in season), and lobster top the menu. After dining on the rich cuisine, take a stroll through the luxuriant grounds, embellished with lawns and lake. ⊠ *2 rue du Château-d'Esclimont, St-Symphorien-le-Château (6 km/4 mi west of Ablis exit on A11 and about 24 km/15 mi from Chartres and Rambouillet),* ☎ *02–37–31–15–15. Reservations essential. Jacket and tie. AE, DC, MC, V.*

$$ ✕ **La Vieille Maison.** Close to Chartres Cathedral, in the same narrow street as Le Buisson Ardent, this intimate spot with a flower-filled patio has a regularly changing menu. Invariably, however, it includes regional specialties such as truffles and asparagus with chicken. Prices, though justified, can be steep; the 170-franc/€26 prix-fixe lunch menu is a good bet. ⊠ *5 rue au Lait,* ☎ *02–37–34–10–67. AE, MC, V. Closed Mon. No dinner Sun.*

$–$$ ✕ **Le Buisson Ardent.** This wood-beamed restaurant on a quaint old street near Chartres Cathedral has two prix-fixe menus, imaginative food, and attentive service. Some of the excellent dishes include chicken ravioli with leeks and rolled beef with spinach. ⊠ *10 rue au Lait,* ☎ *02–37–34–04–66. AE, DC, MC, V. No dinner Sun.*

Chartres A to Z

To research prices, get advice from other travelers, and book travel arrangements, visit www.fodors.com.

CAR TRAVEL
The A10/A11 expressways link Paris to Chartres, 88 km (55 mi) away.

GUIDED TOURS
Cityrama organizes half-day trips to Chartres (275 frs/€42) and combined excursions to Chartres and Versailles (595 frs/€91).
➤ CONTACTS: **Cityrama** (⊠ 4 pl. des Pyramides, Paris, ☎ 01–44–55–61–00).

TRAIN TRAVEL
Trains depart hourly from Paris's Gare Montparnasse to Chartres (travel time is 50–70 minutes, depending on service).

VISITOR INFORMATION
➤ CONTACTS: **Chartres** (⊠ Pl. de la Cathédrale, 28000 Chartres, ☎ 02–37–21–50–00).

DISNEYLAND PARIS

In April 1992 American pop culture secured a mammoth outpost just 32 km (20 mi) east of Paris in the form of Disneyland Paris. On 1,500 acres in Marne-la-Vallée, Disneyland Paris has a convention center, sports facilities, an entertainment and shopping complex, restaurants, thousands of hotel rooms, and, of course, the theme park itself. The theme park is made up of five "lands": Main Street U.S.A., Frontierland, Adventureland, Fantasyland, and Discoveryland. The central theme of each land is relentlessly echoed in every detail, from attractions to restaurant menus to souvenirs.

Main Street U.S.A. is the scene of the Disney Parades held every afternoon and—during holiday periods—every evening, too.

Top attractions at **Frontierland** are the chilling Phantom Manor, haunted by holographic spooks, and the thrilling runaway mine train of Big Thunder Mountain, a roller coaster that plunges wildly through floods and avalanches in a setting meant to evoke Monument Valley.

Whiffs of Arabia, Africa, and the West Indies give **Adventureland** its exotic cachet; the spicy meals and snacks served here rank among the best food in the theme park. Don't miss the Pirates of the Caribbean, an exciting mise-en-scène populated by eerily human computer-driven figures, or Indiana Jones and the Temple of Doom, a breathtaking ride that relives some of our luckless hero's most exciting moments.

Fantasyland charms the youngest park goers with familiar cartoon characters from such Disney classics as *Snow White, Pinocchio, Dumbo,* and *Peter Pan.* The focal point of Fantasyland, and indeed Disneyland Paris, is Le Château de la Belle au Bois Dormant (Sleeping Beauty's Castle), a 140-ft, bubble gum–pink structure topped with 16 blue- and gold-tipped turrets. The castle design was allegedly inspired by illustrations from a medieval Book of Hours. In the dungeon is a scaly, green 2-ton dragon who rumbles and grumbles in his sleep and occasionally rouses to roar—an impressive feat of engineering that terrifies every tot in the crowd!

Discoveryland is a futuristic setting for high-tech Disney entertainment. Robots on roller skates welcome you to Star Tours, a pitching, plunging, sense-confounding ride through intergalactic space. Space Mountain pretends to catapult you through the Milky Way.

For entertainment outside the theme park, check out **Disney Village,** a vast pleasure mall designed by American architect Frank Gehry. Featured are American-style restaurants (crab shack, diner, deli, steak house), a disco, and a dinner theater where Buffalo Bill stages his Wild West Show twice nightly. An 18-hole golf course is open to the public (☎ 01–60–45–68–04 information). WEB *www.disneylandparis.com.* ✉ *Disneyland Paris (prices vary according to season) 170–230 frs/€26–35.* ⊙ *Mid-June–mid-Sept., daily 9 am–10 pm; mid-Sept.–mid-June, daily 10–8.*

Dining

$–$$ ✕ **Disneyland Restaurants.** Disneyland Paris is peppered with places to eat, ranging from snack bars and fast-food joints to five full-service restaurants—each with a distinguishing theme. In addition, all Disney hotels and Festival Disney have restaurants that are open to the public. But since these are outside the theme park, you probably won't want to waste time traveling to them for lunch. Wine and beer are served in the theme park's five sit-down restaurants, as well as in the hotels and restaurants outside the park. Eateries serve nonstop as long as the park is open. *AE, DC, MC, V (at sit-down restaurants; no credit cards at others).*

Disneyland Paris A to Z

BUS TRAVEL

Shuttle buses link Disneyland Paris to Roissy (56 km/35 mi) and Orly (50 km/31 mi) airports. The fare is around 80 francs/€12.30 one-way.

CAR TRAVEL

The Strasbourg-bound A4 expressway leads from Paris to Disneyland Paris, at Marne-la-Vallée, a journey of 32 km (20 mi) that in normal traffic takes about 30 minutes. The 4-km (2½-mi) route from the expressway to the entrance of the theme park is clearly marked. Day visitors must head for the *Parking Visiteurs,* which costs 40 francs/€6 per car and is 600 yards from the theme-park entrance.

TRAIN TRAVEL

Disneyland Paris's suburban train station (Marne-la-Vallée–Chessy) is just 100 yards from the entrance to both the theme park and Festival Disney. Trains run every 10 to 20 minutes from RER-A stations in central Paris: Charles-de-Gaulle–Étoile, Auber, Châtelet–Les Halles, Gare de Lyon, and Nation. The trip takes about 40 minutes and costs 80 francs/€12.30 round-trip (including the métro to the RER). A TGV station next to the RER station at Disneyland Paris offers direct train service to and from Lille, Lyon, and Marseille.

VISITOR INFORMATION

➤ CONTACTS: **Disneyland Paris S.C.A.** (✉ Central Reservations Office, BP 104, 77777 Marne-la-Vallée, Cedex 4, France, ☎ 01–60–30–60–30, ⒻⒶⓍ 01–49–30–71–00). **Walt Disney World Central Reservations** (✉ Box 10, 100 Lake Buena Vista, FL 32830–0100, ☎ 407/934–7639).

FONTAINEBLEAU AND VAUX-LE-VICOMTE

Fontainebleau, with its historic château, is a favorite place for excursions, especially since the superb Baroque château of Vaux-le-Vicomte is close by.

Fontainebleau

Numbers in the text correspond to numbers on the Fontainebleau map.

Like Chambord in the Loire Valley and Compiègne to the north of Paris, Fontainebleau earned royal esteem as a hunting base. As at Versailles, a hunting lodge once stood on the site of the current château, along with a chapel built in 1169 and consecrated by exiled (later murdered and canonized) English priest Thomas à Becket.

The **Château de Fontainebleau** you see today dates from the 16th century, although additions were made by various royal incumbents over the next 300 years. The palace was begun under flamboyant Renaissance King François I, the French contemporary of England's Henry VIII.

The king hired Italian artists Il Rosso (a pupil of Michelangelo) and Primaticcio to embellish his château. In fact, they did much more: by introducing the pagan allegories and elegant lines of Mannerism to France, they revolutionized the realm of French decorative art. Their ❶ extraordinary frescoes and stuccowork can be admired in the **Galerie François-I** (Francis I Gallery) and the crown jewel of the interior, the ❷ **Salle de Bal.** Here in the ceremonial ballroom, which is nearly 100 ft long, you can admire the dazzling 16th-century frescoes and gilding.

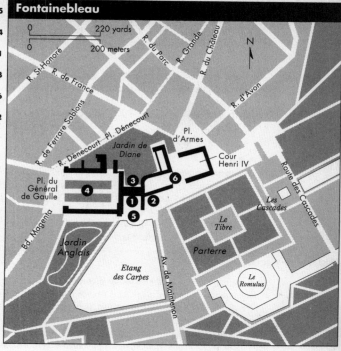

Fontainebleau

Completed under Henri II, François's successor, it is luxuriantly wood paneled, with a parquet floor whose gleaming finish reflects the patterns on the ceiling above. Like the château as a whole, the room exudes a sense of elegance and style—but on a more intimate, human scale than at Versailles: this is Renaissance, not Baroque.

❸ Napoléon's apartments occupied the first floor. You can see a lock of his hair, his Légion d'Honneur medal, his imperial uniform, the hat he wore on his return from Elba in 1815, and one bed in which he definitely did spend a night (almost every town in France boasts a bed in which the emperor supposedly snoozed). There is also a throne room—Napoléon spurned the one at Versailles, a palace he disliked—and the Queen's Boudoir, known as the Room of the Six Maries (occupants included ill-fated Marie-Antoinette and Napoléon's second wife, Marie-Louise). Highlights of other salons include 17th-century tapestries, marble reliefs by Jacquet de Grenoble, and paintings and frescoes by the versatile Primaticcio.

Although Louis XIV's architectural fancy was concentrated on Versailles, he commissioned Mansart to design new pavilions and had André Le Nôtre replant the gardens at Fontainebleau, to which the king and his court returned every fall for the hunting season. But it was Napoléon who made a Versailles out of Fontainebleau, as it were, by spending lavishly to restore it to its former glory. He held Pope Pius VII prisoner here in 1812, signed the second Church-State concordat here in 1813, and, in the cobbled **Cour des Adieux** (Farewell Courtyard), said **❹** good-bye to his Old Guard in 1814 as he began his brief exile on the Mediterranean island of Elba. The famous Horseshoe Staircase that dominates the Cour des Adieux, once the Cour du Cheval Blanc (White Horse Courtyard), was built by Androuet du Cerceau for Louis XIII (1610–43).

⑤ Another courtyard—the **Cour de la Fontaine** (Fountain Courtyard)—was commissioned by Napoléon in 1812 and adjoins the Étang des Carpes (Carp Pond). Ancient carp are alleged to swim here, although Allied soldiers drained the pond in 1915 and ate all the fish, and, in the event they missed some, Hitler's hordes did likewise in 1940.

⑥ The **Porte Dauphine** is the most beautiful of the various gateways that connect the complex of buildings; its name commemorates the fact that the Dauphin—the heir to the throne, later Louis XIII—was christened under its archway in 1606. ⊠ *Pl. du Général-de-Gaulle,* ☎ *01–60–71–50–70.* ▣ *Château 35 frs/€5.34, gardens free.* ☉ *Château Wed.–Mon. 9:30–12:30 and 2–5, gardens daily 9 am–dusk.*

Dining

$$–$$$ ✕ **Le Beauharnais.** Opposite the château, in the Aigle Noir hotel, this restaurant serves classic French fare in a grand setting; especially good is the lamb with thyme and gentian. Prix-fixe menus are 195 and 450 francs/€30 and 69. There's a tranquil garden for alfresco dining in summer. ⊠ *27 pl. Napoléon-Bonaparte,* ☎ *01–60–74–60–00. Jacket and tie. AE, DC, MC, V. Closed last week of Dec.*

Vaux-le-Vicomte

The majestic **Château de Vaux-le-Vicomte,** started in 1656 by court finance wizard Nicolas Fouquet, is one of the most impressive buildings in Ile-de-France. The construction process was monstrous: villages were razed, and then 18,000 workmen were called in to execute the plans of architect Louis Le Vau, decorator Charles Le Brun, and landscape gardener André Le Nôtre. The housewarming party was so lavish that star guest Louis XIV, tetchy at the best of times, threw a jealous fit, hurled Fouquet into the slammer, and promptly began building Versailles to prove just who was boss.

Decoration of the château's landmark feature, the **cupola,** was halted at Fouquet's arrest, and the ceiling of the oval **Grand Salon** beneath remains depressingly blank. Le Brun's major achievement is the ceiling of the **Chambre du Roi** (King's Bedchamber) depicting *Time Bearing Truth Heavenward.* The word "squirrel" in French is *écureuil,* but in local dialect they were known as *fouquets*; they appear here (along the frieze) and throughout the château, a sly visual tribute to the château's hapless founder. Le Brun's other masterwork is the ceiling in the **Salon des Muses** (Salon of the Muses), a brilliant allegorical composition painted in glowing, sensuous colors surpassing anything he achieved at Versailles.

A clever **exhibit,** complete with life-size wax figures, explains the rise and fall of Nicolas Fouquet. Although accused by Louis XIV and subsequent historians of megalomania and shady financial dealings, he was apparently condemned on little evidence by a court eager to please the jealous, irascible monarch. The exhibition continues in the basement, whose cool, dim rooms used to store food and wine and house the château's staff. The **kitchens,** a more cheerful sight with their gleaming copperware and old menus, are also down here.

Le Nôtre's stupendous, studiously restored **gardens** contain statues, waterfalls, and fountains. There is also a **Musée des Équipages** (Carriage Museum)—stocked with carriages, saddles, and a smithy—near the entrance. Check with the chateau office to see if there are any special events scheduled around the time of your visit—candlelight tours, concerts, and other delights sometimes adorn the Vaux-le-Vicomte schedule. ⊠ *Domaine de Vaux-le-Vicomte, 77950 Maincy,* ☎ *01–64–14–41–90,*

WEB *www.vaux-le-vicomte.com.* 🎟 *63 frs/€9.61, grounds and carriage museum only 49 frs/€7.50.* 🕐 *Château Easter–Nov. 11, daily 10–6. Candlelight visits May–Oct., Thurs. and Sat. 8:30–midnight (80 frs/€12.3).*

Dining

$ ✕ **L'Écureuil.** An imposing barn to the right of the château entrance has been transformed into this self-service cafeteria where, beneath the ancient rafters, you can enjoy fine steaks (insist yours is cooked enough), coffee, or a snack. The restaurant is open daily for lunch and tea, and for dinner during candlelit visits. ✉ *Château de Vaux-le-Vicomte. Reservations not accepted. MC, V.*

Fontainebleau and Vaux-le-Vicomte A to Z

CAR TRAVEL

From Paris's Porte d'Orléans or Porte d'Italie, take A6, then N7 to Fontainebleau (total distance 72 km/45 mi). Vaux-le-Vicomte is 21 km (13 mi) north of Fontainebleau. Take N6 to Melun, then N36 northeast (direction Meaux), turning right after 1½ km (1 mi) or so along D215.

GUIDED TOURS

Cityrama runs half-day trips to Fontainebleau. The cost is around 330 francs/€50 and the tours depart Wednesday, Friday, and Sunday at 1 or 1:45. Paris Vision offers half-day trips to Fontainebleau and other sights in the region.

➤ CONTACTS: **Cityrama** (✉ 4 pl. des Pyramides, Paris, ☏ 01–44–55–61–00). **Paris Vision** (✉ 214 rue de Rivoli, Paris, ☏ 01–42–60–30–01).

TRAIN TRAVEL

Fontainebleau is about 50 minutes from Paris's Gare de Lyon; take a bus to complete the 3-km (2-mi) trip from the station (Fontainebleau-Avon) to the château. Vaux-le-Vicomte is a 7-km (4-mi) taxi ride from the nearest station at Melun, served by regular trains from Paris and Fontainebleau. The taxi ride costs about 80–100 francs/€12.30–15.30.

VISITOR INFORMATION

➤ CONTACTS: **Fontainebleau** (✉ 4 rue Royale, 77300 Fontainebleau, ☏ 01–60–74–99–99).

GIVERNY

The village of Giverny has become a place of pilgrimage for art lovers. It was here that Claude Monet lived, for 43 years, until his death in 1926 at the age of 86, adorning his house with a water-lily garden that was, in essence, a three-dimensional Impressionist painting. After decades of neglect, his pretty pink house with green shutters, the **Maison et Jardin de Claude Monet** (Claude Monet House and Garden), his studios, and his garden with its famous lily pond were lovingly restored thanks to gifts from around the world and, in particular, from the United States. Late spring is perhaps the best time to visit, when the apple trees are in blossom and the garden is a riot of color. Try to avoid summer weekends and afternoons in July and August, when the limited capacity of Monet's home and gardens is pushed to the limit by busloads of tourists.

Monet was brought up in Normandy and, like many of the other Impressionists, was attracted by the soft light of the Seine Valley. After several years at Argenteuil, just north of Paris, he moved downriver to Giverny in 1883 along with his two sons, his mistress Alice Hoschedé (whom he later married), and her six children. By 1890, a prospering Monet was able to buy the house outright. Three years later, he purchased another plot of land across the lane to continue his gardening experiments, diverting the Epte River to make a pond.

Monet's house has a warm family feeling that may come as a welcome break after visiting stately French châteaux. The rooms have been restored to Monet's original designs: the kitchen with blue tiles, the buttercup-yellow dining room, and Monet's bedroom on the second floor. Reproductions of his own works, as well as some of the Japanese prints Monet avidly collected, are displayed around the house. His studios are also open for viewing.

The garden, with flowers spilling out across the paths, is as cheerful and natural as the house—quite unlike formal French gardens. The enchanting water garden, with its water lilies, bridges, and rhododendrons, is across the lane that runs to the side of the house and can be reached through a tunnel. The lilies and Japanese bridges became special features of his garden and now help to conjure up an image of a grizzle-bearded Monet dabbing cheerfully at his canvases—capturing changes in light and weather in a way that was to have a major influence on 20th-century art. From Giverny, you may want to continue up the Seine Valley to the site of another of his celebrated painting series: Rouen Cathedral. ⊠ *84 rue Claude-Monet,* ☎ *02–32–51–28–21,* WEB *www.giverny.org.* ⊠ *35 frs/€5.34, gardens only 25 frs/€3.81.* ⊙ *Apr.– Oct., Tues.–Sun. 10–6.*

The spacious, airy **Musée d'Art Américain** (American Art Museum), endowed by Chicago art patrons Daniel and Judith Terra, displays works by American Impressionists who were influenced by—and often studied with—Claude Monet. ⊠ *99 rue Claude-Monet,* ☎ *02–32–51–94– 65.* ⊠ *35 frs/€5.34.* ⊙ *Apr.–Oct., Tues.–Sun. 10–6.*

Dining

$$$ ✕ **Château de Brécourt.** Part of the stylish Relais & Châteaux group, this 17th-century brick château on extensive grounds is outside Giverny (you'll need a car to get here). The menu, serving creative spins on French cuisine, may include smoked salmon-and-crab cakes, turbot with caviar, and pears in a flaky pastry roasted in honey for dessert. ⊠ *Douains (11 km/7 mi west of Giverny via D181),* ☎ *02–32–52–40–50. AE, DC, MC, V.*

$–$$ ✕ **Les Jardins de Giverny.** This commendable restaurant, a few minutes' walk from Monet's house, has an old-fashioned dining room overlooking a rose garden. On the prix-fixe menus (130 francs, 170 francs, and 230 francs/€20, 26, and 35) you may get such inventive dishes as foie gras laced with applejack or seafood terrine with a mild pepper sauce. ⊠ *1 rue Milieu,* ☎ *02–32–21–60–80. AE, MC, V. Closed Mon., Nov. 1–15, and Feb.*

Giverny A to Z

CAR TRAVEL
Take expressway A13 from Paris to the Vernon exit (D181). Cross the Seine in Vernon and follow D5 to Giverny (total distance 84 km/ 52 mi).

GUIDED TOURS
Guided excursions are organized by American Express on either a half-day or full-day basis, combined with trips to Rouen. **Cityrama** run tours to Giverny, lasting about five hours, Tuesday–Saturday; cost is 400 francs/€61.

➤ CONTACTS: **American Express** (✉ 11 rue Scribe, Paris, ☎ 01–47–77–77–07). **Cityrama** (✉ 4 pl. des Pyramides, Paris, ☎ 01–44–55–61–00).

TRAIN TRAVEL

Take the train from Paris's Gare St-Lazare to Vernon (50 minutes). Giverny is 5½ km (3½ mi) away by bus or taxi, which you can get at the train station. Call the Vernon Tourist Office for information.

➤ CONTACTS: **Vernon Tourist Office** (☎ 02–32–51–39–60).

VERSAILLES

Numbers in the text correspond to numbers on the Versailles map.

Paris in the 17th century was a rowdy, rabble-ridden city. Louis XIV hated it and set about in search of a new power base. He settled on Versailles, 20 km (12 mi) west of Paris, where his father had a small château–hunting lodge.

❶ Today the **Château de Versailles** seems monstrously big, but it wasn't large enough for the army of 20,000 noblemen, servants, and hangers-on who moved in with Louis. A new city—a new capital, in fact—had to be constructed from scratch to accommodate them. Tough-thinking town planners promptly dreamt up vast mansions and avenues broader than the Champs-Élysées—all in bicep-flexing Baroque.

It was hardly surprising that Louis XIV's successors rapidly felt out of sync with their architectural inheritance. The Sun King's successors, Louis XV and Louis XVI, preferred to cower in small retreats in the gardens, well out of the mighty château's shadow. The two most famous of these structures are the Petit Trianon, a model of classical harmony and proportion built by Louis XV; and the Hameau, where Marie-Antoinette could play at being a shepherdess amid the ersatz rusticity of her Potemkin hamlet.

The contrast between the majestic and the domesticated is an important part of Versailles's appeal. But pomp and bombast dominate the mood here, and you won't need reminding that you're in the world's grandest palace—or one of France's most popular tourist attractions. The park outside is the ideal place to get your breath back. Le Nôtre's gardens represent formal landscaping at its most rigid and sophisticated.

The château was built under court architects Le Vau and Mansart between 1662 and 1690; the entrance is through the gilt-and-iron gates from huge place d'Armes. In the center of the building, across the sprawling cobbled forecourt, are the rooms that belonged to the king and queen. The two wings were occupied by the royal children and princes; attendants were up in the attics.

One of the highlights of the tour is the **Galerie des Glaces** (Hall of Mirrors), fully restored to its original dazzle. It was here that Bismarck proclaimed the unified German Empire in 1871, and the controversial Treaty of Versailles, asserting Germany's responsibility for World War I, was signed in 1919. The **Grands Appartements** (State Apartments) are formal; the **Petits Appartements** (Private Apartments), where royal family and friends lived, are on a more human scale. The intimate **Opéra Royal,** the first oval hall in France, was designed for Louis XV. Touch the "marble" loges—they're actually painted wood. The chapel, built by Mansart, is a study in white-and-gold solemnity. In 1997 the former state rooms and the sumptuous debate chamber of the **Aile du Midi** (South Wing) were opened to the public, with infrared headphone commentary (available in English) explaining Versailles's parliamentary his-

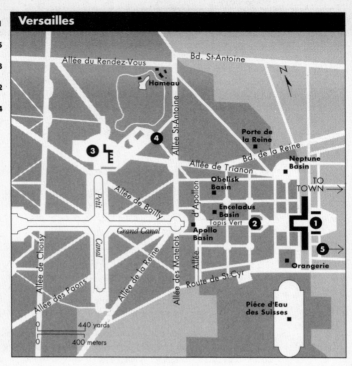

Versailles

tory. ☎ *01–30–83–77–88,* WEB *www.chateauversailles.fr.* ⊠ *Château 46 frs/€7, parliament exhibition 25 frs/€3.81 extra.* ☉ *May–Sept., Tues.–Sun. 9–6:30; Oct.–Apr., Tues.–Sun. 9–5:30. Opéra Royal 9:45– 3:30 (tours every 15 mins).*

❷ The 250-acre **Parc de Versailles** has woods, lawns, flower beds, statues, lakes, and fountains. An extensive tree-replacement scheme—necessary once a century (because the trees get too old, big, and unwieldy)—was launched at the start of 1998 to recapture the full impact of Le Nôtre's artful vistas; the scheme assumed fresh urgency after the ferocious storms of December 1999 decimated the park and felled another 5,000 trees. The fountains are turned on Sunday from May through September, making a fabulous spectacle. ⊠ *Park free, fountains 32 frs/€4.90.* ☉ *Grounds daily 7 am–dusk.*

❸ At one end of the Petit Canal, about 1½ km (1 mi) from the château, stands the **Grand Trianon,** a pink-marble pleasure palace built by Jules Hardouin-Mansart in the late 1680s. ⊠ *30 frs/€4.6 (joint ticket with Petit Trianon).* ☉ *May–Sept., Tues.–Sun. noon–6:30; Oct.–Apr., Tues.–Sun. noon–5:30.*

❹ The **Petit Trianon,** close to the Grand Trianon, is a sumptuously furnished neoclassical mansion erected in the 1760s by architect Jacques Gabriel. Louis XV had a superb botanical garden planted here; some of the trees from that era survive today. Louis XVI presented the Petit Trianon to Marie-Antoinette, who spent lavish sums creating an idealized world nearby, the charming **Hameau,** a hamlet of thatched-roof cottages, complete with water mill, lake, and pigeon loft. Here, the tragic queen played out her happiest days pretending to be a shepherdess tending a flock of perfumed sheep, and here, today, her spirit is stronger than anywhere else in France, making this a must-do for fans of the hapless Toinette. ✏ *30 frs/€4.60 (joint ticket with Grand Trianon).* ☉ *May–Sept., Tues.–Sun. noon–6:30; Oct.–Apr., Tues.–Sun. noon–5:30.*

⑤ Facing the château are the Trojan-size royal stables, the **Grandes Écuries** (Great Stables). Nowadays the **Musée des Carosses** (Carriage Museum) is housed here, with its distinguished array of royal and imperial carriages. ✉ *1 av. de Paris,* ☎ *01–30–21–54–82.* ✏ *20 frs/€3.* ☉ *Weekends 2–6.*

The **town of Versailles** is often overlooked. Although you may be tired from exploring the palace and park, it's worth strolling along the town's broad, leafy boulevards. The majestic scale of many buildings is a reminder that this was, after all, the capital of France from 1682 to 1789 (and again from 1871 to 1879). Visible farther to the right, as you look toward the town from the palace, is the dome of the austere **Cathédrale St-Louis** (✉ Pl. St-Louis), built from 1743 to 1754; it has a fine organ loft and two-tiered facade.

To the left of place d'Armes, beyond elegant, octagonal place Hoche, is the sturdy Baroque church of **Notre-Dame** (✉ At rue Hoche and rue de la Paroisse), built from 1684 to 1686 by Jules Hardouin-Mansart as the parish church for Louis XIV's brand-new town. The street in front of Notre-Dame, rue de la Paroisse, leads up to **place du Marché**, site of a magnificent morning market every Tuesday, Friday, and Sunday. The wide-ranging **Musée Lambinet,** behind Notre-Dame church, is an imposing 18th-century mansion with a maze of cozy rooms furnished with paintings, weapons, fans, and porcelain. ✉ *54 bd. de la Reine,* ☎ *01–39–50–30–32.* ✏ *30 frs/€4.60.* ☉ *Tues.–Sun. 2–5.*

Dining

$$$–$$$$ ✕ **Les Trois Marches.** One of the best-known restaurants in the Paris area, in the Trianon Palace Hotel near an entrance to the château park, serves chef Gérard Vié's creative dishes such as duckling roasted with vinegar and honey. The prix-fixe (320 francs/€49) weekday lunch is the most affordable option. ✉ *1 bd. de la Reine,* ☎ *01–39–50–13–21. Reservations essential. Jacket and tie. AE, DC, MC, V. Closed Aug.*

$$–$$$ ✕ **Café Trianon.** In the Palace Hotel Trianon, chef Benoist Bambaud serves traditional French cuisine: salmon, roast bream, confit de canard, and lamb with rosemary. The prix-fixe menus are your best bet. ✉ *1 bd. de la Reine,* ☎ *01–30–84–38–80. AE, DC, MC, V.*

$$ ✕ **Quai No. 1.** Barometers, sails, and model boats fill this small seafood restaurant. In summer you can enjoy your meal outside on the terrace. Fish with sauerkraut and home-smoked salmon are specialties; any dish on the two prix-fixe menus is a good value. ✉ *1 av. de St-Cloud,* ☎ *01–39–50–42–26. MC, V. Closed Mon. No dinner Sun.*

Versailles A to Z

CAR TRAVEL

From Paris, head west on highway A13 from Porte d'Auteuil (a total distance of 20 km/12 mi). Allow 15–30 minutes, depending on traffic.

GUIDED TOURS

Many guided-tour companies offer excursions to Versailles. **Paris Vision** arranges half- and full-day guided tours of Versailles for around 200 or 400 francs (€30 or 61). **Cityrama** is a popular Versailles tour-company option.

➤ CONTACTS: **Paris Vision** (✉ 214 rue de Rivoli, Paris, ☎ 01–42–60–30–01). **Cityrama** (✉ 4 pl. des Pyramides, Paris, ☎ 01–44–55–61–00).

TRAIN TRAVEL

Three train routes travel between Paris and Versailles (20–30 minutes away). The RER-C to Versailles Rive-Gauche takes you closest to the château (600 yards away via avenue de Sceaux). The other trains run from Paris's Gare St-Lazare to Versailles Rive-Droite (closer to the Trianons and town market but 1 km/½ mi from the château via rue du Maréchal-Foch and avenue de St-Cloud) and from Paris's Gare Montparnasse to Versailles-Chantiers (1 km/½ mi to the château via rue des États-Généraux and avenue de Paris). From Versailles-Chantiers, some trains continue on to Chartres.

VISITOR INFORMATION

➤ CONTACTS: **Versailles Office du Tourisme** (⊠ 7 rue des Reservoirs, 78000 Versailles, ☏ 01–39–50–36–22).

8 BACKGROUND AND ESSENTIALS

Portrait of Paris

Books and Videos

Chronology

Smart Travel Tips A to Z

Vocabulary

Menu Guide

PARIS À LA PARISIENNE

It is midnight at the neighborhood brasserie. Waiters swathed in starchy white glance discreetly at their watches as a family—mother, son, and wife—sip the last of a bottle of Chiroubles and scrape up the remains of their steak tartare on silverware dexterously poised with arched wrists. They are all wearing scarves: the mother's is a classic silk *carré*, tastefully folded at the throat; the wife's is Indian gauze and glitters; the son's is wool and hangs like a prayer shawl over his black turtleneck. Finished, they stir their coffee without looking. They smoke: the mother, Gitanes; the son, Marlboros; the wife rolls her own from a silver case. Alone, they act out their personal theater, uncontrived and unobserved, their Doisneauesque tableau reflected only in the etched-glass mirrors around them, enhanced by the sobriety of their dress and the pallor of their Gallic skin.

Whoever first said that "God found Paris too perfect, so he invented the Parisians" had it wrong. This extraordinary maquette of a city, with its landscape of mansards and chimneys, its low-slung bridges and vast boulevards, is nothing but a rough-sketched stage set that drinks its color from the lifeblood of those infamous Parisians whom everyone claims to hate but whom everyone loves to emulate.

Mythologized for their arrogance, charm, and savoir faire—as well as their disdain for the foreigners they find genetically incapable of sharing these characteristics—the Parisians continue to mesmerize. For the generations of American and English voyeurs who have ventured curiously, enviously into countless mirrored brasseries, downed numerous bottles of *cuvée maison,* fumbled at nautical knots in newly bought scarves, even suffered squashed berets and unfil-tered Gauloises, the Parisian remains inimitable—and infinitely fascinating.

Alternately patronizing and self-effacing, they move through their big-city lives with enviable style and urban grit. They are chronically thin, despite the truckloads of beef stew, pâté, and tart Tatin they consume without blushing. They still make the cigarette look glamorous—and a graceful bit of stage business indispensable to good talk—in spite of the gas-mask levels of smoke they generate. They stride over bridges aloof to the monuments framed in every sweeping perspective, yet they discourse—lightly, charmingly—on Racine, NATO, and the latest ruling of the Académie Française. They are proud, practical, often witty, and always chic, from the thrift-shop style of the Sorbonne student to the Chanel suit on the thin shoulders of a well-boned *dame d'un certain âge.*

Ferociously (with some justice) in love with their own culture—theater, literature, film, art, architecture, haute cuisine, and haute couture—Parisians worship France as ardently as New Yorkers dismiss the rest of America. While Manhattanites berate the nonentities west of the Hudson, Parisians romanticize the rest of France, making an art of the weekend foray and the regional vacation: why should we go *à l'étranger* (abroad) when we have the Dordogne, the Auvergne, and Bretagne?

And for all their vulnerability to what they frame as the "American Assault," for every Disney store, action film, and McDonald's in Paris (not to mention Benetton and Laura Ashley, and France's own Celio, Orcade, and Descamps chains), there is a plethora of unique shops selling all-white blouses, African bracelets, dog jackets, and Art Deco jewelry.

And for every commercial bookstore chain there are five tiny *libraries* selling tooled-leather encyclopedias, collections of out-of-print plays, and yellow paperbacks lovingly pressed in waxed paper. The famous *bouquinistes* hover like squatters along the Seine, their folding metal boxes opening to showcase a treasure trove of old magazines, scholarly journals, and hand-colored botanical prints that flap from clothespins in the wind. Yet they are not nomads, these bouquinistes: dormant through winter, their metal stands are fixtures as permanent and respectable as those of the medieval merchants that built shops along the Pont Neuf. They are determinedly Parisian—individual, independent, and one-of-a-kind.

But in spite of their fierce individuality, Parisians also demand that certain conformities be followed. And here the gap between native and visitor widens. If Parisians treat tourists a bit like occupying forces—disdainfully selling them Beaujolais-Nouveau in July, seating them by the kitchen doors, refusing to understand honest attempts at French—they have formed their opinions based on bitter experience. The waiter who scorches tourists with flared nostrils and firmly turned back was trained to respect his métier—meaning not pouring Coke with foie gras or bringing the check with dessert. The meal is a sacred ritual here, and diverging from the norm is tantamount to disgrace.

Doing as the Parisians do, you can go a long way toward closing the gap of disdain. When dining, for example, give yourself over to the meal. Order a kir as an aperitif, instead of a whiskey or beer. Drink wine or mineral water with your meal. Order coffee *after* dessert, not with it. And accept the fact that diet sodas are rarely available in restaurants.

The wine will come chilled, aired, and ready for tasting with the respect usually reserved for a holy relic. Enjoy each course, sipping, discussing, digesting leisurely; the waiter will not be pressed by hurried tourists. When you're done eating, align your silverware on the plate (a sign for the waiter to clear). Cheese can be the climax of the meal, well worth skipping dessert if necessary, and a magnificent way to finish the wine. Have your coffee after dessert and, without exception, black with sugar; a milky froth will not do on a full stomach. The art of stirring *un express* in Paris rivals the art of scarf-tying.

Ask for *l'addition*; the waiter will not commit the gaffe of bringing the check uninvited. And no matter how deeply you enter into your role as Parisian manqué, avoid saying "*Garçon!*" (Say "*S'il vous plait*" instead.) These are rules that apply at the most unassuming corner bistro and the grandest three-star restaurant; following them can thaw the waiterly chill that can render a meal unforgettable—for all the wrong reasons—and can make for meals that are as memorable as an evening at the Opéra de la Bastille, complete with sets and choreography.

It is this fixed attention to experience and detail that sets the Parisians apart. Desk-eaters they are not: When they work, they work without a coffee break. When they eat, business still grinds to a halt. Weekends are sacred. And oh, do they vacation, all of them at once, all of them abandoning Paris in August with a fierceness of purpose that mirrors their commitment to food—an all-night drive, a rental booked months in advance.

By matching that Parisian passion for the complete, the correct, the comme il faut, your own experience will be all the more authentic. Having eaten with proper reverence, keep your sightseeing agenda at the same lofty level. If you go to the Louvre, spend the day; do not lope through the wide corridors in search of *La Joconde* (*Mona Lisa*). You can leave for a three-hour lunch, if you choose, and come back with the same ticket, even avoiding the lines by reentering via the Passage Richelieu. If time won't allow an all-day survey, do as the locals do: choose an era and immerse yourself. Then take a break and plunge into another. Eavesdrop on a guided tour. Go back and look at a painting again. And take the time to stare at the ceil-

Portrait

ings: the architecture alone of this historic monument merits a day's tour.

As you apply yourself to the Parisian experience in spirit, diverge in fact: walk. The natives may prefer to sit in a café or even hurry straight home by métro (*"métro, boulot, dodo"*— "métro, work, sleep"—as the saying goes). You, as a visitor, are obliged to wander down tortuous medieval streets; up vast boulevards so over-scaled you seem to gain no ground; over bridges that open up broad perspectives on illuminated monuments that outnumber even those in Rome.

They are all there, the clichés of Paris romance: the moon over the Seine reflected in the wake of the Bateaux-Mouches; the steps Leslie Caron blushed down in *An American in Paris*; the lovers kissing under the lime tree pollards. But there are surprises, too: a troop of hunting horns striking unearthly sonorities under a resonant bridge; flocks of wild geese flying low over the towers of Notre-Dame; and a ragged expatriate writer leaving a well-scraped plat du jour on the table as he bolts away from the bill. (*C'est dommage*: he would have been well fed by Ragueneau, the baker-writer in *Cyrano de Bergerac* who opened his Paris pastry shop to starving poets.)

The more resourceful you are, the more surprises you will unearth in your Paris wanderings. Follow the strains of Lully into a chamber orchestra rehearsal in St-Julien-le-Pauvre; if you're quiet and still, you may not be asked to leave. Brave the smoking lounge at intermission at the Comédie-Française and you'll find the battered leather chair that the young actor Molière sat in as L'Invalide Imaginaire. Take the métro to

L'Armée du Salut (Salvation Army) in the 13e arrondissement, and you'll not only find Art Deco percolators and hand-knit stockings but you'll also be inside the futuristic curves of a 1933 Le Corbusier masterwork.

Tear yourself away from the big-name museums and you'll discover a world of small galleries. Go in: you don't have to press your nose to the glass. The exhibits are constantly changing and you can always find one relevant to Paris—Frank Horvat's photos of Pigalle or a Christo retrospective, including the Pont Neuf wrappings. It is worth buying one of the weekly guides—*Pariscope, L'Officiel des Spectacles, Figaroscope*—and browsing through it over your *café crème* and croissant.

Resourcefulness, after all, is a sign of enthusiasm and appreciation—for when you are well informed and acutely tuned in to the nuances of the city, you can approach it as a connoisseur. Then you can peacefully co-exist with Parisians, partaking, in their passion for this marvelous old city, from the same plate of cultural riches. Hemingway, as usual, put it succinctly: "It was always pleasant crossing bridges in Paris." Cultural bridges, too.

Bon séjour à Paris.

— Nancy Coons

Nancy Coons's latest contributions to the Fodor's list are *Provence and the Côte d'Azur* and *Escape to Provence*. She has written on food and culture for *National Geographic Traveler*, the *Wall Street Journal*, *Opera News*, and *European Travel & Life*. Based in Luxembourg and France since 1987, she now works out of her 300-year-old farmhouse in Lorraine, which she shares with her husband and two daughters.

WHAT TO READ AND WATCH BEFORE YOU GO

Books

For a look at American expatriates in Paris between the wars, read *Sylvia Beach and the Lost Generation* by Noel R. Fitch or *A Moveable Feast* by Ernest Hemingway. Flaubert's *Sentimental Education* includes excellent descriptions of Paris and its environs, as do many Zola novels. Other recommended titles include Charles Dickens's *A Tale of Two Cities,* Henry James's *The Ambassadors,* Colette's *The Complete Claudine,* Hemingway's *The Sun Also Rises,* and Gertrude Stein's *Paris, France.* George Orwell's *Down and Out in Paris and London* gives an account of life on a shoestring in these two European capitals. More essays about Paris are excerpted in *A Place in the World Called Paris.* Yet another anthology of essays on Paris is the *Travelers' Tales Guides: Paris.*

Jules Verne's *Paris in the Twentieth Century* provides a view from the past of Paris in the future. A history of Paris from the Revolution to the Belle Epoque is found in Johannes Willms's *Paris: Capital of Europe. A Traveller's History of Paris* by Robert Cole is a good overview. Tyler Stovall's *Paris Noir: African-Americans in the City of Light* is a history of African-Americans in Paris. *Inside Paris* is a photography book of Paris interiors. Two unconventional guides to Paris are Karen Elizabeth Gordon's witty and surreal *Paris Out of Hand* and Lawrence Osborne's *Paris Dreambook.*

Three memoirs by Americans who have lived in Paris are Art Buchwald's *I'll Always Have Paris,* Edmund White's *Our Paris,* and Stanley Karnow's *Paris in the Fifties. Paris Notebooks* by Mavis Gallant is her observations of Paris life. *Between Meals* by A. J. Liebling looks at the art of eating in Paris. *A Corner in the Marais: Memoir of a Paris Neighborhood* is Alex Karmel's history of the neighborhood. More recently, Edmund White and Hubert Sorin weighed in with *Our Paris: Sketches with Memory,* while Adam Gopnik, the distinguished Paris-based correspondent of the *New Yorker* hit the best-seller lists in 2000 with his *Paris to the Moon.*

Videos

For a glimpse of Paris before you go, rent one of the following films: *Gigi* (1958; in English), Hollywood's most opulent valentine to Paris won the Best Picture Oscar, thanks to its memorable Lerner and Loewe musical score and magnificent sets designed by Cecil Beaton; *An American in Paris* (1951; in English), a Hollywood musical with a great Gershwin score stars Gene Kelly and is another Best Picture Oscar winner; *Charade* (1963; in English) is a comic thriller starring Cary Grant and Audrey Hepburn; *How to Steal a Million* (1966; in English) is a chic art-theft caper starring Peter O'Toole, Audrey Hepburn, and many soigné Paris settings; *À Bout de Souffle* (*Breathless,* 1960; in French), by Jean-Luc Godard, is about a car thief who flees with his American girlfriend. Others to try include *Diva* (1981; in French), about a singer in Paris who becomes involved in murder and drug smuggling; *Funny Face* (1957; in English), a Roger Edens musical with Audrey Hepburn and Fred Astaire immortalizing the high-fashion world of 1950s Paris; *Last Tango in Paris* (1972; in English), a Bertolucci film starring Marlon Brando; *Ready to Wear* (1994; in English), a Robert Altman film about the fashion industry; and *Zazie Dans le Métro* (1960; in French), a Louis Malle film about the adventures of a 10-year-old girl in Paris.

PARIS AT A GLANCE

ca. 200 BC   The Parisii—Celtic fishermen—live on the Ile de la Cité.

52   Romans establish a colony, Lutetia, on the Ile de la Cité, which soon spreads to both Seine banks. Under the Romans, Paris becomes a major administrative and commercial center, its situation on a low, defensible crossing point on the Seine making it a natural communications nexus.

ca. AD 250   St. Denis, the first bishop of Paris and France's patron saint, is martyred in Christian persecutions.

451   The hordes of Attila the Hun are said to be halted before reaching Paris by the prayers of St. Geneviève (died 512); in fact they are halted by an army of Romans and mercenaries. Few traces of the Roman era in Paris remain. Most of those that do are from the late empire, including the catacombs of Montparnasse and the baths that form part of the National Museum of the Middle Ages.

The Merovingian Dynasty (486–751)

507   Clovis, king of the Franks and founder of the Merovingian dynasty, makes Paris his capital. Many churches are built, including the abbey that will become St-Germain-des-Prés. Commerce is active; Jewish and Asian communities are founded along the Seine.

The Carolingian Dynasty (751–987)

Under the Carolingians, Paris ceases to be the capital of France and sinks into political insignificance, but it remains a major administrative, commercial, and ecclesiastical center—and, as a result of the last, one of the foremost centers of culture and learning west of Constantinople.

845–87   Parisians restore the fortifications of the city, which are repeatedly sacked by the Vikings (up to 877).

The Capetian Dynasty (987–1328)

987   Hugh Capet, Count of Paris, becomes king. Paris, once more the capital, grows in importance. The Ile de la Cité is the seat of government, commerce makes its place on the Right Bank, and a university develops on the Left Bank.

1140–63   The Gothic style of architecture appears at St-Denis: Notre-Dame, begun in 1163, sees the style come to maturity. In the late 12th century streets are paved.

1200   Philippe-Auguste charters a university, builds walls around Paris, and constructs a fortress, the first Louvre.

1243–þ46   The Sainte-Chapelle is built to house the reputed crown of thorns brought by Louis IX (St. Louis) from Constantinople.

1253   The Sorbonne is founded, to become a major theological center.

The Valois Dynasty (1328–1589)

1348–49   The Black Death and the beginning of the Hundred Years' War bring misery and strife to Paris.

1364–80   Charles V works to restore prosperity to Paris. The Bastille is built to defend new city walls. The Louvre is converted into a royal palace.

1420–37   After the battle of Agincourt, Henry V of England enters Paris. Joan of Arc leads an attempt to recapture the city (1429). Charles VII of France drives out the English (1437).

1469   The first printing house in France is established at the Sorbonne.

1515–47   François I imports Italian artists, including Leonardo da Vinci, to work on his new palace at Fontainebleau, bringing the Renaissance to France. François resumes work on the Louvre and builds the Hôtel de Ville in the new style. The Tour St-Jacques (bell tower) is completed (all that now remains of the church of St-Jacques-de-la-Boucherie).

1562–98   In the Wars of Religion, Paris remains a Catholic stronghold. On August 24, 1572, Protestant leaders are killed in the St. Bartholomew's Day Massacre.

The Bourbon Dynasty (1589–1789)

1598–1610   Henri IV begins his reign after converting to Catholicism, declaring "Paris is worth a mass." He embellishes Paris, laying out the Renaissance place des Vosges, first in a new Parisian style of town planning that will last until the 19th century. In 1610, Henri is assassinated. His widow, Maria de' Medici, begins the Luxembourg Palace and Gardens.

1624   Cardinal Richelieu is appointed minister to Louis XIII and concludes the ongoing religious persecution by strictly imposing Catholicism on the country. In 1629 he begins construction of the Palais-Royal.

1635   The Académie Française is founded.

1643–1715   Reign of Louis XIV, the Sun King. Paris rebels against him in the Fronde uprisings (1648–52). Early in his reign, he creates a new palace at Versailles, away from the Paris mobs. It becomes the largest royal complex in Europe, the symbolic center of a centralized French state. His minister of finance, Colbert, establishes the Gobelins factory-school for tapestries and furniture (1667). André Le Nôtre transforms the Jardin de Tuileries (Tuileries Gardens) and lays out the Champs-Élysées (1660s). Louis founds the Hôtel des Invalides (1670).

1715–89   During the reigns of Louis XV and Louis XVI, Paris becomes the European center of culture and style.

1783   New outer walls of Paris are begun, incorporating customs gatehouses to control the flow of commerce into the city. The walls, which include new parks, triple the area of Paris.

Chronology

The Revolution, Empire and Restoration (1789–1814)

1789-99 The French Revolution begins as the Bastille is stormed on July 14, 1789. The First Republic is established. Louis XVI and his queen, Marie-Antoinette, are guillotined in place de la Concorde. Almost 2,600 others perish in the same way during the Terror (1793–94).

1799-1814 Napoléon begins to convert Paris into a neoclassical city—the Empire style. The Arc de Triomphe and the first iron bridges across the Seine are built. In 1805 he orders the completion of the Louvre Museum.

1815 The Congress of Vienna ensures the restoration of the Bourbon dynasty following the fall of Napoléon.

1828-42 Urban and political discontent causes riots and demonstrations in the streets. Yet another uprising replaces Charles X with Louis-Philippe's liberal monarchy in 1830. Napoléon's remains are returned to Paris in 1840.

The Second Republic and the Second Empire (1848–70)

1852 In 1852 further additions to the Louvre are made. Under Napoléon III, the Alsatian town planner Baron Haussmann guts large areas of medieval Paris to lay out broad boulevards linking important squares. Railroad stations and the vast covered markets at Les Halles are built.

1862 Victor Hugo's *Les Misérables* is published in Paris while the liberal author remains in exile by order of Napoléon III.

1870-71 Franco-Prussian War; Paris is besieged by Prussian troops; starvation is rampant—each week during the winter, 5,000 people die. The Paris Commune, an attempt by the citizens to take power in 1871, results in bloody suppression and much property damage (the Tuileries Palace is razed). Hugo returns to Paris.

The Third Republic (1871–1944)

1875 The Paris Opéra is inaugurated after 14 years of construction.

1889 The Eiffel Tower is built for the Paris World Exhibition.

1900 The International Exhibition in Paris popularizes the curving forms of Art Nouveau with the entrance for the newly opened Paris métro.

1914-18 World War I. The Germans come within 15 km (9 mi) of Paris (so close that Paris taxis are used to carry troops to the front).

1919 The Treaty of Versailles is signed, formally ending World War I.

1925 International Decorative Art exhibition consecrates the restrained, sophisticated design style now known as Art Deco.

1918-39 Between the wars, Paris attracts artists and writers, including Americans Ernest Hemingway and Gertrude Stein. Paris nourishes Existentialism, a philosophical movement, and major modern art movements—Constructivism, Dadaism, Surrealism.

1939–45   World War II. Paris falls to the Germans in 1940. The French government moves to Vichy and collaborates with the Nazis. The Resistance movement uses Paris as a base. The Free French Army, under Charles de Gaulle, joins with the Allies to liberate Paris after D Day, August 1944.

The Fourth and Fifth Republics (1944–present)

1944–46   De Gaulle moves the provisional government to Paris.

1958–69   De Gaulle is president of the Fifth Republic.

1960s–70s   Paris undergoes physical changes: Dirty buildings are cleaned, beltways are built around the city, and expressways are driven through the heart of it. Major new building projects (especially La Défense) are banished to the outskirts.

1962   De Gaulle grants Algeria independence; growing tensions with immigrant workers in Paris and other cities.

1968   Parisian students declare the Sorbonne a commune in riots that lead to de Gaulle's resignation.

1969   Les Halles market is moved and its buildings demolished.

1977   The Centre Pompidou opens to controversy, marking a high point in modern political intervention in the arts and public architecture.

1981   François Mitterrand (1916–96) is elected president. Embarks on a major building program throughout the city.

1986   Musée d'Orsay opens in the former Gare d'Orsay train station.

1989   Paris celebrates the bicentennial of the French Revolution. The Louvre's glass pyramid, the Grande Arche of La Défense, and the Opéra Bastille are completed.

1992   Disneyland Paris opens at Marne-la-Vallée east of Paris.

1994   Paris–London rail link via Channel Tunnel becomes operational.

1995   Paris Mayor Jacques Chirac replaces François Mitterrand as the president of France.

1998   Amid scenes of popular fervor in Paris not seen since the Liberation in 1944, France hosts and wins the Soccer World Cup.

1999   Hurricane on December 26 devastates Bois de Boulogne, Bois de Vincennes, and park of Versailles. New Métro Line (No. 14) links Madeleine to new national library in Tolbiac, southeast Paris.

2000   Paris marks the new millennium with a scintillating new lighting scheme for the Eiffel Tower, a giant wheel on Place de la Concorde, and a huge statue of Charles de Gaulle on the Champs-Élysées. The facade of the Opéra is cleaned and the Centre Pompidou reopens after major renovation. A new pedestrian bridge links the Musée d'Orsay to the Tuileries.

2001   The world-ranking Musée Guimet collection of Asian art reopens after many years. Musée Grevin waxworks museum undergoes $7 million face-lift

ESSENTIAL INFORMATION

ADDRESSES

Addresses in Paris are fairly straight-forward: there is the number, the street name and, often, the location in one of Paris's 20 arrondissements (districts): for instance, Paris 75010 or, simply, the last two digits, 10ᵉ, both of which indicate that the address is in the 10th. Due to its large size, the 16th arrondissement has two numbers assigned to it: 75016 and 75116. For the layout of Paris's arrondissements, consult the map at the end of this section. They are laid out in a spiral, beginning from the area around the Louvre (1ᵉʳ arron-dissement), then moving clockwise through the Marais, the Quartier Latin, St-Germain, and then out from the city center to the outskirts until it reaches Menilmontant/Père-Lachaise (20ᵉ arrondissement). Occasionally you may see an address with a number plus *bis*—for instance, 20 bis rue Vavin. This indicates that 20 bis is the next entrance or door down from 20 rue Vavin. Please note that in France, you enter a building on the ground floor, or *rez-de-chausée* (RC or 0), and go up one floor to the first floor, or *premier étage*. General address terms used in this book to keep in mind are: *av.* (abbreviation for ave-nue); *bd.* (abbreviation for boule-vard); *carrefour* (crossway); *cours* (promenade); *passage* (passageway); *quai* (quay/wharf/pier); *rue* (street); *sq.* (abbreviation for square).

AIR TRAVEL TO & FROM
PARIS

As one of the premier destinations in the world, Paris is serviced by a great many international carriers and a surprising number of U.S.-based companies. **Air France** is the French flag carrier and offers numerous flights (often several per day) between Paris's Charles de Gaulle airport and New York City's JFK airport;

Newark, New Jersey; Washington, D.C.'s Reagan airport; Miami; Chicago; Houston; San Francisco; Los Angeles; Toronto; Montréal; and Mexico City. American-based carriers are usually less expensive but offer, on the whole, fewer nonstop direct flights. **TWA** offers daily nonstop flights to Paris from New York City's JFK; in peak season, flights from Boston's Logan International airport, Washington, D.C., and St. Louis are offered, as well as connecting flights from Los Angeles. **Delta Airlines** is a popular U.S.–France carrier; depar-tures to Paris leave Atlanta, Cincin-nati, and New York City's JFK, while Delta's regional flights link airports through the southeast U.S and the Midwest with its main international hub in Atlanta. Travelers in the north-east and southwest of the United States often use **Continental Airlines,** whose nonstop Paris flights generally depart from Newark and Houston; in peak season, they often offer daily departures. Another popular carrier is **United Airlines,** with nonstop flights to Paris from Chicago, Washington, D.C., and San Francisco. **American Airlines** also offers daily nonstop flights to Paris's Orly airport from numerous cities, including New York City's JFK, Boston, Miami, Chicago, and Dallas/Fort Worth. **Northwest** offers a daily departure to Paris from its hub in Detroit; connections from Seattle, Minneapolis, and numerous other airports link up to Detroit. In Canada, Air France and **Air Canada** are the leading choices for departures from Toronto and Montréal; in peak season, departures are often on a daily basis. From London, Air France, **British Airways,** and **British Midland** are the leading carriers, with up to 15 flights daily in peak season. In addi-tion, direct routes link Manchester, Edinburgh, and Southampton with Paris. Considering the expense of this short flight, however, more and more travelers are using train transport via the Eurostar Express through the Channel Tunnel. Options are more limited for travelers to Paris from Australia and New Zealand, who usually wind up taking British Airways and **Qantas** flights to London, then connections to Paris.

BOOKING

When you book **look for nonstop flights** and **remember that "direct" flights stop at least once.** Try to avoid connecting flights, which require a change of plane. For more booking tips and to check prices and make on-line flight reservations, log on to www.fodors.com.

CARRIERS

➤ MAJOR AIRLINES: **Air Canada** (☎ 800/776–3000 in the U.S. and Canada). **Air France** (☎ 800/237–2747 in the U.S.; 08–02–80–28–02 in France; WEB www.airfrance.com). **American Airlines** (☎ 800/433–7300 in the U.S.; 01–69–32–73–07 in France; WEB www.aa.com). **British Airways** (☎ 800/247–9297 in the U.S.; 0345/222111 in the U.K.; 08–25–82–54–00 in France; WEB www.britishairways.com). **Continental** (☎ 800/231–0856 in the U.S.; 01–42–99–09–09 in France; WEB www.continental.com). **Delta** (☎ 800/241–4141 in the U.S.; 08–00–35–40–80 in France; WEB www.delta.com). **Northwest** (☎ 800/225–2525 in the U.S.; 01–42–66–90–00 in France; WEB www.klm.com). **Qantas** (☎ 800/227–4500 in the U.S.; 08–03–84–68–46 in France; WEB www.qantas.com). **TWA** (☎ 800/892–4141 in the U.S.; 08–01–89–28–92 in France; WEB www.twa.com). **United** (☎ 800/538–2929 in the U.S.; 08–01–72–72–72 in France; WEB www.unitedairlines.com). **US Airways** (☎ 800/428–4322 in the U.S.; 08–20–30–49–23 in France; WEB www.usairways.com).

➤ TRAVEL BETWEEN THE U.K. AND FRANCE: **Air France** (☎ 020/8742–6600 in the U.K.; 08–02–80–28–02 in France; WEB www.airfrance.com). **British Airways** (☎ 0345/222–111 in the U.K.; 08–02–80–29–02 in France; WEB www.britishairways.com). **British Midland** (☎ 020/8754–7321; 0345/554–554 in the U.K.; 01–48–62–55–

65 in France; WEB www.british-midland.com).

➤ TRAVEL WITHIN FRANCE: **Air France** (☎ 800/237–2747 in the U.S.; 08–02–80–28–02 in France; WEB www.airfrance.com). **Air Liberté** (☎ 08–03–80–58–05; WEB www.air-liberte.fr).

CHECK-IN & BOARDING

You can save on air travel within Europe if you plan on traveling to and from Paris aboard Air France. If you **sign up for Air France's Euro Flyer program,** you can buy between three and nine flight coupons, valid on the airline's flights to more than 100 European cities. At $120 each (April–October) and $99 each (November–March), these coupons are a good deal, and the fine print still allows you plenty of freedom.

Assuming that not everyone with a ticket will show up, airlines routinely overbook planes. When everyone does, airlines ask for volunteers to give up their seats. In return, these volunteers usually get a certificate for a free flight and are rebooked on the next flight out. If there are not enough volunteers, the airline must choose who will be denied boarding. The first to get bumped are passengers who checked in late and those flying on discounted tickets, so **get to the gate and check in as early as possible,** especially during peak periods.

Always **bring a government-issued photo ID to the airport;** a passport is best. You may be asked to show it before you are allowed to check in.

CUTTING COSTS

The least expensive airfares to Paris must usually be purchased in advance and are nonrefundable. It's smart to **call a number of airlines, and when you are quoted a good price, book it on the spot**—the same fare may not be available the next day. Always **check different routings** and look into using different airports. Travel agents, especially low-fare specialists, are helpful.

Consolidators are another good source. They buy tickets for scheduled international flights at reduced rates from the airlines, then sell them at prices that beat the best fare available directly from the airlines, usually without restrictions. Sometimes you can even get your money back if you need to return the ticket. Carefully read the fine print detailing penalties for changes and cancellations, and **confirm your consolidator reservation with the airline.**

When you **fly as a courier,** you trade your checked-luggage space for a ticket deeply subsidized by a courier service. There are restrictions on when you can book and how long you can stay.

➤ CONSOLIDATORS: **Cheap Tickets** (☎ 800/377–1000). **Discount Airline Ticket Service** (☎ 800/576–1600). **Unitravel** (☎ 800/325–2222). **Up & Away Travel** (☎ 212/889–2345). **World Travel Network** (☎ 800/409–6753).

➤ COURIERS: **Air Courier Association** (✉ 15000 W. 6th Ave., Suite 203, Golden, CO 80401, ☎ 800/282–1202, WEB www.aircourier.org). **International Association of Air Travel Couriers** (✉ 220 S. Dixie Hwy. No. 3, Box 1349, Lake Worth, FL, 33460, ☎ 561/582–8320, FAX 561/582–1581, WEB www.courier.org). **Now Voyager Travel** (✉ 74 Varick St., Suite 307, New York, NY 10013).

ENJOYING THE FLIGHT

For more legroom, **request an emergency-aisle seat.** Don't sit in the row in front of the emergency aisle or in front of a bulkhead, where seats may not recline. If you have dietary concerns, **ask for special meals when booking.** These can be vegetarian, low-cholesterol, or kosher, for example. On long flights, try to maintain a normal routine, to help fight jet lag. At night, **get some sleep.** By day, **eat light meals, drink water** (not alcohol), and **move around the cabin** to stretch your legs. For additional jet-lag tips consult *Fodor's FYI: Travel Fit & Healthy* (available at bookstores everywhere).

FLYING TIMES

Flying time to Paris is 7 hours from New York, 9½ hours from Chicago, and 11 hours from Los Angeles. Flying time from the United Kingdom to Paris is 1½ hours.

HOW TO COMPLAIN

If your baggage goes astray or your flight goes awry, complain right away. Most carriers require that you **file a claim immediately.**

➤ AIRLINE COMPLAINTS: U.S. Department of Transportation **Aviation Consumer Protection Division** (✉ C-75, Room 4107, Washington, DC 20590, ☎ 202/366–2220, WEB www.dot.gov/airconsumer). **Federal Aviation Administration Consumer Hotline** (☎ 800/322–7873).

AIRPORTS & TRANSFERS

The major airports are Charles de Gaulle (also known as Roissy), 26 km (16 mi) northeast of Paris, and Orly, 16 km (10 mi) south of Paris. It doesn't really matter which one you fly into; both are easily accessible to Paris, though Roissy is the only one with a TGV (high-speed train) station.

➤ AIRPORT INFORMATION: **Charles de Gaulle/Roissy** (☎ 01–48–62–22–80 in English). **Orly** (☎ 01–49–75–15–15, WEB www.french-airports.com).

AIRPORT TRANSFERS

Charles de Gaulle/Roissy: From the Charles de Gaulle airport, **the least expensive way to get into Paris is on the RER-B line,** the suburban express train, which leaves from beneath Terminal 2 (look for signs for the RER in the airport terminal; you may have to catch the free shuttle to get to the RER station, which is only a short ride away). Trains to central Paris (Les Halles, St-Michel, Luxembourg) depart every 15 minutes. The fare (including métro connection) is 49 francs/€7.32, and journey time is about 35 minutes. Note that you have to carry your luggage down to the train tracks, and trains can be crowded if you are traveling during rush hour.

Another way to get into Paris is to **take the Air France bus** between Charles de Gaulle airport and the city (you needn't have flown Air France to use this service). Buses run every 12–20 minutes between the airport and Montparnasse, as well as between the airport and the Arc de Triomphe, with a stop at the Air France air terminal at Porte Maillot. The fare is 65 francs/€9.92, and journey time is about 40 minutes. Another option is to **take Roissybus, operated by the Paris Transit Authority,** which runs between Charles de Gaulle and the Opéra every 15 minutes; the cost is 48 francs/€7.32. Note that you have to hail the bus that you want—it will not stop automatically—and that rush-hour traffic can make the trip slow.

For a comfortable, hassle-free arrival in Paris, you can **arrange a ride with Paris Airports Service or Airport Shuttle,** and a bilingual chauffeur will be waiting with a minivan to drive you directly to your destination. Rates are set so there are no unpleasant surprises due to poor traffic conditions. Prices are economic— approximately 120 francs/€19 for one person and 89 francs/€14 per person for two or more people traveling together, and can be prepaid by credit card. It is best to call, fax, or e-mail your request at least 24 hours in advance, noting your flight number, expected time of arrival, and your address in Paris.

Taxis are your least desirable mode of transportation into the city. If you are traveling at peak tourist times, you may have to stand in a very long line with a lot of other disgruntled European travelers (most of whom smoke). Journey times, and as a consequence, prices, are therefore unpredictable. At best, the journey takes 30 minutes but it can take as long as one hour. The average fare falls between 170 francs/ €26 and 300 francs/€46. You can ask for a quote before getting into the taxi, but it is almost certain that your driver (grumpy) will respond with a shrug. There is also a 6 franc/€.91 supplement per piece of luggage.

Orly: From the Orly airport, **the most economical way to get into Paris is to take the RER-C or Orlyrail line;** catch the free shuttle bus from the terminal to the train station. Trains to Paris leave every 15 minutes. The fare is 30 francs/€4.6, and journey time is about 35 minutes. Another option is to **take the monorail service, Orlyval,** which runs between the Antony RER-B station and Orly airport every

7 minutes. The fare to downtown Paris is 57 francs/€8.70.

You can also **take an Air France bus** from Orly to Les Invalides on the Left Bank and Montparnasse; these run every 12 minutes (you need not have flown on Air France to use this service). The fare is 50 francs/€7.60, and journey time is between 30 and 45 minutes, depending on traffic. The Paris Transit Authority's **Orlybus is yet another option;** buses leave every 15 minutes for the Denfert-Rochereau métro station; the cost is 35 francs/€5.3.

With advance reservations **Paris Airports Service or Airport Shuttle can pick you up at Orly** and drive you directly to your destination. If possible make your reservations at least 24 hours in advance; MasterCard and Visa are accepted and the operators speak English. The fare for one person traveling alone is 89 francs/ €13.60 or 110 francs/€16.80 per person with two or more people traveling together. At best, **taxis take around 25 minutes from Orly to downtown Paris;** the fare falls between 100 francs/€15.25 and 170 francs/€30.55.

➤ TAXIS & SHUTTLES: **Air France Bus** (☎ 01–41–56–89–00 recorded information in English; WEB www.car. airfrance.fr). **Airport Shuttle** (☎ 01– 30–11–11–90; 888/426–2705 toll free from the U.S.; FAX 01–30–11–11–99; WEB www.airportshuttle.fr). **Paris Airports Service** (☎ 08–21–80–08– 01; FAX 01–49–62–78–79; WEB www. parisairportservice.com).

DUTY-FREE SHOPPING

Duty-free shopping is no longer possible within the European Union.

BOAT & FERRY TRAVEL

Linking France and the United Kingdom, a boat or ferry trip across the Channel can range from a mere 40 minutes (via Hovercraft) to 90 minutes (via ferryboat). Trip length also depends on your departure point: popular routes link Boulogne and Folkestone, Dieppe and Newhaven, Le Havre and Portsmouth, and, the most booked passage, Calais and Dover. Driving distances from the French ports to Paris are as follows:

from Calais, 290 km (180 mi); from Boulogne, 243 km (151 mi); from Dieppe, 193 km (120 mi); from Dunkerque, 257 km (160 mi). The fastest routes to Paris from each port are via N43, A26, and A1 from Calais and the Channel Tunnel; via N1 from Boulogne; via N15 from Le Havre; via D915 and N1 from Dieppe; and via A25 and A1 from Dunkerque.

➤ DOVER–CALAIS: **Hoverspeed** (⊠ International Hoverport, Marine Parade, Dover CT17 9TG, ☎ 01304/ 240241, WEB www.hoverspeed.com) operates up to 15 crossings a day by Hovercraft and catamaran. The crossings take 35 minutes (Hovercraft) or 95 minutes (catamaran).

P&O European Ferries (⊠ Channel House, Channel View Rd., Dover, Kent CT17 9TJ, ☎ 020/8575–8555, WEB www.poportsmouth.com) has up to 25 sailings a day; the crossing takes about 75 minutes. **Seafrance** (⊠ 23 rue Louis-le-Grand, Paris 75002, ☎ 01–44–94–40–40, WEB www. seafrance.net) operates up to 15 sailings a day; the crossing takes about 90 minutes.

➤ FOLKESTONE–BOULOGNE: **Hoverspeed** is the sole operator on this route, with ten 35-minute crossings a day.

➤ NEWHAVEN–DIEPPE: **Seafrance** has as many as four sailings a day, and the crossing takes four hours.

➤ PORTSMOUTH–LE HAVRE: **P&O European Ferries** has up to three sailings a day, and the crossing takes 5½ hours by day, 7½ by night.

FARES & SCHEDULES

Schedules and tickets are available at any travel agency throughout France or via the Internet. Travel agencies accept traveler's checks, major credit cards, and cash. Fares vary, but a round-trip from Dover to Calais completed within five days costs 240 francs/€36.65 for one person, 1,450 francs/€221.40 for two adults plus a car. The price doubles if the visit exceeds five days.

BUS TRAVEL AROUND PARIS

Although it's slower than the métro, **traveling by bus is a convenient and scenic way to get around the city.**

Paris buses are green and white; route number and destination are marked in front and major stopping-places along the sides. The brown bus shelters, topped by red and yellow circular signs, contain timetables and route maps; note that buses must be hailed at these larger bus shelters, as they service multiple lines and routes. Smaller stops are designated simply by a pole with bus numbers.

Of Paris's 250 bus routes, three main lines circle the *grands boulevards* and are known as the *petite ceinture* (small belt). These constitute bus numbers PC 1, PC 2, and PC 3, which run in a continuous circle covering the major *portes,* or entryways, into the city center. More than two hundred other bus routes run throughout Paris, reaching virtually every nook and cranny of the city. During weekdays and Saturday, buses run every five minutes (as opposed to the 15- to 20-minute wait on Sunday and national holidays). One ticket will take you anywhere within the city; if you get off at any point, your ticket is no longer viable. Bus transport is ideal for the elderly, women with children (easy access with strollers), and anyone who likes to take the scenic route. Needless to say, seats are more difficult to find during rush hours.

A map of the bus system is on the flip side of every métro map, in all métro stations, and at all bus stops. Maps are also located in each bus. A recorded message announces the name of the next stop. To get off, press the red button located on all the silver poles that run the length of the bus and the *arrêt demandé* (stop requested) light directly behind the driver will light up. Use the rear door to exit.

The Balabus, a public orange-and-white bus that runs between May and September, gives an interesting 50-minute tour around the major sights. You can use your Paris-Visite, Carte Orange, or Mobilis pass, or one to three bus tickets depending on how far you ride. The route runs from La Défense to the Gare de Lyon.

FARES & SCHEDULES

Regular buses accept métro tickets, or you can buy a single ticket on board (exact change appreciated) for 8 francs/€1.20. If you have individual tickets, you should **be prepared to punch your ticket in the red-and-gray machines located at the entrance of the bus.** You need to show (but not punch) weekly, monthly, and Paris-Visite/Mobilis tickets to the driver. Bus tickets can be bought on board buses, in the métro, or in any bar/tabac store sporting one of the lime-green métro symbols above its street sign.

Most routes operate from 7 AM to 8:30 PM (or 20h30 to the French); some continue to midnight. After 8:30 PM you must either take the métro or one of the 18 "Noctambus" lines (which are indicated by a brown owl symbol at bus stops). These bus lines operate hourly (1:30–5:30 AM) between Châtelet and various nearby suburbs; they can be stopped by hailing them at any point on their route. Paris-Visite/Mobilis passes are accepted on the Noctambus. A regular ticket costs 15 fr/€2.30 and allows for one transfer.

➤ BUS INFORMATION: **RATP** (⌧ Pl. de la Madeleine, 75008; 53 bis quai des Grands Augustins, 75006 Paris; ☎ 08–36–68–41–14, ⊞ www.ratp. com).

BUS TRAVEL TO & FROM
PARIS

The excellent national train service in France means that long-distance bus service in the country is practically nonexistent; **regional buses are found mainly where train service is spotty.** Local bus information to the rare rural areas where trains do not have access can be obtained from the SNCF.

The largest international operator is Eurolines France, whose main terminal is in the Parisian suburb of Bagnolet (a half-hour métro ride from central Paris, at the end of métro line 3). Eurolines runs many international routes.

FARES & SCHEDULES

It is possible to take a bus (via ferry) to Paris from the United Kingdom; just be aware that what can save you in money will almost certainly cost you in time—the trip takes about seven hours as opposed to the three it takes on the Eurostar train line (Gare du Nord–Victoria Station). Eurolines operates a service from London's Victoria Coach Station, via the Dover–Calais ferry, to Paris's Porte de Bagnolet. There is a 9 AM departure that arrives in Paris at 4 PM, a 2 PM departure that arrives at 9 PM, and the overnight trip from 9:30 PM, which arrives in Paris at 7 AM. Fares are £60 round-trip (under-25 youth pass £56), £35 one-way. Other Eurolines routes include the following: Amsterdam (7 hours, 450 francs/€69); Barcelona (15 hours, 1020 francs/€155.75); and Berlin (10 hours, 930 francs/€142). There are also international-only arrival-departures from Avignon, Bordeaux, Lille, Lyon, Toulouse, and Tours. Hoverspeed offers up to four daily departures from London's Victoria Coach Station. Fares are £60 round-trip, £38 one-way.

➤ BUS INFORMATION: **Eurolines** (⌧ 28 av. Général-de-Gaulle, Bagnolet, ☎ 08–36–69–52–52 in France; 020/ 7730–3499 in the U.K.; ⊞ www. eurolines.fr). **Hoverspeed** (⌧ International Hoverport, Marine Parade, Dover CT17 9TG, ☎ 01304/240241; ⊞ www.hoverspeed.com). **Paris Vision** (⌧ 1 rue d'Auber, 75009 Paris, ☎ 01–47–42–27–40). **SNCF** (⌧ 88 rue St-Lazare, 75009 Paris, ☎ 08–36–35–35–39 in English).

BUSINESS HOURS

BANKS & OFFICES

On **weekdays, banks are open** generally 9:30 AM–4:30 or 5 PM (note that the Banque de France closes at 3:30), and some banks are also open on Saturday 9–5 as well. In general, government offices and businesses are open 9–5.

GAS STATIONS

Gas stations in the city are generally open 7:30 AM–8 PM, though those near the city's *portes* (or principal entranceways) near the *péripherique* (beltway) are open 24 hours a day.

MUSEUMS & SIGHTS

Most **museums close one day a week**—usually either Monday or Tuesday—and on national holidays. Generally, museums and national monuments are open from 10 AM to 5 or 6 PM. A few close for lunch (noon–2) and are open Sunday only in the afternoon. Many of the large museums have one *nocturne* (nighttime) opening per week when they are open until 9:30 or 10 PM. The Louvre is closed on Tuesday and stays open late on Wednesday until 9:45 PM. The Centre Pompidou is closed on Tuesday and has late opening hours daily until 10 PM. The Musée d'Orsay is closed on Monday and stays open until 9:30 PM on Thursday. The Louvre is open free to the public the first Sunday of every month.

PHARMACIES

Pharmacies are generally open Monday–Saturday 8:30 AM–8 PM. Those pharmacies that are nearby and open late, 24 hours, or on Sunday are listed on the door.

SHOPS

Generally, **large shops are open from 9:30 or 10 AM to 7 or 8 PM** and don't close at lunchtime. Many of the large department stores stay open until 10 PM on Wednesday or Thursday. Smaller shops and many supermarkets often open earlier (8 AM) but take a lengthy lunch break (1 PM–3 PM) and generally close around 8 PM; small food shops are often open Sunday mornings, 9 AM–1 PM. In a bind, there is always a small corner grocery store that stays open late, usually until 11 PM, for basic necessities like diapers, bread, cheese, and fruit (and perhaps the unnecessary bottle of chilled champagne or the disposable plastic rain hat, circa 1950). Note that prices are substantially higher in such outlets than in the larger supermarkets. Most shops close all day Sunday, except in the Marais (where a variety of shops that stand side by side on rue des Francs Bourgeois, from antiques to chic little designers, jewelry to home decoration, open their doors to welcome hordes of Sunday browsers); the Bastille, the Latin Quarter, and the Ile de la Cité also have shops that open on Sunday.

CAMERAS & PHOTOGRAPHY

If you need to get your camera repaired, your best bet is to go to one of the FNAC stores in Paris. Note that it

might take some time to have your camera fixed. The *Kodak Guide to Shooting Great Travel Pictures* (available at bookstores everywhere) is loaded with tips.

➤ CAMERA REPAIR AND PHOTO DEVELOPING: **FNAC** (✉ 26–30 av. des Ternes, 17ᵉ; in the Forum des Halles, 1–7 rue Pierre-Lescot, 1ᵉʳ; 136 rue St-Lazare, 9ᵉ; 157 rue du Faubourg St-Antoine, 11ᵉ).

➤ PHOTO HELP: **Kodak Information Center** (☎ 800/242–2424).

EQUIPMENT PRECAUTIONS

Don't pack film and equipment in checked luggage, where it is much more susceptible to damage. X-ray machines used to view checked luggage are becoming much more powerful and therefore are much more likely to ruin your film. Always **keep film and tape out of the sun.** Carry an extra supply of batteries, and **be prepared to turn on your camera or camcorder** to prove to security personnel that the device is real. Always **ask for hand inspection of film,** which becomes clouded after repeated exposure to airport X-ray machines, and **keep videotapes away from metal detectors.**

FILM & DEVELOPING

The easiest place to get film developed and printed is at one of the various FNAC stores around the city. Keep in mind that it is expensive to have film developed and printed in Paris—around $20 per 36-exposure roll.

VIDEOS

Video systems are not the same all over the world. The United States, for instance, uses NTSC and France uses SECAM. Other European countries, including the United Kingdom, use PAL. This means that you probably won't be able to play video tapes from the United States in France. You should also **bring extra blank video tapes with you from home** for your camcorder as you may not be able to find compatible tapes in France.

CAR RENTAL

Rates in Paris begin at approximately $70 a day and $200 a week for an economy car with air-conditioning, manual transmission, and unlimited mileage. This does not include tax on car rentals, which is 20.6% or, if you pick it up at the airport, the airport tax. To save money, **make reservations before you go**; you can generally get a much better deal. Note that driving in Paris is best avoided, and parking is very difficult to find. You're better off renting a car only when you want to take excursions out of the city.

Renting a car through a local French agency has a number of disadvantages, notably price, as they simply cannot compete with the larger international companies. These giants combine bilingual service, the security of name recognition, extensive services (such as 24-hour hot lines), and fully automatic vehicles. SNAC, a France-based agency, can be useful if you are interested in luxury cars (convertible BMWs) or large family vans (Renault Espace, for example).

➤ MAJOR AGENCIES: **Alamo** (☎ 800/522–9696; 020/8759–6200 in the U.K.). **Avis** (☎ 800/331–1084; 800/879–2847 in Canada; 02/9353–9000 in Australia; 09/525–1982 in New Zealand; 0870/606–0100 in the U.K.). **Budget** (☎ 800/527–0700; 0870/607–5000 in the U.K., through affiliate Europcar). **Dollar** (☎ 800/800–6000; 0124/622–0111 in the U.K., through affiliate Sixt Kenning; 02/9223–1444 in Australia). **Hertz** (☎ 800/654–3001; 800/263–0600 in Canada; 020/8897–2072 in the U.K.; 02/9669–2444 in Australia; 09/256–8690 in New Zealand). **National Car Rental** (☎ 800/227–7368; 020/8680–4800 in the U.K., where it is known as National Europe). **SNAC** (☎ 01–44–05–33–99).

CUTTING COSTS

To get the best deal, **book through a travel agent, who will shop around.** Note that the big international agencies, like Hertz and Avis, offer better prices to their clients who make reservations in their home countries before they arrive in France; prices quoted in France are usually higher. If you need to rent a car while in France, it even pays to call home and have a friend take care of it for you from there.

Do **look into wholesalers,** companies that do not own fleets but rent in bulk from those that do and often offer better rates than traditional car-rental operations. Payment must be made before you leave home.

➤ WHOLESALERS: **Auto Europe** (☎ 207/842–2000 or 800/223–5555, FAX 800/235–6321, WEB www.autoeurope.com). **DER Travel Services** (✉ 9501 W. Devon Ave., Rosemont, IL 60018, ☎ 800/782–2424, FAX 800/282–7474 information; 800/860–9944 brochures, WEB www.dertravel.com).**Europe by Car** (☎ 212/581–3040 or 800/223–1516, FAX 212/246–1458, WEB www.europebycar.com). **Kemwel Holiday Autos** (☎ 800/678–0678, FAX 914/825–3160, WEB www.kemwel.com).

INSURANCE

When driving a rented car you are generally responsible for any damage to or loss of the vehicle. Before you rent, see what coverage your personal auto-insurance policy and credit cards provide.

Before you buy collision coverage, check your existing policies—you may already be covered. However, collision policies that car-rental companies sell for European rentals usually do not include stolen-vehicle coverage.

REQUIREMENTS & RESTRICTIONS

In France, you drive on the right and **yield to drivers coming from streets to the right.** However, this rule does not necessarily apply at roundabouts, where you should watch out for just about everyone. You must **wear your seat belt,** and children under 12 may not travel in the front seat. Speed limits are 130 kph (80 mph) on expressways (*autoroutes*), 110 kph (70 mph) on divided highways (*routes nationales*), 90 kph (55 mph) on other roads (*routes*), 50 kph (30 mph) in cities and towns (*villes et villages*).

In France **your own driver's license is acceptable.** An International Driver's Permit is not necessary unless you are planning on a long-term stay; you can get one from the American or Canadian Automobile Association, and, in the United Kingdom, from the Automobile Association or Royal Automobile Club. You must be 18 years old to drive, but there is no top age limit for those whose faculties are intact. To rent a car you must be 21 or older and have a major credit card, though you are charged a 110 francs/€16.80 per day supplement if you're under 25.

SURCHARGES

Before you pick up a car in one city and leave it in another, **ask about drop-off charges or one-way service fees,** which can be substantial. Note, too, that some rental agencies charge extra if you return the car before the time specified in your contract. To avoid a hefty refueling fee, **fill the tank just before you turn in the car,** but be aware that gas stations near the rental outlet may overcharge.

CAR TRAVEL

France's roads are classified into five types, numbered and prefixed *A* (*autoroute*), *N* (*route nationale*), *D* (*route départmentale*), *C,* or *V.* Roads marked *A* (*autoroutes*) are expressways. There are excellent links between Paris and most French cities. When trying to get around Ile-de-France, it is often difficult to avoid Paris—just **try to steer clear of the rush hours** (7–9:30 AM and 4:30–7:30 PM). A *péage* (toll) must be paid on most expressways: the rate varies but can be steep. Certain booths allow you to pay with your credit card.

There are two major rings that run parallel to each other and encircle Paris: the *périférique intérieur,* the inside ring also known as the *grands boulevards* (not to be confused with the major avenue layout in the center of Paris's Right Bank) and the *périférique extérieur,* the outside ring, which is a major highway and from which *portes* (gates) connect Paris to the major highways of France. The names of these highways function on the same principal as the métro, with the final destination as the determining point in the direction you must take.

Heading north, look for Porte de la Chapelle (direction Lille and Charles de Gaulle airport); east, for Porte de Bagnolet (direction Metz and Nancy); south, for Porte d'Orléans (direction Lyon and Bordeaux); and west, for Porte d'Auteuil (direction Rouen and Chartres) or Porte de St-Cloud.

EMERGENCY SERVICES

If your car breaks down on an expressway, pull your car as far off the road as possible, light your emergency indicators, and, if possible, put the emergency triangle located in the boot of your car at least 30 yards behind your car to warn oncoming traffic; then **go to a roadside emergency telephone.** These phones put you in direct contact with the police, automatically indicating your exact location, and are available every 3 km (2 mi). If you have a breakdown anywhere else, find the nearest garage or contact the police. There are also 24-hour assistance hot lines valid throughout France (available through rental agencies and supplied to you when you rent the car), but do not hesitate in calling the police in case of any roadside emergency, for they are quick and reliable and the phone call is free. There are special phones just for this purpose on all highways—just pick up the phone and dial 17.

➤ CONTACTS: **Police** (☎ 17). **Club Automobile de l'Île de France** (☎ 01–40–55–43–00) is for members only.

FROM THE U.K.

Motorists from the United Kingdom have a choice of either the Channel Tunnel or the ferry services when traveling to the continent. Reservations are essential at peak times and always a good idea, especially when going via the Chunnel. Cars don't drive in the Chunnel but are loaded onto trains.

GASOLINE

Gas is expensive and prices vary enormously; anything from 6.5 francs/€1 to 9 francs/€1.37 per liter. Credit cards are accepted in every gas station. There are very few self-service vending machines for gas in Paris.

PARKING

Finding parking in Paris is very difficult. Meters and ticket machines (pay and display) are common: make sure you **have a supply of 10 franc/€1.52 coins.** If you're planning on spending a lot of time in Paris with a car, **it** might be a good idea to buy a parking card (*carte de stationnement*) for 100 francs/€15.25 or 200 francs/€30.53 at any café sporting the red TABAC sign. This card works like a credit card in the parking meters, allowing you to avoid the inconvenience of finding exact change. After depositing enough money (or using your parking card) in the ticket machine, you will receive a receipt; **be sure to display the receipt on the inside window of the vehicle,** the dashboard on the passenger side being best. Note that in August, parking is free in certain residential areas. However, **only parking meters with a dense yellow circle on them indicate free parking in August; if you do not see the circle, pay.** Parking tickets are expensive and there is no shortage of the blue-uniformed parking police. Parking lots, indicated by a blue sign with a white *P*, are usually underground and are generally expensive (due to the 24-hour surveillance systems).

RULES OF THE ROAD

A native quirk that takes some getting used to is the famous *priorité à droite* law that states that all drivers must yield to any vehicle coming from the right—to be safe, slow down at *all* crosswalks and make sure no one is coming from the right.

Some important traffic terms and signs to note: *Sortie* (Exit); *Sens Unique* (One Way); *Stationnement Interdite* (No Parking); *Cul de Sac* (Dead End). Blue rectangular signs indicate a highway; triangles carry illustrations of a particular traffic hazard; speed limits are indicated in a circle with the maximum speed encircled in red.

THE CHANNEL TUNNEL

Short of flying, taking the "Chunnel" is the fastest way to cross the English Channel: 35 minutes from Folkestone to Calais, 60 minutes from motorway to motorway, or 3 hours from London's Waterloo Station to Paris's Gare du Nord.

➤ CAR TRANSPORT: **Le Shuttle** (☎ 0870/535–3535 in the U.K.).

➤ PASSENGER SERVICE: In the United Kingdom: **Eurostar** (☎ 0870/518–

6186), **InterCity Europe** (☎ 0870/584–8848 for credit-card bookings). In the United States: **BritRail Travel** (☎ 800/677–8585), **Rail Europe** (☎ 800/942–4866).

CHILDREN IN PARIS

If you are renting a car, don't forget to **arrange for a car seat** when you reserve. For general advice about traveling with children, check out the family travel tips in the Family Travel section of www.fodors.com and consult *Fodor's FYI: Travel with Your Baby* (available in bookstores everywhere).

BABY-SITTING

Agencies can provide English-speaking baby-sitters with just a few hours' notice. The hourly rate is approximately 35 francs/€5.35 (three-hour minimum) plus an agency fee of 60 francs/€9.25.

➤ AGENCIES: **Ababa** (✉ 8 av. du Maine, 15ᵉ, ☎ 01-45-49-46-46). **Allo Maman Poule** (✉ 7 Villa Murat, 16ᵉ, ☎ 01-45-20-96-96). **Baby Sitting Service** (✉ 18 rue Tronchet, 8ᵉ, ☎ 01-46-37-51-24).

FLYING

Experts agree that it's a good idea to use safety seats aloft for children weighing less than 40 pounds. Airlines set their own policies: U.S. carriers usually require that the child be ticketed, even if he or she is young enough to ride free, since the seats must be strapped into regular seats. Do **check your airline's policy about using safety seats during takeoff and landing.** And since safety seats are not allowed everywhere in the plane, get your seat assignments early.

When reserving, **request children's meals or a freestanding bassinet** if you need them. But note that bulkhead seats, where you must sit to use the bassinet, may lack an overhead bin or storage space on the floor.

FOOD

The best restaurants in Paris do not welcome small children; except for the traditional family Sunday-noon dinner, fine dining is considered an adult pastime. With kids, **you're best off taking them to more casual** bistros, brasseries, and cafés; these also offer the flexible meal times that children often require. Stick with the familiar when you are ordering; an omelet with fries, a sausage with whipped potatoes, or a ham-and-cheese sandwich are comforting for jet-lagged tummies. Do not expect child-friendly amenities like high chairs, coloring books, a smoke-free atmosphere, or even an indulgent waiter, for that matter. Other restaurant options include one of the many Chinese restaurants that serve favorites such as grilled chicken, shrimp, or spring rolls or one of the American restaurants on the Champs-Élysées or near Les Halles. If it is sunny you can always buy a fresh roasted chicken (have it cut), some cherry tomatoes, and raspberry tarts and have a picnic in the Luxembourg or Tuileries Gardens. Remember though—if you (or they) get desperate, Paris has its share of McDonald's, Pizza Huts, and other fast-food restaurants.

LODGING

Most hotels in Paris allow children under a certain age to stay in their parents' room at no extra charge, but others charge for them as extra adults; be sure to **find out the cutoff age for children's discounts.**

The Novotel chain allows up to two children under 15 to stay free in their parents' room, and many properties have playgrounds. Sofitel hotels offer a free second room for children during July and August and over the Christmas period.

➤ BEST CHOICES: **Novotel** (☎ 800/221–4542 international reservations). **Sofitel** (☎ 800/221–4542 international reservations).

SIGHTS & ATTRACTIONS

Paris has plenty of diversions for the young (noted by a 🦆 duck icon in the margin throughout this book), and **almost all museums and movie theaters offer discounted rates** to children. *Le Pariscope* and *L'Officiel des Spectacles* are two weekly publications that have sections in English about entertainment for children. The **CIDJ**, the Centre d'Information et de Documentation pour la Jeunesse

(Center for Information and Documentation for Young People), also has information about activities and events for youngsters in Paris. *Fodor's Around Paris with Kids* (available in bookstores everywhere) can help you plan your days together.

SUPPLIES & EQUIPMENT

Supermarkets carry several major brands of diapers (*couches à jeter*), universally referred to as Pampers (pronounced "pawm-paires"). Junior sizes are hard to come by, as the French toilet-train early. Baby formula is available in grocery stores or pharmacies. There are two types of formula: *lait premier age,* for infants 0–4 months, and *lait deuxième age,* for 4 months or older. French formulas come in powder form and need to be mixed with a pure, low-mineral-content bottled water like Evian or Volvic (the French *never* mix baby formula with tap water). American formulas do not exist in France. If you're looking for treats for your little ones, some items to keep in mind are *coloriage* (coloring books); *crayons de couleur* (crayons); *pâte à modeler* (modeling clay); and *feutres* (markers).

COMPUTERS ON THE ROAD

If you use a major Internet provider, getting on-line in Paris shouldn't be difficult. Call your Internet provider to get the local access number in Paris. Many hotels have business services with Internet access and even in-room modem lines. You will, however, need an adapter for your computer for the European-style plugs. If you're traveling with a laptop, carry a spare battery and adapter. Never plug your computer into any socket before asking about surge protection. IBM sells a pen-size modem tester that plugs into a telephone jack to check if the line is safe to use.

➤ ACCESS NUMBERS IN PARIS: **AOL** (☎ 01–41–45–81–00). **Compuserve** (☎ 08–03–00–60–00, 08–03–00–80–00, or 08–03–00–90–00).

➤ INTERNET CAFÉS: **Café Orbital** (✉ 17 rue de Médicis, 6ᵉ, ☎ 01–43–25–76–77). **Cybercafé** (✉ 72–74 passage de Choiseul, 2ᵉ, ☎ 01–47–

03–36–12, WEB www.cari.com, métro Opéra). **Cybercafé de Paris** (✉ 15 rue des Halles, 1er, ☎ 01–42–21–11–11). **Les Jardins de l'Internet Cybercafé** (✉ 79 bd. St-Michel, 4e, ☎ 01–44–07–22–20, WEB www.jardin-internet. net, métro Cluny–La Sorbonne). **Web Bar** (✉ 32 rue de Picardie, 3e, ☎ 01–42–72–66–55, WEB www. webbar.fr, métro République).

➤ INTERNET PROVIDER IN ENGLISH: **Almanet** (✉ 8 rue Dupont des Loges, 2e, ☎ 01–44–18–70–70, WEB www. alma-net.net).

CONCIERGES

Concierges, found in many hotels, can help you with theater tickets and dinner reservations: a good one with connections may be able to get you seats for a hot show or prime-time dinner reservations at the restaurant of the moment. You can also turn to your hotel's concierge for help with travel arrangements, sightseeing plans, services ranging from aromatherapy to zipper repair, and emergencies. Always, **always tip** a concierge who has been of assistance.

CONSUMER PROTECTION

Whenever shopping or buying travel services in Paris, **pay with a major credit card,** if possible, so you can cancel payment or get reimbursed if there's a problem. If you're doing business with a particular company for the first time, **contact your local Better Business Bureau and the attorney general's offices** in your state and (for U.S. businesses) the company's home state as well. Have any complaints been filed? Finally, if you're buying a package or tour, always **consider travel insurance** that includes default coverage.

➤ BBBs: **Council of Better Business Bureaus** (✉ 4200 Wilson Blvd., Suite 800, Arlington, VA 22203, ☎ 703/276–0100, FAX 703/525–8277, WEB www.bbb.org).

CUSTOMS & DUTIES

When shopping, **keep receipts** for all purchases. Upon reentering the country, **be ready to show customs officials what you've bought.** If you feel a duty is incorrect or object to the way your clearance was handled, note the inspector's badge number and ask to see a supervisor. If the problem isn't resolved, write to the appropriate authorities, beginning with the port director at your point of entry.

IN AUSTRALIA

Australian residents who are 18 or older may bring home $A400 worth of souvenirs and gifts (including jewelry), 250 cigarettes or 250 grams of tobacco, and 1,125 ml of alcohol (including wine, beer, and spirits). Residents under 18 may bring back $A200 worth of goods. Prohibited items include meat products. Seeds, plants, and fruits need to be declared upon arrival.

➤ INFORMATION: **Australian Customs Service** (Regional Director, ✉ Box 8, Sydney, NSW 2001, Australia, ☎ 02/9213–2000, FAX 02/9213–4000, WEB www.customs.gov.au).

IN CANADA

Canadian residents who have been out of Canada for at least seven days may bring home C$500 worth of goods duty-free. If you've been away fewer than seven days but more than 48 hours, the duty-free allowance drops to C$200; if your trip lasts 24–48 hours, the allowance is C$50. You may not pool allowances with family members. Goods claimed under the C$500 exemption may follow you by mail; those claimed under the lesser exemptions must accompany you. Alcohol and tobacco products may be included in the seven-day and 48-hour exemptions but not in the 24-hour exemption. If you meet the age requirements of the province or territory through which you reenter Canada, you may bring in, duty-free, 1.14 liters (40 imperial ounces) of wine or liquor *or* 24 12-ounce cans or bottles of beer or ale. If you are 16 or older you may bring in, duty-free, 200 cigarettes and 50 cigars. Check ahead of time with Revenue Canada or the Department of Agriculture for policies regarding meat products, seeds, plants, and fruits.

You may send an unlimited number of gifts worth up to C$60 each duty-free to Canada. Label the package UNSOLICITED GIFT—VALUE UNDER $60. Alcohol and tobacco are excluded.

➤ INFORMATION: **Revenue Canada** (✉ 2265 St. Laurent Blvd. S, Ottawa, Ontario K1G 4K3, Canada, ☎ 613/993–0534; 800/461–9999 in Canada, FAX 613/991–4126, WEB www.ccra-adrc.gc.ca).

IN FRANCE

If you're coming from outside the European Union (EU), you may import duty free: (1) 200 cigarettes or 100 cigarillos or 50 cigars or 250 grams of tobacco (twice that if you live outside Europe); (2) 2 liters of wine and, in addition, (a) 1 liter of alcohol over 22% volume (most spirits) or (b) 2 liters of alcohol under 22% volume (fortified or sparkling wine) or (c) 2 more liters of table wine; (3) 50 ml of perfume and 250 ml of toilet water; (4) 200 grams of coffee, 100 grams of tea; and (5) other goods to the value of 300 francs/€46 (100 francs/€15.3 for those under 15).

If you're arriving from an EU country, you may be required to declare all goods and prove that anything over the standard limit is for personal consumption. But there is no limit or customs tariff imposed on goods carried within the EU.

Any amount of French or foreign currency may be brought into France, but foreign currencies converted into francs may be reconverted into a foreign currency only up to the equivalent of 5,000 francs/€769.

➤ INFORMATION: **Direction des Douanes** (✉ 16 rue Yves Toudic, 10ᵉ, ☎ 01–40–40–39–00).

IN NEW ZEALAND

Homeward-bound residents 17 or older may bring back $700 worth of souvenirs and gifts. Your duty-free allowance also includes 4.5 liters of wine or beer; one 1,125-ml bottle of spirits; and either 200 cigarettes, 250 grams of tobacco, 50 cigars, or a combination of the three up to 250 grams. Prohibited items include meat products, seeds, plants, and fruits.

➤ INFORMATION: **New Zealand Customs** (Custom House, ✉ 50 Anzac Ave., Box 29, Auckland, New Zealand, ☎ 09/300–5399, FAX 09/359–6730, WEB www.customs.govt.nz).

IN THE U.K.

If you are a U.K. resident and your journey was wholly within the European Union (EU), you won't have to pass through customs when you return to the United Kingdom. If you plan to bring back large quantities of alcohol or tobacco, check EU limits beforehand. From countries outside the EU, you may bring home, duty-free, 200 cigarettes or 50 cigars; 1 liter of spirits or 2 liters of fortified or sparkling wine or liqueurs; 2 liters of still table wine; 60 ml of perfume; 250 ml of toilet water; plus £136 worth of other goods, including gifts and souvenirs. If returning from outside the EU, prohibited items include meat products, seeds, plants, and fruits.

➤ INFORMATION: **HM Customs and Excise** (✉ Dorset House, Stamford St., Bromley, Kent BR1 1XX, U.K., ☎ 020/7202–4227, WEB www.hmce.gov.uk).

IN THE U.S.

U.S. residents who have been out of the country for at least 48 hours (and who have not used the $400 allowance or any part of it in the past 30 days) may bring home $400 worth of foreign goods duty-free.

U.S. residents 21 and older may bring back 1 liter of alcohol duty-free. In addition, regardless of your age, you are allowed 200 cigarettes and 100 non-Cuban cigars. Antiques, which the U.S. Customs Service defines as objects more than 100 years old, enter duty-free, as do original works of art done entirely by hand, including paintings, drawings, and sculptures.

You may also mail or ship packages home duty-free: up to $200 worth of goods for personal use, with a limit of one parcel per addressee per day (except alcohol or tobacco products or perfume worth more than $5); label the package PERSONAL USE and attach a list of its contents and their retail value. Do not label the package UNSOLICITED GIFT or your duty-free exemption will drop to $100. Mailed items do not affect your duty-free allowance on your return.

➤ INFORMATION: **U.S. Customs Service** (✉ 1300 Pennsylvania Ave. NW, Washington, DC 20229, WEB www. customs.gov; inquiries ☎ 202/354–1000; complaints c/o ✉ 1300 Pennsylvania Ave. NW, Room 5.4D, Washington, DC 20229; registration of equipment c/o ✉ Resource Management, ☎ 202/927–0540).

DINING

For information on mealtimes, reservations, what to wear, and specific restaurants, *see* Chapter 3. The restaurants we list are the cream of the crop in each price category.

DISABILITIES & ACCESSIBILITY

Although the city of Paris is doing much to ensure that public facilities accommodate people with mobility difficulties, it still has a long way to go. Some sidewalks now have low curbs, and many arrondissements have public rest rooms and telephone boxes that are accessible to travelers using wheelchairs.

➤ LOCAL RESOURCES: **Association des Paralysés de France** (✉ 17 bd. Auguste-Blanqui, 75013 Paris, ☎ 01–44–16–83–83) is a very helpful organization. **Comité Nationale Français de Liaison pour la Réadaptation des Handicapés** (✉ 236 bis rue de Tolbiac, 75013 Paris, ☎ 01–53–80–66–66) publishes an extensive guide in English entitled "Paris for Everyone" that costs 60 francs/€9.2 and has in-depth information on hotels, transportation, and interesting, accessible activities in the capital.

RESERVATIONS

When discussing accessibility with an operator or reservations agent, **ask hard questions.** Are there any stairs, inside *or* out? Are there grab bars next to the toilet *and* in the shower/tub? How wide is the doorway to the room? To the bathroom? For the most extensive facilities meeting the latest legal specifications, **opt for newer accommodations.**

TRANSPORTATION

The Paris métro is a labyrinth of winding stairs, malfunctioning doors, and hordes of scurrying Parisians, all of which make it a less than ideal mode of transport for travelers with disabilities. In addition, very few métro and RER stations are wheelchair-accessible with the exception of the new, fully automated line Météor. For those with walking difficulties, all stairs have handrails, and nearly two-thirds of the stations have at least one escalator. Avoid peak hours between 8 and 9 AM and 6 and 7 PM. Bus lines Nos. 38, 62, 68, and 91 are wheelchair-accessible, but note that you will be more comfortable traveling with someone who can help you. For information about accessibility, **get the RER and métro access guide,** available at most stations and from the Paris Transit Authority. The SNCF has special accommodations in the first-class departments of trains that are reserved exclusively for people using wheelchairs (and are available for the second-class price). **It is essential to reserve special train tickets in advance—this not only assures a comfortable seat but guarantees assistance at the station.** Taxi drivers are required by law to assist travelers with disabilities in and out of their vehicles.

The Airhop shuttle company runs adapted vehicles to and from the airports; Orly–Paris costs 180 francs/€27.50 and Charles de Gaulle–Paris costs 250 francs/€38.15; this service is available weekdays only. Reservations (in French) must be made in advance. Note that you must pay 15 francs/€2.40 for every 15 minutes there is a delay.

➤ LOCAL RESOURCES: **Airhop** (☎ 01–41–29–01–29). **G.I.H.P.** (✉ 98 rue de la Porte Jaune, 92210 St-Cloud, ☎ 01–41–83–15–15). **Paris Transit Authority** (RATP) (✉ 54 quai de la Rapée, 75599 Cedex 12, ☎ 08–36–68–77–14, WEB www.ratp.com).

➤ COMPLAINTS: **Aviation Consumer Protection Division** for airline-related problems. **Civil Rights Office** (✉ U.S. Department of Transportation, Departmental Office of Civil Rights, S-30, 400 7th St. SW, Room 10215, Washington, DC 20590, ☎ 202/366–4648, FAX 202/366–9371, WEB www.dot.gov/ost/docr/index.htm) for problems with surface transportation. **Disability Rights Section** (✉ U.S. Department of Justice, Civil Rights

Division, Box 66738, Washington, DC 20035-6738, ☎ 202/514–0301 or 800/514–0301; 202/514–0383 TTY; 800/514–0383 TTY, FAX 202/307–1198, WEB www.usdoj.gov/crt/ada/adahom1.htm) for general complaints.

TRAVEL AGENCIES

In the United States, the Americans with Disabilities Act requires that travel firms serve the needs of all travelers. Some agencies specialize in working with people with disabilities.

➤ TRAVELERS WITH MOBILITY PROBLEMS: **Access Adventures** (✉ 206 Chestnut Ridge Rd., Scottsville, NY 14624, ☎ 716/889–9096, dltravel@prodigy.net), run by a former physical-rehabilitation counselor. **Accessible Vans of America** (✉ 9 Spielman Rd., Fairfield, NJ 07004, ☎ 877/282–8267, FAX 973/808–9713, WEB www.accessiblevans.com). **CareVacations** (✉ 5-5110 50th Ave., Leduc, Alberta T9E 6V4, Canada, ☎ 780/986–6404 or 877/478–7827, FAX 780/986–8332, WEB www.carevacations.com), for group tours and cruise vacations. **Flying Wheels Travel** (✉ 143 W. Bridge St., Box 382, Owatonna, MN 55060, ☎ 507/451–5005 or 800/535–6790, FAX 507/451–1685, WEB www.flyingwheelstravel.com).

DISCOUNTS & DEALS

Be a smart shopper and **compare all your options** before making decisions. A plane ticket bought with a promotional coupon from travel clubs, coupon books, and direct-mail offers or on the Internet may not be cheaper than the least expensive fare from a discount ticket agency. And always keep in mind that what you get is just as important as what you save.

Paris Tourist Offices, railroad stations, major métro stations, and participating museums sell the *Carte Musées et Monuments* (Museums and Monuments Pass), which offers unlimited access to more than 65 museums and monuments in Paris over a one-, three-, or five- consecutive day period; the cost, respectively, is 80 francs/€12.20, 160 francs/€24.40, and 240 francs/€36.59. Temporary exhibitions are not included in this pass. The pass is most beneficial if

you are going to visit many museums and monuments in a short amount of time; however, it also allows access to museums and monuments without having to wait in line (something to consider if you're going to make the Louvre your second home-away-from-home). If you don't plan on seeing that many museums or monuments, you may be better off paying per site.

DISCOUNT RESERVATIONS

To save money, **look into discount reservations services** with toll-free numbers, which use their buying power to get a better price on hotels, airline tickets, even car rentals. When booking a room, always **call the hotel's local toll-free number** (if one is available) rather than the central reservations number—you'll often get a better price. Always ask about special packages or corporate rates.

When shopping for the best deal on hotels and car rentals, **look for guaranteed exchange rates,** which protect you against a falling dollar. With your rate locked in, you won't pay more, even if the price goes up in the local currency.

➤ AIRLINE TICKETS: ☎ **800/FLY–ASAP.**

➤ HOTEL ROOMS: **Hotel Reservations Network** (☎ 800/964–6835, WEB www.hoteldiscount.com). **International Marketing & Travel Concepts** (☎ 800/790–4682, imtc@mindspring.com). **Players Express Vacations** (☎ 800/458–6161, WEB www.playersexpress.com). **Steigenberger Reservation Service** (☎ 800/223–5652, WEB www.srs-worldhotels.com). **Travel Interlink** (☎ 800/888–5898, WEB www.travelinterlink.com). **Turbotrip.com** (☎ 800/473–7829, WEB www.turbotrip.com).

PACKAGE DEALS

Don't confuse packages and guided tours. When you buy a package, you travel on your own, just as though you had planned the trip yourself. Fly-drive packages, which combine airfare and car rental, are often a good deal. In cities, ask the local visitors' bureau about hotel packages that include tickets to major museum exhibits or other special events.

ELECTRICITY

To use your U.S.-purchased electric-powered equipment, **bring a converter and adapter.** The electrical current in Paris is 220 volts, 50 cycles alternating current (AC); wall outlets take continental-type plugs, with two round prongs.

If your appliances are dual-voltage, you'll need only an adapter. Don't use 110-volt outlets marked FOR SHAVERS ONLY for high-wattage appliances such as blow-dryers. Most laptops operate equally well on 110 and 220 volts and so require only an adapter.

EMBASSIES

➤ AUSTRALIA: ✉ 4 rue Jean-Rey, Paris, 15ᵉ, ☎ 01–40–59–33–00, métro Bir Hakeim, open weekdays 9:15–12:15.

➤ CANADA: ✉ 35 av. Montaigne, Paris, 8ᵉ, ☎ 01–44–43–29–00, métro Franklin-D.-Roosevelt, open weekdays 8:30–11.

➤ NEW ZEALAND: ✉ 7 ter rue Léonardo da Vinci, Paris, 16ᵉ, ☎ 01–45–00–24–11, métro Victor Hugo, open weekdays 9–1.

➤ UNITED KINGDOM: ✉ 35 rue du Faubourg-St-Honoré, Paris, 8ᵉ, ☎ 01–44–51–31–00, métro Madeleine, open weekdays 9:30–12:30 and 2:30–5.

➤ UNITED STATES: ✉ 2 rue St-Florentin, Paris, 1ᵉʳ, ☎ 01–43–12–22–22 in English; 01–43–12–23–47 in emergencies, métro Concorde), open weekdays 9–3.

EMERGENCIES

The French National Health Care system has been organized to provide fully equipped, fully staffed hospitals within 30 minutes of every resident in Paris. For signage, hospitals are indicated by a rectangular blue box with a white cross. This guide book does not list the major Paris hospitals, as the French government prefers an emergency operator to make the judgment call and assign you the best and most convenient option for your emergency. Note that if you are able to walk into a hospital emergency room by yourself, you are often considered "low priority" and the

wait can be interminable. So if time is of the essence, the best thing to do is to call the **fire department** (18); a fully trained team of paramedics will usually arrive within five minutes. You may also dial for a **Samu ambulance** (15); there is usually an English-speaking physician available who will help you assess the situation and either dispatch an ambulance immediately or advise you as to your best course of action.

In a less urgent situation, do what the French do and call **SOS Doctor** or **SOS Dental** services; like magic, a certified, experienced doctor or dentist arrives at the door well within an hour, armed with an old leather doctor case filled with the essentials to diagnose and treat the patient (at an average cost of 350 francs/ €53.45). He or she may or may not be bilingual but will, at worst, have a rudimentary understanding of English. This is a very helpful 24-hour service to use for common benign illnesses that need to be treated quickly for comfort, such as high fevers, toothaches, or stomach flus (which seem to have the unfortunate habit of announcing themselves late at night).

The **American Hospital** and the **Hertford British Hospital** both have 24-hour emergency hot lines with bilingual doctors and nurses who can provide advice. For small problems, go to a **pharmacy,** marked by a green neon cross. Pharmacists have the right to administer first aid and recommend over-the-counter drugs, and they can be very helpful in advising you in English or sending you to the nearest English-speaking pharmacist.

Call the **police** (17) if there has been a crime or an act of violence. On the street, some French phrases that may be needed in an emergency are as follows: *Au secours!* (Help!), *urgence* (emergency), *samu* (ambulance), *pompiers* (firemen), *poste de station* (police station), *médicin* (doctor), and *hôpital* (hospital).

➤ DOCTORS & DENTISTS: **SOS Dentists** (☎ 01–43–37–51–00). **SOS Doctors** (☎ 01–47–07–77–77).

➤ EMERGENCY SERVICES: **Ambulance** (☎ 15). **Fire Department** (☎ 18).

Police (☎ 17). These numbers are toll-free and can be dialed from any phone.

➤ HOSPITALS: **The American Hospital** (✉ 63 bd. Victor-Hugo, Neuilly, ☎ 01–47–47–70–15). **The Hertford British Hospital** (✉ 3 rue Barbès, Levallois-Perret, ☎ 01–46–39–22–22).

➤ HOT LINES: **FACTS–Line I** ☎ 01–47–23–80–8), open Monday, Wednesday, and Friday 6–10 PM, offers HIV/AIDS support in English. **SOS Help** (☎ 01–47–23–80–80), open 3–11 PM, is an English-language crisis and information hot line.

➤ LATE-NIGHT AND 24-HOUR PHARMACIES: **Dhéry** (✉ Galerie des Champs, 84 av. des Champs-Élysées, 8ᵉ, ☎ 01–45–62–02–41) is open 24 hours. **Pharmacie des Arts** (✉ 106 bd. Montparnasse, 14ᵉ) is open daily until midnight. **Pharmacie Matignon** (✉ rue Jean-Mermoz, at the Rond-Point de Champs-Élysées, 8ᵉ) is open daily until 2 AM.

ENGLISH-LANGUAGE MEDIA

BOOKS

For information about bookstores in Paris, *see* Specialty Shops *in* Chapter 6. The American Library in Paris is another resource for English-language books; it's open Tuesday–Saturday 10–7.

➤ BOOKSTORES

See the listings in Chapter 6, Shopping.

Library: **AMERICAN LIBRARY** (✉ 10 rue du Général Ganou, 7e, ☎ 01–53–59–12–60). There is a 70-franc/€10.7 per-day fee for nonmembers.

NEWSPAPERS & MAGAZINES

A number of free magazines in English, with all kinds of listings, including events, bars, restaurants, shops, films, and museums, are available in Paris. Look for *Time Out Paris, FUSAC, The Paris Free Voice,* and *Irish Eyes,* which are available at both tourist offices and all Anglo-American restaurants, bars, and bookshops. Besides a large variety of French newspapers and magazines, all kinds of English-language newspapers and magazines can be found at news-

stands, especially in major tourist areas, including the *International Herald Tribune, USA Today,* the *New York Times,* the *European Financial Times,* the *Times* of London, *Newsweek, The Economist, Vogue,* and *Elle.*

RADIO & TELEVISION

Radio in France is an eclectic mix, with more variety of music than you'd expect. Most stations broadcast in French. A number play Top 40 music, including Cherie FM (91.3), Skyrock (96), NRJ (100.3), Radio Nova (101.5), and Fun Radio (101.9). A variety of music can be found on FIP (105.1); classical on Radio Classique (101.1); '60s–'90s on Nostalgie (90.4); techno on Radio FG (98.2); and the news (in French) on France Info (105.5).

Turn on the television and you'll notice many American shows dubbed into French (Canal Jimmy, Channel 8, shows American shows in their original, undubbed format). France has both national stations (TF1, France 2, France 3, La Cinq/Arte, and M6) and cable stations (most notably CanalPlus, France's version of HBO). Every morning at 7:05 AM, ABC News (from the night before) is aired. You can also find CNN, BBC World, and BBC Prime on cable.

GAY & LESBIAN TRAVEL

In Paris, several gay and lesbian organizations provide information on events, medical care, and counseling to one of the largest homosexual communities in the world. A number of informative newspapers and magazines that cover the Parisian gay-lesbian scene are available at stores and kiosks in the city, including *TETU, Gai Guide, Gai Pied Hebdo,* and *Lesbia.*

➤ ORGANIZATIONS: **Agora** (✉ 33 bd. Picpus, 12ᵉ, ☎ 01–43–42–19–02) provides information on events, meetings, and rallies. **Association des Médecins Gais** (☎ 01–48–05–81–71) and **Écoute Gaie** (☎ 01–44–93–01–02 after 6 PM) give advice and information over the phone. **Centre Gai et Lesbien** (✉ 3 rue Keller, 11ᵉ, ☎ 01–43–57–21–47). **Les Mots à la Bouche** (✉ 6 rue Ste-Croix-de-la-Bretonnerie,

4e, ☎ 01–42–78–88–30) is Paris's largest gay bookstore and is always a rich resource for current happenings and literature.

➤ GAY- & LESBIAN-FRIENDLY TRAVEL AGENCIES: **Different Roads Travel** (✉ 8383 Wilshire Blvd., Suite 902, Beverly Hills, CA 90211, ☎ 323/651–5557 or 800/429–8747, FAX 323/651–3678, lgernert@tzell.com). **Kennedy Travel** (✉ 314 Jericho Turnpike, Floral Park, NY 11001, ☎ 516/352–4888 or 800/237–7433, FAX 516/354–8849, WEB www.kennedytravel.com). **Now Voyager** (✉ 4406 18th St., San Francisco, CA 94114, ☎ 415/626–1169 or 800/255–6951, FAX 415/626–8626, WEB www.nowvoyager.com). **Skylink Travel and Tour** (✉ 1006 Mendocino Ave., Santa Rosa, CA 95401, ☎ 707/546–9888 or 800/225–5759, FAX 707/546–9891, WEB www.skylinktravel.com), serving lesbian travelers.

GUIDEBOOKS

Plan well and you won't be sorry. Guidebooks are excellent tools—and you can take them with you. You may want to check out *Fodor's Exploring Paris* (full color), the pocket-size *Citypack Paris,* and *Fodor's upCLOSE Paris* (budget travel)—all available at on-line retailers and bookstores everywhere.

LANGUAGES FOR TRAVELERS

A phrase book and language-tape set can help get you started. *Fodor's French for Travelers* (available at bookstores everywhere) is excellent.

HEALTH

For information on doctors and hospitals in Paris, *see* Emergencies, *above.*

HOLIDAYS

With 11 national holidays (*jours feriés*) and five weeks of paid vacation, the French have their share of repose. In May, there is a holiday nearly every week, so be prepared for stores, banks, and museums to shut their doors for days at a time. If a holiday falls on a Tuesday or Thursday, many businesses *font le pont* (make the bridge) and close on that Monday or Friday as well. But some exchange booths in tourist areas,

small grocery stores, restaurants, cafés, and bakeries usually remain open. Bastille Day (July 14) is observed in true French form. Celebrations begin on the evening of the 13th, when city firemen open the doors to their stations, often classed as historical monuments, to host their much-acclaimed all-night balls and finish the next day with the annual military parade and air show.

Note that these dates are for the calendar year 2002: January 1 (New Year's Day); March 31 (Easter Sunday); May 1 (Labor Day); May 8 (VE Day); May 9 (Ascension); May 19 (Pentecost Sunday); July 14 (Bastille Day); August 15 (Assumption); November 1 (All Saints); November 11 (Armistice); December 25 (Christmas).

INSURANCE

The most useful travel-insurance plan is a comprehensive policy that includes coverage for trip cancellation and interruption, default, trip delay, and medical expenses (with a waiver for preexisting conditions).

Without insurance you will lose all or most of your money if you cancel your trip, regardless of the reason. Default insurance covers you if your tour operator, airline, or cruise line goes out of business. Trip-delay covers expenses that arise because of bad weather or mechanical delays. Study the fine print when comparing policies.

If you're traveling internationally, a key component of travel insurance is coverage for medical bills incurred if you get sick on the road. Such expenses are not generally covered by Medicare or private policies. U.K. residents can buy a travel-insurance policy valid for most vacations taken during the year in which it's purchased (but check preexisting-condition coverage). British and Australian citizens need extra medical coverage when traveling overseas. British citizens need extra medical coverage when traveling abroad. Australian citizens need extra medical coverage when traveling abroad.

Always **buy travel policies directly from the insurance company;** if you buy them from a cruise line, airline, or tour operator that goes out of business you probably will not be covered for the agency or operator's default, a major risk. Before making any purchase, **review your existing health and homeowner's policies** to find what they cover away from home.

➤ TRAVEL INSURERS: In the United States: **Access America** (✉ 6600 W. Broad St., Richmond, VA 23230, ☎ 804/285–3300 or 800/284–8300, FAX 804/673–1586, WEB www.previewtravel.com), **Travel Guard International** (✉ 1145 Clark St., Stevens Point, WI 54481, ☎ 715/345–0505 or 800/826–1300, FAX 800/955–8785, WEB www.noelgroup.com).

➤ INSURANCE INFORMATION: In the United Kingdom: **Association of British Insurers** (✉ 51–55 Gresham St., London EC2V 7HQ, U.K., ☎ 020/7600–3333, FAX 020/7696–8999, WEB www.abi.org.uk). In Canada: **Voyager Insurance** (✉ 44 Peel Center Dr., Brampton, Ontario L6T 4M8, Canada, ☎ 905/791–8700, 800/668–4342 in Canada). In Australia: **Insurance Council of Australia** (✉ Level 3, 56 Pitt St., Sydney NSW 2000, ☎ 03/9614–1077, FAX 03/9614–7924). In New Zealand: **Insurance Council of New Zealand** (✉ Box 474, Wellington, New Zealand, ☎ 04/472–5230, FAX 04/473–3011, WEB www.icnz.org.nz).

LANGUAGES FOR TRAVELERS

The French may appear prickly at first to English-speaking visitors. But it usually helps if you **make an effort to speak a little French.** A simple, friendly *bonjour* (hello) will do, as will asking if the person you are greeting speaks English (*Parlez-vous anglais?*). Be patient, and speak English slowly. *See* the French Vocabulary and Menu Guide at the back of the book for more suggestions.

A phrase book and language-tape set can help get you started.

➤ PHRASE BOOKS & LANGUAGE-TAPE SETS: *Fodor's French for Travelers* (☎ 800/733–3000 in the U.S.; 800/668–4247 in Canada; $7 for phrase book, $16.95 for audio set plus $5.50 for shipping).

LODGING

The lodgings we list are the cream of the crop in each price category. We always list the facilities that are available—but we don't specify whether they cost extra: when pricing accommodations, always ask what's included and what costs extra. Assume that hotels operate on the **European Plan** (with no meals) unless we specify otherwise.

APARTMENT RENTALS

If you want a home base that's roomy enough for a family and comes with cooking facilities, **consider a furnished rental.** These can save you money, especially if you're traveling with a group. Home-exchange directories sometimes list rentals as well as exchanges. You might also look in the bimonthly journal *France-USA Contacts* (known as *FUSAC*), which lists rentals as well as apartment exchanges.

➤ INTERNATIONAL AGENTS: **At Home Abroad** (✉ 405 E. 56th St., Suite 6H, New York, NY 10022, ☎ 212/421–9165, FAX 212/752–1591, WEB member.aol.com/athomabrod/index.html). **Drawbridge to Europe** (✉ 102 Granite St., Ashland, OR 97520, ☎ 541/482–7778 or 888/268–1148, FAX 541/482–7779, WEB www.drawbridgetoeurope.com). **Hideaways International** (✉ 767 Islington St., Portsmouth, NH 03801, ☎ 603/430–4433 or 800/843–4433, FAX 603/430–4444, WEB www.hideaways.com; membership $129). **Hometours International** (✉ Box 11503, Knoxville, TN 37939, ☎ 865/690–8484 or 800/367–4668, WEB thor.he.net/~hometour/). **Interhome** (✉ 1990 N.E. 163rd St., Suite 110, N. Miami Beach, FL 33162, ☎ 305/940–2299 or 800/882–6864, FAX 305/940–2911, WEB www.interhome.com). **Vacation Home Rentals Worldwide** (✉ 235 Kensington Ave., Norwood, NJ 07648, ☎ 201/767–9393 or 800/633–3284, FAX 201/767–5510, WEB www.vhrww.com). **Villanet** (✉ 11556 First Ave. NW, Seattle, WA 98177, ☎ 206/417–3444 or 800/964–1891, FAX 206/417–1832, WEB www.rentavilla.com). **Villas and Apartments Abroad** (✉ 1270 Ave. of the Americas, 15th floor, New York, NY 10020, ☎ 212/897–5045 or 800/433–3020,

FAX 212/897–5039, WEB www.vaanyc.
com). **Villas International** (✉ 950
Northgate Dr., Suite 206, San Rafael,
CA 94903, ☎ 415/499–9490 or
800/221–2260, FAX 415/499–9491,
WEB www.villasintl.com).

➤ LOCAL AGENTS: *See* Chapter 3.

HOME EXCHANGES

If you would like to exchange your
home for someone else's, **join a home-
exchange organization,** which will
send you its updated listings of available exchanges for a year and will
include your own listing in at least
one of them. It's up to you to make
specific arrangements.

➤ EXCHANGE CLUBS: **HomeLink
International** (✉ Box 47747, Tampa,
FL 33647, ☎ 813/975–9825 or
800/638–3841, FAX 813/910–8144,
WEB www.homelink.org; $98 per
year). **Intervac U.S.** (✉ Box 590504,
San Francisco, CA 94159, ☎ 800/
756–4663, FAX 415/435–7440,
WEB www.intervacus.com; $93 yearly
fee includes one catalogue and
on-line access).

HOSTELS

No matter what your age, you can
**save on lodging costs by staying at
hostels.** In some 5,000 locations in
more than 70 countries around the
world, Hostelling International (HI),
the umbrella group for a number of
national youth-hostel associations,
offers single-sex, dorm-style beds and,
at many hostels, rooms for couples
and family accommodations. Membership in any HI national hostel
association, open to travelers of all
ages, allows you to stay in HI-affili-
ated hostels at member rates; one-
year membership is about $25 for
adults (C$26.75 in Canada, £9.30 in
the United Kingdom, $30 in Aus-
tralia, and $30 in New Zealand);
hostels run about $10–$25 per night.
Members have priority if the hostel is
full; they're also eligible for discounts
around the world, even on rail and
bus travel in some countries.

Most of Paris's hostels and *foyers*
(student hostels) are bargains at 100
francs/€15.25–170 francs/€25.95 a
night for a bed with free showers and
a baguette-and-coffee wake-up call;
some are even located in top city
locales. In summer, you should reserve in writing a month in advance
(deposits are often taken via credit
card, usually MasterCard and Visa,
for advance reservations); if you don't
have a reservation, it's a good idea to
check in as early as 8 AM. Some foyers
have age restrictions and tend to
house young workers and students in
dormlike accommodations, but other
foyers accommodate travelers of all
ages. Paris's major public hostels are
run by the Féderation Unie des
Auberges de Jeunesse (FUAJ)—for
about 130 francs/€19.85, a bed,
sheets, shower, and breakfast are
provided, with beds usually three to
four to a room. Maisons Interna-
tionales des Jeunes Étudiants (MIJE)
have the plushest hostels, sometimes
in historic mansions. Private hostels
have accommodations that run from
pleasant, if spartan, double rooms to
dormlike arrangements.

➤ BEST OPTIONS: Near Père-Lachaise:
**Auberge de Jeunesse d'Artagnan
FUAJ** (✉ 80 rue Vitruve, 3ᵉ, ☎ 01–
40–32–34–56, FAX 01–40–32–34–55).
Near the Eiffel Tower: **Aloha Hostel**
(✉ 1 rue Borromée,, 75015, ☎ 01–
42–73–03–03, FAX 01–42–73–14–14).
Near Montmartre: **Village** (✉ 20 rue
d'Orsel, 75018, ☎ 01–42–64–22–02,
FAX 01–42–64–22–04). In the Latin
Quarter: **Young and Happy Youth
Hostel** (✉ 80 rue Mouffetard, 75005,
☎ 01–45–35–09–53). In the Marais:
Hôtel le Fauconnier MIJE (✉ 11 rue
de Fauconnier, 75004, ☎ 01–42–74–
23–45, FAX 01–42–74–08–93).

➤ ORGANIZATIONS: **Australian Youth
Hostel Association** (✉ 10 Mallett St.,
Camperdown, NSW 2050, Australia,
☎ 02/9565–1699, FAX 02/9565–1325,
WEB www.yha.com.au). **Féderation
Unie des Auberges de Jeunesse** (FUAJ/
Hostelling International; ✉ FUAJ
Beaubourg: 9 rue Brantôme, 3ᵉ, Paris,
☎ 01–48–04–70–40, WEB www.fuaj.
org; Centre National: ✉ 27 rue Pajol,
18ᵉ, Paris, ☎ 01–44–89–87–27).
**Hostelling International—American
Youth Hostels** (✉ 733 15th St. NW,
Suite 840, Washington, DC 20005,
☎ 202/783–6161, FAX 202/783–6171,
WEB www.hiayh.org). **Hostelling
International—Canada** (✉ 400–205
Catherine St., Ottawa, Ontario K2P
1C3, Canada, ☎ 613/237–7884,

FAX 613/237–7868, WEB www. hostellingintl.ca). **Youth Hostel Association of England and Wales** (✉ Trevelyan House, 8 St. Stephen's Hill, St. Albans, Hertfordshire AL1 2DY, U.K., ☎ 0870/870–8808, FAX 01727/844126, WEB www.yha.org.uk). **Youth Hostels Association of New Zealand** (✉ Box 436, Christchurch, New Zealand, ☎ 03/379–9970, FAX 03/365–4476, WEB www.yha.org.nz).

HOTELS

It's always a good idea to **make hotel reservations in Paris as far in advance as possible,** especially in late spring, summer, and fall. E-mailing is probably the easiest way to contact a hotel if the hotel has Internet connections; faxing is another convenient way to contact the hotel (the staff is probably more likely to read English than to understand it over the phone long distance), though calling also works. In your e-mail or fax (or over the phone), specify the exact dates that you want to stay at the hotel (when you will arrive and when you will check out); the size of the room you want and how many people will be sleeping there; what kind of bed you want (single or double, twin beds or double, etc.); and whether you want a bathroom with a shower or bathtub (or both). You might also ask if a deposit (or your credit card number) is required and, if so, what happens if you cancel. Request that the hotel fax you back so that you have a written confirmation of your reservation in hand when you arrive at the hotel.

Here are some French words that can come in handy when booking a room: air-conditioning (*climatisation*); private baths (*salle de bain privée*); bathtub (*baignoire*); shower (*douche*).

If you arrive in Paris without a reservation, one of the two tourist offices may be able to help you. You may be able to get a better rate per night if you are staying a week or longer; ask. Note that the quality of accommodations, particularly older properties and even in luxury hotels, can vary from room to room; **if you don't like the room you're given, ask to see another.** You'll often see a sign outside a hotel with a painted shield bearing one to four stars based on a government rating system. At the bottom end are one-star hotels, where you might have to share a bathroom and do without an elevator. Two- and three-star hotels generally have private bathrooms, elevators, and in-room televisions. The ratings are sometimes misleading, however, since many hotels prefer to be understarred for tax reasons.

In addition to smaller properties and luxury hotels, Paris has—but is not dominated by—big chains. Examples in the upper price bracket are Frantel, Hilton, Hyatt, Marriott, and Novotel. The Best Western, Campanile, Climat de France, Holiday Inn, Ibis, and Timhotel chains are more moderate. Typically, chains offer a more consistent standard of modern features (modern bathrooms, TV, etc.) but tend to lack atmosphere.

All hotels listed have private bath unless otherwise noted.

➤ TOLL-FREE NUMBERS: **Best Western** (☎ 800/528–1234, WEB www. bestwestern.com). **Choice** (☎ 800/221–2222, WEB www.hotelchoice.com). **Clarion** (☎ 800/252–7466, WEB www. hotelchoice.com). **Comfort** (☎ 800/228–5150, WEB www.comfortinn. com). **Forte** (☎ 800/225–5843, WEB www.forte-hotels.com). **Four Seasons** (☎ 800/332–3442, WEB www. fourseasons.com). **Hilton** (☎ 800/445–8667, WEB www.hilton.com). **Holiday Inn** (☎ 800/465–4329, WEB www.basshotels.com). **Hyatt Hotels & Resorts** (☎ 800/233–1234, WEB www.hyatt.com). **Inter-Continental** (☎ 800/327–0200, WEB www. interconti.com). **Le Meridien** (☎ 800/543–4300, WEB www.forte-hotels. com). **Logis de France** (☎ 01–45–84–70–00, FAX 01–44–24–08–74). **Marriott** (☎ 800/228–9290, WEB www. marriott.com). **Le Meridien** (☎ 800/543–4300, WEB www.lemeridien-hotels. com). **Nikko Hotels International** (☎ 800/645–5687, WEB www. nikkohotels.com). **Quality Inn** (☎ 800/228–5151, WEB www.qualityinn.com). **Radisson** (☎ 800/333–3333, WEB www. radisson.com). **Relais & Châteaux** (☎ 01–45–72–96–50 in France; 212/856–0115; 800/860–4930 in the U.S., FAX 01–45–72–96–69 in France; 212/856–0193 in the U.S., WEB www.

relaischateaux.com).**Renaissance Hotels & Resorts** (☎ 800/468–3571, WEB www.renaissancehotels.com/). **Sheraton** (☎ 800/325–3535, WEB www. starwood.com). **Small Luxury Hotels of the World** (☎ 713/522–9512; 800/525–4800 in the U.S.; 44/01372–361873 in the U.K., FAX 713/524–7412 in the U.S.; 44/01372–361874 in the U.K.).

MAIL & SHIPPING

Post offices, or PTT, are scattered throughout every arrondissement and are recognizable by a yellow LA POSTE sign. They are usually open weekdays 8 AM–7 PM, Saturday 8 AM–noon.

➤ POST OFFICES: **Main office** (✉ 52 rue du Louvre, 1er), open 24 hours seven days a week. **Champs-Élysées office** (✉ 10 rue Balzac, 8e), Monday to Saturday, open until 7 PM.

OVERNIGHT SERVICES

Sending overnight mail from Paris is relatively easy. Besides DHL, Federal Express, and UPS, the French post office has an overnight mail service called Chronopost that has special prepaid boxes for international use (and also boxes specifically made to mail wine). All agencies listed can be used as drop-off points and all have information in English.

➤ MAJOR SERVICES: **DHL** (✉ 6 rue des Colonnes, 7e, ☎ 01–55–35–30–30, WEB www.dhl.com; ✉ 59 rue Iéna, 16e, ☎ 01–45–01–91–00). **Federal Express** (✉ 63 bd. Haussmann, 8e, ☎ 01–40–06–90–16, www.fedex. com/fr; ✉ 2 rue 29 Juillet, 1er, ☎ 01–49–26–04–66; 08–00–12–38–00 information in English about pickups, 01–49–26–04–66; 08–00–12–38–00 information in English about pick-ups; WEB www.ups.com). **UPS** (✉ 34 bd. Malesherbes, 8e; ✉ 107 rue Réaumur, 2e; ☎ 08–00–87–78–77 for both).

POSTAL RATES

Airmail letters to the United States and Canada cost 4.40 francs/€.67 for 20 grams, 8.20 francs/€1.25 for 40 grams, and 13 francs/€1.98 for 60 grams. Letters to the United Kingdom cost 3 francs/€.45 for up to 20 grams, as they do within France. Postcards cost 3 francs/€.45 within France and EU countries and 4.40 francs/€.67 to the United States and Canada. Stamps can be bought in post offices and cafés sporting a red TABAC sign.

RECEIVING MAIL

If you're uncertain where you'll be staying, have mail sent to American Express (if you're a card member) or to "poste restante" at any post office.

MÉTRO

Métro stations are recognizable either by a large yellow *M* within a circle or by the distinctive curly green Art Nouveau railings and archway bearing the full title (Métropolitain). Taking **the métro is the most efficient way to get around Paris.** *See* the métro map at the end of Smart Travel Tips A to Z.

Fourteen métro and two RER (Réseau Express Régional, or the Regional Express Network) lines crisscross Paris and the suburbs, and you are seldom more than 500 yards from the nearest station. The métro network connects at several points in Paris with the RER, the commuter trains that go from the city center to the suburbs. RER trains crossing Paris on their way from suburb to suburb can be great time-savers because they only make a few stops in the city (you can use the same tickets for both the métro and the RER within Paris).

It's essential to **know the name of the last station on the line you take,** as this name appears on all signs. A connection (you can make as many as you like on one ticket) is called a *correspondance.* At junction stations, illuminated orange signs bearing the name of the line terminus appear over the correct corridors for each correspondance. Illuminated blue signs marked *sortie* indicate the station exit. Note that tickets are only valid inside the gates, or *limites.*

Métro service starts at 5:30 AM and continues until 1 AM, when the last train on each line reaches its terminus. Some lines and stations in Paris are a bit risky at night, in particular Lines 2 and 13. But in general, the métro is relatively safe throughout, providing you **don't walk around with your wallet hanging out of your** back pocket or travel alone late at night.

FARES & SCHEDULES

All **métro tickets and passes are valid not only for the métro but also for all RER and bus travel within Paris.** Métro tickets cost 8 francs/€1.20 each; a *carnet* (10 tickets for 55 francs/€8.40) is a better value. The best deal is the weekly (*coupon jaune*) or monthly (*carte orange*) ticket, sold according to zone. Zones 1 and 2 cover the entire métro network; tickets cost 85 francs/€13 a week or 285 francs/€43.45 a month. If you plan to take suburban trains to visit places in Ile-de-France, consider a four-zone (Versailles, St-Germain-en-Laye; 142 francs/€21.65 a week) or six-zone (Rambouillet, Fontainebleau; 184 francs/€28.10 a week) ticket. For these weekly/monthly tickets, you need a pass (available from rail and major métro stations) and a passport-size photograph (many stations have photo booths).

A one-day (Mobilis) and the two- to five-day (Paris-Visite) tickets assure unlimited travel on the entire RATP network: métro, RER, bus, tram, funicular (Montmartre), and noctambus (night bus). Unlike the coupon jaune, which is good from Monday morning to Sunday evening, Mobilis and Paris-Visite passes are valid starting any day of the week and give you discounts on a limited number of museums and tourist attractions. The price is 55 francs/€8.40 (one-day), 90 francs/€13.70 (two-day), 120 francs/€18.30 (three-day), and 175 francs/€26.70 (five-day) for Paris only. Rates for children ages 4–11 are approximately half of these prices. Suburbs such as Versailles and St-Germain-en-Laye cost 155 francs/€23.60 (one-day). EuroDisney costs 155 francs/€23.60, 225 francs/€34.30, 280 francs/€42.70, and 350 francs/€53.35 respectively for a one-to four-day pass.

Access to métro and RER platforms is through an automatic ticket barrier. Slide your ticket in and pick it up as it pops out. Be certain to **keep your ticket during your journey;** you'll need it to leave the RER system and in case you run into any green-clad ticket inspectors, who will impose a big fine if you can't produce your ticket.

➤ MÉTRO INFORMATION: **RATP** (✉ Pl. de la Madeleine, 8ᵉ 53 bis quai des Grands-Augustins, 6ᵉ; ☎ 08-36-68-41-14, WEB www.ratp.fr), open daily 9–5.

MONEY MATTERS

Like many capital cities, **Paris is expensive**; the good news is that it is, at press time (Spring 2001), less expensive than New York City, London, and Tokyo. If you avoid the obvious tourist traps, you can find affordable places to eat and shop. Prices tend to reflect the standing of an area in the eyes of Parisians; much sought-after residential arrondissements such as the 7ᵉ, 16ᵉ, and 17ᵉ—of limited tourist interest—are far more expensive than the student-oriented, much-visited Latin Quarter. The tourist area where value for money is most difficult to find is the 8ᵉ arrondissement, on and around the Champs-Élysées. Places where you can generally be certain to shop, eat, and stay without overpaying include the streets surrounding Montmartre (not the Butte, or hilltop, itself); the St-Michel/Sorbonne area on the Left Bank; the mazelike streets around Les Halles and the Marais in central Paris; in Montparnasse, south of the boulevard; and the Bastille, République (especially the trendy rue Oberkamp), and Belleville areas of eastern Paris.

Note that in cafés, bars, and some restaurants, **it's less expensive to eat or drink standing at the counter than it is to sit at a table.** Two prices are listed—*au comptoir* (at the counter) and *à salle* (at a table)—and sometimes a third for the terrace. A cup of coffee, standing at a bar, costs from 7 francs/€1.06; if you sit, it will cost 10 francs/€1.50–40 francs/€6.10. A glass of beer costs from 10 francs/€1.50 standing and from 15 francs/€2.30 to 40 francs/€6.10 sitting; a soft drink costs between 10 francs/€1.50 and 20 francs/€3.05. A ham sandwich will cost between 17 francs/€2.60 and 30 francs/€4.60.

Expect to pay 40 francs/€6.10–70 francs/€10.70 for a short taxi ride. Museum entry is 20 francs/€3.05–45 francs/€6.90, though there are hours or days of the week when admission is reduced or free.

Prices throughout this guide are given for adults. Substantially reduced fees are almost always available for children, students, and senior citizens.

ATMS

ATMs are one of the easiest ways to get francs. Although transaction fees may be higher abroad than at home, banks usually offer excellent, wholesale exchange rates through ATMs. You may, however, have to look around for Cirrus and Plus locations; it's a good idea to get a list of locations from your bank before you go. Note, too, that you may have better luck with ATMs if you're using a credit card or debit card that is also a Visa or MasterCard, rather than just your bank card.

To get cash at ATMs in Paris, **your PIN must be four digits long,** If you are having trouble remembering your pin, do not try more than twice, because at the third attempt, the machine will eat your card and you will have to go back the next morning to retrieve it. Note, too, that you may be charged by your bank for using ATMs overseas; inquire at your bank about charges.

CREDIT CARDS

Throughout this guide, the following abbreviations are used: **AE,** American Express; **DC,** Diners Club; **MC,** MasterCard; and **V,** Visa.

➤ REPORTING LOST CARDS: **American Express** (☎ 336/939–1111 or 336/668–5309); call collect. **Diners Club** (☎ 303/799–1504); call collect. **MasterCard** (☎ 0800/90–1387). **Visa** (☎ 0800/90–1179; 410/581–9994 collect).

CURRENCY

On January 1, 2002, the new single European Union (EU) currency, the euro, will finally become the official currency of the 11 countries participating in the European Monetary Union (with the notable exceptions of Great Britain, Denmark, Sweden, and Greece). In France, the long-awaited physical debut of the euro will begin somewhat confusingly: all banks, businesses, and money machines will be stocked in euros as of the first of January but French francs will *also* be valid until midnight February 17, 2002—a six-week period when you can still buy your newspaper with francs but receive your change in euros. Until that point, people can continue to use the franc in their day-to-day transactions and travelers will continue to exchange their money for its colorful 500-, 200-, 100-, 50-, and 20-franc banknotes; the 20-, 10-, 5-, 2-, and 1-franc coins will weigh down their pockets and the tiny 20-, 10-, and 5-centime coins will find their way to the bottom of their luggage as they always do. Your best bet is to change your remaining francs (or any other EU currency) into euros the minute you arrive in France, and for once it doesn't really matter where you do so because the rate between the franc (or other Monetary Union currencies) and the euro was irrevocably fixed in late 1999 (1 euro = 6.55 francs), thus eliminating any fluctuations in the market and any need for commission. If anyone tries to charge you a commission when you are changing French francs (or any other EU currency) into euros, stop the transaction immediately.

On the other hand, the U.S. dollar (and all other currencies that are not part of the EU community) and the euro are in direct competition. In fact, this is the reason why the euro was created in the first place, so it could box with the big boys. Here the gloves are off and you do have to pay close attention to where you change your money, thus following the old guidelines for exchanging currencies—**shop around for the best exchange rates (and also check the rates before leaving home) when it comes to non-EU currencies, such as the U.S dollar, the Japanese yen, and the British pound.** To reiterate: there is a big difference between exchanging old francs (set rate/no commission/no worries) and changing dollars (competition/fluctuation/diverse commission).

Although it might take Europeans a little getting used to, the euro will make your life much, much easier. Gone are the days when a day trip to Germany meant changing money into yet another currency and paying whatever supplementary commission thereon. Before, a trip to Europe meant carting home a small plastic bag of faded notes in all colors of the rainbow and hundreds of coins you had to examine carefully to find the origin; now with the euro, crossing borders will just be that much easier: first, you won't have to take all that time and energy following your trusty guidebook's expert advice on the best exchange locations; second, there won't be that awkward moment when you find you don't have enough local currency to buy a piece of gum; and third, you won't have to do all that math (hooray!). The euro was created as a direct competitor with the U.S. dollar which means that their rates are quite similar: at press time (Spring 2001), one euro =.91 US$. The rates of conversion between the euro and other local currencies have been irrevocably fixed: 1 euro = 6.55 French francs; 1.95 German marks; 1.39 Canadian dollars; 0.78 Irish punts; 13.76 Austrian schillings; 1.79 Australian dollars; 2.14 New Zealand dollars; 1936.26 Italian liras; 40.33 Belgian francs; 166.38 Spanish pesetas; 2.20 Dutch guilders; 200.48 Portuguese escudos; 40.33 Luxembourg francs; 5.94 Finnish markkas; and 0.62 English pounds.

The euro system is classic; there are eight coins: 1 and 2 euros, plus 1, 2, 5, 10, 20, and 50 centimes, or cents, of the euro. All coins have one side that has the value of the euro on it and the other side with each countries' own unique national symbol. There are seven colorful notes: 5, 10, 20, 50, 100, 200, and 500 euros. Notes have the principal architectural styles from antiquity onwards on one side and the map and the flag of Europe on the other and are the same for all countries. Notes are the same for all countries. Don't be alarmed if you forgot some rumpled francs at home this trip as there is an ample grace period; you have until midnight February 17, 2005 to change coins and until midnight February 17, 2012 to change notes at the Banque of France—but after these dates you may as well frame those remaining francs and hang them on the wall.

CURRENCY EXCHANGE

These days, the **easiest way to get euros—and, up to February 17, 2002, francs (at some machines)—is through ATMs**; you can find them in airports, train stations, and throughout the city. ATM rates are excellent because they are based on wholesale rates offered only by major banks. It's a good idea, however, to bring some euros—or, if you wish, francs (up to February 17, 2002)—with you from home and always to have some cash and traveler's checks as backup. For the best deal when exchanging currencies not within the Monetary Union purview (the U.S. dollar, the yen, and the English pound are examples), compare rates at banks (which usually have the most favorable rates) and booths and look for exchange booths that clearly state "no commission." At exchange booths always confirm the rate with the teller before exchanging money. You won't do as well at exchange booths in airports or rail and bus stations, in hotels, in restaurants, or in stores. Of all the banks in Paris, Banque de Paris generally has the best rates. To avoid lines at airport exchange booths, **get euros—or a bit of local currency—before you leave home.**

➤ EXCHANGE SERVICES: **International Currency Express** (☎ 888/278–6628 orders, WEB www.foreignmoney.com). **Thomas Cook Currency Services** (☎ 800/287–7362 telephone orders and retail locations, WEB www.us. thomascook.com).

TRAVELER'S CHECKS

Do you need traveler's checks? It depends on where you're headed. If you're going to rural areas and small towns, go with cash; traveler's checks are best used in cities. Lost or stolen checks can usually be replaced within 24 hours. To ensure a speedy refund, buy your own traveler's checks—don't let someone else pay for them: irregularities like this can cause delays. The person who bought the checks should make the call to request a refund.

PACKING

In your carry-on luggage, **pack an extra pair of eyeglasses or contact** lenses and **enough of any medication you take** to last the entire trip. You may also ask your doctor to write a spare prescription using the drug's generic name, since brand names may vary from country to country. In luggage to be checked, **never pack prescription drugs or valuables.** To avoid customs delays, carry medications in their original packaging. And don't forget to carry with you the addresses of offices that handle refunds of lost traveler's checks. Check *Fodor's How to Pack* (available in bookstores everywhere) for more tips.

CHECKING LUGGAGE

How many carry-on bags you can bring with you is up to the airline. Most allow two, but not always, so make sure that everything you carry aboard will fit under your seat or in the overhead bin, and get to the gate early. Note that if you have a seat at the back of the plane, you'll probably board first, while the overhead bins are still empty.

If you are flying internationally, note that baggage allowances may be determined not by piece but by weight—generally 88 pounds (40 kilograms) in first class, 66 pounds (30 kilograms) in business class, and 44 pounds (20 kilograms) in economy.

Airline liability for baggage is limited to $1,250 per person on flights within the United States. On international flights it amounts to $9.07 per pound or $20 per kilogram for checked baggage (roughly $640 per 70-pound bag) and $400 per passenger for unchecked baggage. You can buy additional coverage at check-in for about $10 per $1,000 of coverage, but it excludes a rather extensive list of items, shown on your airline ticket.

Before departure, **itemize your bags' contents** and their worth, and label the bags with your name, address, and phone number. (If you use your home address, cover it so potential thieves can't see it readily.) Inside each bag, **pack a copy of your itinerary.** At check-in, **make sure that each bag is correctly tagged** with the destination airport's three-letter code. If your bags arrive damaged or fail to arrive at all, file a written report with the airline before leaving the airport.

PASSPORTS & VISAS

When traveling internationally, **carry your passport** even if you don't need one (it's always the best form of I.D.) and **make two photocopies of the data page** (one for someone at home and another for you, carried separately from your passport). If you lose your passport, promptly call the nearest embassy or consulate and the local police.

ENTERING FRANCE

All citizens of Australia, Canada, New Zealand, the United States, and the United Kingdom, even infants, need only a valid passport to enter France for stays of up to 90 days. If you lose your passport, promptly call the nearest embassy or consulate and the local police.

➤ AUSTRALIAN CITIZENS: **Australian Passport Office** (☎ 131–232, WEB www.dfat.gov.au/passports).

➤ CANADIAN CITIZENS: **Passport Office** (☎ 819/994–3500; 800/567–6868 in Canada, WEB www.dfait-maeci.gc.ca/passport).

➤ NEW ZEALAND CITIZENS: **New Zealand Passport Office** (☎ 04/494–0700, WEB www.passports.govt.nz).

➤ U.K. CITIZENS: **London Passport Office** (☎ 0870/521–0410, WEB www.ukpa.gov.uk) for fees and documentation requirements and to request an emergency passport.

➤ U.S. CITIZENS: **National Passport Information Center** (☎ 900/225–5674; calls are 35¢ per minute for automated service, $1.05 per minute for operator service; WEB www.travel.state.gov/npicinfo.html).

REST ROOMS

Use of public toilet facilities in cafés and bars is usually reserved for the customer. Bathrooms are often located downstairs and are usually unisex, which may mean walking by a men's urinal to reach the cubicle. Turkish toilets—holes in the ground surrounded by porcelain pads for your feet—still exist. Stand as far away as possible when you press the flushing mechanism in order to avoid water damage to your shoes. In certain cafés, the lights will not come on in the bathroom until the cubicle door is locked. These lights work on a three-minute timer to save electricity. Simply press the button again if the lights go out. Clean public toilets are available in fast-food chains, department stores, and public parks. You can also find pay-per-use toilet units on the street, which require 2 francs/€.30 (small children, however, should not use these alone, as the self-sanitizing system works with weight-related sensors that might not detect a child's presence). There are bathrooms in the larger métro stations and in all train stations for a cost of 1 franc/€.15–2 francs/€.30.

SAFETY

Paris is one of the safest big cities in the world, good news for the traveling lone female. Although times are changing, the idea still exists that women traveling alone are fair game for troublesome comments and the like; however, *dragueurs* (men who persistently profess their undying love to hapless female passersby) are a dying breed in this increasingly politically correct world. Certain neighborhoods can pose problems, thanks to the night trade that goes on around Les Halles and St-Denis and on boulevard Clichy in Pigalle. Some off-the-beaten-path neighborhoods—particularly the outlying suburban communities around Paris, heavily populated by working-class and immigrant populations—may deserve extra precaution. Note that smiling automatically out of politeness is not part of French culture and can be quickly misinterpreted. If you encounter a problem, don't be afraid to show your irritation. When in doubt, stick to the boulevards, memorize the time of the last métro train to your station, ride in the first car by the conductor, and just use your common sense. Paris is a giant metropolis, so it is always best to be streetwise and aware.

SENIOR-CITIZEN TRAVEL

Travelers 60 years or older to Paris can take advantage of many discounts, such as reduced admissions of 20%–50% to museums and movie theaters. For rail travel outside of Paris, the Carte Senior entitles travelers 60 years and older to discounts.

To qualify for age-related discounts, **mention your senior-citizen status up front** when booking hotel reservations (not when checking out) and before you're seated in restaurants (not when paying the bill). When renting a car, ask about promotional car-rental discounts, which can be cheaper than senior-citizen rates.

➤ EDUCATIONAL PROGRAMS: **Elderhostel** (✉ 11 Ave. de Lafayette, Boston, MA 02111-1746, ☎ 877/426–8056, FAX 877/426–2166, WEB www.elderhostel.org). **Interhostel** (✉ University of New Hampshire, 6 Garrison Ave., Durham, NH 03824, ☎ 603/862–1147 or 800/733–9753, FAX 603/862–1113, WEB www.learn.unh.edu).

SIGHTSEEING TOURS

There are many ways to see Paris on a guided tour.

BIKE TOURS

A number of companies organize bike tours around Paris and its environs (Versailles, Chantilly, and Fontainebleau) for about 150 francs/€23–200 francs/€30 per person.

➤ INFORMATION: **Butterfield & Robinson** (✉ 70 Bond St., Toronto, Canada M5B 1X3, ☎ 416/864–1354 or 800/678–1147). **Paris Bike** (✉ 83 rue Daguerre, 14e, ☎ 01–45–38–58–58). **Paris à Vélo, C'est Sympa** (✉ 37 bd. Bourdon, 4e, ☎ 01–48–87–60–01).

BOAT TOURS

Boat trips along the Seine run throughout the day and evening for a cost of 40 francs/€6.10–100 francs/€15.25. Many of the tours include lunch or dinner for an average cost of 300 francs/€45.80–600 francs/€91.60. Reservations for meals are usually essential, and some require jacket and tie.

Bateaux Mouches boats depart from the Pont de l'Alma (Right Bank) 10–noon, 2–7, and 8:30–10:30. Lunch is served at 1 PM and dinner at 8:30 PM. Bateaux Parisiens–Tour Eiffel boats depart from the Pont d'Iéna (Left Bank) every half hour in summer and every hour in winter, starting at 10 AM. The last boat leaves at 9 PM (11 PM in summer). There are lunch and dinner cruises. Bat-O-Bus's trip along the Seine without commentary gives you the advantage of being able to get on and off at any one of five stops along the river, including Trocadéro, Musée d'Orsay, the Louvre, Notre-Dame, and Hôtel de Ville. Take it one stop for 20 francs/€3.05, pay 60 francs/€9.15 for a full-day ticket, or buy a season ticket for 250 francs/€38.15. Note that it operates from April 15 to October 31 and departs every half hour between 10 and 6. Canauxrama organizes leisurely canal tours in flat-bottom barges along the St-Martin and Ourcq canals in East Paris. Departures from the quai de la Loire are at 9:15 and 2:45, and departures from the Bassin de l'Arsenal (opposite 50 boulevard de la Bastille) are at 9:30 and 2:30. The trip lasts about 2½ hours. Reservations should be made. Paris Canal runs three-hour trips with bilingual commentary between the Musée d'Orsay and the Parc de La Villette, between April and mid-November only. Reservations are essential. Vedettes du Pont Neuf boats depart every half hour from square du Vert Galant, 10–noon, 1:30–6:30, and 9–10:30 from March to October. Yachts de Paris organizes 2½-hour "gourmet cruises" (for about 890 francs/€135.90) year-round.

➤ FEES & SCHEDULES: **Bateaux Mouches** (✉ Pont de l'Alma, 8ᵉ, ☎ 01–42–25–96–10, WEB www.bateauxmouches.com). **Bateaux Parisiens-Tour Eiffel** (✉ Pont d'Iéna, 7ᵉ, ☎ 01–44–11–33–44, WEB www.bateauxparisiens.com). **Bat-O-Bus** (✉ Pont d'Iéna, 7ᵉ, ☎ 01–44–11–33–44 or 01–44–11–33–99, WEB www.ratp.com). **Canauxrama** (✉ 5 bis quai de la Loire, 19ᵉ; Bassin de l'Arsenal, 12ᵉ; ☎ 01–42–39–15–00; WEB www.canauxrama.com). **Paris Canal** (✉ 19 quai de la Loire, 19ᵉ; ☎ 01–42–40–96–97). **Vedettes du Pont Neuf** (✉ Ile de la Cité, 1ᵉʳ, ☎ 01–46–33–98–38). **Yachts de Paris** (✉ Port de Javel, ☎ 01–44–54–14–70, WEB www.yachtsdeparis.com).

BUS TOURS

For a two-hour orientation tour by bus, the standard price is about 150 francs/€23. The two largest bus-tour operators are Cityrama and Paris Vision; for a more intimate—albeit expensive—tour of the city, Cityrama also runs several minibus excursions per day. Paris Bus gives tours in a London-style double-decker bus. You can catch the bus at any of nine pickup points; tickets cost 125 francs/€19.08 and allow you unlimited use for two days. For 145 francs/€22.10 the "Paris Open Tour" gives you two (consecutive) days of freedom to visit Paris in a double-decker bus with an open top. The bilingual tour lasts about two hours, but you can get on and off as you please, since the bus stops at more than 20 spots along a circular route. A copy of the timetables for these tours is available from the main Paris Tourist Office. RATP (Paris Transit Authority) also gives guide-accompanied excursions in and around Paris by bus.

➤ FEES & SCHEDULES: **Cityrama** (✉ 4 pl. des Pyramides, 1ᵉʳ, ☎ 01–44–55–61–00). **Paris Bus** (☎ 01–42–30–55–50). **Paris Vision** (✉ 214 rue de Rivoli, 1ᵉʳ, ☎ 01–42–60–31–25). **RATP** (✉ Pl. de la Madeleine, 8ᵉ; 53 bis quai des Grands-Augustins, 6ᵉ, ☎ 08–36–68–41–14).

HELICOPTER TOURS

For a spectacular aerial view of Paris, Delta Lima offers a helicopter tour; it takes off from Toussus le Noble (15 minutes from Paris). Tours last 35 minutes and cost 962 francs/€146.85 per person.

➤ FEES & SCHEDULES: **Delta Lima** (☎ 01–40–68–01–23).

MINIBUS TOURS

Paris Bus and Paris Major Limousine organize tours of Paris and environs by luxury minibuses (for 4 to 15 passengers) for a minimum of four hours. The price varies from 1,700 francs/€260 to 2,600 francs/€397. Reservations are essential.

➤ INFORMATION: **Paris Bus** (✉ 22 rue de la Prévoyance, Vincennes, ☎ 01–43–65–55–55, WEB www.touring-france.com). **Paris Major**

Limousine (✉ 6 pl. de la Madeleine, 8ᵉ, ☎ 01–44–52–50–00, WEB www. paris-limousine.fr).

WALKING TOURS

There are a number of English-language walking tours of Paris. Walking tours generally last about two hours and cost about 60 francs/€9.15. Paris Contact arranges walking tours of popular sights such as the Louvre and Versailles and unique theme tours, such as "Jefferson's Paris" and "The Paris of Proust," and can, upon request, do individually organized tours. Paris Walking Tours offers a wide variety of tours, from neighborhood visits to museum tours and theme tours (such as "Hemingway's Paris"). Bohemian Paris organizes a stroll on the Left Bank, filled with literary discussion, biographical information, and gossipy anecdotes about Paris in the '20s; this tour, led by a university professor and writer, costs 200 francs/€30.55 and lasts 2½ hours. Black Paris Tours organizes a variety of tours exploring the places made famous by African-American musicians, writers, artists, and political exiles.

Tours include a four- to five-hour walking-bus-métro tour (350 francs/€53.45) that offers first-time visitors a city orientation and a primer in the history of African-Americans in Paris. Other options include "Montmartre/Pigalle: The 1920s Harlem of Paris" and tours of top African and soul-food restaurants. A list of walking tours is also available from the Caisse Nationale des Monuments Historiques, in the weekly magazine *Pariscope,* and in *L'Officiel des Spectacles,* which lists walking tours under the heading "*Conférences*" (most are in French, unless otherwise noted).

➤ FEES & SCHEDULES: **Black Paris Tours** (☎ 01–46–37–03–96). **Bohemian Paris** (☎ 01–56–24–36–00). **Butterfield & Robinson** (✉ 70 Bond St., Toronto, Canada M5B 1X3, ☎ 416/864–1354 or 800/678–1147). **Caisse Nationale des Monuments Historiques** (✉ Bureau des Visites/Conférences, Hôtel de Sully, 62 rue St-Antoine, 4ᵉ, ☎ 01–44–61–21–70). **Paris Contact** (☎ 01–42–51–08–40). **Paris Walking Tours** (☎ 01–48–09–21–40, WEB www.paris-walks.com).

STUDENTS IN PARIS

For a detailed listing of deals for students in Paris, ask for the brochure *"Jeunes à Paris"* from the main tourist office. *"France-USA Contacts"* ("*FUSAC*"), a twice-monthly publication available free in restaurants and bookstores, also has useful information.

➤ IDs & SERVICES: **Council Travel** (CIEE; ✉ 205 E. 42nd St., 15th floor, New York, NY 10017, ☎ 212/822–2700 or 888/268–6245, FAX 212/822–2699, WEB www.councilexchanges.org) for mail orders only, in the United States. **Travel Cuts** (✉ 187 College St., Toronto, Ontario M5T 1P7, Canada, ☎ 416/979–2406 or 800/667–2887 in Canada, FAX 416/979–8167, WEB www.travelcuts.com).

TAXES

All taxes must be included in affixed prices in France. Prices in **restaurants and hotel prices must by law include taxes and service charges:** if these appear as additional items on your bill, you should complain.

VALUE-ADDED TAX

VAT (value-added tax, known in France as TVA), at a standard rate of 19.6% (33% for luxury goods), is included in the price of many goods, but foreigners are often entitled to a refund. To be eligible for the VAT, an item (or items) must be purchased in one day in one place and must equal or exceed 1,200 francs (€182.2). You cannot combine purchases from different shops to total the required amount, nor combine purchases from various days to total the required amount. The VAT for services (restaurants/theater, etc.) are not refundable for the leisure traveler. To receive the VAT, request a refund form from the business, fill it out on the spot, noting your preferred means of receiving the VAT payment (credit card or a bankers check in U.S.

dollars). The business must complete the form and stamp it, then mail it in a provided stamped-addressed envelope. Alternatively, you can process your VAT refund at the airport. Go to the airport's VAT or (TVA) counter (at your last point of departure from the European Union) and be ready to show the customs official your goods. The customs official will then (all-importantly) stamp your forms and put the letter into any one of the mail boxes at the airport. Your refund will arrive either as a credit to your credit card or as a check in U.S. dollars. You can also go to the French consulate with your plane tickets, your VAT forms, and the items you purchased to receive the stamp (which costs $21) that will ensure the VAT refund; there is a three month (after date of purchase) time limit. Finally, there are commercial companies which facilitate this process for you: Global Refund is among the largest.

➤ VAT REFUNDS: **Global Refund** (☎ 800/566–9828, FAX 845/348–1549, WEB www.globalrefund.com).

TAXIS

Taxi rates are based on location and time. Daytime rates, A (7 AM–7 PM), within Paris are 3.63 francs/€.55 per kilometer, and nighttime rates, B, are around 6.05 francs/€.92 per kilometer. Suburban zones and airports, C, are 7.16 francs/€1.09 per kilometer. There is a basic hire charge of 13 francs/€1.98 for all rides, a 6-franc/€.91 supplement per piece of luggage, and a 5-franc/€.76 supplement if you're picked up at an SNCF station. Waiting time is charged at 130 francs/€19.84 per hour. The easiest way to get a taxi is to **ask your hotel or a restaurant to call a taxi for you or go to the nearest taxi stand** (you can find one every couple of blocks); cabs with their signs lit can be hailed but are annoyingly difficult to spot (and they are not all one, uniform color). Note that taxis seldom take more than three people at a time. Tip the driver about 10%.

TELEPHONES

AREA & COUNTRY CODES

The country code for France is 33. The first two digits of French numbers are a prefix determined by zone: Paris and Ile-de-France, 01; the northwest, 02; the northeast, 03; the southeast, 04; and the southwest, 05. Pay close attention to numbers beginning with 08. Calls that begin with 08 followed by 00 are toll-free, but calls that begin with 08 followed by 36—like the information lines for the SNCF for example–cost 2.27 francs/€.34 per minute, so be careful. Numbers that begin with 06 are reserved for cell phones.

Note that **when dialing France from abroad, drop the initial 0 from the telephone number** (all numbers listed in this book include the initial 0, which is used for calling numbers *from within* France). To call a telephone number in Paris from the United States, dial 011–33 plus the phone number minus the initial 0 (phone numbers in this book are listed with the full 10 digits, which you use to make local calls). To call France from the United Kingdom, dial 00–33, then dial the number in France minus the initial 0.

DIRECTORY & OPERATOR ASSISTANCE

To find a number in France, **dial 12 for information.** For international inquiries, dial 00–33 plus the country code. These calls have a fixed rate of 4 francs/€.61.

Another source of information is the Minitel, an on-line network similar to the Internet. You can use one—they look like small computer terminals—free in most post offices. To access the on-line phone book, hit the *appel* (call) key, then type the name you are looking for, and hit *envoi* (return). It is also useful for tracking down services: tap in *piscine* (swimming pool) under *activité* (activity), for example, and it will give you a list of all the pools in Paris. Go to other lines or pages by hitting the *suite* (next) key. Newer models will connect automatically when you hit the book-icon key. To disconnect, hit *fin* (end).

INTERNATIONAL CALLS

To make a direct international call out of France, dial 00 and wait for the tone; then dial the country code (1 for the United States and Canada, 44 for the United Kingdom, 61 for Australia, and 64 for New Zealand) and the area code (minus any initial 0) and number.

Expect to be overcharged if you make calls from your hotel. Approximate daytime rates, per minute, are 2.25 francs/€.34 to the United States and Canada (8 AM–9:30 PM) and 2.10 francs/€.32 for the United Kingdom (2 PM–8 PM); reduced rates at other time intervals, per minute, are 1.80 francs/€.27 to the United States and Canada and 1.65 franc/€.25 to the United Kingdom.

To call home with the help of an operator, dial 00–33 plus the country code. There is an automatic 44.5 francs/€6.79 service charge.

Telephone cards are sold that enable you to make long-distance and international calls from pay phones.

LOCAL CALLS

When making a local call in Paris or to Ile-de-France, **dial the full 10-digit number, including the initial 0.** A local call costs 74 centimes/€.11 for every three minutes.

LONG-DISTANCE CALLS

To call from region to region within France, **dial the full 10-digit number, including the initial 0.**

LONG-DISTANCE SERVICES

AT&T, MCI, and Sprint access codes make calling long distance relatively convenient, but you may find the local access number blocked in many hotel rooms. First ask the hotel operator to connect you. If the hotel operator balks, ask for an international operator, or dial the international operator yourself. One way to improve your odds of getting connected to your long-distance carrier is to travel with more than one company's calling card (a hotel may block Sprint, for example, but not MCI). If all else fails, call from a pay phone.

➤ ACCESS CODES: AT&T Direct (☎ 08–00–99–00–11; 08–00–99–01–11; 800/222–0300 information). **MCI WorldPhone** (☎ 08–00–99–00–19; 800/444–4444 information). **Sprint International Access** (☎ 08–00–99–00–87; 800/793–1153 information).

PHONE CARDS

Most **French pay phones are operated by** *télécartes* (phone cards), which you can buy from post offices, tabacs, and métro stations. These phone cards will save you money and hassle, since it is almost impossible to find phones that take change these days. There are two types of cards: the *télécarte international,* which allows you to make local calls and offers greatly reduced rates on international calls (instructions are in English and the cost is 50 francs/€7.63 for 60 units and 100 francs/€15.26 for 120 units); and the simple *télécarte,* which allows you to make calls in France (the cost is 49 francs/€7.48 for 50 units; 97.5 francs/€14.80 for 120 units). You can also use your credit card in much the same way as a télécarte.

In the rare cafés you may still be able to find pay phones that operate with 1-, 2-, and 5-franc coins (1.5 francs for local calls). Lift the receiver, place your coin(s) in the appropriate slots, and dial.

PUBLIC PHONES

Public **telephone booths can almost always be found in post offices, métro stations, bus stops, and in many cafés,** as well as on the street.

TIME

The time difference between New York and Paris is 6 hours (so when it's 1 PM in New York, it's 7 PM in Paris). The time difference between London and Paris is 1 hour; between Sydney and Paris, 8–9 hours; and between Auckland and Paris, 12 hours. All schedules, be it train, plane, or theater, work on a 24-hour or "continual" clock in France, which means that 8 AM is 8h00 but 8 pm is 20h00. Midnight is 24h00.

TIPPING

Bills in bars and restaurants must, by law, include service, but **it is customary to round out your bill with some small change** unless you're dissatisfied. The amount varies—from 50 centimes or 1 franc/€.15 for a beer to 10 francs/€1.52–15 francs/2.30 after a meal. In expensive restaurants, it's common to leave an additional 5% of the bill on the table.

Tip taxi drivers and hairdressers about 10% of the bill. Give theater and cinema ushers a couple of francs. In some theaters and hotels, cloak-room attendants may expect nothing (watch for signs that say *pourboire interdit*—tipping forbidden); other-wise, give them 5 francs/€.75. Wash-room attendants usually get 2 francs/€.30, though the sum is often posted.

If you stay more than two or three days in a hotel, it is customary to leave something for the chamber-maid—about 10 francs/€1.50 per day. Expect to pay about 10 francs/€1.50 (5 francs/€.75 in a moderately priced hotel) to the person who carries your bags or who hails you a taxi. In hotels providing room service, give 5 francs/€.75 to the waiter (this does not apply if breakfast is rou-tinely served in your room). If the chambermaid does some pressing or laundering for you, give her 5 francs/€.75–10 francs/€1.50 on top of the bill. If the concierge has been very helpful, it is customary to leave a tip of 50 francs/€7.60–100 francs/€15.25, depending on the type of hotel and the level of service.

Service station attendants get nothing for pumping gas or checking oil but 5 francs/€.75 or 10 francs/€1.50 for checking tires. Train and airport porters get a fixed sum (6 francs/€.90–10 francs/€1.50) per bag. Museum guides should get 5 francs/€.75–10 francs/€1.50 after a guided tour. It is standard practice to tip bus drivers about 10 francs/€1.50 after an excursion.

TOURS & PACKAGES

Because everything is prearranged on a prepackaged tour or independent vacation, you spend less time plan-ning—and often get it all at a good price.

For hundreds of out-of-the-ordinary tour options click on "Adventure Travel" at www.fodors.com.

BOOKING WITH AN AGENT

Travel agents are excellent resources. But it's a good idea to collect bro-chures from several agencies, as some agents' suggestions may be influenced by relationships with tour and pack-age firms that reward them for vol-ume sales. If you have a special interest, **find an agent with expertise in that area**; ASTA has a database of specialists worldwide.

Make sure your travel agent knows the accommodations and other ser-vices of the place they're recommend-ing. Ask about the hotel's location, room size, beds, and whether it has a pool, room service, or programs for children, if you care about these. Has your agent been there in person or sent others whom you can contact?

Do some homework on your own, too: local tourism boards can provide information about lesser-known and small-niche operators, some of which may sell only direct.

BUYER BEWARE

Each year consumers are stranded or lose their money when tour opera-tors—even large ones with excellent reputations—go out of business. So **check out the operator.** Ask several travel agents about its reputation, and try to **book with a company that has a consumer-protection program.** (Look for information in the com-pany's brochure.) In the United States, members of the National Tour Association and the United States Tour Operators Association are required to set aside funds to cover your payments and travel arrange-ments in the event that the company defaults. It's also a good idea to choose a company that participates in the American Society of Travel Agents' Tour Operator Program (TOP); ASTA will act as mediator in any disputes between you and your tour operator.

Remember that the more your pack-age or tour includes the better you can predict the ultimate cost of your vacation. Make sure you know ex-actly what is covered, and **beware of hidden costs.** Are taxes, tips, and transfers included? Entertainment and excursions? These can add up.

➤ TOUR-OPERATOR RECOMMENDA-
TIONS: **American Society of Travel
Agents** (☞ Travel Agencies, *below*).
National Tour Association (NTA;
✉ 546 E. Main St., Lexington, KY
40508, ☎ 859/226–4444 or 800/
682–8886, WEB www.ntaonline.com).
**United States Tour Operators Associ-
ation** (USTOA; ✉ 342 Madison Ave.,
Suite 1522, New York, NY 10173,
☎ 212/599–6599 or 800/468–7862,
FAX 212/599–6744, WEB www.ustoa.
com).

TRAIN TRAVEL TO & FROM PARIS

The SNCF, France's rail system, is
fast, punctual, comfortable, and
comprehensive. There are various
options: local trains, overnight trains
with sleeping accommodations, and
the high-speed TGV, or *Trains à
Grande Vitesse* (averaging 255 kph/
160 mph on the Lyon/southeast line
and 300 kph/190 mph on the Lille
and Bordeaux/southwest lines).

The TGVs, the fastest way to get
around the country, operate between
Paris and Lille/Calais, Paris and Lyon/
Switzerland/the Riviera, Paris and
Angers/Nantes, Paris and Tours/
Poitiers/Bordeaux, Paris and Brussels,
and Paris and Amsterdam. As with
other main-line trains, a small supplement may be assessed at peak hours.

Paris has six international rail stations: Gare du Nord (northern
France, northern Europe, and England via Calais or Boulogne); Gare
St-Lazare (Normandy, England via
Dieppe); Gare de l'Est (Strasbourg,
Luxembourg, Basel, and central Europe); Gare de Lyon (Lyon, Marseille,
the Riviera, Geneva, Italy); and Gare
d'Austerlitz (Loire Valley, southwest
France, Spain). Note that Gare Montparnasse has taken over as the main
terminus for trains bound for southwest France since the introduction of
the new TGV-Atlantique service.

CUTTING COSTS

To save money, **look into rail passes.**
But be aware that if you don't plan to
cover many miles you may come out
ahead by buying individual tickets.

RAIL PASSES

If you plan to travel outside of Paris
by train, **consider purchasing a France
Rail Pass,** which allows three days of
unlimited train travel in a one-month
period. If you travel solo, first class
will run you $210, while second class
is $180: you can add up to six days
on this pass for $30 a day. For two
people traveling together on a Saver
Pass, the cost is $171, while in second
class, it is $146; additional days (up
to 6) cost $30 each. Other options
include the France Rail 'n Drive Pass
(combining rail and rental car),
France Rail 'n Fly Pass (rail travel and
one air-travel journey within France),
and the France Fly Rail 'n Drive Pass
(a rail, air, and rental-car program all
in one).

France is one of 17 countries in which
you can use EurailPasses, which
provide unlimited first-class rail
travel, in all of the participating
countries, for the duration of the
pass. If you plan to rack up the miles,
get a standard pass. These are available for 15 days ($554), 21 days
($718), one month ($890), two
months ($1,260), and three months
($1,558). If your plans call for only
limited train travel, **look into a Europass,** which costs less money than a
EurailPass. Unlike with the Eurail-
Passes, however, you get a limited
number of travel days, in a limited
number of countries, during a specified time period. For example, a two-
month Europass ($348–$728) allows
between 5 and 15 days of rail travel
but costs around $200 less than the
least expensive EurailPass. Keep in
mind, however, that the Europass is
good only in France, Germany, Italy,
Spain, and Switzerland, and the
number of countries you can visit is
further limited by the type of pass you
buy.

In addition to standard EurailPasses,
ask about special rail-pass plans.
Among these are the Eurail Youthpass
(for those under age 26), the Eurail
Saver Pass (which gives a discount for
two or more people traveling together), a Eurail Flexipass (which
allows a certain number of travel days
within a set period), the Euraildrive
Pass, and the Europass Drive (train
and rental car).

Whichever of the above passes you choose, remember that **you must purchase your Eurail and Euro passes at home before leaving for France.**

Another option is to **purchase one of the discount rail passes available only for sale in France** from SNCF.

When traveling together, **two people (who don't have to be a couple) can save money with the Prix Découverte à Deux.** You'll get a 25% discount during "*périodes bleus*" (blue periods: weekdays and not on or near any holidays). Note that you have to be with the person you said you would be traveling with.

You can **get a reduced fare if you're a senior citizen (over 60).** There are two options: for the Prix Découverte Senior, all you have to do is show a valid ID with your age and you're entitled to up to a 25% reduction in fares in first and second class. The second, the Carte Senior, is better if you're planning on spending a lot of time traveling; it costs 290 francs/€44.20, is valid for one year, and entitles you to up to a 50% reduction on most trains with a guaranteed minimum reduction of 25%. It also entitles you to a 30% discount on trips outside of France.

With the Carte Enfant Plus, for 350 francs/€53.35 **children under 12 and up to four accompanying adults can get up to 50% off on most trains for an unlimited number of trips.** This card is perfect if you're planning on spending a lot of time traveling in France with your children, as it's valid for one year. You can also opt for the Prix Découverte Enfant Plus: when you buy your ticket, simply show a valid ID with your child's age and you can get a significant discount for your child and a 25% reduction for up to four accompanying adults.

If you purchase an individual ticket from SNCF in France and you're under 26, you automatically get a 25% reduction (a valid ID, such as an ISIC card or your passport, is necessary). If you're going to be using the train quite a bit during your stay in France and **if you're under 26, consider buying the Carte 12–25** (270 francs/€41.15), which offers unlim-

ited 50% reductions for one year (provided that there's space available at that price; otherwise you'll just get the standard 25% discount).

If you don't benefit from any of these reductions and **if you plan on traveling at least 200 km (132 mi) round-trip and don't mind staying over a Saturday night, look into the Prix Découverte Séjour.** This ticket gives you a 25% reduction.

Don't assume that your rail pass guarantees you a seat on the train you wish to ride. You need to **book seats ahead even if you're using a rail pass.**

FARES & SCHEDULES

You can **call for train information or reserve tickets in any Paris station,** irrespective of destination. If you know what station you'll depart from, you can get a free schedule there (while supplies last), or you can access the new, multilingual computerized-schedule information network at any Paris station. You can also make reservations and buy your ticket while at the computer. Go to the Grandes Lignes counter for travel within France and to the Billets Internationaux desk if you're heading out of the country. Note that calling the SNCF's 08 number costs 2.21 francs/€.35 per minute, which quickly adds up; to save this cost, either go to the nearest station and make the reservations in person or visit the SNCF Web site, www.sncf.fr.

Seat reservations are required on TGVs and are a good idea on trains that may be crowded—particularly in summer and holidays on popular routes. You also need a reservation for sleeping accommodations.

➤ TRAIN INFORMATION: **BritRail Travel** (☎ 800/677–8585 in the U.S.; 020/7834–2345 in the U.K.). **Eurostar** (☎ 08–36–35–35–39 in France; 0345/881881 in the U.K.; WEB www.eurostar.com). **InterCity Europe** (✉ Victoria Station, London, ☎ 020/7834–2345; 020/7828–0892; 0990/848–848 credit-card bookings). **Rail Europe** (☎ 800/942–4866 in the U.S., WEB www.raileurope.com). **SNCF** (✉ 88 rue St-Lazare, 75009 Paris, ☎ 08–36–35–35–35, WEB www.sncf.fr).

BETWEEN THE U.K. AND FRANCE

Short of flying, taking the "Chunnel" is the fastest way to cross the English Channel: 3 hours from London's central Waterloo Station to Paris's central Gare du Nord, 35 minutes from Folkestone to Calais, and 60 minutes from motorway to motorway. There is a vast range of prices for Eurostar—round-trip tickets range from 3,400 francs/€520 for first class to 690 francs/€105.35 for second class depending on when you travel. It's a good idea to **make a reservation if you're traveling with your car on a Chunnel train**; cars without reservations, if they can get on at all, are charged 20% extra.

British Rail also has four daily departures from London's Victoria Station, all linking with the Dover–Calais/Boulogne ferry services through to Paris. There is also an overnight service on the Newhaven–Dieppe ferry. Journey time is about eight hours. Credit-card bookings are accepted by phone or in person at a British Rail Travel Centre.

➤ CAR TRANSPORT: **Le Shuttle** (☎ 0990/353–535 in the U.K.; 03–21–00–61–00 in France; WEB www.eurotunnel.co.uk).

➤ PASSENGER SERVICE: **BritRail Travel** (☎ 800/677–8585 in the U.S.; 020/7834–2345 in the U.K.). **Eurostar** (☎ 0990/186–186 in the U.K.; 08–36–35–35–39 in France; WEB www.eurostar.com). **InterCity Europe** (✉ Victoria Station, London, ☎ 020/7834–2345; 020/7828–0892; 0990/848–848 credit-card bookings). **Rail Europe** (☎ 800/942–4866 in the U.S., WEB www.raileurope.com).

TRAVEL AGENCIES

A good travel agent puts your needs first. Look for an agency that has been in business at least five years, emphasizes customer service, and has someone on staff who specializes in your destination. In addition, **make sure the agency belongs to a professional trade organization.** The American Society of Travel Agents (ASTA), with 27,000 agents in some 170 countries, is the largest and most influential in the field. Operating under the motto "Integrity in Travel," it maintains and enforces a strict code of ethics and will step in to help mediate any agent-client disputes if necessary. ASTA also maintains a Web site that includes a directory of agents. (If a travel agency is also acting as your tour operator, *see* Buyer Beware *in* Tours & Packages, *above*.)

➤ LOCAL AGENT REFERRALS: **American Society of Travel Agents** (ASTA; ☎ 800/965–2782 24-hr hot line, FAX 703/739–7642, WEB www.astanet.com). **Association of British Travel Agents** (✉ 68–71 Newman St., London W1T 3AH, U.K., ☎ 020/7637–2444, FAX 020/7637–0713, WEB www.abtanet.com). **Association of Canadian Travel Agents** (✉ 130 Albert St., Ste. 1705, Ottawa, Ontario K1P 5G4, Canada, ☎ 613/237–3657, FAX 613/237–7502, WEB www.acta.net). **Australian Federation of Travel Agents** (✉ Level 3, 309 Pitt St., Sydney, NSW 2000, Australia, ☎ 02/9264–3299, FAX 02/9264–1085, WEB www.afta.com.au). **Travel Agents' Association of New Zealand** (✉ Box 1888, Wellington 10033, New Zealand, ☎ 04/499–0104, FAX 04/499–0827, WEB www.taanz.org.nz).

➤ PARIS AGENCIES: **American Express** (✉ 11 rue Scribe, 8e, ☎ 01–47–77–77–07; ✉ 38 av. de Wagram, 8e, ☎ 01–42–27–58–80). **Nouvelles Frontières** (✉ 5 av. de l'Opéra, 1er, métro Pyramides, ☎ 08–03–33–33–33). **Soltours** (✉ 48 rue de Rivoli, 4e, métro Hôtel-de-Ville, ☎ 01–42–71–24–34).

VISITOR INFORMATION

FRANCE TOURIST INFORMATION

France On-Call (☎ 410/286–8310 weekdays 9–7, WEB www.francetourism.com). **Chicago** (✉ 676 N. Michigan Ave., Chicago, IL 60611, fgto@mcs.net). **Los Angeles** (✉ 9454 Wilshire Blvd., Suite 715, Beverly Hills, CA 90212, fgto@gte.net). **New York City** (✉ 444 Madison Ave., 16th floor, New York, NY 10022, info@francetourism.com). **Canada** (✉ 1981 av. McGill College, Suite 490, Montréal, Québec H3A 2W9). **U.K.** (✉ 178 Piccadilly, London W1V OAL, ☎ 020/76399–3500, FAX 020/76493–6594).

LOCAL TOURISM INFORMATION

Espace du Tourisme d'Ile-de-France (⊠ Carrousel du Louvre, 99 rue de Rivoli, Paris 75001, ☎ 08–03–81–80–00 or 01–44–50–19–98). **Office du Tourisme de la Ville de Paris** (⊠ Paris Tourist Office, 127 av. des Champs-Élysées, ☎ 01–49–52–53–54, 01–49–52–53–56 recorded information in English).

➤ U.S. GOVERNMENT ADVISORIES: **U.S. Department of State** (⊠ Overseas Citizens Services Office, Room 4811 N.S., 2201 C St. NW, Washington, DC 20520, ☎ 202/647–5225 interactive hot line, WEB http://travel. state.gov/travel/html); enclose a self-addressed, stamped, business-size envelope.

➤ PARIS/FRANCE WEB SITES: For more specific information on Paris, visit one of the following: **Eurostar** (WEB www. eurail.com/ www.eurostar.com). **Eurostar** (WEB www.eurail.com/ www. eurostar.com). **Louvre Museum** (WEB mistral.culture.fr/louvre/louvrea. htm). **French Embassy** (WEB www. france.diplomatie.fr). **French Government Tourist Office** (WEB www.france-tourism.com). **French Ministry of Culture** (WEB www.culture.fr). **Paris Tourist Office** (WEB www.paris.org). **Rail Europe** (WEB www.raileurope.com). **RATP** (WEB www.ratp.fr). **SNCF** (WEB www.sncf.fr).

WEB SITES

Do check out the World Wide Web when planning your trip. You'll find everything from weather forecasts to virtual tours of famous cities. Be sure to **visit Fodors.com** (www.fodors. com), a complete travel-planning site. You can research prices, check out bargains, read late-breaking travel news, and book plane tickets, hotel rooms, rental cars, vacation packages, and more. In addition, you can post your pressing questions in the Travel Talk section and, in the site's Rants & Raves section, read comments about some of the restaurants and hotels in this book—and chime in yourself. Other planning tools include a currency converter and weather reports, and there are loads of links to travel resources.

WHEN TO GO

The major tourist season in France stretches from Easter to mid-September, but **Paris has much to offer in every season.** Paris in the early spring can be disappointingly damp, though it's relatively tourist free; May and June are delightful, with good weather and plenty of cultural and other attractions. July and August can be sultry. Moreover, many theaters and some of the smaller restaurants and shops close for the entire month of August. If you're undeterred by the hot weather and the pollution, you'll notice a fairly relaxed atmosphere around the city, as this is the month when most Parisians are on vacation. September is ideal. Cultural life revives after the summer break, and sunny weather often continues through the first half of October. The ballet and theater are in full swing in November, but the weather is part wet and cold, part bright and sunny. December is dominated by the *fêtes de fin d'année* (end-of-year festivities) and a busy theater, ballet, and opera season into January.

CLIMATE

The following are the average daily maximum and minimum temperatures for Paris.

➤ FORECASTS: **Weather Channel Connection** (☎ 900/932–8437), 95¢ per minute from a Touch-Tone phone.

Jan.	43F	6C	May	68F	20C	Sept.	70F	21C
	34	1		49	10		53	12
Feb.	45F	7C	June	73F	23C	Oct.	60F	16C
	34	1		55	13		46	8
Mar.	54F	12C	July	76F	25C	Nov.	50F	10C
	39	4		58	14		40	5
Apr.	60F	16C	Aug.	75F	24C	Dec.	44F	7C
	43	6		58	14		36	2

FESTIVALS AND SEASONAL EVENTS

➤ Nov. 11: **Armistice Day** ceremonies at the Arc de Triomphe include a military parade down the Champs-Élysées.

➤ 3RD THURS. IN NOV.: **Beaujolais Nouveau,** that light, fruity wine from the Beaujolais region of France, is officially released at midnight on Wednesday; its arrival is celebrated on the third Thursday in November in true Dionysian form in cafés and restaurants around the city.

➤ LATE NOV.: **Salon des Caves Particulières** brings French producers to the exhibition center at Porte de Versailles for a wine-tasting jamboree. Galleries and museums also will open their doors for the "Le Mois de la Photo" (Photo Month) event.

➤ LATE NOV.–LATE DEC.: The festive **Christmas Market** (✉ Pl. du 11-Novembre-1918, 10ᵉ, métro Gare de l'Est) features crafts, gifts, and toys from every region of France.

➤ LATE DEC.: **Christmas** is highlighted by illuminations throughout the city, particularly on the Champs-Élysées, avenue Montaigne, and boulevard Haussmann. In the Jardin des Tuileries there's a fair with a Ferris wheel, and outside the Hôtel de Ville is a giant **crèche plus an ice-skating rink free to the public.**

➤ DEC. 31: For New Year's Eve **L'An 2002** (The Year 2002) big events are planned; contact the French Tourist Office for more information.

➤ FEB.: **Foire à la Feraille de Paris** is an antiques and bric-a-brac fair held in the Bois de Vincennes.

➤ MAR.: **Salon du Livre,** an international book exposition, is held annually at the end of the month.

➤ MAR.–APR.: **Foire du Trône,** an amusement park, is set up in the Bois de Vincennes.

➤ MAR.–APR.: The **Prix du Président de la République** takes place at the Auteuil Racecourse.

➤ LATE APR.: The **International Marathon of Paris** runs through the city and large parks on the outskirts.

➤ EARLY MAY: At the **Foire de Paris** hundreds of booths display everything from crafts to wines. The **Novotel-Perrier French Open** takes place at the national golf course in les Yvelines just outside of Paris.

➤ END OF MAY: The **Course des Garçons de Café** is an entertaining race through the streets of Paris by waiters bearing full trays of drinks; it begins and ends at the Hôtel de Ville.

➤ MAY–LATE SEPT.: **Grandes Eaux Musicales** is a fountain display at the Château de Versailles (Sunday only).

➤ LATE MAY–EARLY JUNE: The **Festival de Jazz de Boulogne-Billancourt** attracts big names and varied styles of jazz in Boulogne-Billancourt, a suburb of Paris.

➤ LATE MAY–EARLY JUNE: The **French Open Tennis Championships** take place at Roland Garros Stadium. The **Grand Steeple Chase** takes place at the Porte D'Auteuil racetrack.

➤ MID-JUNE–MID-JULY: **Festival du Marais** features everything from music to dance to theater in the churches and historic mansions of the Marais (tickets: ✉ 44 rue François-Miron, 4ᵉ, ☎ 01–48–87–60–08, métro St-Paul). A similar celebration takes place at the **Butte Montmartre Festival** (☎ 01–42–62–46–22). Just outside Paris, the **Festival de St-Denis** takes place this year with live music, theatre, dance, and a Robert Wilson creation in the Gothic basilica.

➤ JUNE: **Paris Air Show,** which takes place in odd-numbered years only, is a display of old and new planes at Le Bourget Airport. The colorful **Gay Pride Parade** takes place mid-month.

➤ LATE JUNE: The **Grand Prix de Paris,** is held on the flat at Longchamp Racecourse. The **45th International Air Show** takes place in Le Bourget.

➤ JULY 13: **Bals des Sapeurs-Pompiers** (Firemen's Balls), held to celebrate the start of Bastille Day the next day, spill into the streets of every arrondissement. Head to any *casern* (fire station) in Paris and dance the night away to live music; spectacular party locations also include historic landmarks in the Marais and a barge on the Seine.

➤ JULY 14: **Bastille Day** celebrates the storming of the Bastille prison in 1789. There's a military parade along the Champs-Élysées in the morning and fireworks at night at Trocadéro.

➤ LATE JULY: The **Tour de France**, the world's leading bicycle race, speeds to a Sunday finish on the Champs-Élysées.

➤ LATE JULY–END AUG.: The **Fête Musique en l'Ile** (☎ 01–45–23–18–25 for details) is a series of concerts held in the picturesque 17th-century Église St-Louis on Ile St-Louis.

➤ MID–LATE SEPT.: **Biennale des Antiquaires** (even-numbered years only), an antiques fair, takes place at the Carrousel du Louvre.

➤ LATE SEPT.: On the **Journée du Patrimonie,** the third Sunday in September, normally closed historic buildings—such as the state residences of the President and Prime Minister—are open to the public. The world class (second only to Tokyo) **Salon Mondial de l'Automobile** auto show takes place this month. The

(very) loud **Techno Parade** winds its way through the streets of Paris to finish at Trocadéro.

➤ EARLY OCT.: **Fêtes des Vendanges,** held the first Saturday of October, marks the grape harvest in the Montmartre vineyard, at the corner of rue des Saules and rue St-Vincent.

➤ EARLY OCT.: **FIAC** (International Fair of Contemporary Art) takes place at Porte de Versailles.

➤ EARLY OCT.: **Prix de l'Arc de Triomphe,** Europe's top flat race, is the first Sunday of the month at Longchamp Racecourse.

➤ OCT.: **Paris Auto Show** (even-numbered years only) takes place at the Porte de Versailles.

➤ MID-OCT.–EARLY NOV.: The **Fête de Jazz de Paris** (☎ 01–47–83–33–58 for information) is a two-week celebration that includes lots of big-name musicians.

➤ OCT.–NOV.: The **Fête d'Art Sacré** (☎ 01–42–77–92–26 for information) is a series concerts and exhibitions held in churches throughout the city.

Paris Métro

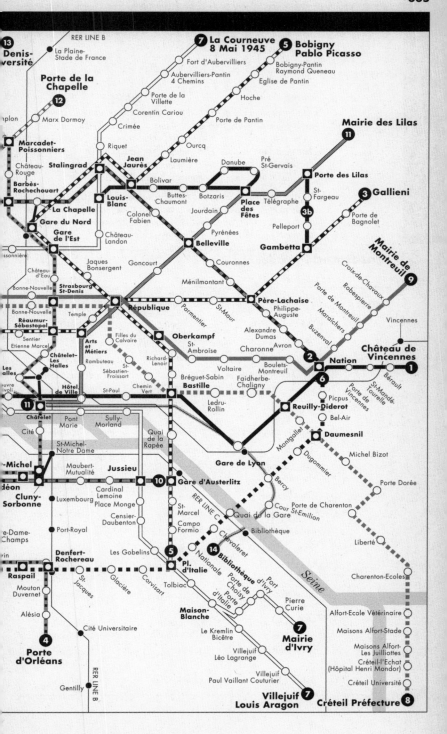

WORDS AND PHRASES

One of the trickiest French sounds to pronounce is the nasal final *n* sound (whether or not the *n* is actually the last letter of the word). You should try to pronounce it as a sort of nasal grunt—as in "huh." The vowel that precedes the *n* will govern the vowel sound of the word, and in this list we precede the final *n* with an *h* to remind you to be nasal.

Another problem sound is the ubiquitous but untransliterable *eu*, as in *bleu* (blue) or *deux* (two), and the very similar sound in *je* (I), *ce* (this), and *de* (of). The closest equivalent might be the vowel sound in "put," but rounded.

Words and Phrases

	English	French	Pronunciation
Basics			
	Yes/no	Oui/non	wee/nohn
	Please	S'il vous plaît	seel voo play
	Thank you	Merci	mair-**see**
	You're welcome	De rien	deh ree-**ehn**
	That's all right	Il n'y a pas de quoi	eel nee ah pah de kwah
	Excuse me, sorry	Pardon	pahr-**dohn**
	Sorry!	Désolé(e)	day-zoh-**lay**
	Good morning/ afternoon	Bonjour	bohn-**zhoor**
	Good evening	Bonsoir	bohn-**swahr**
	Goodbye	Au revoir	o ruh-**vwahr**
	Mr. (Sir)	Monsieur	muh-**syuh**
	Mrs. (Ma'am)	Madame	ma-**dam**
	Miss	Mademoiselle	mad-mwa-**zel**
	Pleased to meet you	Enchanté(e)	ohn-shahn-**tay**
	How are you?	Comment allez-vous?	kuh-mahn-tahl-ay **voo**
	Very well, thanks	Très bien, merci	tray bee-ehn, mair-**see**
	And you?	Et vous?	ay voo?
Numbers			
	one	un	uhn
	two	deux	deuh
	three	trois	twah
	four	quatre	**kaht**-ruh

five	cinq	sank
six	six	seess
seven	sept	set
eight	huit	wheat
nine	neuf	nuf
ten	dix	deess
eleven	onze	ohnz
twelve	douze	dooz
thirteen	treize	trehz
fourteen	quatorze	kah-torz
fifteen	quinze	kanz
sixteen	seize	sez
seventeen	dix-sept	deez-**set**
eighteen	dix-huit	deez-**wheat**
nineteen	dix-neuf	deez-**nuf**
twenty	vingt	vehn
twenty-one	vingt-et-un	vehnt-ay-**uhn**
thirty	trente	trahnt
forty	quarante	ka-**rahnt**
fifty	cinquante	sang-**kahnt**
sixty	soixante	swa-**sahnt**
seventy	soixante-dix	swa-sahnt-**deess**
eighty	quatre-vingts	kaht-ruh-**vehn**
ninety	quatre-vingt-dix	kaht-ruh-vehn-**deess**
one hundred	cent	sahn
one thousand	mille	meel

Colors

black	noir	nwahr
blue	bleu	bleuh
brown	brun/marron	bruhn/mar-**rohn**
green	vert	vair
orange	orange	o-**rahnj**
pink	rose	rose
red	rouge	rouge
violet	violette	vee-o-**let**
white	blanc	blahnk
yellow	jaune	zhone

Days of the Week

Sunday	dimanche	dee-**mahnsh**
Monday	lundi	luhn-**dee**
Tuesday	mardi	mahr-**dee**
Wednesday	mercredi	mair-kruh-**dee**
Thursday	jeudi	zhuh-**dee**
Friday	vendredi	vawn-druh-**dee**
Saturday	samedi	sahm-**dee**

Months

January	janvier	zhahn-vee-**ay**
February	février	feh-vree-**ay**
March	mars	marce
April	avril	a-**vreel**
May	mai	meh
June	juin	zhwehn
July	juillet	zhwee-**ay**
August	août	ah-**oo**
September	septembre	sep-**tahm**-bruh
October	octobre	awk-**to**-bruh
November	novembre	no-**vahm**-bruh
December	décembre	day-**sahm**-bruh

Useful Phrases

Do you speak English?	Parlez-vous anglais?	par-lay **voo** **ahn**-glay
I don't speak . . . French	Je ne parle pas . . . français	zhuh nuh parl pah frahn-**say**
I don't understand	Je ne comprends pas	zhuh nuh kohm-**prahn** pah
I understand	Je comprends	zhuh kohm-**prahn**
I don't know	Je ne sais pas	zhuh nuh say **pah**
I'm American/ British	Je suis américain/ anglais	zhuh sweez a-may-ree-**kehn**/ahn-**glay**
What's your name?	Comment vous ap-pelez-vous?	ko-mahn voo za-pell-ay-**voo**
My name is . . .	Je m'appelle . . .	zhuh ma-**pell** . . .
What time is it?	Quelle heure est-il?	kel air eh-**teel**
How?	Comment?	ko-**mahn**
When?	Quand?	kahn
Yesterday	Hier	yair
Today	Aujourd'hui	o-zhoor-**dwee**
Tomorrow	Demain	duh-**mehn**
This morning/ afternoon	Ce matin/cet après-midi	suh ma-**tehn**/ set ah-pray-mee-**dee**
Tonight	Ce soir	suh **swahr**
What?	Quoi?	kwah
What is it?	Qu'est-ce que c'est?	kess-kuh-**say**

Why?	Pourquoi?	**poor**-kwa
Who?	Qui?	kee
Where is . . .	Où est . . .	oo ay
the train station?	la gare?	la gar
the subway station?	la station de métro?	la sta-**syon** duh may-**tro**
the bus stop?	l'arrêt de bus?	la-**ray** duh **booss**
the terminal (airport)?	l'aérogare?	lay-ro-**gar**
the post office?	la poste?	la post
the bank?	la banque?	la bahnk
the . . . hotel?	l'hôtel . . .?	lo-**tel**
the store?	le magasin?	luh ma-ga-**zehn**
the cashier?	la caisse?	la **kess**
the . . . museum?	le musée . . .?	luh mew-**zay**
the hospital?	l'hôpital?	lo-pee-**tahl**
the elevator?	l'ascenseur?	la-sahn-**seuhr**
the telephone?	le téléphone?	luh tay-lay-**phone**
Where are the restrooms?	Où sont les toilettes?	oo sohn lay twah-**let**
Here/there	Ici/là	ee-**see**/la
Left/right	A gauche/à droite	a goash/a draht
Straight ahead	Tout droit	too drwah
Is it near/far?	C'est près/loin?	say pray/ lwehn
I'd like . . .	Je voudrais . . .	zhuh voo-**dray**
a room	une chambre	ewn **shahm**-bruh
the key	la clé	la clay
a newspaper	un journal	uhn zhoor-**nahl**
a stamp	un timbre	uhn **tam**-bruh
I'd like to buy . . .	Je voudrais acheter . . .	zhuh voo-**dray ahsh**-tay
a cigar	un cigare	uhn see-**gar**
cigarettes	des cigarettes	day see-ga-**ret**
matches	des allumettes	days a-loo-**met**
dictionary	un dictionnaire	uhn deek-see-oh-**nare**
soap	du savon	dew sah-**vohn**
city map	un plan de ville	uhn plahn de **veel**
road map	une carte routière	ewn cart roo-tee-**air**
magazine	une revue	ewn reh-**vu**
envelopes	des enveloppes	dayz ahn-veh-**lope**
writing paper	du papier à lettres	dew pa-pee-**ay** a **let**-ruh

postcard	une carte postale	ewn cart pos-**tal**
How much is it?	C'est combien?	say comb-bee-**ehn**
It's expensive/cheap	C'est cher/pas cher	say share/pa share
A little/a lot	Un peu/beaucoup	uhn peuh/bo-**koo**
More/less	Plus/moins	plu/mwehn
Enough/too (much)	Assez/trop	a-say/tro
I am ill/sick	Je suis malade	zhuh swee ma-**lahd**
Call a . . .	Appelez un . . .	a-play uhn
doctor	docteur	dohk-**tehr**
Help!	Au secours!	o suh-**koor**
Stop!	Arrêtez!	a-reh-**tay**
Fire!	Au feu!	o fuh
Caution!/Look out!	Attention!	a-tahn-see-**ohn**

Dining Out

A bottle of . . .	une bouteille de . . .	ewn boo-**tay** duh
A cup of . . .	une tasse de . . .	ewn tass duh
A glass of . . .	un verre de . . .	uhn vair duh
Ashtray	un cendrier	uhn sahn-dree-**ay**
Bill/check	l'addition	la-dee-see-**ohn**
Bread	du pain	dew pan
Breakfast	le petit-déjeuner	luh puh-**tee** day-zhuh-**nay**
Butter	du beurre	dew burr
Cheers!	A votre santé!	ah vo-truh sahn-**tay**
Cocktail/aperitif	un apéritif	uhn ah-pay-ree-**teef**
Dinner	le dîner	luh dee-**nay**
Dish of the day	le plat du jour	luh plah dew **zhoor**
Enjoy!	Bon appétit!	bohn a-pay-**tee**
Fixed-price menu	le menu	luh may-**new**
Fork	une fourchette	ewn four-**shet**
I am diabetic	Je suis diabétique	zhuh swee dee-ah-bay-**teek**
I am on a diet	Je suis au régime	zhuh sweez oray-**jeem**

I am vegetarian	Je suis végé-tarien(ne)	zhuh swee vay-zhay-ta-ree-**en**
I cannot eat . . .	Je ne peux pas manger de . . .	zhuh nuh **puh** pah mahn-**jay** deh
I'd like to order	Je voudrais commander	zhuh voo-**dray** ko-mahn-**day**
I'm hungry/thirsty	J'ai faim/soif	zhay fahm/swahf
Is service/the tip included?	Est-ce que le service est compris?	ess kuh luh sair-**veess** ay comb-**pree**
It's good/bad	C'est bon/mauvais	say bohn/mo-**vay**
It's hot/cold	C'est chaud/froid	say sho/frwah
Knife	un couteau	uhn koo-**toe**
Lunch	le déjeuner	luh day-zhuh-**nay**
Menu	la carte	la cart
Napkin	une serviette	ewn sair-vee-**et**
Pepper	du poivre	dew **pwah**-vruh
Plate	une assiette	ewn a-see-**et**
Please give me . . .	Donnez-moi . . .	doe-nay-**mwah**
Salt	du sel	dew sell
Spoon	une cuillère	ewn kwee-**air**
Sugar	du sucre	dew **sook**-ruh
Waiter!/Waitress!	Monsieur!/Mademoiselle!	muh-**syuh**/mad-mwa-**zel**
Wine list	la carte des vins	la cart day an

KEY WORDS ON THE MENU

French	English
General Dining	
Entrée	Appetizer/Starter
Garniture au choix	Choice of vegetable side
Plat du jour	Dish of the day
Selon arrivage	When available
Supplément/En sus	Extra charge
Sur commande	Made to order
Petit Déjeuner (Breakfast)	
Confiture	Jam
Miel	Honey
Oeuf à la coque	Boiled egg
Oeufs sur le plat	Fried eggs
Oeufs brouillés	Scrambled eggs
Tartine	Bread with butter
Poissons/Fruits de Mer (Fish/Seafood)	
Anchois	Anchovies
Bar	Bass
Brandade de morue	Creamed salt cod
Brochet	Pike
Cabillaud/Morue	Fresh cod
Calmar	Squid
Coquilles St-Jacques	Scallops
Crevettes	Shrimp
Cuisses de grenouilles	Frogs' legs
Daurade	Sea bream
Ecrevisses	Prawns/Crayfish
Harengs	Herring
Homard	Lobster
Huîtres	Oysters
Langoustine	Prawn/Lobster
Lotte	Monkfish
Maquereau	Mackerel
Moules	Mussels
Palourdes	Clams
Saumon	Salmon
Thon	Tuna
Truite	Trout
Viande (Meat)	
Agneau	Lamb
Boeuf	Beef
Boudin	Sausage
Boulettes de viande	Meatballs
Brochettes	Kabobs

Cassoulet	Casserole of white beans, meat
Cervelle	Brains
Chateaubriand	Double fillet steak
Choucroute garnie	Sausages with sauerkraut
Côtelettes	Chops
Côte/Côte de boeuf	Rib/T-bone steak
Cuisses de grenouilles	Frogs' legs
Entrecôte	Rib or rib-eye steak
Épaule	Shoulder
Escalope	Cutlet
Foie	Liver
Gigot	Leg
Porc	Pork
Ris de veau	Veal sweetbreads
Rognons	Kidneys
Saucisses	Sausages
Selle	Saddle
Tournedos	Tenderloin of T-bone steak
Veau	Veal

Methods of Preparation

A point	Medium
A l'étouffée	Stewed
Au four	Baked
Ballotine	Boned, stuffed, and rolled
Bien cuit	Well-done
Bleu	Very rare
Frit	Fried
Grillé	Grilled
Rôti	Roast
Saignant	Rare
Sauté/Poêlée	Sautéed

Volailles/Gibier (Poultry/Game)

Blanc de volaille	Chicken breast
Canard/Caneton	Duck/Duckling
Cerf/Chevreuil	Venison (red/roe)
Coq au vin	Chicken stewed in red wine
Dinde/Dindonneau	Turkey/Young turkey
Faisan	Pheasant
Lapin/Lièvre	Rabbit/Wild hare
Oie	Goose
Pintade/Pintadeau	Guinea fowl/Young guinea fowl
Poulet/Poussin	Chicken/Spring chicken

Légumes (Vegetables)

Artichaut	Artichoke
Asperge	Asparagus
Aubergine	Eggplant
Carottes	Carrots
Champignons	Mushrooms

Chou-fleur	Cauliflower
Chou (rouge)	Cabbage (red)
Laitue	Lettuce
Oignons	Onions
Petits pois	Peas
Pomme de terre	Potato
Tomates	Tomatoes

Fruits/Noix (Fruits/Nuts)

Abricot	Apricot
Amandes	Almonds
Ananas	Pineapple
Cassis	Blackcurrants
Cerises	Cherries
Citron/Citron vert	Lemon/Lime
Fraises	Strawberries
Framboises	Raspberries
Pamplemousse	Grapefruit
Pêche	Peach
Poire	Pear
Pomme	Apple
Prunes/Pruneaux	Plums/Prunes
Raisins/Raisins secs	Grapes/Raisins

Desserts

Coupe (glacée)	Sundae
Crème Chantilly	Whipped cream
Gâteau au chocolat	Chocolate cake
Glace	Ice cream
Tarte tatin	Caramelized apple tart
Tourte	Layer cake

Drinks

A l'eau	With water
Avec des glaçons	On the rocks
Bière	Beer
Blonde/brune	Light/dark
Café noir/crème	Black coffee/with steamed milk
Chocolat chaud	Hot chocolate
Eau-de-vie	Brandy
Eau minérale	Mineral water
gazeuse/non gazeuse	*carbonated/still*
Jus de . . .	. . . juice
Lait	Milk
Sec	Straight or dry
Thé	Tea
au lait/au citron	*with milk/lemon*
Vin	Wine
blanc	*white*
doux	*sweet*
léger	*light*
brut	*very dry*
rouge	*red*

INDEX

FODOR'S PARIS 2002

EDITOR: Robert I. C. Fisher

Editorial Contributors: Simon Hewitt, Rosa Jackson, Nicola Keegan, Christopher Mooney, Ian Phillips

Editorial Production: Stacey Kulig

Maps: David Lindroth, *cartographer;* Bob Blake and Rebecca Baer, *map editors*

Design: Fabrizio La Rocca, *creative director;* Guido Caroti, *art director;* Jolie Novak, *senior picture editor;* Melanie Marin, *photo editor*

Cover Design: Pentagram

Production/Manufacturing: Angela L. McLean

COPYRIGHT

SPECIAL SALES

Fodor's Travel Publications are available at special discounts for bulk purchases for sales promotions or premiums. Special editions, including personalized covers, excerpts of existing guides, and corporate imprints, can be created in large quantities for special needs. For more information, contact your local bookseller or write to Special Markets, Fodor's Travel Publications, 280 Park Avenue, New York, NY 10017. Inquiries from Canada should be directed to your local Canadian bookseller or sent to Random House of Canada, Ltd., Marketing Department, 2775 Matheson Boulevard East, Mississauga, Ontario L4W 4P7. Inquiries from the United Kingdom should be sent to Fodor's Travel Publications, 20 Vauxhall Bridge Road, London SW1V 2SA, England.

IMPORTANT TIP

Although all prices, opening times, and other details in this book are based on information supplied to us at press time, changes occur all the time in the travel world, and Fodor's cannot accept responsibility for facts that become outdated or for inadvertent errors or omissions. So always confirm information when it matters, especially if you're making a detour to visit a specific place.

PHOTOGRAPHY

Corbis, *Robert Holmes,* cover (Right Bank book stall).

Corbis Images: *3 top left, 3 top right, 3 bottom left, 8F, 26 top, 26 bottom, 27, 28 top, 28 center, 29, 30F, 30G, 30H.* Owen Franken, *16A, 30A.*

DIAF: *Jean Gabanou, 12A, 15E. G. Guittot, 19C. Rosine Mazin, 18B, 20A, 24A, 24B. Giovanni Simeone, 4-5. Daniel Thierry, 9 center, 12B, 19E.*

Christian Dior, *15F.*

Alain Ducasse: *P. Hussenot, 2 top right.*

Familia Hôtel, *30B.*

Emmanuel Ferrand, *25F.*

Owen Franken, *7D, 10A, 10 bottom right, 10B, 11D, 14A, 16 top, 16 bottom, 17B, 17C, 21C, 22A, 22 bottom, 23D, 25E.*

Galeries Lafayette, *14B, 14C.*

Hôtel Caron de Beaumarchais, *30J.*

Hôtel Ritz Paris, *2 bottom center.*

Hôtel de Vendôme, *30E.*

The Image Bank: *Daniel Barbier, 6C. Alain Choisnet, 6A. Greg Christensen, 30C. Antony Edwards, 11E. Herb Hartmann, 25C. F. Hidalgo, 9H. Mahaux Photography, 18A. Marvin E. Newman, 7E, 13C, 13D, 14D, 19D, 21D, 22B. Pascal Perret, 1. Andrea Pistolesi, 11C, 32. Bernard Roussel, 9G. Harald Sund, 21E. Matthew Weinreb, 13F. Hans Wolf, 30I.*

Catherine Karnow, *13E, 17 center, 20B, 23C.*

La Tuile a Loup, *3 bottom right.* James Lemass, *6B, 25D.*

Le Relais Saint Germain, *30D.*

Paris Convention and Visitors Bureau: *Frédéric Buxin, 2 bottom right.*

Sonia Rykiel, *2 bottom left.*

Sebastian Sousser, *2 top left.*

ABOUT OUR WRITERS

The more you know before you go, the better your trip will be. Paris's newest museum could be just around the corner from your hotel, but if you don't know it's there, it might as well be on the other side of the globe. That's where this book comes in. Here at Fodor's, and at our on-line arm, Fodors.com, our focus is on providing you with information that's not only useful but accurate and on target. And to direct you to the places that are truly worth your time and money, we've rallied a team of endearingly picky know-it-alls we're pleased to call our writers. There's no substitute for advice from a like-minded friend who has just come back from where you're going, but our critics, having seen all corners of Paris, are the next best thing. They're the kind of people you'd poll for tips yourself if you knew them.

Simon Hewitt, headed to Paris straight from studying French and art history at Oxford. It was a return to base: His grandmother was French, as are his wife and daughter. He moved to Versailles a few years ago to gain a different perspective on life in and around the French capital. When not contemplating the Sun King's bicep-flexing Baroque, his thoughts often turn to cricket—he is captain of the French national team.

Nicola Keegan was born in Ireland and raised in Iowa. But after spending one year at the Sorbonne, she knew Paris was going to be her home forever. Now famous for crossing the city on foot even in the worst storms, and her uncanny knowledge of where to purchase absolute necessities from truffle oil to that perfect pair of gold-hued boots, she brings all her hard earned "savoir faire" to Chapter 8's Smart Travel Tips section.

Nancy Coons has lived in France for many years and has written many books for Fodor's, including *Provence and the Côte d'Azur, Escape to Provence,* and *Escape to the Riviera.*

Robert I. C. Fisher, editor of *Fodor's Paris 2002,* succeeded in getting one foot in the caviar when he was sent to the French capital to write up the Hôtel Lambert—the noted Ile St-Louis residence of Baron and Baroness Guy de Rothschild—for the April 1988 issue of *Town & Country.* He still fondly recalls a pre-dawn hike up to the Sacré-Coeur to catch the sun come up over Paris.

Rosa Jackson's love affair with French pastries began at age four, when she spent her first year in Paris before returning to the Canadian north. Early experiments with eclairs and croissants led her to enroll in the Paris Cordon Bleu, where she learned that even great chefs make mistakes. A food writer for the past ten years and a Parisian since 1995, Rosa has eaten in hundreds of Paris restaurants—and always has room for dessert.

Christopher Mooney originally came to Paris to study French philosophy, smoke Gîtanes cigarettes, and hang out in cafés. Ten years later he's still there, but his taste for Gallic thought and tobacco has given way to an unslakeable thirst for fine Burgundy vintages. A passionate writer (his pet computer often doubles as an additional pillow when he's traveling on the road), he devotes his efforts to finding the best Parisian hotels.

Ian Phillips originally moved from Britain to Paris by mistake. He had applied for a job in the Mediterranean, following his dream of sailing yachts, but ended up taking Bateaux Mouches down the Seine instead. Today, he writes on culture and fashion for many publications, including the American and English editions of *House & Garden,* the English and Italian editions of *Vogue,* the French edition of *Architectural Digest,* and *Tatler.*

Don't Forget to Write

Your experiences—positive and negative—matter to us. We follow up on all suggestions. Contact the Paris editor at editors@fodors.com or c/o Fodor's, 280 Park Avenue, New York, NY 10017. Have a fabulous trip!

Karen Cure
Editorial Director